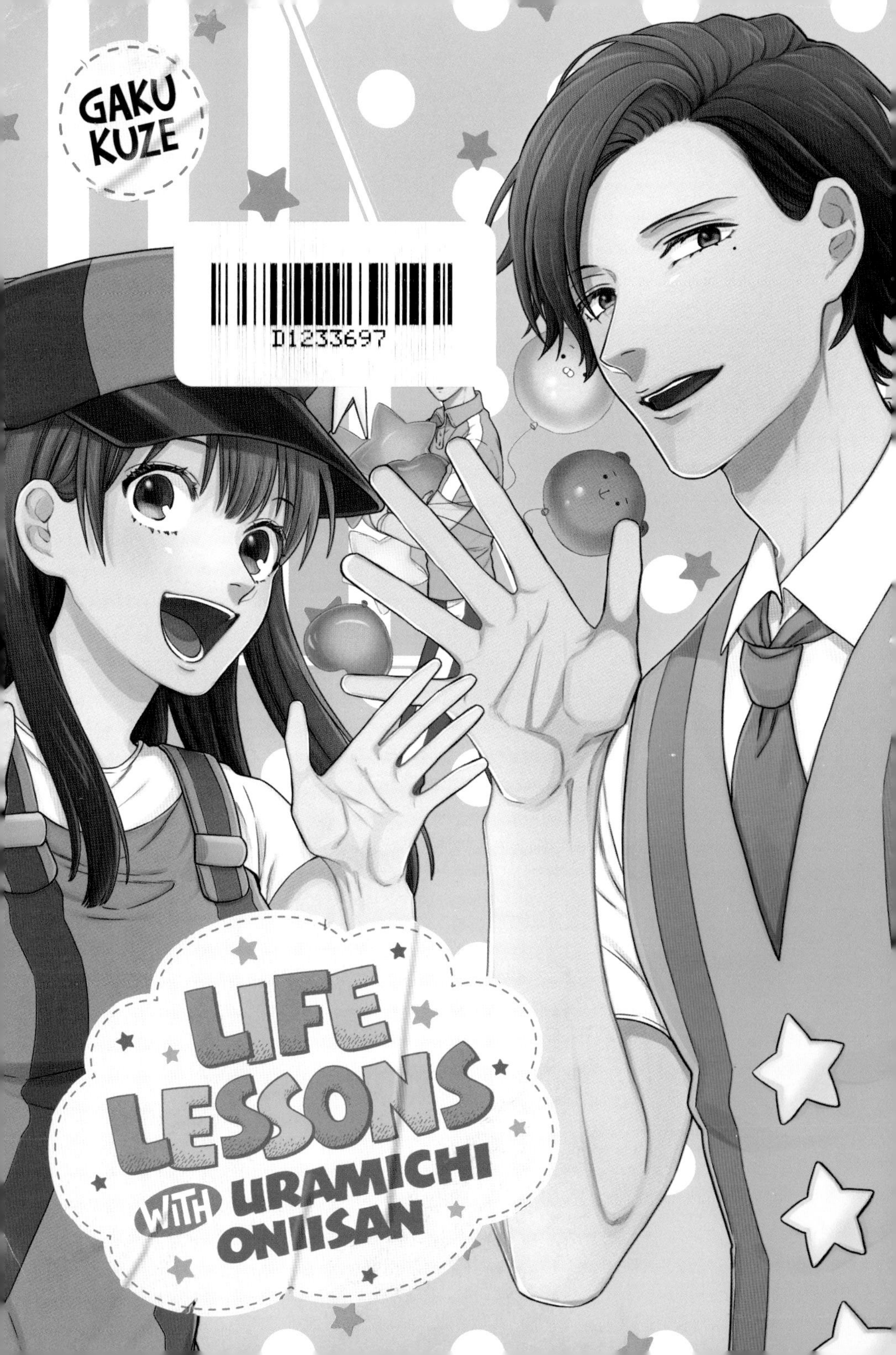
GAKU KUZE
LIFE LESSONS WITH URAMICHI ONIISAN

Contents

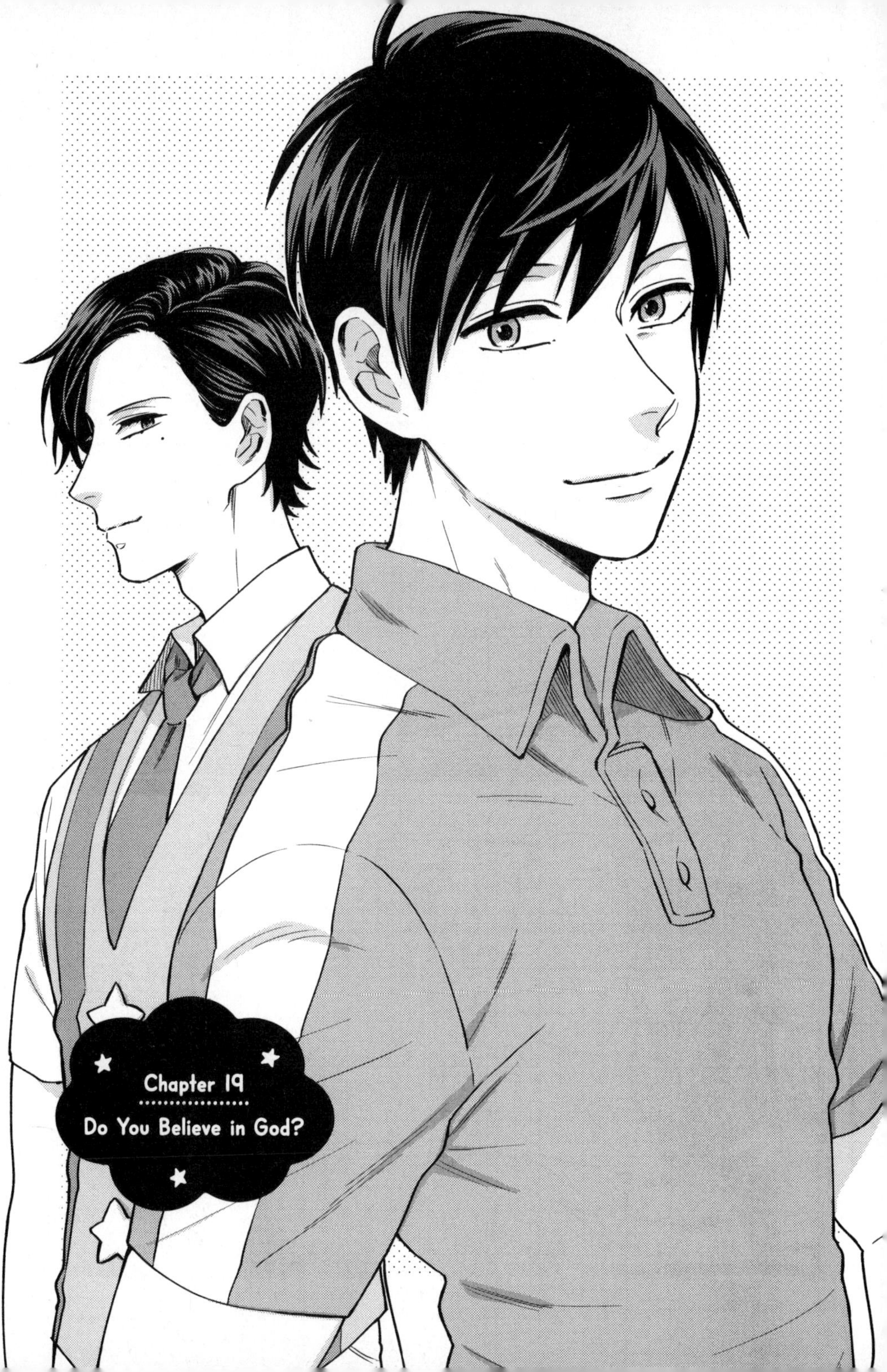
Chapter 19
Do You Believe in God?

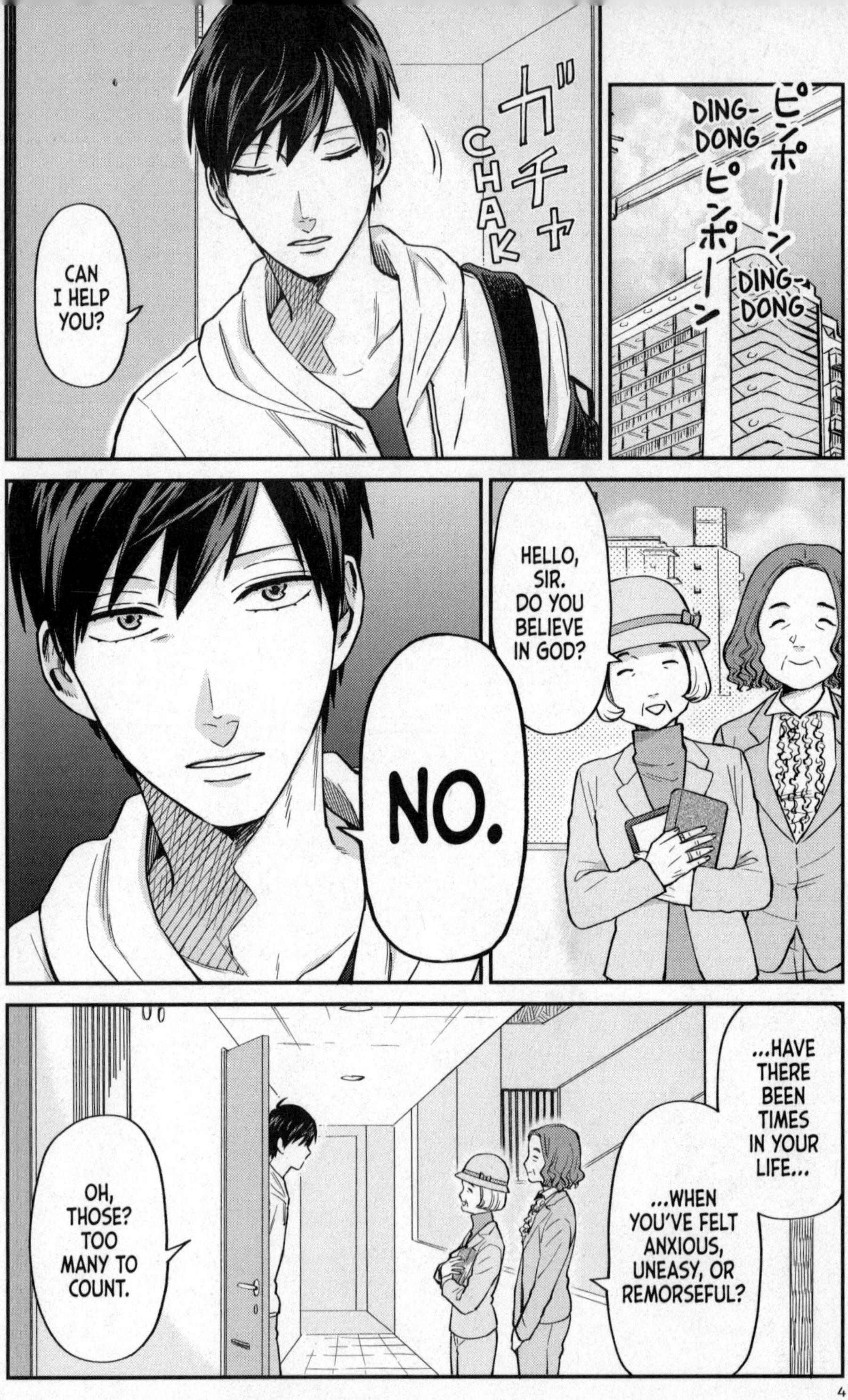
ピンポーン
DING-DONG
ピンポーン
DING-DONG
ガチャ
CHAK
CAN I HELP YOU?
HELLO, SIR. DO YOU BELIEVE IN GOD?
NO.
...HAVE THERE BEEN TIMES IN YOUR LIFE...
...WHEN YOU'VE FELT ANXIOUS, UNEASY, OR REMORSEFUL?
OH, THOSE? TOO MANY TO COUNT.

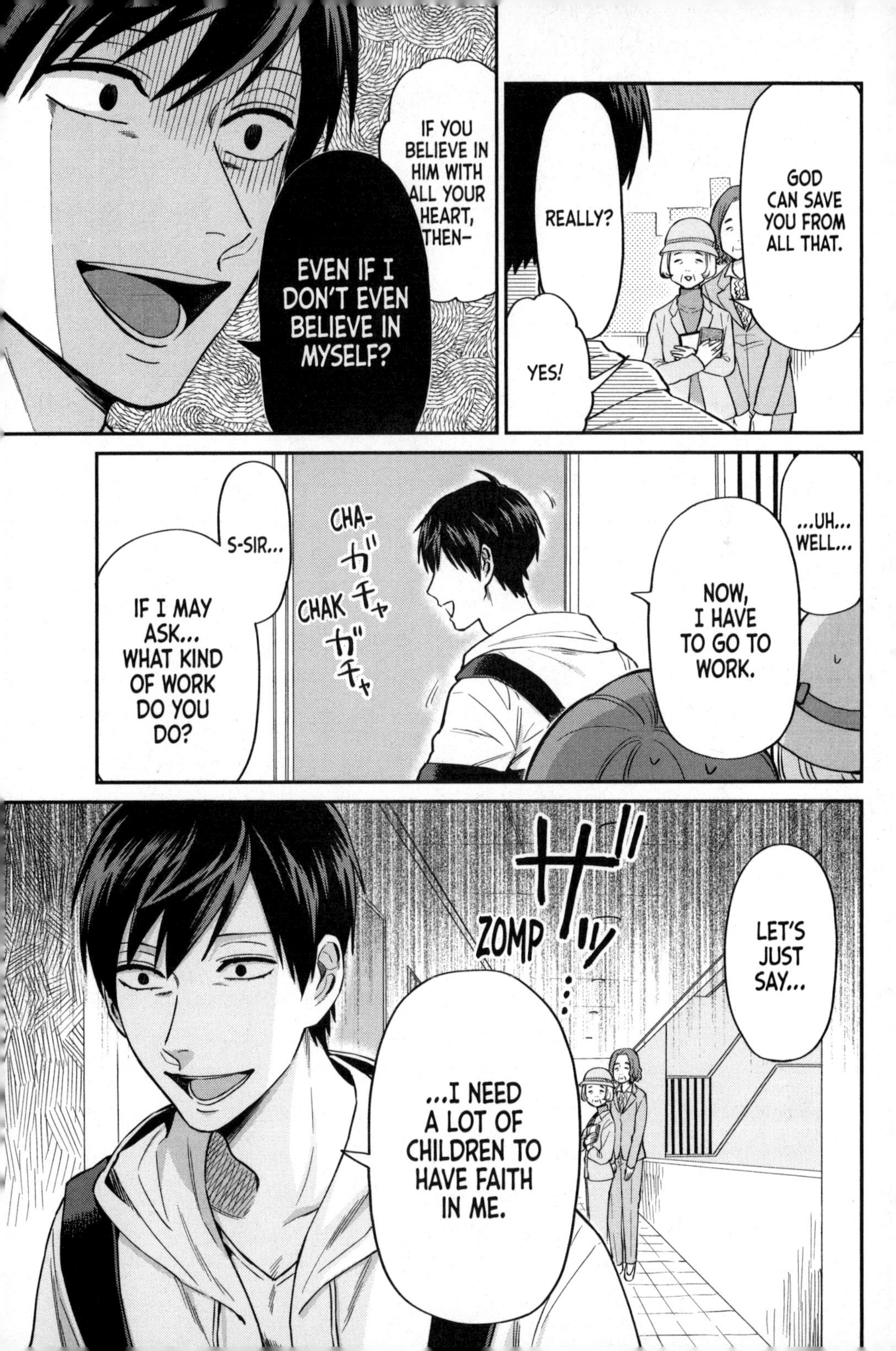
GOD CAN SAVE YOU FROM ALL THAT.
REALLY?
YES!
IF YOU BELIEVE IN HIM WITH ALL YOUR HEART, THEN—
EVEN IF I DON'T EVEN BELIEVE IN MYSELF?
...UH... WELL...
NOW, I HAVE TO GO TO WORK.
ガチャ ガチャ
CHA-
CHAK
S-SIR...
IF I MAY ASK... WHAT KIND OF WORK DO YOU DO?
LET'S JUST SAY...
ザッ
ZOMP
...I NEED A LOT OF CHILDREN TO HAVE FAITH IN ME.

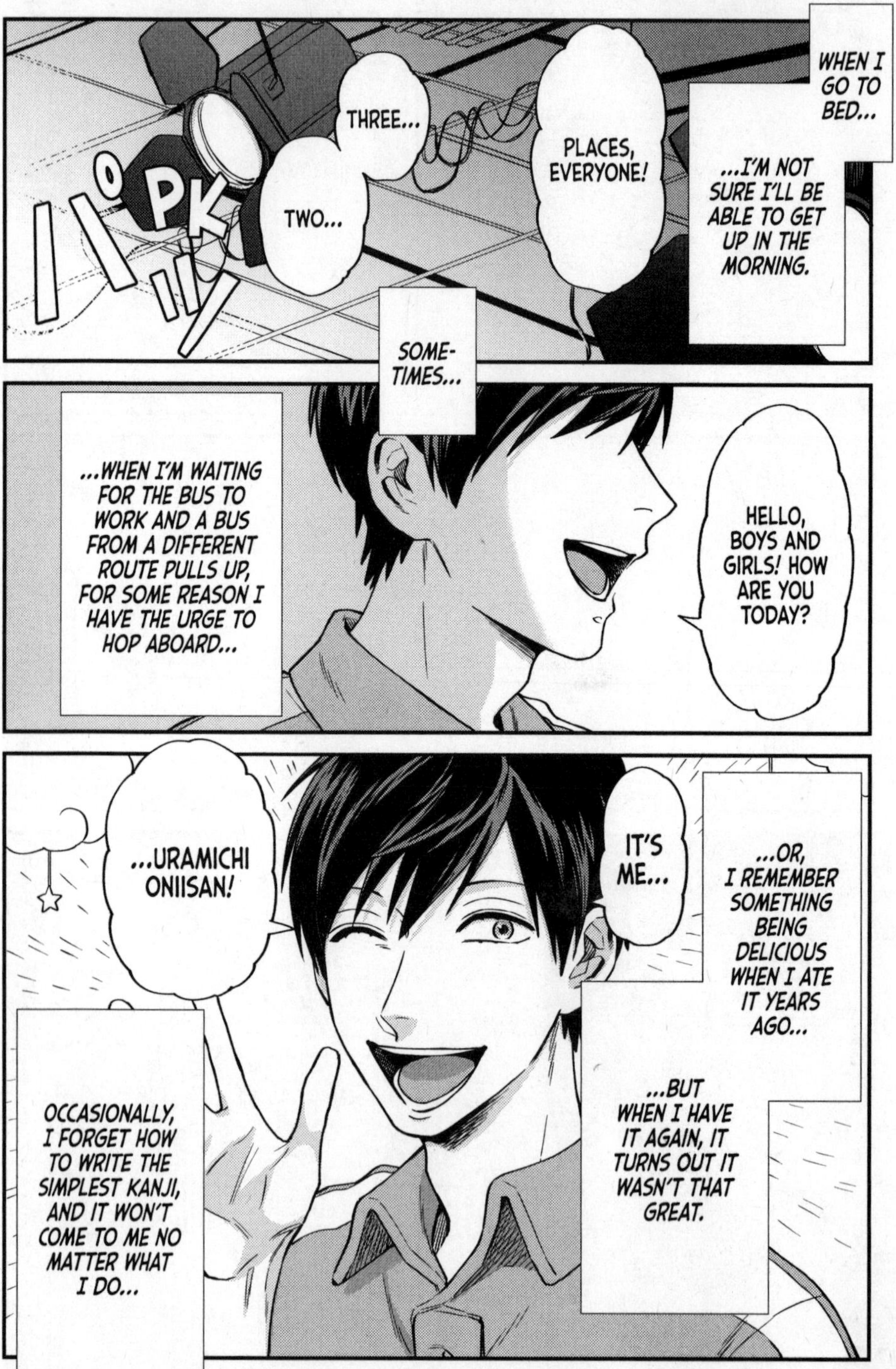
WHEN I GO TO BED...
...I'M NOT SURE I'LL BE ABLE TO GET UP IN THE MORNING.
PLACES, EVERYONE!
THREE...
TWO...
PK
SOME-TIMES...
HELLO, BOYS AND GIRLS! HOW ARE YOU TODAY?
...WHEN I'M WAITING FOR THE BUS TO WORK AND A BUS FROM A DIFFERENT ROUTE PULLS UP, FOR SOME REASON I HAVE THE URGE TO HOP ABOARD...
...OR, I REMEMBER SOMETHING BEING DELICIOUS WHEN I ATE IT YEARS AGO...
IT'S ME...
...URAMICHI ONIISAN!
...BUT WHEN I HAVE IT AGAIN, IT TURNS OUT IT WASN'T THAT GREAT.
OCCASIONALLY, I FORGET HOW TO WRITE THE SIMPLEST KANJI, AND IT WON'T COME TO ME NO MATTER WHAT I DO...

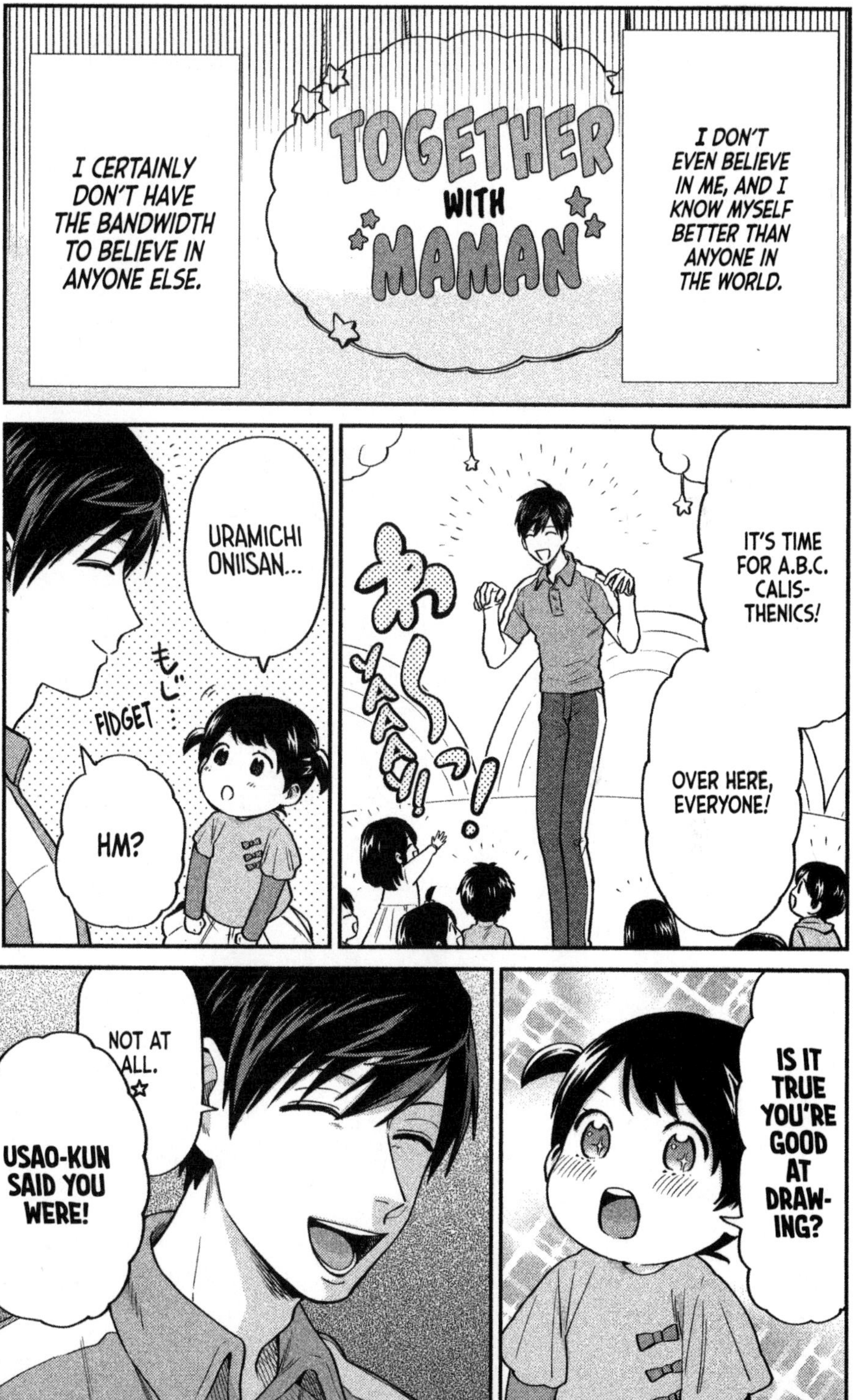
I DON'T EVEN BELIEVE IN ME, AND I KNOW MYSELF BETTER THAN ANYONE IN THE WORLD.
TOGETHER WITH MAMAN
I CERTAINLY DON'T HAVE THE BANDWIDTH TO BELIEVE IN ANYONE ELSE.
IT'S TIME FOR A.B.C. CALIS-THENICS!
わ〜いっ!
OVER HERE, EVERYONE!
URAMICHI ONIISAN...
もじ…
FIDGET
HM?
IS IT TRUE YOU'RE GOOD AT DRAW-ING?
NOT AT ALL. ☆
USAO-KUN SAID YOU WERE!

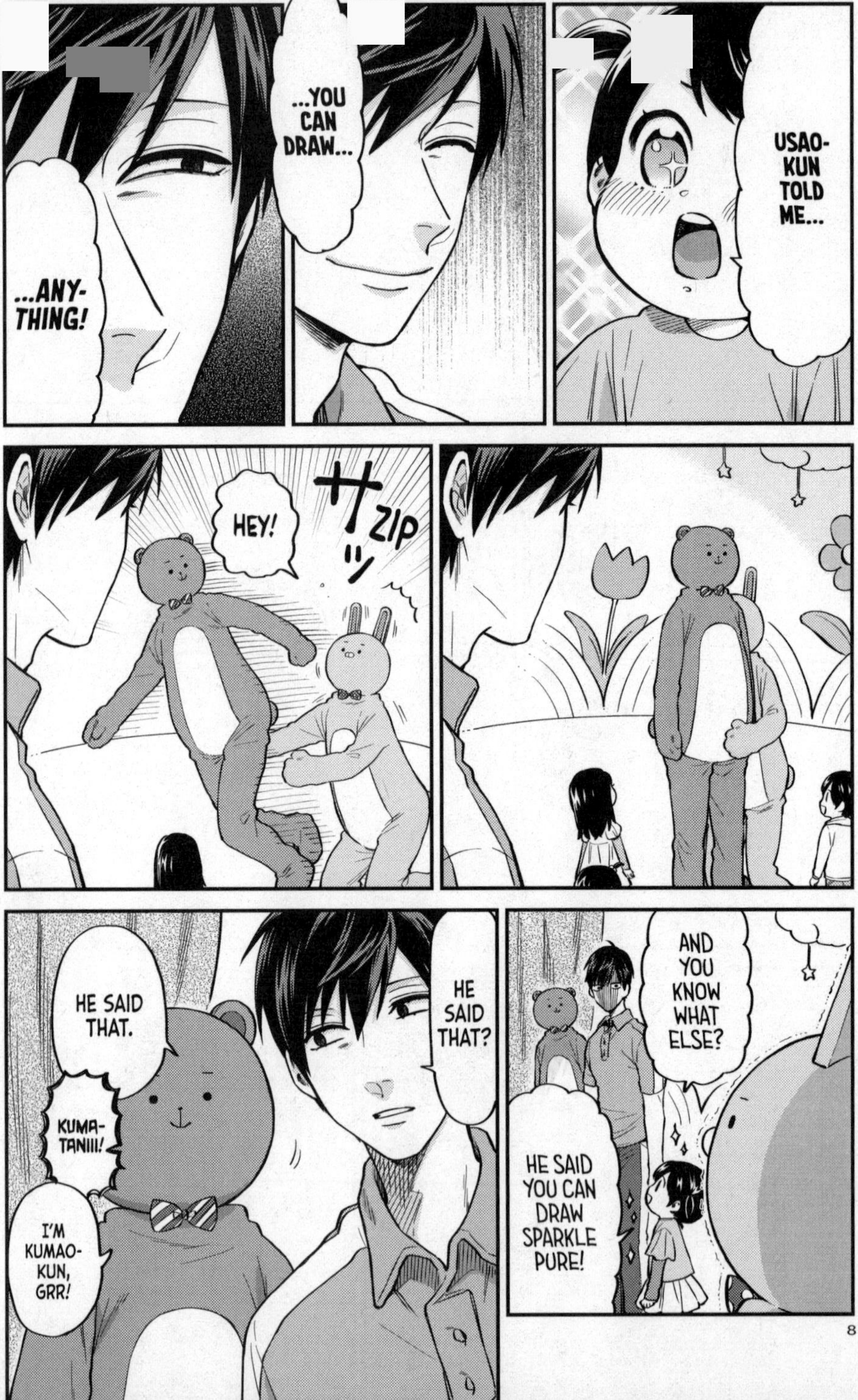
USAO-KUN TOLD ME...
...YOU CAN DRAW...
...ANY-THING!
HEY!
サ ZIP ッ
AND YOU KNOW WHAT ELSE?
HE SAID YOU CAN DRAW SPARKLE PURE!
HE SAID THAT?
HE SAID THAT.
KUMA-TANIII!
I'M KUMAO-KUN, GRR!

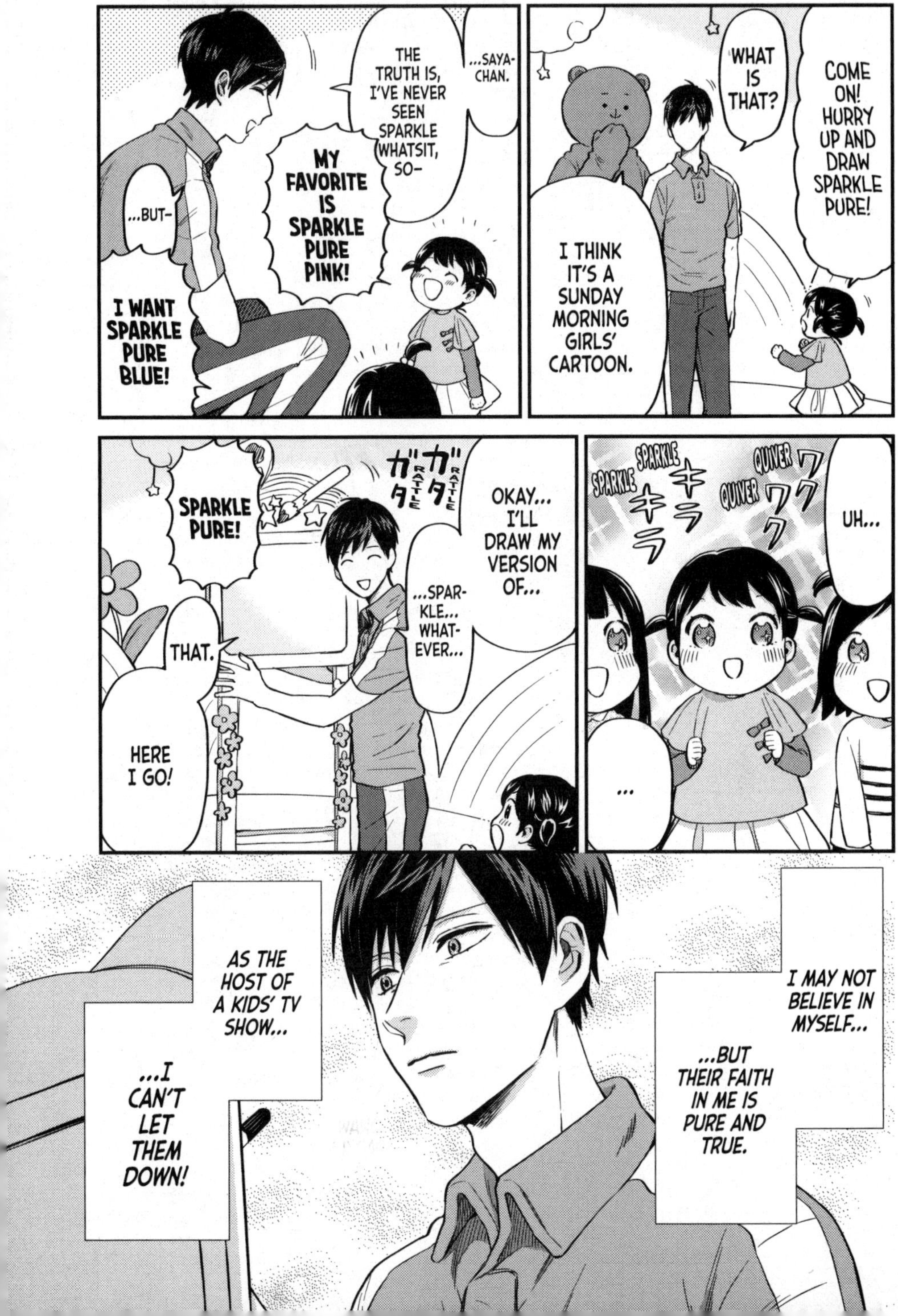
COME ON! HURRY UP AND DRAW SPARKLE PURE!
WHAT IS THAT?
I THINK IT'S A SUNDAY MORNING GIRLS' CARTOON.
...SAYA-CHAN.
THE TRUTH IS, I'VE NEVER SEEN SPARKLE WHATSIT, SO–
MY FAVORITE IS SPARKLE PURE PINK!
...BUT–
I WANT SPARKLE PURE BLUE!
UH...
ワクワク QUIVER QUIVER
キラキラ SPARKLE SPARKLE
...
OKAY... I'LL DRAW MY VERSION OF...
...SPARKLE... WHATEVER...
ガタガタ RATTLE RATTLE
SPARKLE PURE!
THAT.
HERE I GO!
I MAY NOT BELIEVE IN MYSELF...
...BUT THEIR FAITH IN ME IS PURE AND TRUE.
AS THE HOST OF A KIDS' TV SHOW...
...I CAN'T LET THEM DOWN!

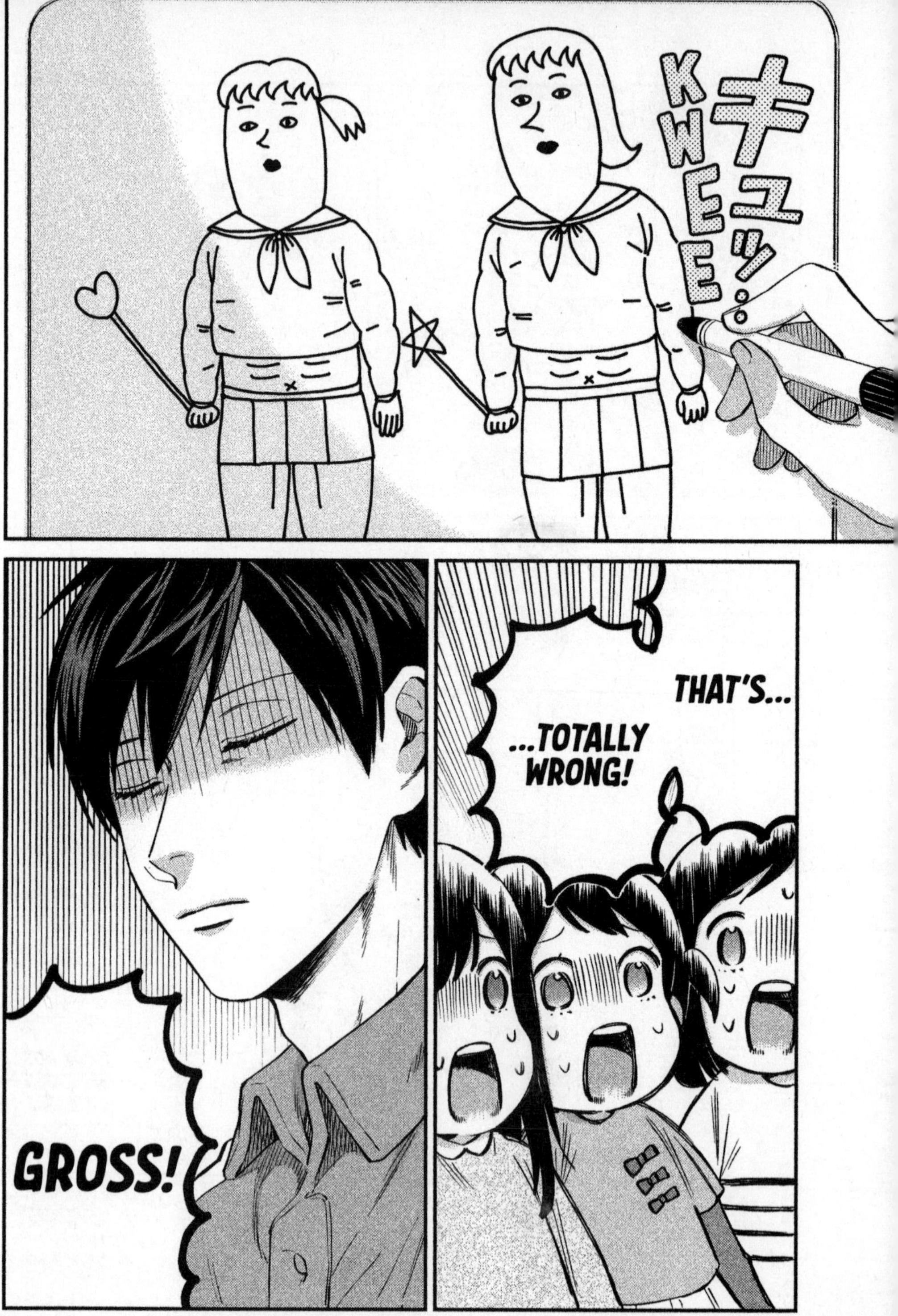
キュッ!
KWEE
THAT'S...
...TOTALLY WRONG!
GROSS!

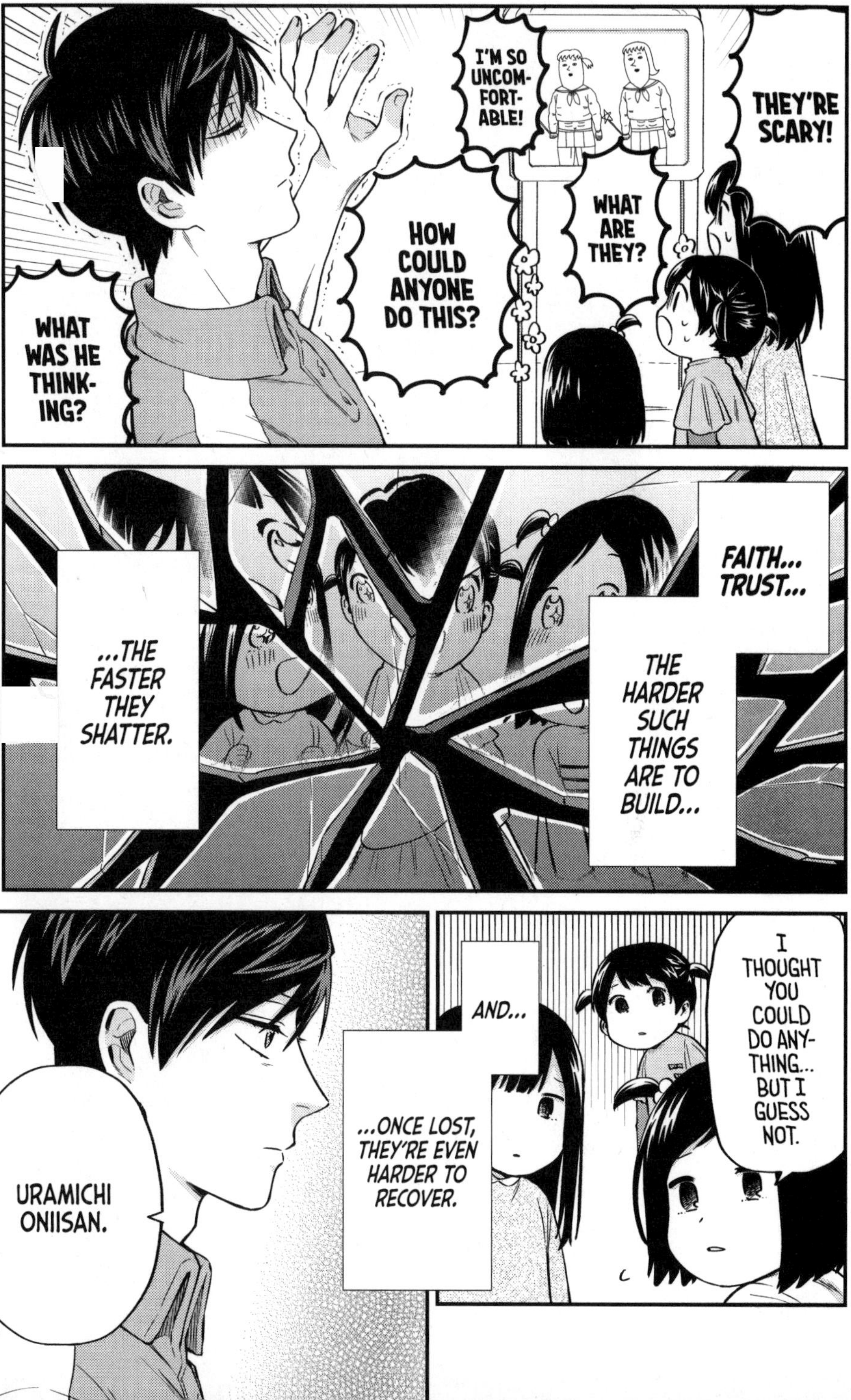

THEY'RE SCARY!
I'M SO UNCOM-FORT-ABLE!
WHAT ARE THEY?
HOW COULD ANYONE DO THIS?
WHAT WAS HE THINK-ING?
FAITH... TRUST...
THE HARDER SUCH THINGS ARE TO BUILD...
...THE FASTER THEY SHATTER.
I THOUGHT YOU COULD DO ANY-THING... BUT I GUESS NOT.
AND...
...ONCE LOST, THEY'RE EVEN HARDER TO RECOVER.
URAMICHI ONIISAN.

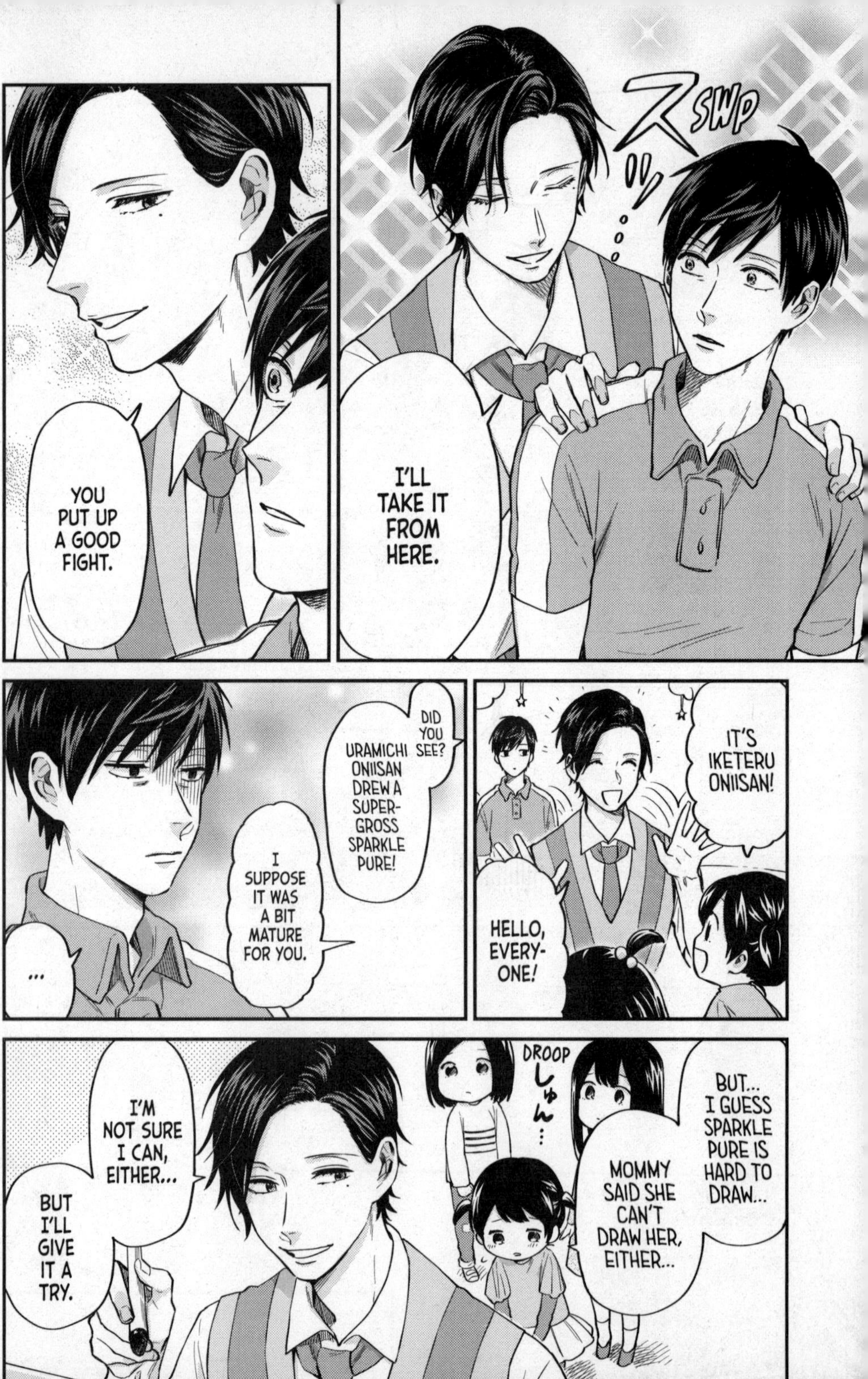
ス SWP
I'LL TAKE IT FROM HERE.
YOU PUT UP A GOOD FIGHT.
IT'S IKETERU ONIISAN!
HELLO, EVERYONE!
DID YOU SEE?
URAMICHI ONIISAN DREW A SUPER-GROSS SPARKLE PURE!
I SUPPOSE IT WAS A BIT MATURE FOR YOU.
...
BUT... I GUESS SPARKLE PURE IS HARD TO DRAW...
DROOP しゅん…
MOMMY SAID SHE CAN'T DRAW HER, EITHER...
I'M NOT SURE I CAN, EITHER...
BUT I'LL GIVE IT A TRY.

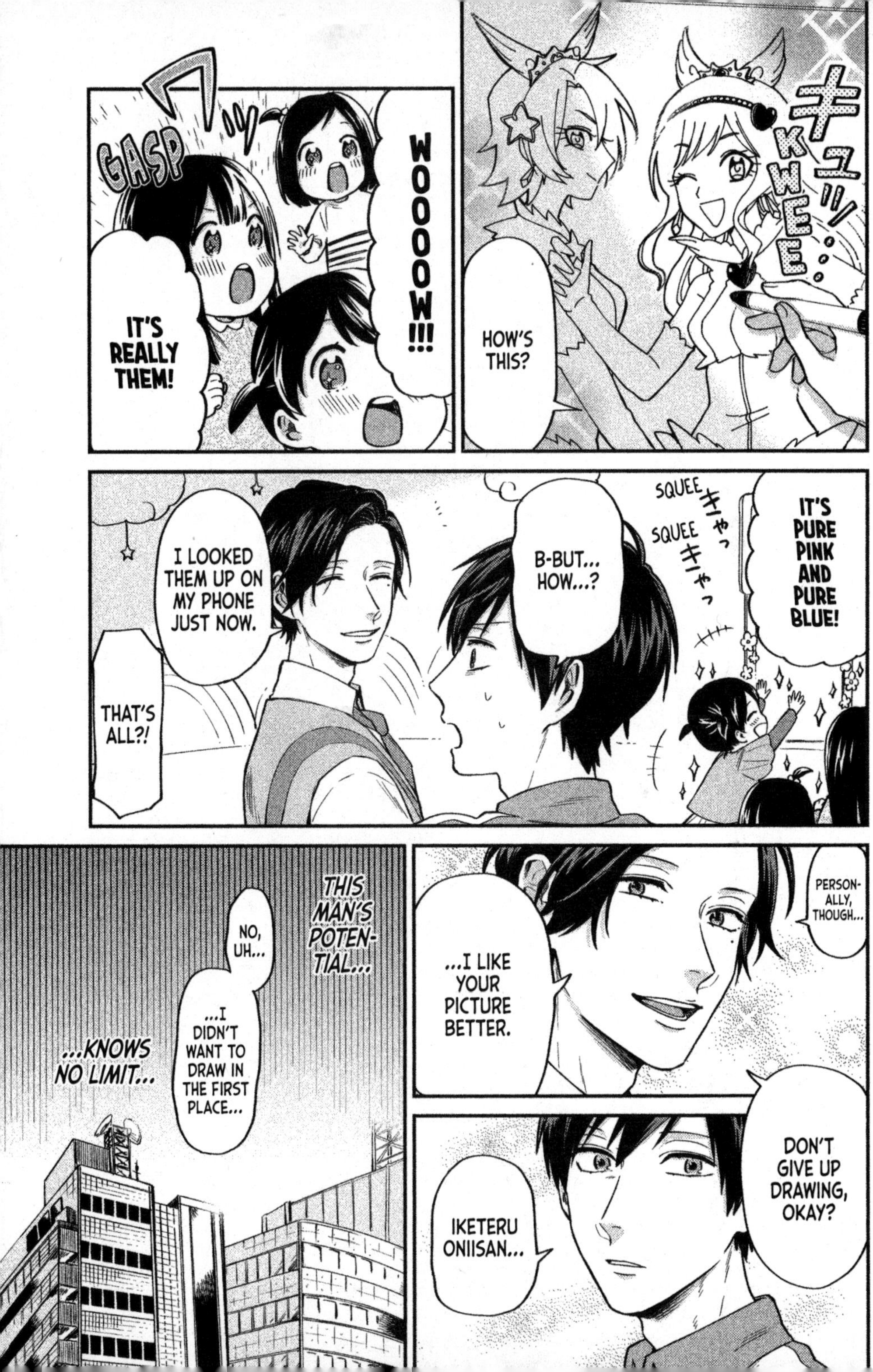

KWEE...
HOW'S THIS?
WOOOOOW!!!
GASP
IT'S REALLY THEM!
IT'S PURE PINK AND PURE BLUE!
SQUEE
SQUEE
B-BUT... HOW...?
I LOOKED THEM UP ON MY PHONE JUST NOW.
THAT'S ALL?!
PERSON-ALLY, THOUGH...
...I LIKE YOUR PICTURE BETTER.
DON'T GIVE UP DRAWING, OKAY?
IKETERU ONIISAN...
THIS MAN'S POTEN-TIAL...
NO, UH...
...I DIDN'T WANT TO DRAW IN THE FIRST PLACE...
...KNOWS NO LIMIT...

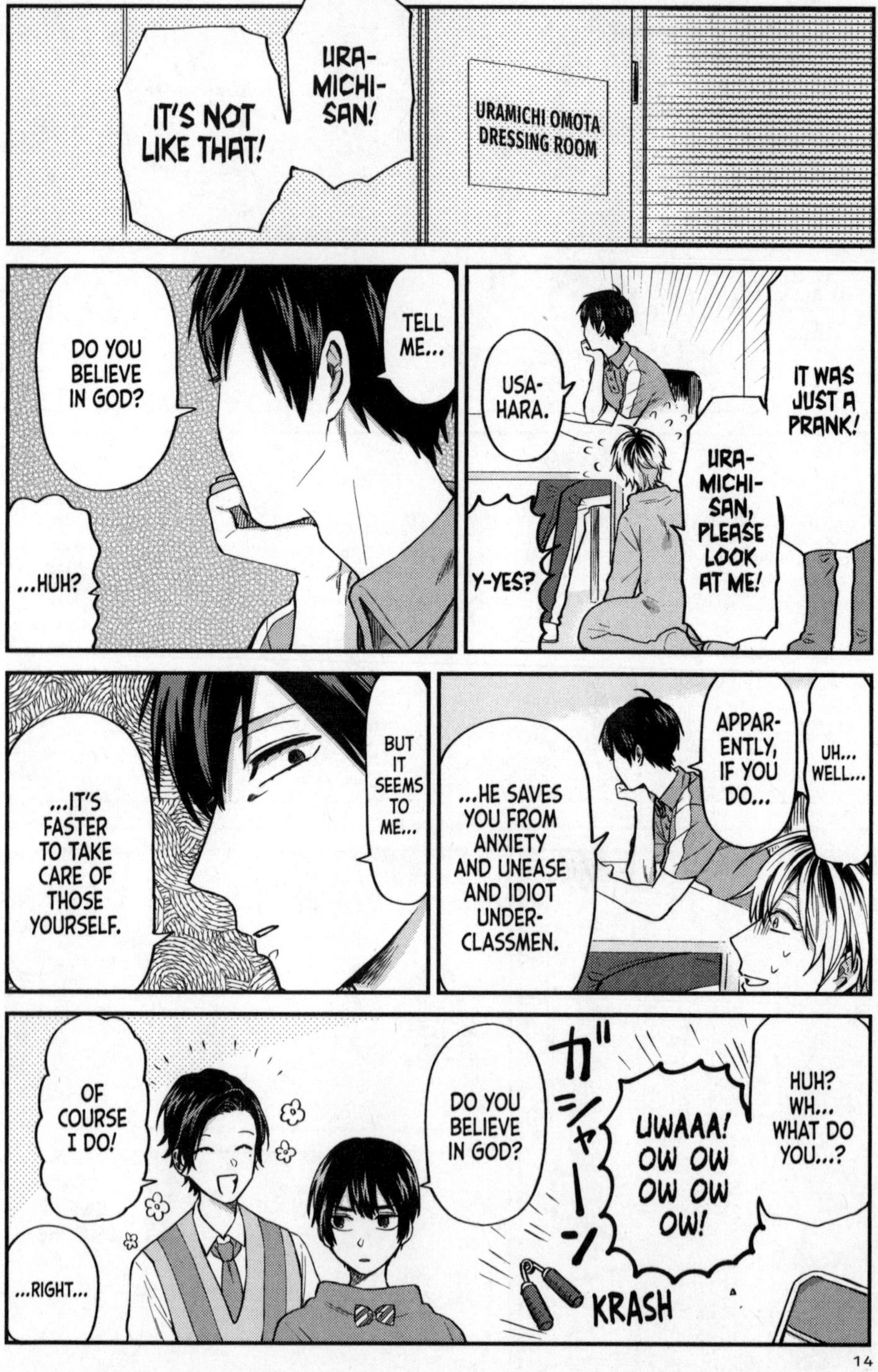
URAMICHI OMOTA DRESSING ROOM
URA-MICHI-SAN!
IT'S NOT LIKE THAT!
IT WAS JUST A PRANK!
URA-MICHI-SAN, PLEASE LOOK AT ME!
USA-HARA.
Y-YES?
TELL ME...
DO YOU BELIEVE IN GOD?
...HUH?
UH... WELL...
APPAR-ENTLY, IF YOU DO...
...HE SAVES YOU FROM ANXIETY AND UNEASE AND IDIOT UNDER-CLASSMEN.
BUT IT SEEMS TO ME...
...IT'S FASTER TO TAKE CARE OF THOSE YOURSELF.
HUH? WH... WHAT DO YOU...?
ガシャーン
UWAAA! OW OW OW OW OW!
KRASH
DO YOU BELIEVE IN GOD?
OF COURSE I DO!
...RIGHT...

Life Lessons with
Uramichi Oniisan

When I Put My Hand Up, A Taxi Stopped

Sung by Iketeru Oniisan and Utano Oneesan

I asked who was coming to the next bar
But when I put my hand up, a taxi stopped

They never stop when you want a ride

Sorry, no... I didn't—
Right... This isn't—

That one cute girl had no plans to come to the bar
That one cute girl hopped right into the cab

It never works out how you intend
I'm never organizing a group night out again

"I'd like a chance to talk to you properly"
I guess that was a big fat lie

It's burned in my mind
The night I entertained clients, got so drunk I almost died
The taxi that passed me by

I was even ready to pay the 20% late-night fee
I raised my hand bravely, but the cab ignored me

Why did a taxi have to stop now?
Is she going to the next bar, yes or no?

I asked who was coming to the next bar
But when I put my hand up, a taxi stopped

I stand and watch the receding white light
Carrying that one cute girl into the night

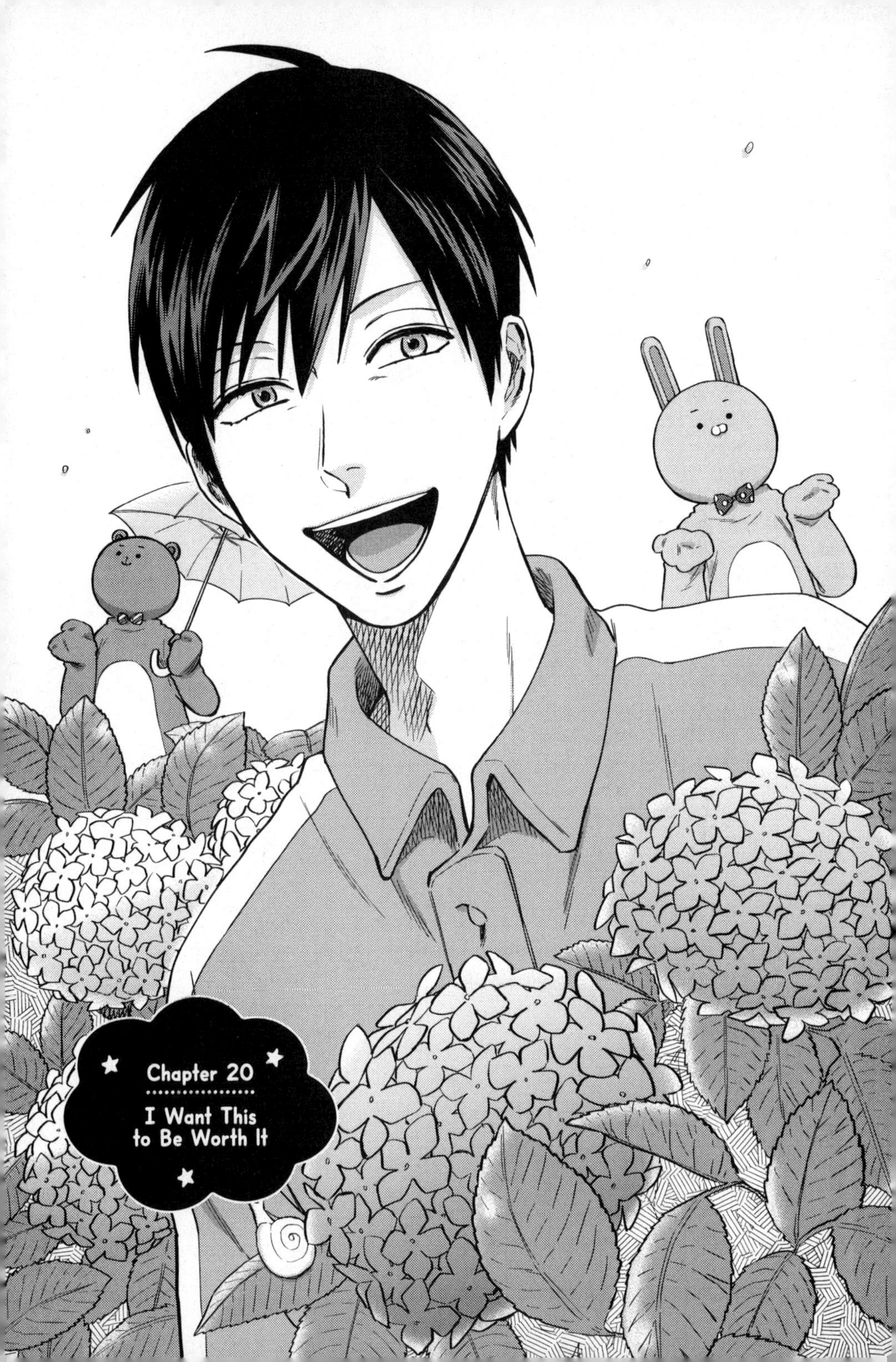
Chapter 20
I Want This to Be Worth It

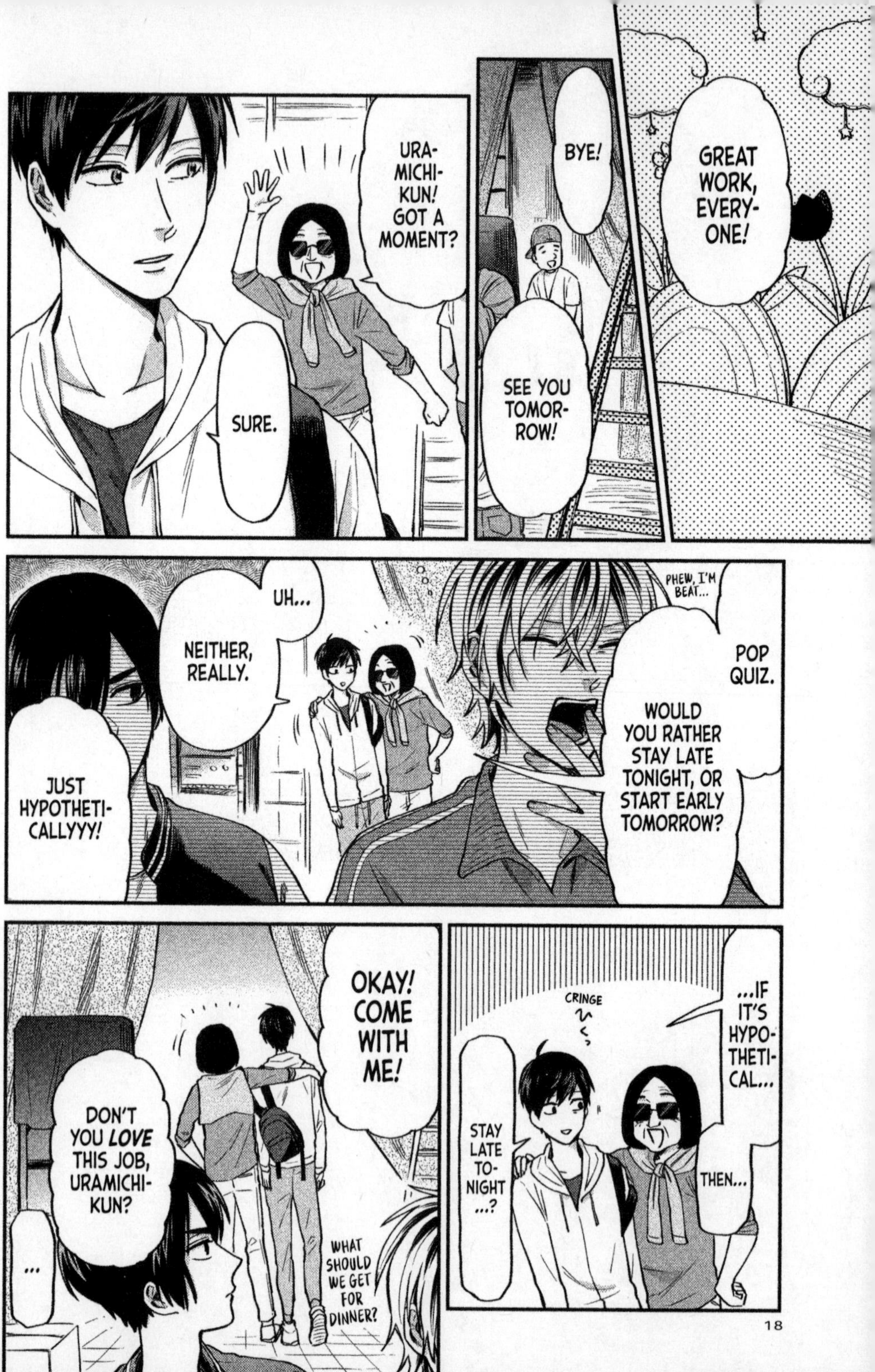
GREAT WORK, EVERYONE!
BYE!
SEE YOU TOMORROW!
URA-MICHI-KUN! GOT A MOMENT?
SURE.
PHEW, I'M BEAT...
POP QUIZ.
WOULD YOU RATHER STAY LATE TONIGHT, OR START EARLY TOMORROW?
UH...
NEITHER, REALLY.
JUST HYPOTHETI-CALLYYY!
...IF IT'S HYPO-THETI-CAL...
CRINGE
THEN...
STAY LATE TO-NIGHT ...?
OKAY! COME WITH ME!
DON'T YOU *LOVE* THIS JOB, URAMICHI-KUN?
WHAT SHOULD WE GET FOR DINNER?
...

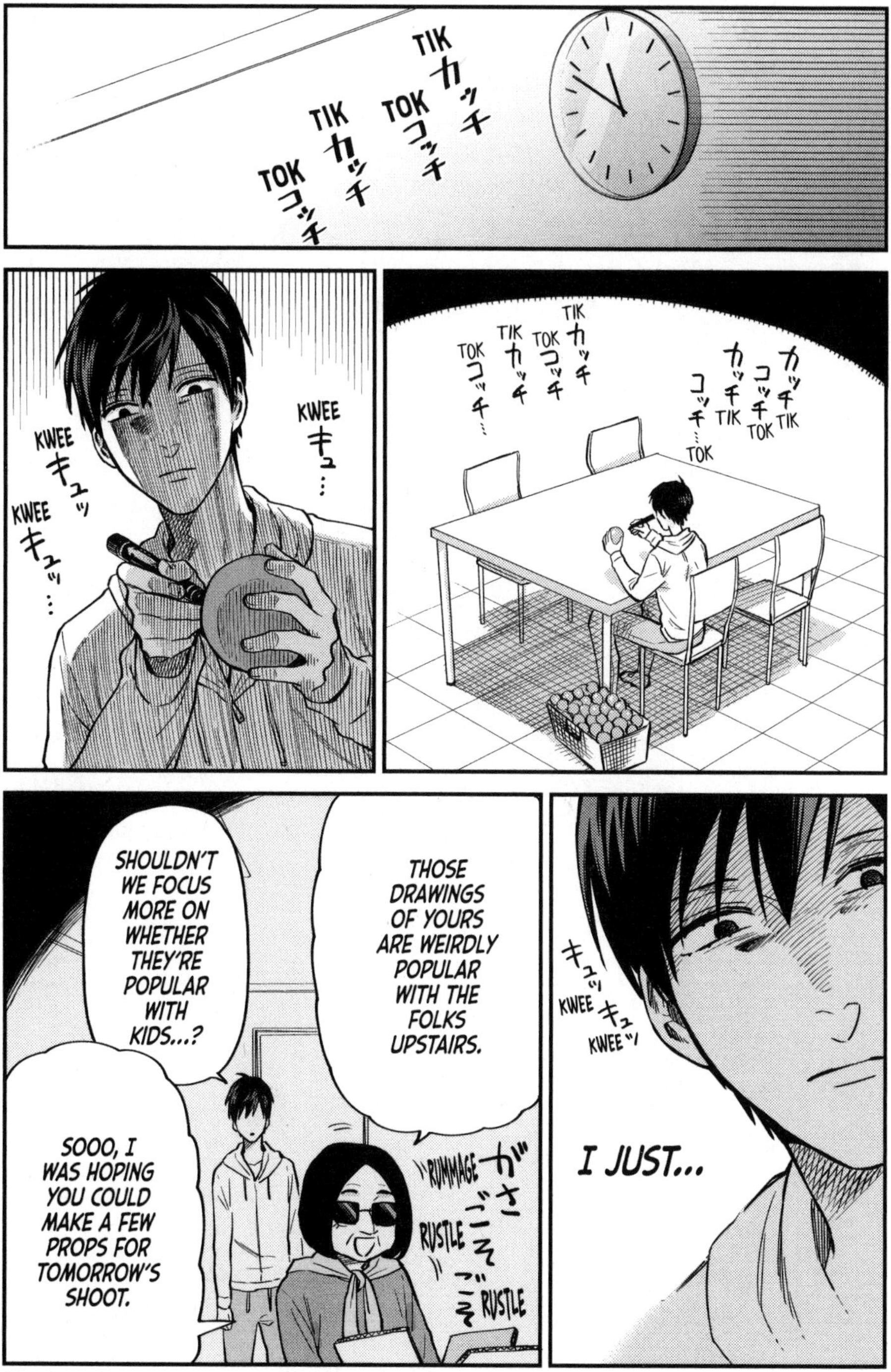
TIK カッチ
TOK コッチ
TIK カッチ
TOK コッチ
カッチ TIK
コッチ TOK
カッチ TIK
コッチ… TOK
TIK カッチ
TOK コッチ
TIK カッチ
TOK コッチ…
KWEE キュ…
KWEE キュッ
KWEE キュッ…
キュッ KWEE
キュッ KWEE
I JUST...
THOSE DRAWINGS OF YOURS ARE WEIRDLY POPULAR WITH THE FOLKS UPSTAIRS.
SHOULDN'T WE FOCUS MORE ON WHETHER THEY'RE POPULAR WITH KIDS...?
RUMMAGE がさ
RUSTLE ごそ
RUSTLE ごそ
SOOO, I WAS HOPING YOU COULD MAKE A FEW PROPS FOR TOMORROW'S SHOOT.

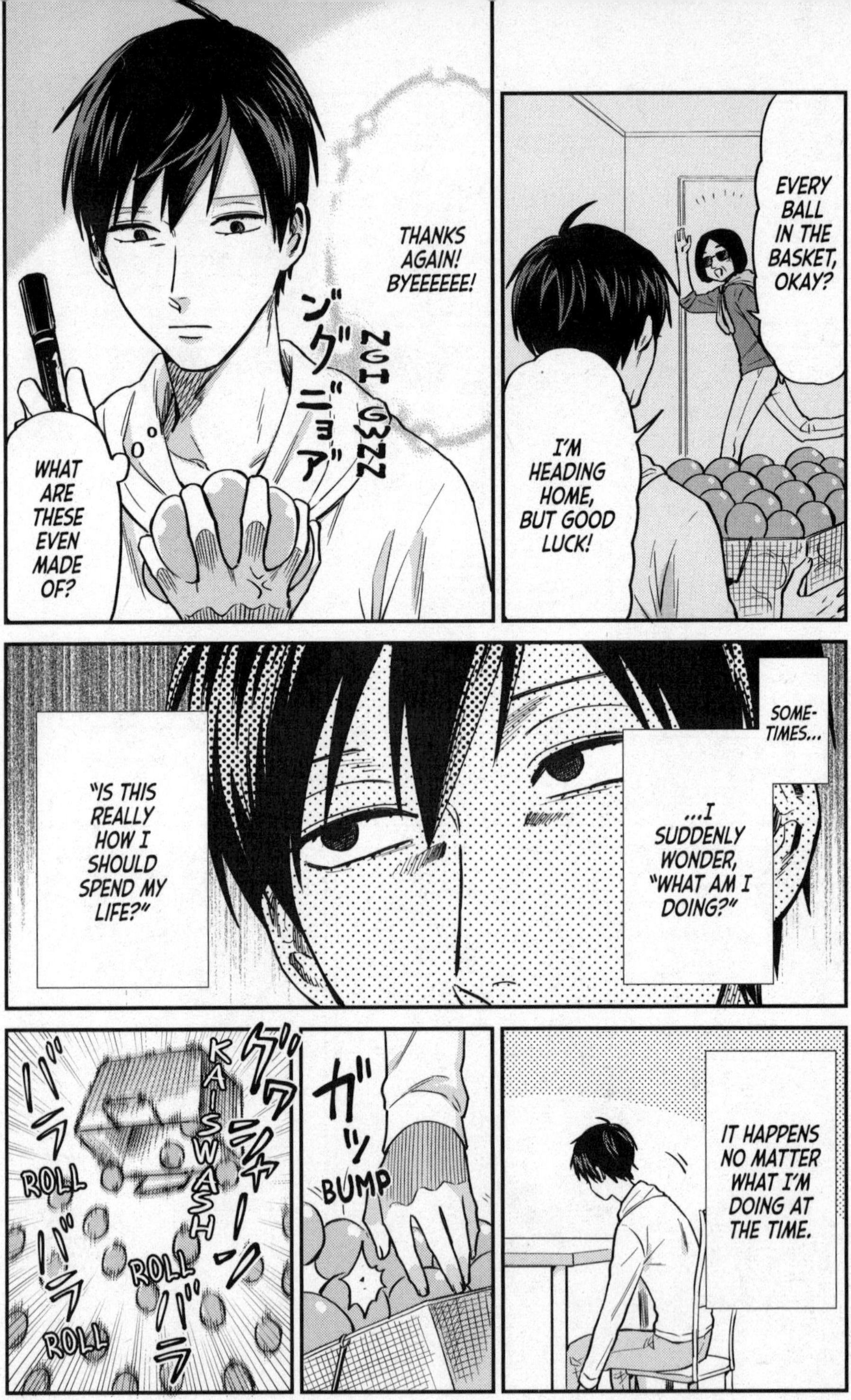

EVERY BALL IN THE BASKET, OKAY?
I'M HEADING HOME, BUT GOOD LUCK!
THANKS AGAIN! BYEEEEEE!
ングニョア
NGH GWNN
WHAT ARE THESE EVEN MADE OF?
SOME-TIMES...
...I SUDDENLY WONDER, "WHAT AM I DOING?"
"IS THIS REALLY HOW I SHOULD SPEND MY LIFE?"
IT HAPPENS NO MATTER WHAT I'M DOING AT THE TIME.
ガッ
BUMP
グワシャーン
KAISWASH
バラ
ROLL
バラ
ROLL
バラ
ROLL

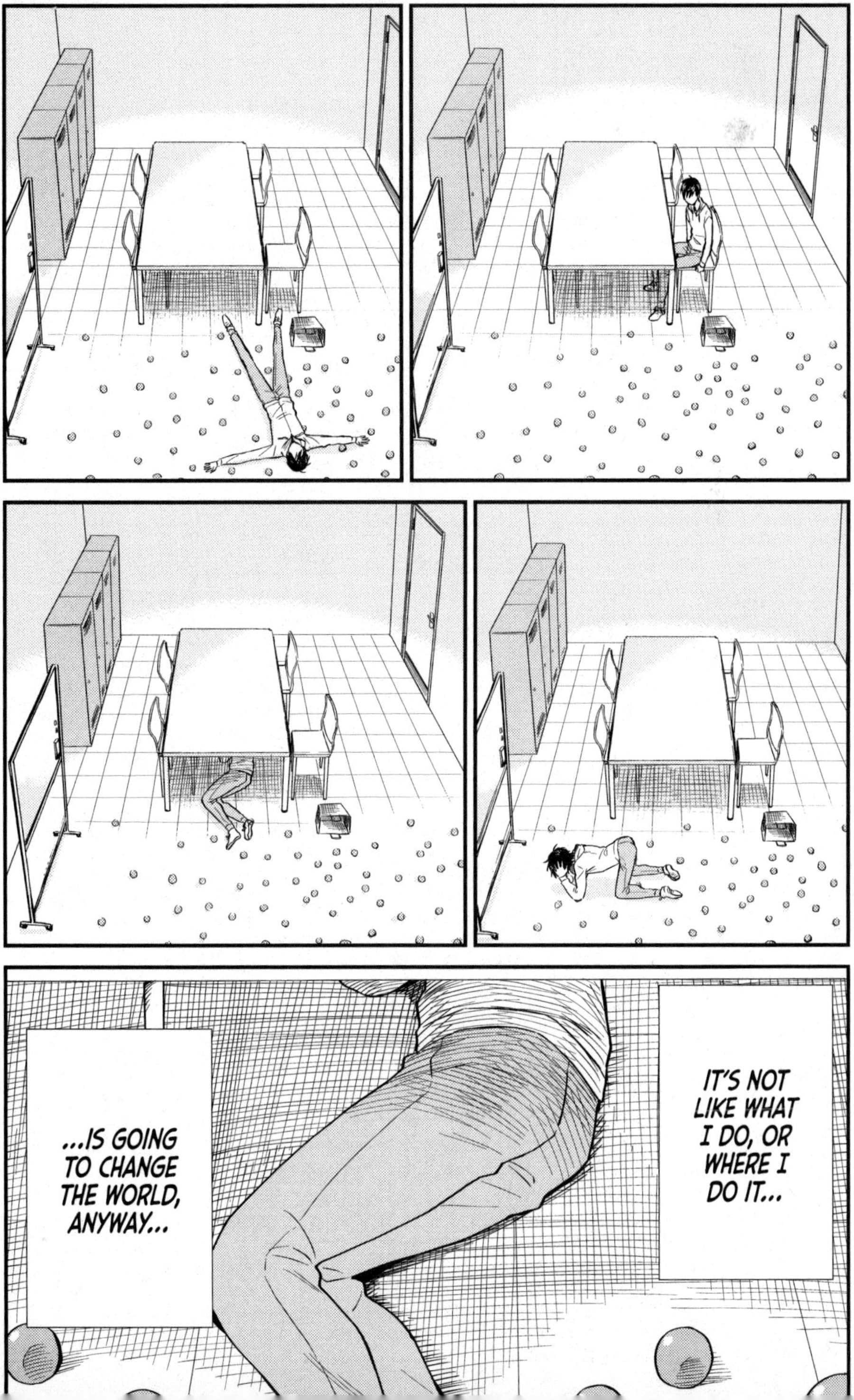
IT'S NOT LIKE WHAT I DO, OR WHERE I DO IT...
...IS GOING TO CHANGE THE WORLD, ANYWAY...

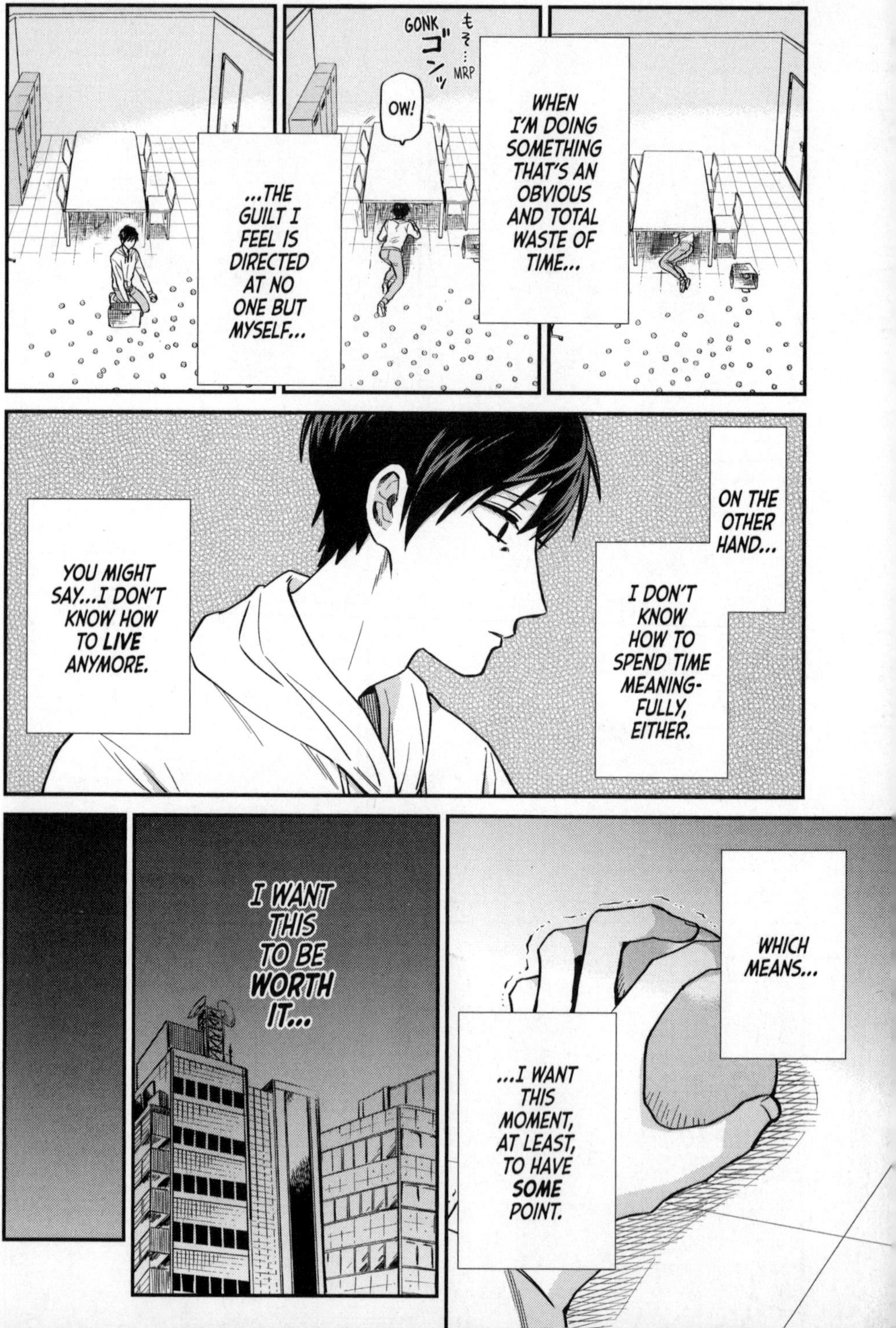
WHEN I'M DOING SOMETHING THAT'S AN OBVIOUS AND TOTAL WASTE OF TIME...
もぞ…
MRP
ゴンッ
GONK
OW!
...THE GUILT I FEEL IS DIRECTED AT NO ONE BUT MYSELF...
ON THE OTHER HAND...
I DON'T KNOW HOW TO SPEND TIME MEANING-FULLY, EITHER.
YOU MIGHT SAY...I DON'T KNOW HOW TO LIVE ANYMORE.
WHICH MEANS...
...I WANT THIS MOMENT, AT LEAST, TO HAVE SOME POINT.
I WANT THIS TO BE WORTH IT...

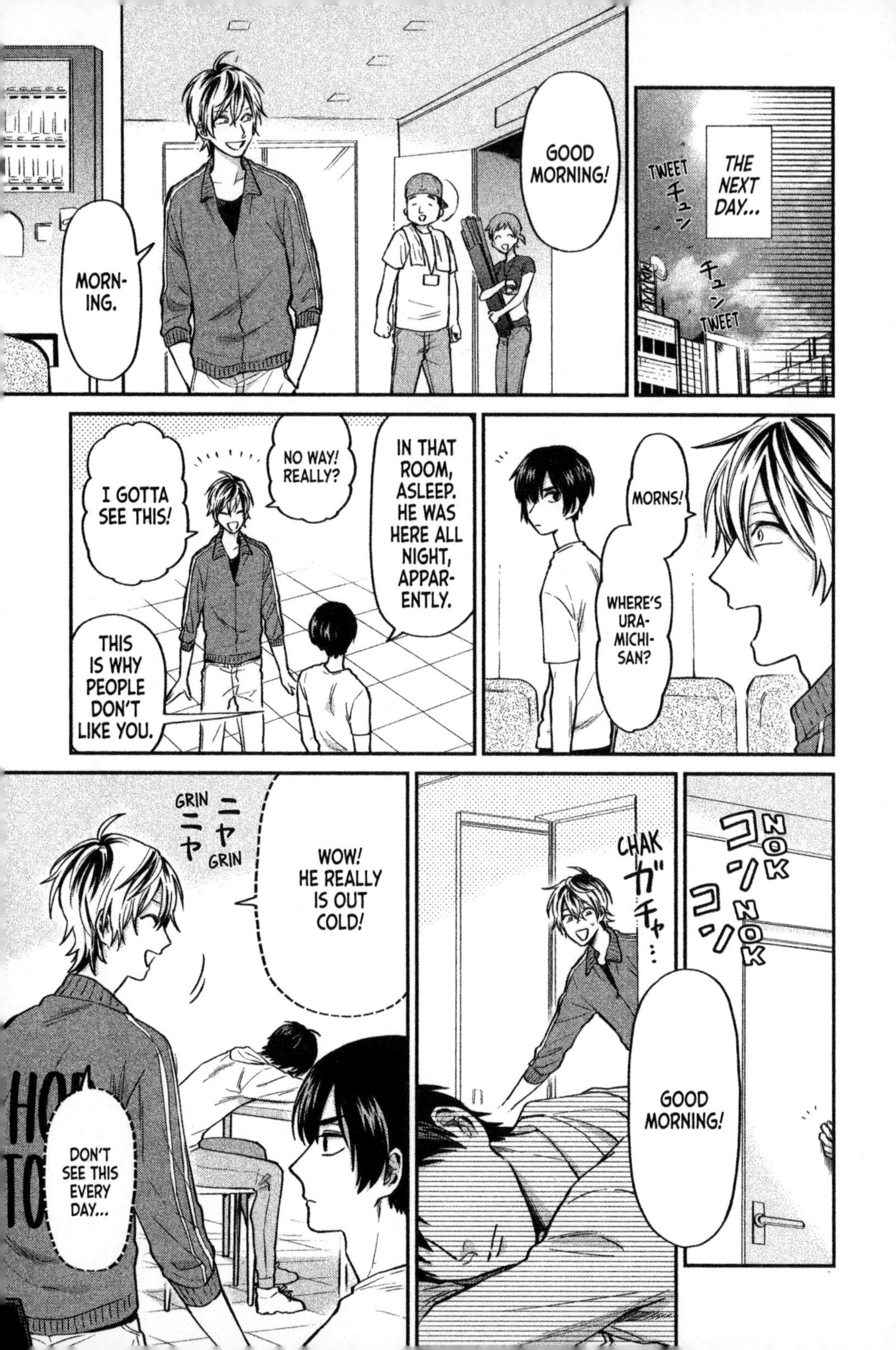
THE NEXT DAY...
TWEET チュン
チュン TWEET
GOOD MORNING!
MORN-ING.
MORNS!
WHERE'S URA-MICHI-SAN?
IN THAT ROOM, ASLEEP. HE WAS HERE ALL NIGHT, APPARENTLY.
NO WAY! REALLY?
I GOTTA SEE THIS!
THIS IS WHY PEOPLE DON'T LIKE YOU.
NOK コン
NOK コン
CHAK ガチャ...
GOOD MORNING!
GRIN ニヤ
GRIN ニヤ
WOW! HE REALLY IS OUT COLD!
DON'T SEE THIS EVERY DAY...

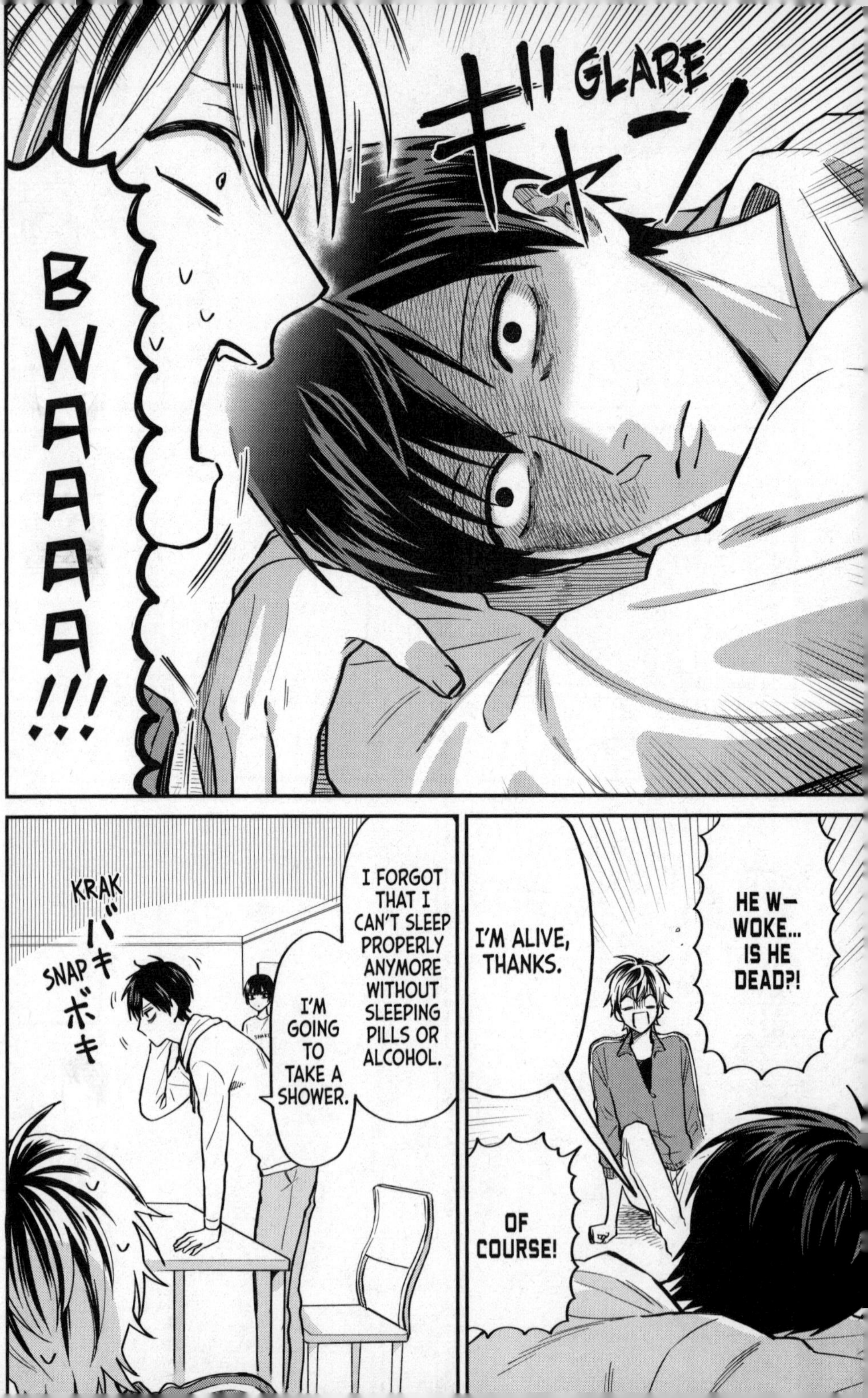

キャー!
GLARE
BWAAAAA!!!
HE W— WOKE... IS HE DEAD?!
I'M ALIVE, THANKS.
OF COURSE!
I FORGOT THAT I CAN'T SLEEP PROPERLY ANYMORE WITHOUT SLEEPING PILLS OR ALCOHOL.
I'M GOING TO TAKE A SHOWER.
バキ
KRAK
ボキ
SNAP

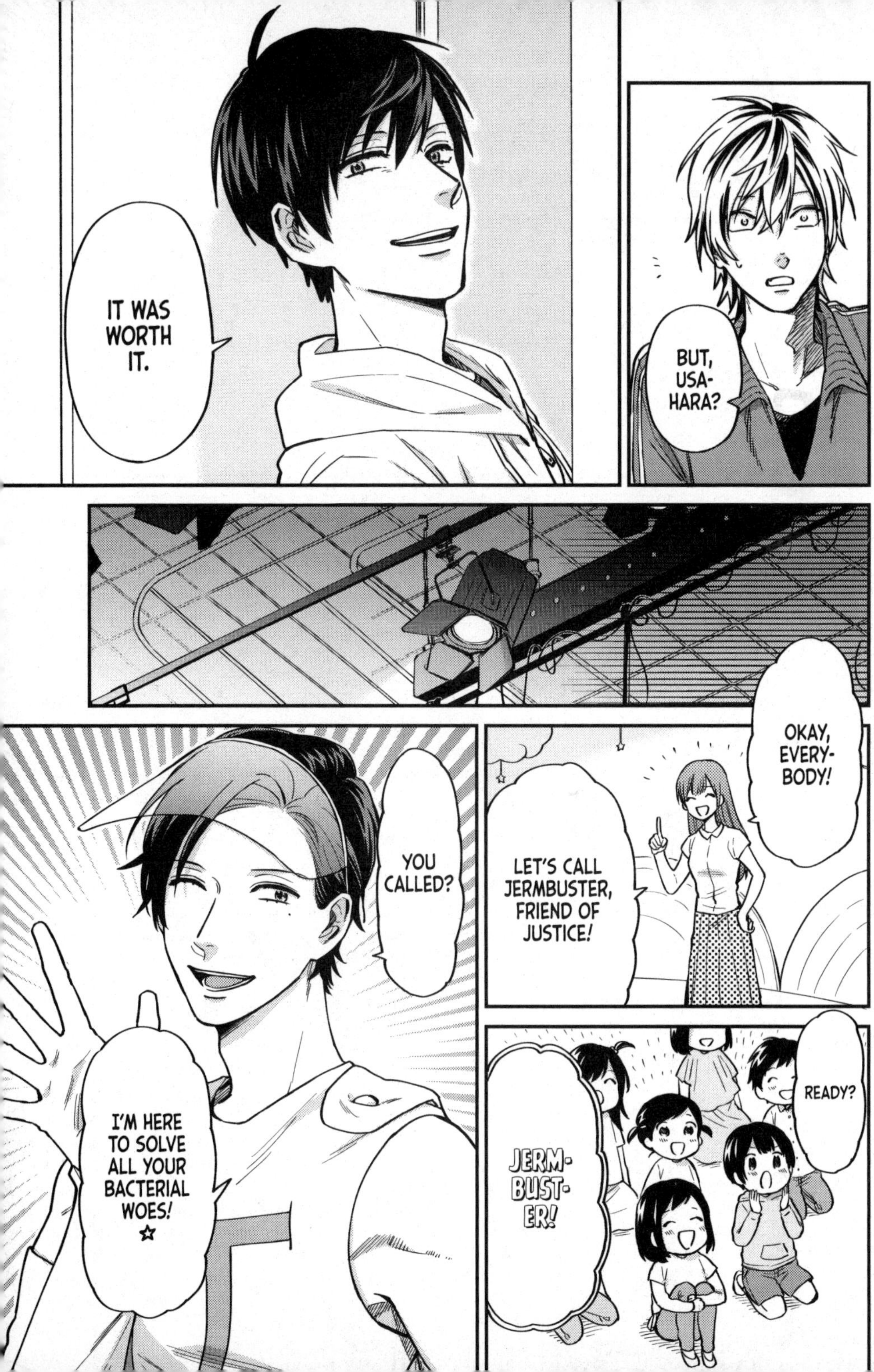
BUT, USA-HARA?
IT WAS WORTH IT.
OKAY, EVERY-BODY!
LET'S CALL JERMBUSTER, FRIEND OF JUSTICE!
READY?
JERM-BUST-ER!
YOU CALLED?
I'M HERE TO SOLVE ALL YOUR BACTERIAL WOES! ☆

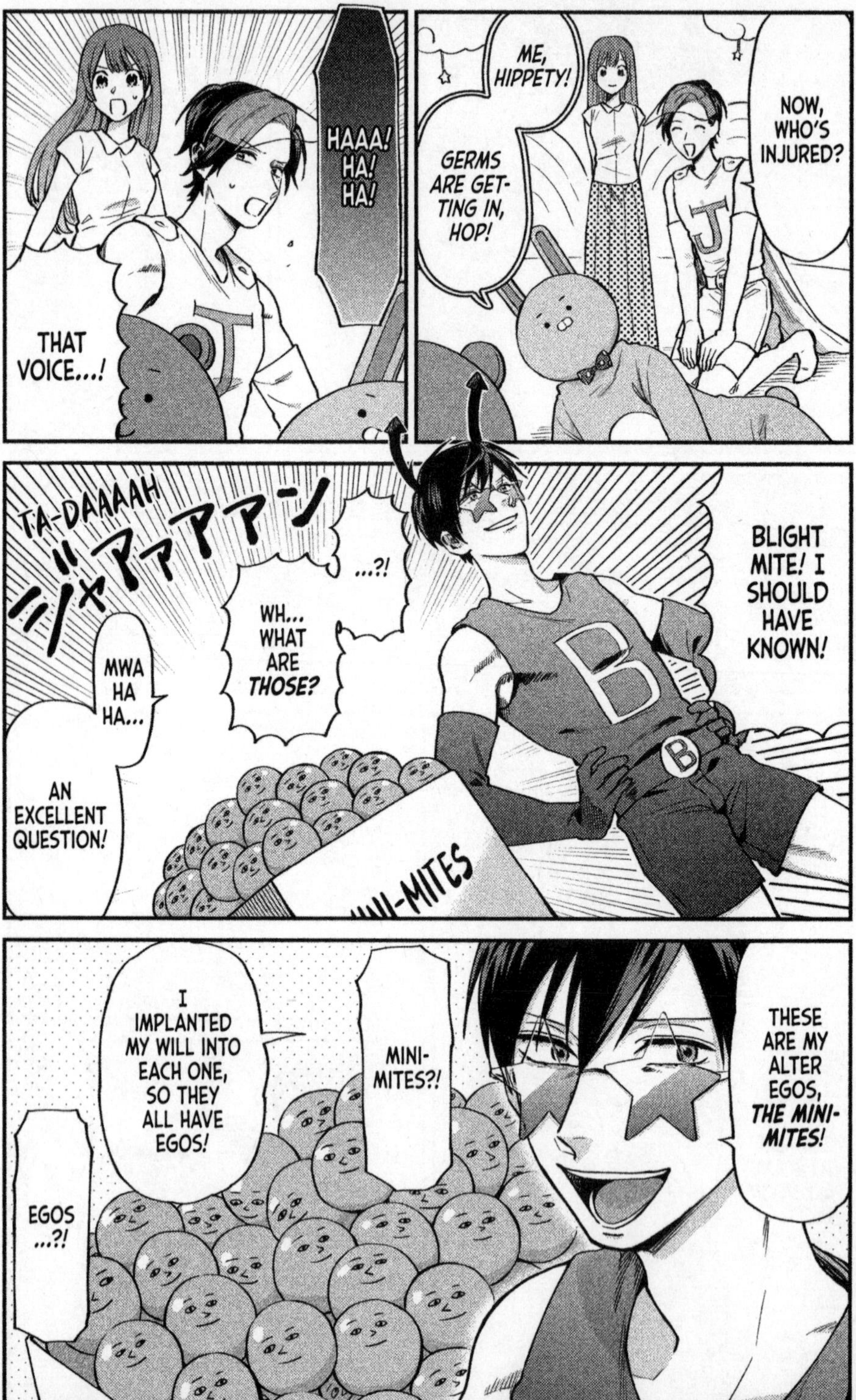
NOW, WHO'S INJURED?
ME, HIPPETY!
GERMS ARE GETTING IN, HOP!
HAAA! HA! HA!
THAT VOICE...!
BLIGHT MITE! I SHOULD HAVE KNOWN!
TA-DAAAAH
ジャァアアーン
...?!
WH... WHAT ARE THOSE?
MWA HA HA...
AN EXCELLENT QUESTION!
NI-MITES
THESE ARE MY ALTER EGOS, THE MINI-MITES!
MINI-MITES?!
I IMPLANTED MY WILL INTO EACH ONE, SO THEY ALL HAVE EGOS!
EGOS ...?!

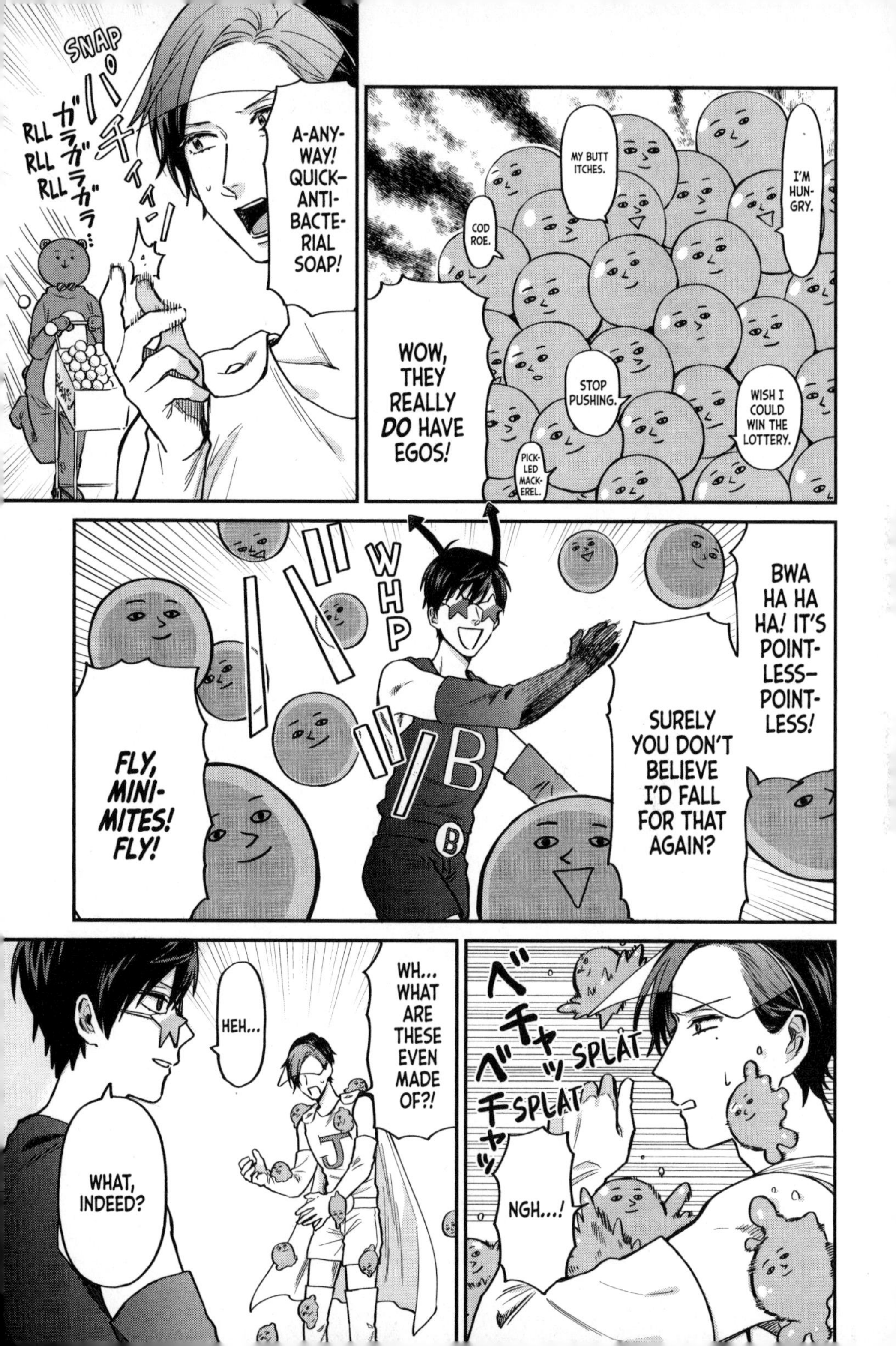
I'M HUNGRY.
MY BUTT ITCHES.
COD ROE.
WISH I COULD WIN THE LOTTERY.
STOP PUSHING.
WOW, THEY REALLY DO HAVE EGOS!
PICKLED MACKEREL.
A-ANYWAY! QUICK-ANTI-BACTERIAL SOAP!
SNAP
RLL RLL RLL
BWA HA HA HA! IT'S POINTLESS-POINTLESS!
SURELY YOU DON'T BELIEVE I'D FALL FOR THAT AGAIN?
WHP
FLY, MINIMITES! FLY!
SPLAT
SPLAT
NGH...!
WH... WHAT ARE THESE EVEN MADE OF?!
HEH...
WHAT, INDEED?

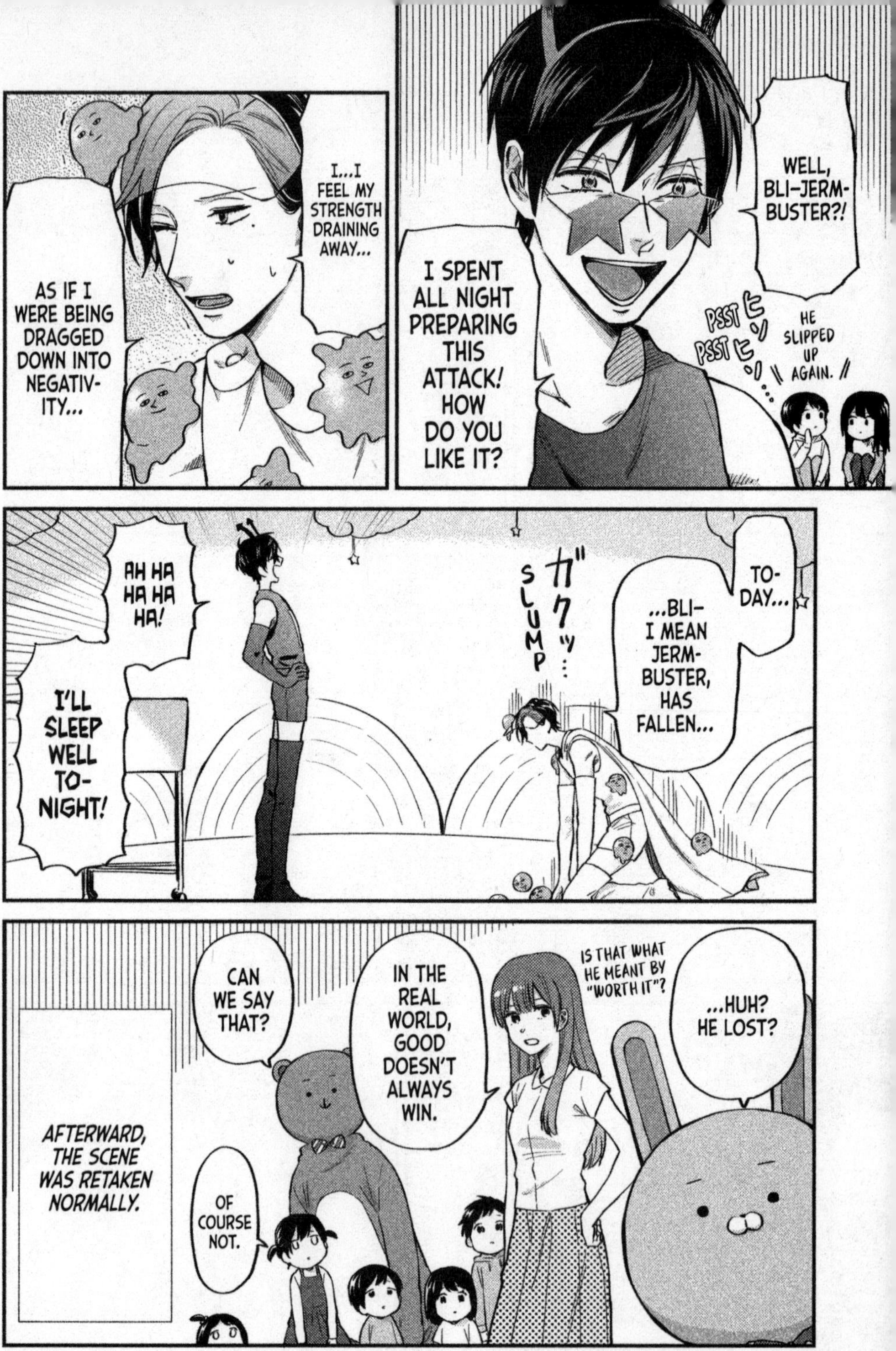
WELL, BLI-JERM-BUSTER?!
I SPENT ALL NIGHT PREPARING THIS ATTACK! HOW DO YOU LIKE IT?
PSSST ヒソ PSSST ヒソ
HE SLIPPED UP AGAIN.
I...I FEEL MY STRENGTH DRAINING AWAY...
AS IF I WERE BEING DRAGGED DOWN INTO NEGATIV-ITY...
TO-DAY...
...BLI- I MEAN JERM-BUSTER, HAS FALLEN...
ガクッ… SLUMP
AH HA HA HA HA!
I'LL SLEEP WELL TO-NIGHT!
...HUH? HE LOST?
IS THAT WHAT HE MEANT BY "WORTH IT"?
IN THE REAL WORLD, GOOD DOESN'T ALWAYS WIN.
CAN WE SAY THAT?
OF COURSE NOT.
AFTERWARD, THE SCENE WAS RETAKEN NORMALLY.

Life Lessons with
Uramichi Oniisan

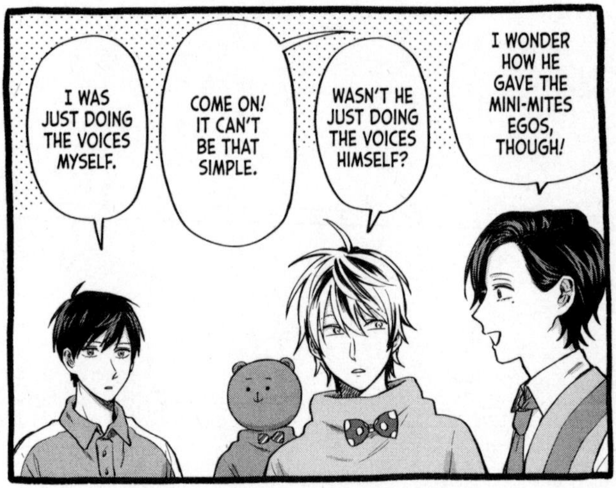
I WONDER HOW HE GAVE THE MINI-MITES EGOS, THOUGH!
WASN'T HE JUST DOING THE VOICES HIMSELF?
COME ON! IT CAN'T BE THAT SIMPLE.
I WAS JUST DOING THE VOICES MYSELF.

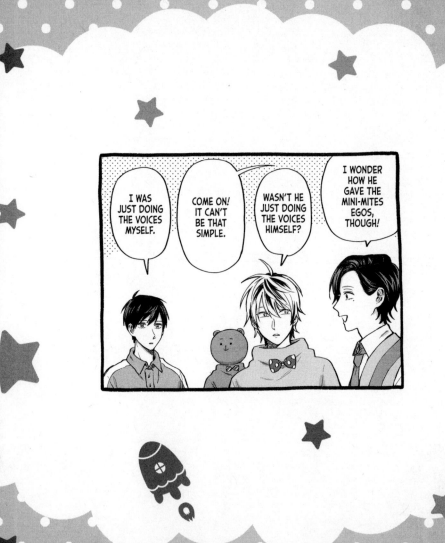

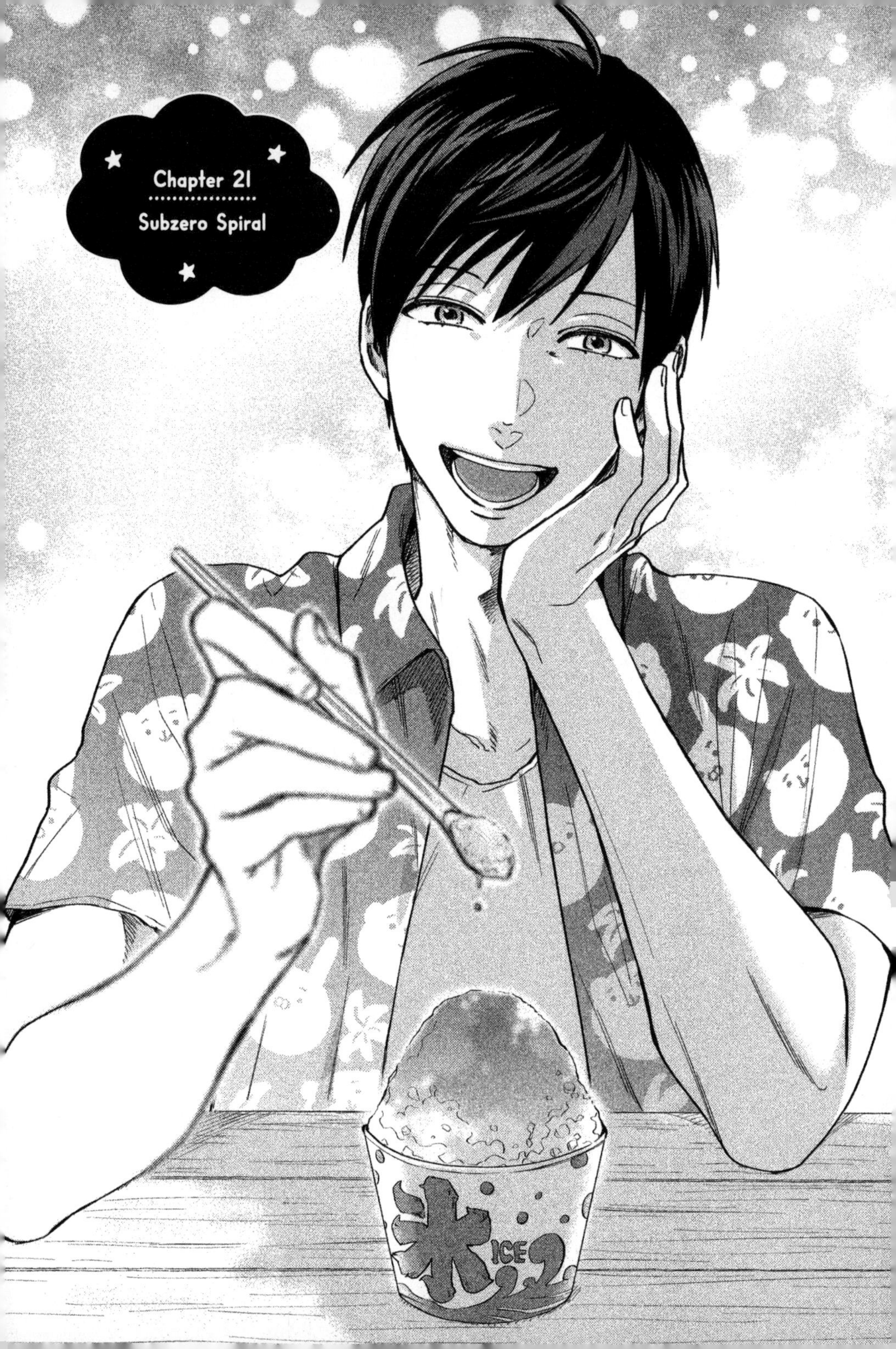
Chapter 21
Subzero Spiral
氷
ICE

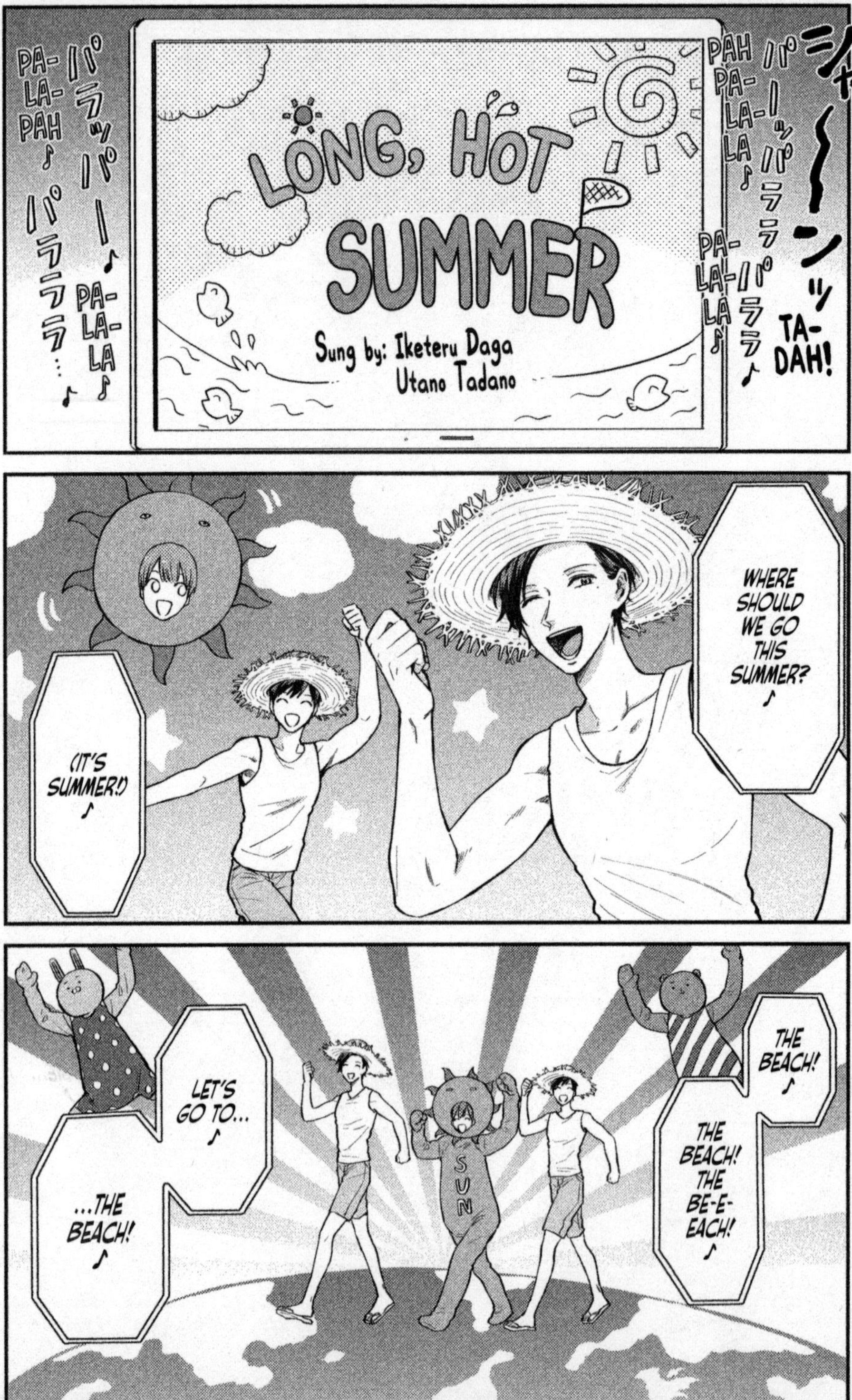
ジャ〜〜ンッ
TA-DAH!
パーッパパラララ♪
PAH PA-LA-LA♪
パラララ♪
PA-LA-LA♪
LONG, HOT SUMMER
Sung by: Iketeru Daga Utano Tadano
パラッパー♪
PA-LA-PAH♪
パラララ…♪
PA-LA-LA♪
WHERE SHOULD WE GO THIS SUMMER? ♪
(IT'S SUMMER!) ♪
THE BEACH! ♪
LET'S GO TO… ♪
THE BEACH! THE BEACH! THE BE-E-EACH! ♪
…THE BEACH! ♪

IT'S SUM-MER, AFTER ALL... ♪
(SUM-MER, AFTER ALL...) ♪
LET'S GET STUPID ON THE BEACH! ♪
WE CAN HAVE A BARBECUE... ♪
PRETEND TO HAVE FUN, SO NOBODY CAN TELL... ♪
...THAT I SPEND MY LIFE... ♪
...WORRIED WHAT OTHER PEOPLE THINK! ♪
AA-AH, THIS ACT DOESN'T SUIT ME... ♪
OH, WELL, HERE IT COMES, BETTER START ACTING DUMBER- ♪
THE LONG, HOT SUMMER! ♪

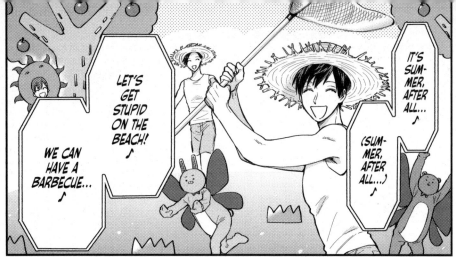

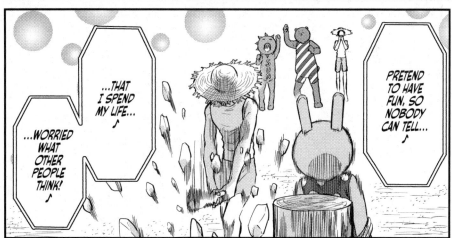

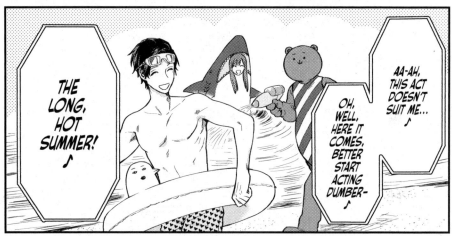

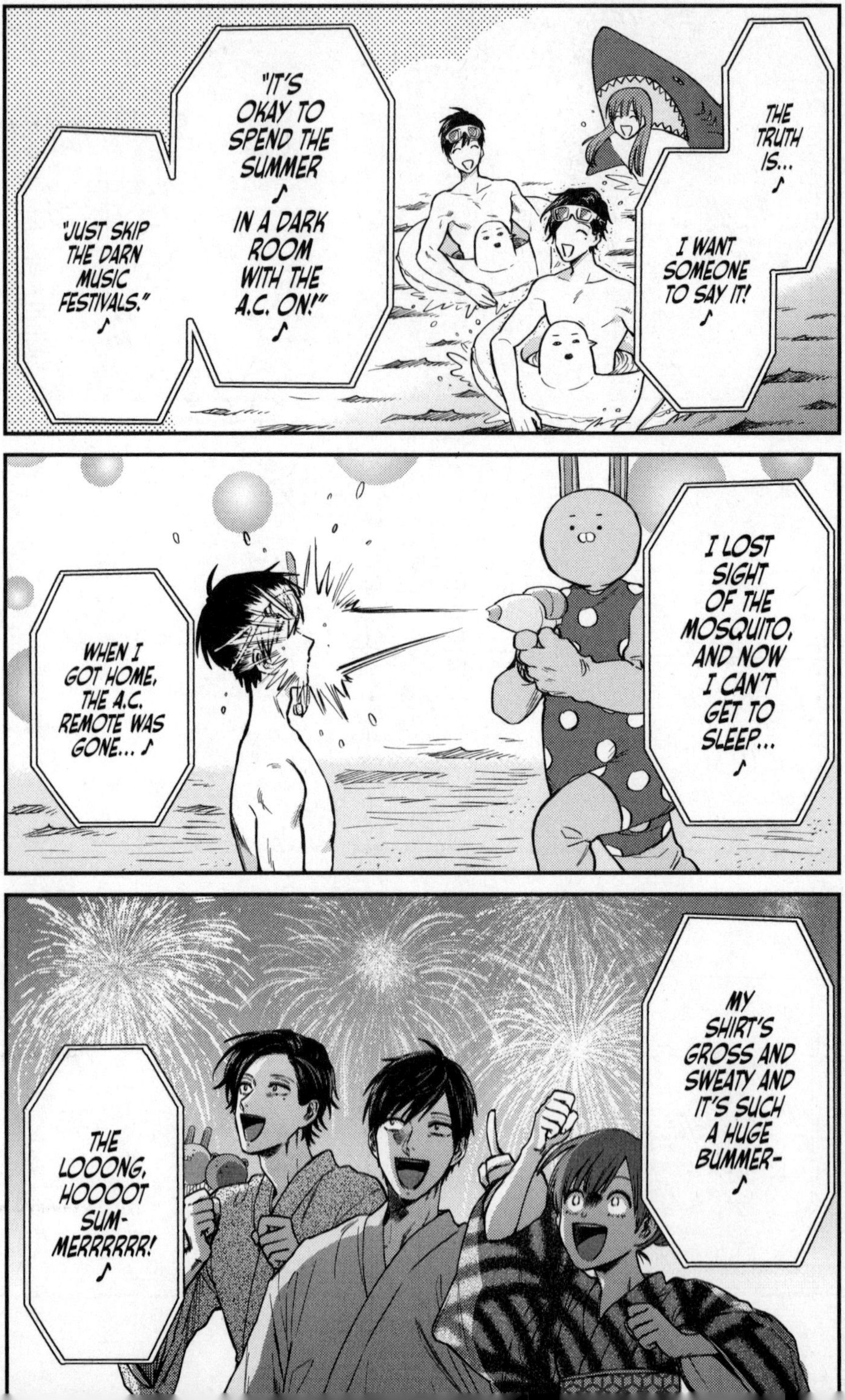
THE TRUTH IS... ♪ I WANT SOMEONE TO SAY IT! ♪
"IT'S OKAY TO SPEND THE SUMMER ♪ IN A DARK ROOM WITH THE A.C. ON!" ♪
"JUST SKIP THE DARN MUSIC FESTIVALS." ♪
I LOST SIGHT OF THE MOSQUITO, AND NOW I CAN'T GET TO SLEEP... ♪
WHEN I GOT HOME, THE A.C. REMOTE WAS GONE... ♪
MY SHIRT'S GROSS AND SWEATY AND IT'S SUCH A HUGE BUMMER- ♪
THE LOOONG, HOOOOT SUM-MERRRRRR! ♪

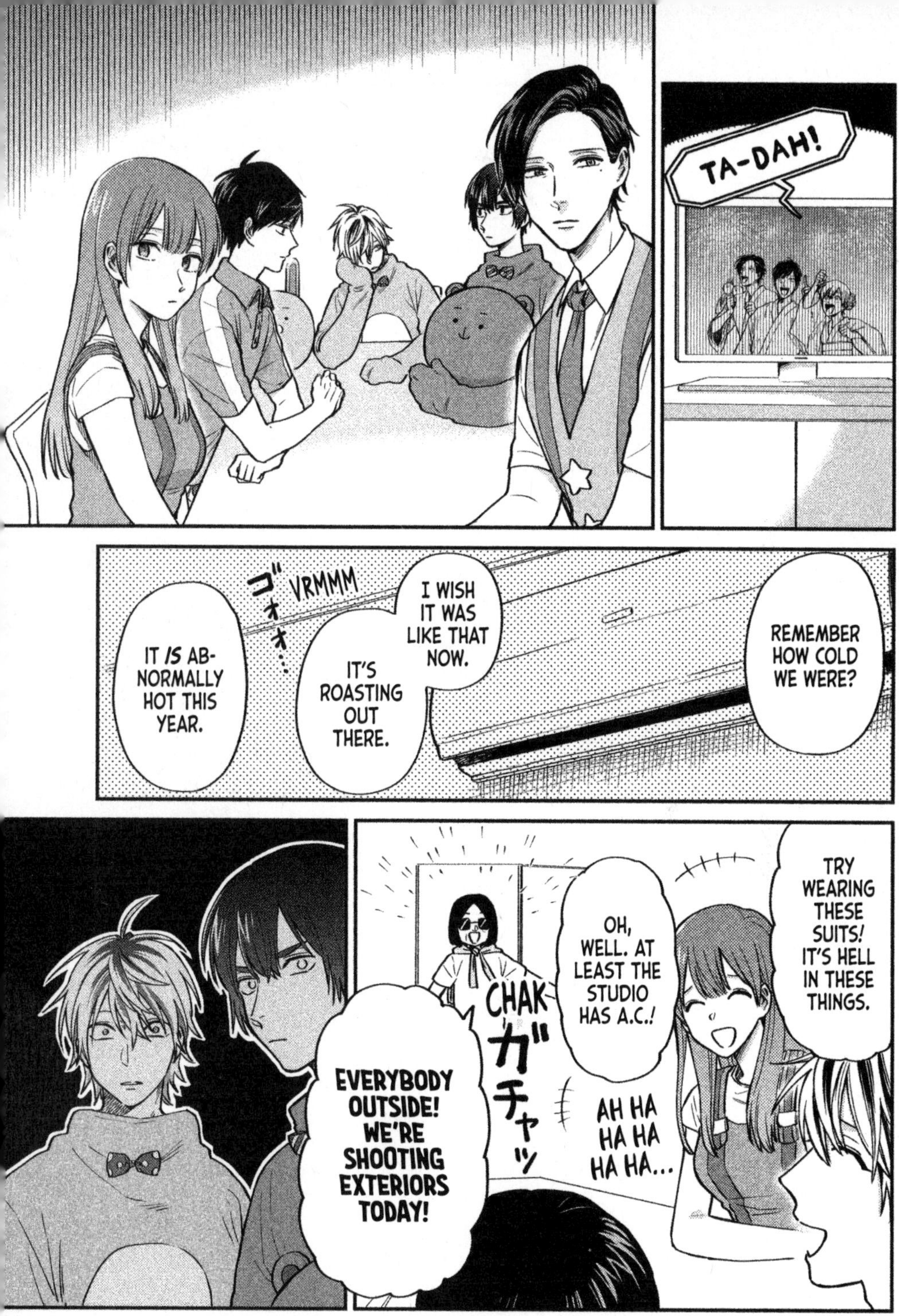
TA-DAH!
REMEMBER HOW COLD WE WERE?
I WISH IT WAS LIKE THAT NOW.
IT'S ROASTING OUT THERE.
VRMMM
ゴォォ…
IT IS ABNORMALLY HOT THIS YEAR.
TRY WEARING THESE SUITS! IT'S HELL IN THESE THINGS.
OH, WELL. AT LEAST THE STUDIO HAS A.C.!
AH HA HA HA HA HA...
CHAK
ガチャッ
EVERYBODY OUTSIDE! WE'RE SHOOTING EXTERIORS TODAY!

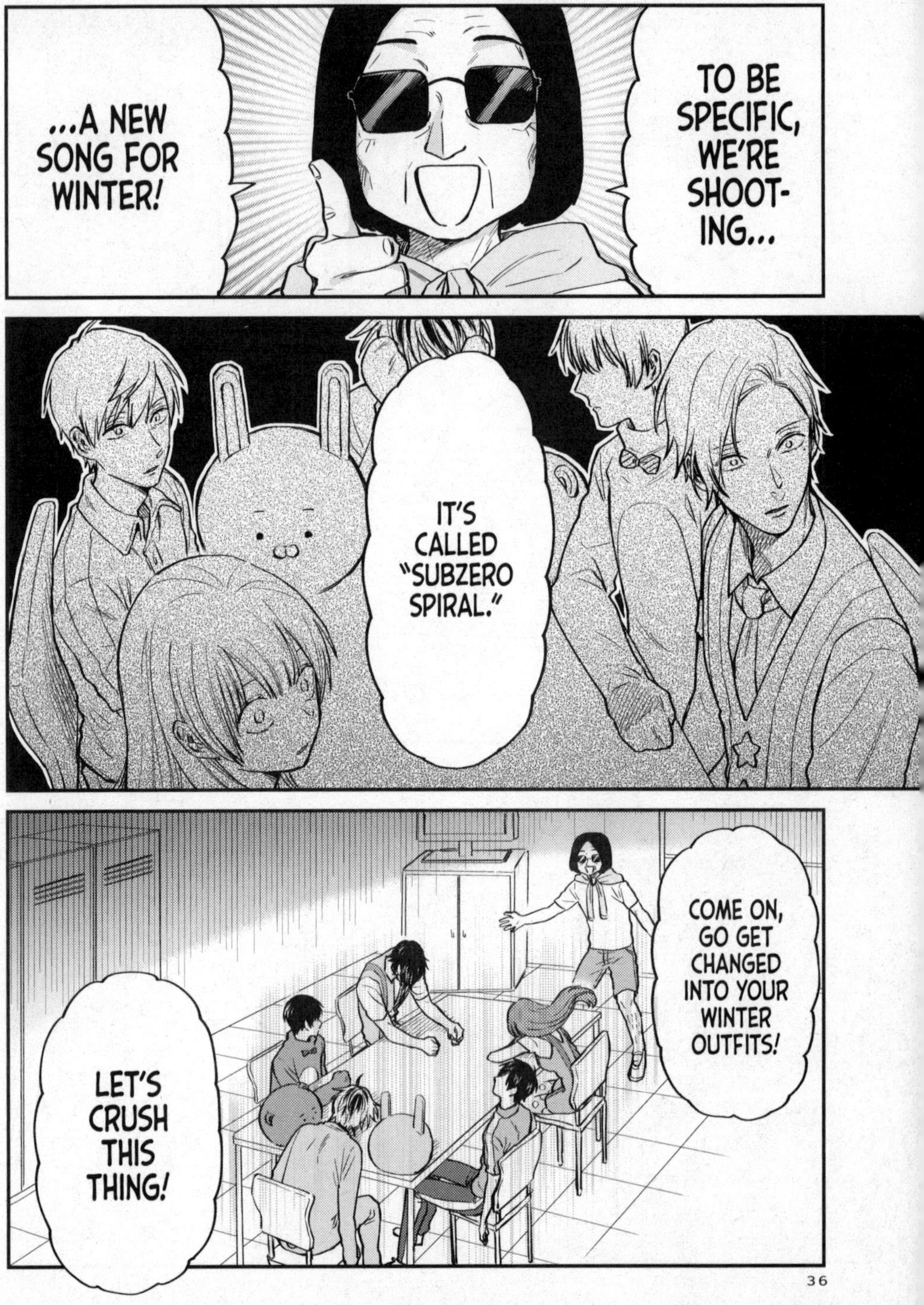
TO BE SPECIFIC, WE'RE SHOOT-ING...
...A NEW SONG FOR WINTER!
IT'S CALLED "SUBZERO SPIRAL."
COME ON, GO GET CHANGED INTO YOUR WINTER OUTFITS!
LET'S CRUSH THIS THING!

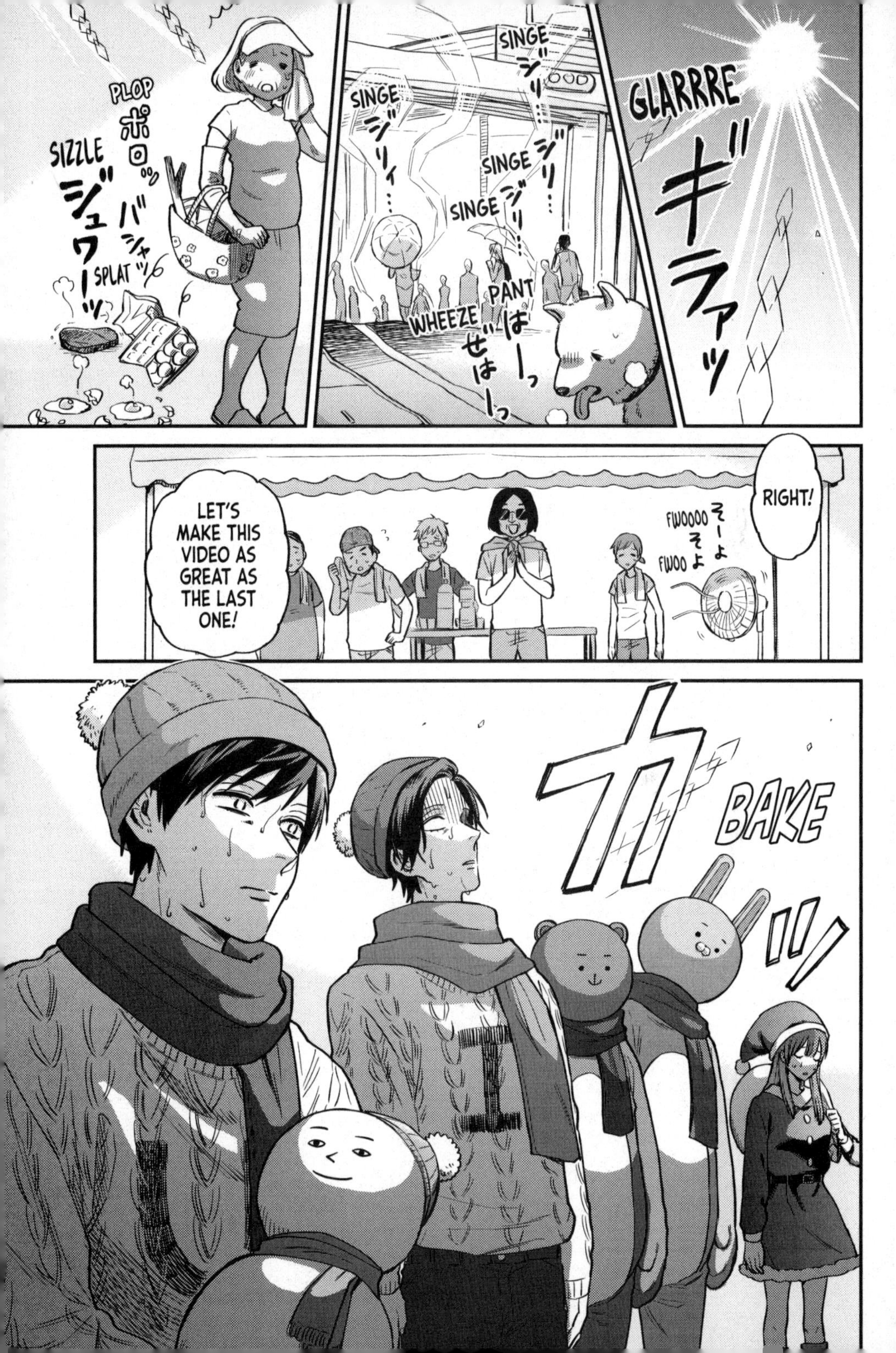
GLARRE
ギラァッ
SINGE
ジリ…
SINGE
ジリィ…
SINGE
ジリ…
SINGE
ジリ…
PANT
はーっ
WHEEZE
ぜはーっ
PLOP
ポロ
SPLAT
バシャッ
SIZZLE
ジュワーッ
RIGHT!
FWOOOO
そーよ
FWOO
そよ
LET'S MAKE THIS VIDEO AS GREAT AS THE LAST ONE!
BAKE
カッ

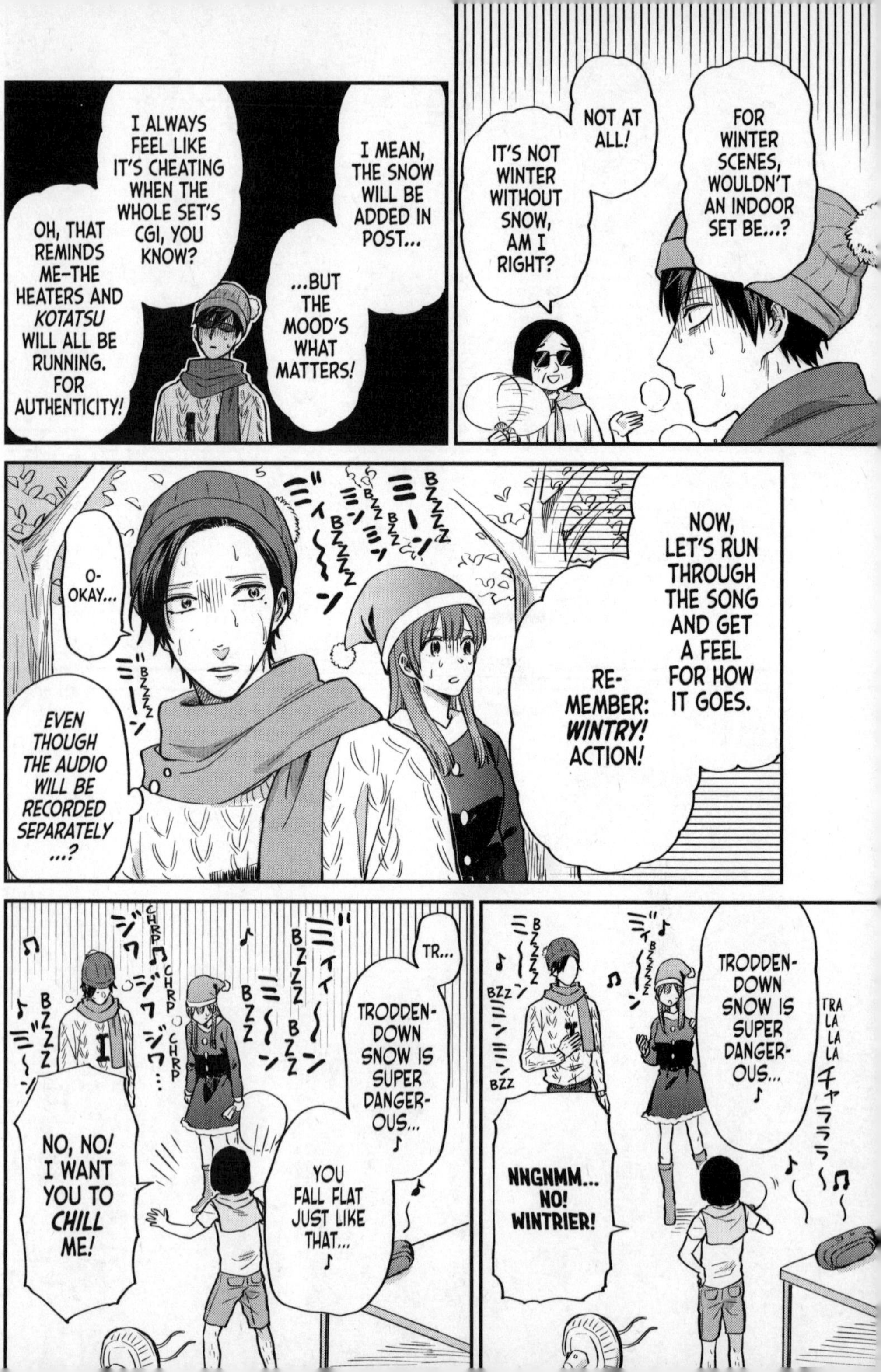

FOR WINTER SCENES, WOULDN'T AN INDOOR SET BE...?
NOT AT ALL!
IT'S NOT WINTER WITHOUT SNOW, AM I RIGHT?
I MEAN, THE SNOW WILL BE ADDED IN POST...
...BUT THE MOOD'S WHAT MATTERS!
I ALWAYS FEEL LIKE IT'S CHEATING WHEN THE WHOLE SET'S CGI, YOU KNOW?
OH, THAT REMINDS ME—THE HEATERS AND *KOTATSU* WILL ALL BE RUNNING. FOR AUTHENTICITY!
NOW, LET'S RUN THROUGH THE SONG AND GET A FEEL FOR HOW IT GOES.
RE-MEMBER: ***WINTRY!*** ACTION!
BZZZZ BZZ BZZ BZZZZ
O-OKAY...
BZZZZ
EVEN THOUGH THE AUDIO WILL BE RECORDED SEPARATELY ...?
TRODDEN-DOWN SNOW IS SUPER DANGER-OUS... ♪
TRA LA LA LA
BZZZZ BZZ BZZ
NNGNMM... NO! WINTRIER!
TR...
TRODDEN-DOWN SNOW IS SUPER DANGER-OUS... ♪
YOU FALL FLAT JUST LIKE THAT... ♪
BZZ BZZ CHRP CHRP CHRP
NO, NO! I WANT YOU TO ***CHILL*** ME!

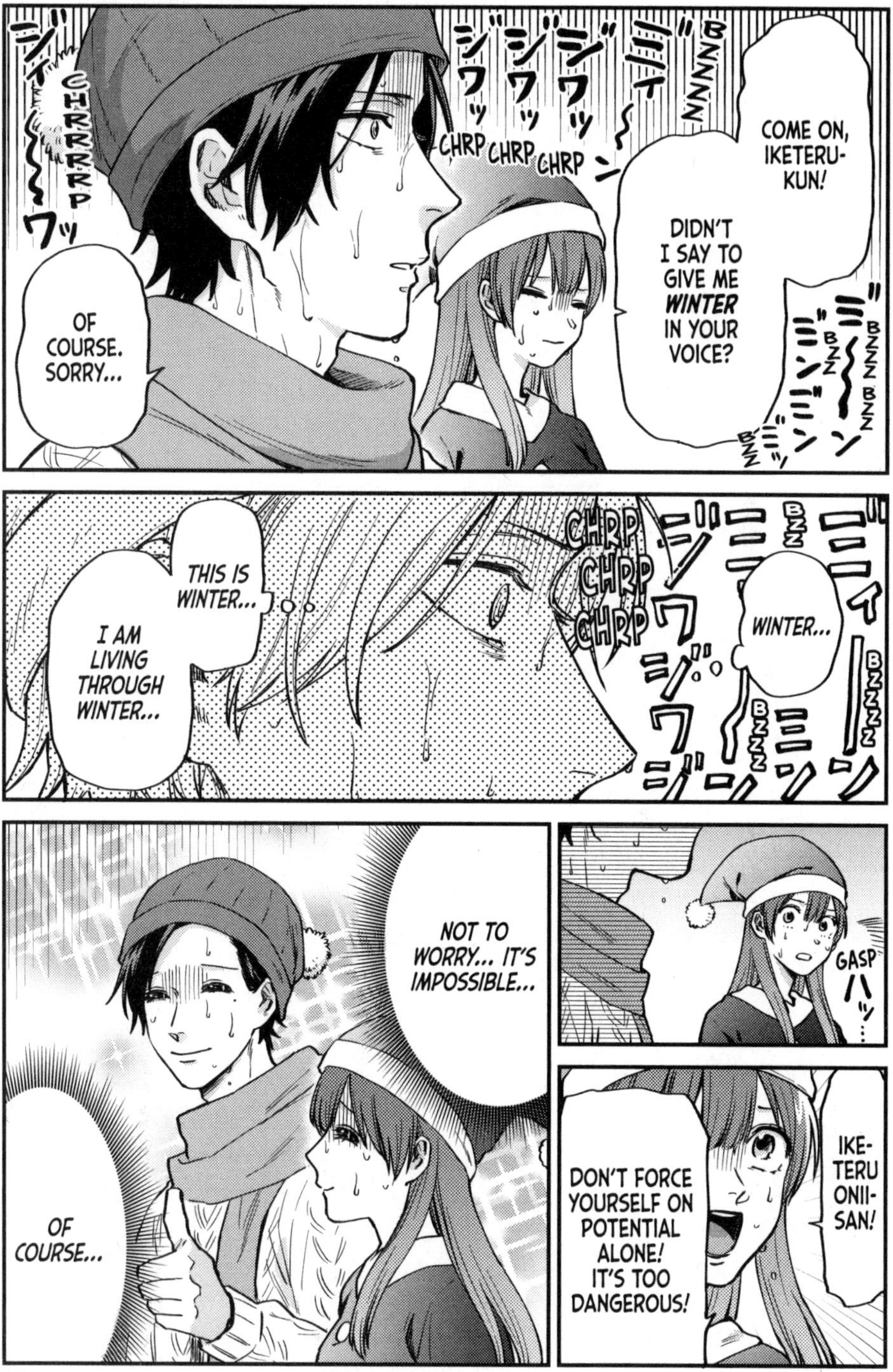
BZZZZZ
COME ON, IKETERU-KUN!
DIDN'T I SAY TO GIVE ME ***WINTER*** IN YOUR VOICE?
CHRP CHRP CHRP
BZZ BZZ BZZ BZZ
CHRRRRP
OF COURSE. SORRY...
BZZ
BZZZZ
WINTER...
BZZZ
CHRP CHRP CHRP
THIS IS WINTER...
I AM LIVING THROUGH WINTER...
GASP
IKE-TERU ONII-SAN!
DON'T FORCE YOURSELF ON POTENTIAL ALONE! IT'S TOO DANGEROUS!
NOT TO WORRY... IT'S IMPOSSIBLE...
OF COURSE...

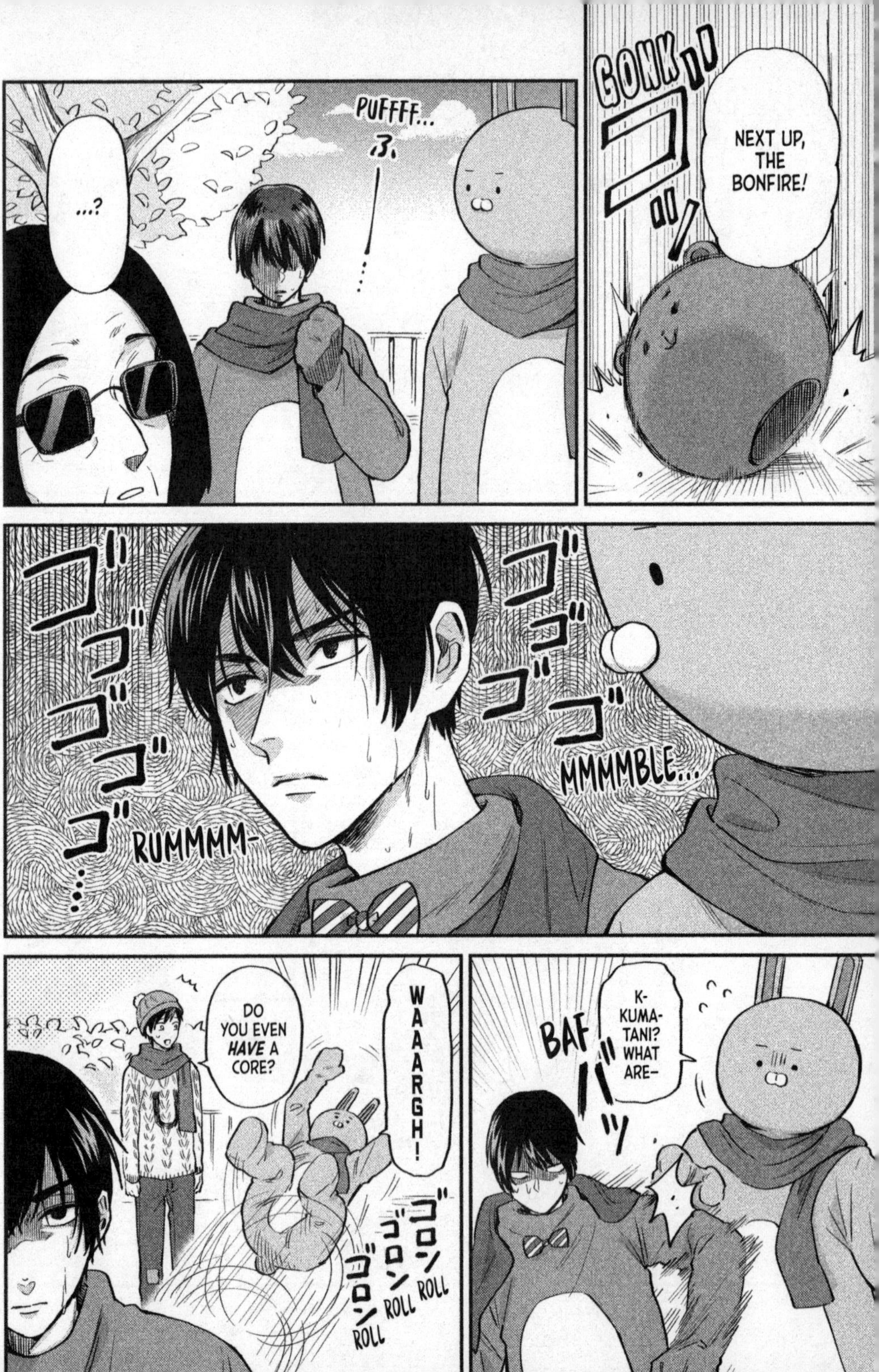
NEXT UP, THE BONFIRE!
GONK ゴッ
PUFFFF... ふー...
...?
ゴゴゴ
MMMMBLE...
ゴゴゴゴ...
RUMMMM-
K-KUMATANI? WHAT ARE—
BAF バッ
WAAAARGH!
DO YOU EVEN *HAVE* A CORE?
ゴロン ROLL
ゴロン ROLL
ゴロン ROLL

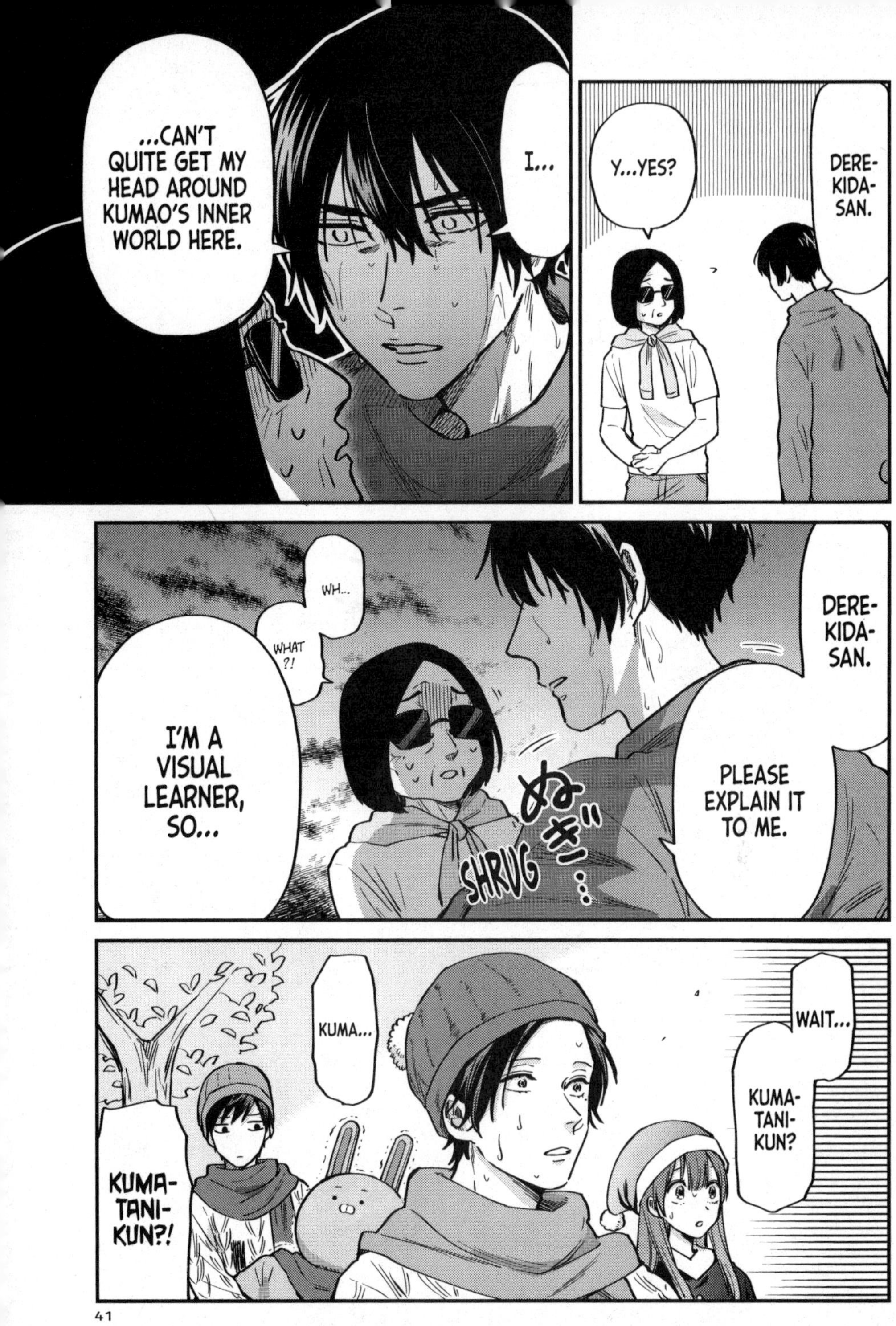
DERE-KIDA-SAN.
Y...YES?
I...
...CAN'T QUITE GET MY HEAD AROUND KUMAO'S INNER WORLD HERE.
DERE-KIDA-SAN.
PLEASE EXPLAIN IT TO ME.
ぬぎ…
SHRUG
WH...
WHAT?!
I'M A VISUAL LEARNER, SO...
WAIT...
KUMA-TANI-KUN?
KUMA...
KUMA-TANI-KUN?!

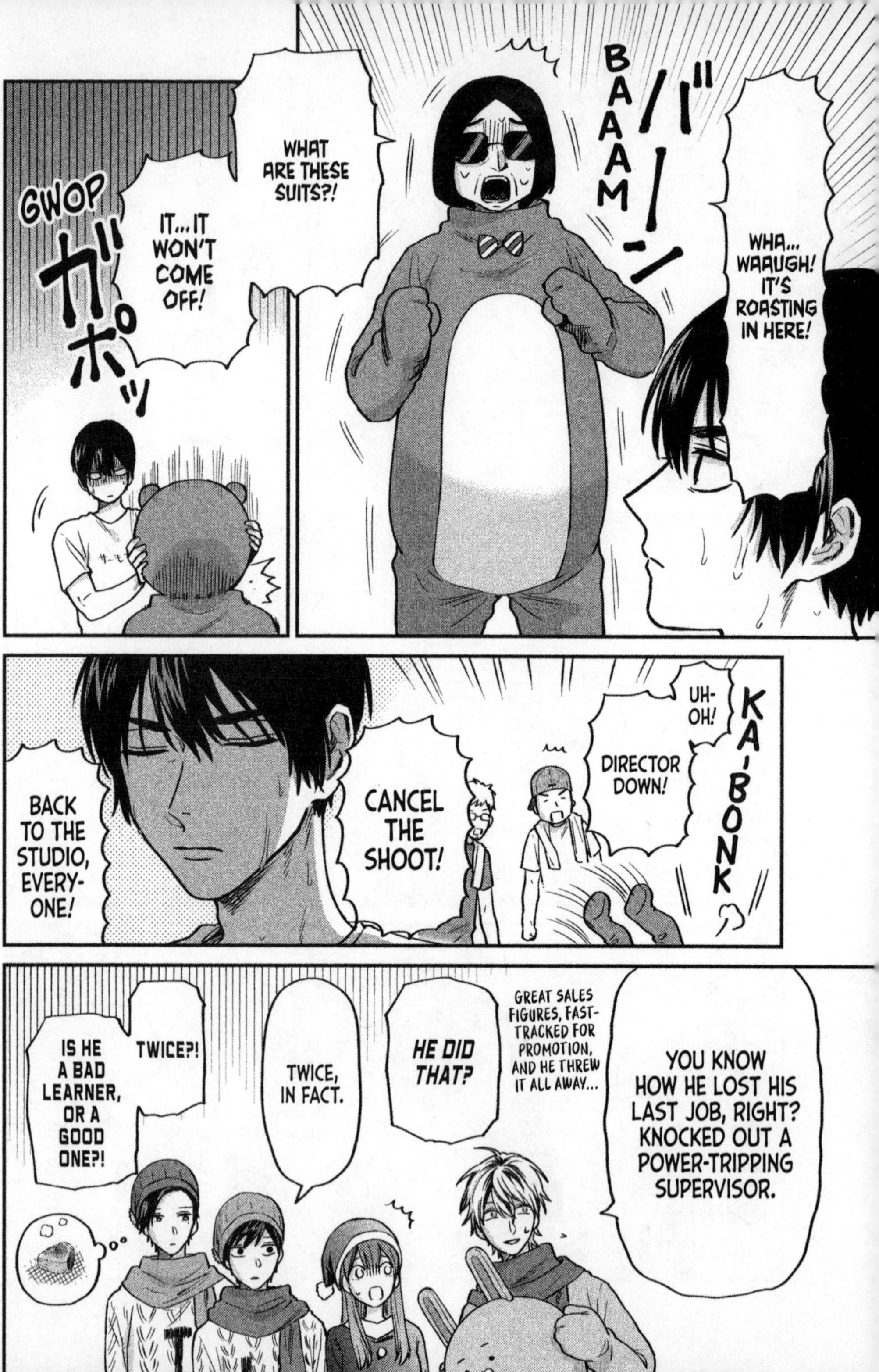
BAAAAM
バーン
WHA... WAAUGH! IT'S ROASTING IN HERE!
WHAT ARE THESE SUITS?!
IT... IT WON'T COME OFF!
GWOP
ガポッ
KA-BONK
UH-OH!
DIRECTOR DOWN!
CANCEL THE SHOOT!
BACK TO THE STUDIO, EVERY-ONE!
YOU KNOW HOW HE LOST HIS LAST JOB, RIGHT? KNOCKED OUT A POWER-TRIPPING SUPERVISOR.
GREAT SALES FIGURES, FAST-TRACKED FOR PROMOTION, AND HE THREW IT ALL AWAY...
HE DID THAT?
TWICE, IN FACT.
TWICE?!
IS HE A BAD LEARNER, OR A GOOD ONE?!

Life Lessons with
Uramichi Oniisan

Long, Hot Summer

Sung by Iketeru Oniisan and Utano Oneesan

Where should we go this summer? (It's summer!)

The beach! The beach! The be-e-each! Let's go to the beach!

It's summer, after all (Summer, after all)

Let's get stupid on the beach
We can have a barbecue

Pretend to have fun, so nobody can tell
That I spend my life
Worried what other people think

Aa-ah, this act doesn't suit me
Oh, well, here it comes, better start acting dumber—

The long, hot summer

The truth is, I want someone to say it

"It's okay to spend the summer
In a dark room with the A.C. on"

"Just skip the darn music festivals"

I lost sight of the mosquito,
and now I can't get to sleep

When I got home, the A.C. remote was gone
My shirt's gross and sweaty and it's such a huge bummer—

The long, hot summer!

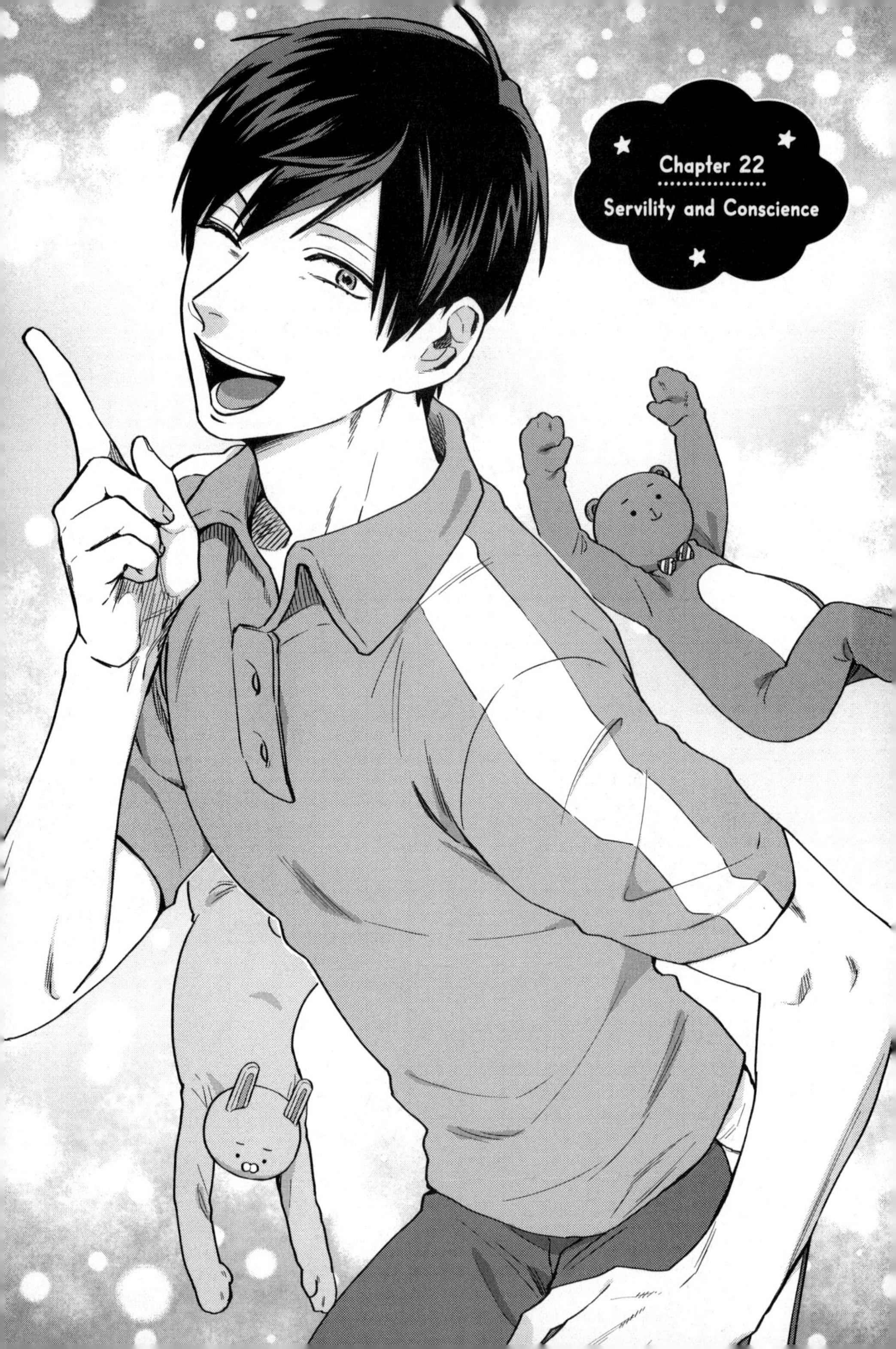
Chapter 22
Servility and Conscience

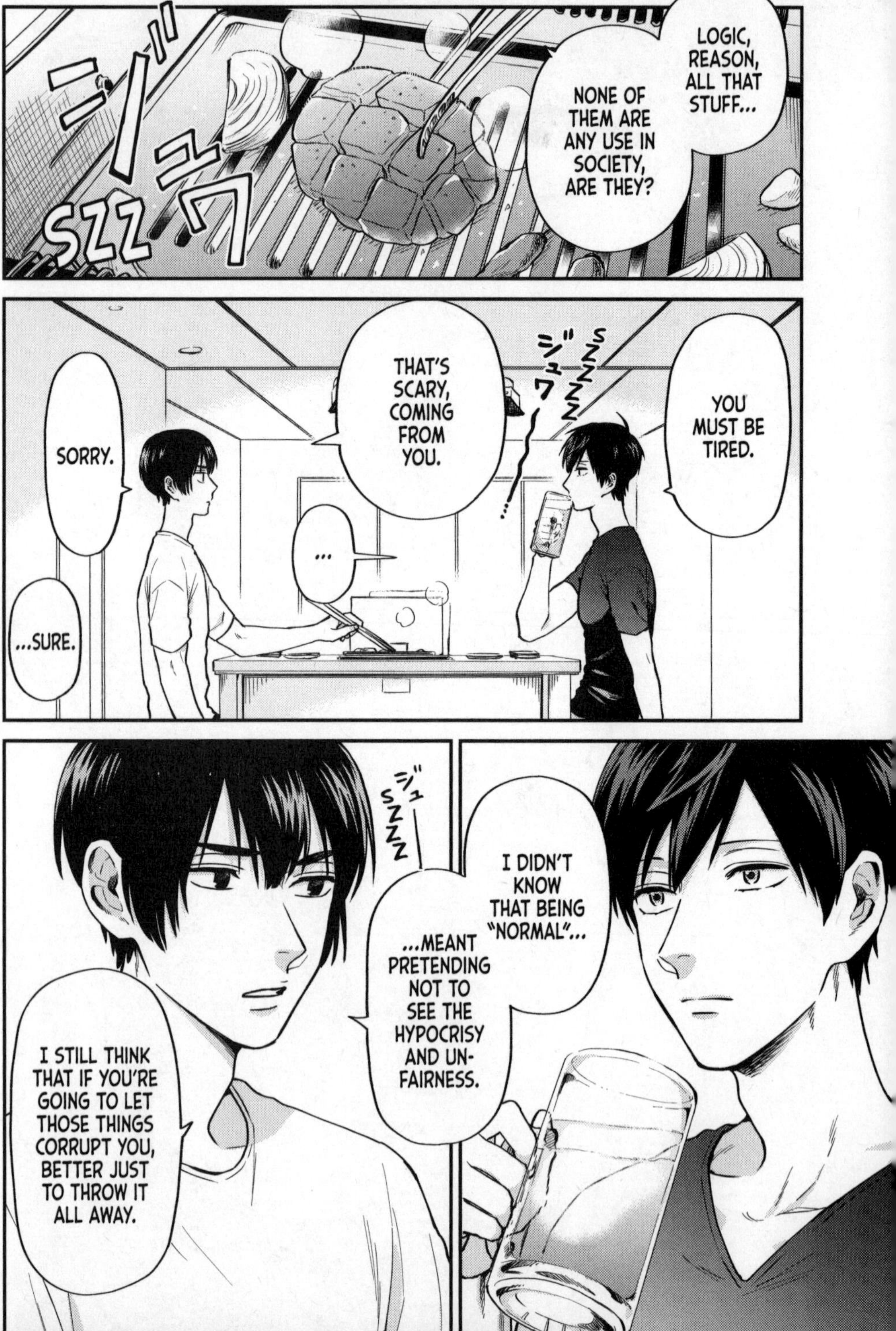
LOGIC, REASON, ALL THAT STUFF...
NONE OF THEM ARE ANY USE IN SOCIETY, ARE THEY?
ジュワ
SZZ
YOU MUST BE TIRED.
ジュワ
SZZZZ
THAT'S SCARY, COMING FROM YOU.
SORRY.
...
...SURE.
I DIDN'T KNOW THAT BEING "NORMAL"...
...MEANT PRETENDING NOT TO SEE THE HYPOCRISY AND UN-FAIRNESS.
ジュ
SZZZ
I STILL THINK THAT IF YOU'RE GOING TO LET THOSE THINGS CORRUPT YOU, BETTER JUST TO THROW IT ALL AWAY.

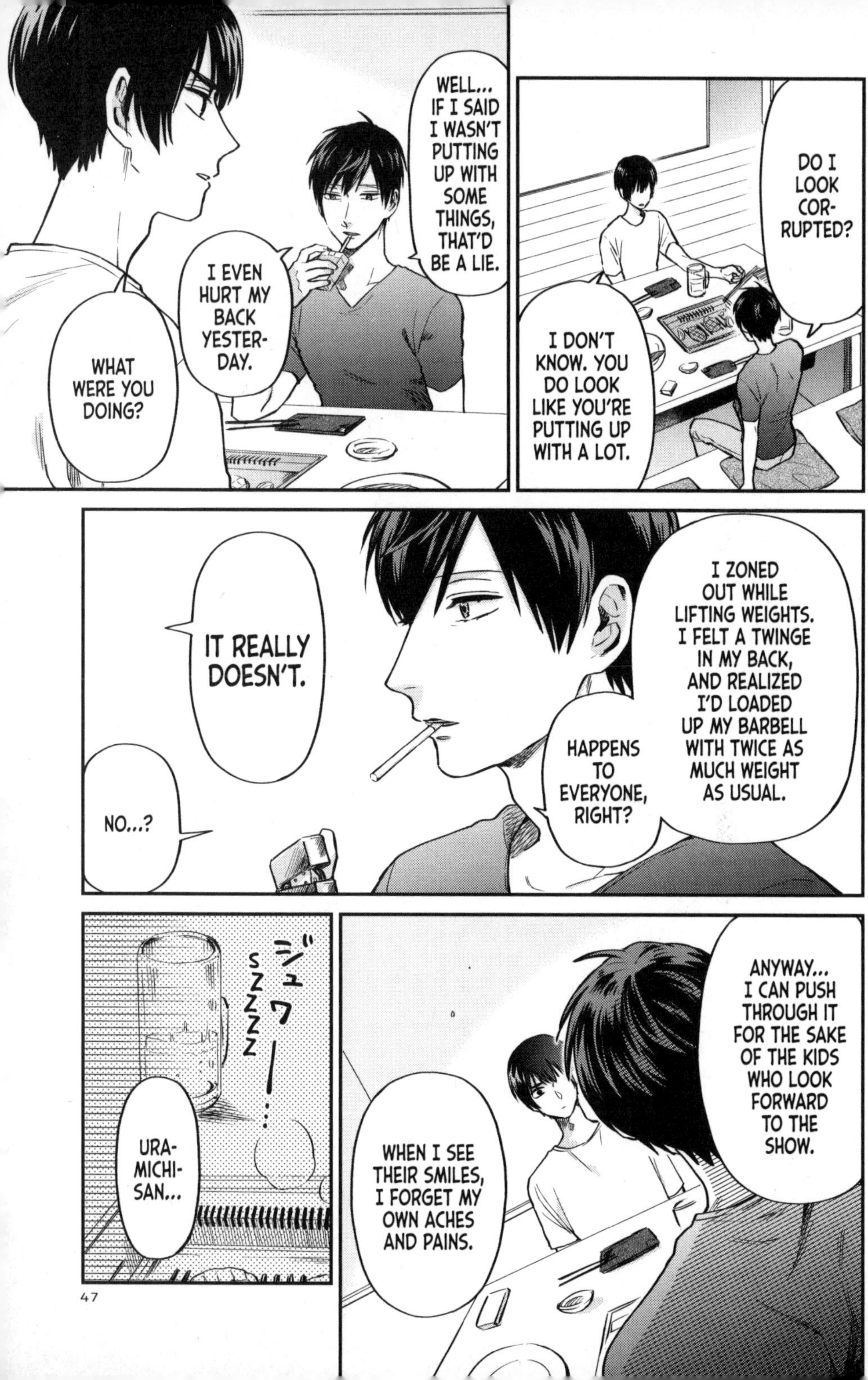
DO I LOOK COR-RUPTED?
I DON'T KNOW. YOU DO LOOK LIKE YOU'RE PUTTING UP WITH A LOT.
WELL... IF I SAID I WASN'T PUTTING UP WITH SOME THINGS, THAT'D BE A LIE.
I EVEN HURT MY BACK YESTER-DAY.
WHAT WERE YOU DOING?
I ZONED OUT WHILE LIFTING WEIGHTS. I FELT A TWINGE IN MY BACK, AND REALIZED I'D LOADED UP MY BARBELL WITH TWICE AS MUCH WEIGHT AS USUAL.
HAPPENS TO EVERYONE, RIGHT?
IT REALLY DOESN'T.
NO...?
ANYWAY... I CAN PUSH THROUGH IT FOR THE SAKE OF THE KIDS WHO LOOK FORWARD TO THE SHOW.
WHEN I SEE THEIR SMILES, I FORGET MY OWN ACHES AND PAINS.
ジュワー…
SZZZZ
URA-MICHI-SAN...

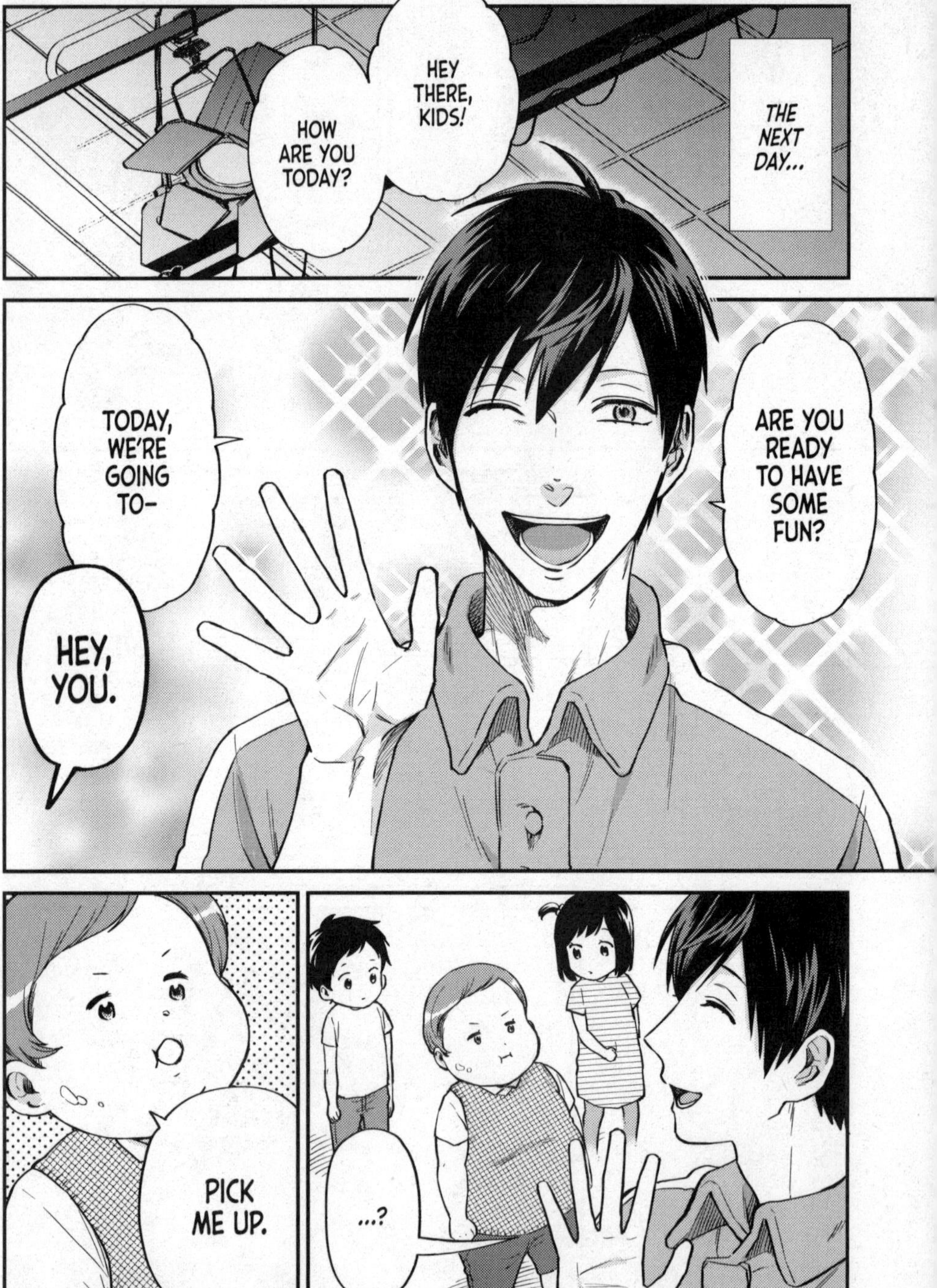
THE NEXT DAY...
HEY THERE, KIDS!
HOW ARE YOU TODAY?
ARE YOU READY TO HAVE SOME FUN?
TODAY, WE'RE GOING TO–
HEY, YOU.
...?
PICK ME UP.

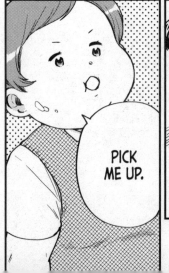

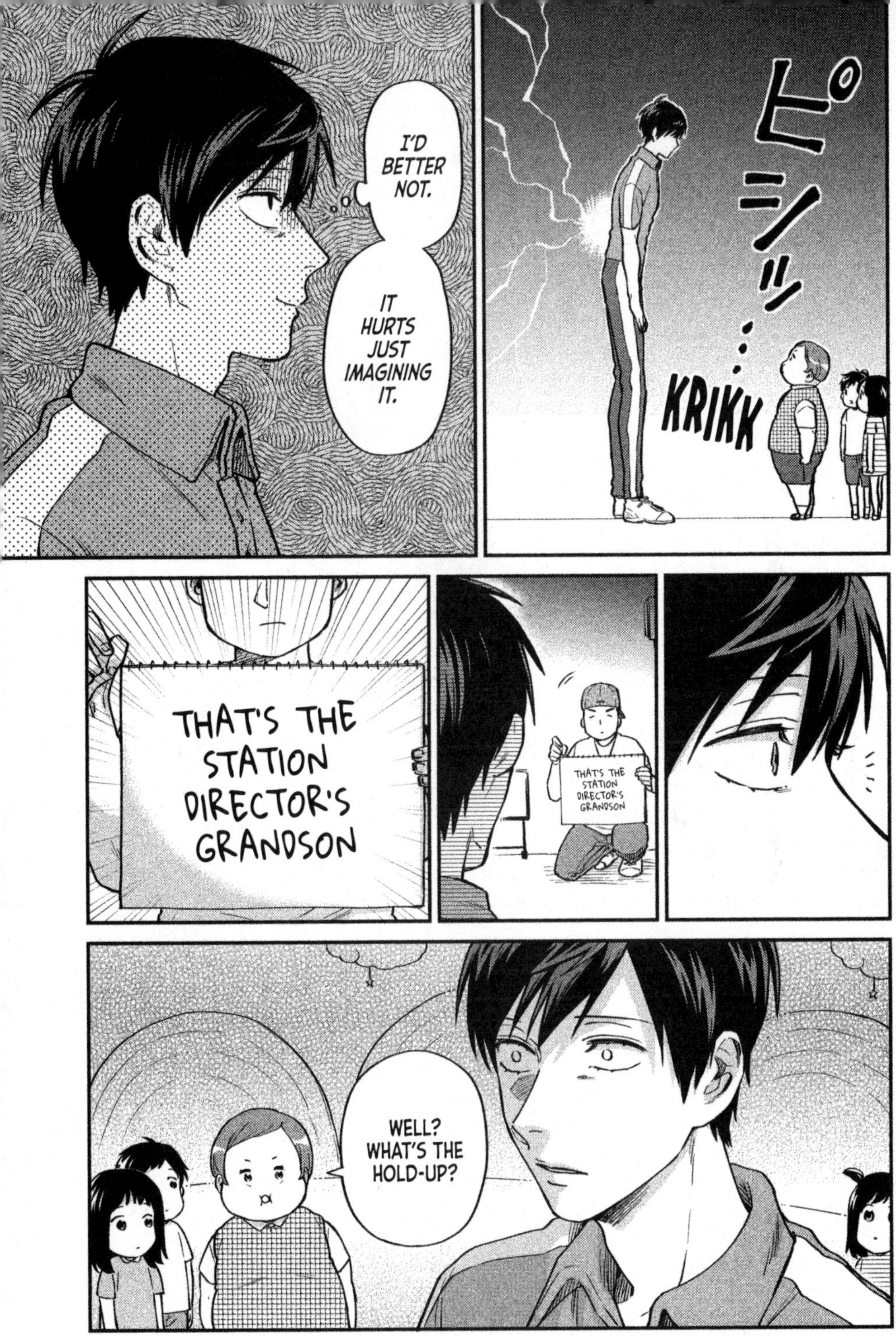
ピシッ…
KRIKK
I'D BETTER NOT.
IT HURTS JUST IMAGINING IT.
THAT'S THE STATION DIRECTOR'S GRANDSON
THAT'S THE STATION DIRECTOR'S GRANDSON
WELL? WHAT'S THE HOLD-UP?

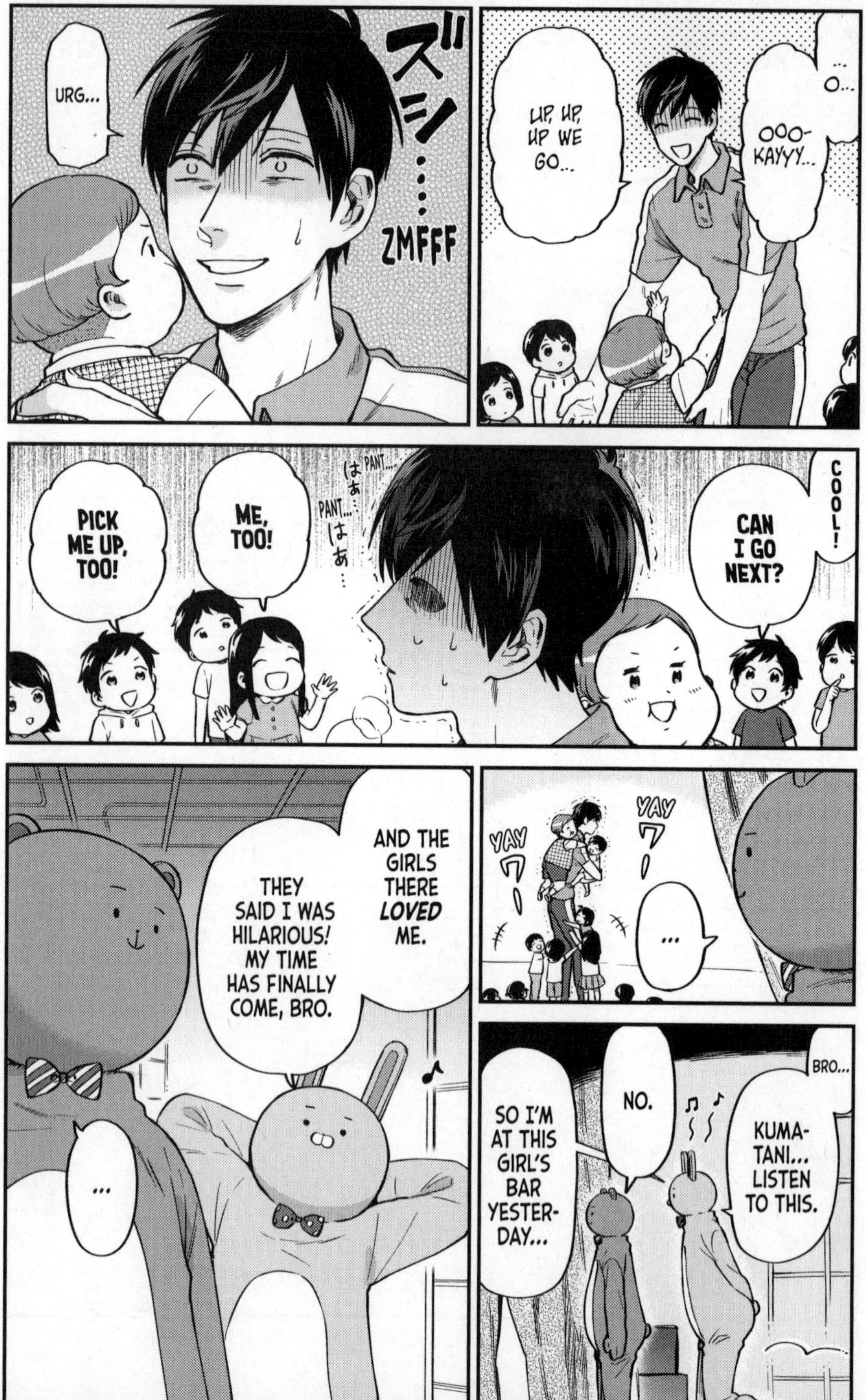
... O... OOO-KAYYY...
UP, UP, UP WE GO...
ズシ... ZMFFF
URG...
COOL!
CAN I GO NEXT?
はぁ... PANT...
はぁ... PANT...
ME, TOO!
PICK ME UP, TOO!
ワー YAY
ワー YAY
...
BRO...
KUMATANI... LISTEN TO THIS.
NO.
SO I'M AT THIS GIRL'S BAR YESTERDAY...
AND THE GIRLS THERE *LOVED* ME.
THEY SAID I WAS HILARIOUS! MY TIME HAS FINALLY COME, BRO.
...

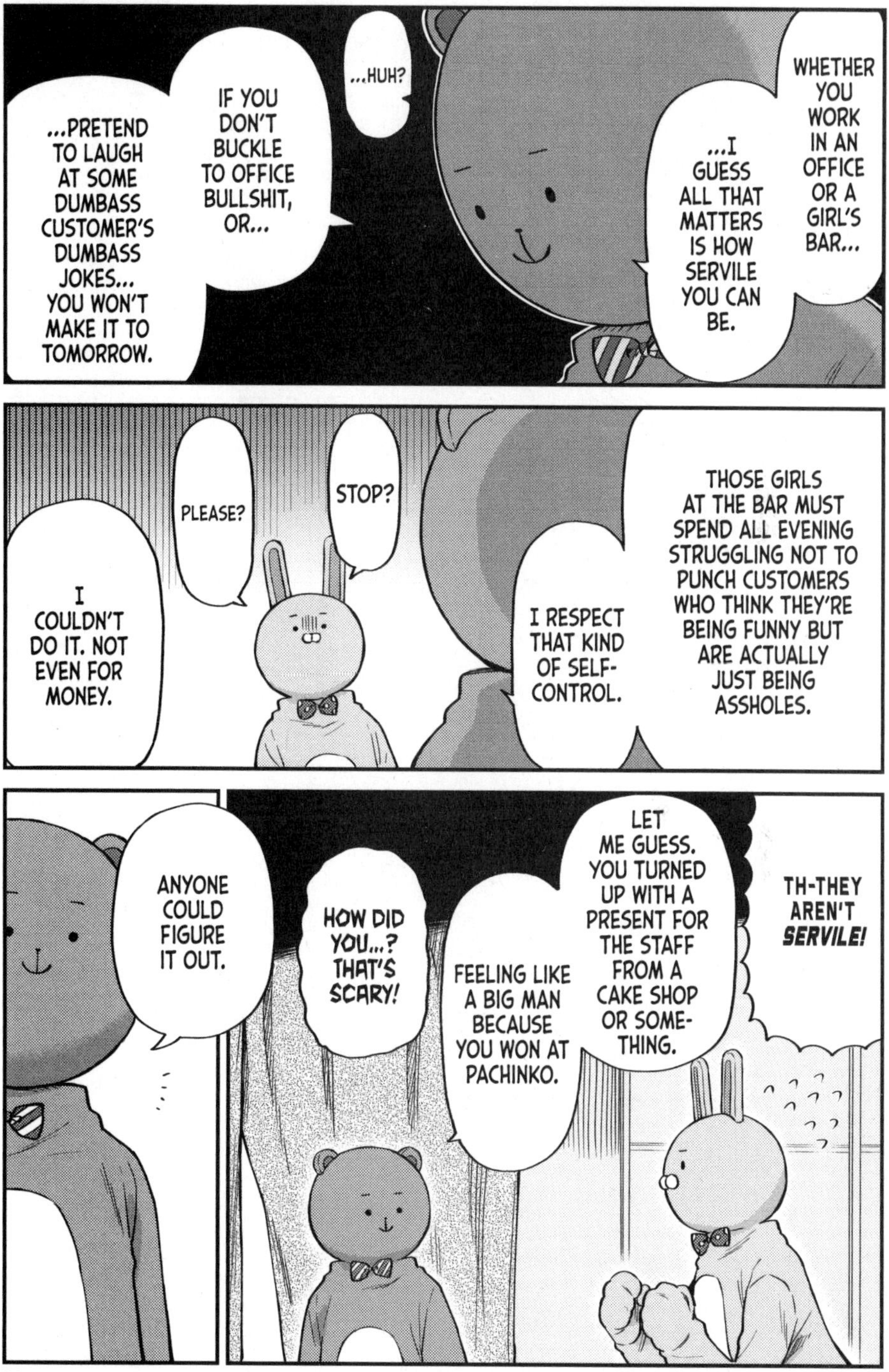
WHETHER YOU WORK IN AN OFFICE OR A GIRL'S BAR...
...I GUESS ALL THAT MATTERS IS HOW SERVILE YOU CAN BE.
...HUH?
IF YOU DON'T BUCKLE TO OFFICE BULLSHIT, OR...
...PRETEND TO LAUGH AT SOME DUMBASS CUSTOMER'S DUMBASS JOKES... YOU WON'T MAKE IT TO TOMORROW.
THOSE GIRLS AT THE BAR MUST SPEND ALL EVENING STRUGGLING NOT TO PUNCH CUSTOMERS WHO THINK THEY'RE BEING FUNNY BUT ARE ACTUALLY JUST BEING ASSHOLES.
I RESPECT THAT KIND OF SELF-CONTROL.
STOP?
PLEASE?
I COULDN'T DO IT. NOT EVEN FOR MONEY.
TH-THEY AREN'T SERVILE!
LET ME GUESS. YOU TURNED UP WITH A PRESENT FOR THE STAFF FROM A CAKE SHOP OR SOME-THING.
FEELING LIKE A BIG MAN BECAUSE YOU WON AT PACHINKO.
HOW DID YOU...? THAT'S SCARY!
ANYONE COULD FIGURE IT OUT.

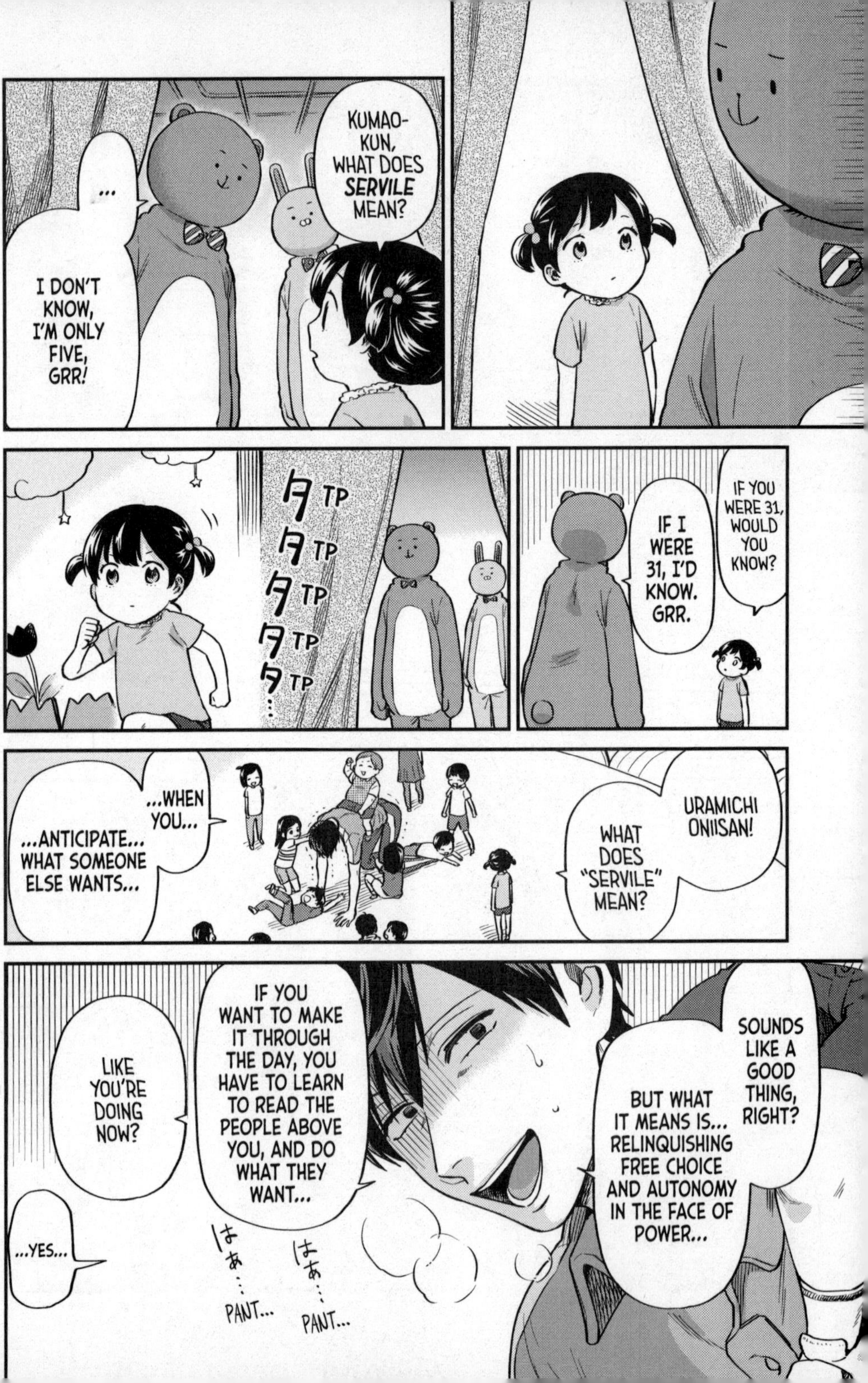
KUMAO-KUN, WHAT DOES SERVILE MEAN?
...
I DON'T KNOW, I'M ONLY FIVE, GRR!
IF YOU WERE 31, WOULD YOU KNOW?
IF I WERE 31, I'D KNOW. GRR.
タ TP タ TP タ TP タ TP タ TP...
URAMICHI ONIISAN!
WHAT DOES "SERVILE" MEAN?
...WHEN YOU...
...ANTICIPATE... WHAT SOMEONE ELSE WANTS...
SOUNDS LIKE A GOOD THING, RIGHT?
BUT WHAT IT MEANS IS... RELINQUISHING FREE CHOICE AND AUTONOMY IN THE FACE OF POWER...
IF YOU WANT TO MAKE IT THROUGH THE DAY, YOU HAVE TO LEARN TO READ THE PEOPLE ABOVE YOU, AND DO WHAT THEY WANT...
LIKE YOU'RE DOING NOW?
はぁ… PANT...
はぁ… PANT...
...YES...

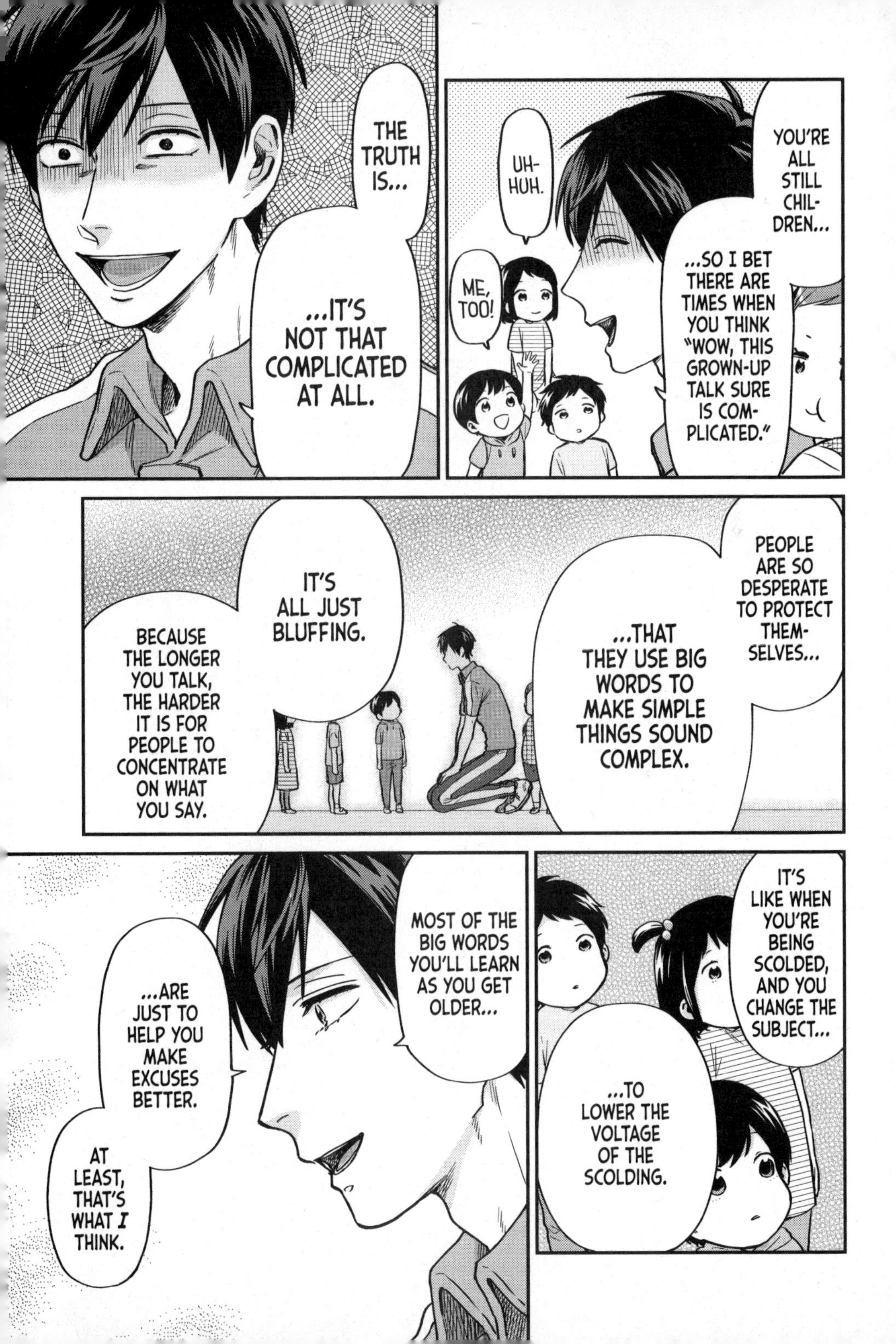
YOU'RE ALL STILL CHIL-DREN...
UH-HUH.
ME, TOO!
...SO I BET THERE ARE TIMES WHEN YOU THINK "WOW, THIS GROWN-UP TALK SURE IS COM-PLICATED."
THE TRUTH IS...
...IT'S NOT THAT COMPLICATED AT ALL.
PEOPLE ARE SO DESPERATE TO PROTECT THEM-SELVES...
...THAT THEY USE BIG WORDS TO MAKE SIMPLE THINGS SOUND COMPLEX.
IT'S ALL JUST BLUFFING.
BECAUSE THE LONGER YOU TALK, THE HARDER IT IS FOR PEOPLE TO CONCENTRATE ON WHAT YOU SAY.
IT'S LIKE WHEN YOU'RE BEING SCOLDED, AND YOU CHANGE THE SUBJECT...
...TO LOWER THE VOLTAGE OF THE SCOLDING.
MOST OF THE BIG WORDS YOU'LL LEARN AS YOU GET OLDER...
...ARE JUST TO HELP YOU MAKE EXCUSES BETTER.
AT LEAST, THAT'S WHAT *I* THINK.

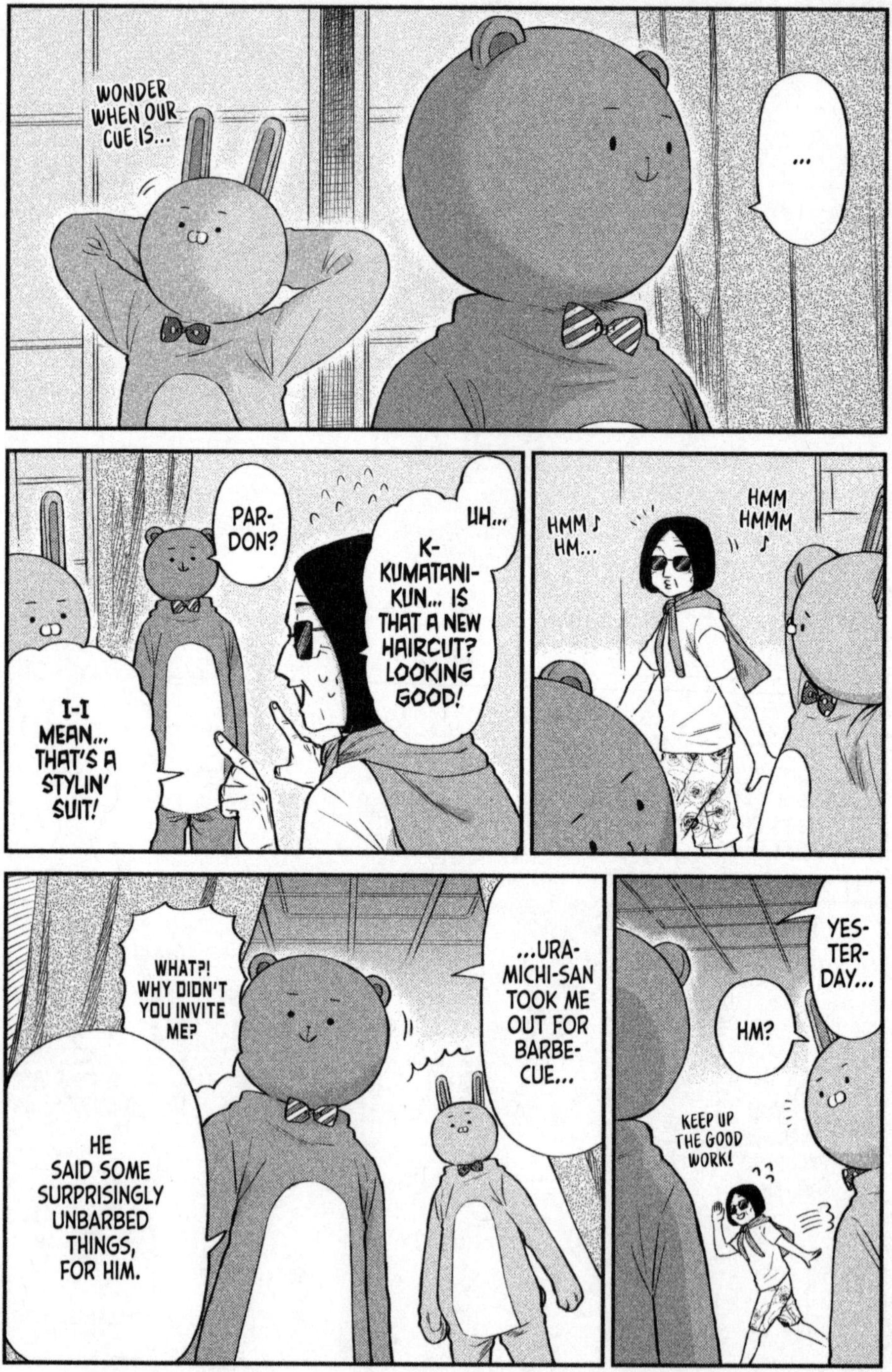
WONDER WHEN OUR CUE IS...
...
HMM HMMM ♪
HMM ♪ HM...
UH... K-KUMATANI-KUN... IS THAT A NEW HAIRCUT? LOOKING GOOD!
PARDON?
I-I MEAN... THAT'S A STYLIN' SUIT!
YES-TER-DAY...
HM?
KEEP UP THE GOOD WORK!
...URA-MICHI-SAN TOOK ME OUT FOR BARBE-CUE...
WHAT?! WHY DIDN'T YOU INVITE ME?
HE SAID SOME SURPRISINGLY UNBARBED THINGS, FOR HIM.

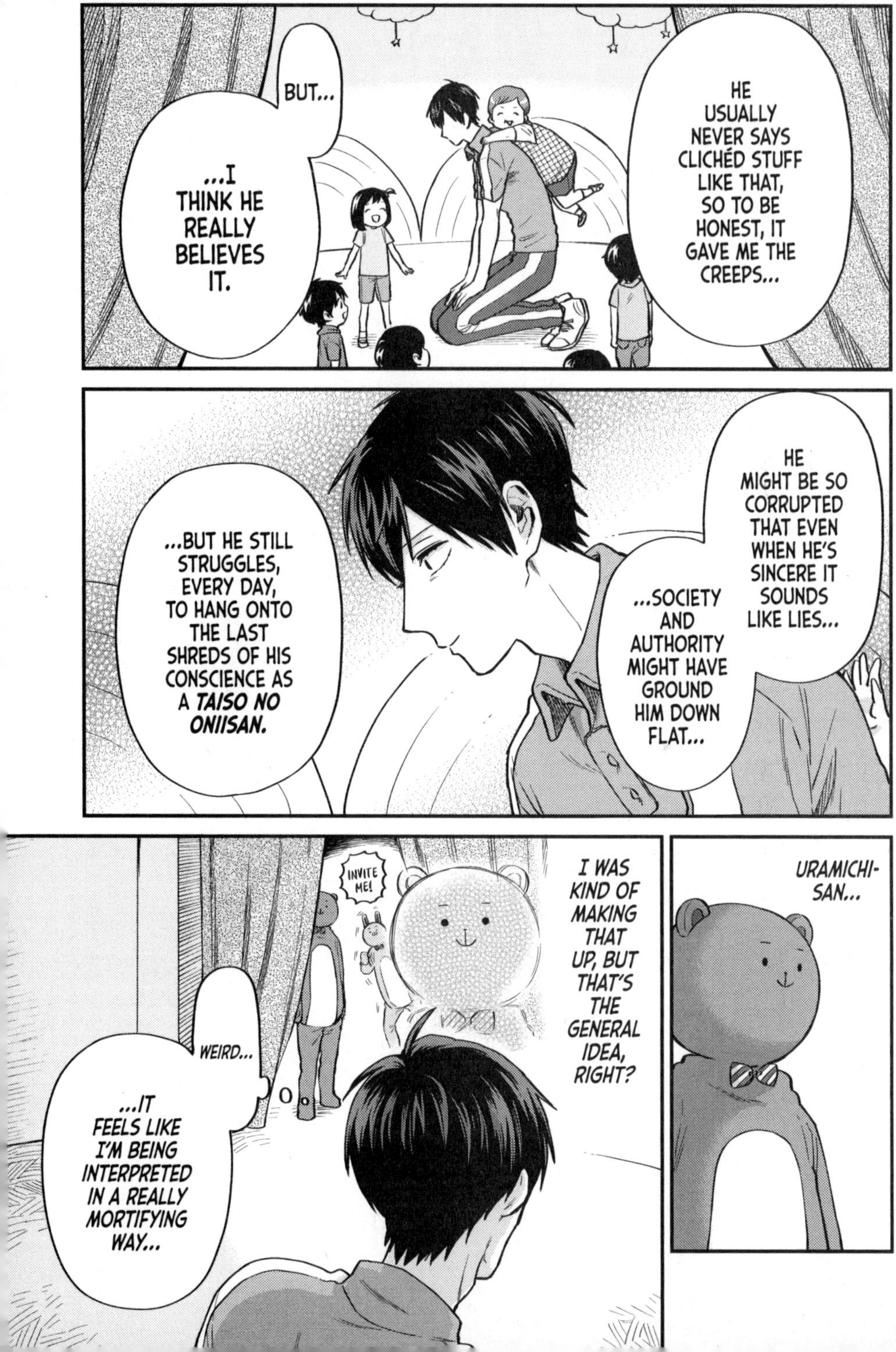
HE USUALLY NEVER SAYS CLICHÉD STUFF LIKE THAT, SO TO BE HONEST, IT GAVE ME THE CREEPS...
BUT...
...I THINK HE REALLY BELIEVES IT.
HE MIGHT BE SO CORRUPTED THAT EVEN WHEN HE'S SINCERE IT SOUNDS LIKE LIES...
...SOCIETY AND AUTHORITY MIGHT HAVE GROUND HIM DOWN FLAT...
...BUT HE STILL STRUGGLES, EVERY DAY, TO HANG ONTO THE LAST SHREDS OF HIS CONSCIENCE AS A *TAISO NO ONIISAN.*
URAMICHI-SAN...
I WAS KIND OF MAKING THAT UP, BUT THAT'S THE GENERAL IDEA, RIGHT?
INVITE ME!
WEIRD...
...IT FEELS LIKE I'M BEING INTERPRETED IN A REALLY MORTIFYING WAY...

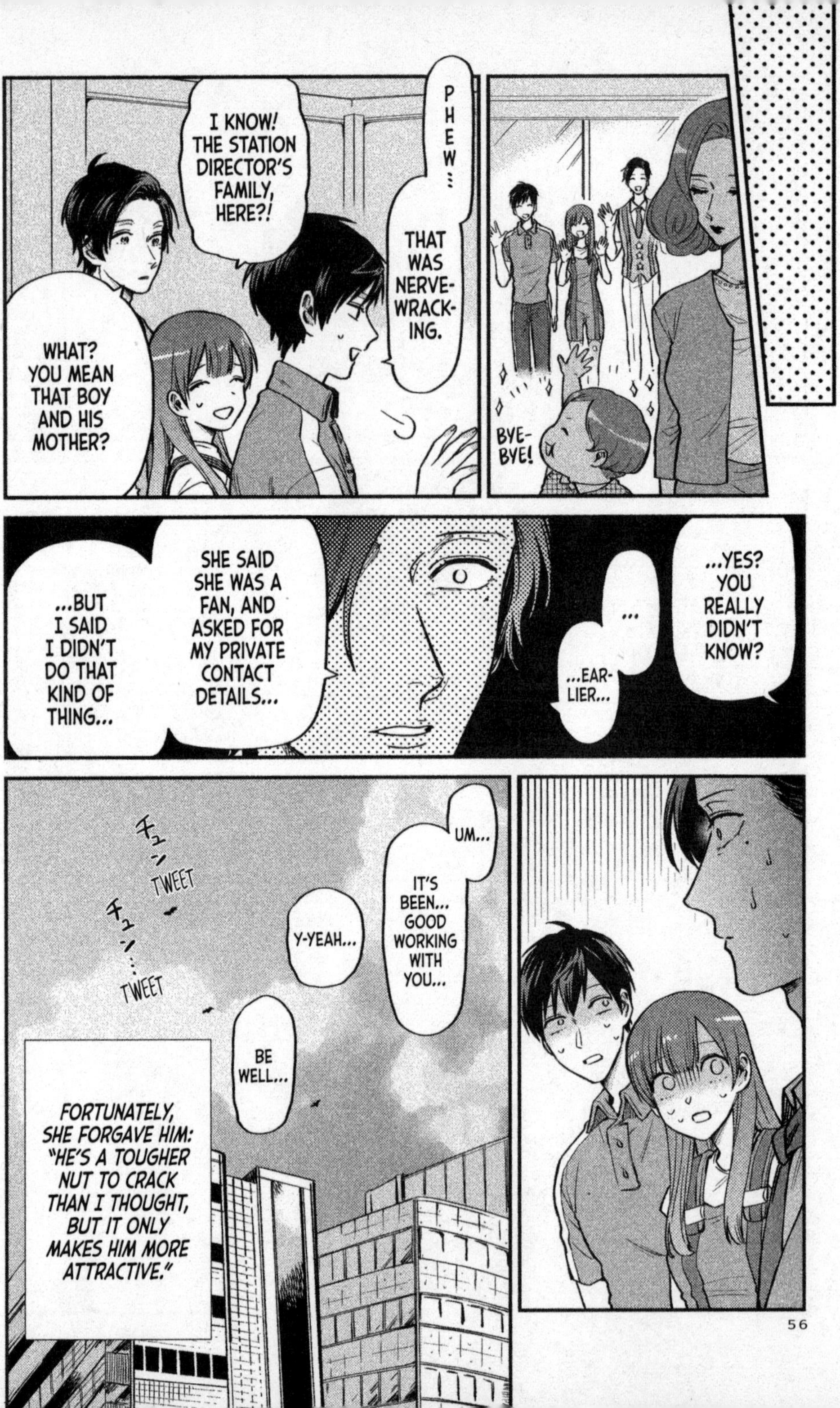

BYE-BYE!
PHEW... THAT WAS NERVE-WRACKING.
I KNOW! THE STATION DIRECTOR'S FAMILY, HERE?!
WHAT? YOU MEAN THAT BOY AND HIS MOTHER?
...YES? YOU REALLY DIDN'T KNOW?
...
...EAR-LIER...
SHE SAID SHE WAS A FAN, AND ASKED FOR MY PRIVATE CONTACT DETAILS...
...BUT I SAID I DIDN'T DO THAT KIND OF THING...
UM...
IT'S BEEN... GOOD WORKING WITH YOU...
Y-YEAH...
BE WELL...
チュン TWEET
チュン... TWEET
FORTUNATELY, SHE FORGAVE HIM: "HE'S A TOUGHER NUT TO CRACK THAN I THOUGHT, BUT IT ONLY MAKES HIM MORE ATTRACTIVE."

Life Lessons with
Uramichi Oniisan

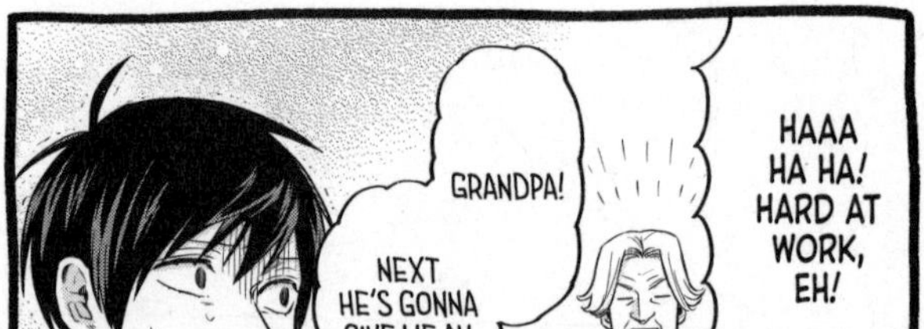
HAAA HA HA! HARD AT WORK, EH!
STATION DIRECTOR
GRANDPA!
NEXT HE'S GONNA GIVE ME AN AIRPLANE RIDE!

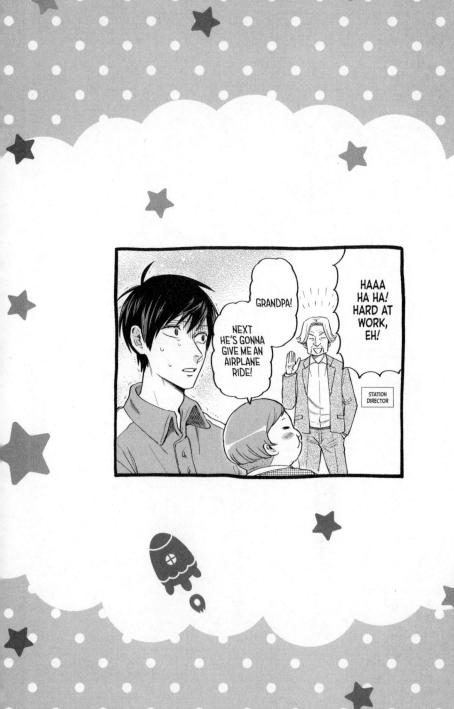

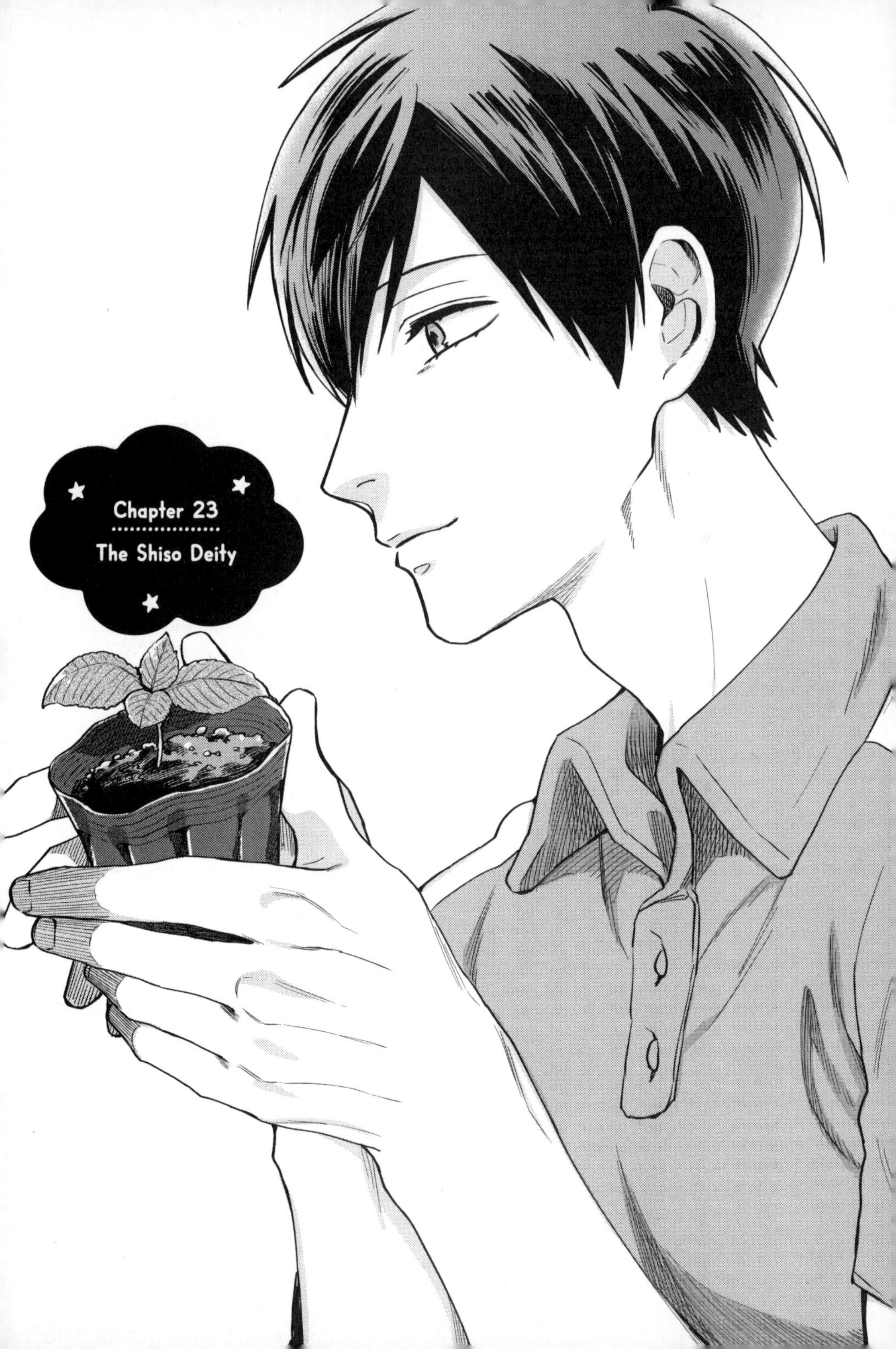
Chapter 23
The Shiso Deity

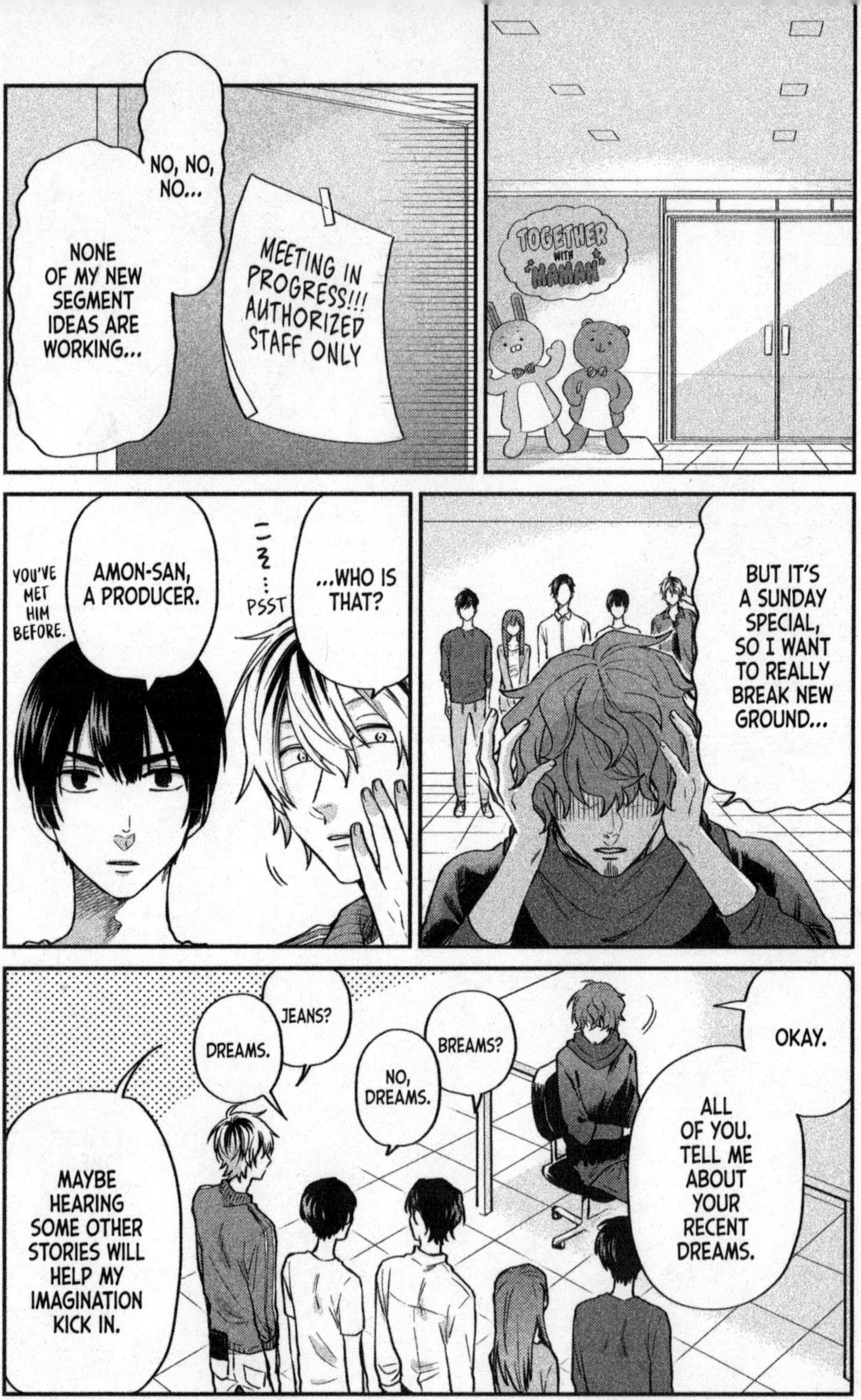
TOGETHER WITH MAMAN
NO, NO, NO...
NONE OF MY NEW SEGMENT IDEAS ARE WORKING...
MEETING IN PROGRESS!!! AUTHORIZED STAFF ONLY
BUT IT'S A SUNDAY SPECIAL, SO I WANT TO REALLY BREAK NEW GROUND...
...WHO IS THAT?
PSST
AMON-SAN, A PRODUCER.
YOU'VE MET HIM BEFORE.
OKAY.
ALL OF YOU. TELL ME ABOUT YOUR RECENT DREAMS.
BREAMS?
NO, DREAMS.
JEANS?
DREAMS.
MAYBE HEARING SOME OTHER STORIES WILL HELP MY IMAGINATION KICK IN.

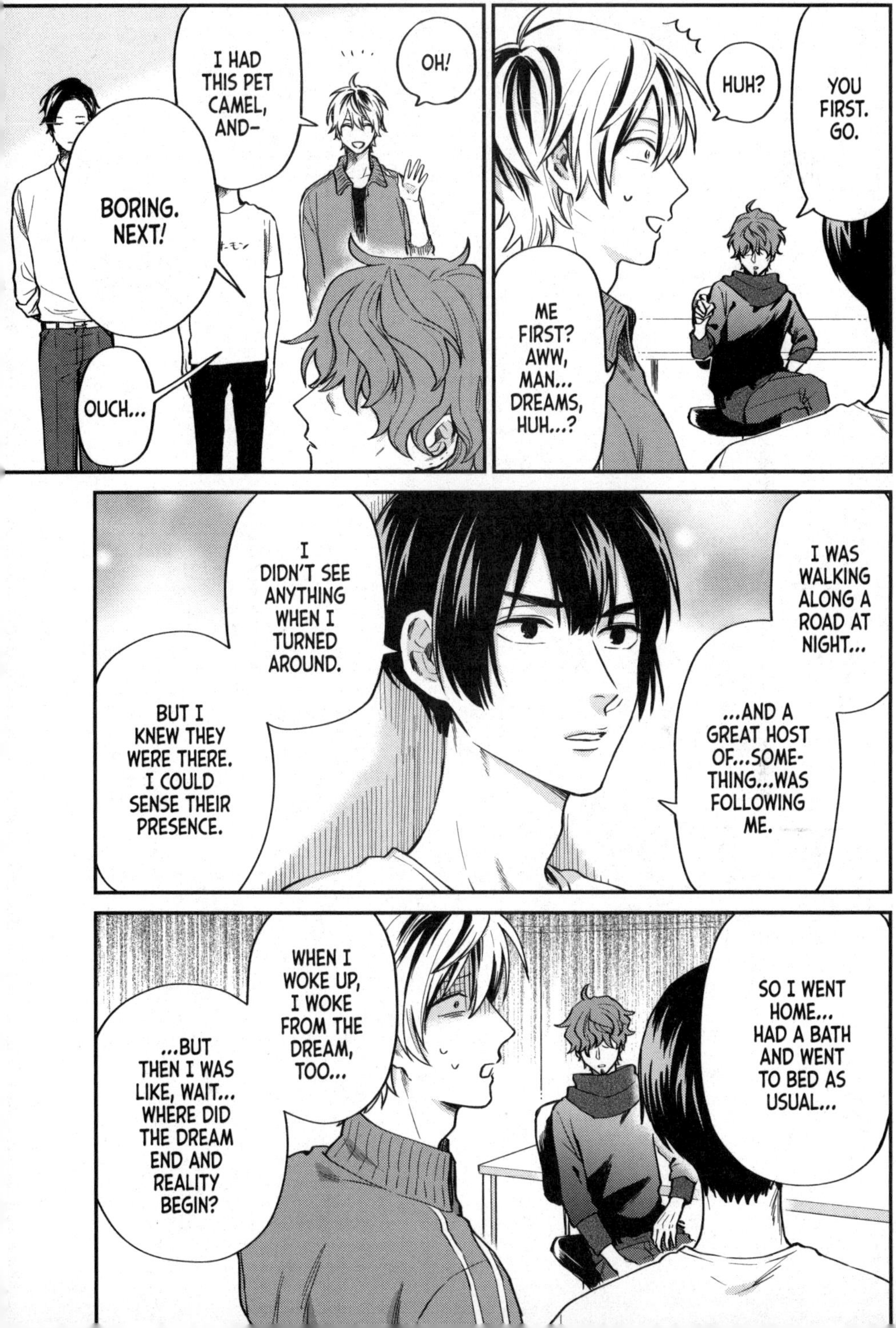
YOU FIRST. GO.
HUH?
ME FIRST? AWW, MAN... DREAMS, HUH...?
OH!
I HAD THIS PET CAMEL, AND–
BORING. NEXT!
OUCH...
I WAS WALKING ALONG A ROAD AT NIGHT...
...AND A GREAT HOST OF...SOME-THING...WAS FOLLOWING ME.
I DIDN'T SEE ANYTHING WHEN I TURNED AROUND.
BUT I KNEW THEY WERE THERE. I COULD SENSE THEIR PRESENCE.
SO I WENT HOME... HAD A BATH AND WENT TO BED AS USUAL...
WHEN I WOKE UP, I WOKE FROM THE DREAM, TOO...
...BUT THEN I WAS LIKE, WAIT... WHERE DID THE DREAM END AND REALITY BEGIN?

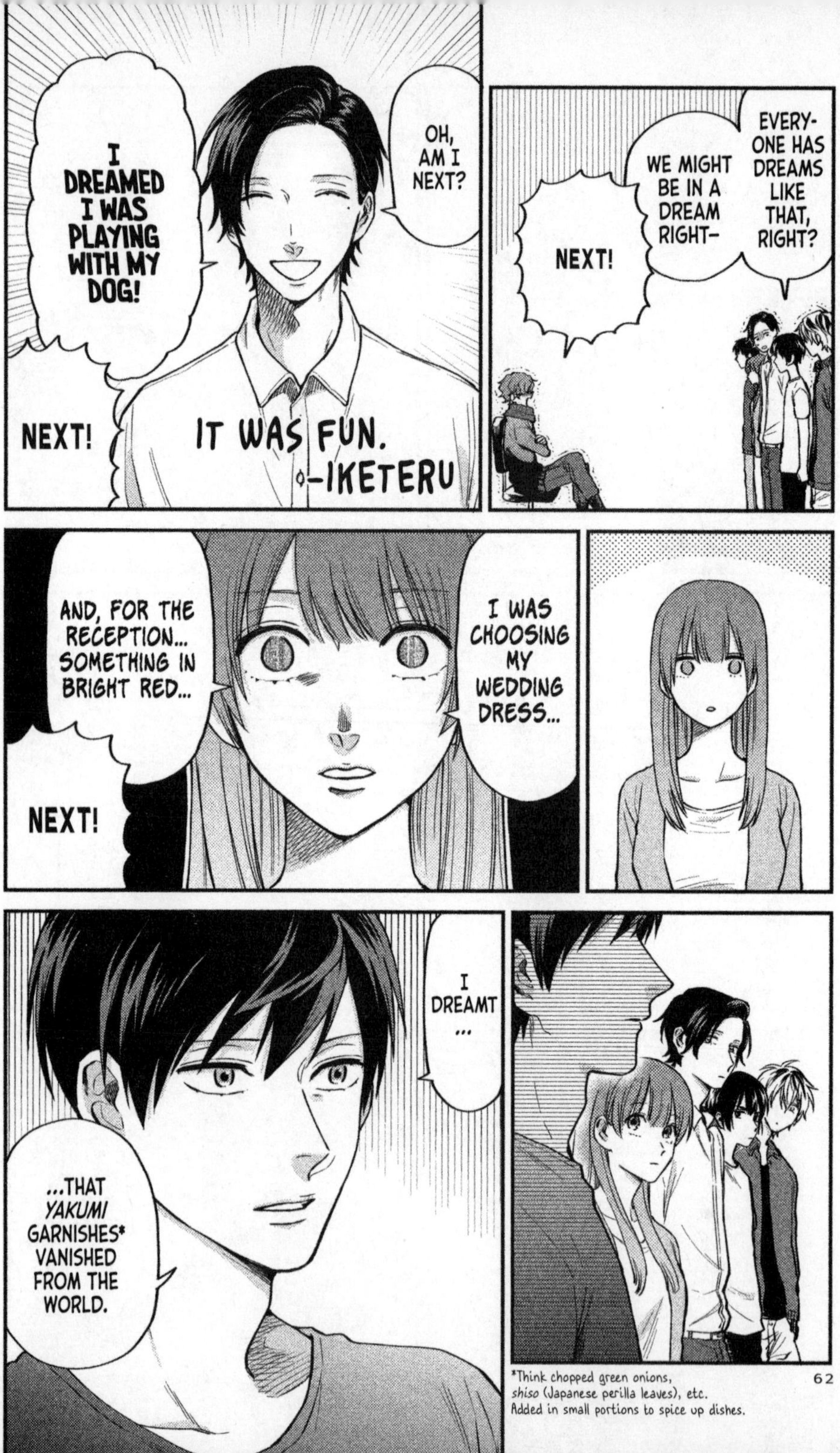
EVERY-ONE HAS DREAMS LIKE THAT, RIGHT?
WE MIGHT BE IN A DREAM RIGHT-
NEXT!
OH, AM I NEXT?
I DREAMED I WAS PLAYING WITH MY DOG!
IT WAS FUN. -IKETERU
NEXT!
I WAS CHOOSING MY WEDDING DRESS...
AND, FOR THE RECEPTION... SOMETHING IN BRIGHT RED...
NEXT!
I DREAMT...
...THAT *YAKUMI* GARNISHES* VANISHED FROM THE WORLD.

*Think chopped green onions, *shiso* (Japanese perilla leaves), etc. Added in small portions to spice up dishes.

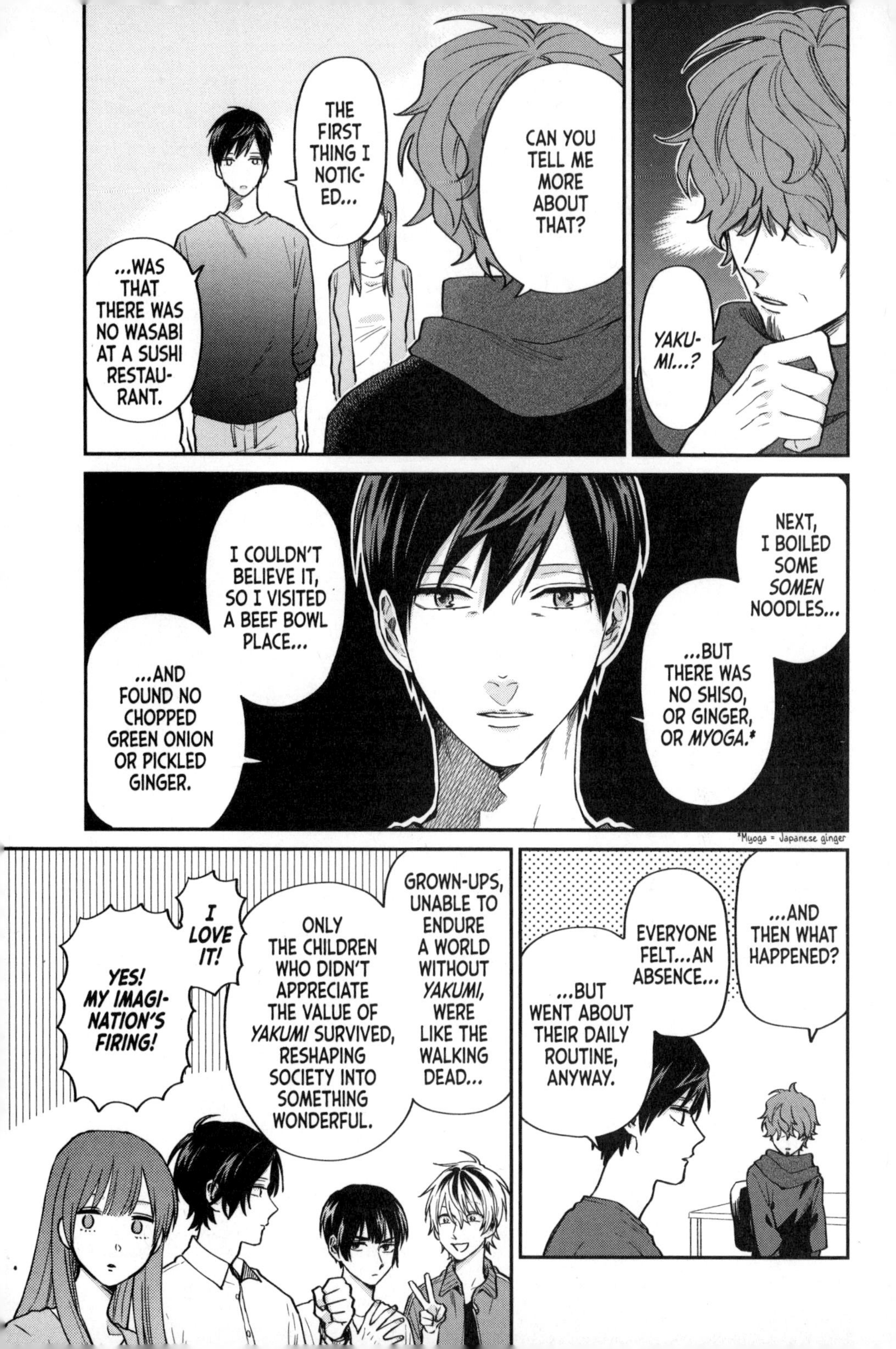
YAKUMI...?
CAN YOU TELL ME MORE ABOUT THAT?
THE FIRST THING I NOTICED...
...WAS THAT THERE WAS NO WASABI AT A SUSHI RESTAURANT.
NEXT, I BOILED SOME *SOMEN* NOODLES...
...BUT THERE WAS NO SHISO, OR GINGER, OR *MYOGA*.*
I COULDN'T BELIEVE IT, SO I VISITED A BEEF BOWL PLACE...
...AND FOUND NO CHOPPED GREEN ONION OR PICKLED GINGER.
...AND THEN WHAT HAPPENED?
EVERYONE FELT...AN ABSENCE...
...BUT WENT ABOUT THEIR DAILY ROUTINE, ANYWAY.
GROWN-UPS, UNABLE TO ENDURE A WORLD WITHOUT *YAKUMI*, WERE LIKE THE WALKING DEAD...
ONLY THE CHILDREN WHO DIDN'T APPRECIATE THE VALUE OF *YAKUMI* SURVIVED, RESHAPING SOCIETY INTO SOMETHING WONDERFUL.
I LOVE IT!
YES! MY IMAGINATION'S FIRING!

*Myoga = Japanese ginger

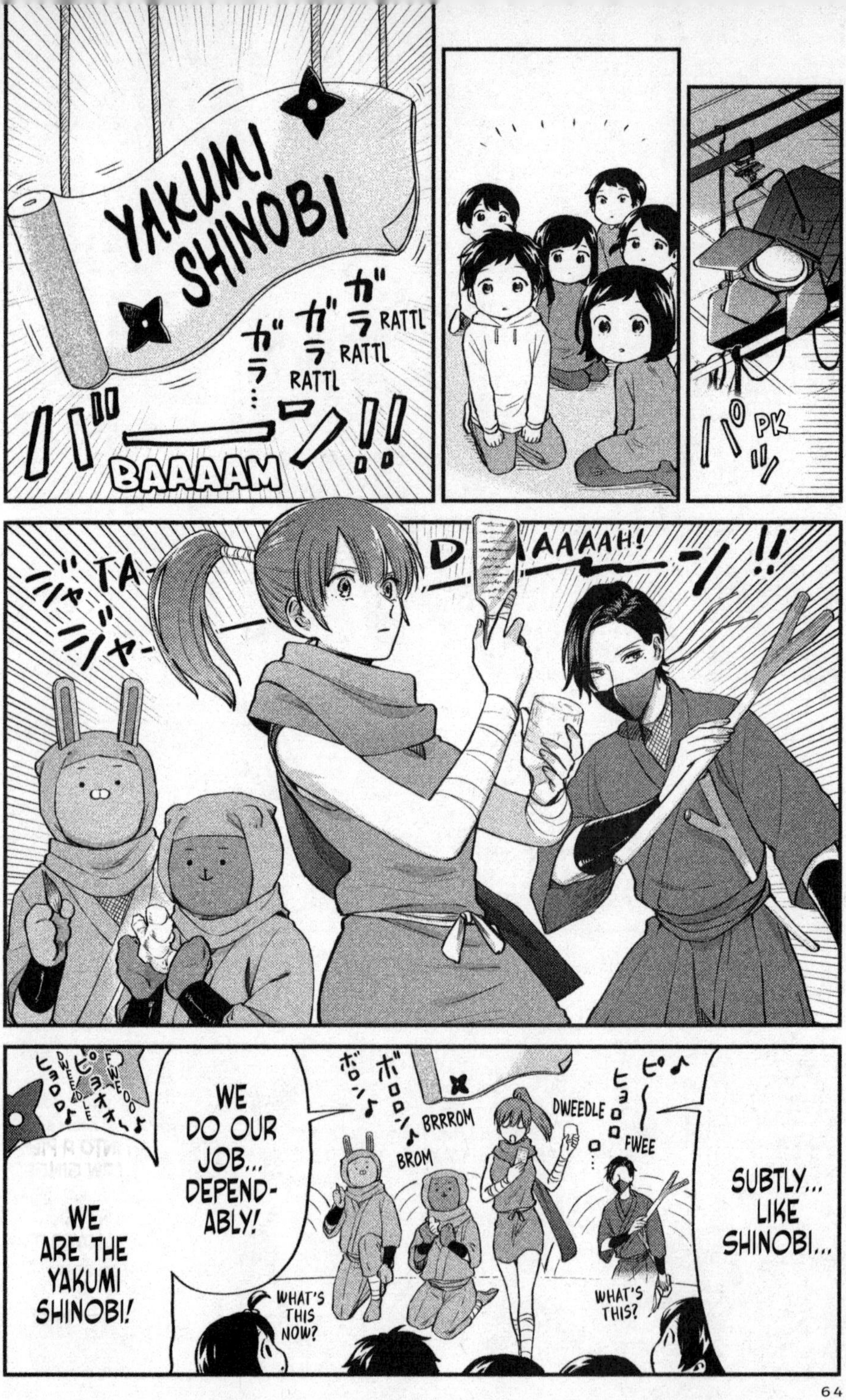
パッ PK
YAKUMI SHINOBI
ガラ RATTL
ガラ RATTL
ガラ… RATTL
バ——ン!! BAAAAM
TA—DAAAAAH!!
ジャジャー
ピ〜♪ ヒョロロ… DWEEDLE FWEE
SUBTLY... LIKE SHINOBI...
WHAT'S THIS?
ボロロン♪ BRRROM
ボロン♪ BROM
WE DO OUR JOB... DEPENDABLY!
WHAT'S THIS NOW?
ピヨオ〜♪ FWEOO
ヒョロロ♪ DWEEDLE
WE ARE THE YAKUMI SHINOBI!

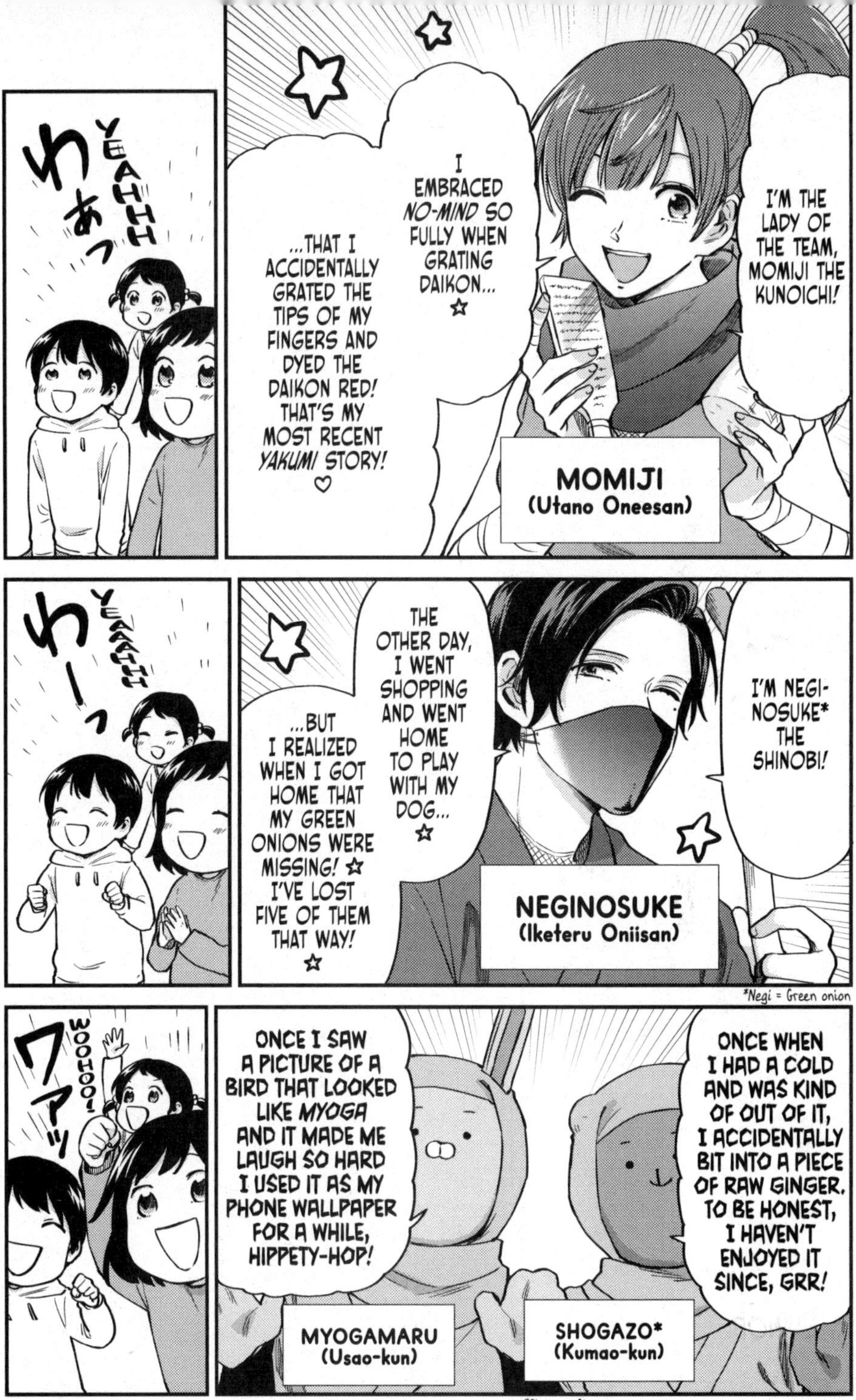
I'M THE LADY OF THE TEAM, MOMIJI THE KUNOICHI!
I EMBRACED *NO-MIND* SO FULLY WHEN GRATING DAIKON... ☆
...THAT I ACCIDENTALLY GRATED THE TIPS OF MY FINGERS AND DYED THE DAIKON RED! THAT'S MY MOST RECENT *YAKUMI* STORY! ♡
MOMIJI
(Utano Oneesan)
わあっ
YEAHHH
I'M NEGI-NOSUKE* THE SHINOBI!
THE OTHER DAY, I WENT SHOPPING AND WENT HOME TO PLAY WITH MY DOG... ☆
...BUT I REALIZED WHEN I GOT HOME THAT MY GREEN ONIONS WERE MISSING! ☆ I'VE LOST FIVE OF THEM THAT WAY! ☆
NEGINOSUKE
(Iketeru Oniisan)
わーっ
YEAAAHHH
ONCE WHEN I HAD A COLD AND WAS KIND OF OUT OF IT, I ACCIDENTALLY BIT INTO A PIECE OF RAW GINGER. TO BE HONEST, I HAVEN'T ENJOYED IT SINCE, GRR!
ONCE I SAW A PICTURE OF A BIRD THAT LOOKED LIKE *MYOGA* AND IT MADE ME LAUGH SO HARD I USED IT AS MY PHONE WALLPAPER FOR A WHILE, HIPPETY-HOP!
SHOGAZO*
(Kumao-kun)
MYOGAMARU
(Usao-kun)
ワァッ
WOOHOO!

*Negi = Green onion

*Shoga = Ginger

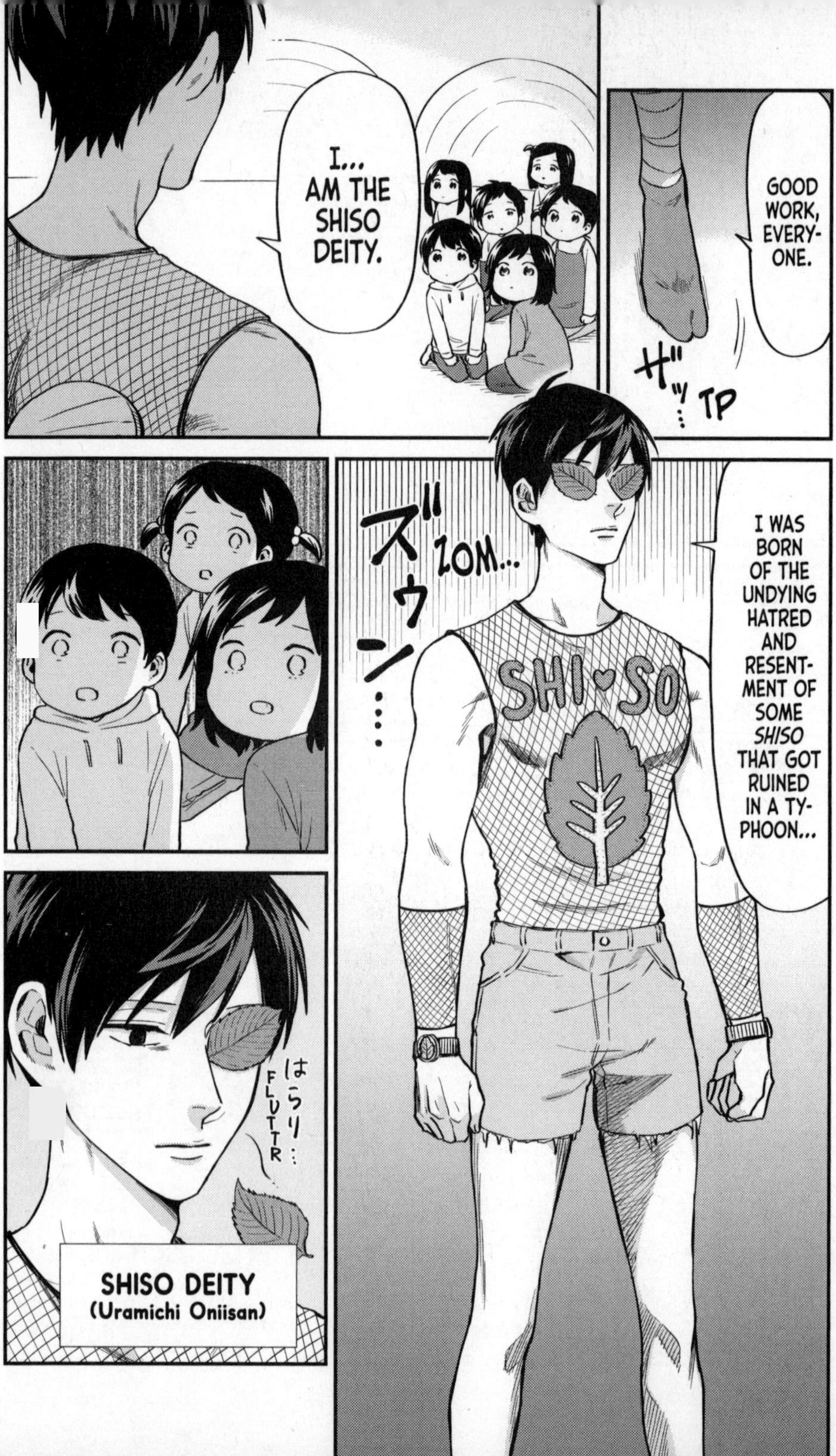
GOOD WORK, EVERY-ONE.
ザッ TP
I... AM THE SHISO DEITY.
ズゥーン… ZOM...
I WAS BORN OF THE UNDYING HATRED AND RESENT-MENT OF SOME *SHISO* THAT GOT RUINED IN A TY-PHOON...
SHI♥SO
はらり… FLUTTR
SHISO DEITY
(Uramichi Oniisan)

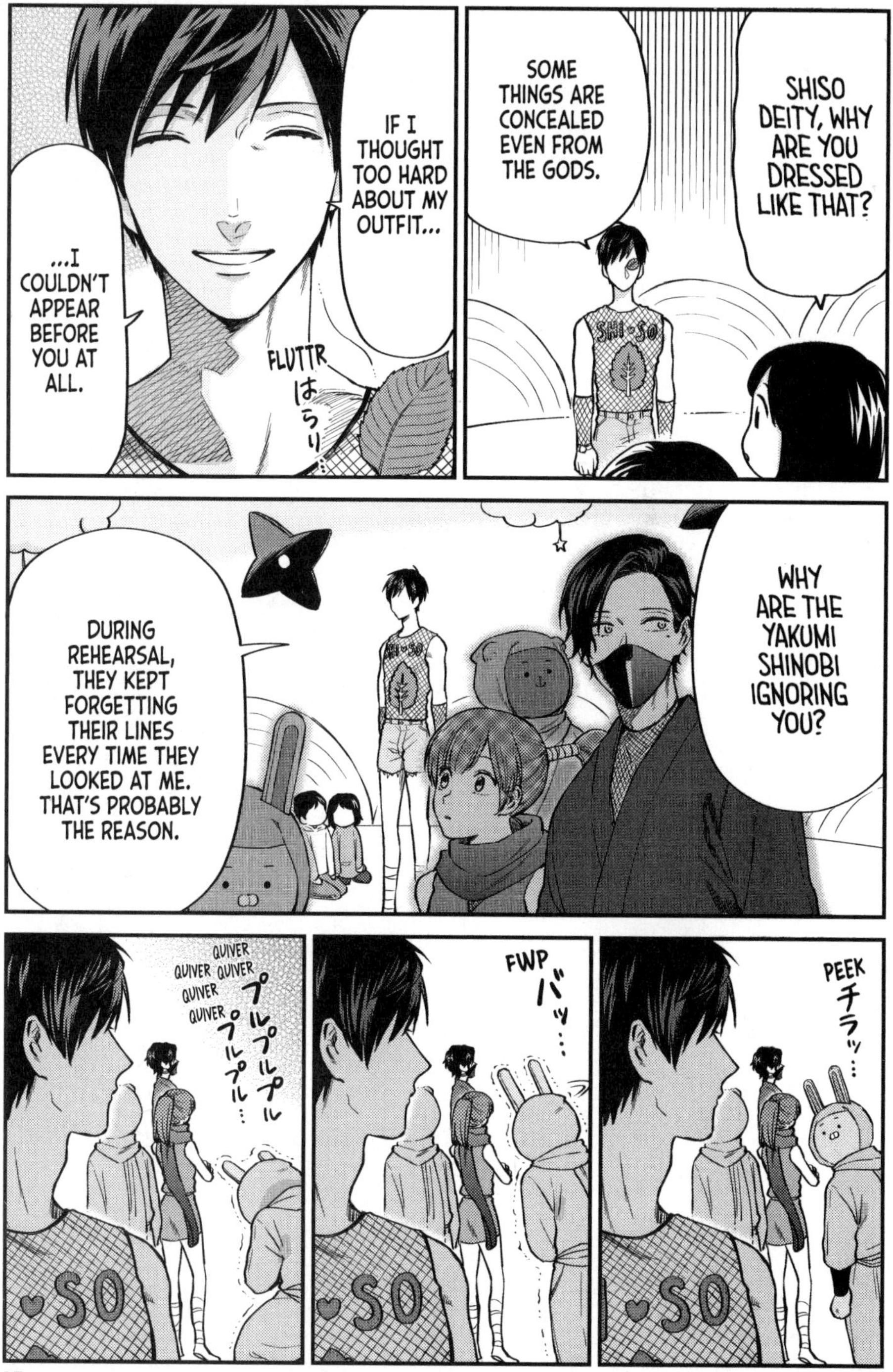
SHISO DEITY, WHY ARE YOU DRESSED LIKE THAT?
SOME THINGS ARE CONCEALED EVEN FROM THE GODS.
IF I THOUGHT TOO HARD ABOUT MY OUTFIT...
...I COULDN'T APPEAR BEFORE YOU AT ALL.
FLUTTR
はらり…
WHY ARE THE YAKUMI SHINOBI IGNORING YOU?
DURING REHEARSAL, THEY KEPT FORGETTING THEIR LINES EVERY TIME THEY LOOKED AT ME. THAT'S PROBABLY THE REASON.
PEEK
チラッ…
FWP
バッ…
QUIVER QUIVER QUIVER QUIVER QUIVER
プルプルプル
プルプル…

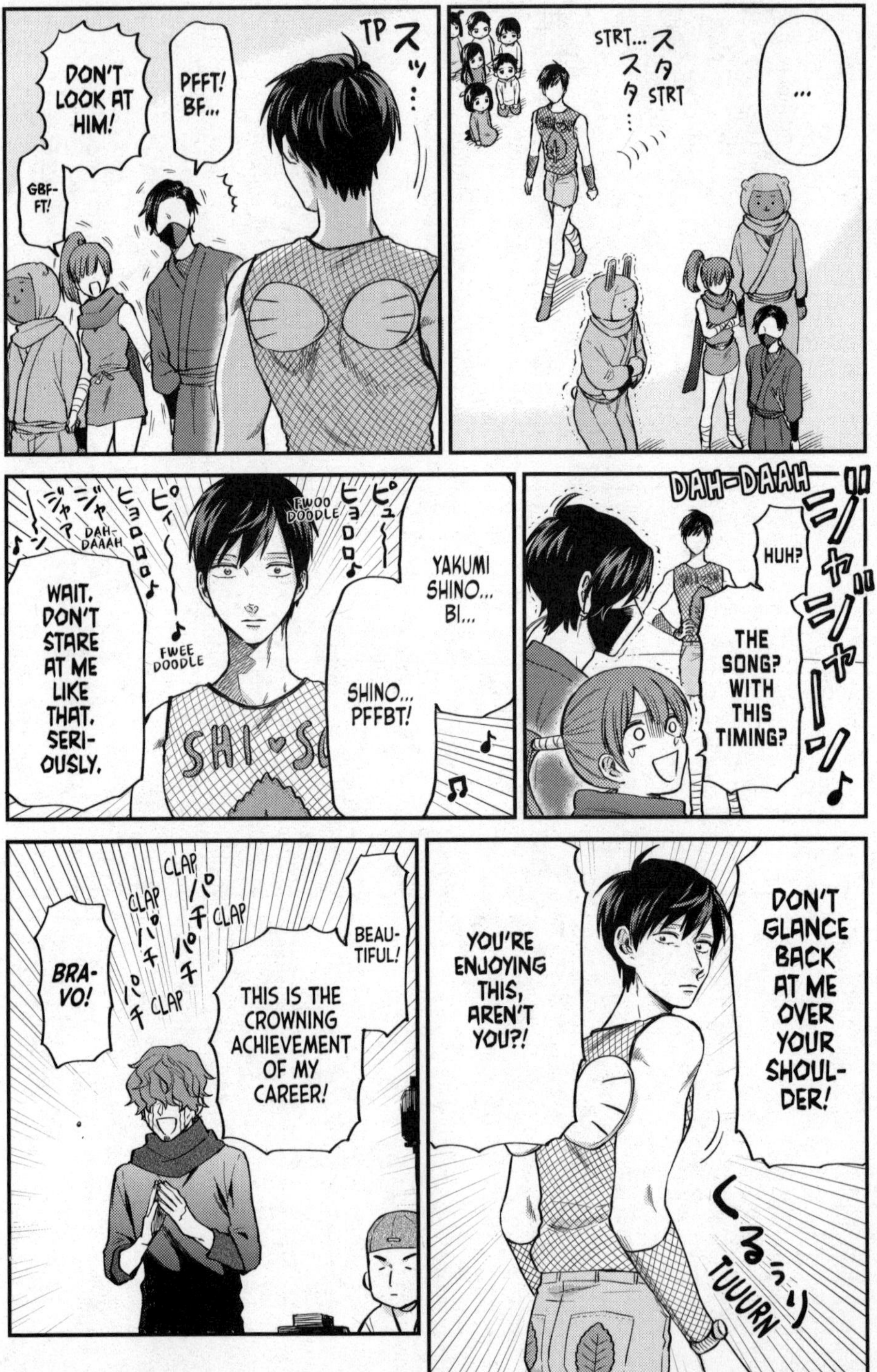
STRT... スタ スタ STRT
...
TP スッ...
PFFT! BF...
DON'T LOOK AT HIM!
GBF-FT!
DAH-DAAH ジャジャーン♪
HUH?
THE SONG? WITH THIS TIMING?
ピュ~ ヒョロロ♪ FWOO DOODLE
YAKUMI SHINO... BI...
SHINO... PFFBT!
ピィ~ ヒョロロロ♪ FWEE DOODLE
ジャジャア~ン♪ DAH-DAAAH
WAIT. DON'T STARE AT ME LIKE THAT. SERI-OUSLY.
DON'T GLANCE BACK AT ME OVER YOUR SHOUL-DER!
YOU'RE ENJOYING THIS, AREN'T YOU?!
くるぅり TUUURN
BEAU-TIFUL!
THIS IS THE CROWNING ACHIEVEMENT OF MY CAREER!
パチ パチ パチ パチ CLAP CLAP CLAP CLAP
BRA-VO!

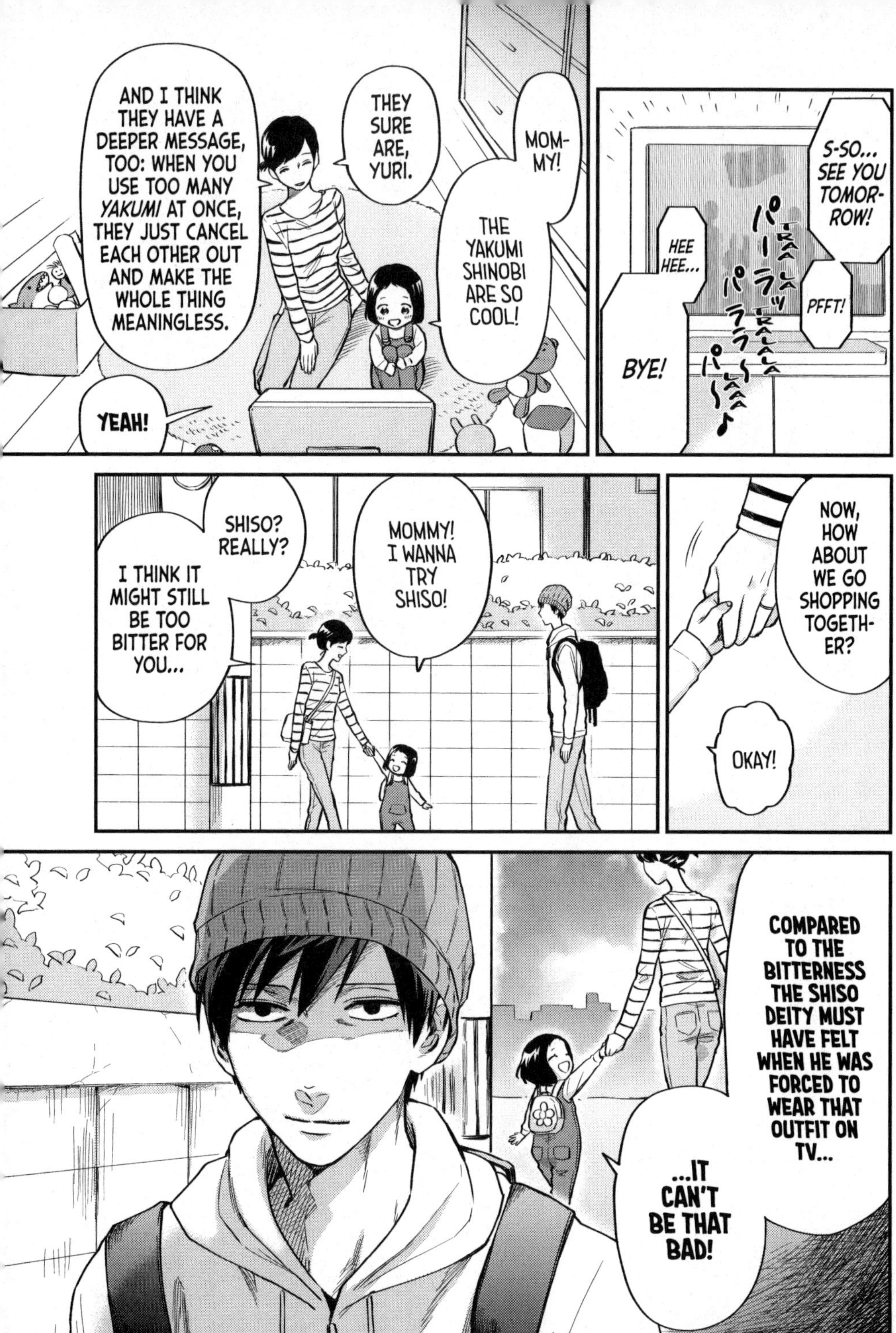
S-SO... SEE YOU TOMORROW!
PFFT!
パーラッパラララ〜パー〜♪
TRAA LA TRALALA LAAA
HEE HEE...
BYE!
MOMMY!
THE YAKUMI SHINOBI ARE SO COOL!
THEY SURE ARE, YURI.
AND I THINK THEY HAVE A DEEPER MESSAGE, TOO: WHEN YOU USE TOO MANY *YAKUMI* AT ONCE, THEY JUST CANCEL EACH OTHER OUT AND MAKE THE WHOLE THING MEANINGLESS.
YEAH!
NOW, HOW ABOUT WE GO SHOPPING TOGETHER?
OKAY!
MOMMY! I WANNA TRY SHISO!
SHISO? REALLY?
I THINK IT MIGHT STILL BE TOO BITTER FOR YOU...
COMPARED TO THE BITTERNESS THE SHISO DEITY MUST HAVE FELT WHEN HE WAS FORCED TO WEAR THAT OUTFIT ON TV...
...IT CAN'T BE THAT BAD!

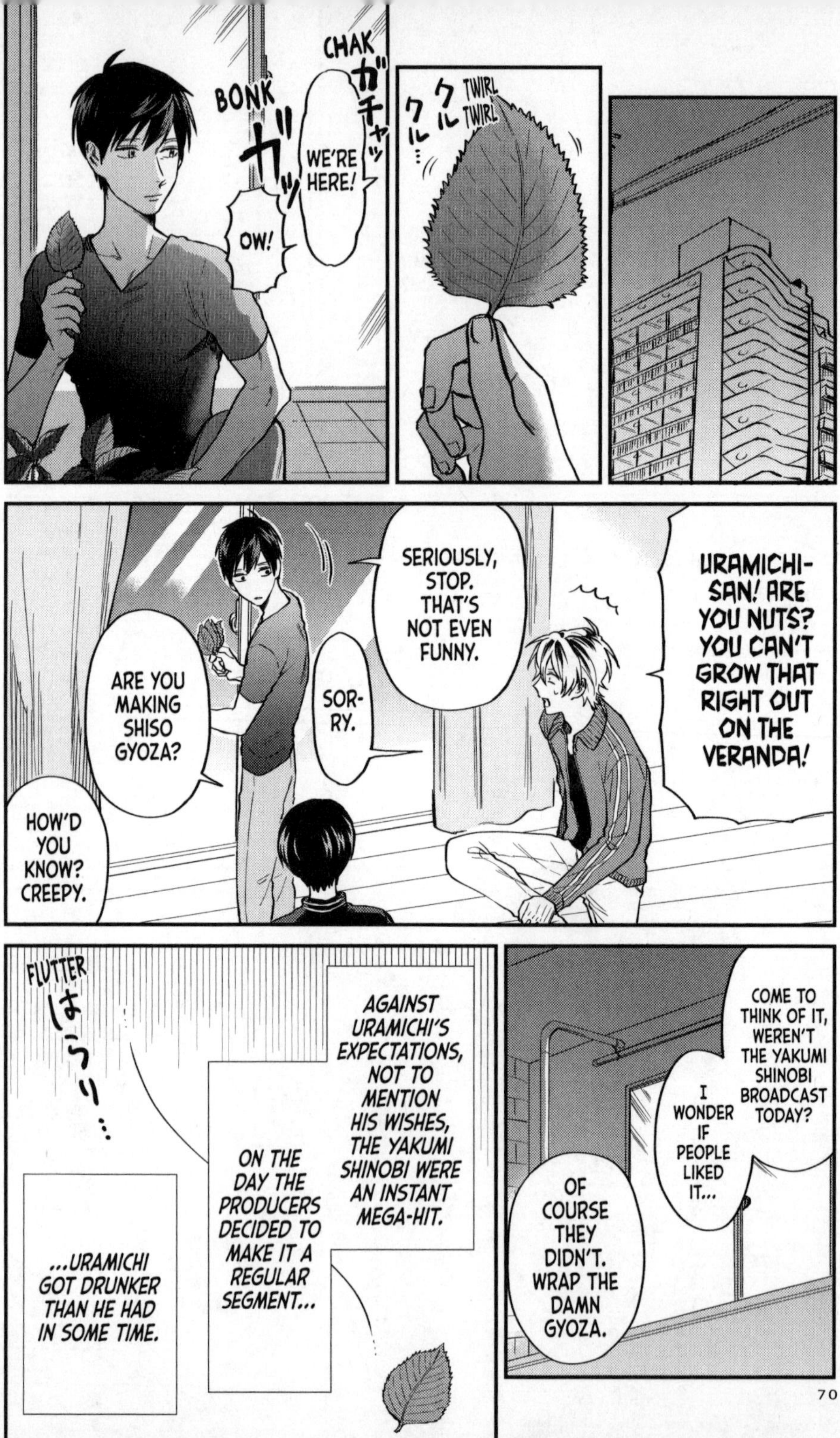
クル クル…
TWIRL TWIRL
CHAK
ガチャッ
WE'RE HERE!
BONK
ガッ
OW!
URAMICHI-SAN! ARE YOU NUTS? YOU CAN'T GROW THAT RIGHT OUT ON THE VERANDA!
SERIOUSLY, STOP. THAT'S NOT EVEN FUNNY.
SOR-RY.
ARE YOU MAKING SHISO GYOZA?
HOW'D YOU KNOW? CREEPY.
COME TO THINK OF IT, WEREN'T THE YAKUMI SHINOBI BROADCAST TODAY?
I WONDER IF PEOPLE LIKED IT...
OF COURSE THEY DIDN'T. WRAP THE DAMN GYOZA.
AGAINST URAMICHI'S EXPECTATIONS, NOT TO MENTION HIS WISHES, THE YAKUMI SHINOBI WERE AN INSTANT MEGA-HIT.
ON THE DAY THE PRODUCERS DECIDED TO MAKE IT A REGULAR SEGMENT...
FLUTTER
はらり…
...URAMICHI GOT DRUNKER THAN HE HAD IN SOME TIME.

Life Lessons with
Uramichi Oniisan

Yakumi Shinobi

Sung by Iketeru Oniisan and Utano Oneesan

Subtly...like shinobi
We do our job...dependably

We are the Yakumi Shinobi!

Turn off the lights
Erase your presence
Close off your mind
Melt into the darkness of the world

On tiptoe...like a shadow
We add a hint of flavor...and then go

But even so
At times, we're a necessary part of the show

Dreaming, skygazing, reading the vibe
Watching the world from off to one side

We are the Yakumi Shinobi!

Spicy with a tingle,
numb like pins and needles
The stimulation's habit-forming
If everything were sweet,
the world would be boring

Running up your sinuses
Stabbing at your tear ducts

The fragrant vistas of the grown-up world

That's us, the Yakumi Shinobi

We are the Yakumi Shinobi!

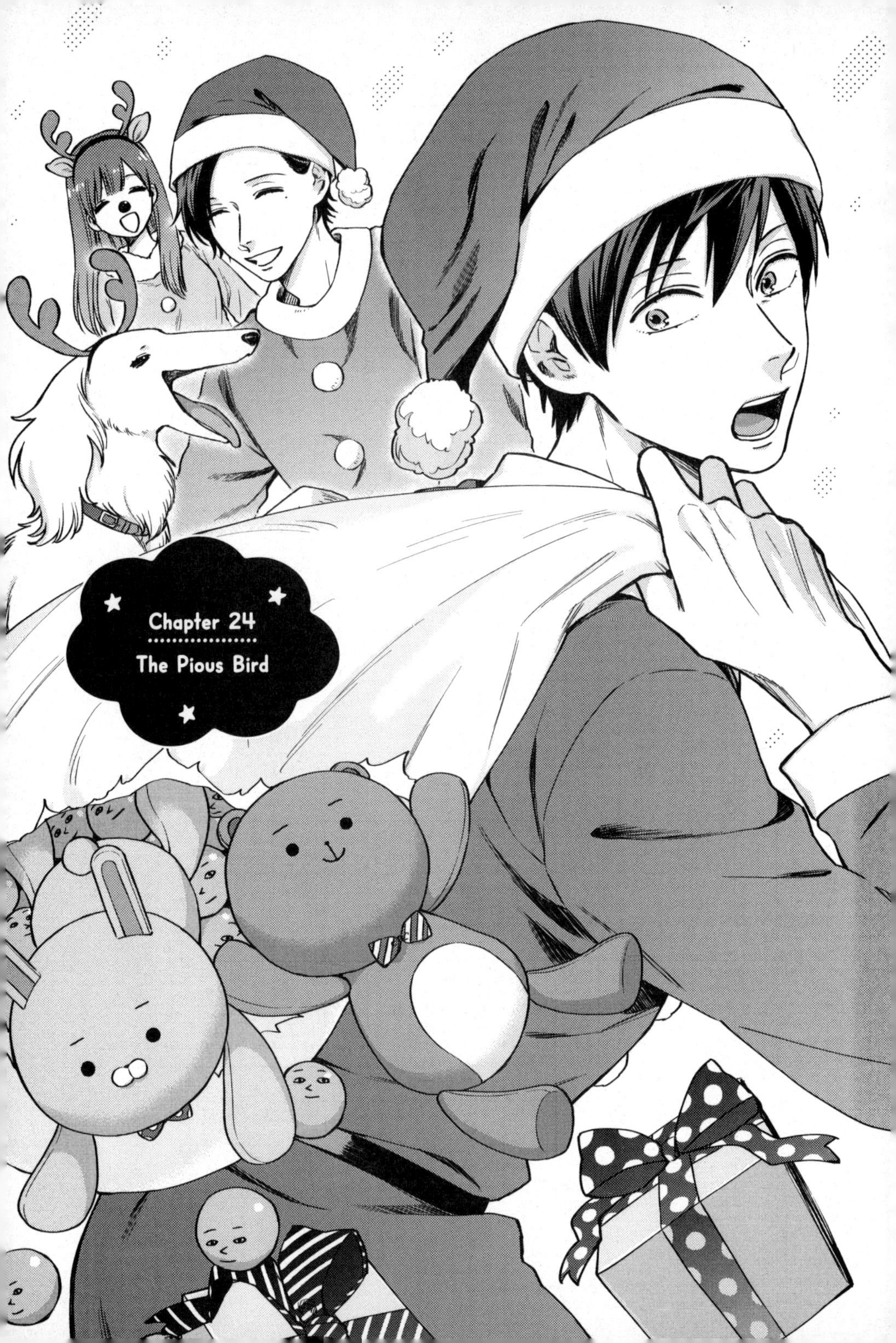
Chapter 24
The Pious Bird

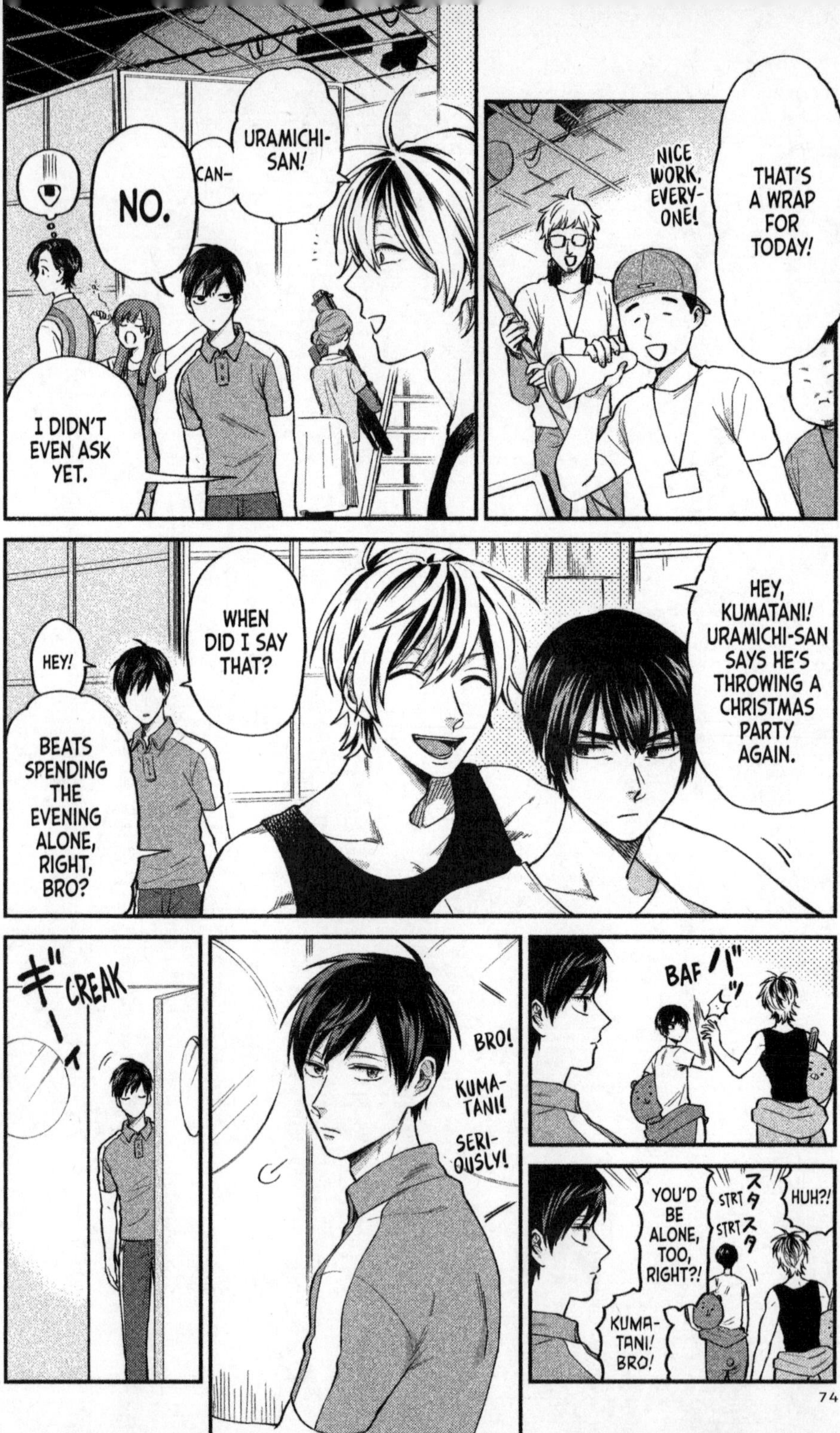
THAT'S A WRAP FOR TODAY!
NICE WORK, EVERY-ONE!
URAMICHI-SAN!
CAN–
NO.
I DIDN'T EVEN ASK YET.
HEY, KUMATANI! URAMICHI-SAN SAYS HE'S THROWING A CHRISTMAS PARTY AGAIN.
WHEN DID I SAY THAT?
HEY!
BEATS SPENDING THE EVENING ALONE, RIGHT, BRO?
BAF
HUH?!
STRT STRT
YOU'D BE ALONE, TOO, RIGHT?!
KUMA-TANI! BRO!
BRO!
KUMA-TANI!
SERI-OUSLY!
CREAK

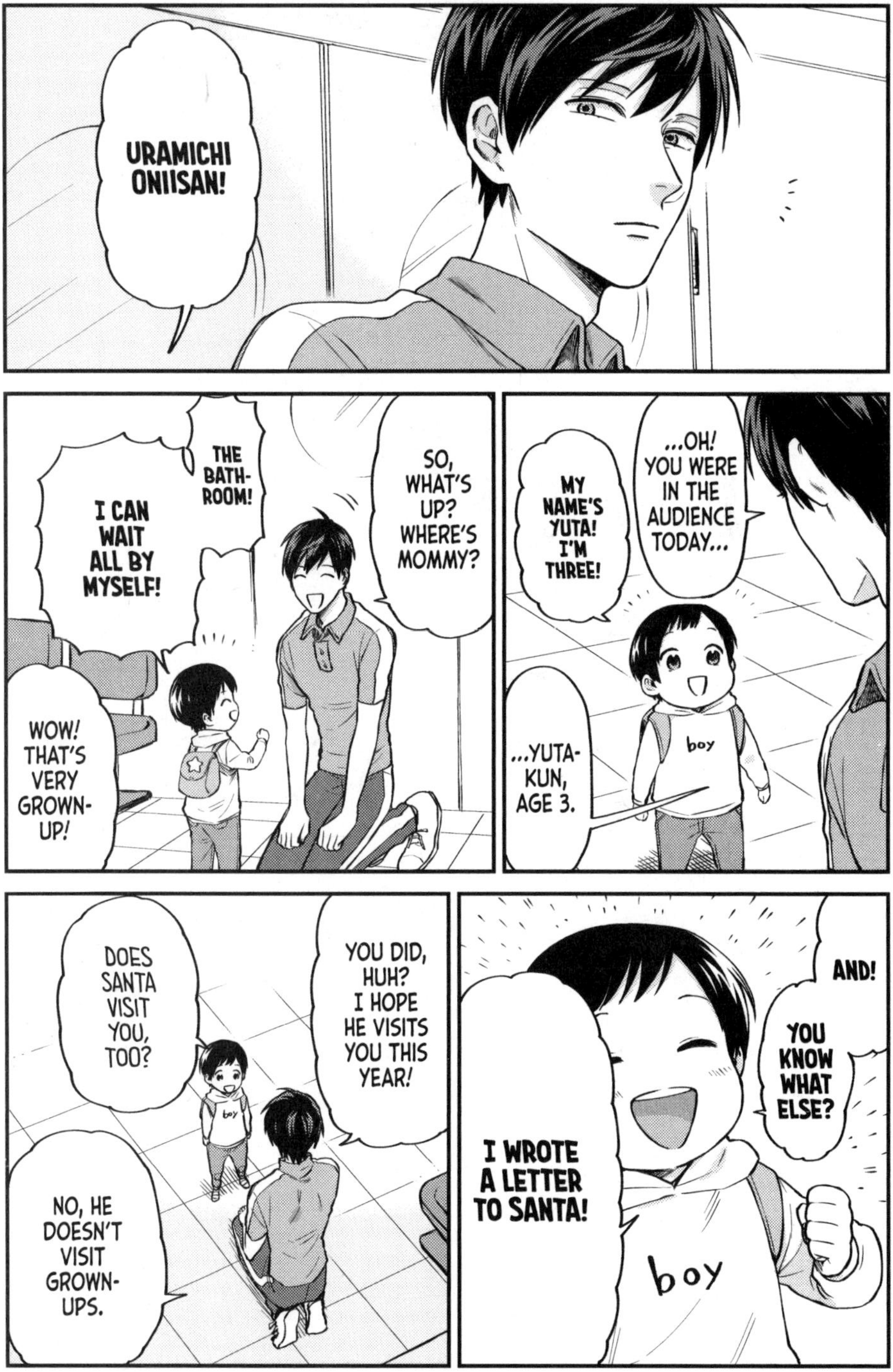
URAMICHI ONIISAN!
...OH! YOU WERE IN THE AUDIENCE TODAY...
MY NAME'S YUTA! I'M THREE!
boy
...YUTA-KUN, AGE 3.
SO, WHAT'S UP? WHERE'S MOMMY?
THE BATHROOM!
I CAN WAIT ALL BY MYSELF!
WOW! THAT'S VERY GROWN-UP!
AND!
YOU KNOW WHAT ELSE?
I WROTE A LETTER TO SANTA!
boy
YOU DID, HUH? I HOPE HE VISITS YOU THIS YEAR!
DOES SANTA VISIT YOU, TOO?
boy
NO, HE DOESN'T VISIT GROWN-UPS.

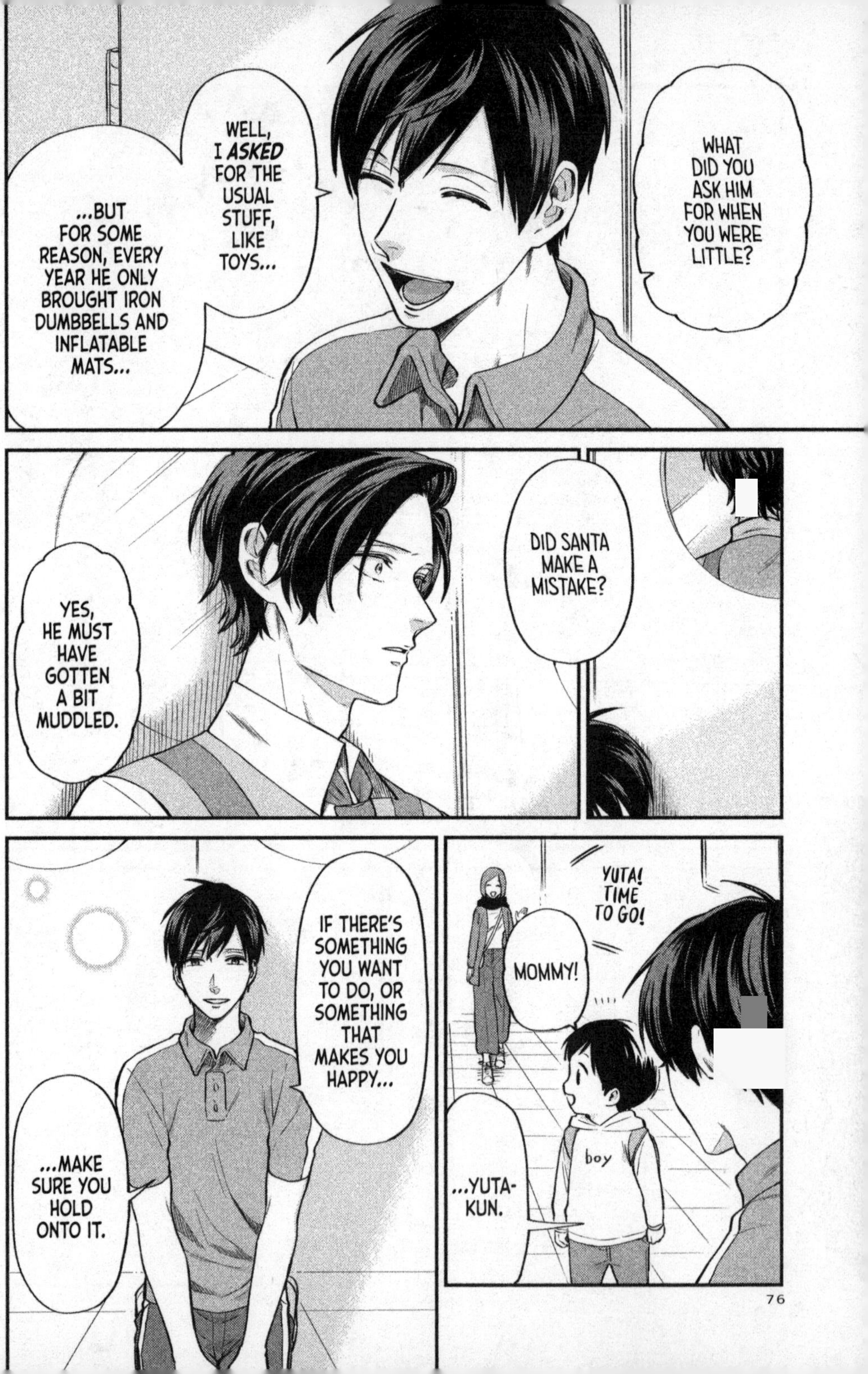
WHAT DID YOU ASK HIM FOR WHEN YOU WERE LITTLE?
WELL, I *ASKED* FOR THE USUAL STUFF, LIKE TOYS...
...BUT FOR SOME REASON, EVERY YEAR HE ONLY BROUGHT IRON DUMBBELLS AND INFLATABLE MATS...
DID SANTA MAKE A MISTAKE?
YES, HE MUST HAVE GOTTEN A BIT MUDDLED.
YUTA! TIME TO GO!
MOMMY!
boy
...YUTA-KUN.
IF THERE'S SOMETHING YOU WANT TO DO, OR SOMETHING THAT MAKES YOU HAPPY...
...MAKE SURE YOU HOLD ONTO IT.

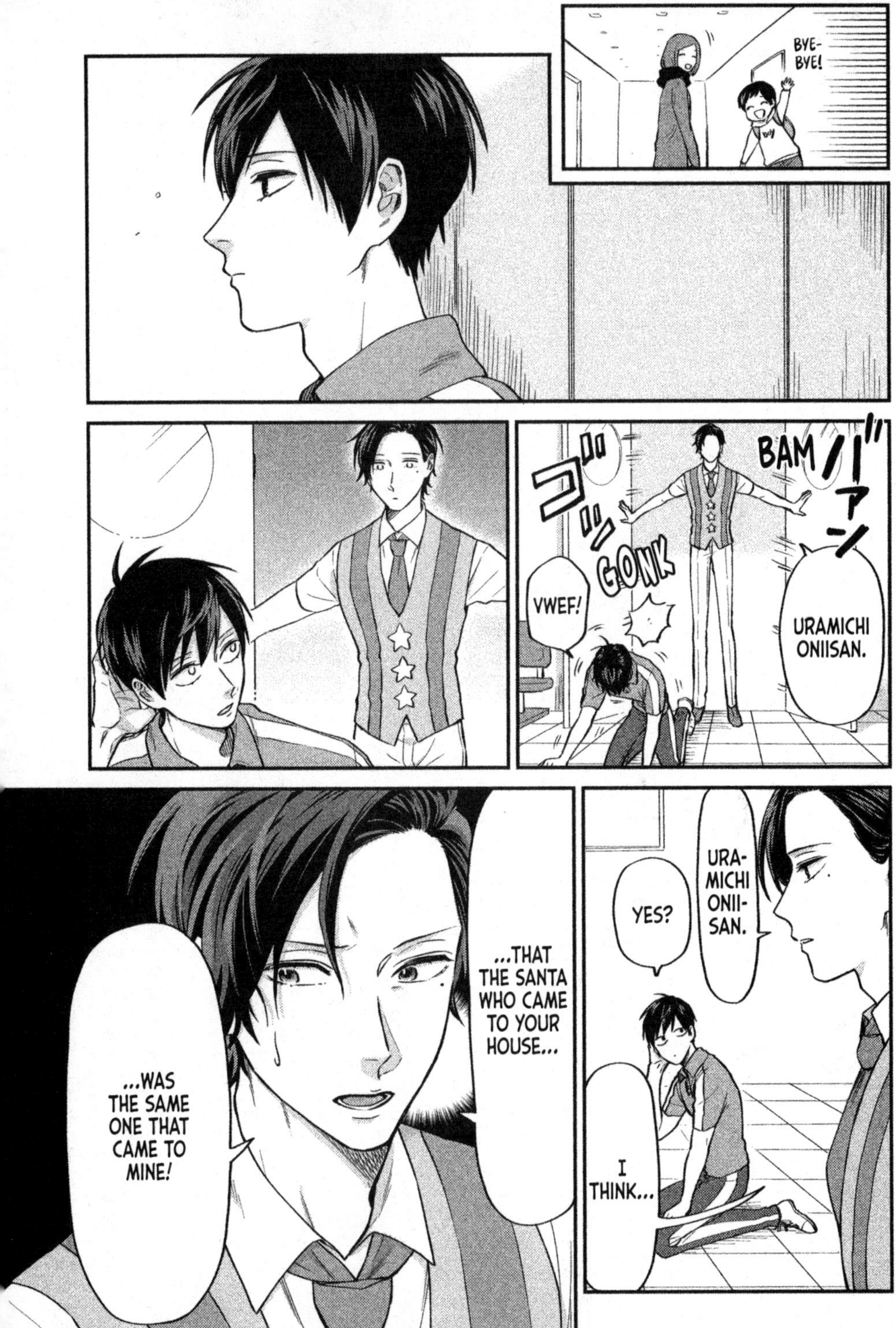
BYE-BYE!
BAM
バーン
URAMICHI ONIISAN.
ゴッ
GONK
VWEF!
URA-MICHI ONII-SAN.
YES?
I THINK...
...THAT THE SANTA WHO CAME TO YOUR HOUSE...
...WAS THE SAME ONE THAT CAME TO MINE!

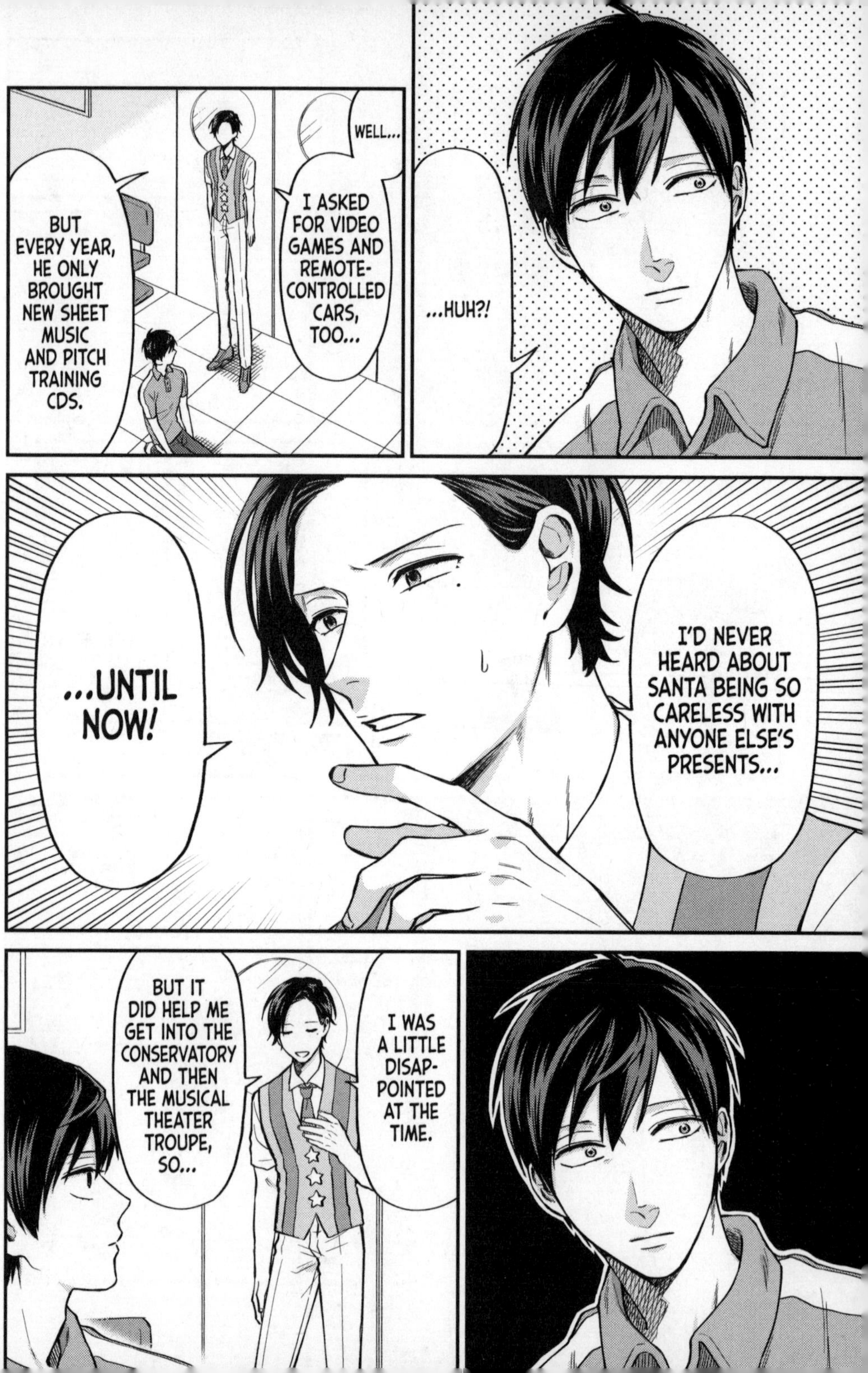
...HUH?!
WELL...
I ASKED FOR VIDEO GAMES AND REMOTE-CONTROLLED CARS, TOO...
BUT EVERY YEAR, HE ONLY BROUGHT NEW SHEET MUSIC AND PITCH TRAINING CDS.
I'D NEVER HEARD ABOUT SANTA BEING SO CARELESS WITH ANYONE ELSE'S PRESENTS...
...UNTIL NOW!
I WAS A LITTLE DISAPPOINTED AT THE TIME.
BUT IT DID HELP ME GET INTO THE CONSERVATORY AND THEN THE MUSICAL THEATER TROUPE, SO...

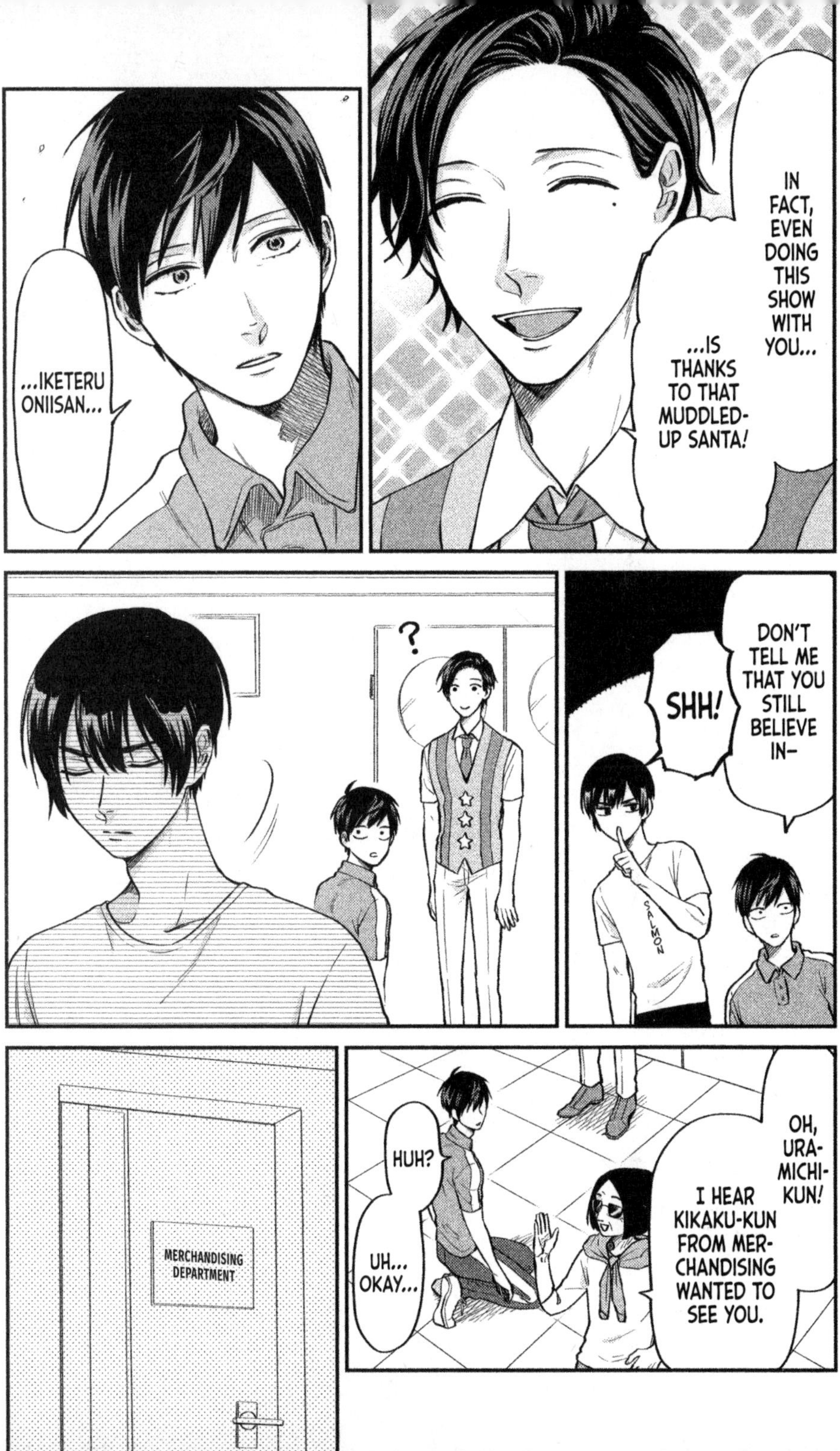
IN FACT, EVEN DOING THIS SHOW WITH YOU...
...IS THANKS TO THAT MUDDLED-UP SANTA!
...IKETERU ONIISAN...
DON'T TELL ME THAT YOU STILL BELIEVE IN–
SHH!
SALMON
?
OH, URA-MICHI-KUN!
I HEAR KIKAKU-KUN FROM MER-CHANDISING WANTED TO SEE YOU.
HUH?
UH... OKAY...
MERCHANDISING DEPARTMENT

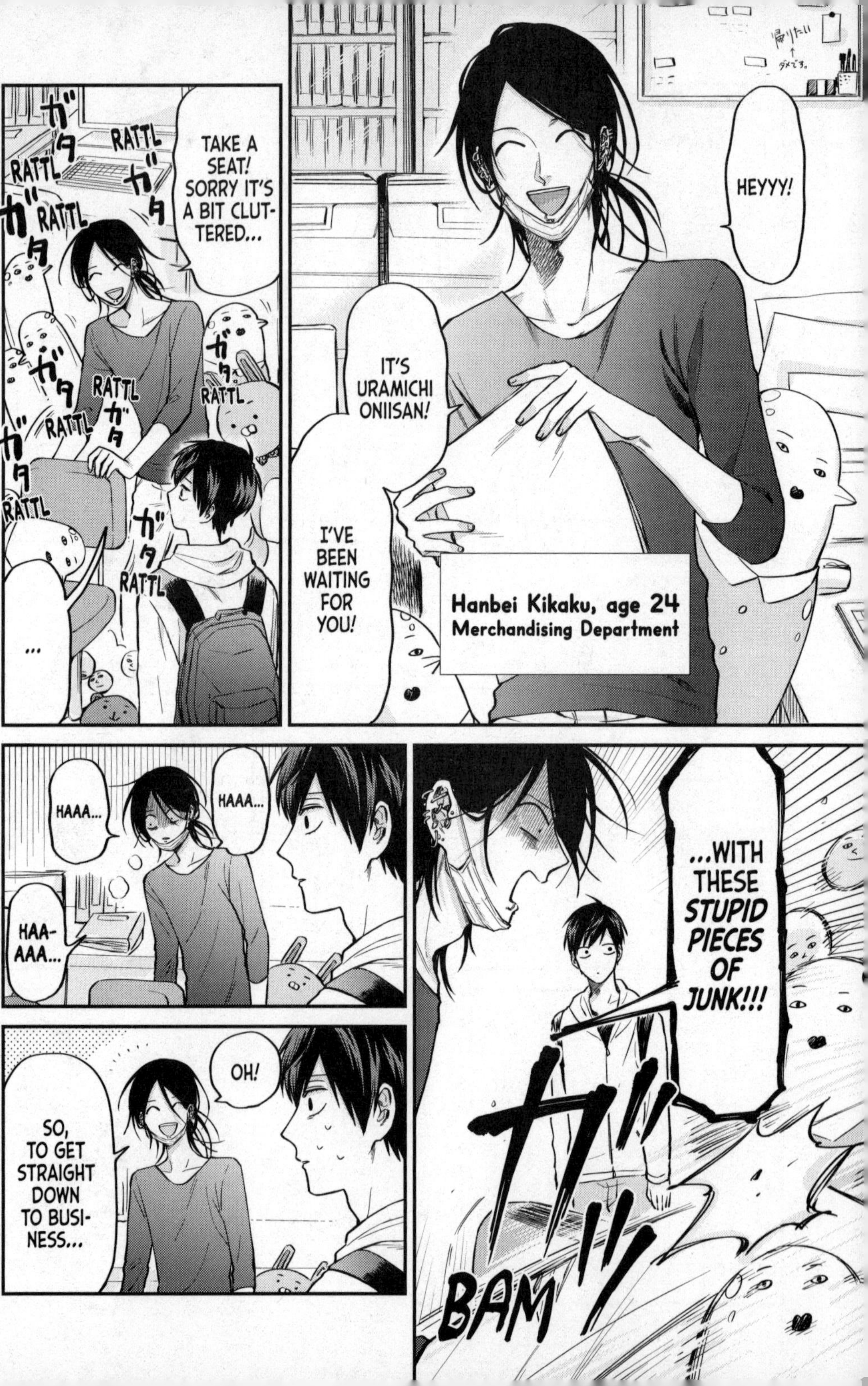
帰りたい
↑
ダメです。
HEYYY!
IT'S URAMICHI ONIISAN!
I'VE BEEN WAITING FOR YOU!
Hanbei Kikaku, age 24
Merchandising Department
TAKE A SEAT! SORRY IT'S A BIT CLUTTERED...
RATTL
RATTL
RATTL
RATTL
RATTL
RATTL
RATTL
RATTL
...
...WITH THESE STUPID PIECES OF JUNK!!!
BAM
HAAA...
HAAA...
HAA-AAA...
OH!
SO, TO GET STRAIGHT DOWN TO BUSINESS...

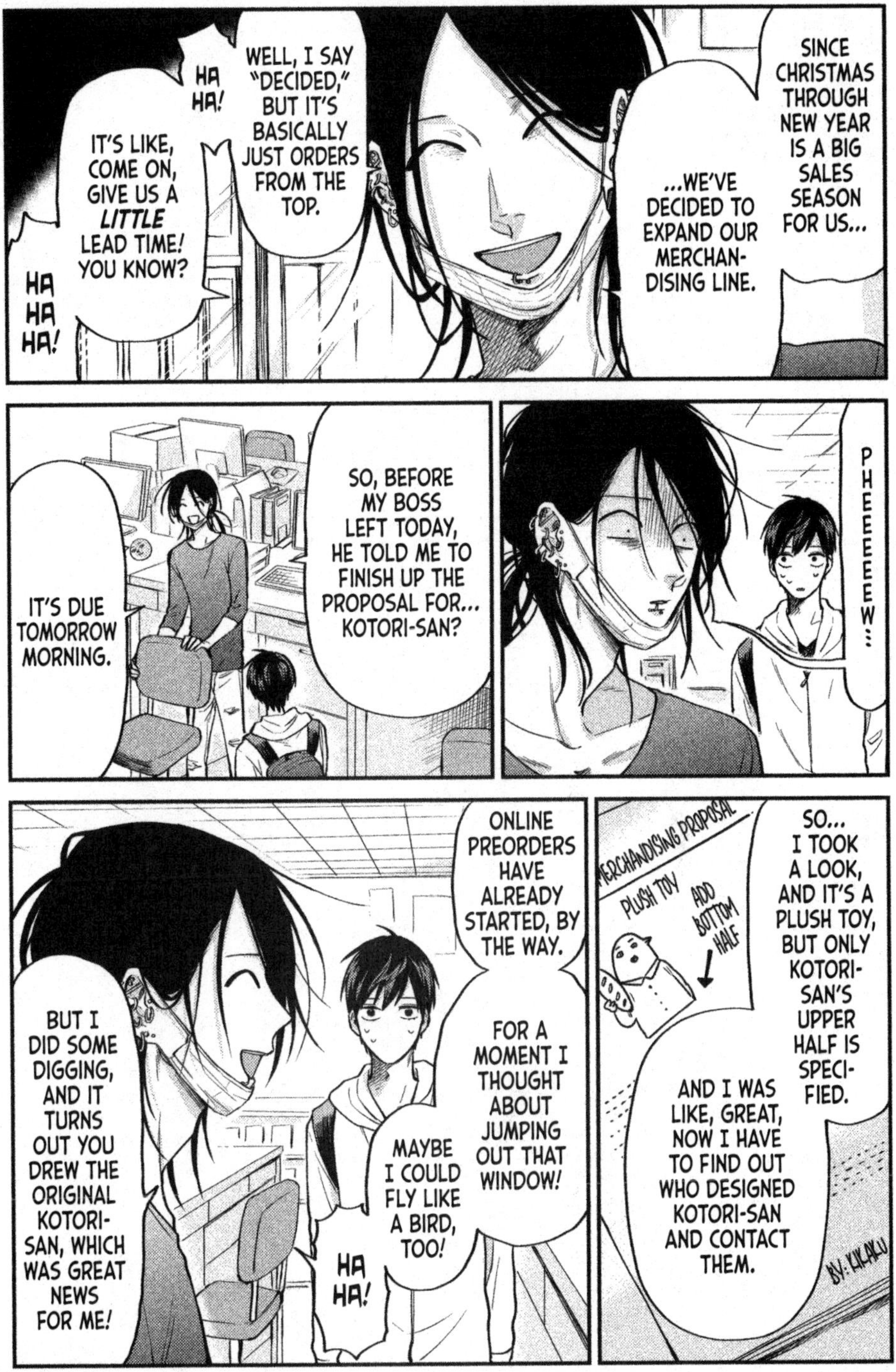
SINCE CHRISTMAS THROUGH NEW YEAR IS A BIG SALES SEASON FOR US...
...WE'VE DECIDED TO EXPAND OUR MERCHANDISING LINE.
WELL, I SAY "DECIDED," BUT IT'S BASICALLY JUST ORDERS FROM THE TOP.
HA HA!
IT'S LIKE, COME ON, GIVE US A *LITTLE* LEAD TIME! YOU KNOW?
HA HA HA!
PHEEEEEEW...
SO, BEFORE MY BOSS LEFT TODAY, HE TOLD ME TO FINISH UP THE PROPOSAL FOR... KOTORI-SAN?
IT'S DUE TOMORROW MORNING.
MERCHANDISING PROPOSAL
PLUSH TOY
ADD BOTTOM HALF
BY: KIKAKU
SO... I TOOK A LOOK, AND IT'S A PLUSH TOY, BUT ONLY KOTORI-SAN'S UPPER HALF IS SPECIFIED.
AND I WAS LIKE, GREAT, NOW I HAVE TO FIND OUT WHO DESIGNED KOTORI-SAN AND CONTACT THEM.
ONLINE PREORDERS HAVE ALREADY STARTED, BY THE WAY.
FOR A MOMENT I THOUGHT ABOUT JUMPING OUT THAT WINDOW!
MAYBE I COULD FLY LIKE A BIRD, TOO!
HA HA!
BUT I DID SOME DIGGING, AND IT TURNS OUT YOU DREW THE ORIGINAL KOTORI-SAN, WHICH WAS GREAT NEWS FOR ME!

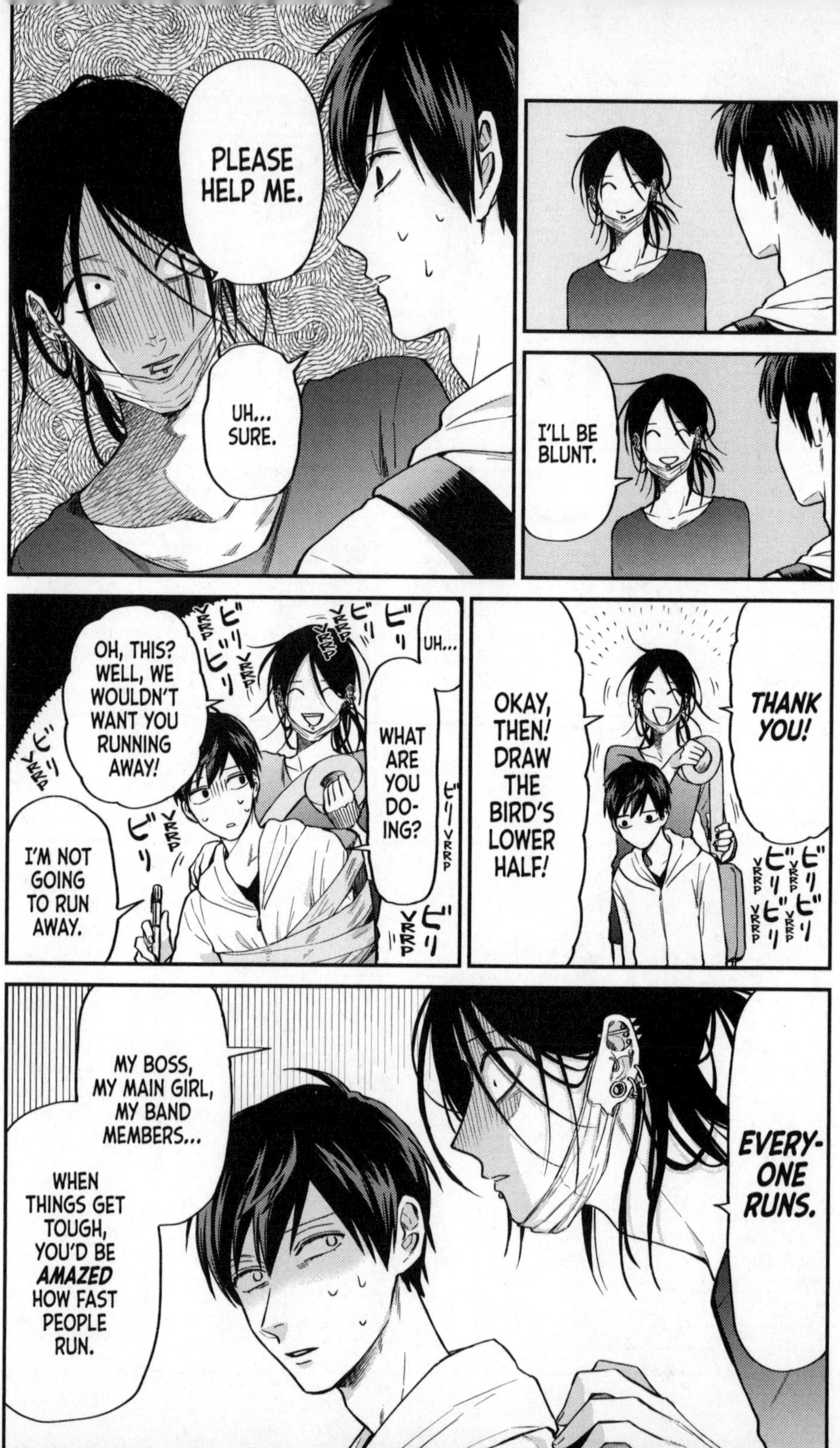
I'LL BE BLUNT.
PLEASE HELP ME.
UH... SURE.
THANK YOU!
OKAY, THEN! DRAW THE BIRD'S LOWER HALF!
ビリ VRRP ビリ VRRP ビリ VRRP ビリ VRRP
UH...
WHAT ARE YOU DOING?
ビリ VRRP ビリ VRRP
ビリ VRRP ビリ VRRP
OH, THIS? WELL, WE WOULDN'T WANT YOU RUNNING AWAY!
ビリ VRRP ビリ VRRP ビリ VRRP
I'M NOT GOING TO RUN AWAY.
EVERY-ONE RUNS.
MY BOSS, MY MAIN GIRL, MY BAND MEMBERS...
WHEN THINGS GET TOUGH, YOU'D BE AMAZED HOW FAST PEOPLE RUN.

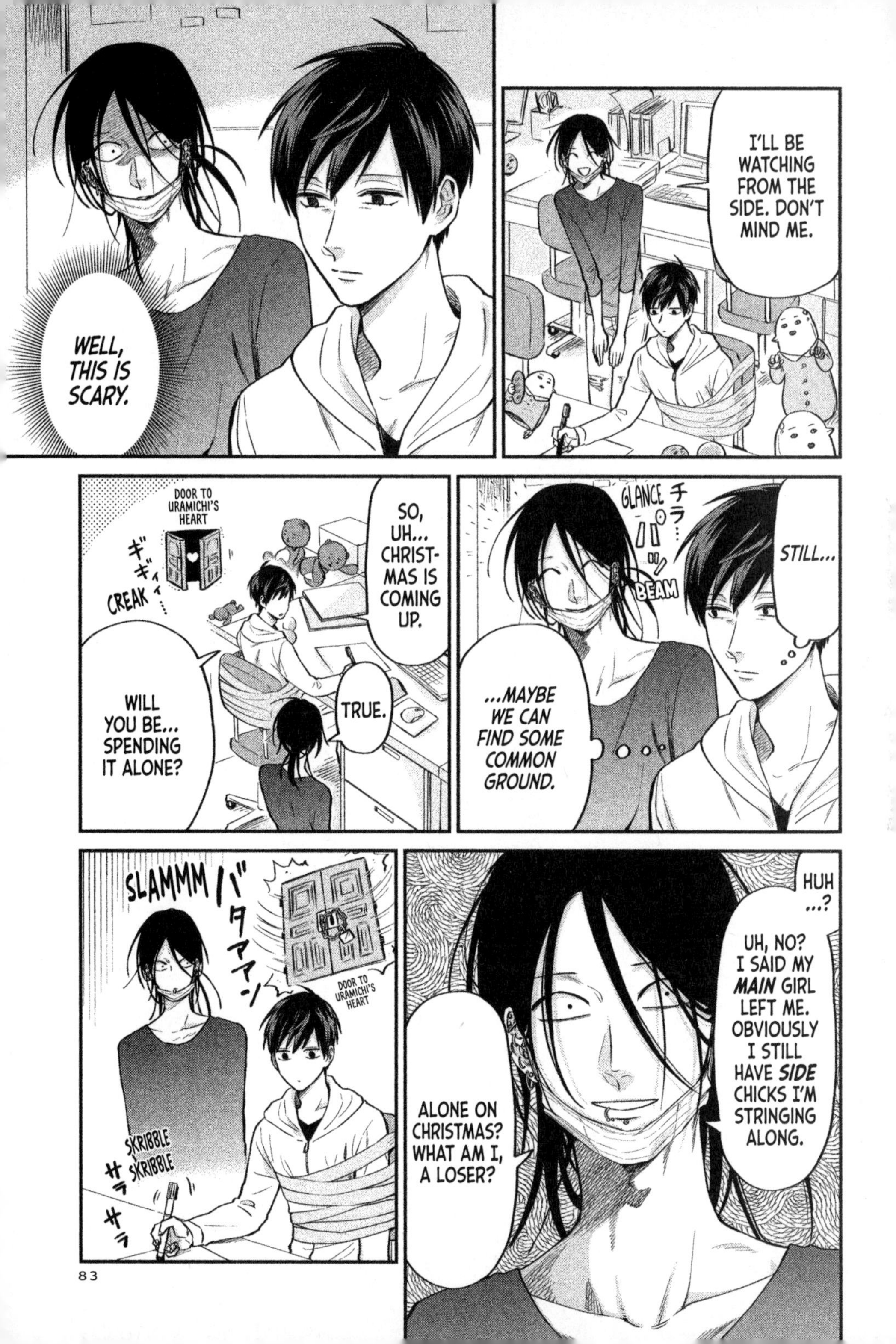
I'LL BE WATCHING FROM THE SIDE. DON'T MIND ME.
WELL, THIS IS SCARY.
GLANCE チラ…
BEAM
STILL...
...MAYBE WE CAN FIND SOME COMMON GROUND.
DOOR TO URAMICHI'S HEART
ギィィ…
CREAK
SO, UH... CHRISTMAS IS COMING UP.
TRUE.
WILL YOU BE... SPENDING IT ALONE?
HUH ...?
UH, NO? I SAID MY *MAIN* GIRL LEFT ME. OBVIOUSLY I STILL HAVE *SIDE* CHICKS I'M STRINGING ALONG.
ALONE ON CHRISTMAS? WHAT AM I, A LOSER?
SLAMMM
DOOR TO URAMICHI'S HEART
SKRIBBLE SKRIBBLE
サラ サラ

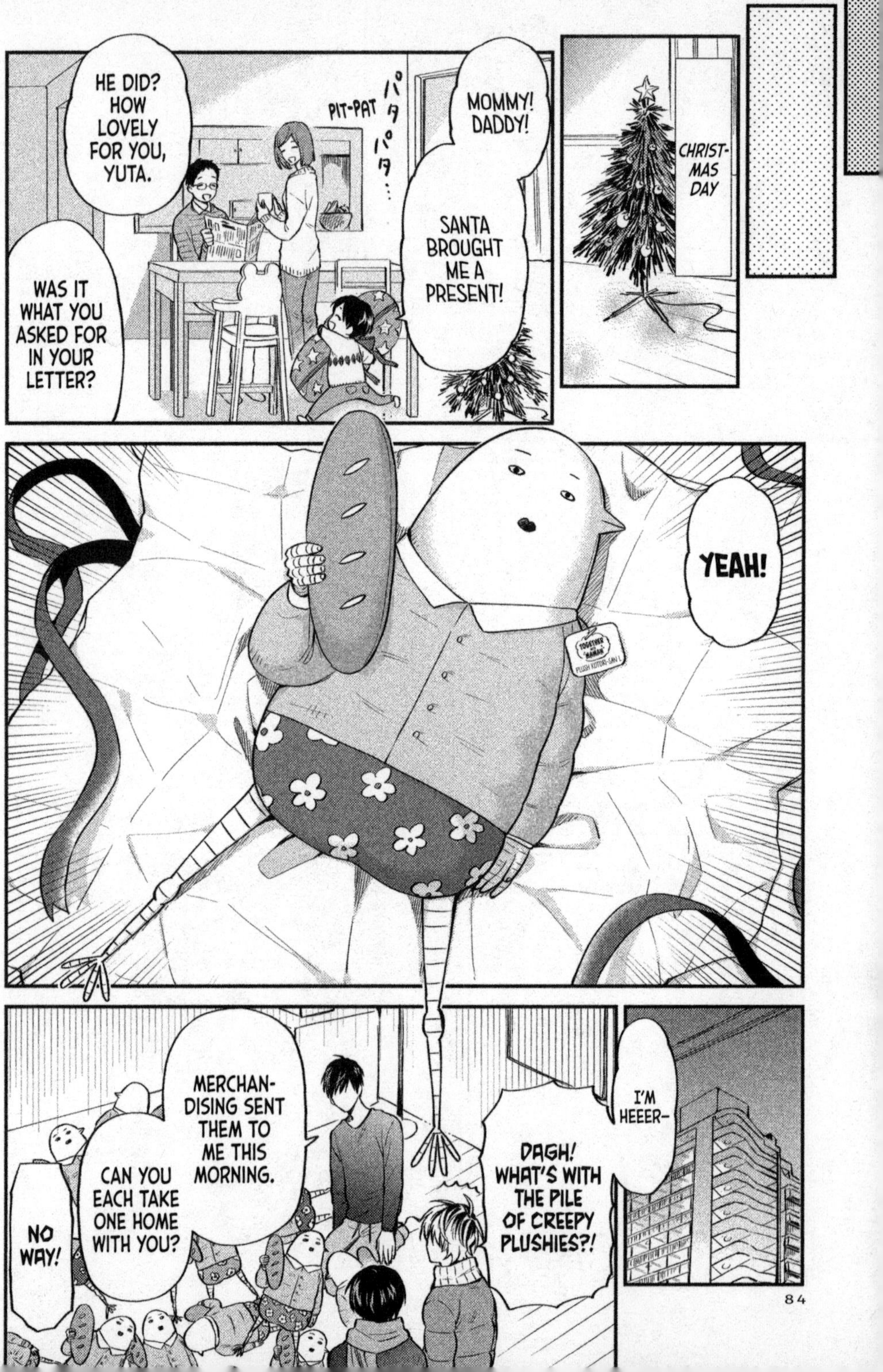
CHRIST-MAS DAY
MOMMY! DADDY!
SANTA BROUGHT ME A PRESENT!
パタパタ…
PIT-PAT
HE DID? HOW LOVELY FOR YOU, YUTA.
WAS IT WHAT YOU ASKED FOR IN YOUR LETTER?
YEAH!
I'M HEEER–
DAGH! WHAT'S WITH THE PILE OF CREEPY PLUSHIES?!
MERCHAN-DISING SENT THEM TO ME THIS MORNING.
CAN YOU EACH TAKE ONE HOME WITH YOU?
NO WAY!

Life Lessons with
Uramichi Oniisan

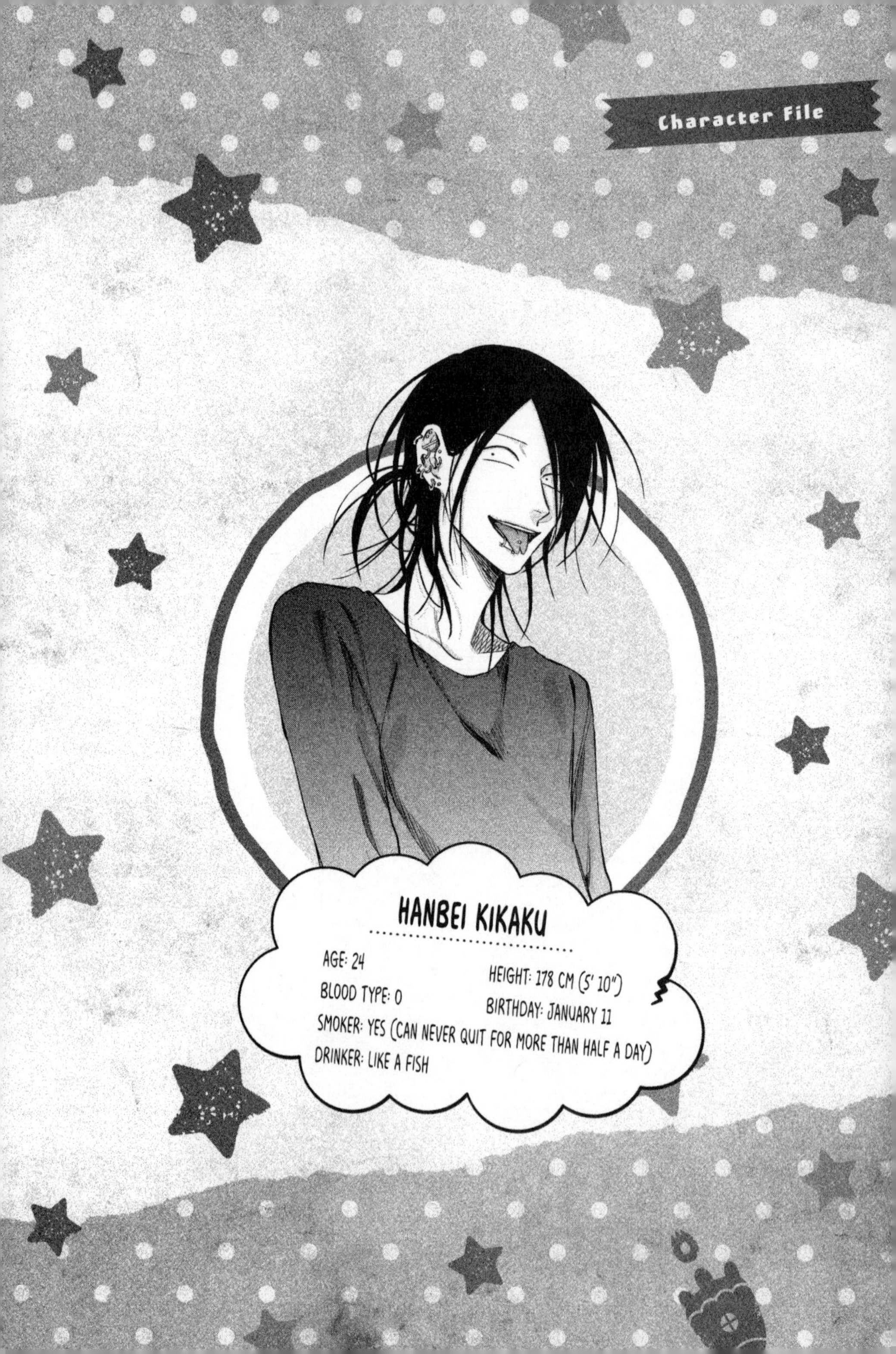
Character File
HANBEI KIKAKU
AGE: 24
HEIGHT: 178 CM (5' 10")
BLOOD TYPE: O
BIRTHDAY: JANUARY 11
SMOKER: YES (CAN NEVER QUIT FOR MORE THAN HALF A DAY)
DRINKER: LIKE A FISH

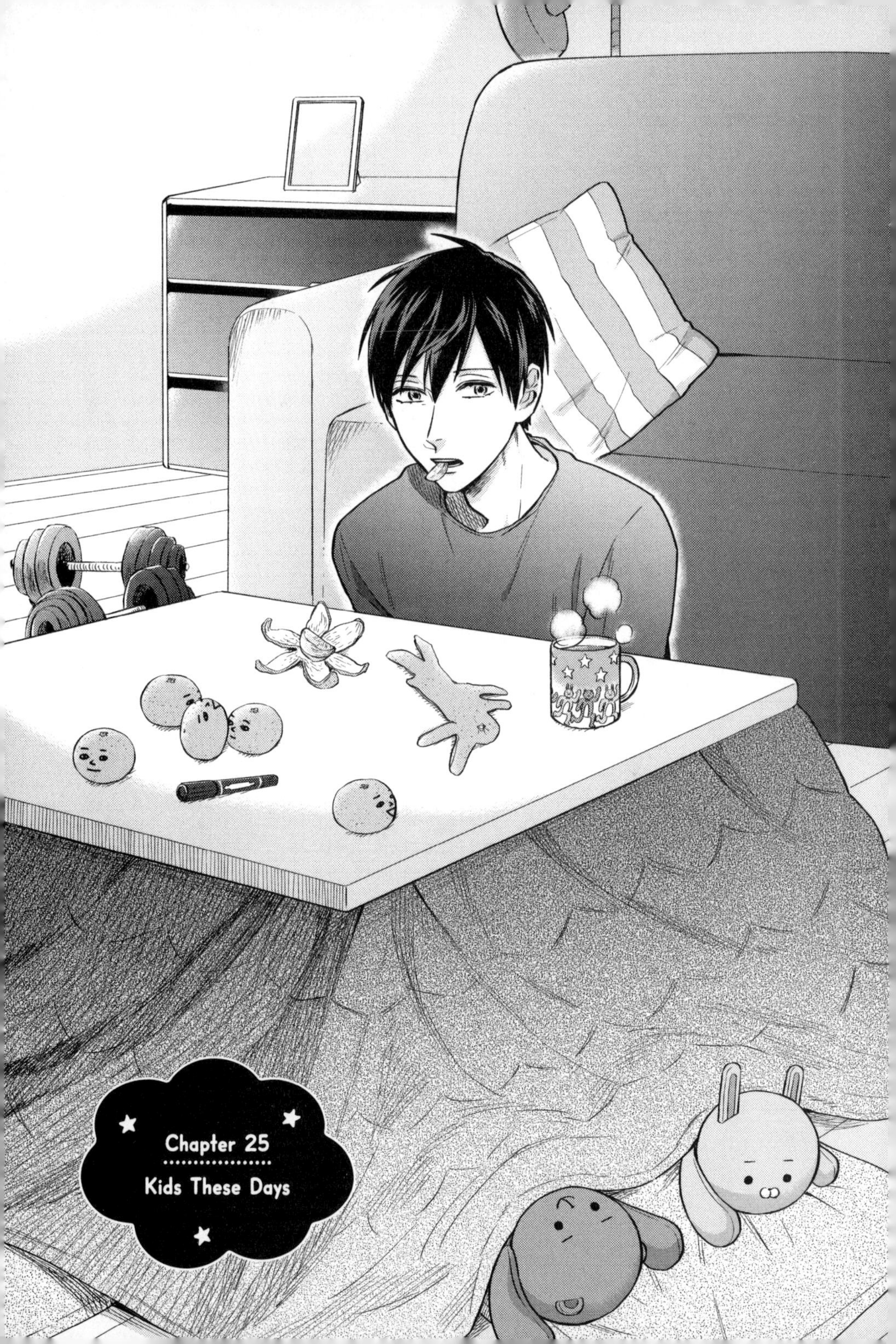
Chapter 25
Kids These Days

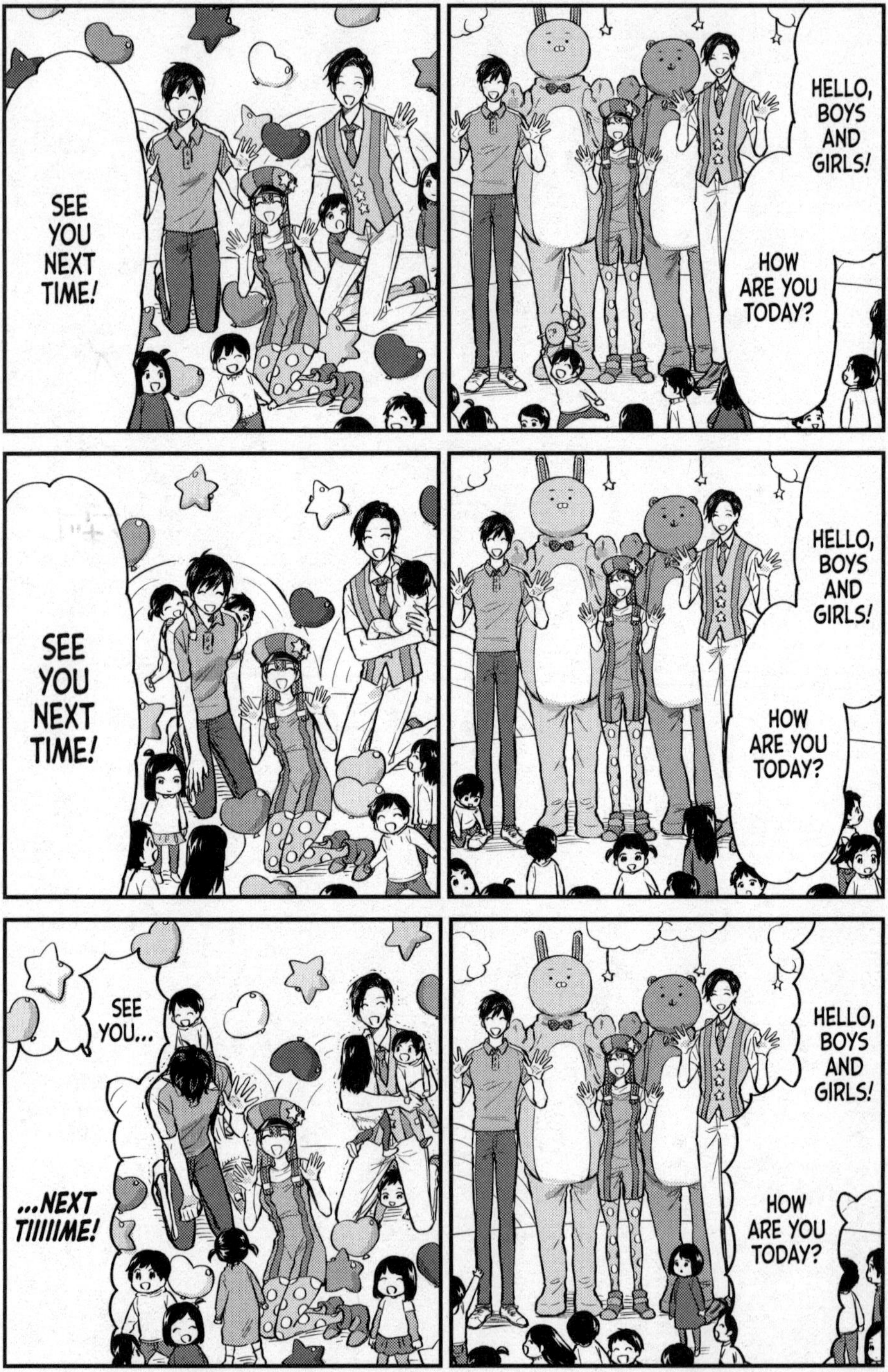
HELLO, BOYS AND GIRLS!
HOW ARE YOU TODAY?
SEE YOU NEXT TIME!
HELLO, BOYS AND GIRLS!
HOW ARE YOU TODAY?
SEE YOU NEXT TIME!
HELLO, BOYS AND GIRLS!
HOW ARE YOU TODAY?
SEE YOU...
...NEXT TIIIIIME!

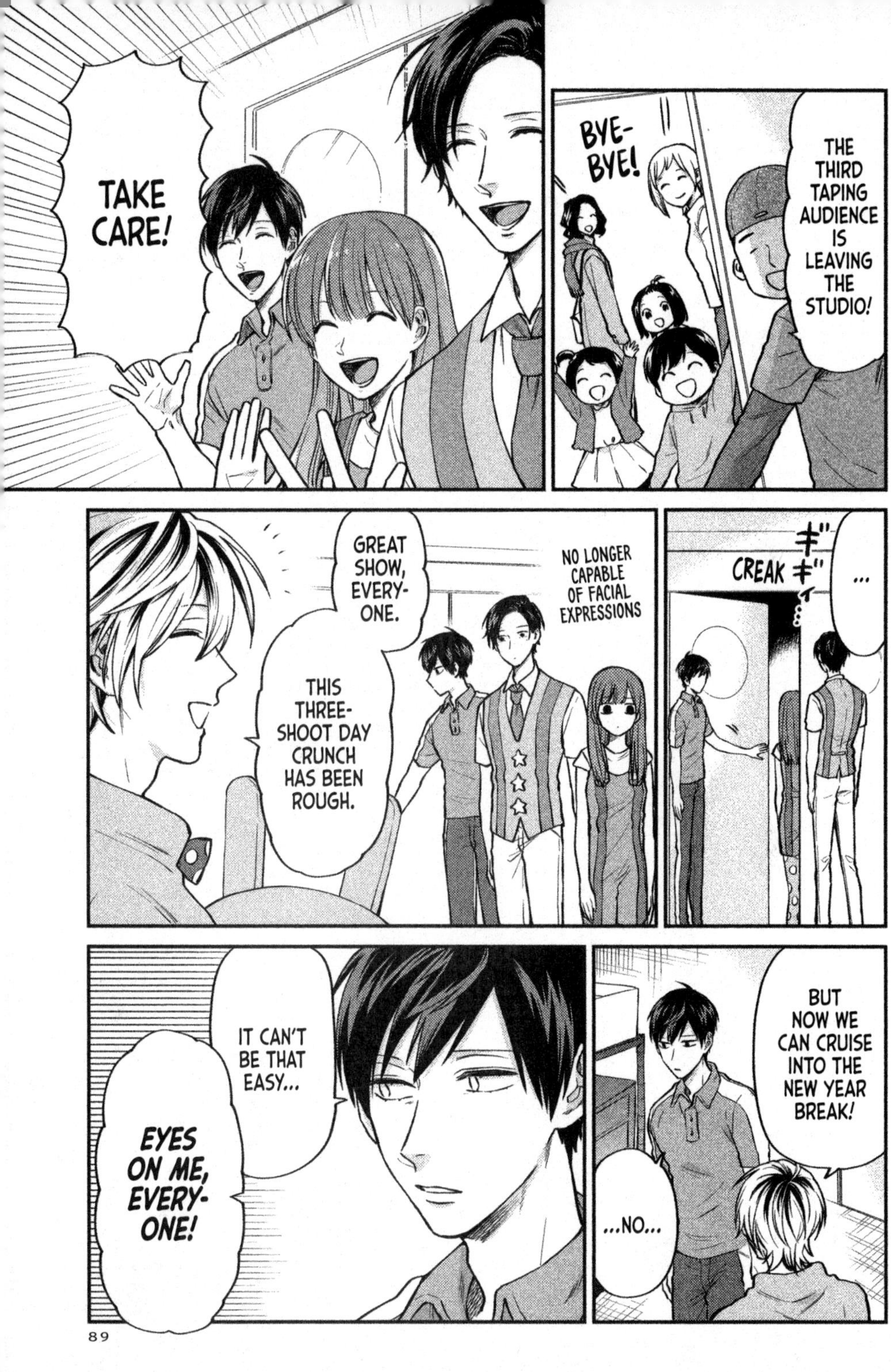
THE THIRD TAPING AUDIENCE IS LEAVING THE STUDIO!
BYE-BYE!
TAKE CARE!
...
CREAK ギィ…
NO LONGER CAPABLE OF FACIAL EXPRESSIONS
GREAT SHOW, EVERYONE.
THIS THREE-SHOOT DAY CRUNCH HAS BEEN ROUGH.
BUT NOW WE CAN CRUISE INTO THE NEW YEAR BREAK!
...NO...
IT CAN'T BE THAT EASY...
EYES ON ME, EVERYONE!

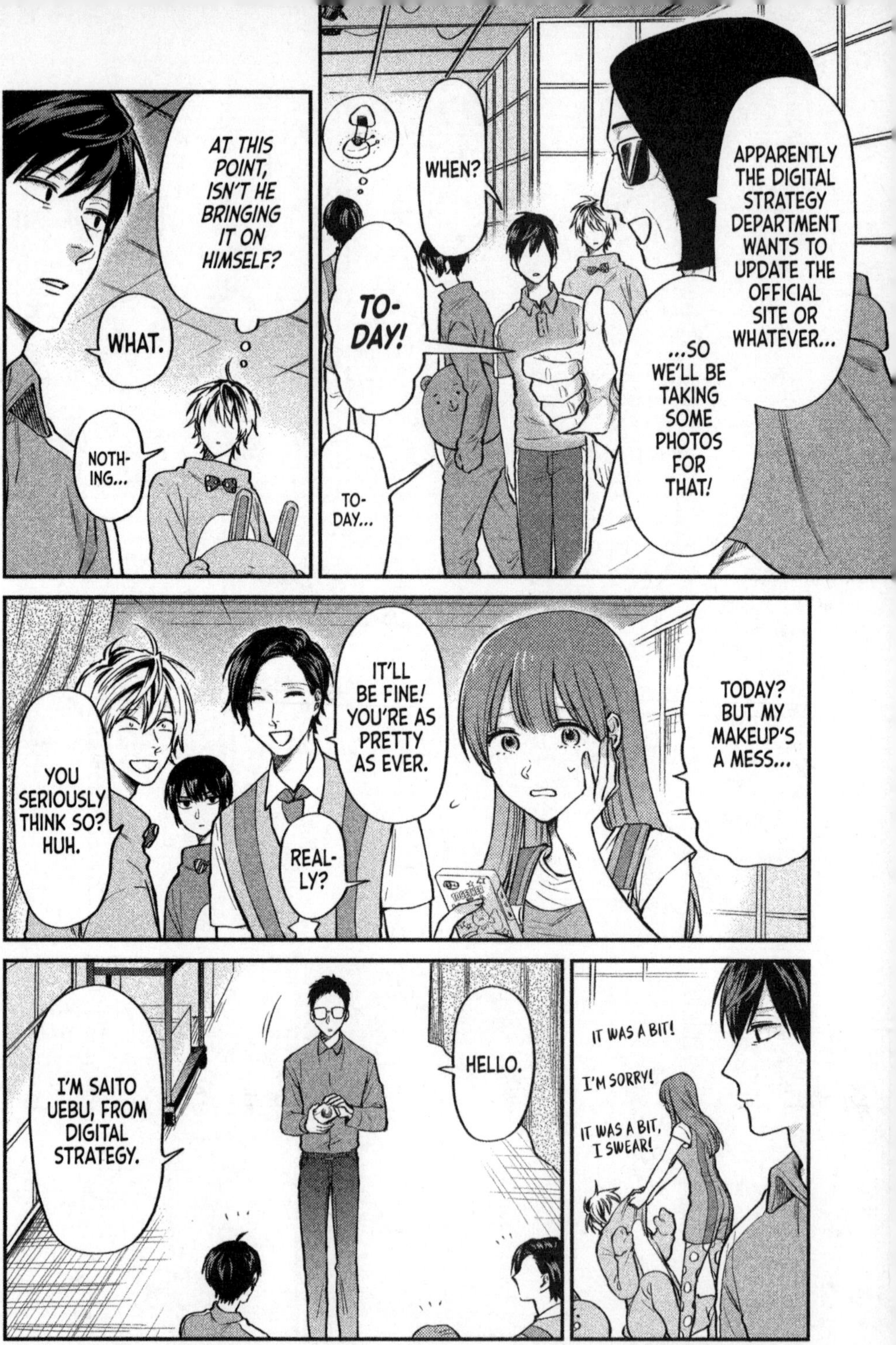
APPARENTLY THE DIGITAL STRATEGY DEPARTMENT WANTS TO UPDATE THE OFFICIAL SITE OR WHATEVER...
...SO WE'LL BE TAKING SOME PHOTOS FOR THAT!
WHEN?
TO-DAY!
TO-DAY...
AT THIS POINT, ISN'T HE BRINGING IT ON HIMSELF?
WHAT.
NOTHING...
TODAY? BUT MY MAKEUP'S A MESS...
IT'LL BE FINE! YOU'RE AS PRETTY AS EVER.
REALLY?
YOU SERIOUSLY THINK SO? HUH.
IT WAS A BIT!
I'M SORRY!
IT WAS A BIT, I SWEAR!
HELLO.
I'M SAITO UEBU, FROM DIGITAL STRATEGY.

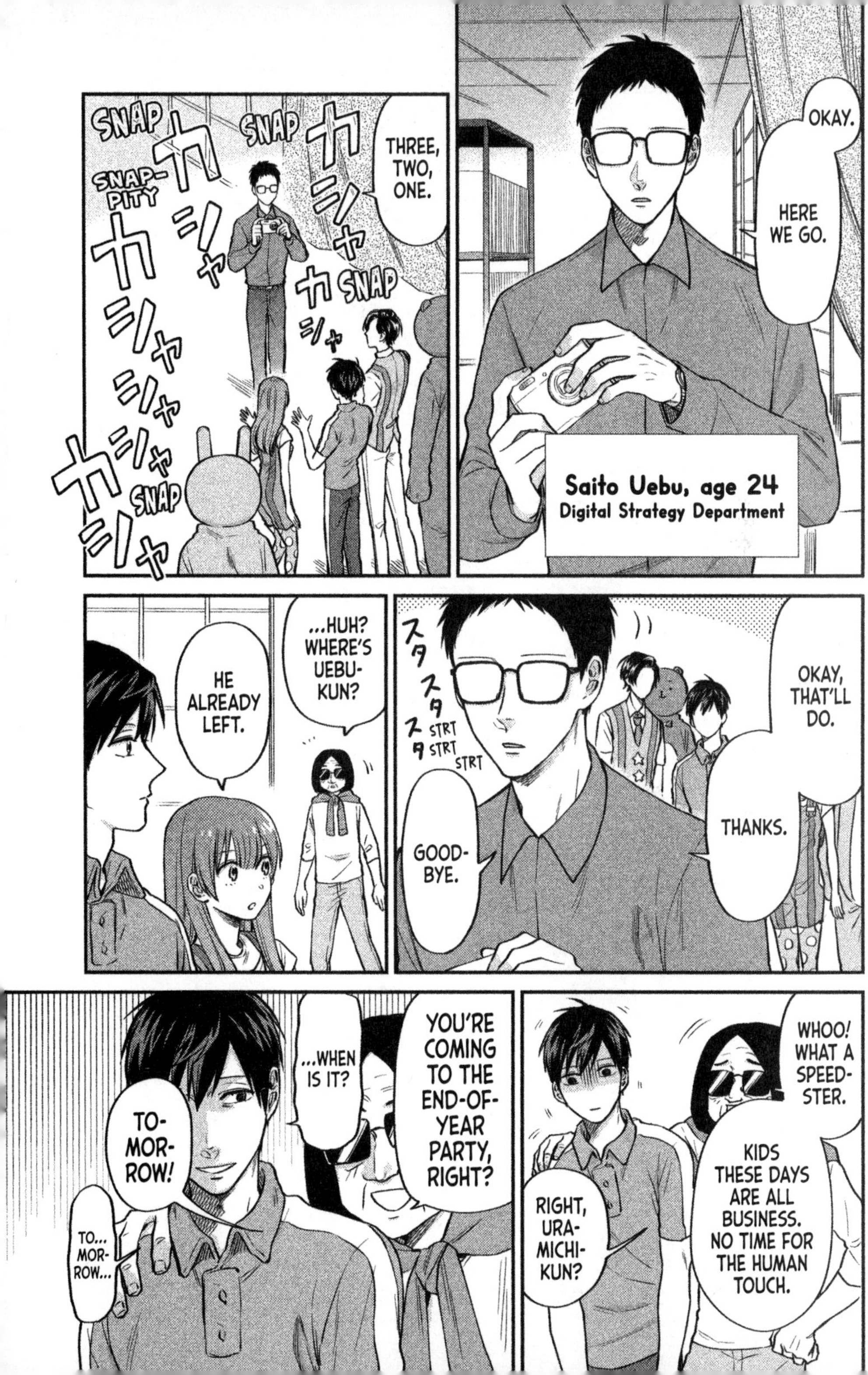
OKAY.
HERE WE GO.
Saito Uebu, age 24
Digital Strategy Department
THREE, TWO, ONE.
SNAP
SNAP
SNAP-PITY
SNAP
SNAP
OKAY, THAT'LL DO.
THANKS.
GOOD-BYE.
STRT STRT STRT
...HUH? WHERE'S UEBU-KUN?
HE ALREADY LEFT.
WHOO! WHAT A SPEEDSTER.
KIDS THESE DAYS ARE ALL BUSINESS. NO TIME FOR THE HUMAN TOUCH.
RIGHT, URA-MICHI-KUN?
YOU'RE COMING TO THE END-OF-YEAR PARTY, RIGHT?
...WHEN IS IT?
TO-MOR-ROW!
TO... MOR-ROW...

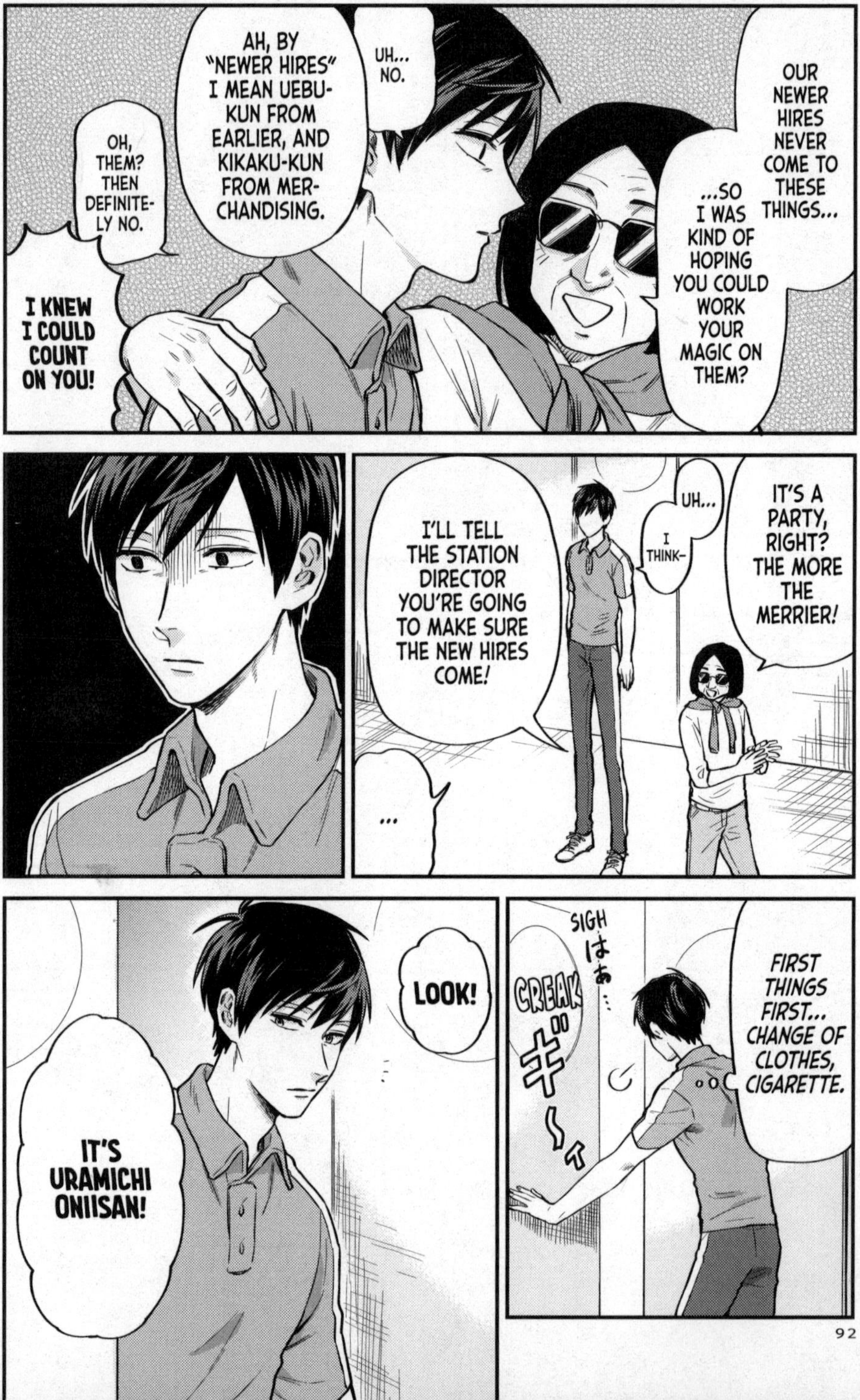
OUR NEWER HIRES NEVER COME TO THESE THINGS...
...SO I WAS KIND OF HOPING YOU COULD WORK YOUR MAGIC ON THEM?
UH... NO.
AH, BY "NEWER HIRES" I MEAN UEBU-KUN FROM EARLIER, AND KIKAKU-KUN FROM MER-CHANDISING.
OH, THEM? THEN DEFINITE-LY NO.
I KNEW I COULD COUNT ON YOU!
IT'S A PARTY, RIGHT? THE MORE THE MERRIER!
UH...
I THINK–
I'LL TELL THE STATION DIRECTOR YOU'RE GOING TO MAKE SURE THE NEW HIRES COME!
...
FIRST THINGS FIRST... CHANGE OF CLOTHES, CIGARETTE.
...
SIGH はぁ…
CREAK ギィ〜ィ
LOOK!
IT'S URAMICHI ONIISAN!

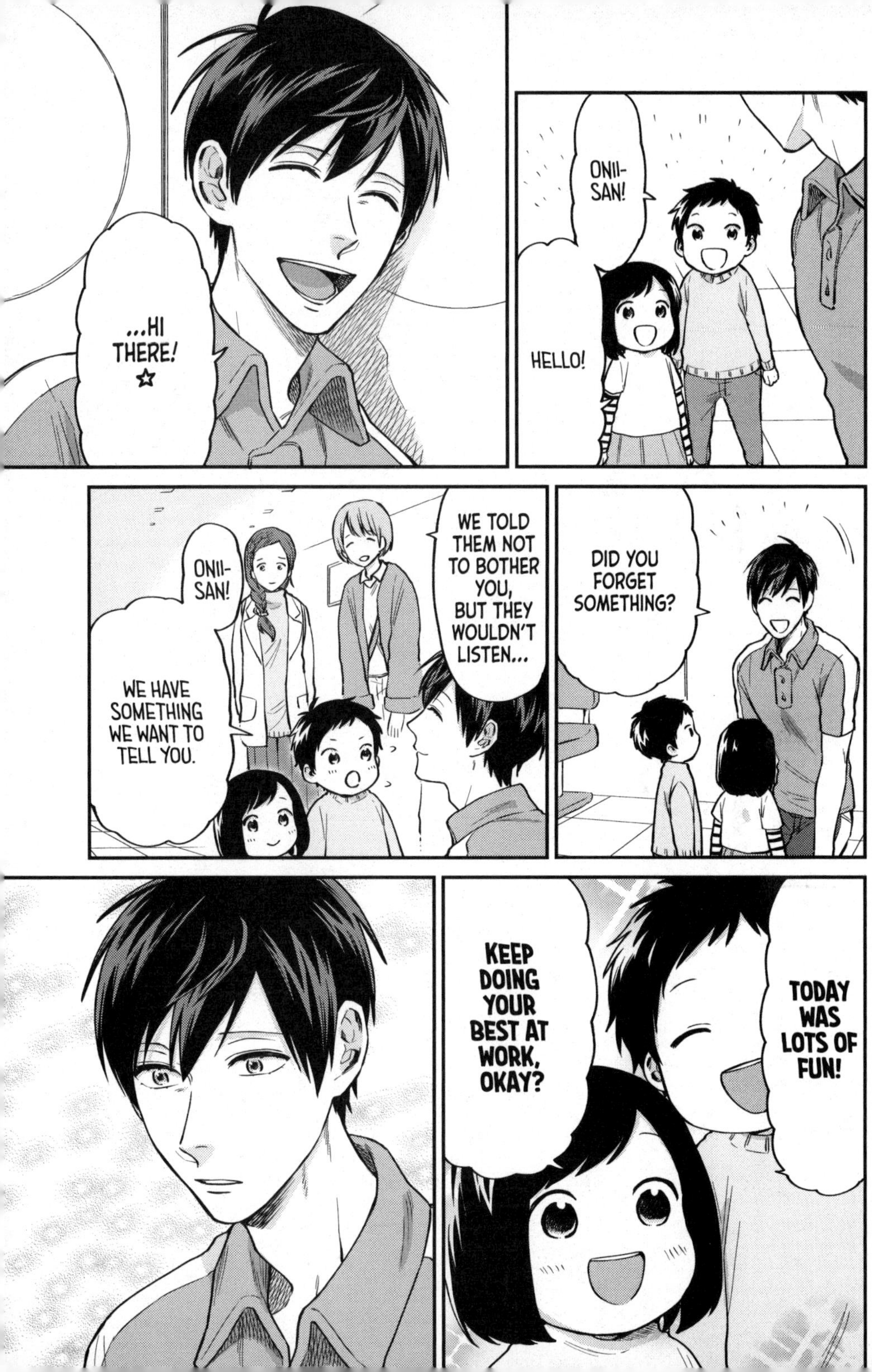
ONII-SAN!
HELLO!
...HI THERE! ☆
DID YOU FORGET SOMETHING?
WE TOLD THEM NOT TO BOTHER YOU, BUT THEY WOULDN'T LISTEN...
ONII-SAN!
WE HAVE SOMETHING WE WANT TO TELL YOU.
TODAY WAS LOTS OF FUN!
KEEP DOING YOUR BEST AT WORK, OKAY?

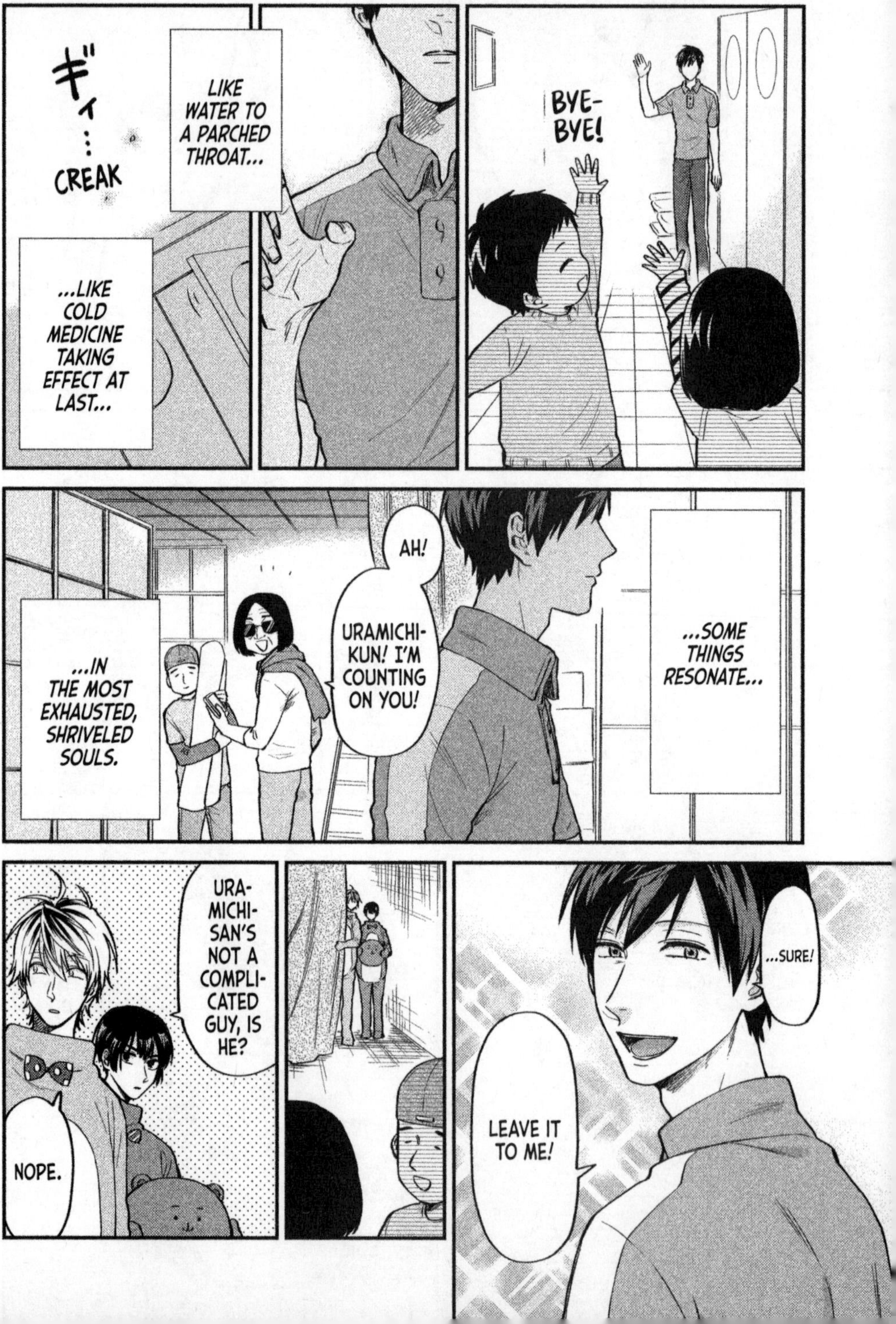
BYE-BYE!
LIKE WATER TO A PARCHED THROAT...
ギィ...
CREAK
...LIKE COLD MEDICINE TAKING EFFECT AT LAST...
...SOME THINGS RESONATE...
AH!
URAMICHI-KUN! I'M COUNTING ON YOU!
...IN THE MOST EXHAUSTED, SHRIVELED SOULS.
...SURE!
LEAVE IT TO ME!
URAMICHI-SAN'S NOT A COMPLICATED GUY, IS HE?
NOPE.

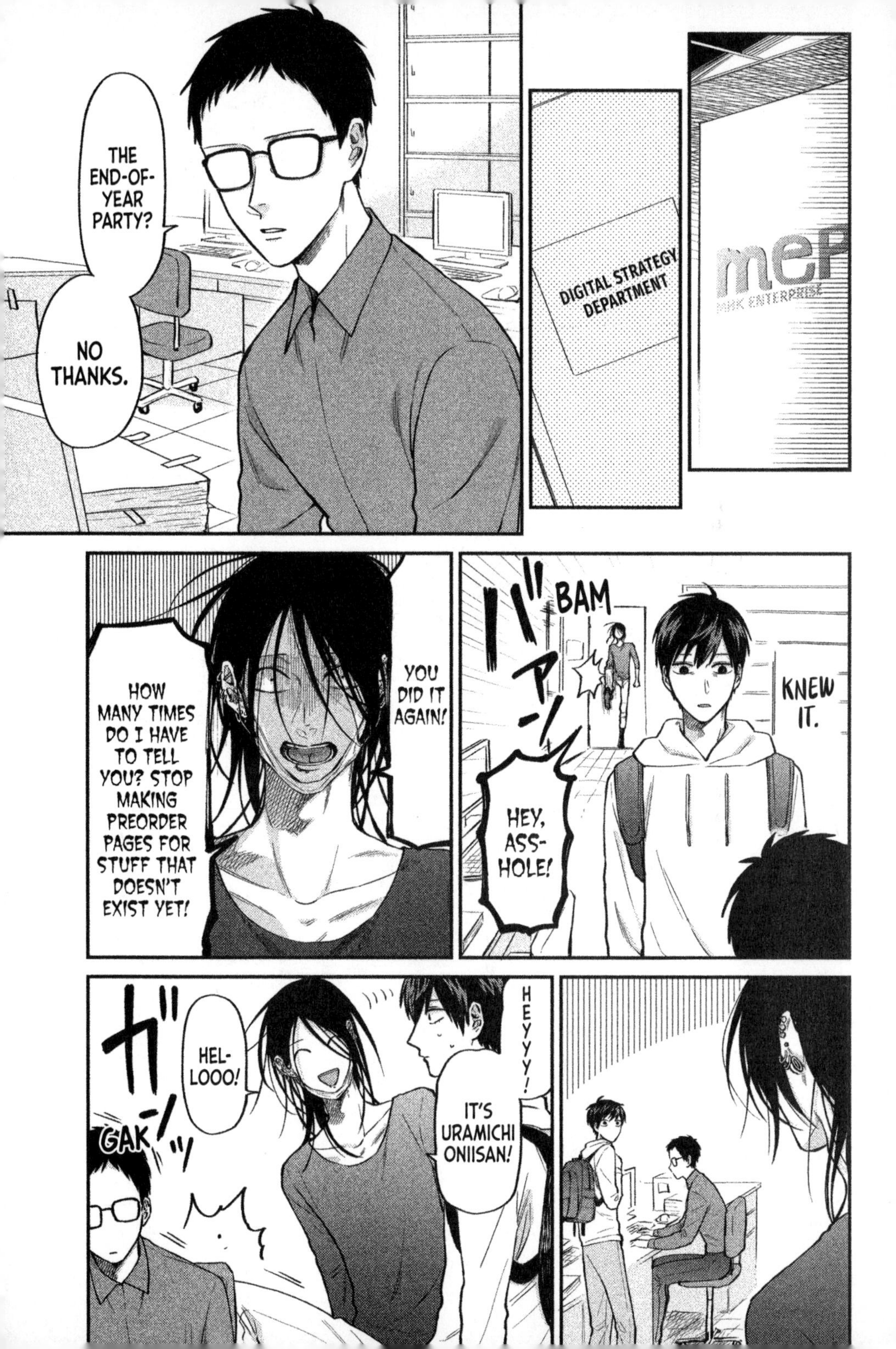
mep
MNK ENTERPRISE
DIGITAL STRATEGY DEPARTMENT
THE END-OF-YEAR PARTY?
NO THANKS.
KNEW IT.
BAM
HEY, ASS-HOLE!
YOU DID IT AGAIN!
HOW MANY TIMES DO I HAVE TO TELL YOU? STOP MAKING PREORDER PAGES FOR STUFF THAT DOESN'T EXIST YET!
HEYYY!
IT'S URAMICHI ONIISAN!
HEL-LOOO!
GAK

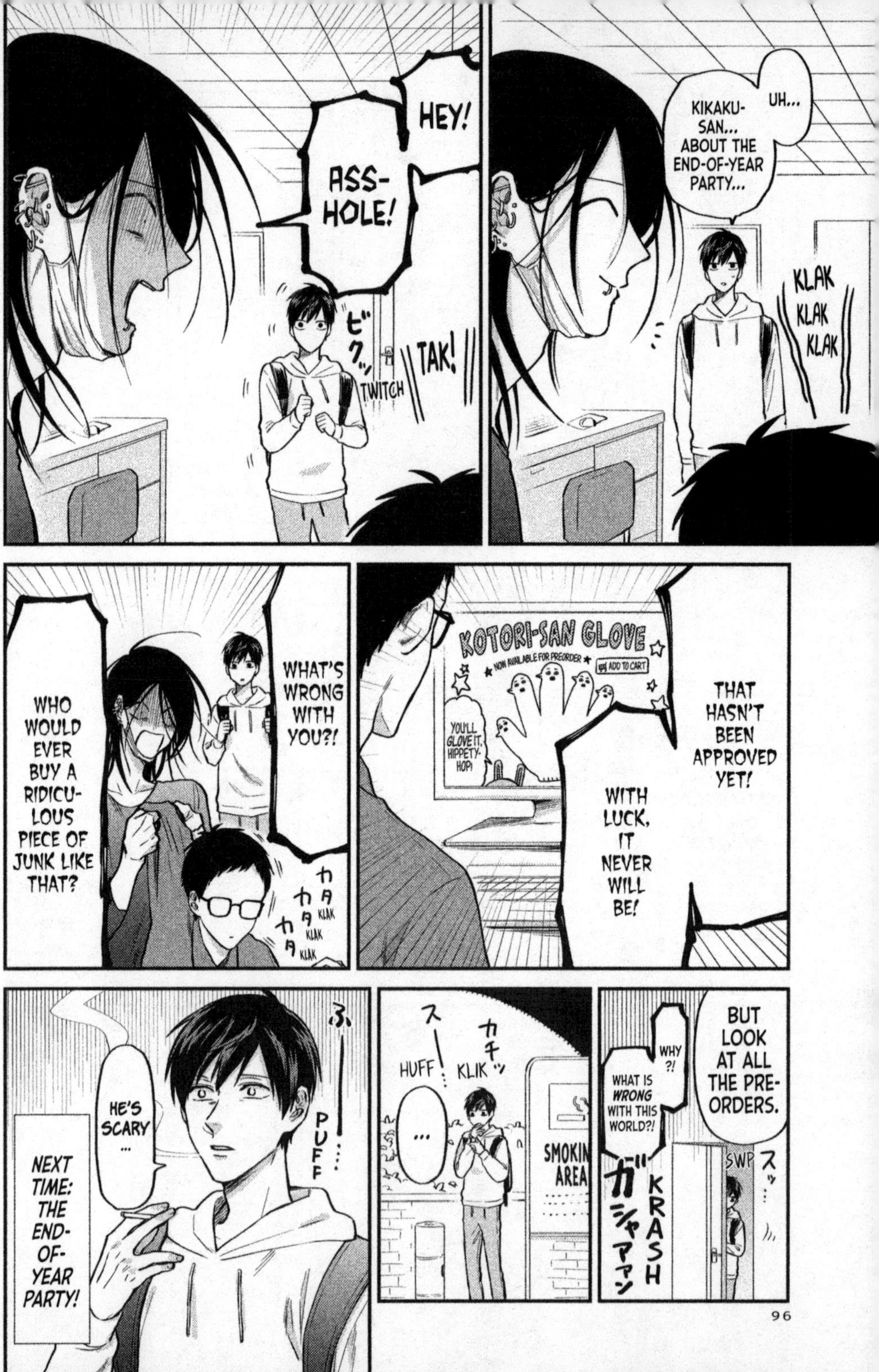
UH...
KIKAKU-SAN... ABOUT THE END-OF-YEAR PARTY...
KLAK KLAK KLAK
HEY!
ASS-HOLE!
ビクッ
TWITCH
TAK!
KOTORI-SAN GLOVE
NOW AVAILABLE FOR PREORDER
ADD TO CART
YOU'LL GLOVE IT, HIPPETY-HOP!
THAT HASN'T BEEN APPROVED YET!
WITH LUCK, IT NEVER WILL BE!
WHAT'S WRONG WITH YOU?!
WHO WOULD EVER BUY A RIDICULOUS PIECE OF JUNK LIKE THAT?
カタ KLAK
カタ KLAK
カタ KLAK
BUT LOOK AT ALL THE PRE-ORDERS.
WHY?!
WHAT IS *WRONG* WITH THIS WORLD?!
ガシャアアン
KRASH
スッ
SWP
カチッ
KLIK
スー
HUFF
...
SMOKIN
AREA
ふー
PUFF
HE'S SCARY...
NEXT TIME: THE END-OF-YEAR PARTY!

Life Lessons with
Uramichi Oniisan

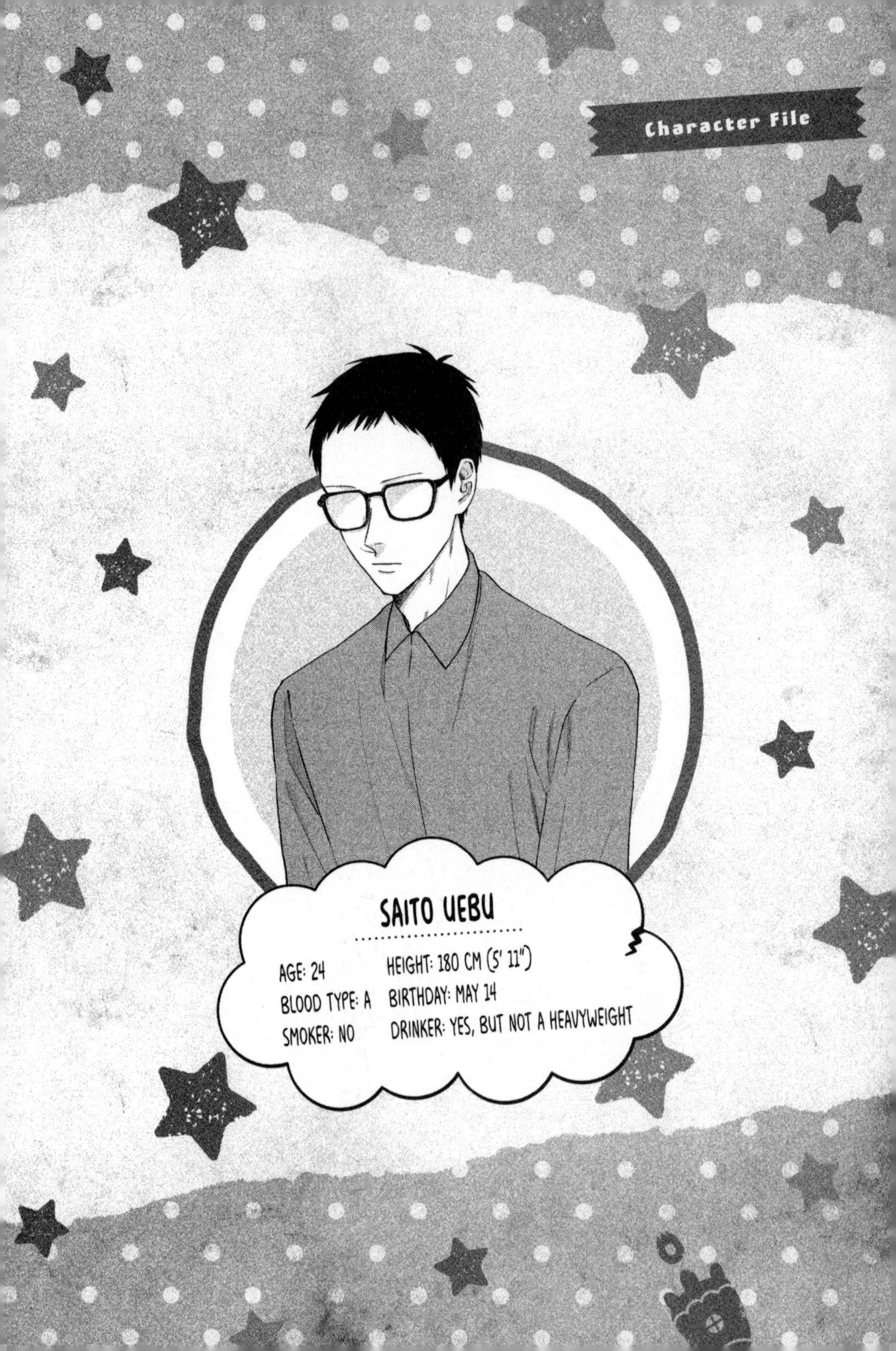
Character File
SAITO UEBU
AGE: 24
HEIGHT: 180 CM (5' 11")
BLOOD TYPE: A
BIRTHDAY: MAY 14
SMOKER: NO
DRINKER: YES, BUT NOT A HEAVYWEIGHT

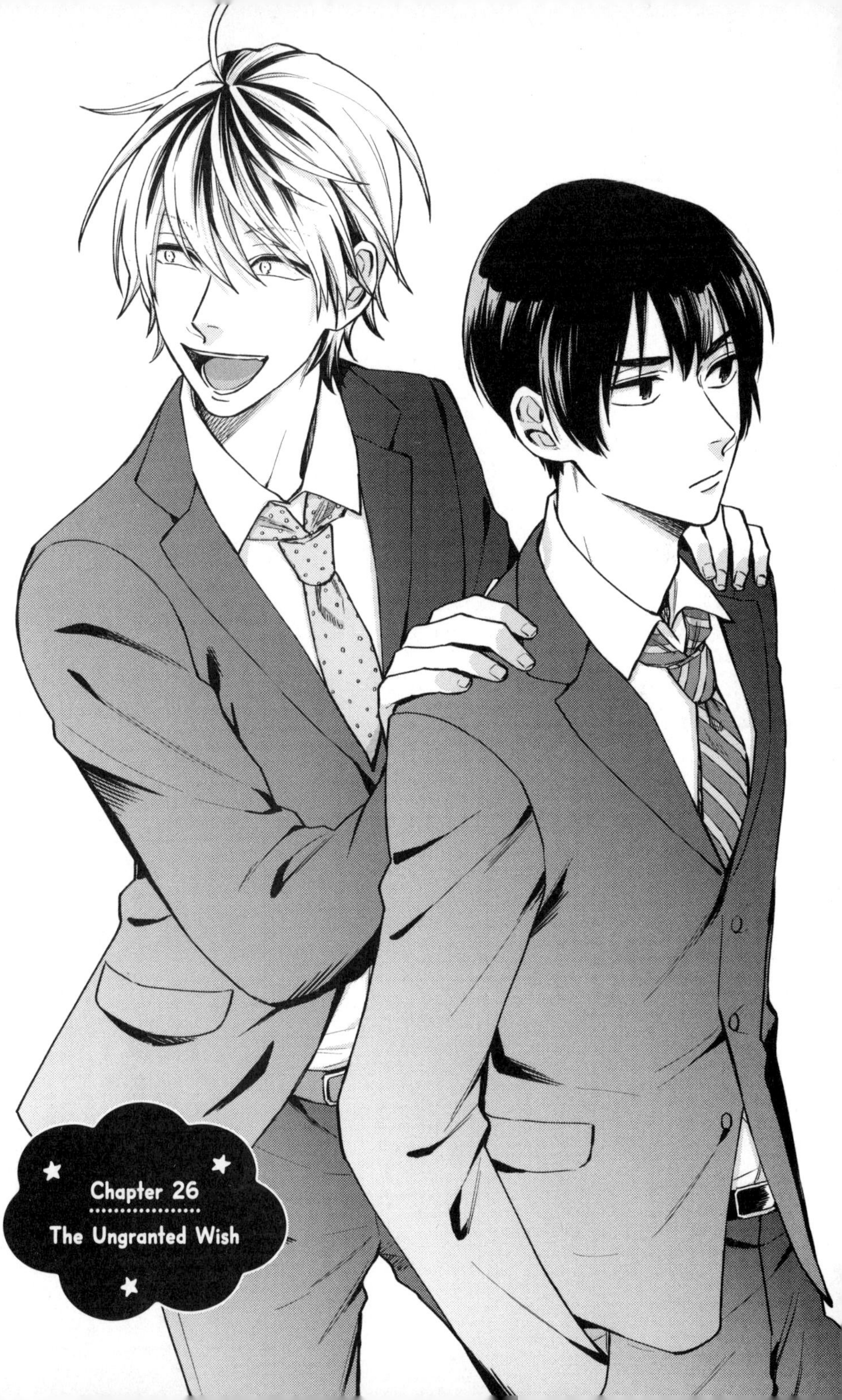
Chapter 26
The Ungranted Wish

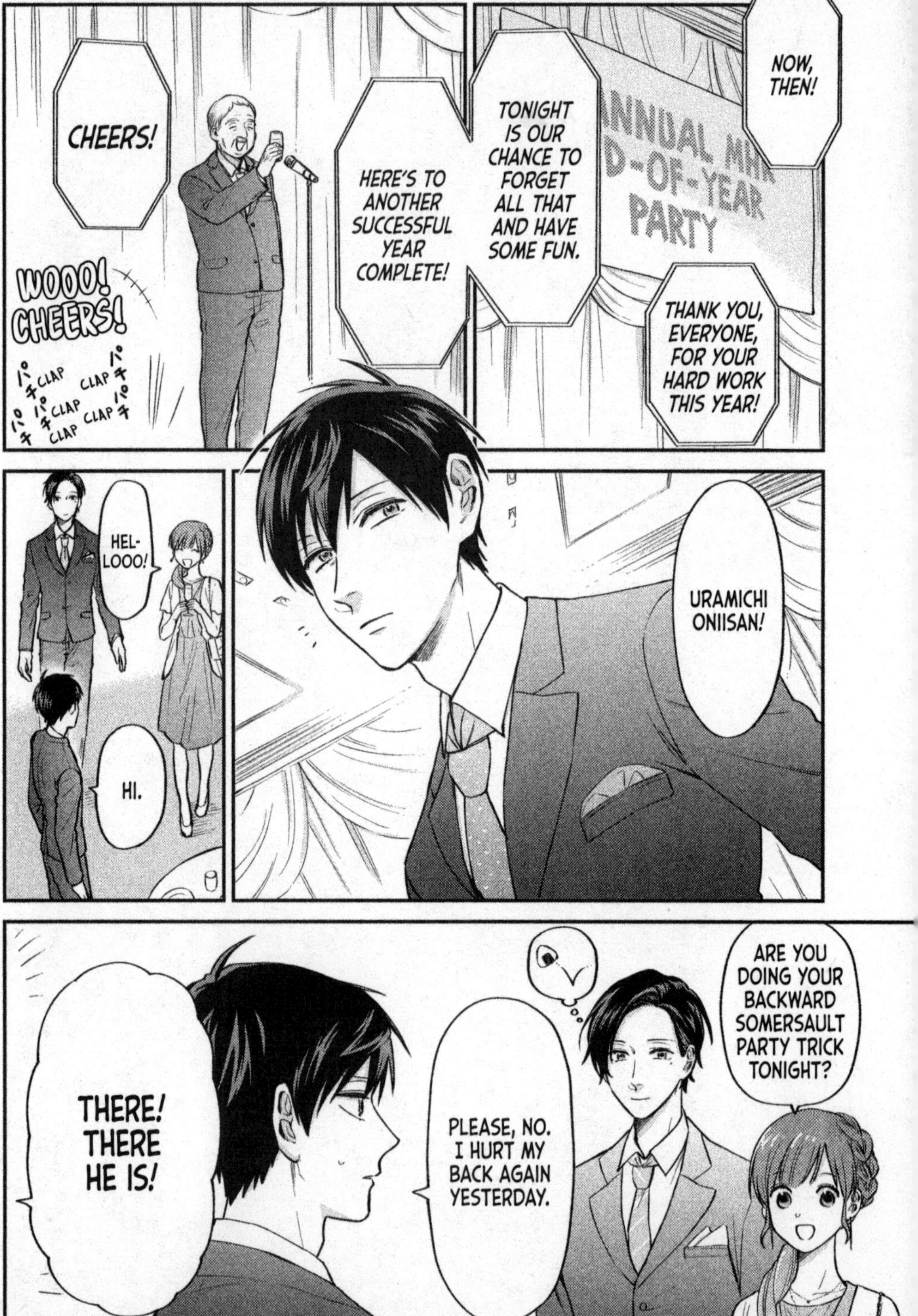
NOW, THEN!
THANK YOU, EVERYONE, FOR YOUR HARD WORK THIS YEAR!
PARTY
TONIGHT IS OUR CHANCE TO FORGET ALL THAT AND HAVE SOME FUN.
HERE'S TO ANOTHER SUCCESSFUL YEAR COMPLETE!
CHEERS!
WOOO! CHEERS!
パチ CLAP
パチ CLAP
パチ CLAP
パチ CLAP
CLAP
CLAP
URAMICHI ONIISAN!
HEL-LOOO!
HI.
ARE YOU DOING YOUR BACKWARD SOMERSAULT PARTY TRICK TONIGHT?
PLEASE, NO. I HURT MY BACK AGAIN YESTERDAY.
THERE! THERE HE IS!

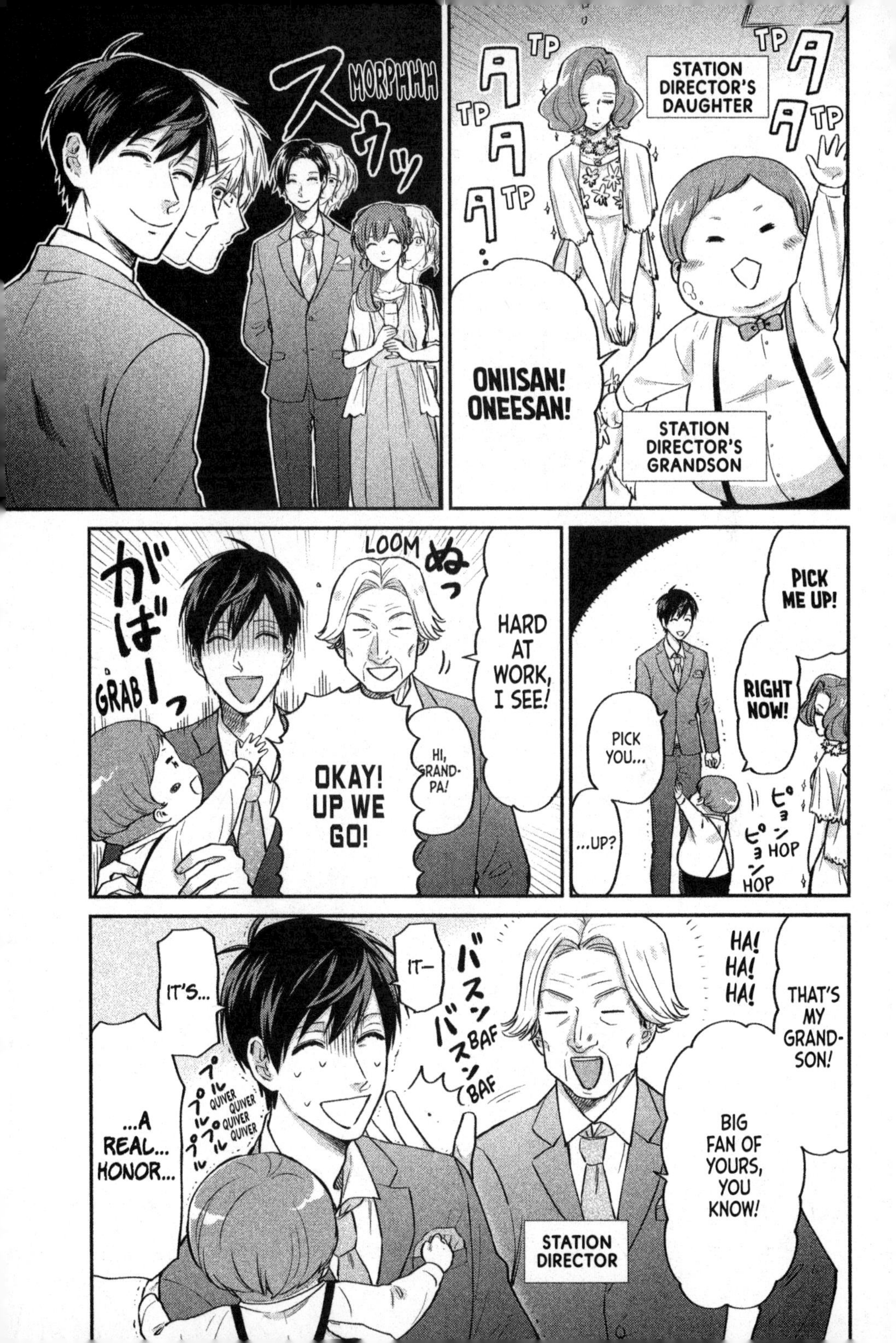

TP タ
TP タ
TP タ
TP タ
TP タ
TP
STATION DIRECTOR'S DAUGHTER
ONIISAN! ONEESAN!
STATION DIRECTOR'S GRANDSON
MORPHHH スウッ
PICK ME UP!
RIGHT NOW!
PICK YOU...
...UP?
ピョン HOP
ピョン HOP
LOOM ぬっ
HARD AT WORK, I SEE!
HI, GRAND-PA!
OKAY! UP WE GO!
がばーっ GRAB
HA! HA! HA!
THAT'S MY GRAND-SON!
BIG FAN OF YOURS, YOU KNOW!
STATION DIRECTOR
バスッ BAF
バスン BAF
IT—
IT'S...
プルプル QUIVER QUIVER
プルプル QUIVER QUIVER
...A REAL... HONOR...

*See Chapter 22

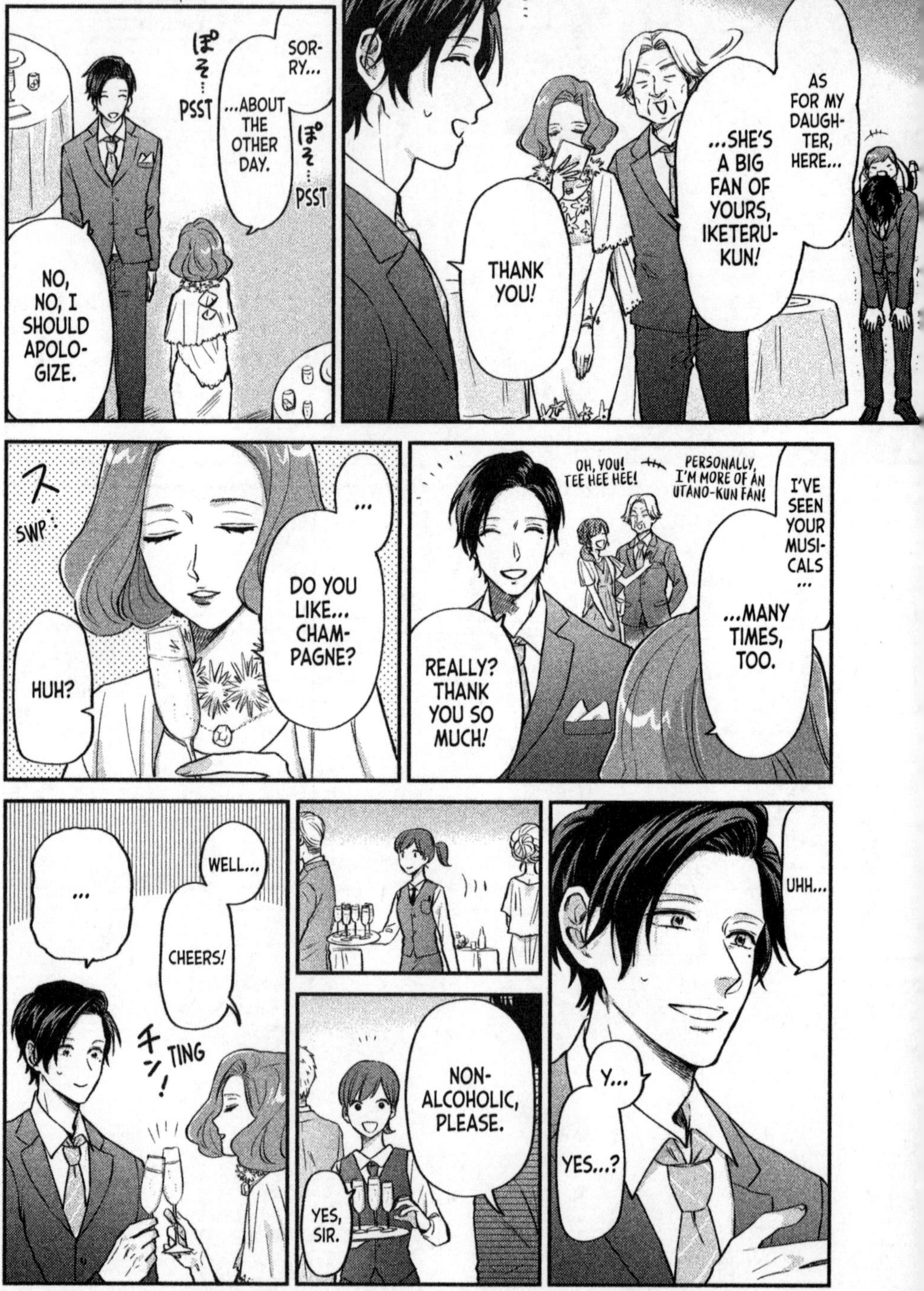
AS FOR MY DAUGHTER, HERE...
...SHE'S A BIG FAN OF YOURS, IKETERU-KUN!
THANK YOU!
SORRY...
ぽそ… PSST
...ABOUT THE OTHER DAY.
ぽそ… PSST
NO, NO, I SHOULD APOLOGIZE.
I'VE SEEN YOUR MUSICALS...
...MANY TIMES, TOO.
PERSONALLY, I'M MORE OF AN UTANO-KUN FAN!
OH, YOU! TEE HEE HEE!
REALLY? THANK YOU SO MUCH!
...
DO YOU LIKE... CHAMPAGNE?
ス SWP
HUH?
UHH...
Y...
YES...?
NON-ALCOHOLIC, PLEASE.
YES, SIR.
...
WELL...
CHEERS!
チン! TING

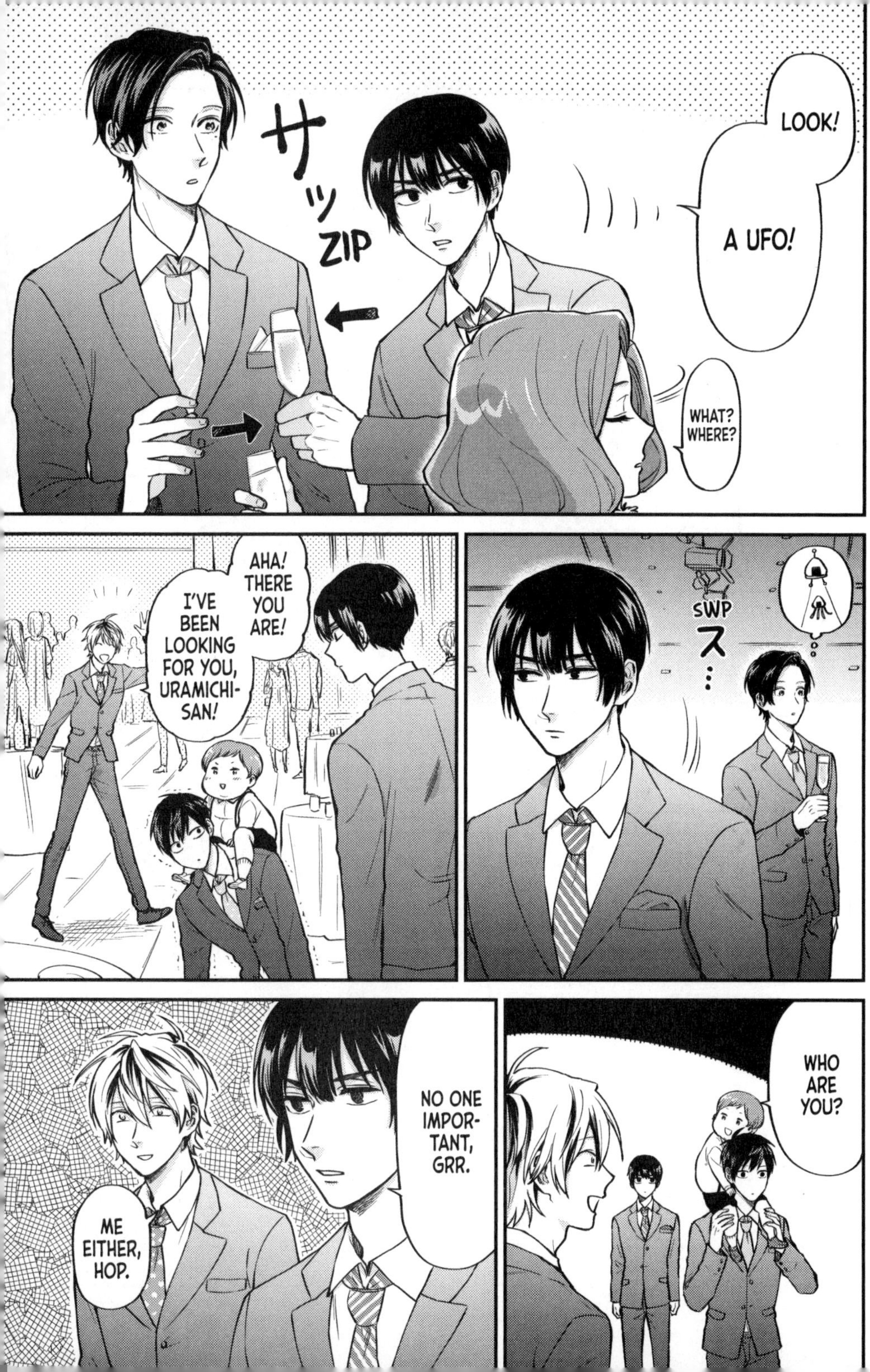
LOOK! A UFO!
サッ
ZIP
WHAT? WHERE?
SWP
ス…
AHA! THERE YOU ARE!
I'VE BEEN LOOKING FOR YOU, URAMICHI-SAN!
WHO ARE YOU?
NO ONE IMPOR-TANT, GRR.
ME EITHER, HOP.

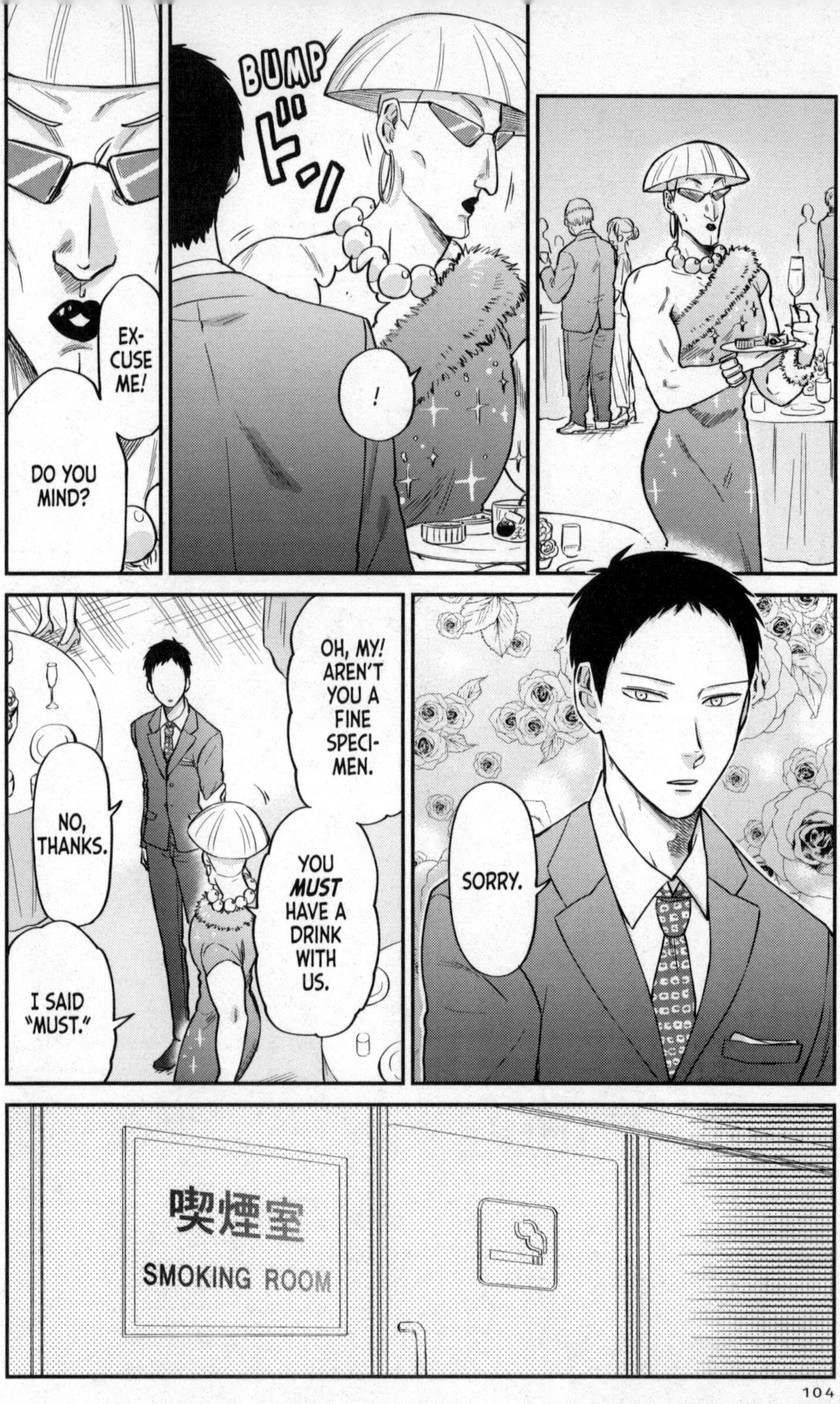
BUMP
ドーッ
!
EX-CUSE ME!
DO YOU MIND?
SORRY.
OH, MY! AREN'T YOU A FINE SPECI-MEN.
YOU *MUST* HAVE A DRINK WITH US.
NO, THANKS.
I SAID "MUST."
喫煙室
SMOKING ROOM

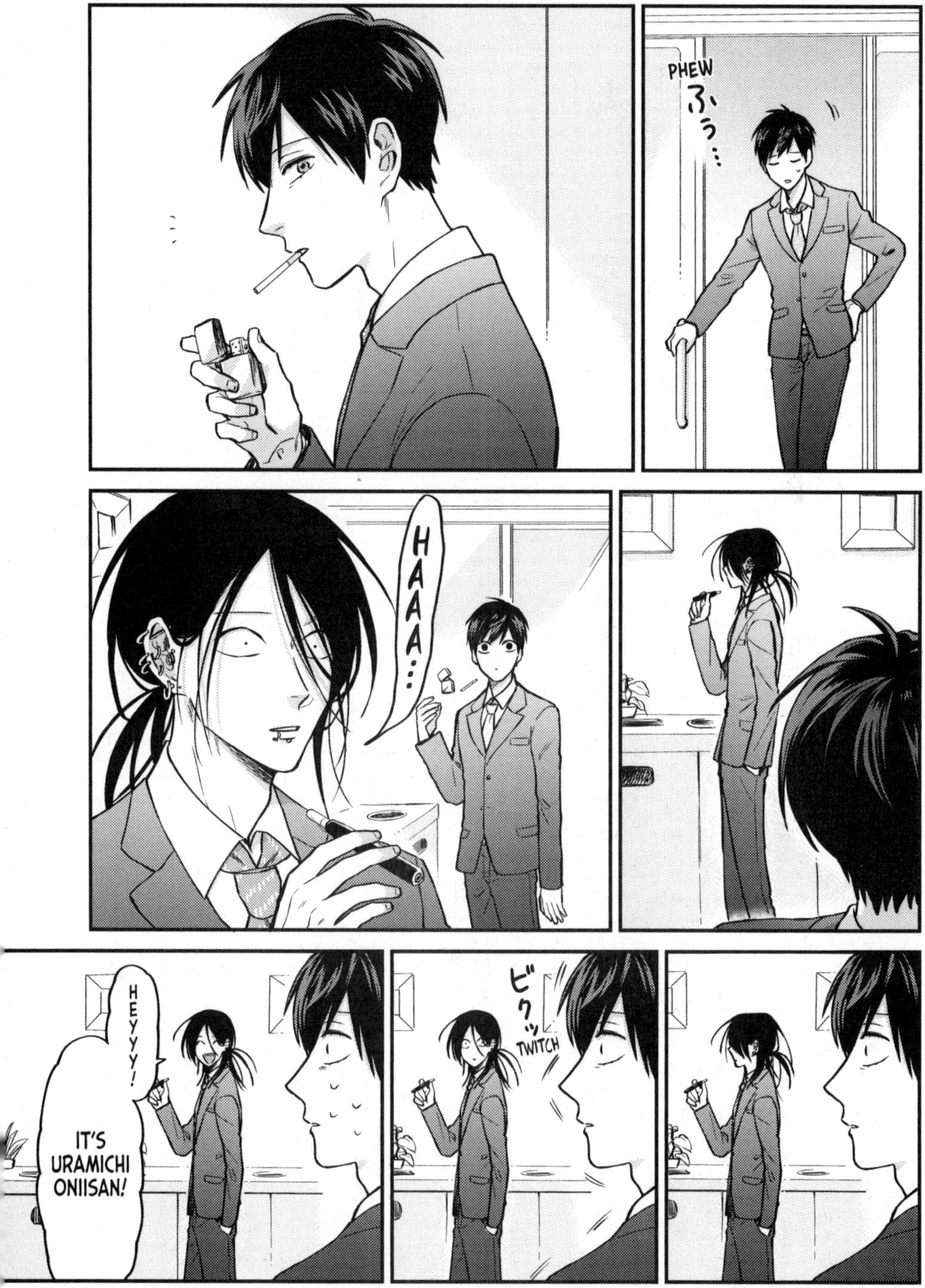
PHEW
ふぅ…
HAAAA...
ビクッ
TWITCH
HEYYY!
IT'S URAMICHI ONIISAN!

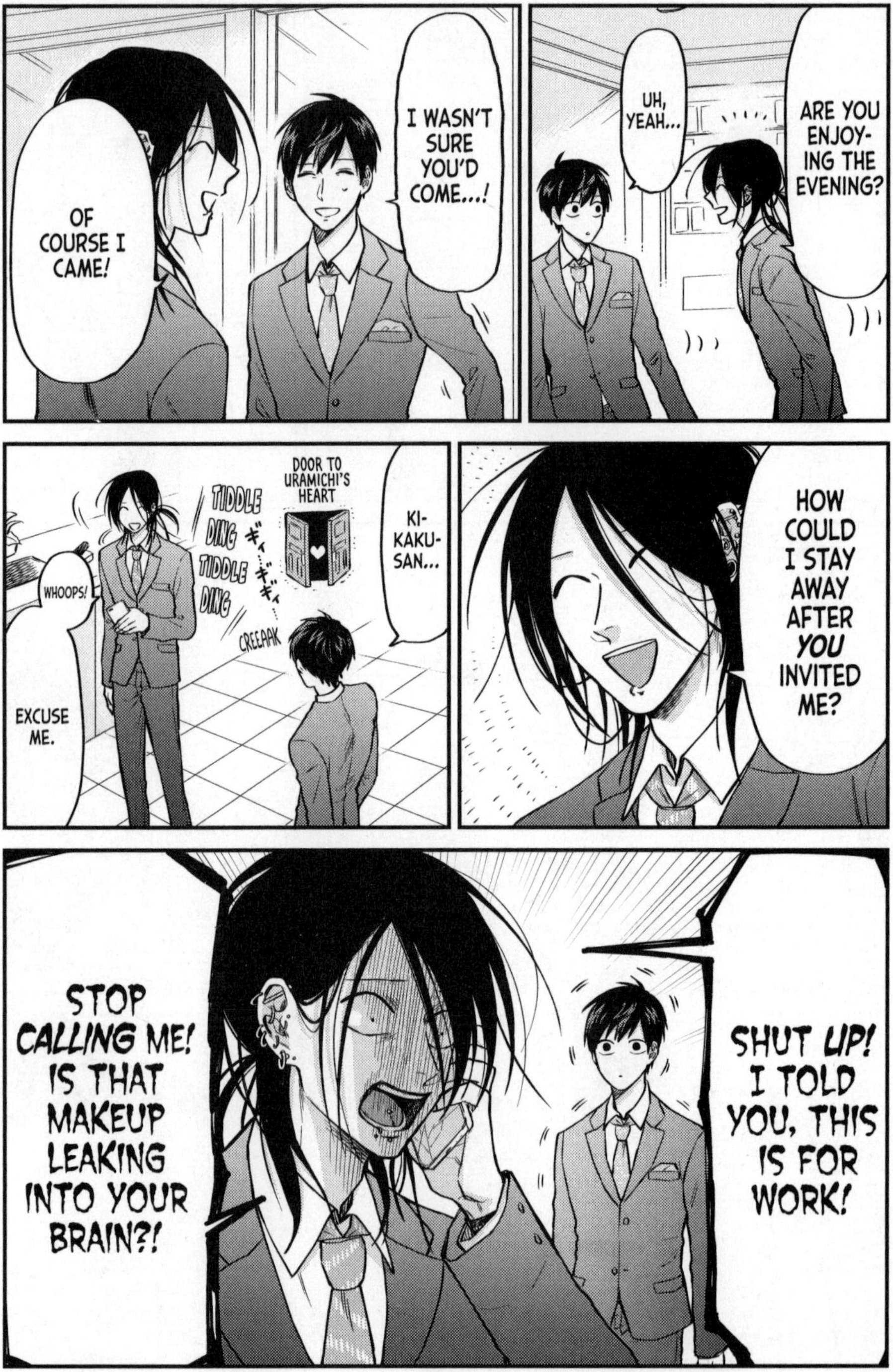
ARE YOU ENJOY-ING THE EVENING?
UH, YEAH...
I WASN'T SURE YOU'D COME...!
OF COURSE I CAME!
HOW COULD I STAY AWAY AFTER YOU INVITED ME?
KI-KAKU-SAN...
DOOR TO URAMICHI'S HEART
TIDDLE DING TIDDLE DING
ギィ…ギィ…
CREEAAK
WHOOPS!
EXCUSE ME.
SHUT UP! I TOLD YOU, THIS IS FOR WORK!
STOP CALLING ME! IS THAT MAKEUP LEAKING INTO YOUR BRAIN?!

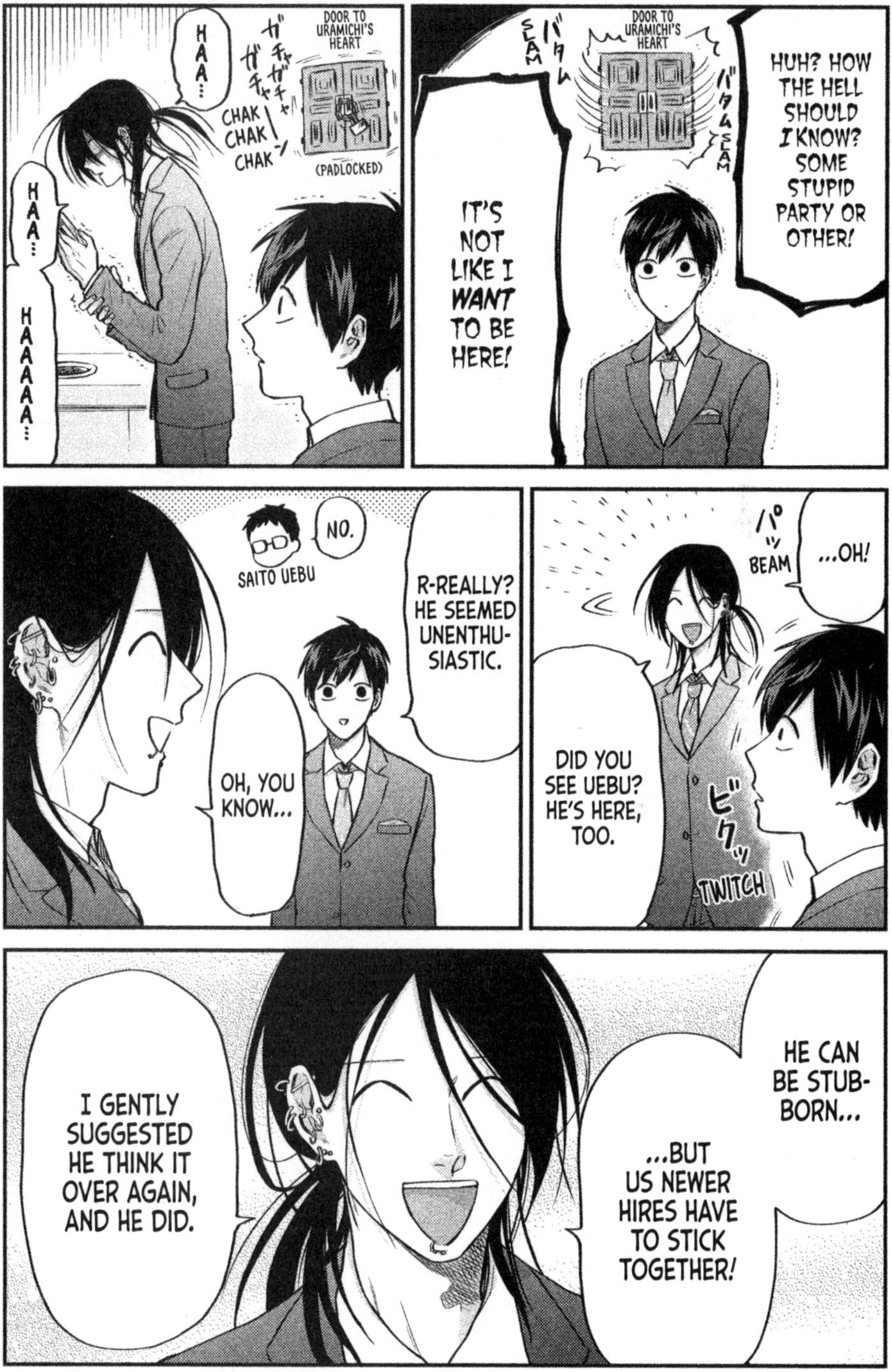
HUH? HOW THE HELL SHOULD I KNOW? SOME STUPID PARTY OR OTHER!
バタム SLAM
DOOR TO URAMICHI'S HEART
バタム SLAM
IT'S NOT LIKE I WANT TO BE HERE!
DOOR TO URAMICHI'S HEART
ガチャガチャ CHAK CHAK CHAK
(PADLOCKED)
HAA...
HAA...
HAAAAAA...
...OH!
パッ BEAM
DID YOU SEE UEBU? HE'S HERE, TOO.
ビクッ TWITCH
R-REALLY? HE SEEMED UNENTHUSIASTIC.
NO.
SAITO UEBU
OH, YOU KNOW...
HE CAN BE STUBBORN...
...BUT US NEWER HIRES HAVE TO STICK TOGETHER!
I GENTLY SUGGESTED HE THINK IT OVER AGAIN, AND HE DID.

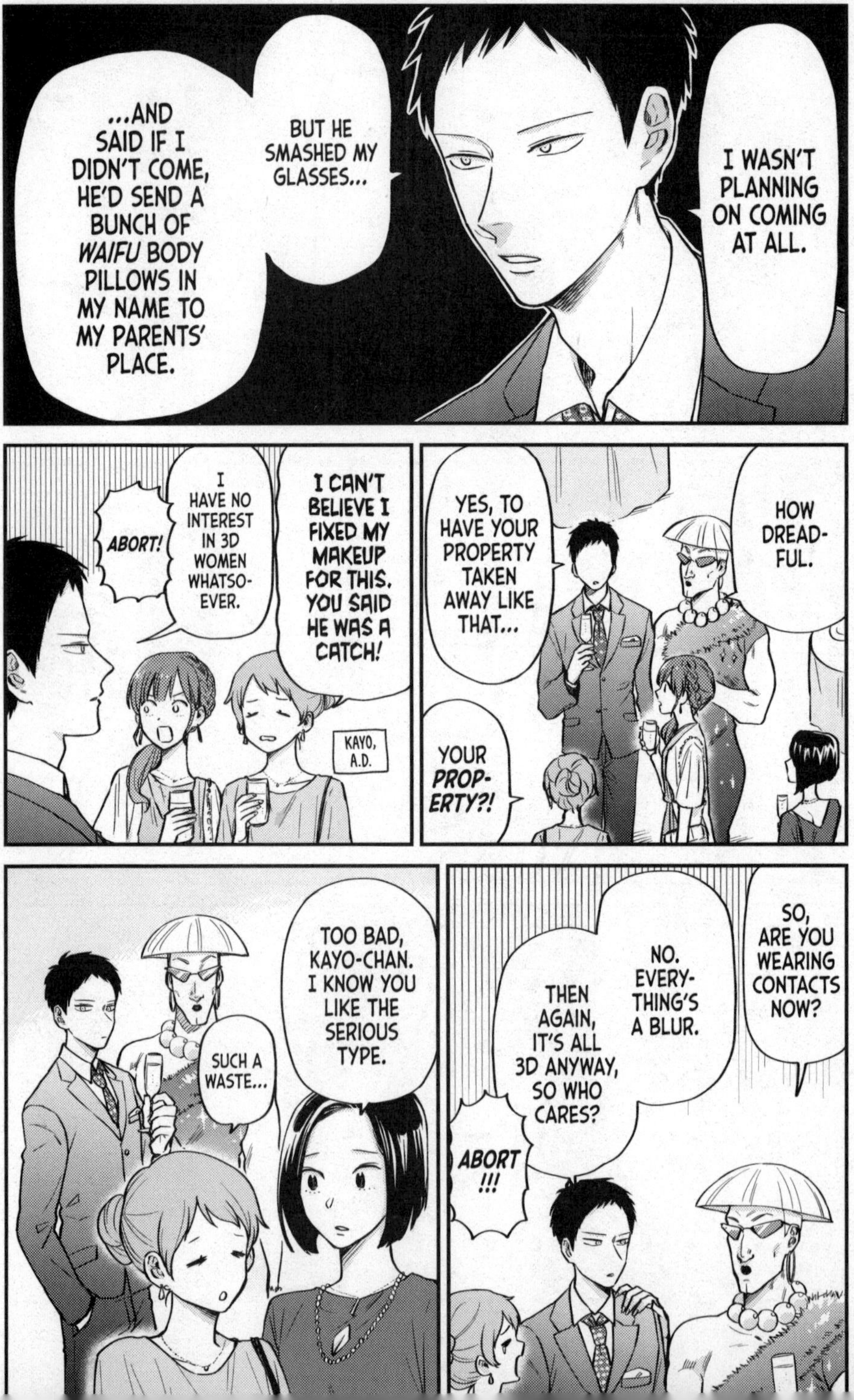

I WASN'T PLANNING ON COMING AT ALL.
BUT HE SMASHED MY GLASSES...
...AND SAID IF I DIDN'T COME, HE'D SEND A BUNCH OF *WAIFU* BODY PILLOWS IN MY NAME TO MY PARENTS' PLACE.
HOW DREADFUL.
YES, TO HAVE YOUR PROPERTY TAKEN AWAY LIKE THAT...
YOUR *PROPERTY?!*
I CAN'T BELIEVE I FIXED MY MAKEUP FOR THIS. YOU SAID HE WAS A CATCH!
I HAVE NO INTEREST IN 3D WOMEN WHATSOEVER.
ABORT!
KAYO, A.D.
SO, ARE YOU WEARING CONTACTS NOW?
NO. EVERYTHING'S A BLUR.
THEN AGAIN, IT'S ALL 3D ANYWAY, SO WHO CARES?
ABORT !!!
TOO BAD, KAYO-CHAN. I KNOW YOU LIKE THE SERIOUS TYPE.
SUCH A WASTE...

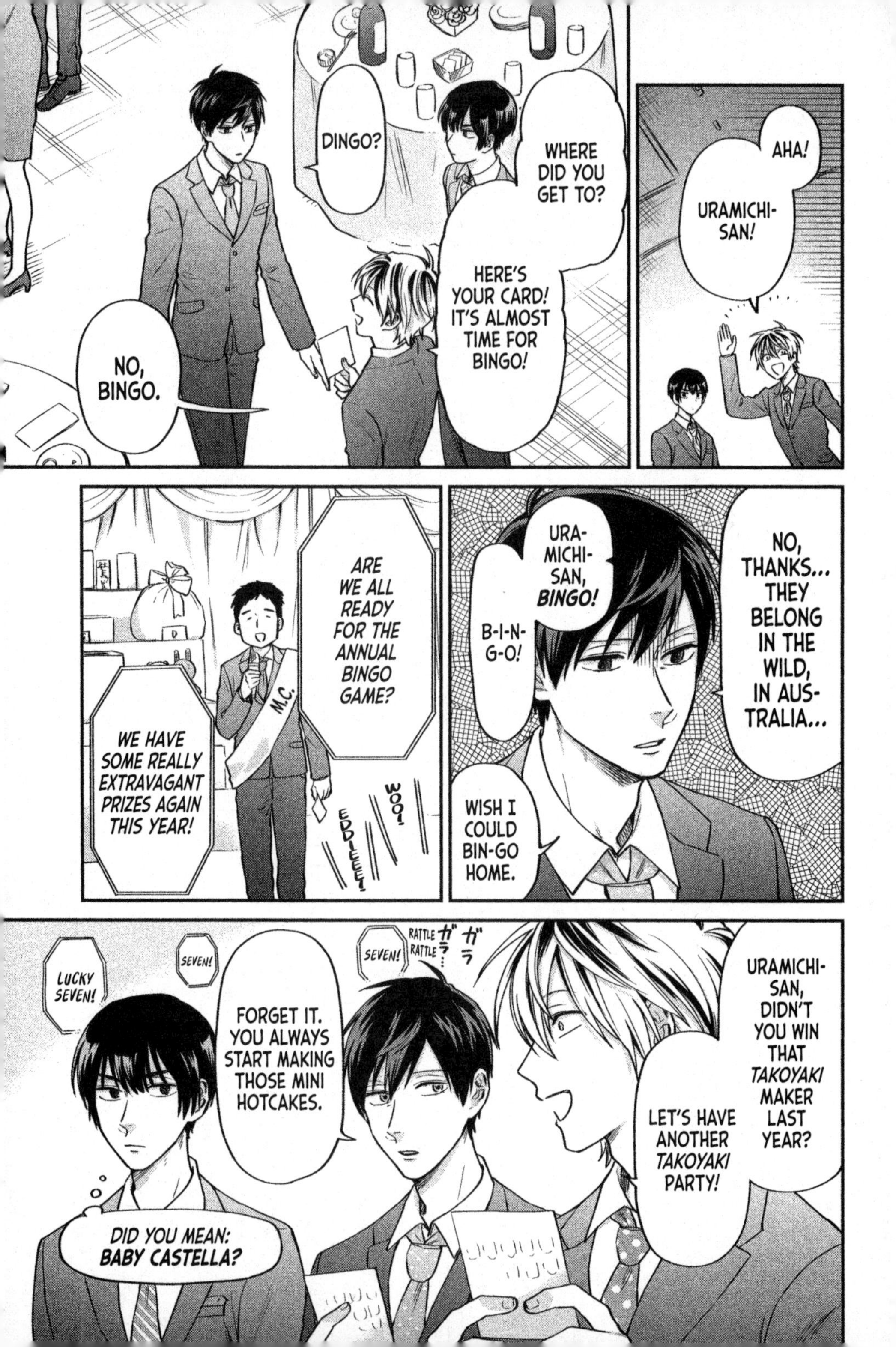
AHA!
URAMICHI-SAN!
WHERE DID YOU GET TO?
HERE'S YOUR CARD! IT'S ALMOST TIME FOR BINGO!
DINGO?
NO, BINGO.
NO, THANKS... THEY BELONG IN THE WILD, IN AUSTRALIA...
URA-MICHI-SAN, BINGO!
B-I-N-G-O!
WISH I COULD BIN-GO HOME.
ARE WE ALL READY FOR THE ANNUAL BINGO GAME?
WOO!
EDDIEEE!
WE HAVE SOME REALLY EXTRAVAGANT PRIZES AGAIN THIS YEAR!
URAMICHI-SAN, DIDN'T YOU WIN THAT TAKOYAKI MAKER LAST YEAR?
LET'S HAVE ANOTHER TAKOYAKI PARTY!
RATTLE RATTLE
SEVEN!
FORGET IT. YOU ALWAYS START MAKING THOSE MINI HOTCAKES.
SEVEN!
LUCKY SEVEN!
DID YOU MEAN: BABY CASTELLA?

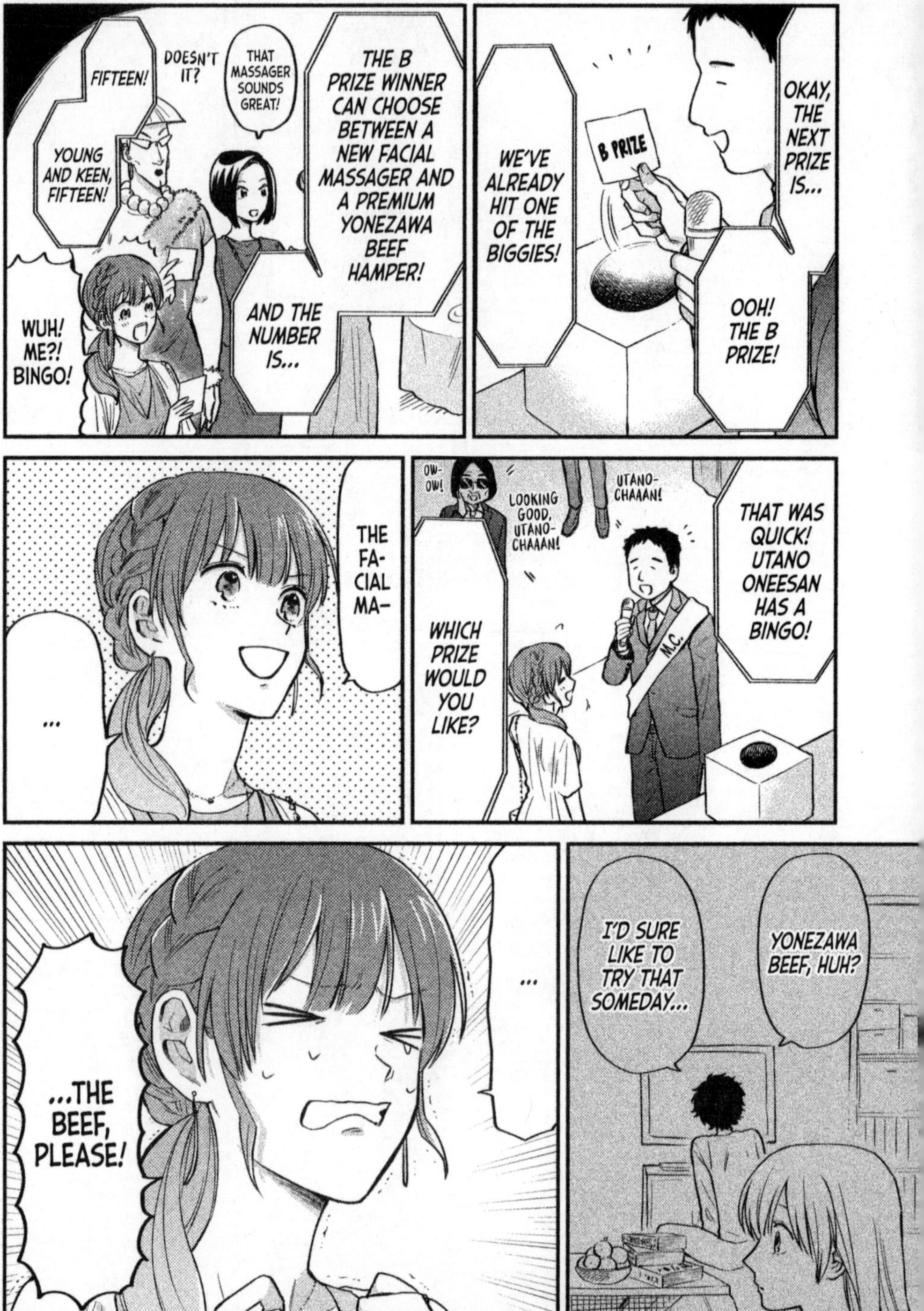
OKAY, THE NEXT PRIZE IS...
B PRIZE
OOH! THE B PRIZE!
WE'VE ALREADY HIT ONE OF THE BIGGIES!
THE B PRIZE WINNER CAN CHOOSE BETWEEN A NEW FACIAL MASSAGER AND A PREMIUM YONEZAWA BEEF HAMPER!
THAT MASSAGER SOUNDS GREAT!
DOESN'T IT?
AND THE NUMBER IS...
FIFTEEN!
YOUNG AND KEEN, FIFTEEN!
WUH! ME?! BINGO!
THAT WAS QUICK! UTANO ONEESAN HAS A BINGO!
UTANO-CHAAAN!
LOOKING GOOD, UTANO-CHAAAN!
OW-OW!
WHICH PRIZE WOULD YOU LIKE?
THE FA-CIAL MA-
...
YONEZAWA BEEF, HUH?
I'D SURE LIKE TO TRY THAT SOMEDAY...
...
...THE BEEF, PLEASE!

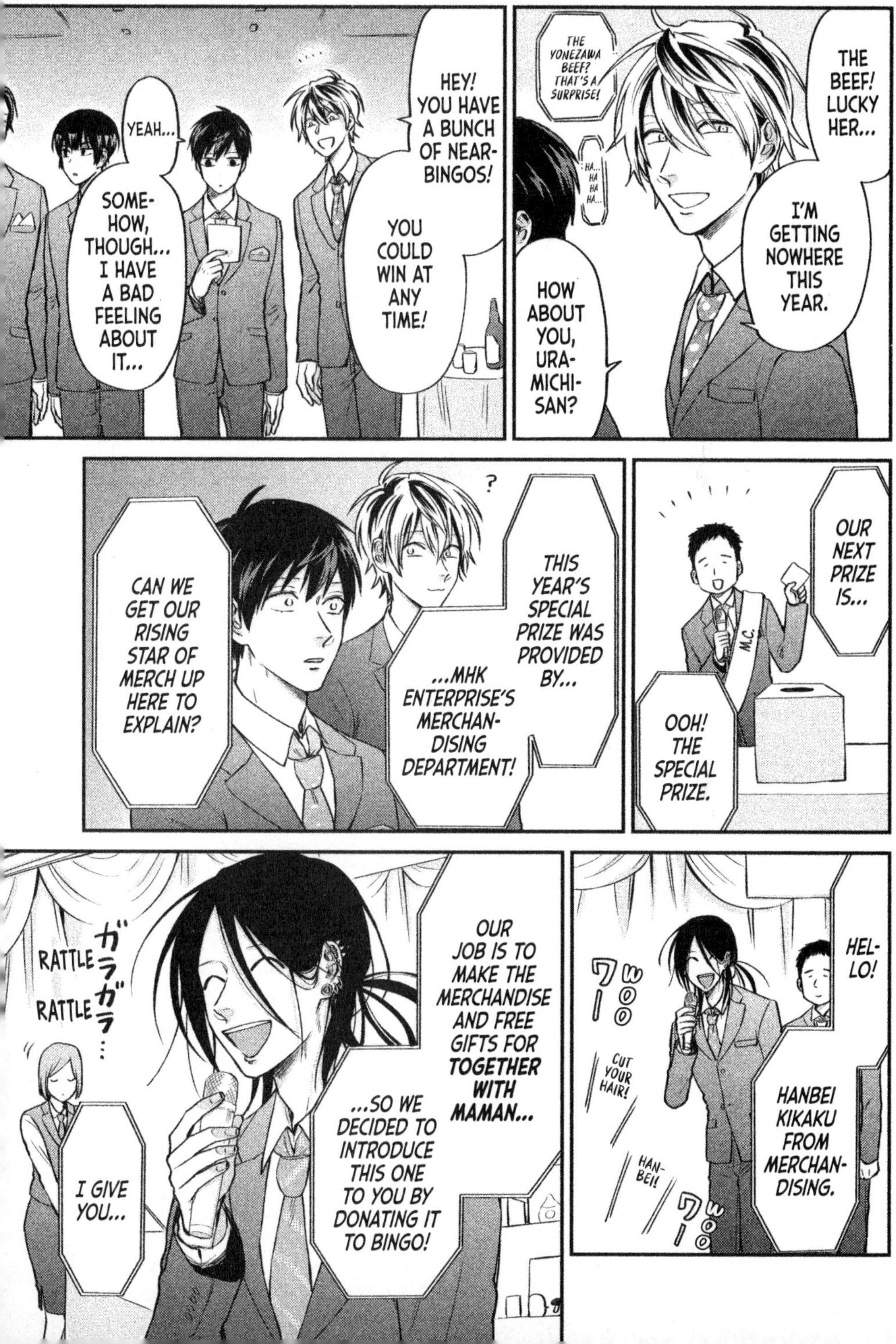
THE BEEF! LUCKY HER...
I'M GETTING NOWHERE THIS YEAR.
THE YONEZAWA BEEF? THAT'S A SURPRISE!
HA... HA HA HA...
HOW ABOUT YOU, URA-MICHI-SAN?
HEY! YOU HAVE A BUNCH OF NEAR-BINGOS!
YOU COULD WIN AT ANY TIME!
YEAH...
SOME-HOW, THOUGH... I HAVE A BAD FEELING ABOUT IT...
OUR NEXT PRIZE IS...
OOH! THE SPECIAL PRIZE.
M.C.
?
THIS YEAR'S SPECIAL PRIZE WAS PROVIDED BY...
...MHK ENTERPRISE'S MERCHAN-DISING DEPARTMENT!
CAN WE GET OUR RISING STAR OF MERCH UP HERE TO EXPLAIN?
HEL-LO!
HANBEI KIKAKU FROM MERCHAN-DISING.
ワー WOO
CUT YOUR HAIR!
HAN-BEI!
ワー WOO
OUR JOB IS TO MAKE THE MERCHANDISE AND FREE GIFTS FOR **TOGETHER WITH MAMAN...**
...SO WE DECIDED TO INTRODUCE THIS ONE TO YOU BY DONATING IT TO BINGO!
ガラガラ… RATTLE RATTLE
I GIVE YOU...

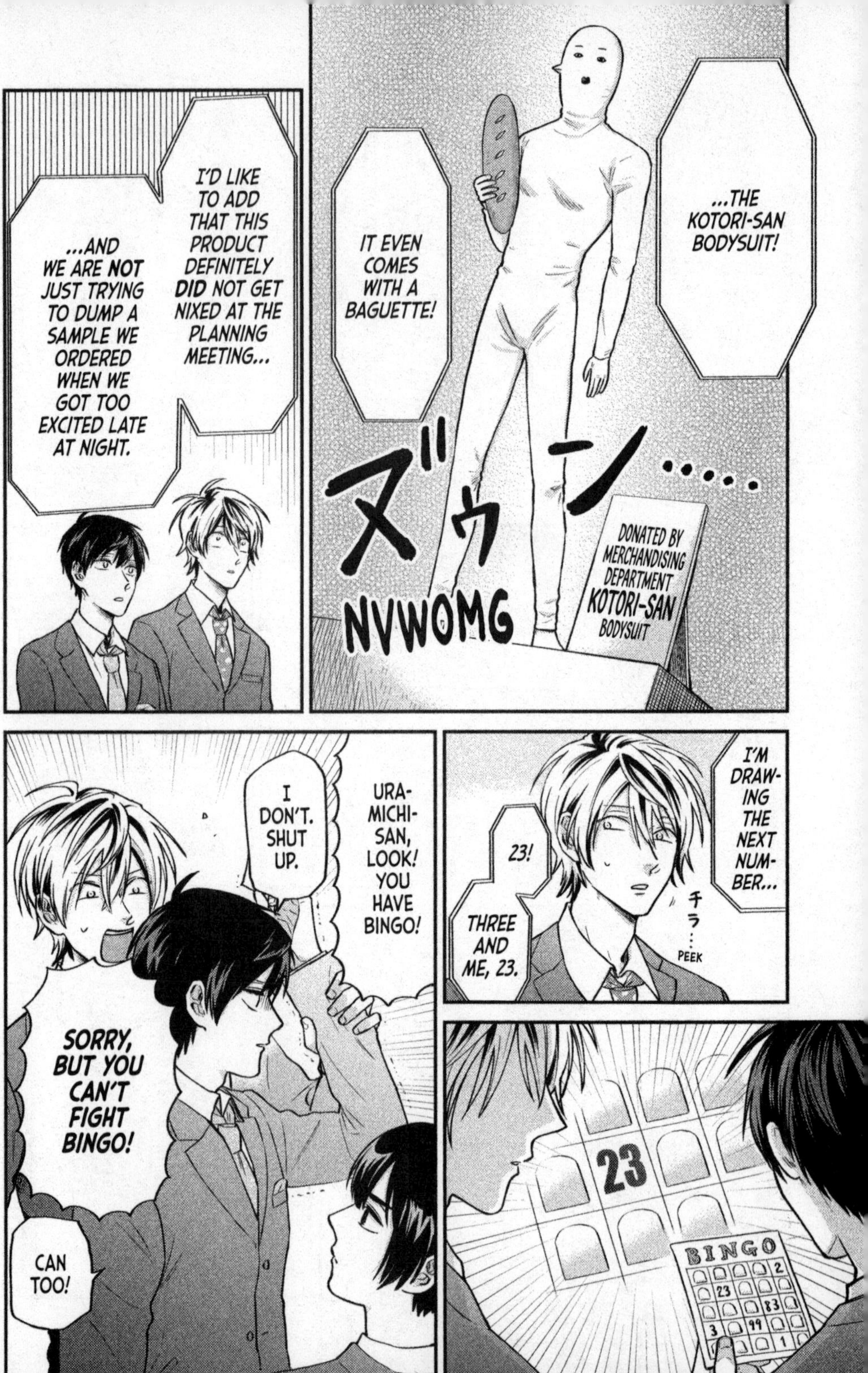
...THE KOTORI-SAN BODYSUIT!
IT EVEN COMES WITH A BAGUETTE!
ヌゥーン.....
NVWOMG
DONATED BY MERCHANDISING DEPARTMENT KOTORI-SAN BODYSUIT
I'D LIKE TO ADD THAT THIS PRODUCT DEFINITELY **DID** NOT GET NIXED AT THE PLANNING MEETING...
...AND WE ARE **NOT** JUST TRYING TO DUMP A SAMPLE WE ORDERED WHEN WE GOT TOO EXCITED LATE AT NIGHT.
I'M DRAWING THE NEXT NUMBER...
23!
THREE AND ME, 23.
チラ…
PEEK
23
BINGO
2
23
83
3
99
1
URA-MICHI-SAN, LOOK! YOU HAVE BINGO!
I DON'T. SHUT UP.
SORRY, BUT YOU CAN'T FIGHT BINGO!
CAN TOO!

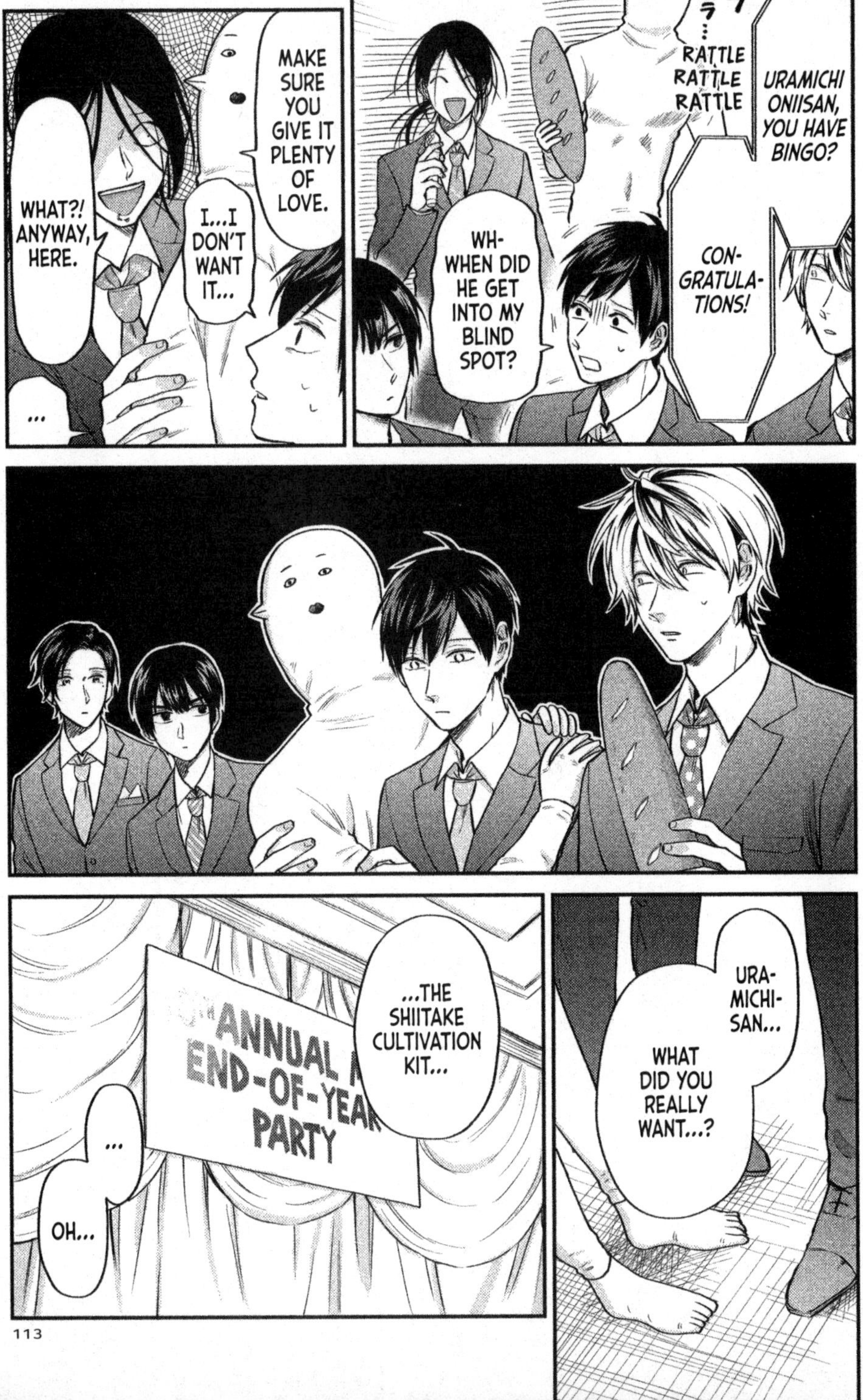
ガラガラガラ…
RATTLE RATTLE RATTLE
URAMICHI ONIISAN, YOU HAVE BINGO?
CON-GRATULA-TIONS!
WH-WHEN DID HE GET INTO MY BLIND SPOT?
MAKE SURE YOU GIVE IT PLENTY OF LOVE.
I...I DON'T WANT IT...
WHAT?! ANYWAY, HERE.
...
URA-MICHI-SAN...
WHAT DID YOU REALLY WANT...?
...THE SHIITAKE CULTIVATION KIT...
ANNUAL
END-OF-YEA
PARTY
...
OH...

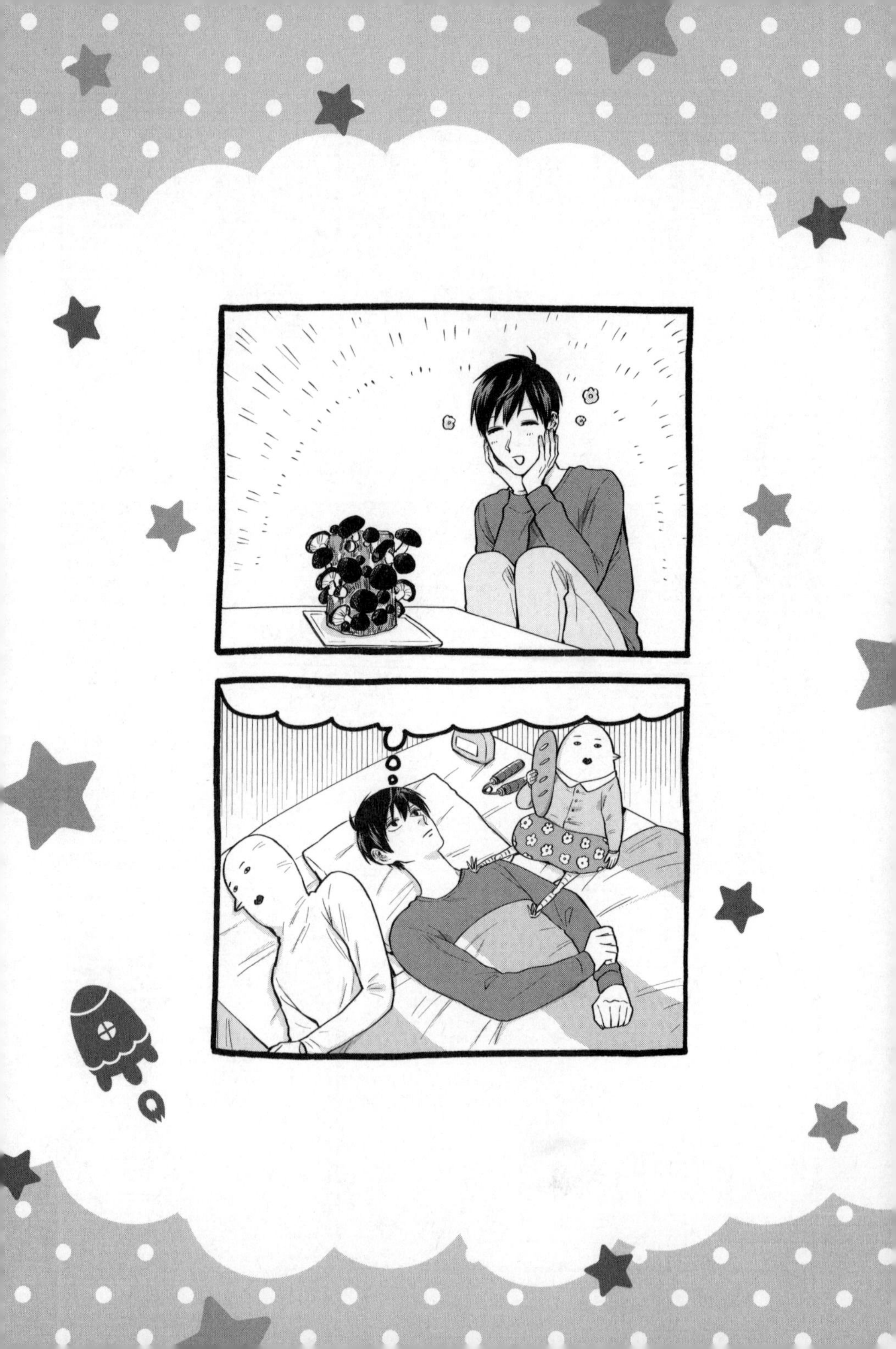

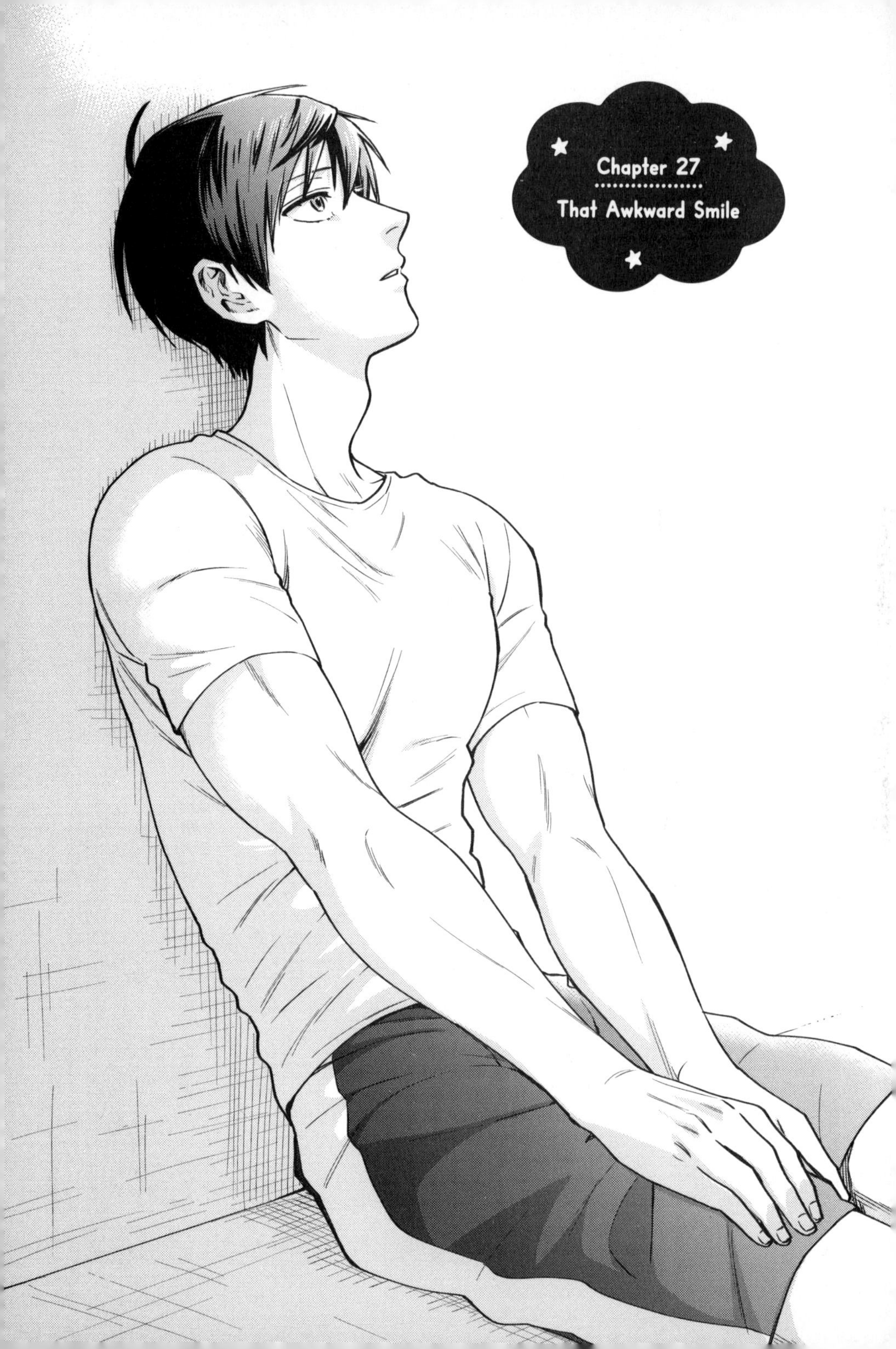
Chapter 27
That Awkward Smile

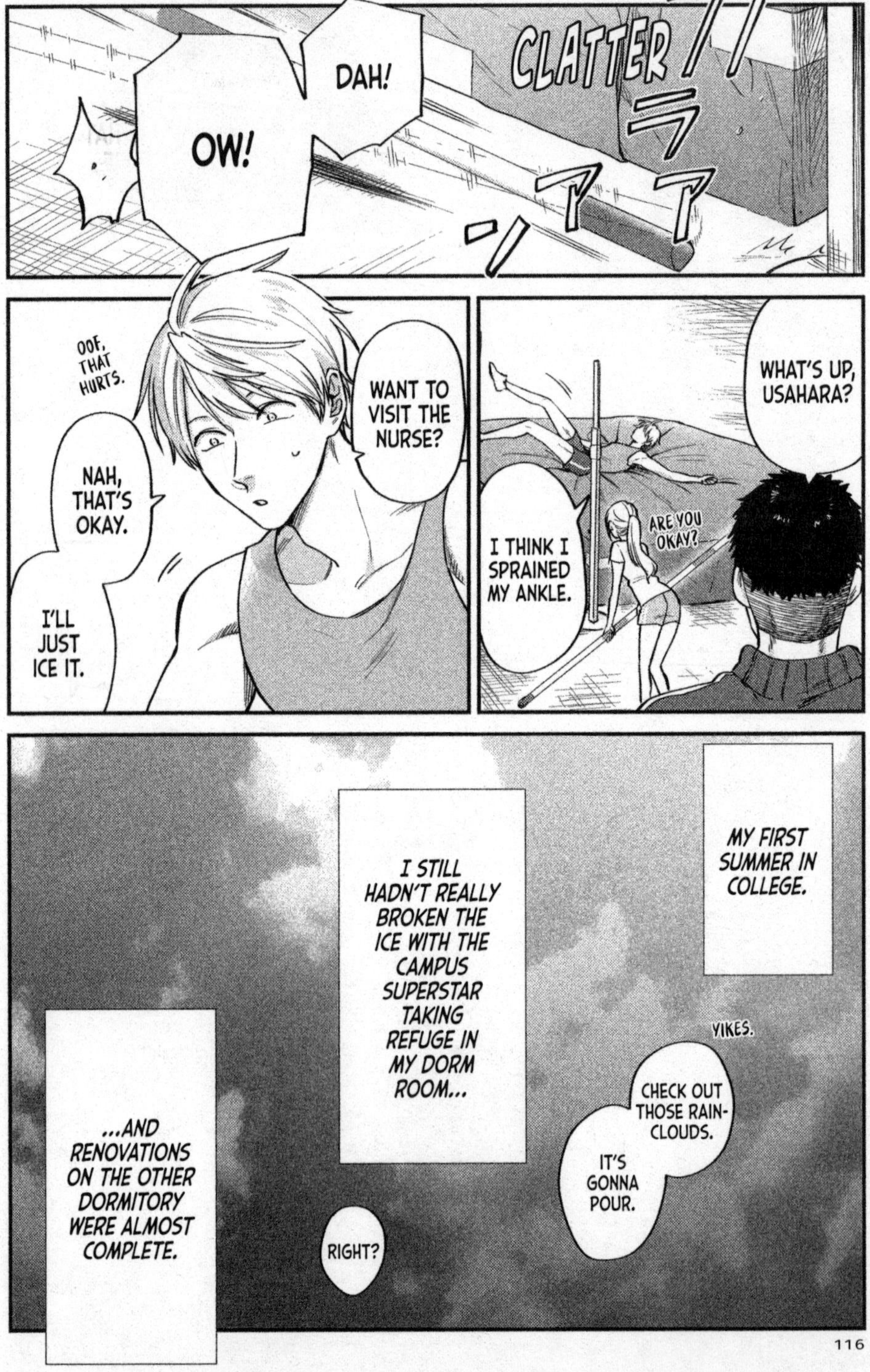
CLATTER
DAH!
OW!
WHAT'S UP, USAHARA?
I THINK I SPRAINED MY ANKLE.
ARE YOU OKAY?
WANT TO VISIT THE NURSE?
OOF, THAT HURTS.
NAH, THAT'S OKAY.
I'LL JUST ICE IT.
MY FIRST SUMMER IN COLLEGE.
I STILL HADN'T REALLY BROKEN THE ICE WITH THE CAMPUS SUPERSTAR TAKING REFUGE IN MY DORM ROOM...
YIKES.
CHECK OUT THOSE RAIN-CLOUDS.
IT'S GONNA POUR.
RIGHT?
...AND RENOVATIONS ON THE OTHER DORMITORY WERE ALMOST COMPLETE.

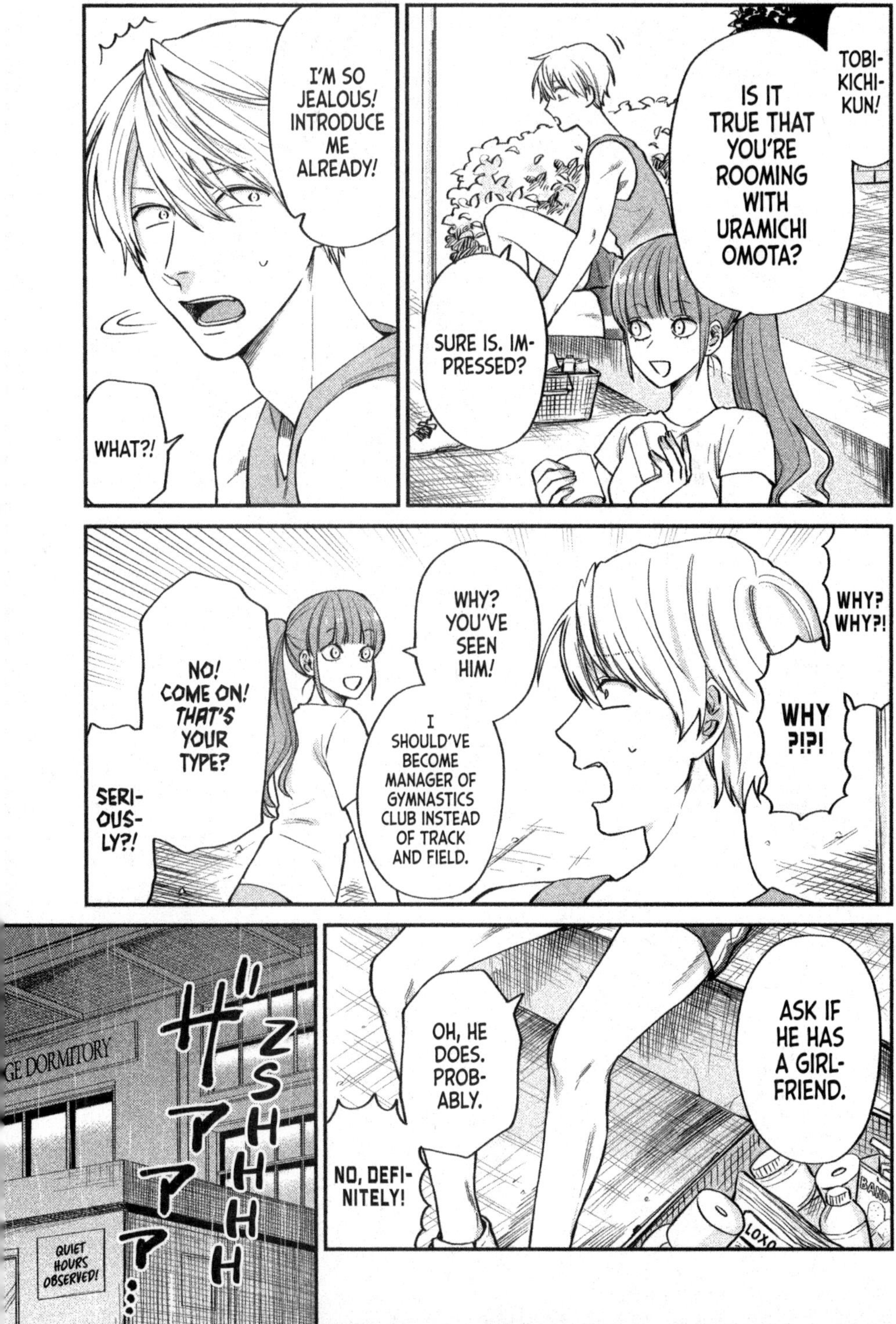
TOBI-KICHI-KUN!
IS IT TRUE THAT YOU'RE ROOMING WITH URAMICHI OMOTA?
SURE IS. IM-PRESSED?
I'M SO JEALOUS! INTRODUCE ME ALREADY!
WHAT?!
WHY? WHY?!
WHY ?!?!
WHY? YOU'VE SEEN HIM!
I SHOULD'VE BECOME MANAGER OF GYMNASTICS CLUB INSTEAD OF TRACK AND FIELD.
NO! COME ON! THAT'S YOUR TYPE?
SERI-OUS-LY?!
ASK IF HE HAS A GIRL-FRIEND.
OH, HE DOES. PROB-ABLY.
NO, DEFI-NITELY!
ZSHHHHH
ザァァ…
GE DORMITORY
QUIET HOURS OBSERVED!

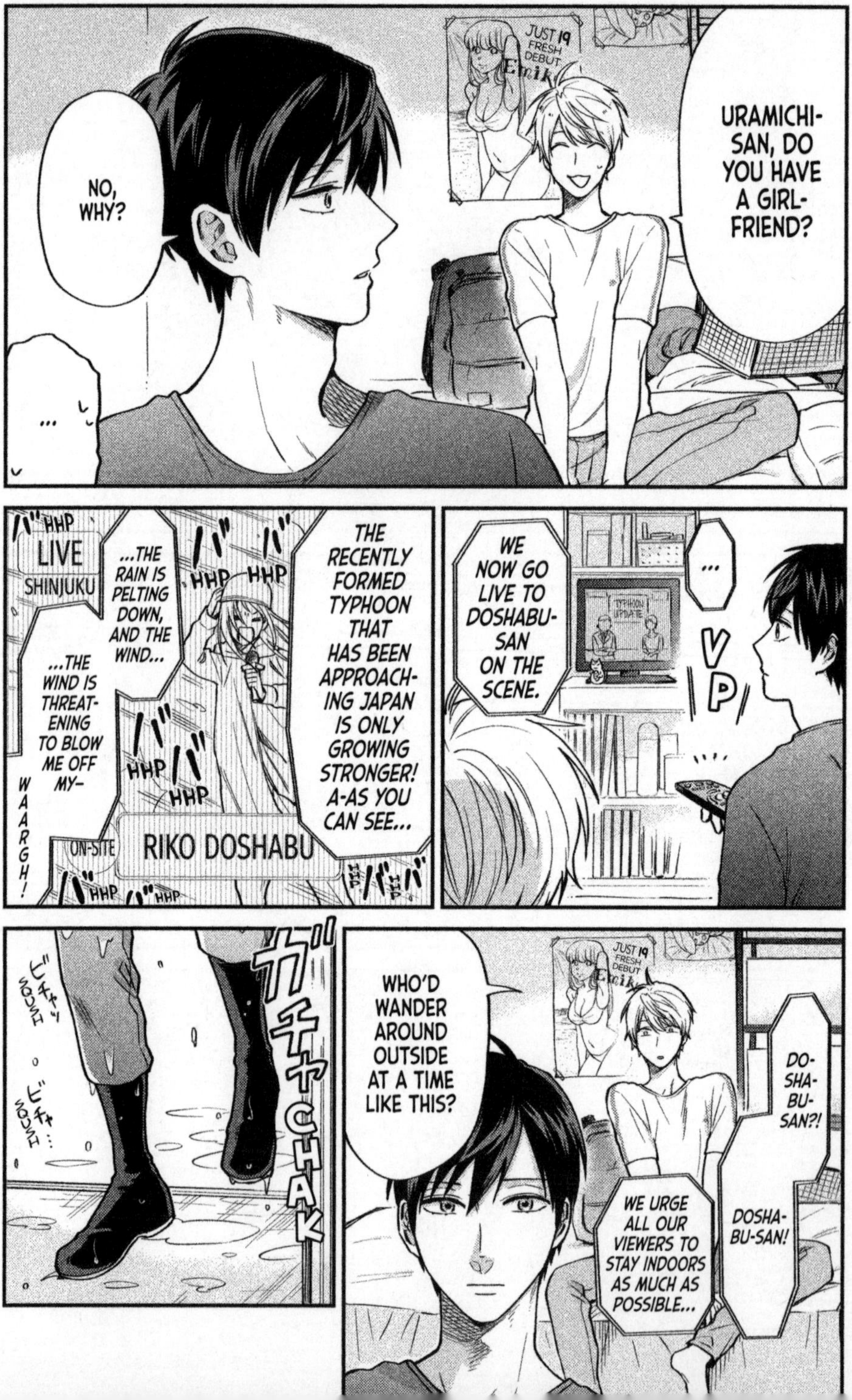
URAMICHI-SAN, DO YOU HAVE A GIRL-FRIEND?
JUST 19 FRESH DEBUT
NO, WHY?
...
...
VP
WE NOW GO LIVE TO DOSHABU-SAN ON THE SCENE.
TYPHOON UPDATE
THE RECENTLY FORMED TYPHOON THAT HAS BEEN APPROACHING JAPAN IS ONLY GROWING STRONGER! A-AS YOU CAN SEE...
バ HHP バ HHP
LIVE SHINJUKU
...THE RAIN IS PELTING DOWN, AND THE WIND...
...THE WIND IS THREATENING TO BLOW ME OFF MY—
WAAARGH!
ON-SITE
RIKO DOSHABU
バ HHP バ HHP
DO-SHA-BU-SAN?!
WHO'D WANDER AROUND OUTSIDE AT A TIME LIKE THIS?
JUST 19 FRESH DEBUT
DOSHA-BU-SAN!
WE URGE ALL OUR VIEWERS TO STAY INDOORS AS MUCH AS POSSIBLE...
ガチャ CHAK
ビチャッ SQUSH
ビチャ… SQUSH

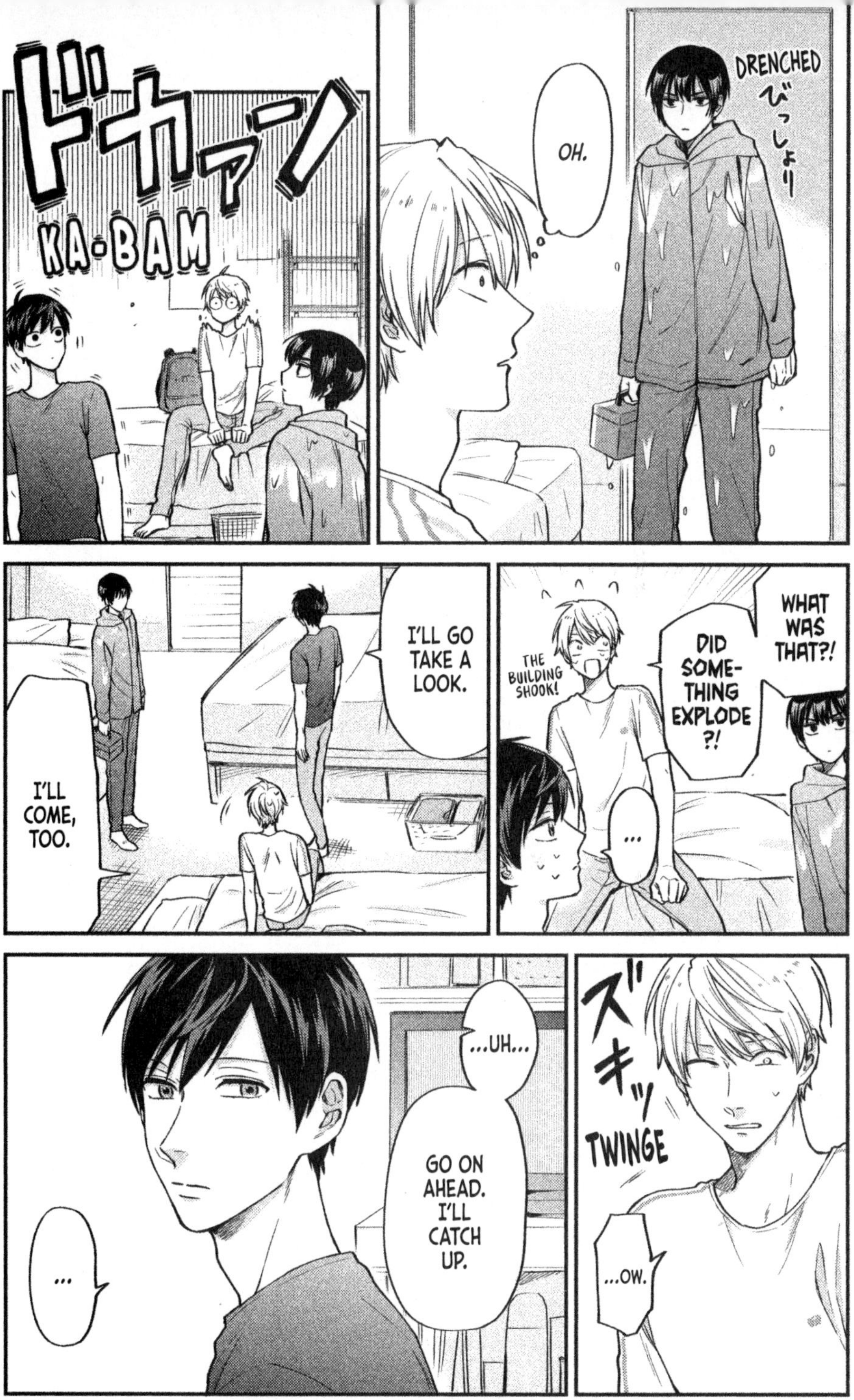
DRENCHED
びっしょり
OH.
ドカァーン
KA-BAM
WHAT WAS THAT?!
DID SOMETHING EXPLODE?!
THE BUILDING SHOOK!
...
I'LL GO TAKE A LOOK.
I'LL COME, TOO.
ズキッ
TWINGE
...OW.
...UH...
GO ON AHEAD. I'LL CATCH UP.
...

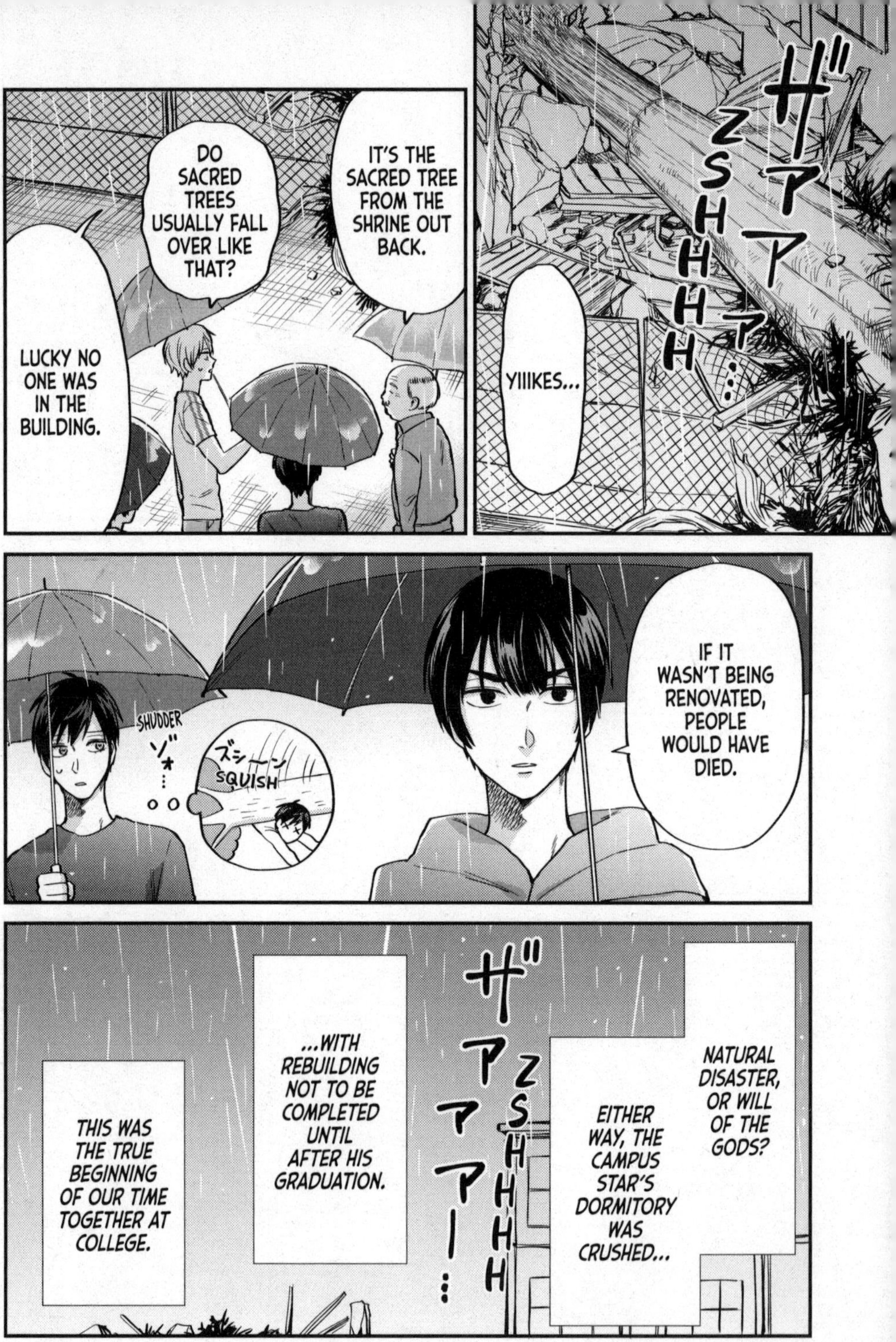
ZSHHHH
YIIIKES...
IT'S THE SACRED TREE FROM THE SHRINE OUT BACK.
DO SACRED TREES USUALLY FALL OVER LIKE THAT?
LUCKY NO ONE WAS IN THE BUILDING.
IF IT WASN'T BEING RENOVATED, PEOPLE WOULD HAVE DIED.
SHUDDER
SQUISH
NATURAL DISASTER, OR WILL OF THE GODS?
EITHER WAY, THE CAMPUS STAR'S DORMITORY WAS CRUSHED...
ZSHHH
...WITH REBUILDING NOT TO BE COMPLETED UNTIL AFTER HIS GRADUATION.
THIS WAS THE TRUE BEGINNING OF OUR TIME TOGETHER AT COLLEGE.

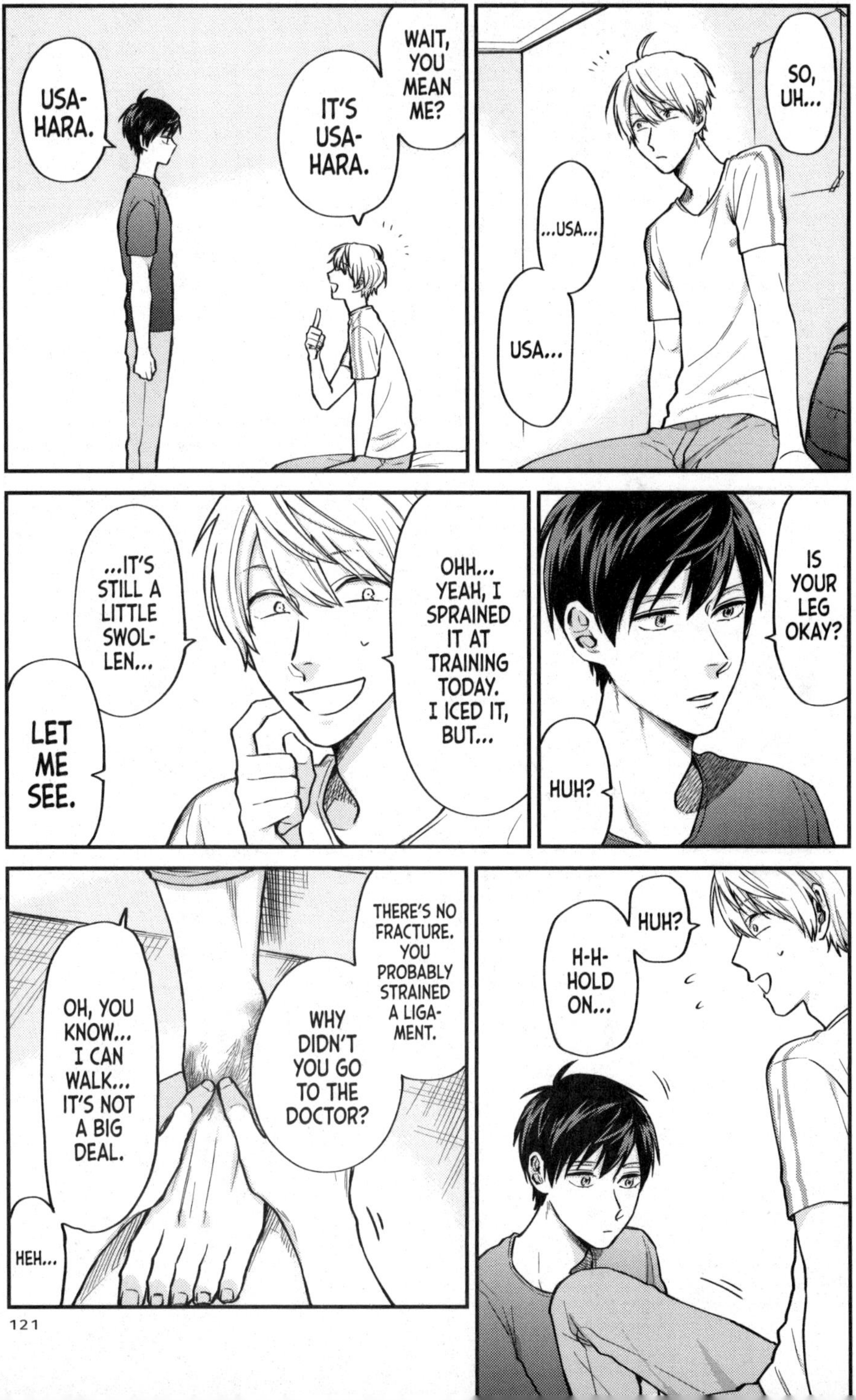
SO, UH...
...USA...
USA...
WAIT, YOU MEAN ME?
IT'S USA-HARA.
USA-HARA.
IS YOUR LEG OKAY?
HUH?
OHH... YEAH, I SPRAINED IT AT TRAINING TODAY. I ICED IT, BUT...
...IT'S STILL A LITTLE SWOL-LEN...
LET ME SEE.
HUH?
H-H-HOLD ON...
THERE'S NO FRACTURE. YOU PROBABLY STRAINED A LIGA-MENT.
WHY DIDN'T YOU GO TO THE DOCTOR?
OH, YOU KNOW... I CAN WALK... IT'S NOT A BIG DEAL.
HEH...

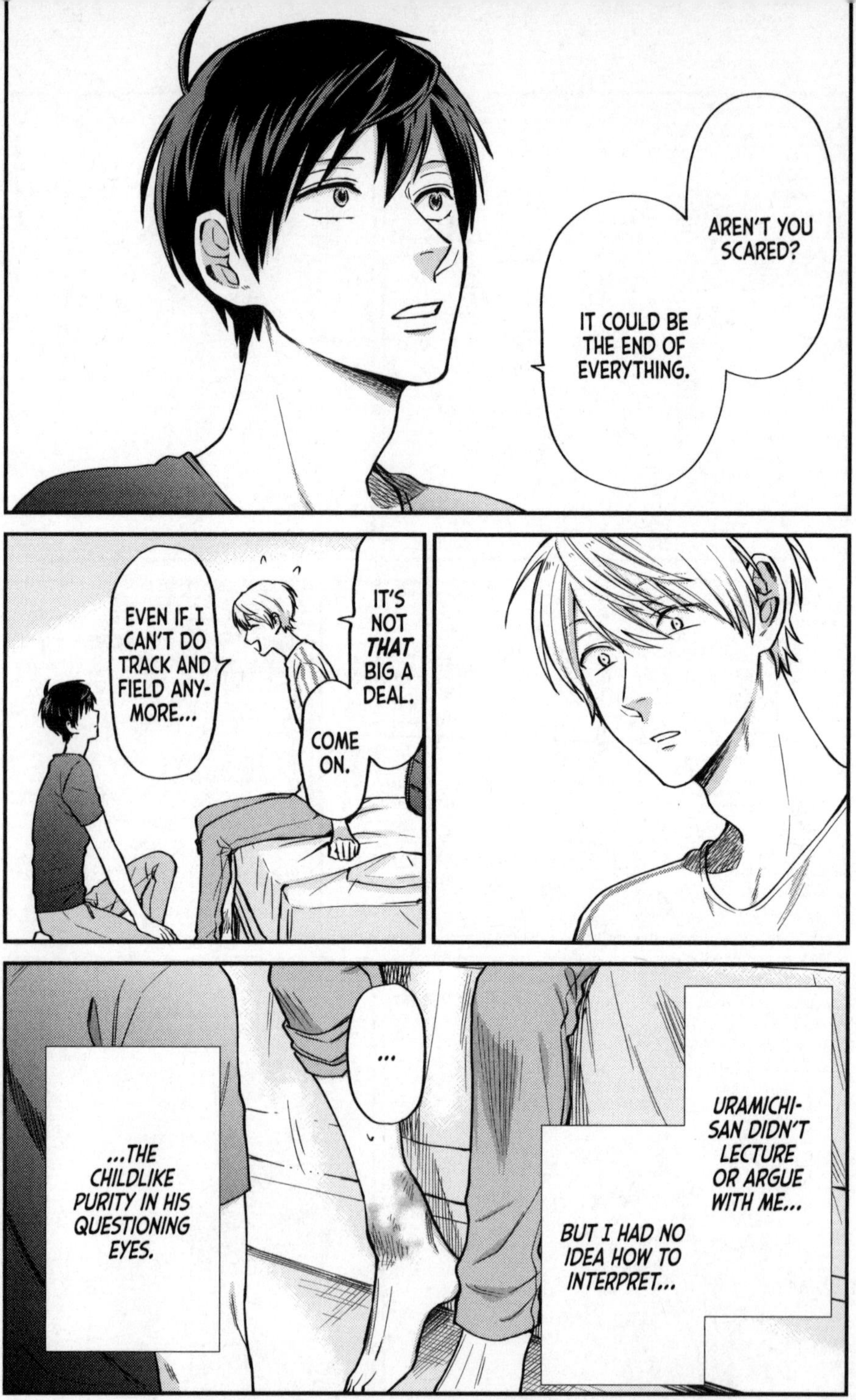

AREN'T YOU SCARED?
IT COULD BE THE END OF EVERYTHING.
IT'S NOT *THAT* BIG A DEAL.
COME ON.
EVEN IF I CAN'T DO TRACK AND FIELD ANY-MORE...
...
URAMICHI-SAN DIDN'T LECTURE OR ARGUE WITH ME...
BUT I HAD NO IDEA HOW TO INTERPRET...
...THE CHILDLIKE PURITY IN HIS QUESTIONING EYES.

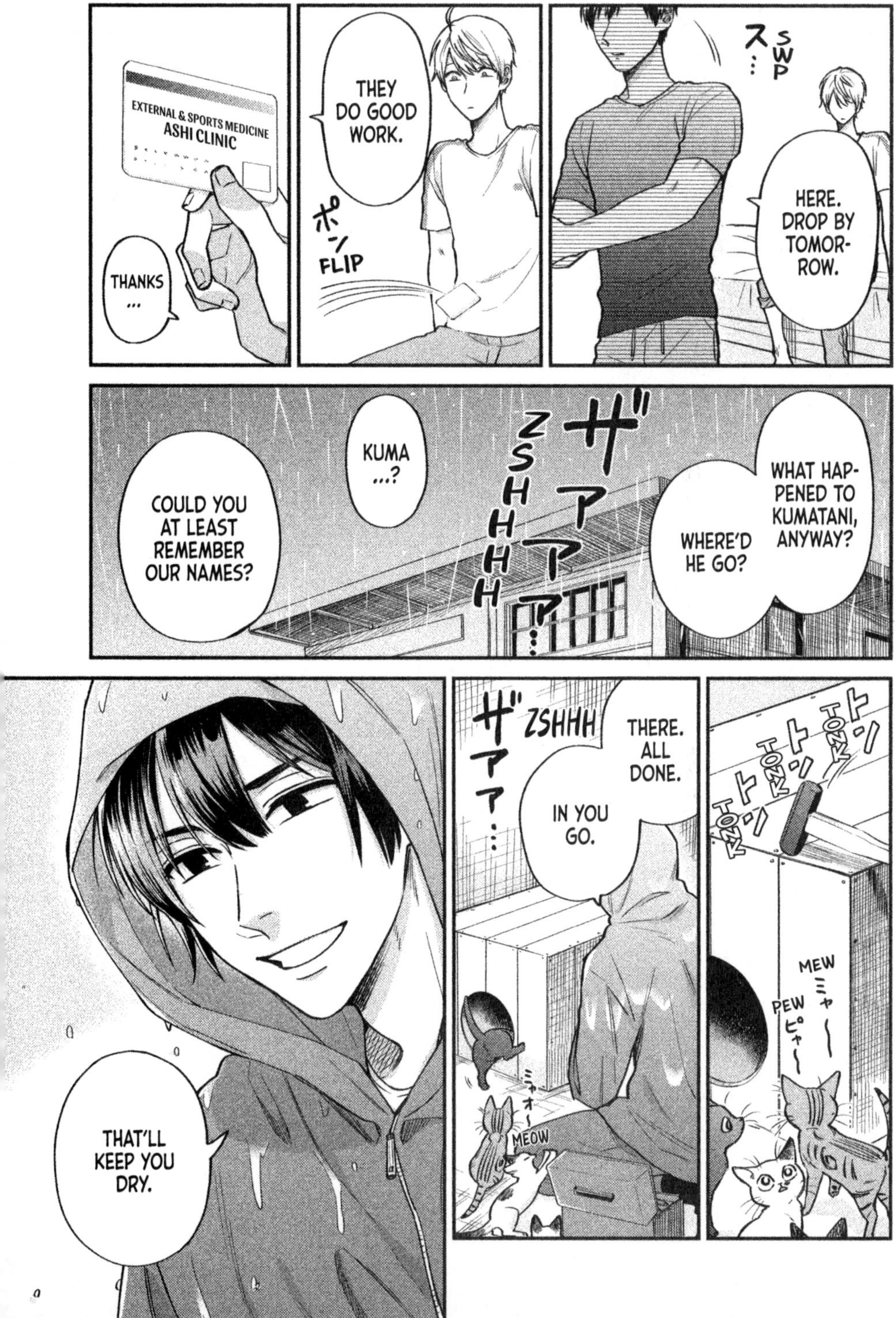
ス… SWP
HERE. DROP BY TOMORROW.
THEY DO GOOD WORK.
ポン FLIP
EXTERNAL & SPORTS MEDICINE
ASHI CLINIC
THANKS…
WHAT HAPPENED TO KUMATANI, ANYWAY?
WHERE'D HE GO?
ザアアア… ZSHHHHH
KUMA…?
COULD YOU AT LEAST REMEMBER OUR NAMES?
トン TONK
トン TONK
トン TONK
MEW ミャ〜
PEW ピャ〜
ザアア… ZSHHH
THERE. ALL DONE.
IN YOU GO.
ミャオ〜 MEOW
THAT'LL KEEP YOU DRY.

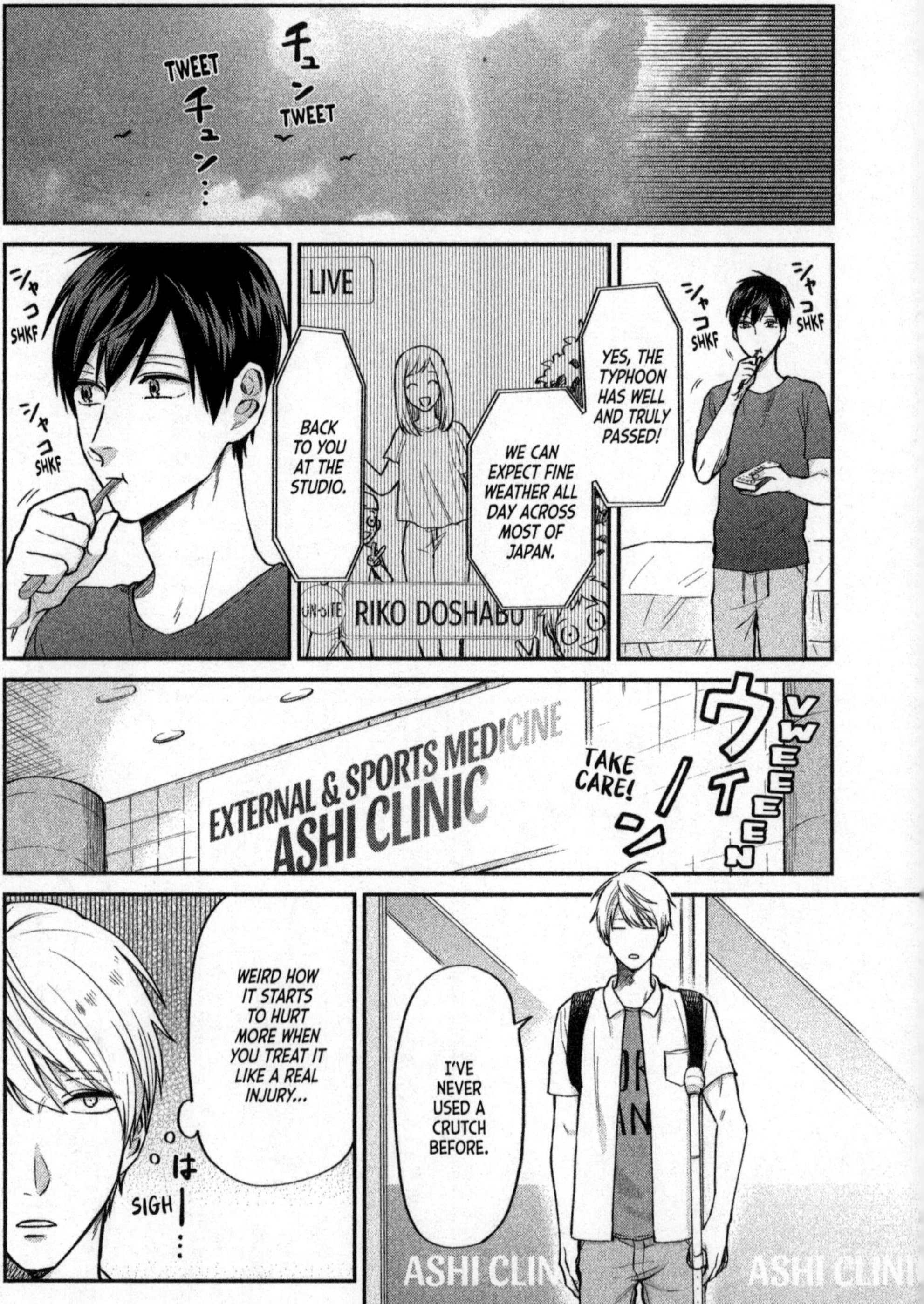
チュン
TWEET
TWEET
チュン…
シャコ
SHKF
シャコ
SHKF
LIVE
YES, THE TYPHOON HAS WELL AND TRULY PASSED!
WE CAN EXPECT FINE WEATHER ALL DAY ACROSS MOST OF JAPAN.
BACK TO YOU AT THE STUDIO.
ON-SITE
RIKO DOSHABU
シャコ
SHKF
シャコ
SHKF
ウィーン
VWEEEEN
TAKE CARE!
EXTERNAL & SPORTS MEDICINE
ASHI CLINIC
I'VE NEVER USED A CRUTCH BEFORE.
ASHI CLINI
ASHI CLIN
WEIRD HOW IT STARTS TO HURT MORE WHEN YOU TREAT IT LIKE A REAL INJURY...
はー…
SIGH

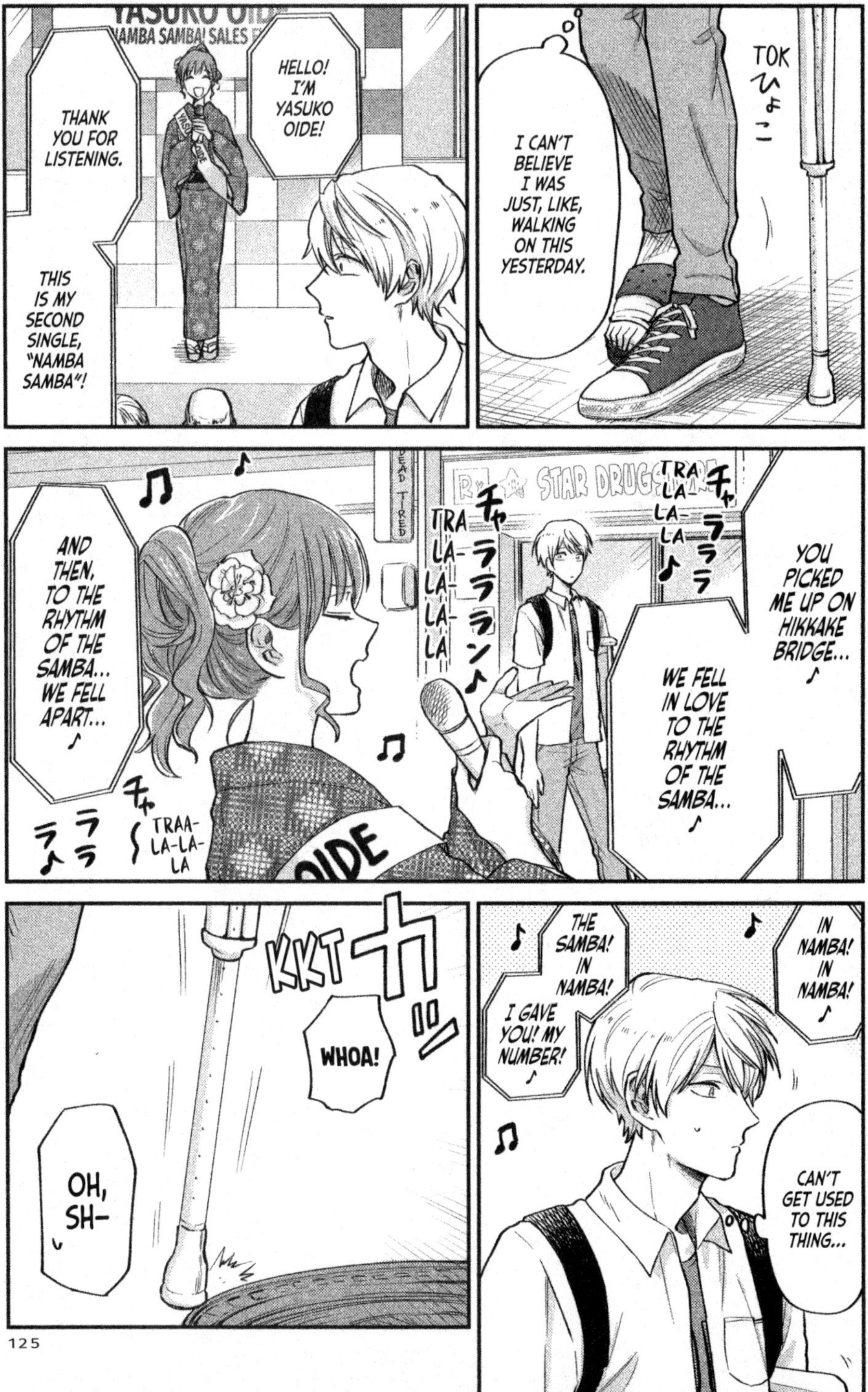
TOK
ひょこ
I CAN'T BELIEVE I WAS JUST, LIKE, WALKING ON THIS YESTERDAY.
HELLO! I'M YASUKO OIDE!
THANK YOU FOR LISTENING.
THIS IS MY SECOND SINGLE, "NAMBA SAMBA"!
YOU PICKED ME UP ON HIKKAKE BRIDGE... ♪
WE FELL IN LOVE TO THE RHYTHM OF THE SAMBA... ♪
TRA LA-LA-LA ♪
チャラララ
STAR DRUGSTORE
TRA LA-LA-LA-LA
チャラララン♪
AND THEN, TO THE RHYTHM OF THE SAMBA... WE FELL APART... ♪
TRAA-LA-LA-LA
チャ〜ララ♪
OIDE
IN NAMBA! IN NAMBA! ♪
THE SAMBA! IN NAMBA! I GAVE YOU! MY NUMBER! ♪
CAN'T GET USED TO THIS THING...
KKT
カッ
WHOA!
OH, SH—

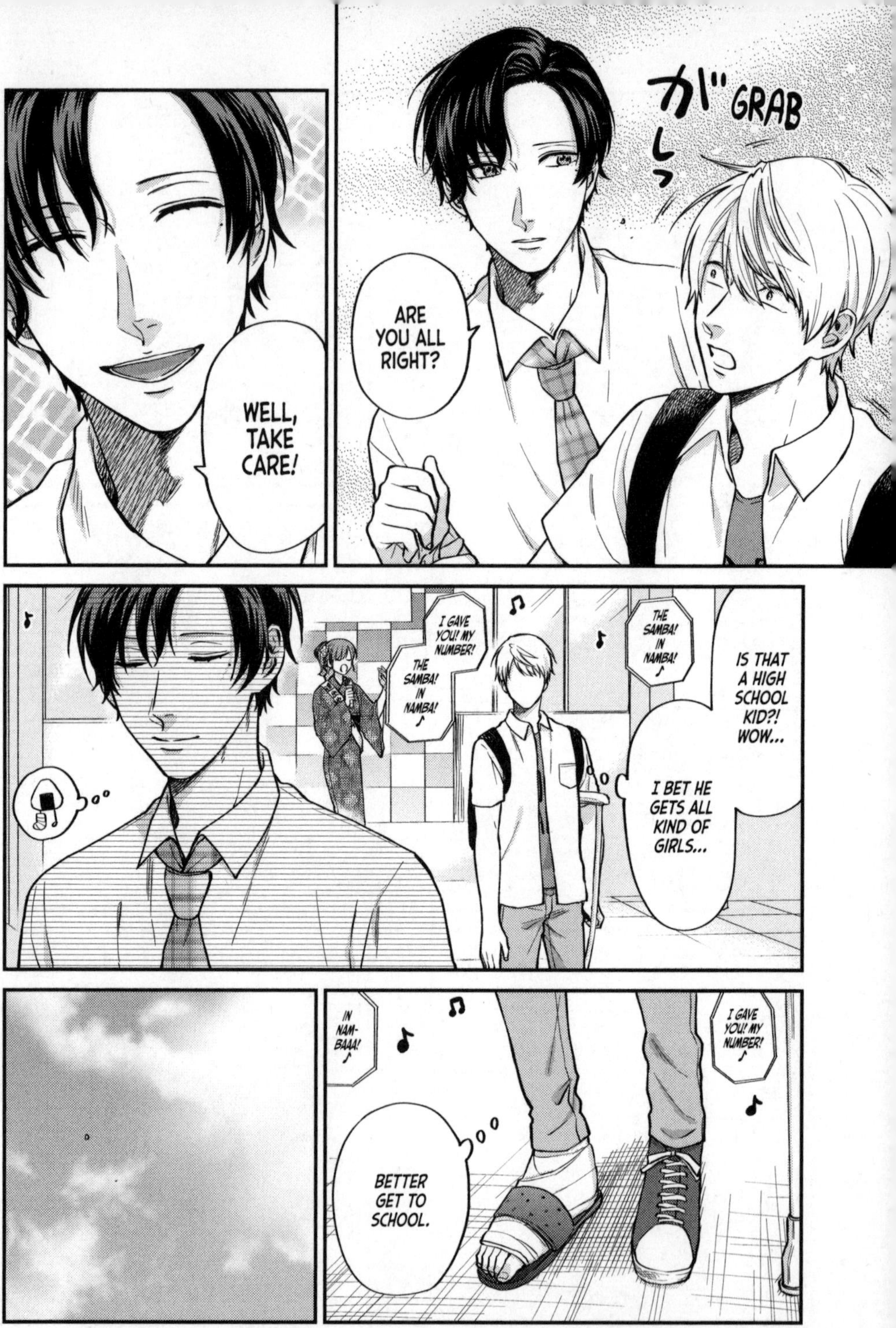
ガしっ
GRAB
ARE YOU ALL RIGHT?
WELL, TAKE CARE!
IS THAT A HIGH SCHOOL KID?! WOW...
I BET HE GETS ALL KIND OF GIRLS...
THE SAMBA! IN NAMBA! ♪
I GAVE YOU! MY NUMBER!
THE SAMBA! IN NAMBA! ♪
I GAVE YOU! MY NUMBER! ♪
IN NAM-BAAA! ♪
BETTER GET TO SCHOOL.

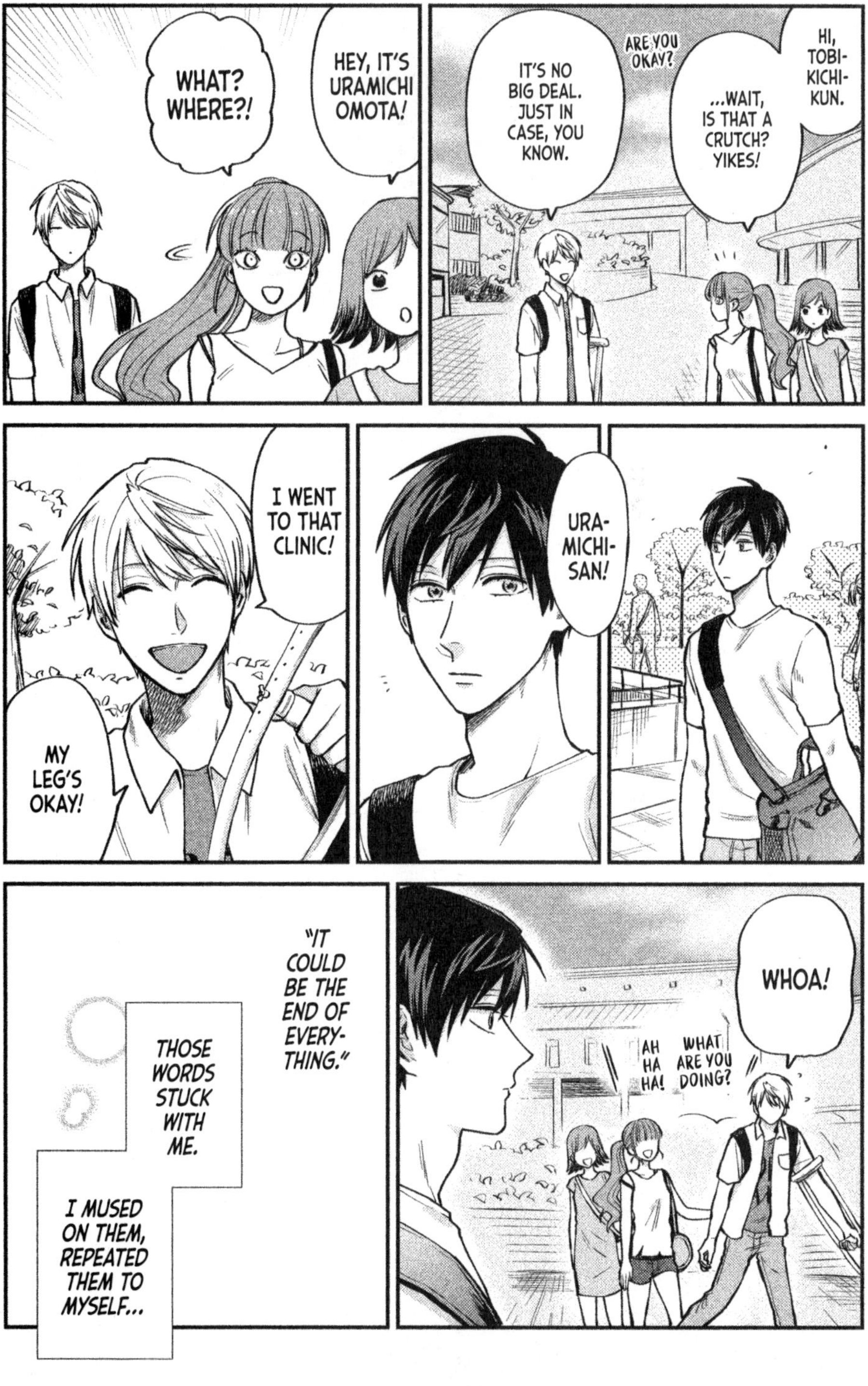
HI, TOBI-KICHI-KUN.
...WAIT, IS THAT A CRUTCH? YIKES!
ARE YOU OKAY?
IT'S NO BIG DEAL. JUST IN CASE, YOU KNOW.
HEY, IT'S URAMICHI OMOTA!
WHAT? WHERE?!
URA-MICHI-SAN!
I WENT TO THAT CLINIC!
MY LEG'S OKAY!
WHOA!
WHAT ARE YOU DOING?
AH HA HA!
"IT COULD BE THE END OF EVERY-THING."
THOSE WORDS STUCK WITH ME.
I MUSED ON THEM, REPEATED THEM TO MYSELF...

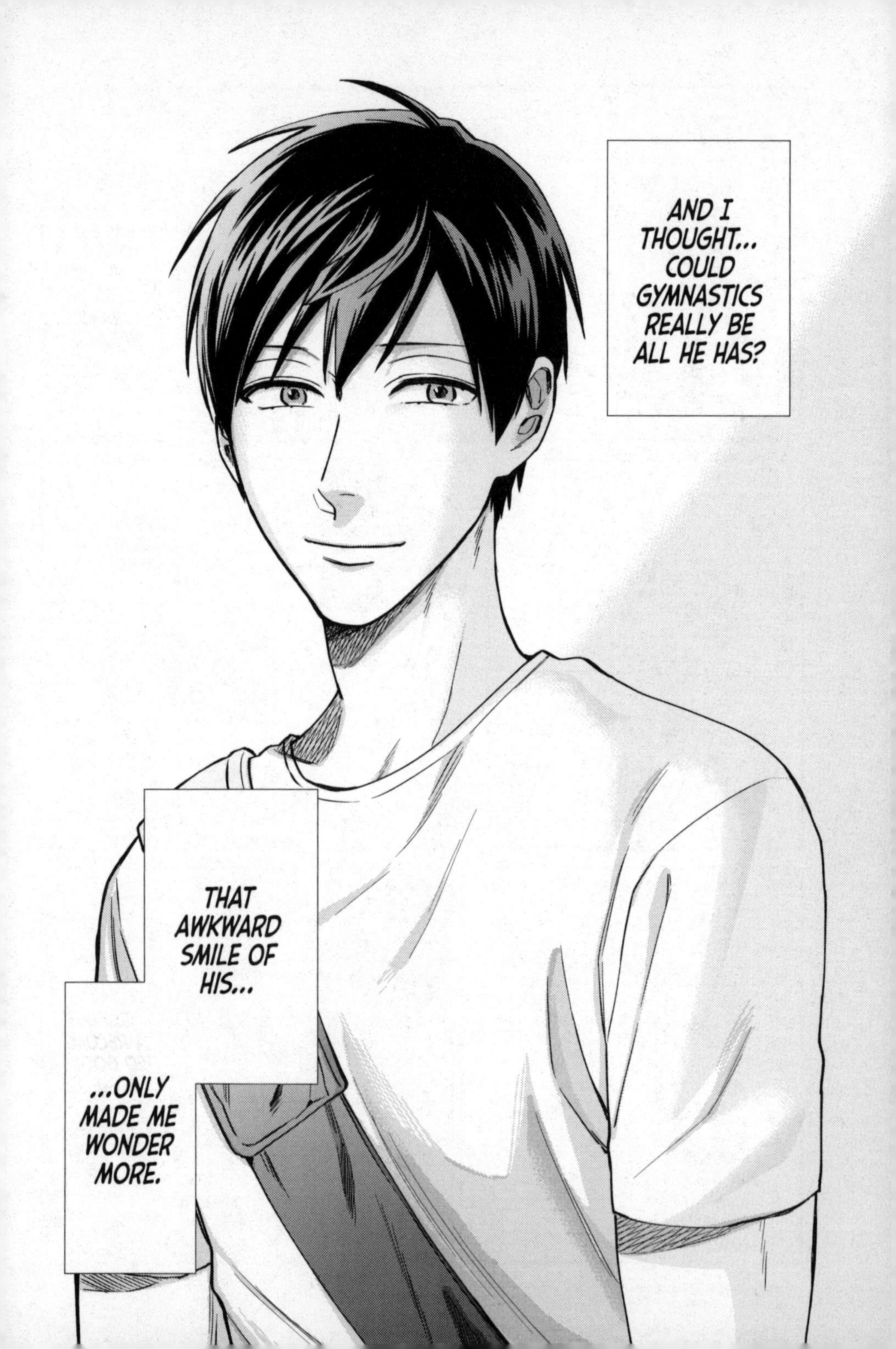
AND I THOUGHT... COULD GYMNASTICS REALLY BE ALL HE HAS?
THAT AWKWARD SMILE OF HIS...
...ONLY MADE ME WONDER MORE.

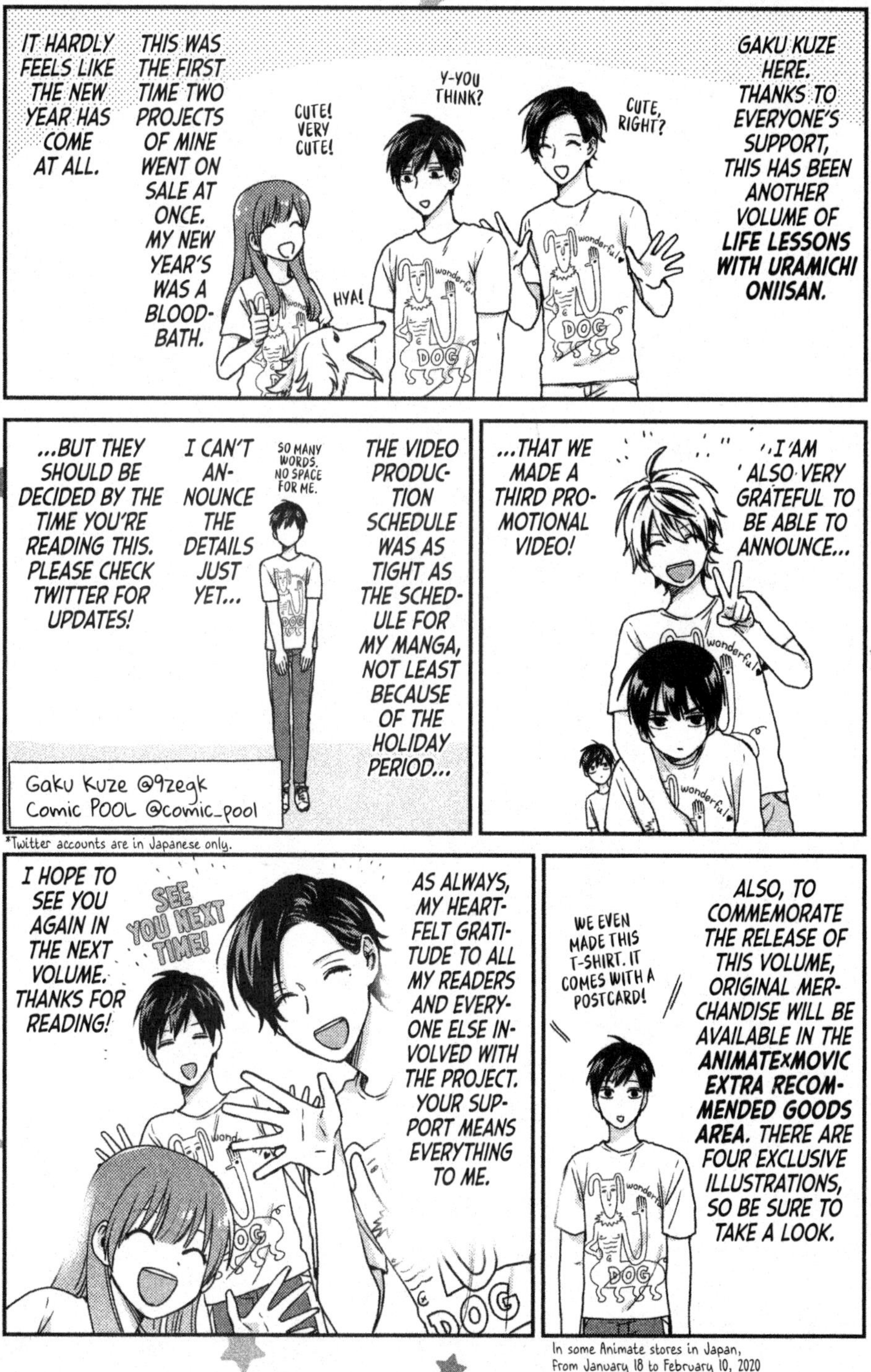
GAKU KUZE HERE. THANKS TO EVERYONE'S SUPPORT, THIS HAS BEEN ANOTHER VOLUME OF LIFE LESSONS WITH URAMICHI ONIISAN.
CUTE, RIGHT?
Y-YOU THINK?
CUTE! VERY CUTE!
HYA!
THIS WAS THE FIRST TIME TWO PROJECTS OF MINE WENT ON SALE AT ONCE. MY NEW YEAR'S WAS A BLOOD-BATH.
IT HARDLY FEELS LIKE THE NEW YEAR HAS COME AT ALL.
I AM ALSO VERY GRATEFUL TO BE ABLE TO ANNOUNCE...
...THAT WE MADE A THIRD PRO-MOTIONAL VIDEO!
THE VIDEO PRODUC-TION SCHEDULE WAS AS TIGHT AS THE SCHED-ULE FOR MY MANGA, NOT LEAST BECAUSE OF THE HOLIDAY PERIOD...
SO MANY WORDS. NO SPACE FOR ME.
I CAN'T AN-NOUNCE THE DETAILS JUST YET...
...BUT THEY SHOULD BE DECIDED BY THE TIME YOU'RE READING THIS. PLEASE CHECK TWITTER FOR UPDATES!
Gaku Kuze @9zegk
Comic POOL @comic_pool
ALSO, TO COMMEMORATE THE RELEASE OF THIS VOLUME, ORIGINAL MER-CHANDISE WILL BE AVAILABLE IN THE ANIMATE×MOVIC EXTRA RECOM-MENDED GOODS AREA. THERE ARE FOUR EXCLUSIVE ILLUSTRATIONS, SO BE SURE TO TAKE A LOOK.
WE EVEN MADE THIS T-SHIRT. IT COMES WITH A POSTCARD!
AS ALWAYS, MY HEART-FELT GRATI-TUDE TO ALL MY READERS AND EVERY-ONE ELSE IN-VOLVED WITH THE PROJECT. YOUR SUP-PORT MEANS EVERYTHING TO ME.
SEE YOU NEXT TIME!
I HOPE TO SEE YOU AGAIN IN THE NEXT VOLUME. THANKS FOR READING!

*Twitter accounts are in Japanese only.

In some Animate stores in Japan, From January 18 to February 10, 2020

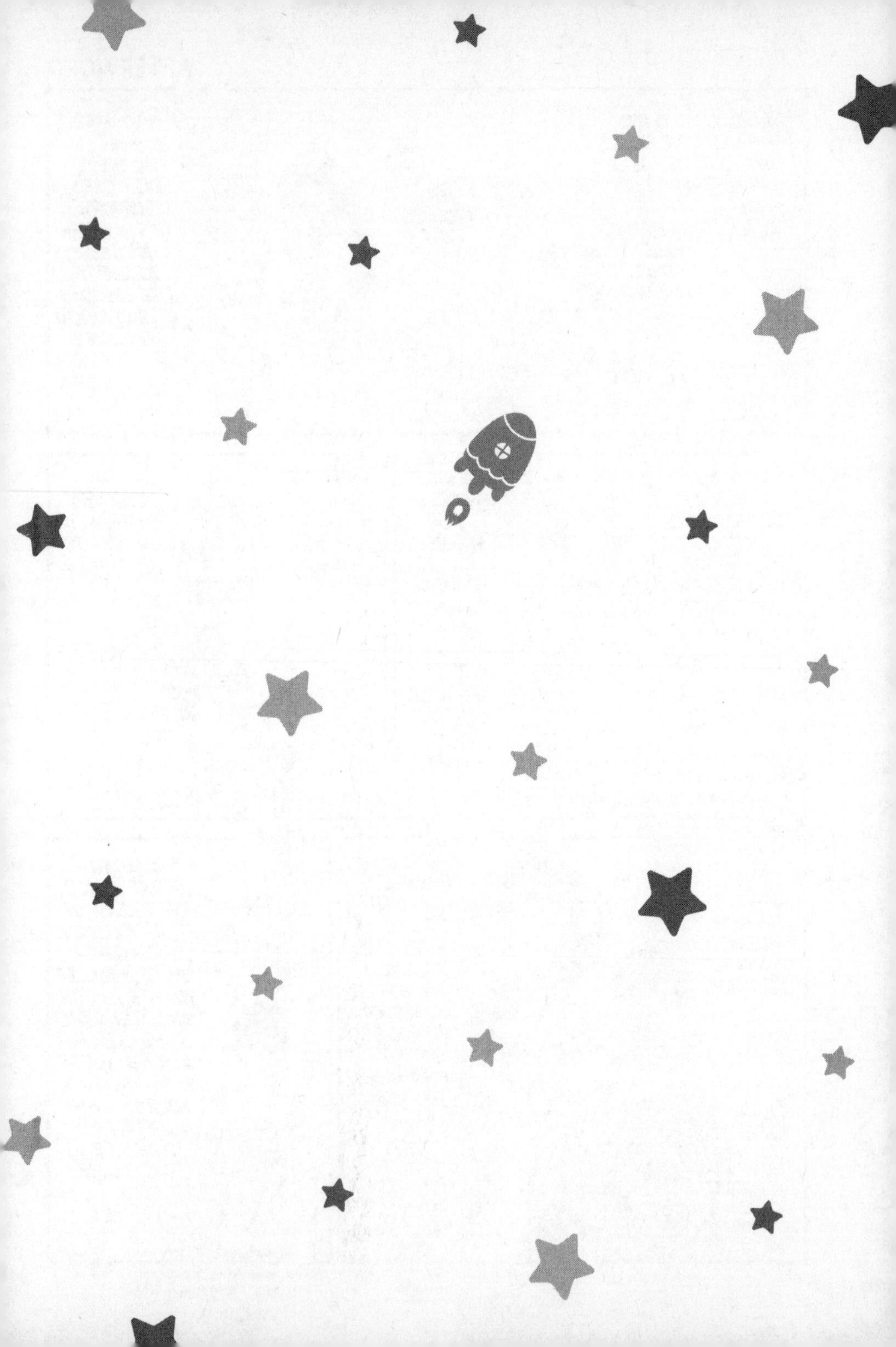

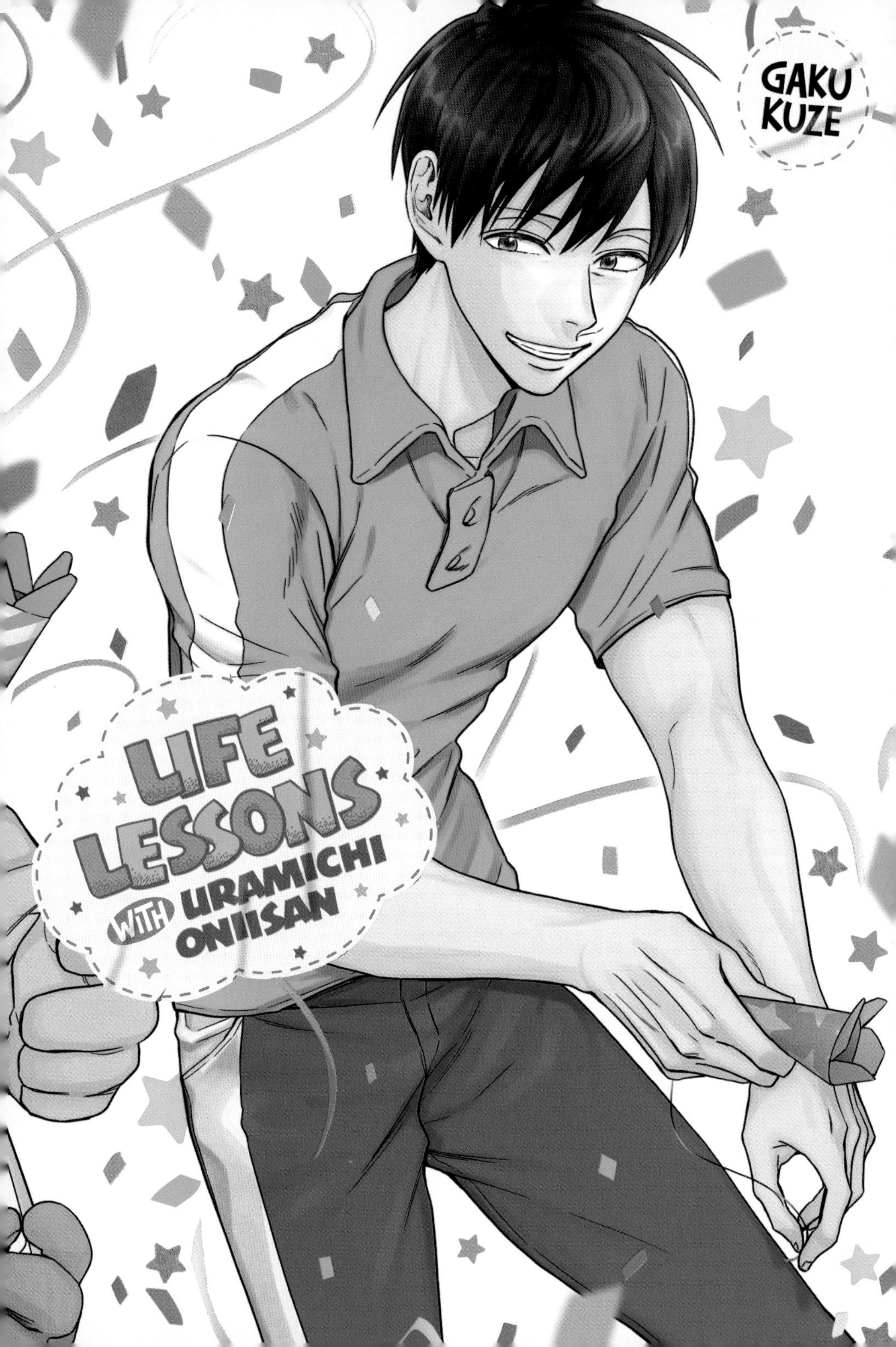
GAKU KUZE
LIFE LESSONS WITH URAMICHI ONIISAN

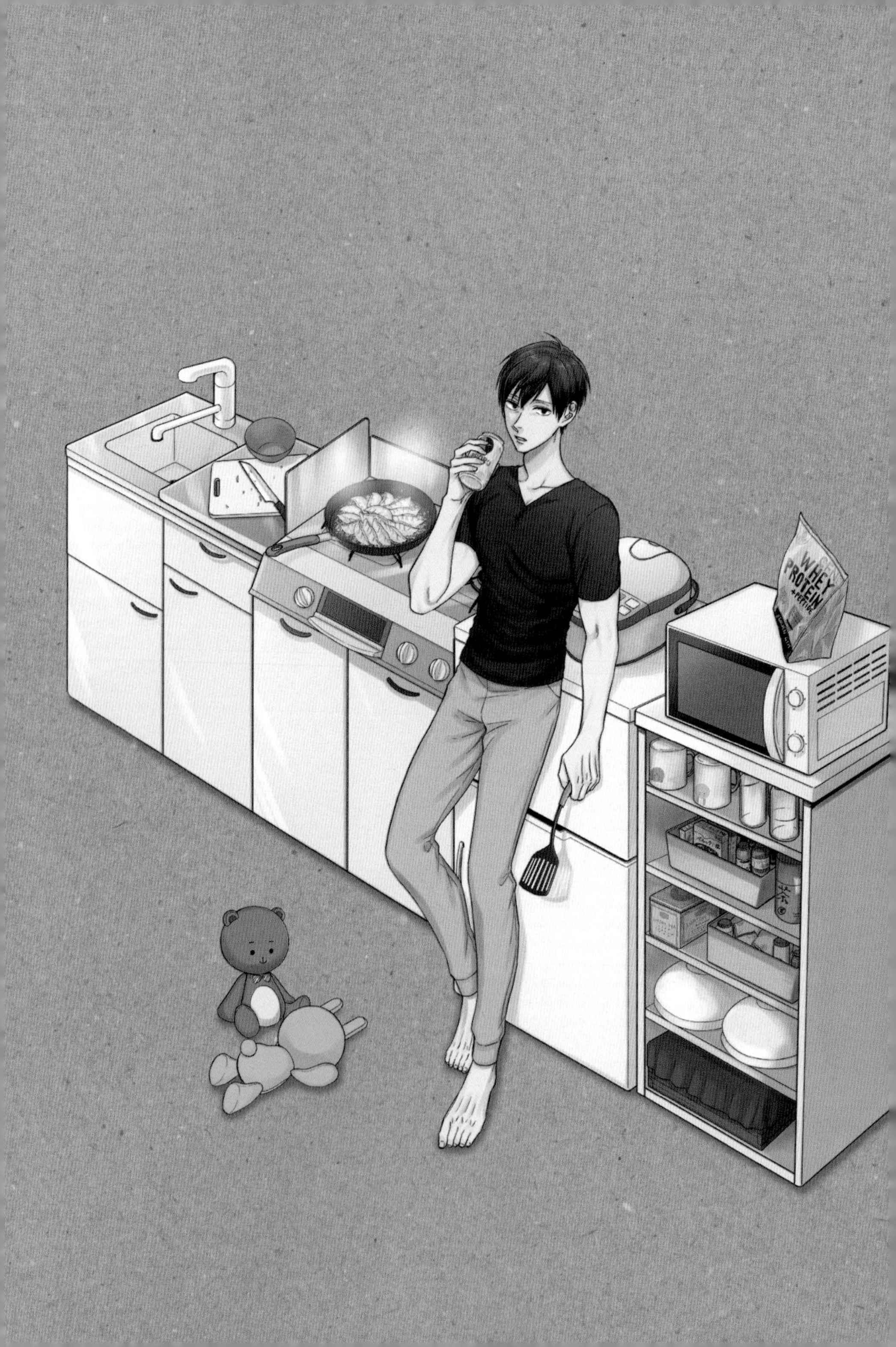
WHEY
PROTEIN
+PEPTIDE

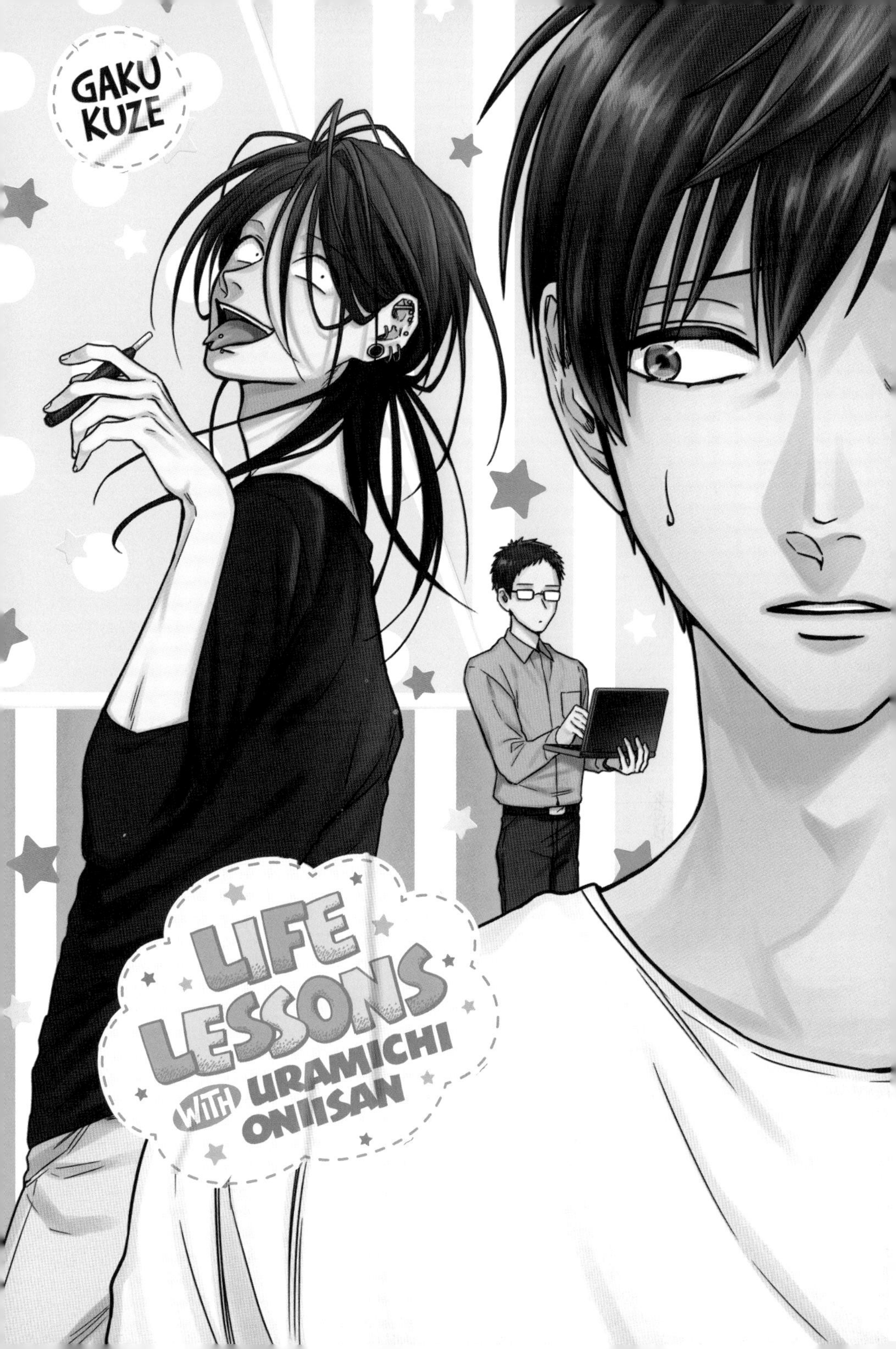
GAKU KUZE
LIFE LESSONS WITH URAMICHI ONIISAN

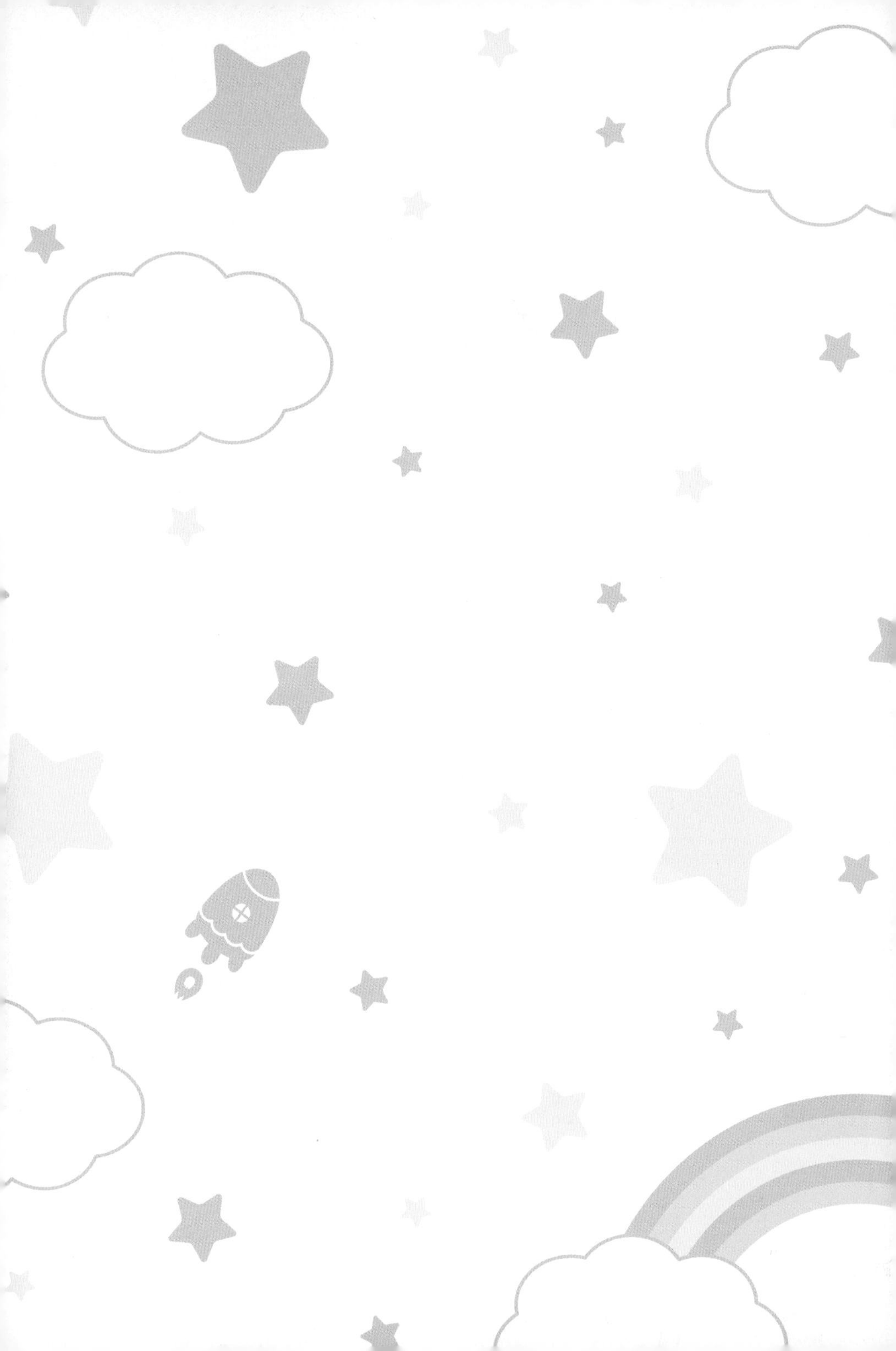

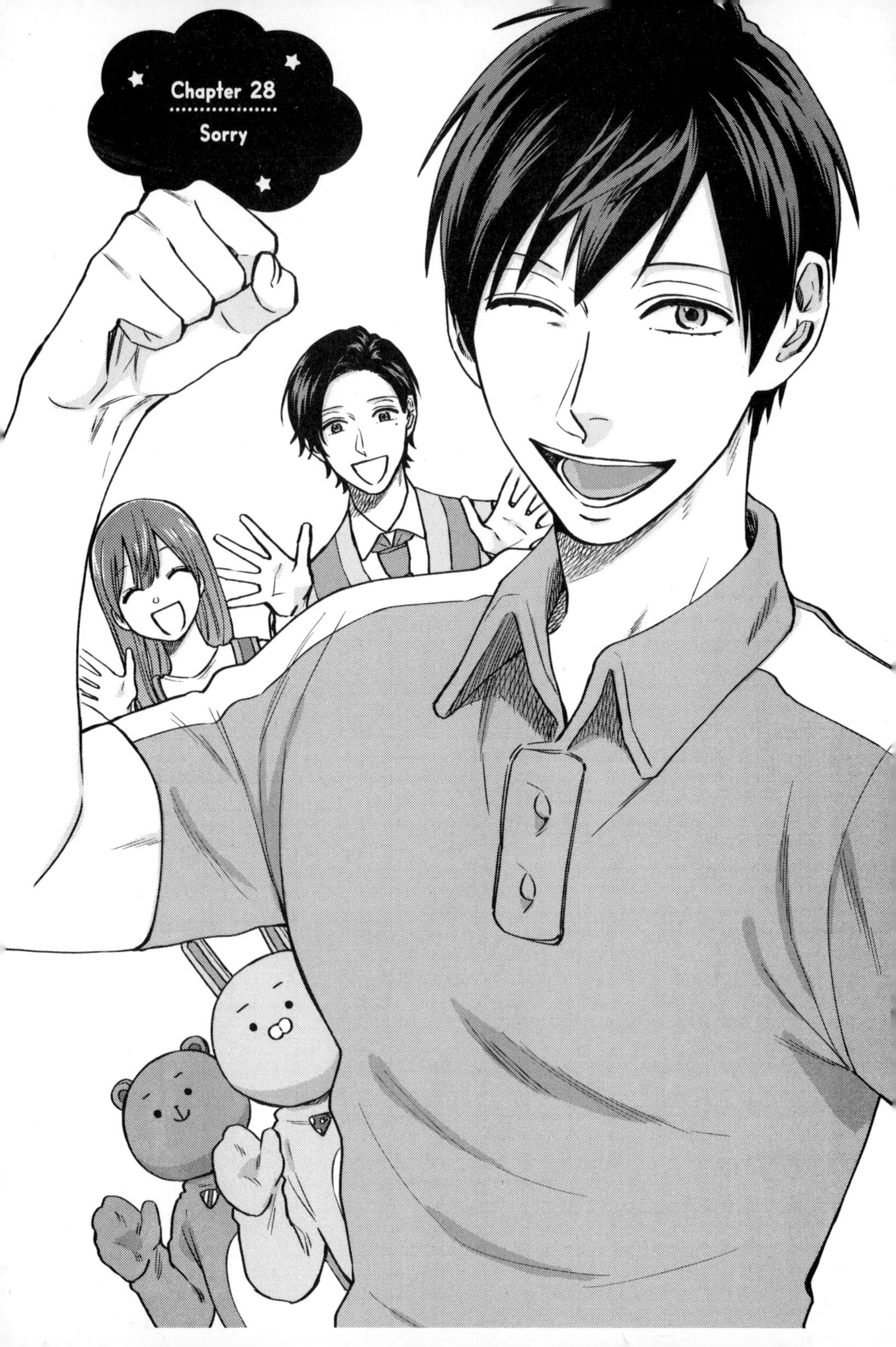
Chapter 28
Sorry

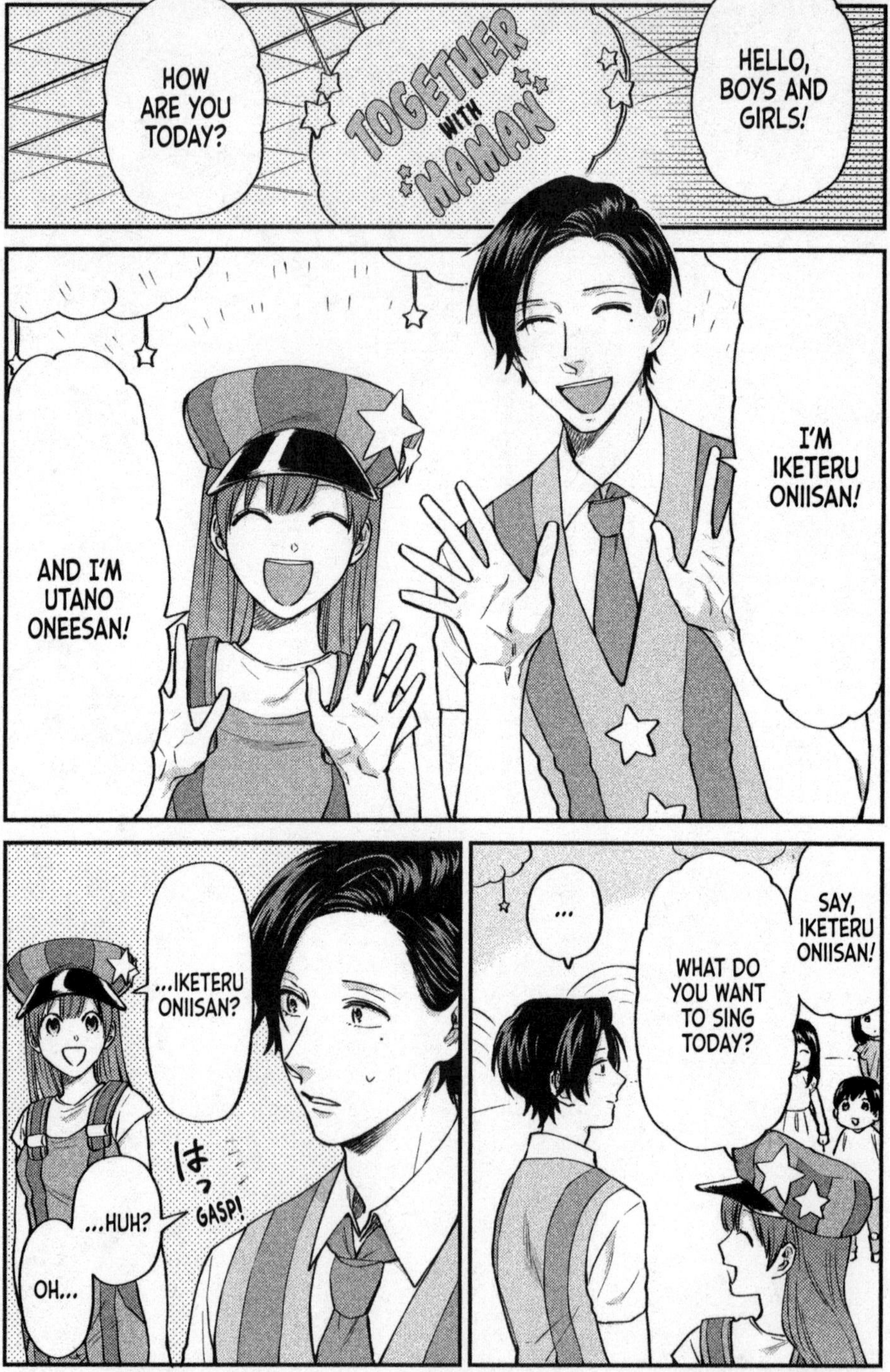

HELLO, BOYS AND GIRLS!
TOGETHER WITH MAMAN
HOW ARE YOU TODAY?
I'M IKETERU ONIISAN!
AND I'M UTANO ONEESAN!
SAY, IKETERU ONIISAN!
WHAT DO YOU WANT TO SING TODAY?
...
...IKETERU ONIISAN?
はっ
GASP!
...HUH?
OH...

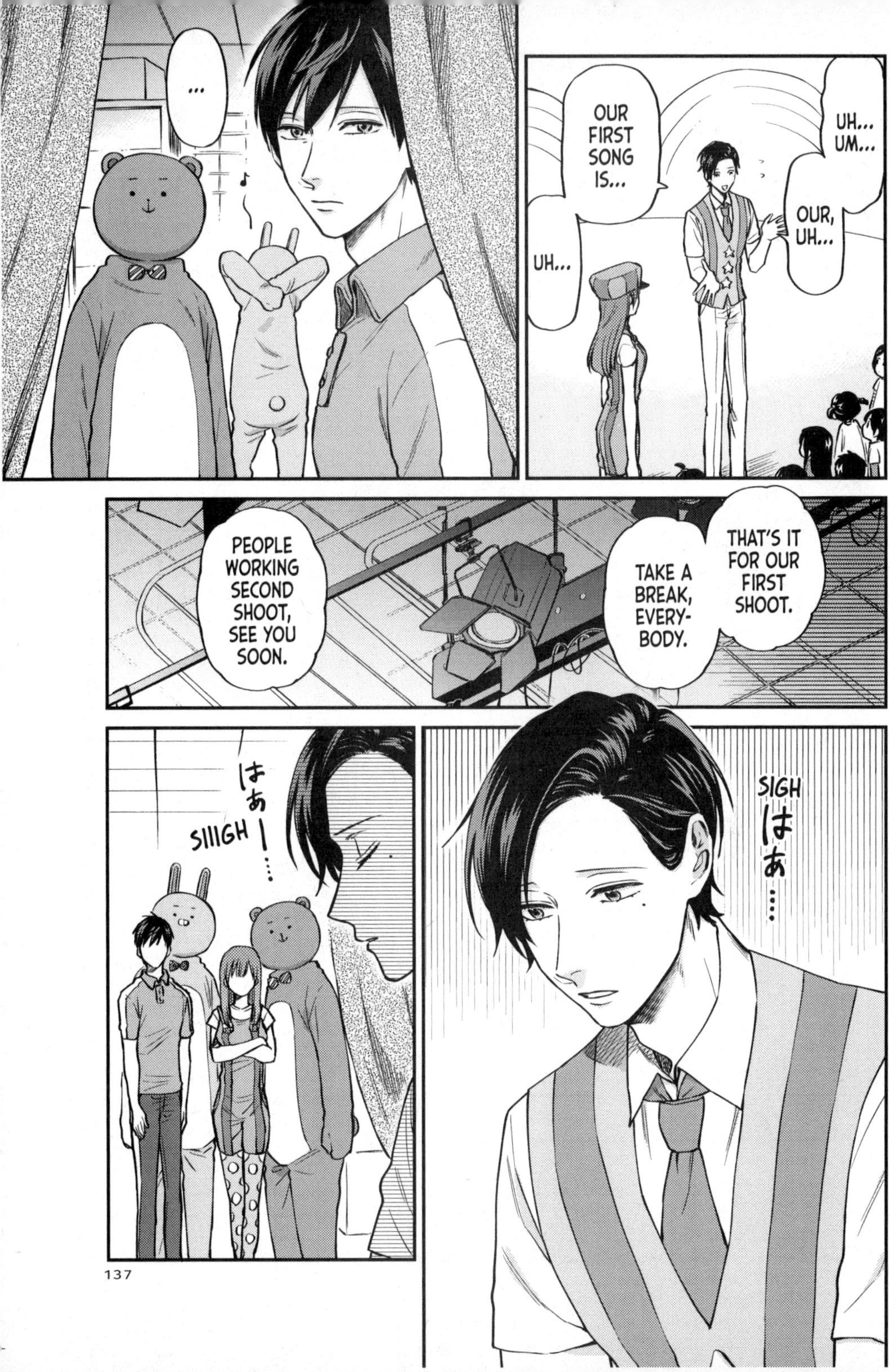
UH... UM...
OUR, UH...
OUR FIRST SONG IS...
UH...
...
THAT'S IT FOR OUR FIRST SHOOT.
TAKE A BREAK, EVERY-BODY.
PEOPLE WORKING SECOND SHOOT, SEE YOU SOON.
SIGH
はあ…
はあー…
SIIIGH

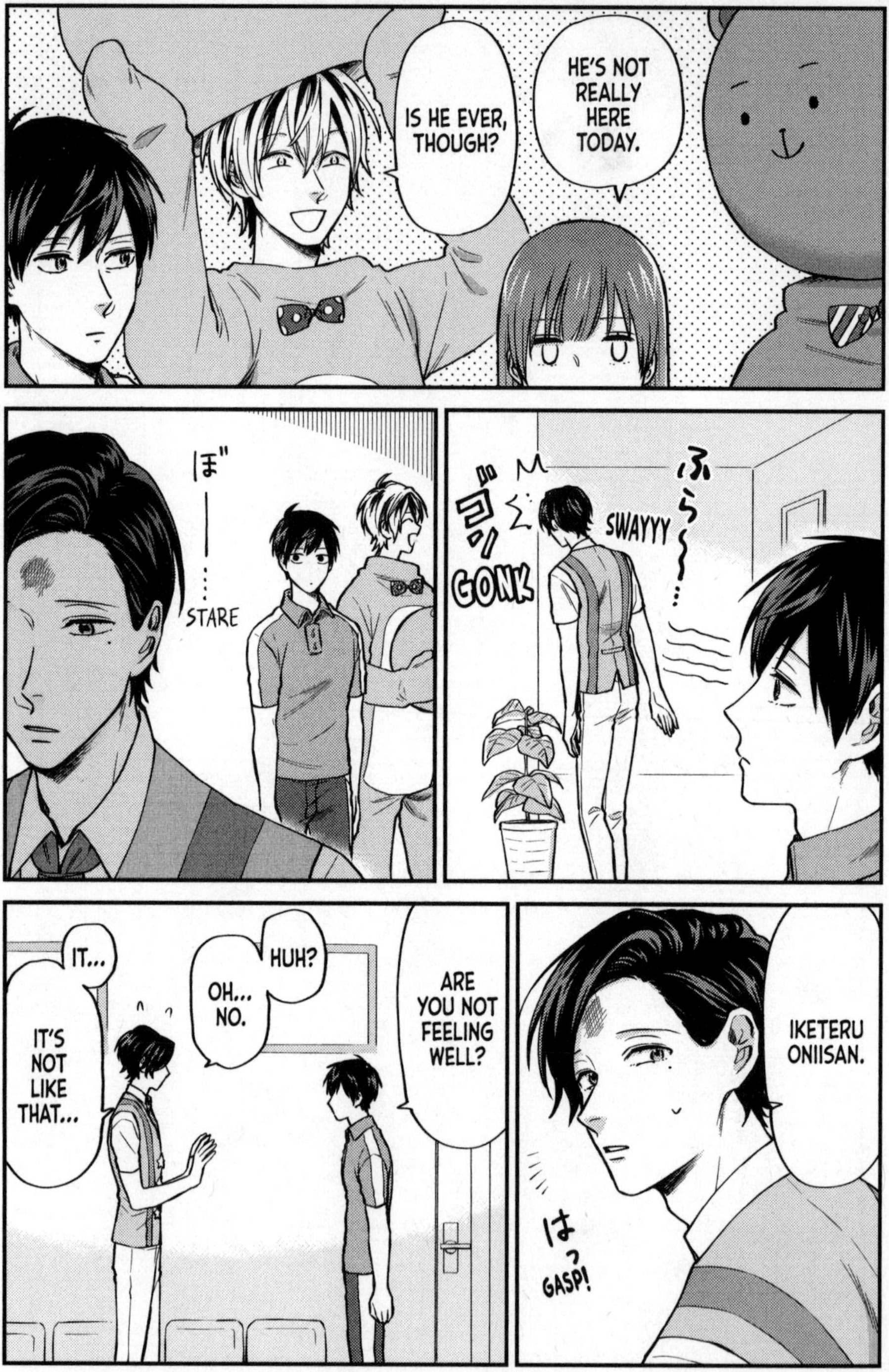
HE'S NOT REALLY HERE TODAY.
IS HE EVER, THOUGH?
ふら〜〜…
SWAYYY
ゴン
GONK
ぼ―――……
STARE
IKETERU ONIISAN.
はっ
GASP!
ARE YOU NOT FEELING WELL?
HUH?
OH... NO.
IT...
IT'S NOT LIKE THAT...

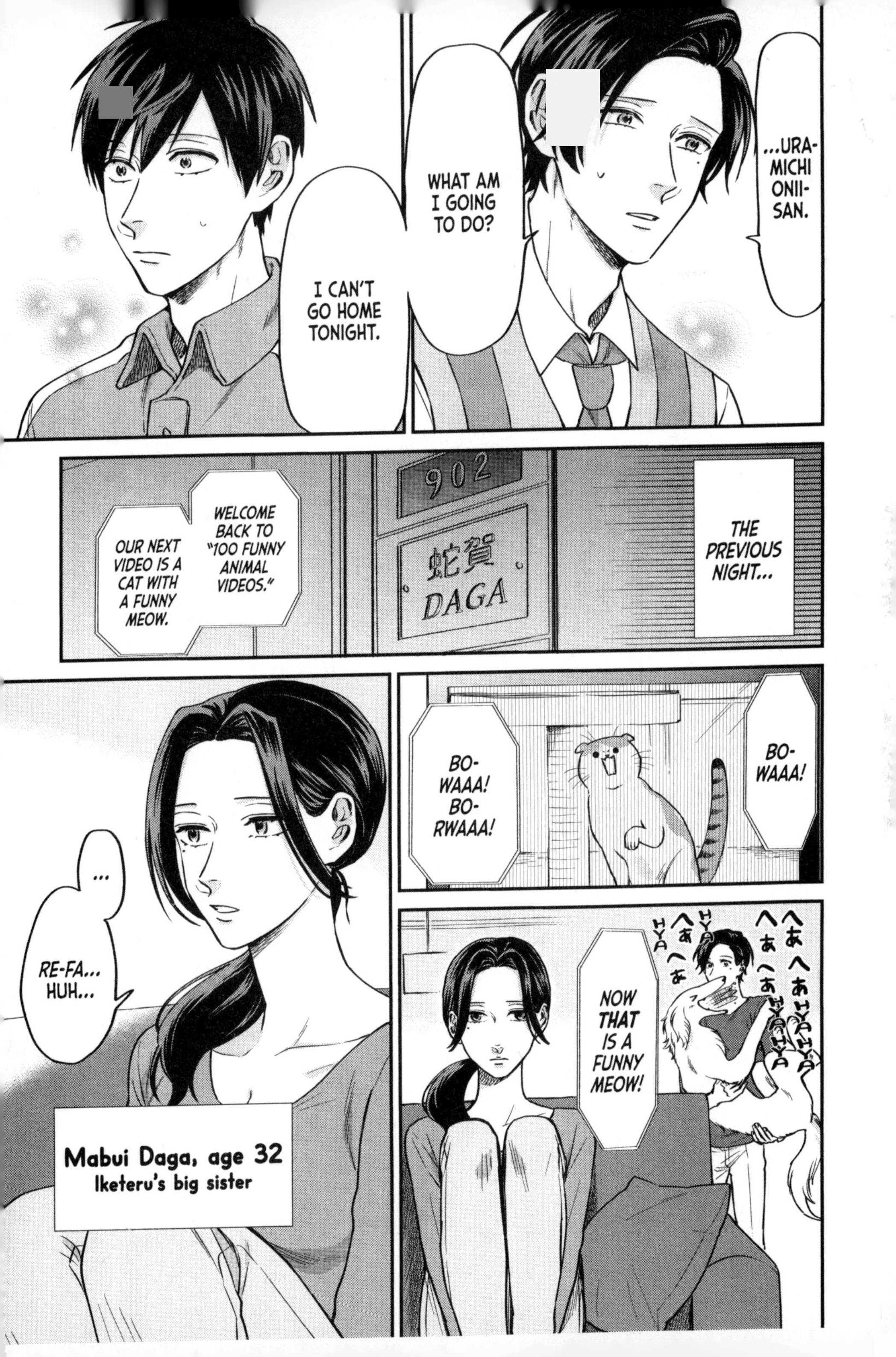
...URA-MICHI ONII-SAN.
WHAT AM I GOING TO DO?
I CAN'T GO HOME TONIGHT.
THE PREVIOUS NIGHT...
902
蛇賀 DAGA
WELCOME BACK TO "100 FUNNY ANIMAL VIDEOS."
OUR NEXT VIDEO IS A CAT WITH A FUNNY MEOW.
BO-WAAA!
BO-WAAA! BO-RWAAA!
NOW THAT IS A FUNNY MEOW!
...
RE-FA... HUH...
Mabui Daga, age 32
Iketeru's big sister

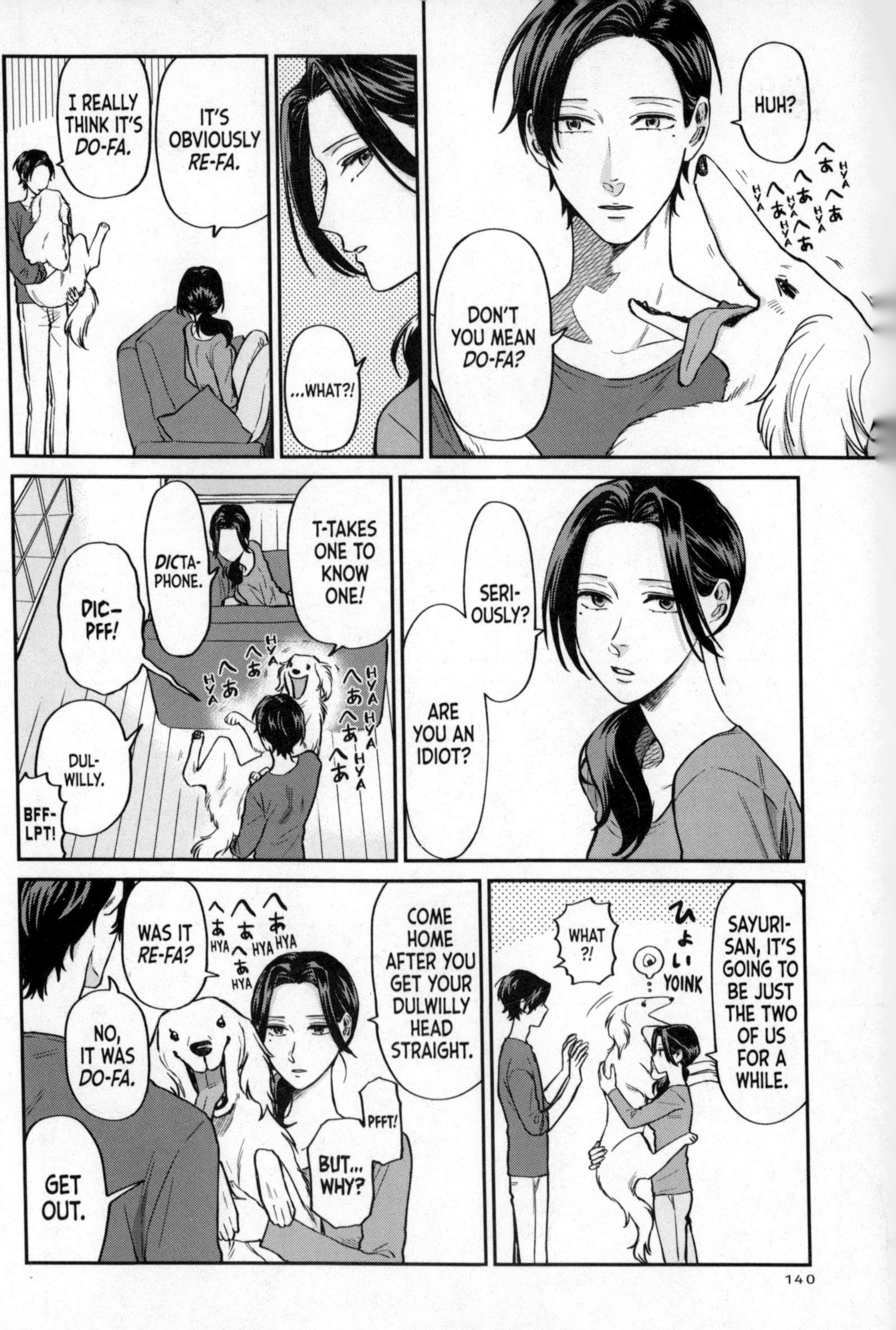
HUH?
へあ へあ へあ へあ へあ
HYA HYA HYA HYA HYA
DON'T YOU MEAN DO-FA?
...WHAT?!
IT'S OBVIOUSLY RE-FA.
I REALLY THINK IT'S DO-FA.
SERIOUSLY?
ARE YOU AN IDIOT?
T-TAKES ONE TO KNOW ONE!
DICTAPHONE.
DIC— PFF!
へあ へあ へあ へあ へあ
HYA HYA HYA HYA HYA
DUL-WILLY.
BFF-LPT!
SAYURI-SAN, IT'S GOING TO BE JUST THE TWO OF US FOR A WHILE.
ひょい
YOINK
WHAT?!
COME HOME AFTER YOU GET YOUR DULWILLY HEAD STRAIGHT.
へあ へあ へあ へあ
HYA HYA HYA HYA
WAS IT RE-FA?
NO, IT WAS DO-FA.
PFFT!
BUT... WHY?
GET OUT.

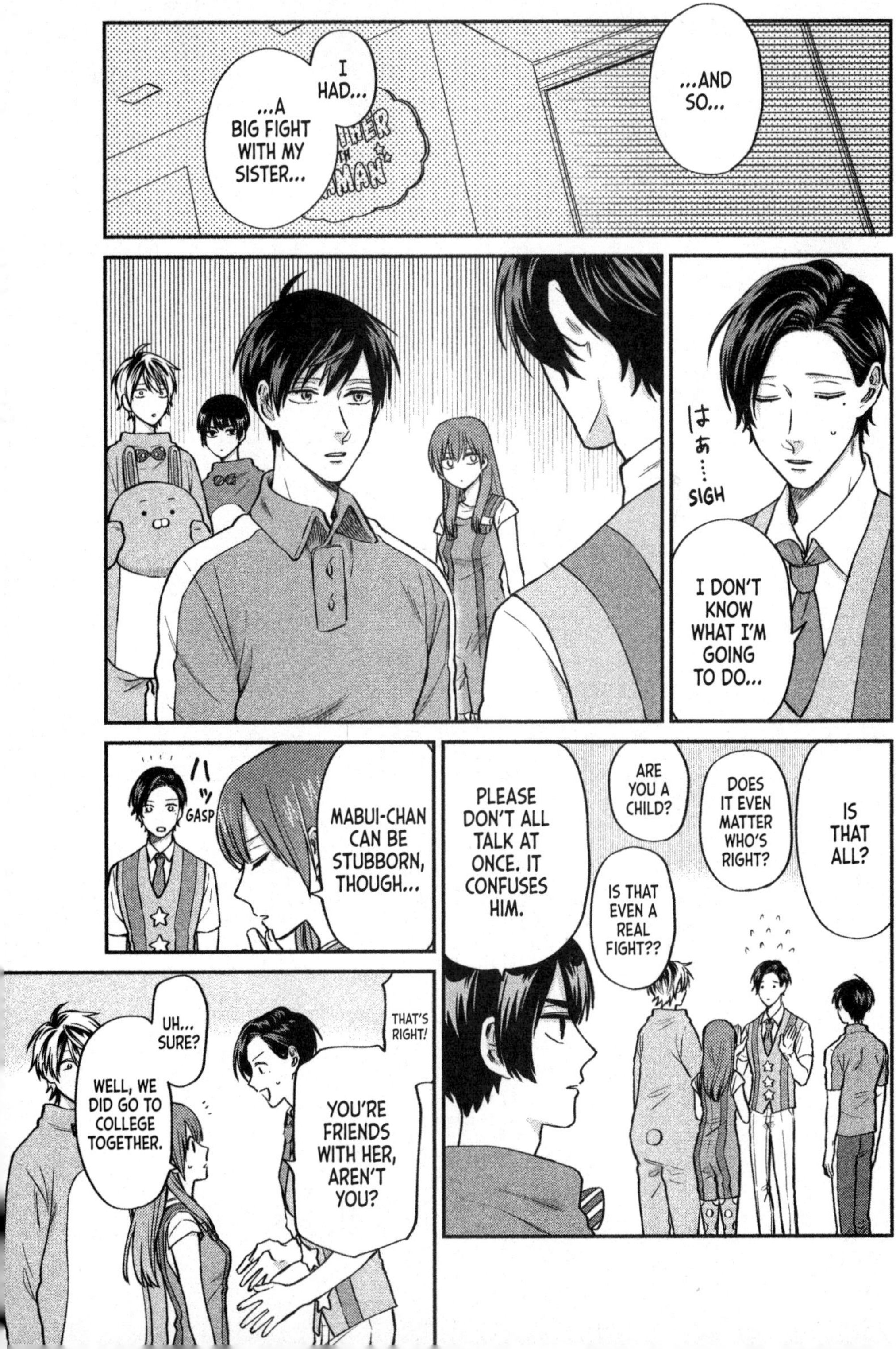
...AND SO...
I HAD...
...A BIG FIGHT WITH MY SISTER...
はぁ… SIGH
I DON'T KNOW WHAT I'M GOING TO DO...
IS THAT ALL?
DOES IT EVEN MATTER WHO'S RIGHT?
ARE YOU A CHILD?
IS THAT EVEN A REAL FIGHT??
PLEASE DON'T ALL TALK AT ONCE. IT CONFUSES HIM.
MABUI-CHAN CAN BE STUBBORN, THOUGH...
ハッ GASP
YOU'RE FRIENDS WITH HER, AREN'T YOU?
THAT'S RIGHT!
UH... SURE?
WELL, WE DID GO TO COLLEGE TOGETHER.

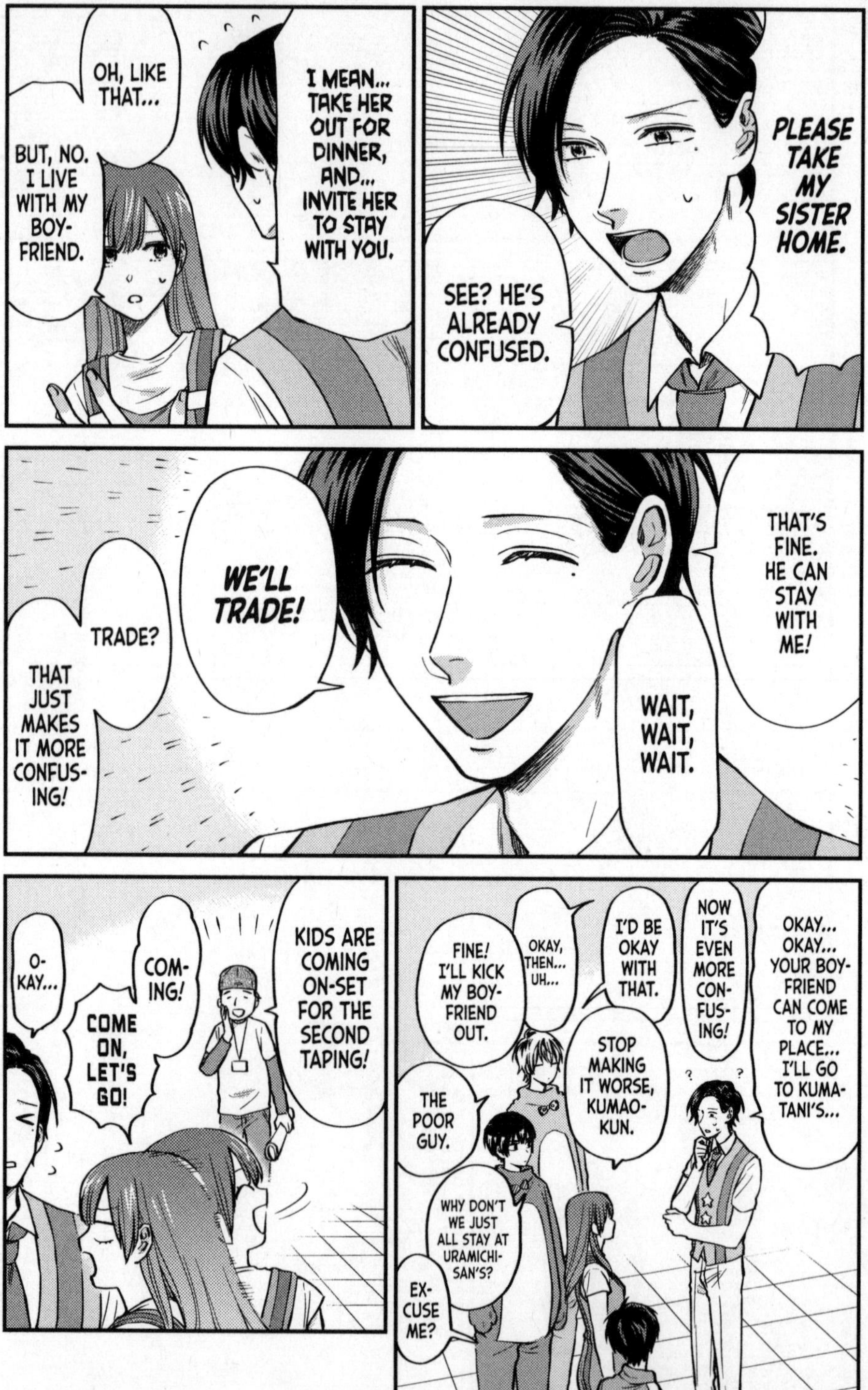
PLEASE TAKE MY SISTER HOME.
SEE? HE'S ALREADY CONFUSED.
I MEAN... TAKE HER OUT FOR DINNER, AND... INVITE HER TO STAY WITH YOU.
OH, LIKE THAT...
BUT, NO. I LIVE WITH MY BOY-FRIEND.
THAT'S FINE. HE CAN STAY WITH ME!
WAIT, WAIT, WAIT.
WE'LL TRADE!
TRADE?
THAT JUST MAKES IT MORE CONFUS-ING!
OKAY... OKAY... YOUR BOY-FRIEND CAN COME TO MY PLACE... I'LL GO TO KUMA-TANI'S...
NOW IT'S EVEN MORE CON-FUS-ING!
I'D BE OKAY WITH THAT.
STOP MAKING IT WORSE, KUMAO-KUN.
OKAY, THEN... UH...
FINE! I'LL KICK MY BOY-FRIEND OUT.
THE POOR GUY.
WHY DON'T WE JUST ALL STAY AT URAMICHI-SAN'S?
EX-CUSE ME?
KIDS ARE COMING ON-SET FOR THE SECOND TAPING!
COM-ING!
COME ON, LET'S GO!
O-KAY...

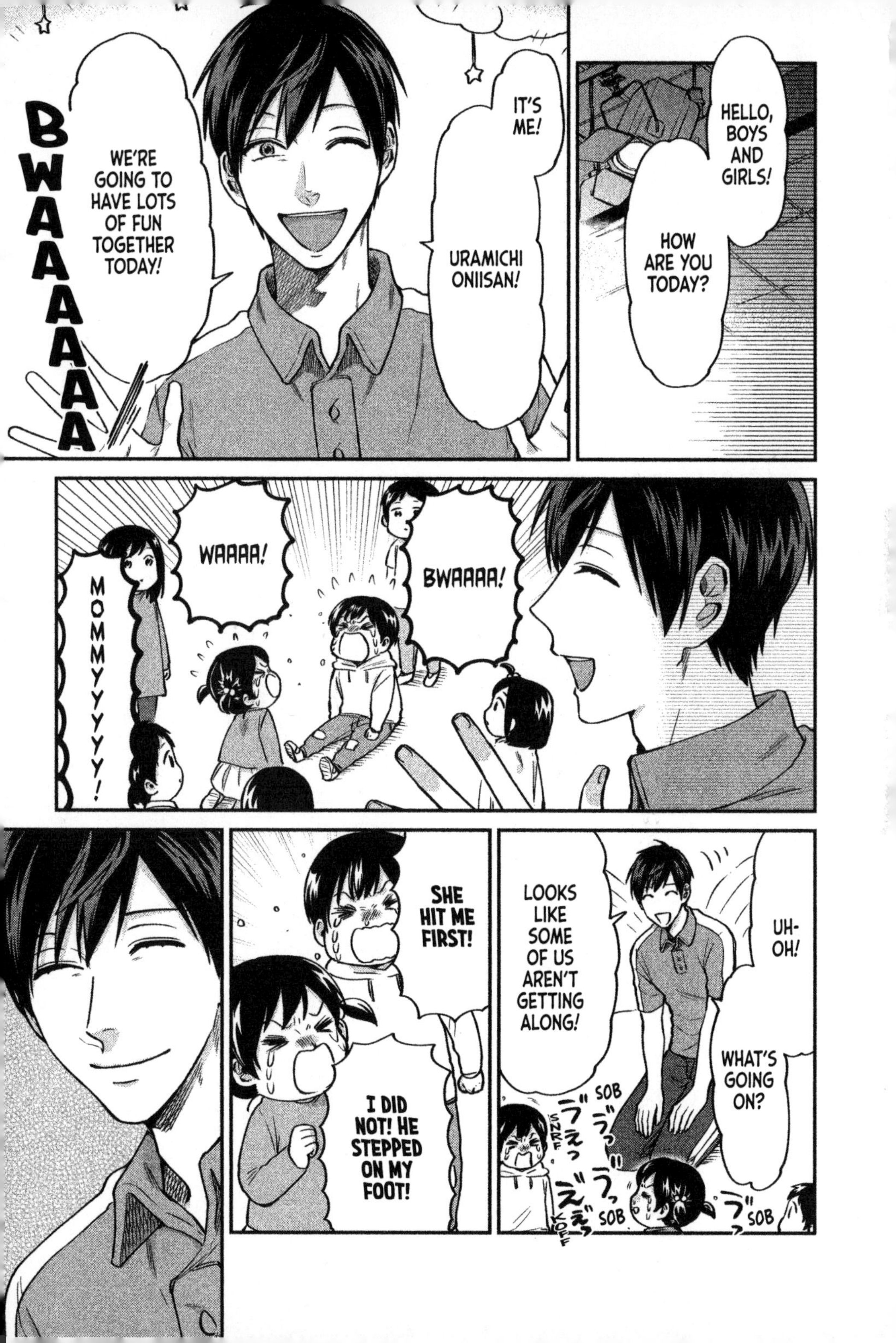
HELLO, BOYS AND GIRLS!
HOW ARE YOU TODAY?
IT'S ME!
URAMICHI ONIISAN!
WE'RE GOING TO HAVE LOTS OF FUN TOGETHER TODAY!
BWAAAAAAA
BWAAAAA!
WAAAA!
MOMMYYYYYY!
UH-OH!
LOOKS LIKE SOME OF US AREN'T GETTING ALONG!
WHAT'S GOING ON?
SOB
SNRF
SOB
KOFF
SOB
SHE HIT ME FIRST!
I DID NOT! HE STEPPED ON MY FOOT!

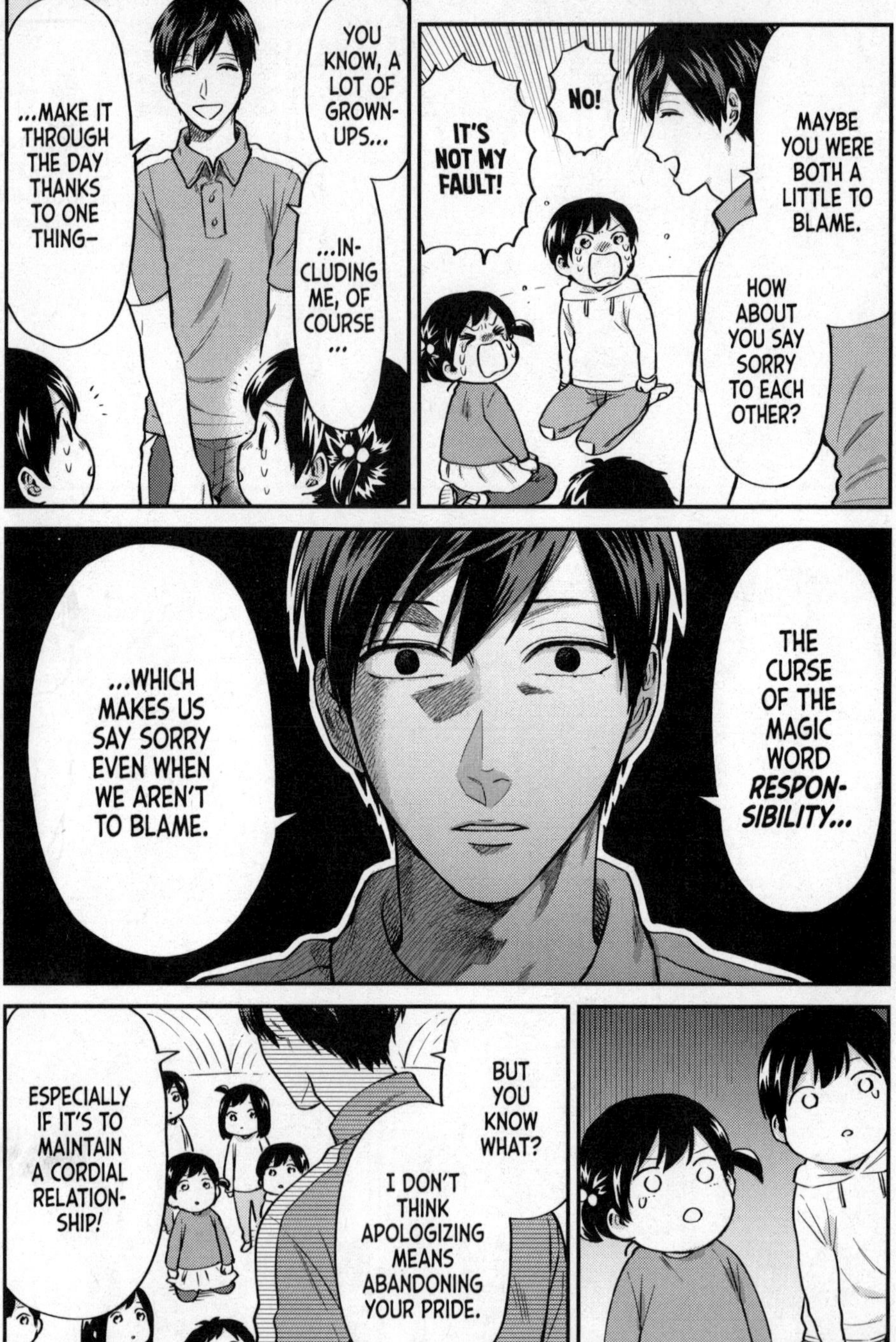
MAYBE YOU WERE BOTH A LITTLE TO BLAME.
HOW ABOUT YOU SAY SORRY TO EACH OTHER?
NO!
IT'S NOT MY FAULT!
YOU KNOW, A LOT OF GROWN-UPS...
...INCLUDING ME, OF COURSE...
...MAKE IT THROUGH THE DAY THANKS TO ONE THING—
THE CURSE OF THE MAGIC WORD *RESPONSIBILITY...*
...WHICH MAKES US SAY SORRY EVEN WHEN WE AREN'T TO BLAME.
ESPECIALLY IF IT'S TO MAINTAIN A CORDIAL RELATIONSHIP!
BUT YOU KNOW WHAT?
I DON'T THINK APOLOGIZING MEANS ABANDONING YOUR PRIDE.

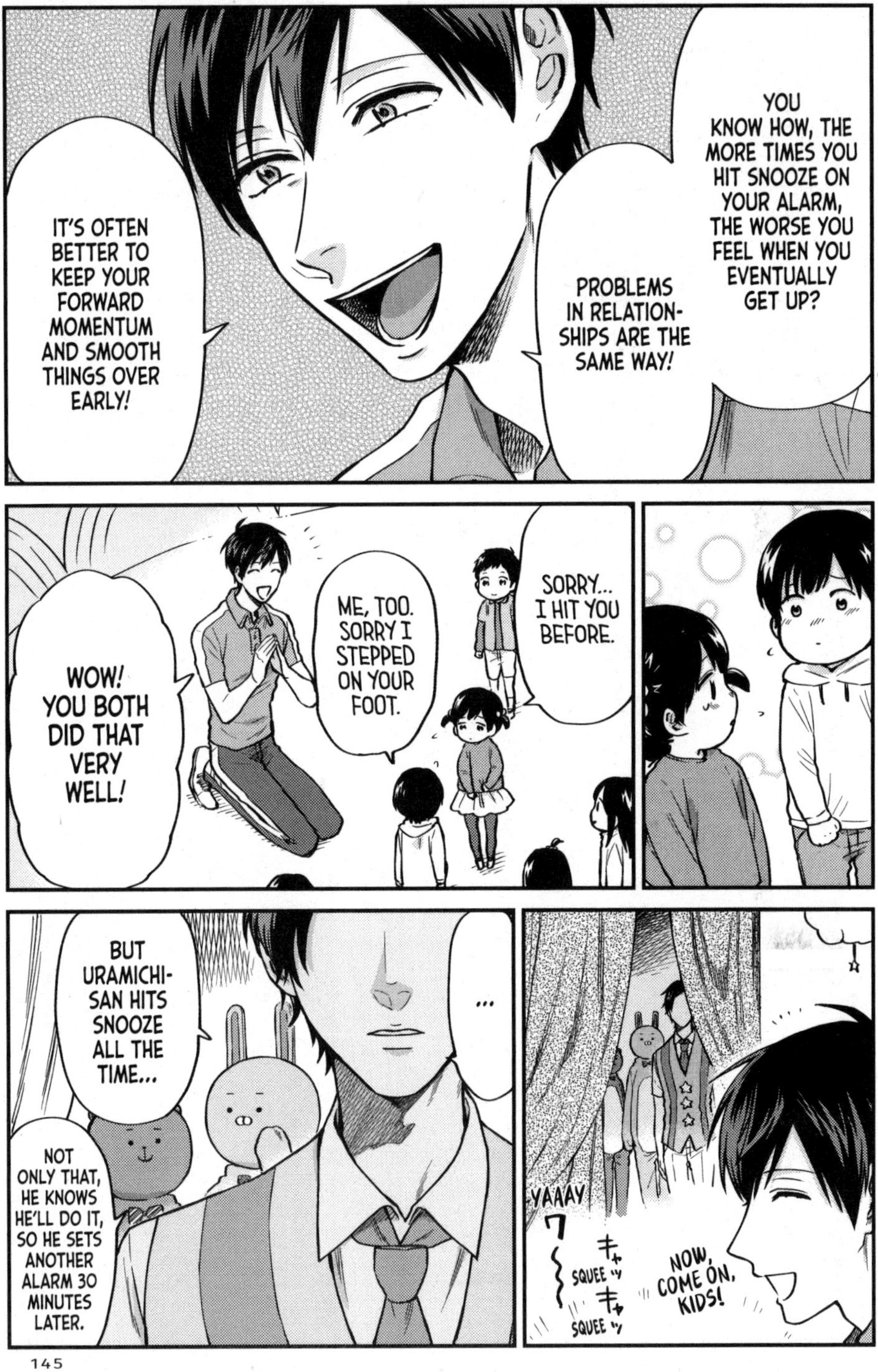
YOU KNOW HOW, THE MORE TIMES YOU HIT SNOOZE ON YOUR ALARM, THE WORSE YOU FEEL WHEN YOU EVENTUALLY GET UP?
PROBLEMS IN RELATIONSHIPS ARE THE SAME WAY!
IT'S OFTEN BETTER TO KEEP YOUR FORWARD MOMENTUM AND SMOOTH THINGS OVER EARLY!
SORRY... I HIT YOU BEFORE.
ME, TOO. SORRY I STEPPED ON YOUR FOOT.
WOW! YOU BOTH DID THAT VERY WELL!
NOW, COME ON, KIDS!
SQUEE キャッ
SQUEE キャッ
YAAAY ワ～
...
BUT URAMICHI-SAN HITS SNOOZE ALL THE TIME...
NOT ONLY THAT, HE KNOWS HE'LL DO IT, SO HE SETS ANOTHER ALARM 30 MINUTES LATER.

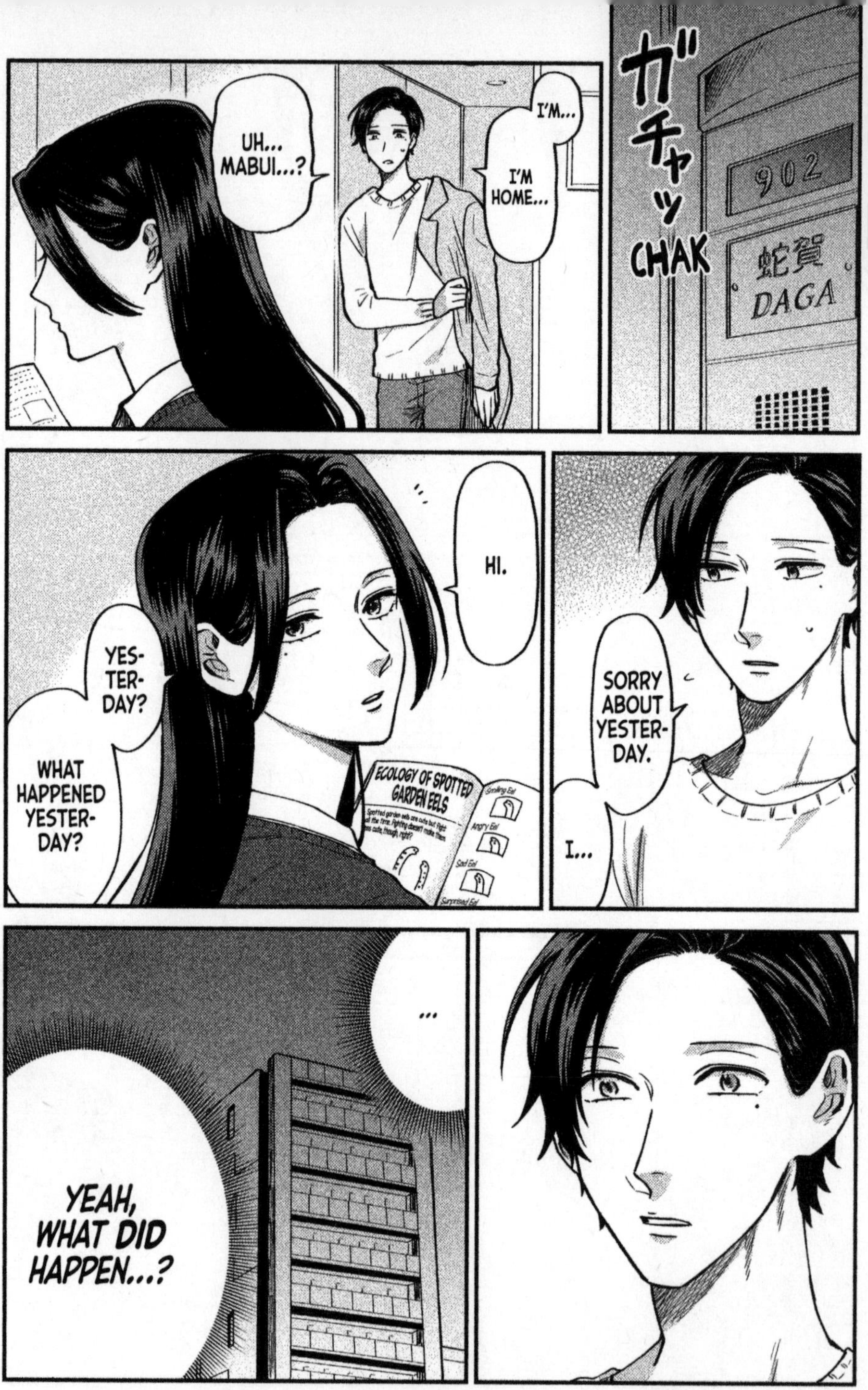
ガチャッ
CHAK
902
蛇賀
DAGA
I'M...
I'M HOME...
UH... MABUI...?
SORRY ABOUT YESTERDAY.
I...
HI.
YES-TER-DAY?
WHAT HAPPENED YESTER-DAY?
ECOLOGY OF SPOTTED GARDEN EELS
Spotted garden eels are cute but fight
the time. Fighting doesn't make them
cute, though, right?
Smiling Eel
Angry Eel
Sad Eel
Surprised Eel
...
YEAH, WHAT DID HAPPEN...?

Life Lessons with
Uramichi Oniisan

MABUI DAGA

AGE: 32   HEIGHT: 169 CM (5' 7")

BLOOD TYPE: O   BIRTHDAY: MAY 7

SMOKER: NO

DRINKER: YES (FAIRLY LIGHTWEIGHT)

Life Lessons with
Uramichi Oniisan

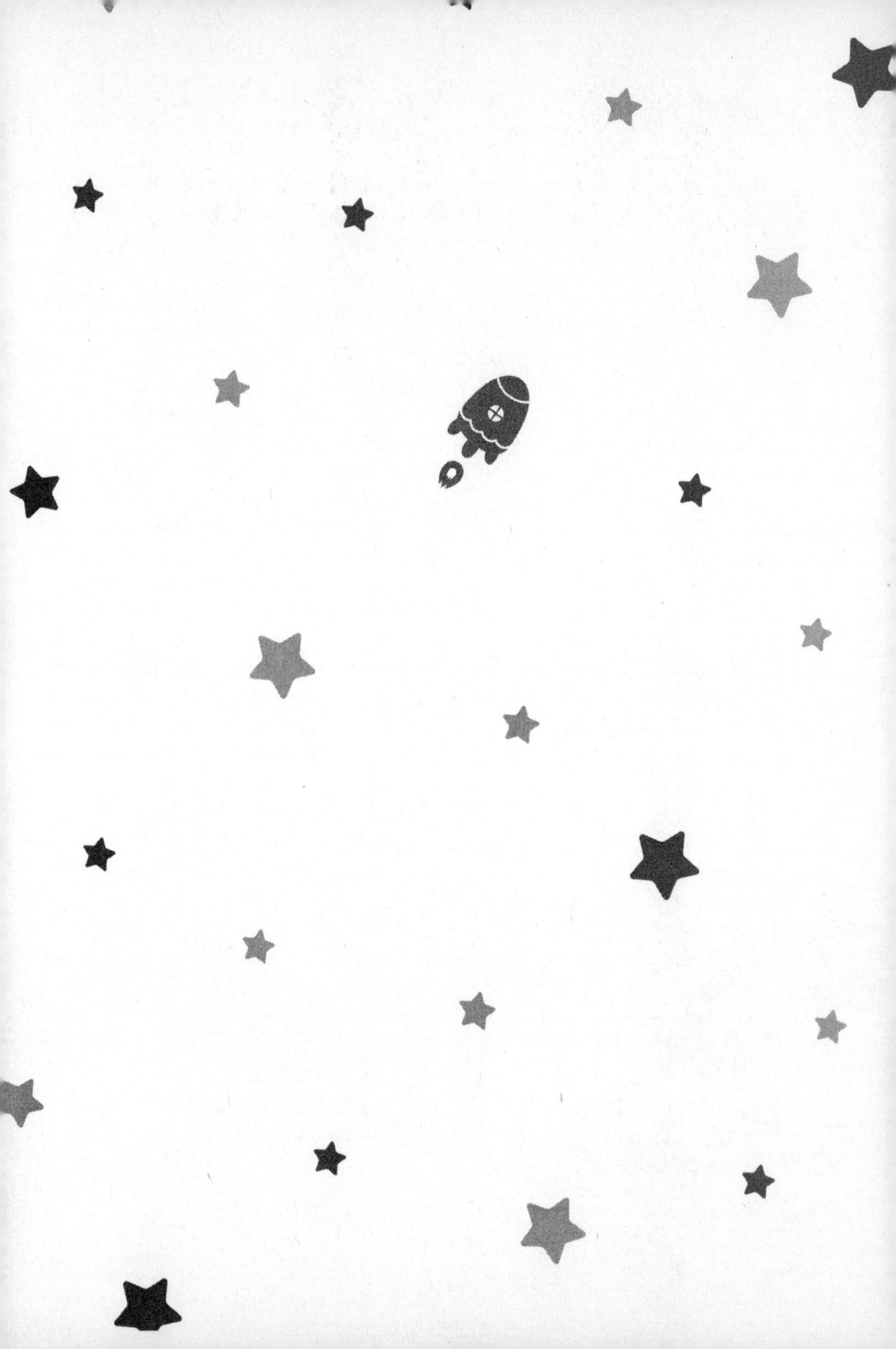

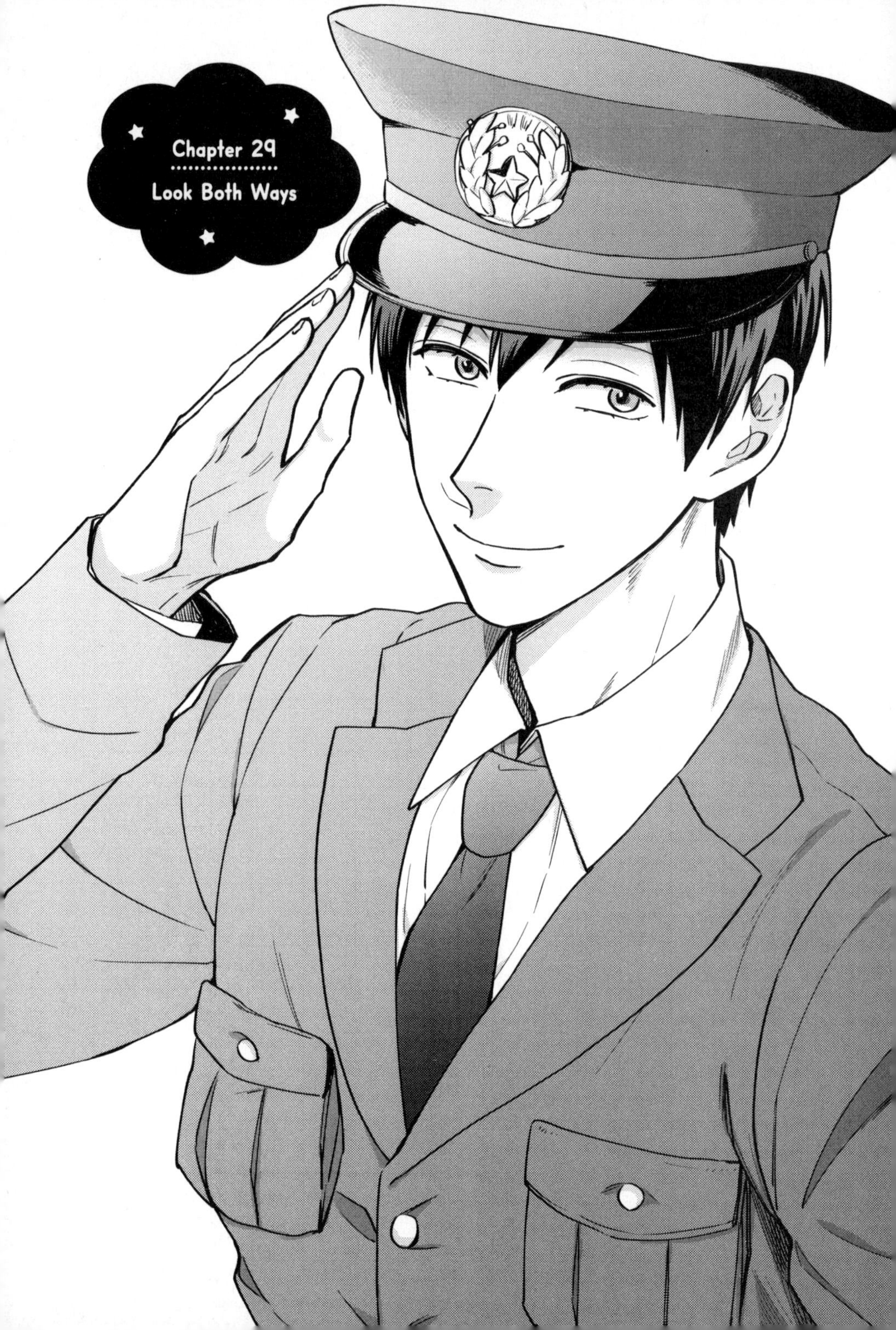
Chapter 29
Look Both Ways

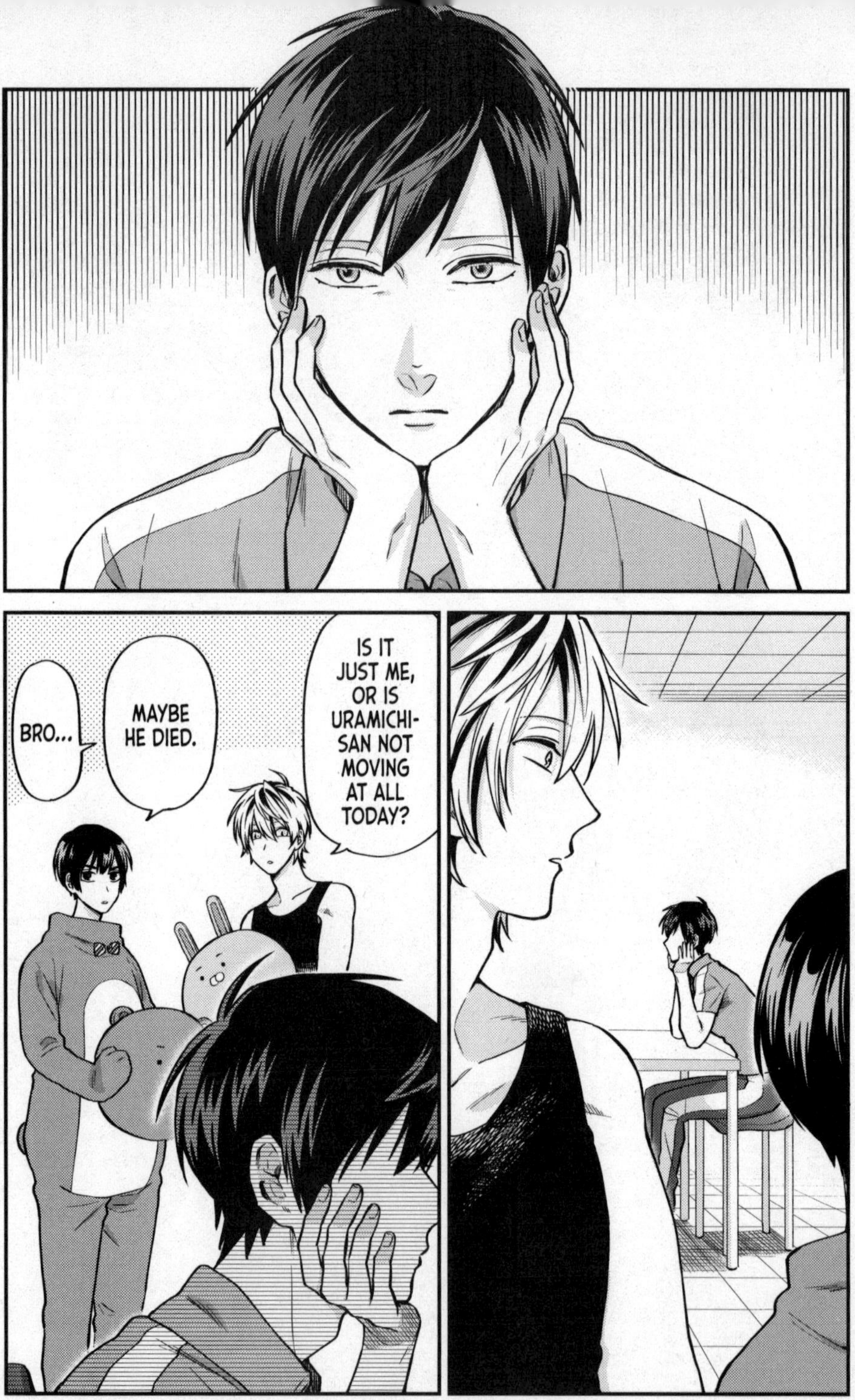
IS IT JUST ME, OR IS URAMICHI-SAN NOT MOVING AT ALL TODAY?
MAYBE HE DIED.
BRO...

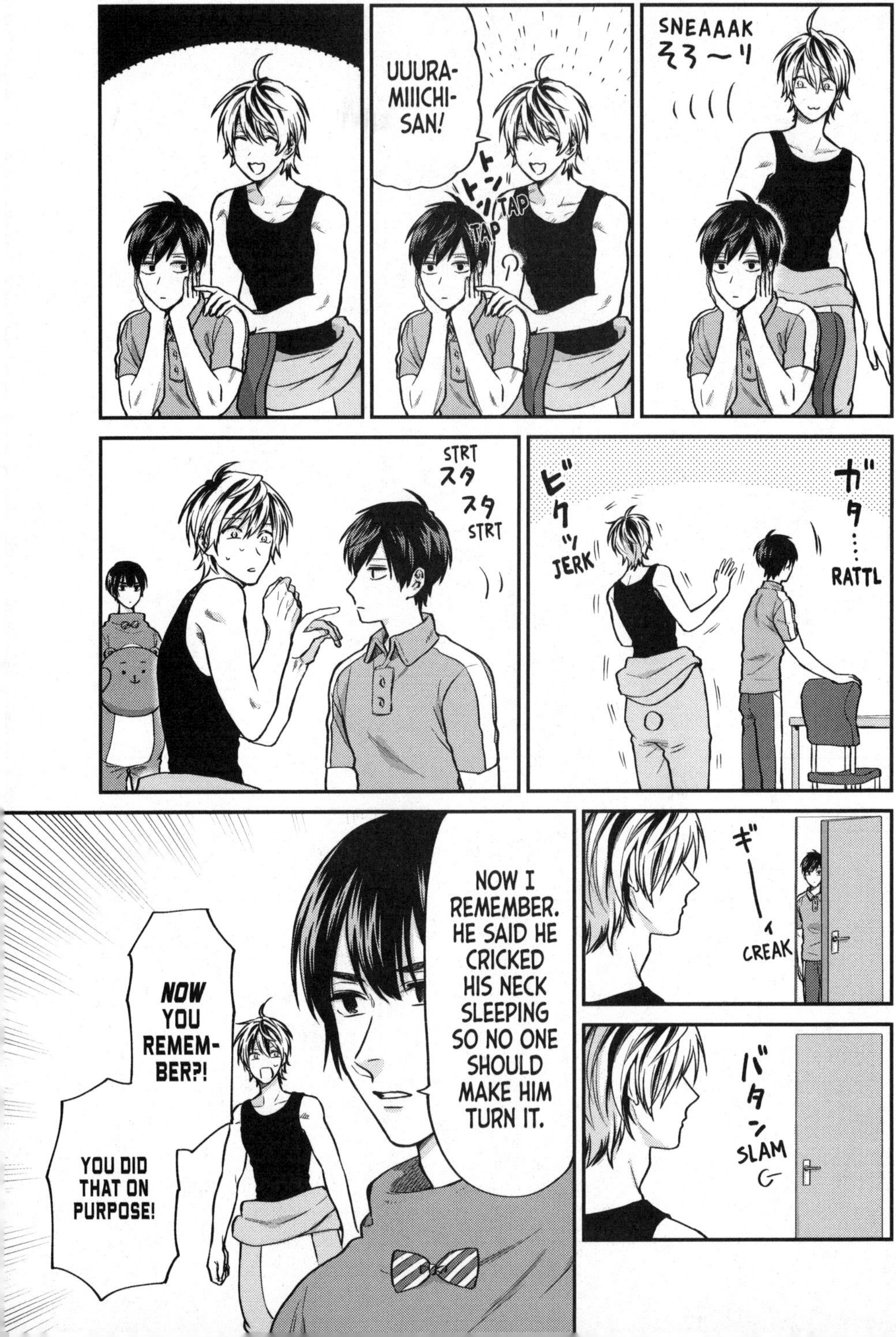
SNEAAAK
そろ～リ
UUURA-MIIICHI-SAN!
トン
トン
TAP
TAP
ガタ…
RATTL
ビクッ
JERK
スタ
STRT
スタ
STRT
ギーィ
CREAK
バタン
SLAM
NOW I REMEMBER. HE SAID HE CRICKED HIS NECK SLEEPING SO NO ONE SHOULD MAKE HIM TURN IT.
NOW YOU REMEMBER?!
YOU DID THAT ON PURPOSE!

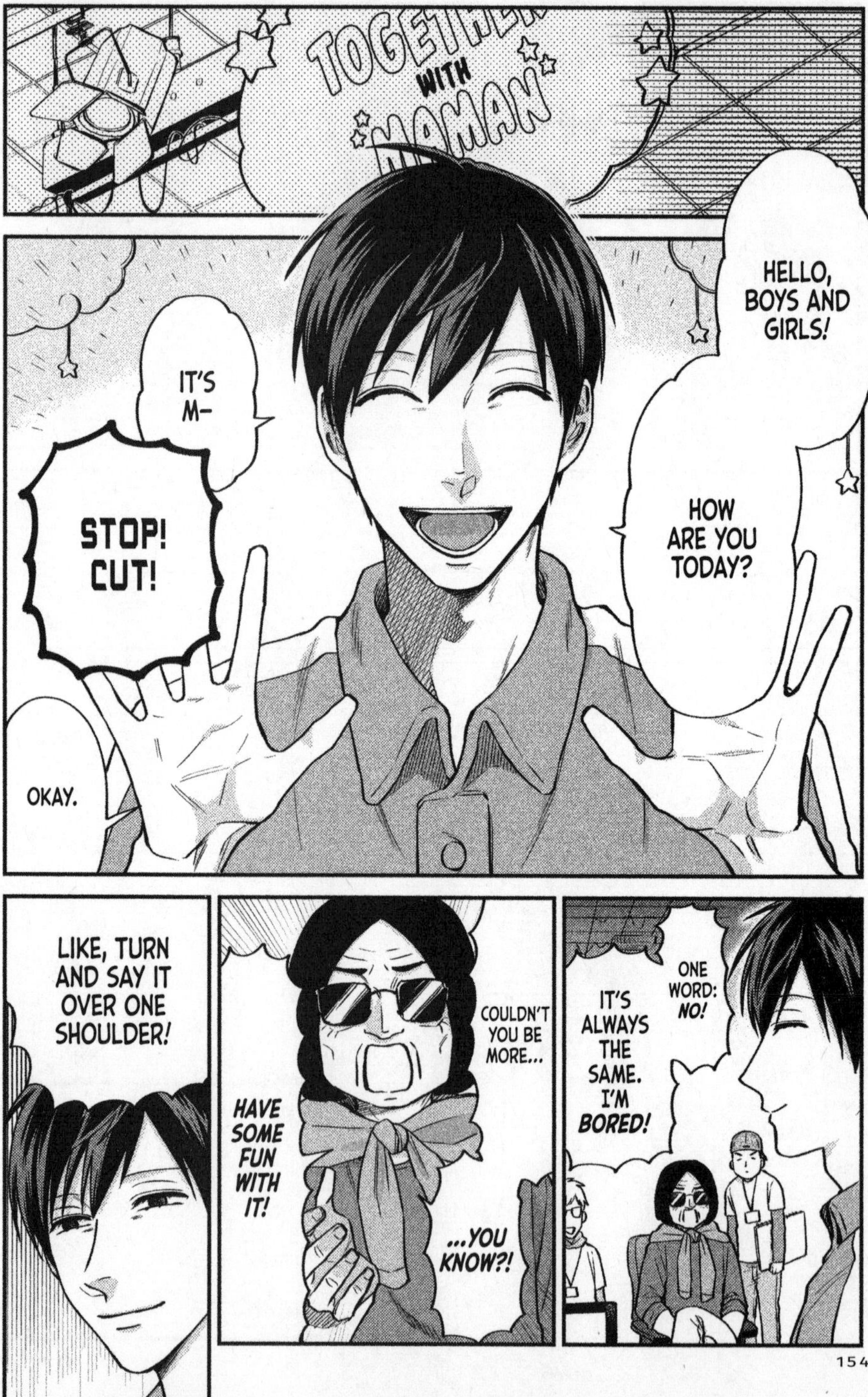
TOGETHE
WITH
MAMAN
HELLO, BOYS AND GIRLS!
HOW ARE YOU TODAY?
IT'S M–
STOP! CUT!
OKAY.
ONE WORD: NO!
IT'S ALWAYS THE SAME. I'M BORED!
COULDN'T YOU BE MORE...
HAVE SOME FUN WITH IT!
...YOU KNOW?!
LIKE, TURN AND SAY IT OVER ONE SHOULDER!

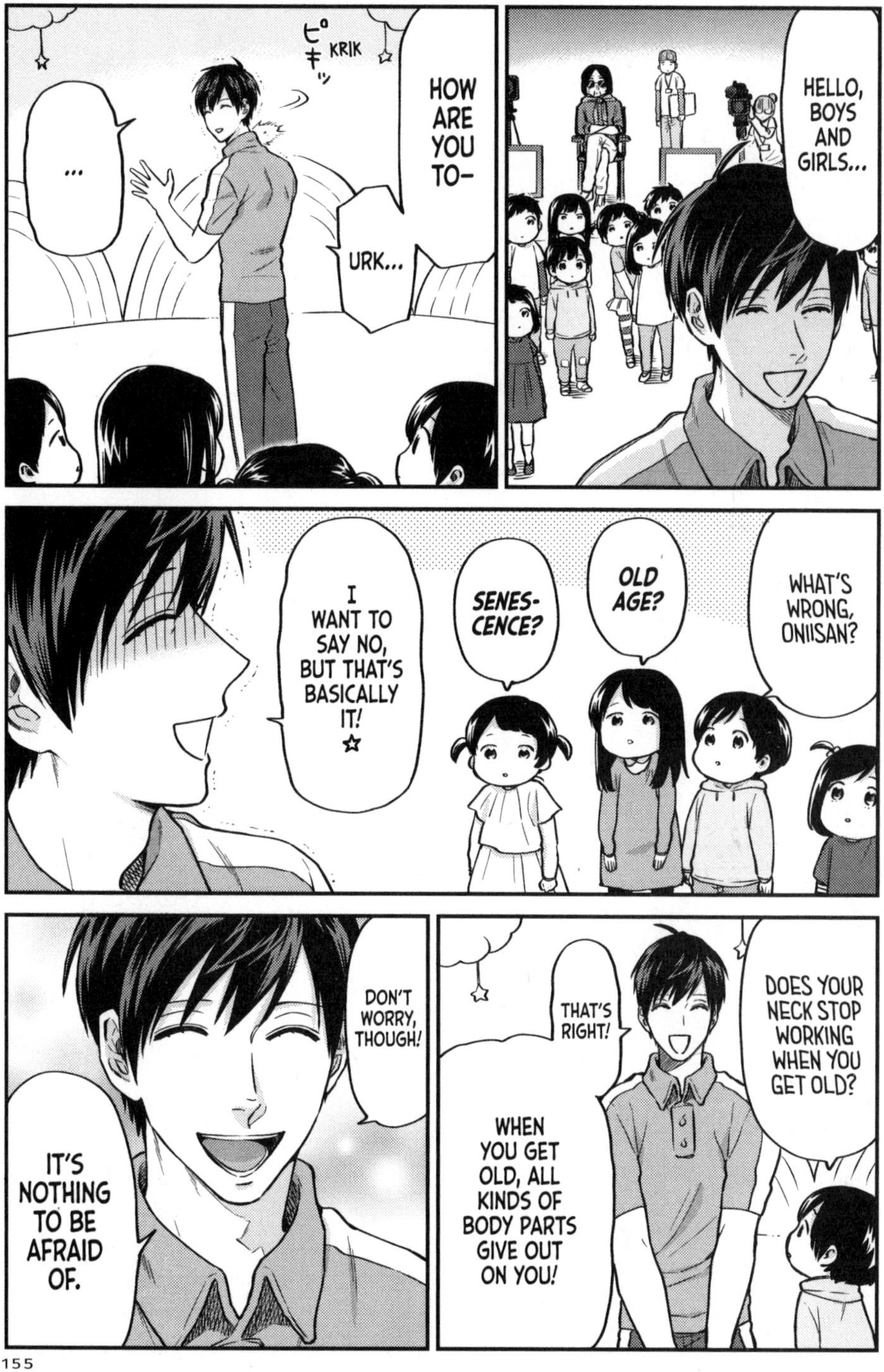
HELLO, BOYS AND GIRLS...
HOW ARE YOU TO–
ピキッ KRIK
URK...
...
WHAT'S WRONG, ONIISAN?
OLD AGE?
SENES-CENCE?
I WANT TO SAY NO, BUT THAT'S BASICALLY IT! ☆
DOES YOUR NECK STOP WORKING WHEN YOU GET OLD?
THAT'S RIGHT!
WHEN YOU GET OLD, ALL KINDS OF BODY PARTS GIVE OUT ON YOU!
DON'T WORRY, THOUGH!
IT'S NOTHING TO BE AFRAID OF.

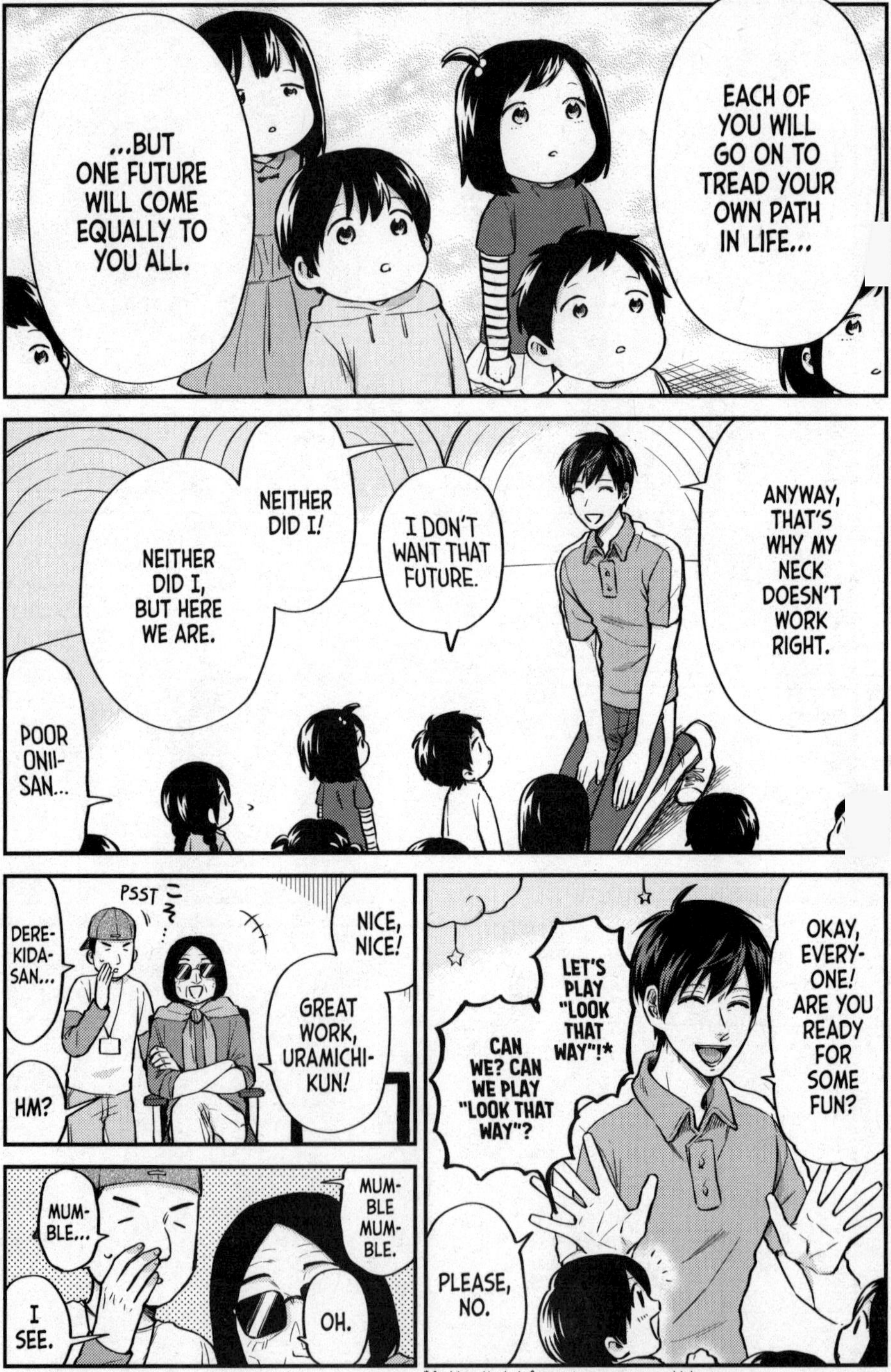
EACH OF YOU WILL GO ON TO TREAD YOUR OWN PATH IN LIFE...
...BUT ONE FUTURE WILL COME EQUALLY TO YOU ALL.
ANYWAY, THAT'S WHY MY NECK DOESN'T WORK RIGHT.
I DON'T WANT THAT FUTURE.
NEITHER DID I!
NEITHER DID I, BUT HERE WE ARE.
POOR ONII-SAN...
OKAY, EVERY-ONE! ARE YOU READY FOR SOME FUN?
LET'S PLAY "LOOK THAT WAY"!*
CAN WE? CAN WE PLAY "LOOK THAT WAY"?
PLEASE, NO.
NICE, NICE!
GREAT WORK, URAMICHI-KUN!
PSST
DERE-KIDA-SAN...
HM?
MUM-BLE MUM-BLE.
MUM-BLE...
OH.
I SEE.

*Acchi muite hoi: Game where you guess which way the leader will point and try to look the other way.

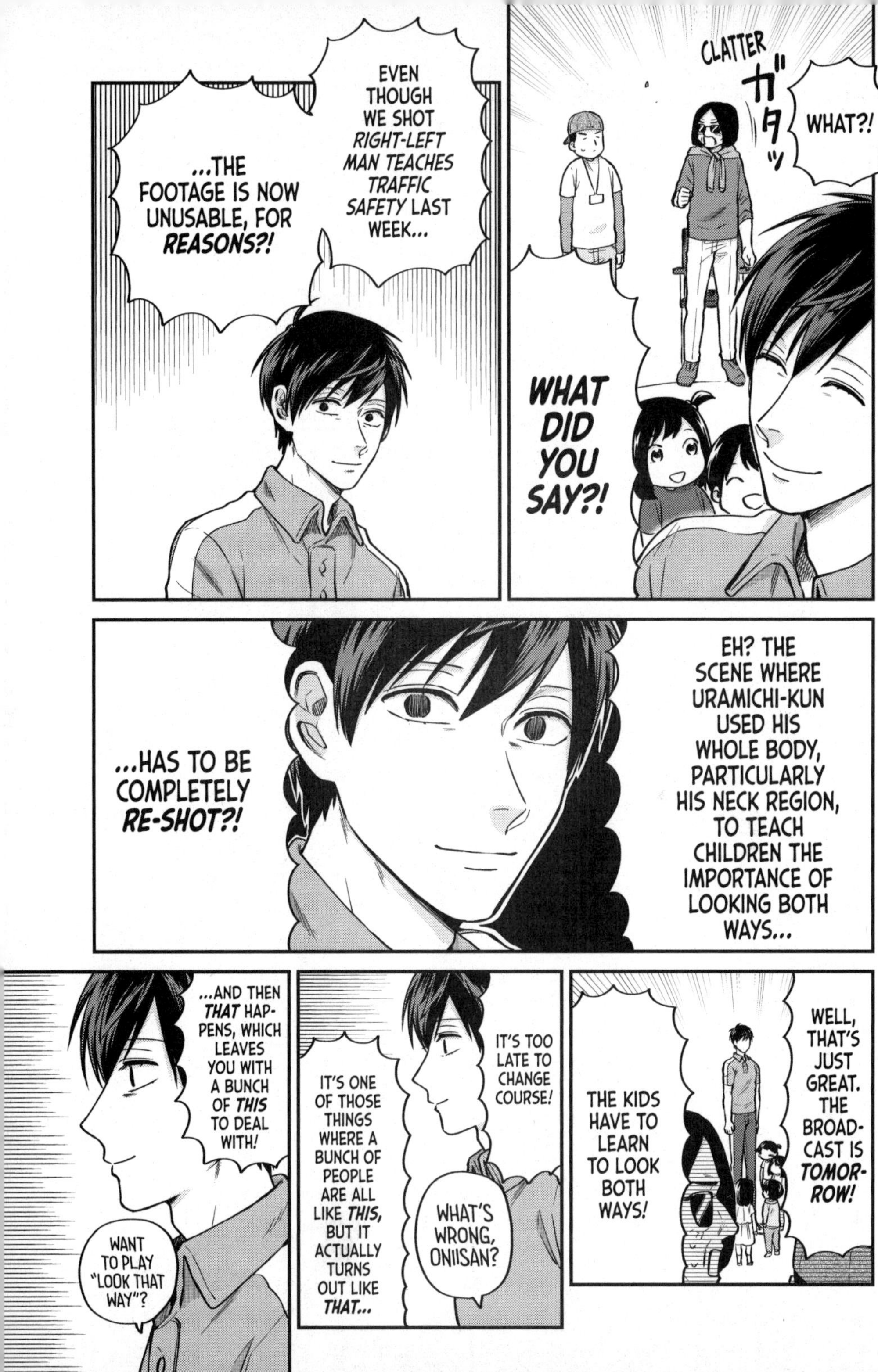
CLATTER
ガタッ
WHAT?!
WHAT DID YOU SAY?!
EVEN THOUGH WE SHOT RIGHT-LEFT MAN TEACHES TRAFFIC SAFETY LAST WEEK...
...THE FOOTAGE IS NOW UNUSABLE, FOR REASONS?!
EH? THE SCENE WHERE URAMICHI-KUN USED HIS WHOLE BODY, PARTICULARLY HIS NECK REGION, TO TEACH CHILDREN THE IMPORTANCE OF LOOKING BOTH WAYS...
...HAS TO BE COMPLETELY RE-SHOT?!
WELL, THAT'S JUST GREAT. THE BROADCAST IS TOMORROW!
THE KIDS HAVE TO LEARN TO LOOK BOTH WAYS!
IT'S TOO LATE TO CHANGE COURSE!
IT'S ONE OF THOSE THINGS WHERE A BUNCH OF PEOPLE ARE ALL LIKE THIS, BUT IT ACTUALLY TURNS OUT LIKE THAT...
WHAT'S WRONG, ONIISAN?
...AND THEN THAT HAPPENS, WHICH LEAVES YOU WITH A BUNCH OF THIS TO DEAL WITH!
WANT TO PLAY "LOOK THAT WAY"?

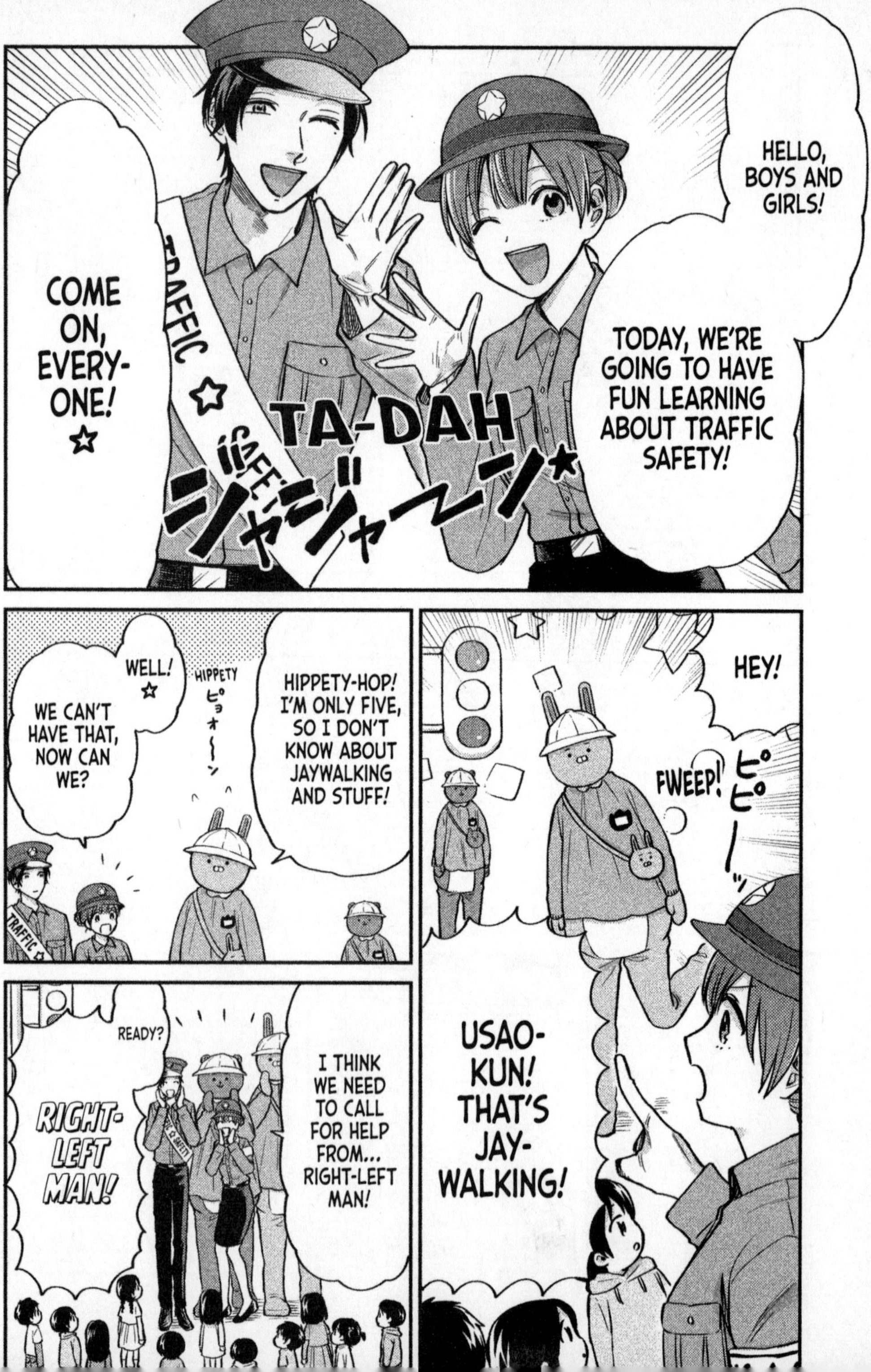
HELLO, BOYS AND GIRLS!
TODAY, WE'RE GOING TO HAVE FUN LEARNING ABOUT TRAFFIC SAFETY!
COME ON, EVERY-ONE! ☆
TA-DAH
ジャジャーン
TRAFFIC ☆
HEY!
FWEEP!
ピピーッ
USAO-KUN! THAT'S JAY-WALKING!
HIPPETY-HOP! I'M ONLY FIVE, SO I DON'T KNOW ABOUT JAYWALKING AND STUFF!
HIPPETY
ピョオ～ン
WELL! ☆
WE CAN'T HAVE THAT, NOW CAN WE?
TRAFFIC ☆
I THINK WE NEED TO CALL FOR HELP FROM... RIGHT-LEFT MAN!
READY?
RIGHT-LEFT MAN!

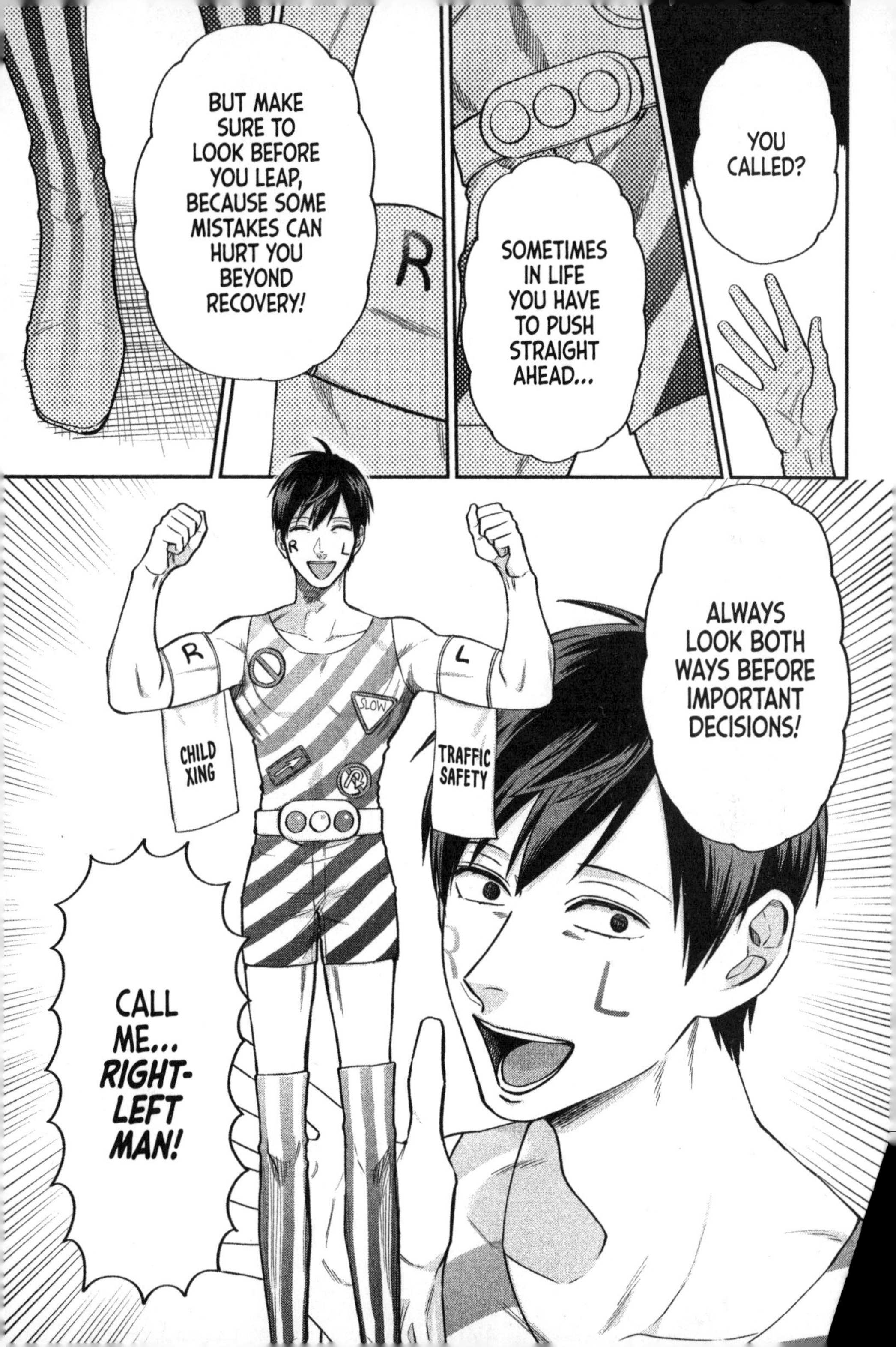
YOU CALLED?
SOMETIMES IN LIFE YOU HAVE TO PUSH STRAIGHT AHEAD...
BUT MAKE SURE TO LOOK BEFORE YOU LEAP, BECAUSE SOME MISTAKES CAN HURT YOU BEYOND RECOVERY!
ALWAYS LOOK BOTH WAYS BEFORE IMPORTANT DECISIONS!
TRAFFIC SAFETY
SLOW
CHILD XING
CALL ME... RIGHT-LEFT MAN!

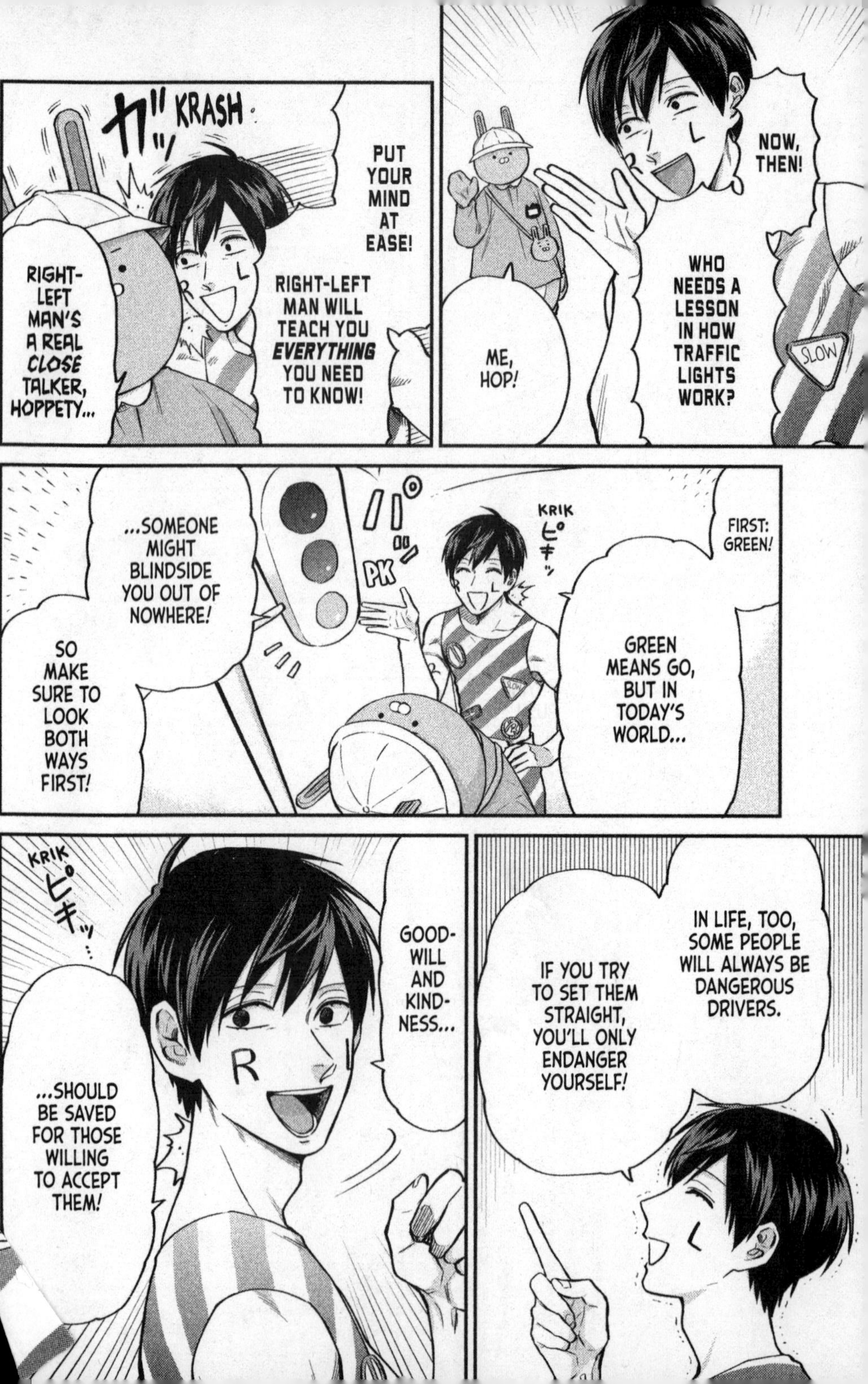
NOW, THEN!
WHO NEEDS A LESSON IN HOW TRAFFIC LIGHTS WORK?
ME, HOP!
カ" KRASH
PUT YOUR MIND AT EASE!
RIGHT-LEFT MAN WILL TEACH YOU *EVERYTHING* YOU NEED TO KNOW!
RIGHT-LEFT MAN'S A REAL *CLOSE* TALKER, HOPPETY...
FIRST: GREEN!
KRIK ピキッ
GREEN MEANS GO, BUT IN TODAY'S WORLD...
パ PK
...SOMEONE MIGHT BLINDSIDE YOU OUT OF NOWHERE!
SO MAKE SURE TO LOOK BOTH WAYS FIRST!
IN LIFE, TOO, SOME PEOPLE WILL ALWAYS BE DANGEROUS DRIVERS.
IF YOU TRY TO SET THEM STRAIGHT, YOU'LL ONLY ENDANGER YOURSELF!
KRIK ピキッ...
GOOD-WILL AND KIND-NESS...
...SHOULD BE SAVED FOR THOSE WILLING TO ACCEPT THEM!

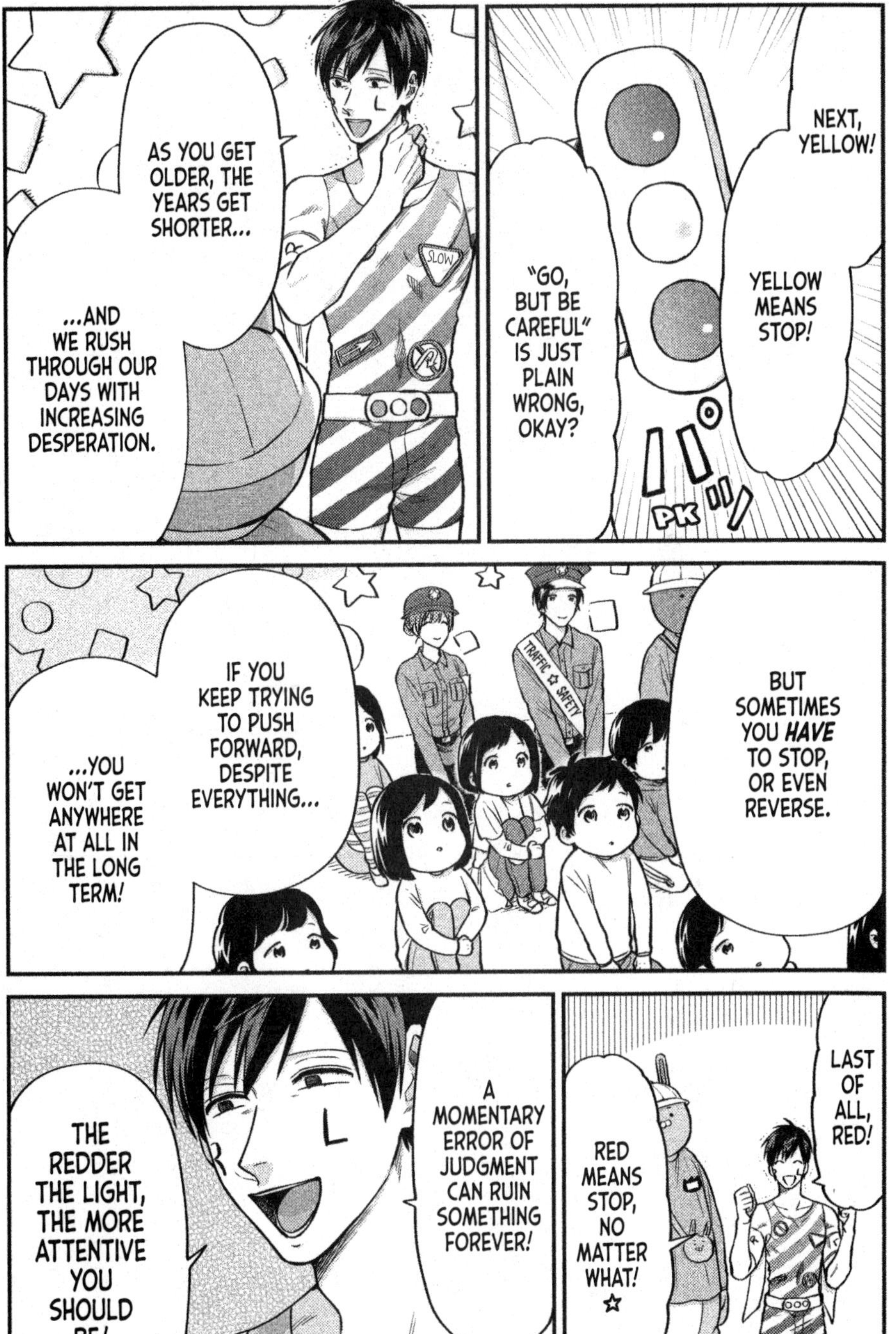
NEXT, YELLOW!
YELLOW MEANS STOP!
"GO, BUT BE CAREFUL" IS JUST PLAIN WRONG, OKAY?
PK
AS YOU GET OLDER, THE YEARS GET SHORTER...
SLOW
...AND WE RUSH THROUGH OUR DAYS WITH INCREASING DESPERATION.
BUT SOMETIMES YOU *HAVE* TO STOP, OR EVEN REVERSE.
TRAFFIC ☆ SAFETY
IF YOU KEEP TRYING TO PUSH FORWARD, DESPITE EVERYTHING...
...YOU WON'T GET ANYWHERE AT ALL IN THE LONG TERM!
LAST OF ALL, RED!
RED MEANS STOP, NO MATTER WHAT! ☆
A MOMENTARY ERROR OF JUDGMENT CAN RUIN SOMETHING FOREVER!
THE REDDER THE LIGHT, THE MORE ATTENTIVE YOU SHOULD BE!

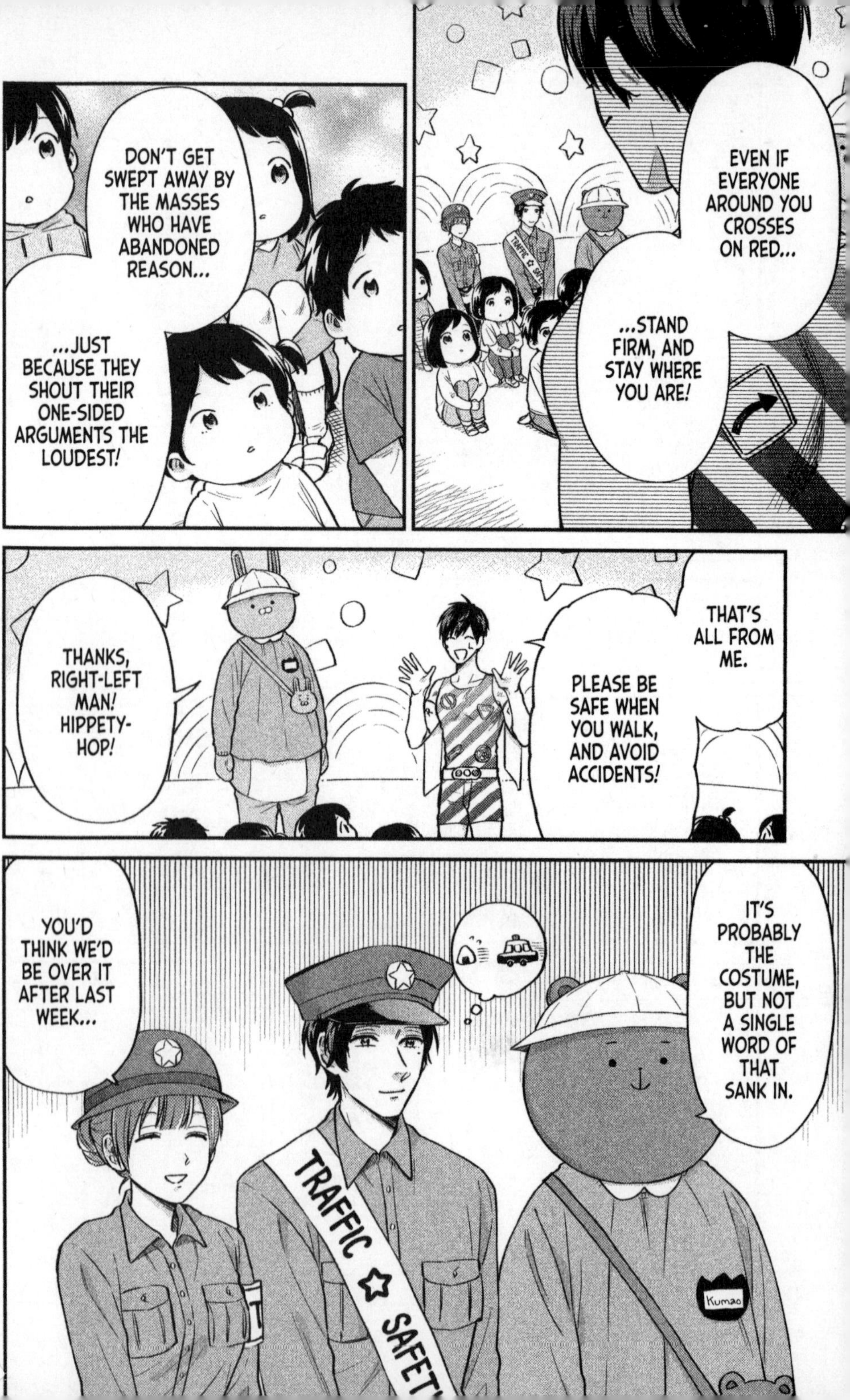
EVEN IF EVERYONE AROUND YOU CROSSES ON RED...
...STAND FIRM, AND STAY WHERE YOU ARE!
DON'T GET SWEPT AWAY BY THE MASSES WHO HAVE ABANDONED REASON...
...JUST BECAUSE THEY SHOUT THEIR ONE-SIDED ARGUMENTS THE LOUDEST!
THAT'S ALL FROM ME.
PLEASE BE SAFE WHEN YOU WALK, AND AVOID ACCIDENTS!
THANKS, RIGHT-LEFT MAN! HIPPETY-HOP!
IT'S PROBABLY THE COSTUME, BUT NOT A SINGLE WORD OF THAT SANK IN.
YOU'D THINK WE'D BE OVER IT AFTER LAST WEEK...
TRAFFIC
SAFET
Kumao

Life Lessons with
Uramichi Oniisan

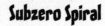

Subzero Spiral

Sung by Iketeru Oniisan and Utano Oneesan

Trodden-down snow is super dangerous
You fall flat just like that

Can't get up
Can't stand up
It's super dangerous, super dangerous
I ache in every part of my body and my heart (They ache!)

Speaking up at the morning meeting was super scary
My proposal fell flat just like that

We need new ideas
Don't be afraid (Say)
Say what you think—isn't that what you told me?
The air in the room froze white
Like a cloudy midwinter sky (Sky)

I just wanted warmth (That's all)
My hand had the shivers
I aimed for "Hot" (Hot)
But I hit the wrong button (Hit)
And what was delivered...was "Cold" (Cold)

Trodden-down snow is super dangerous
You fall flat just like that

A campfire couldn't even start
To thaw my numb, frozen heart

Ice-cold (my heart)
Wind whistles through (my wallet)
And echoes emptily in the night
(the bragging of the older staff)

La la la, doo de doo
La la la la la... (Doo de doo de doo)

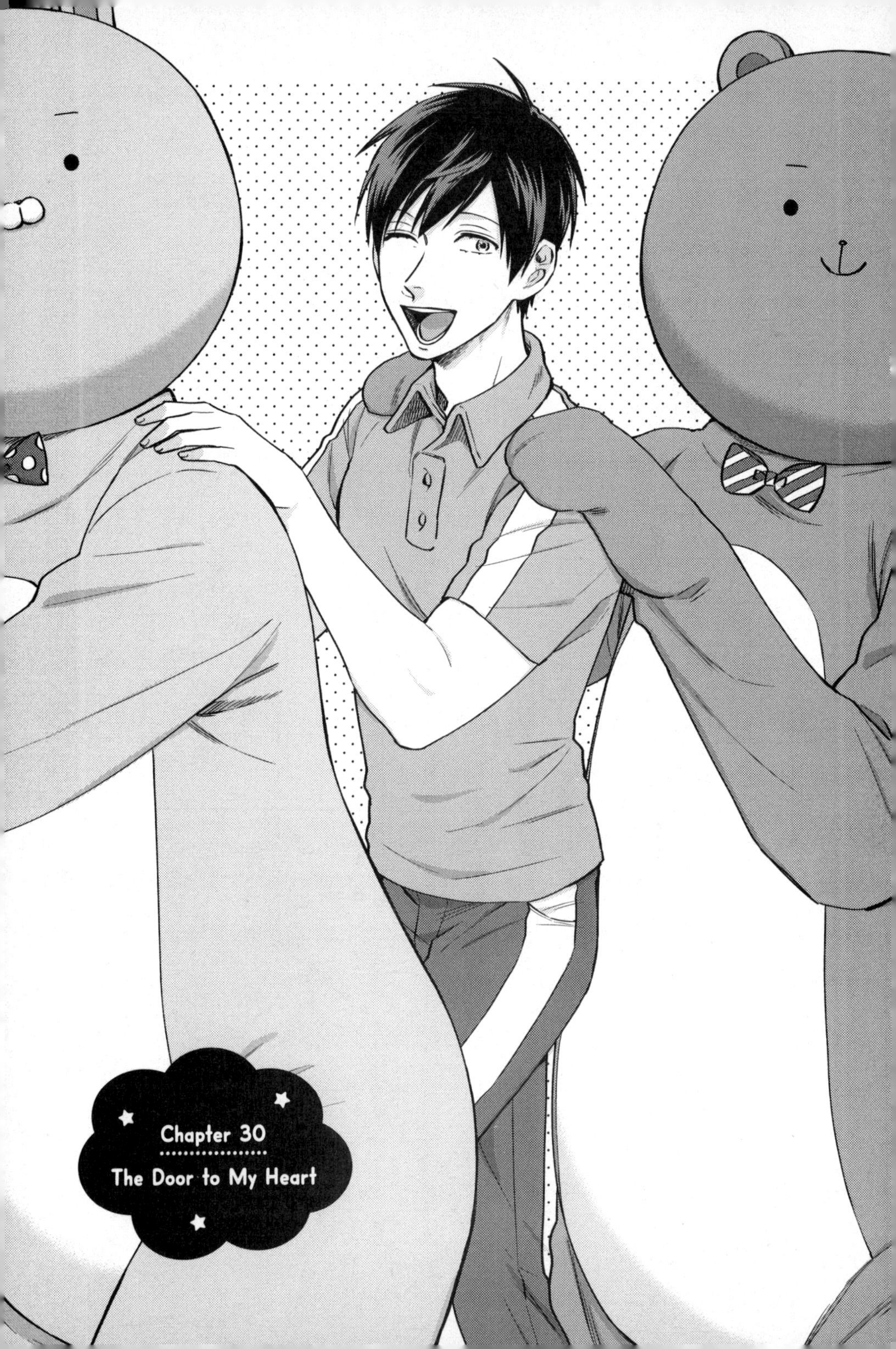
Chapter 30
The Door to My Heart

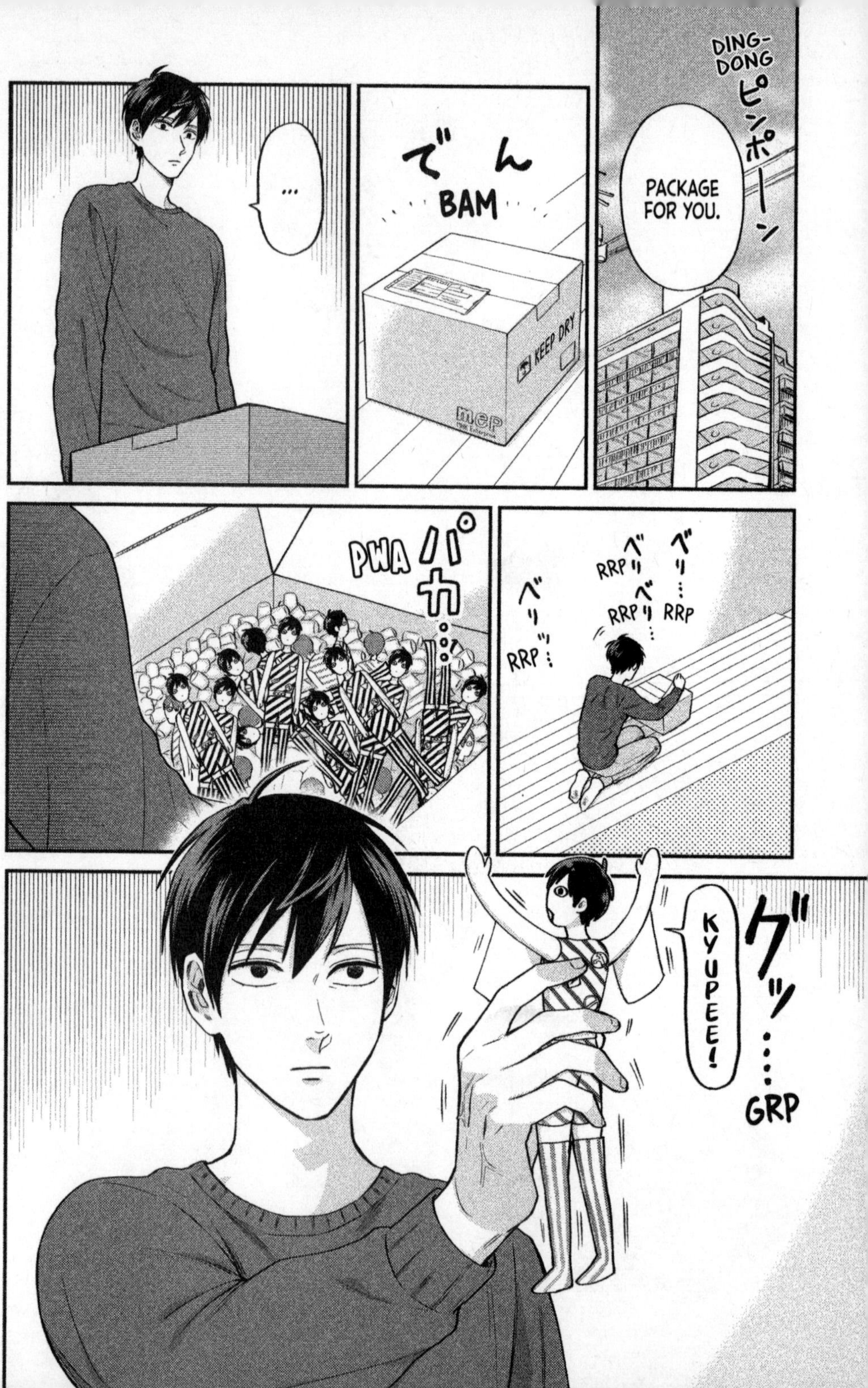
DING-DONG
ピンポーン
PACKAGE FOR YOU.
でん
BAM
...
ベリ…
RRP
ベリ
RRP
ベリベリ…
RRP
ベリッ…
RRP
パカ…
PWA
KYUPEE!
グッ…
GRP

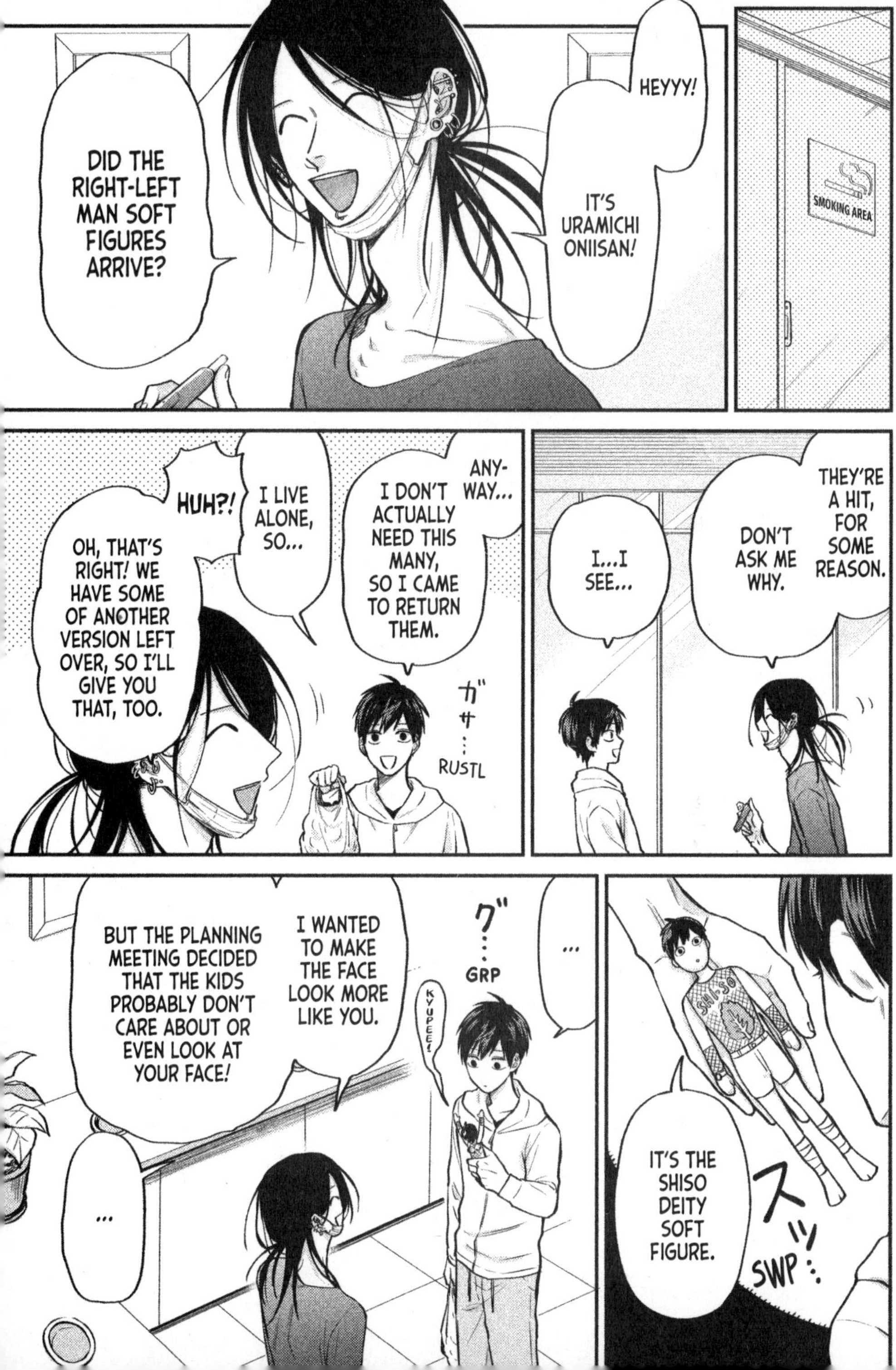
SMOKING AREA
HEYYY!
IT'S URAMICHI ONIISAN!
DID THE RIGHT-LEFT MAN SOFT FIGURES ARRIVE?
THEY'RE A HIT, FOR SOME REASON.
DON'T ASK ME WHY.
I...I SEE...
ANY-WAY...
I DON'T ACTUALLY NEED THIS MANY, SO I CAME TO RETURN THEM.
I LIVE ALONE, SO...
HUH?!
OH, THAT'S RIGHT! WE HAVE SOME OF ANOTHER VERSION LEFT OVER, SO I'LL GIVE YOU THAT, TOO.
ガサ… RUSTL
スッ… SWP
SHI-SO
IT'S THE SHISO DEITY SOFT FIGURE.
...
グ… GRP
I WANTED TO MAKE THE FACE LOOK MORE LIKE YOU.
KYUPEE!
BUT THE PLANNING MEETING DECIDED THAT THE KIDS PROBABLY DON'T CARE ABOUT OR EVEN LOOK AT YOUR FACE!
...

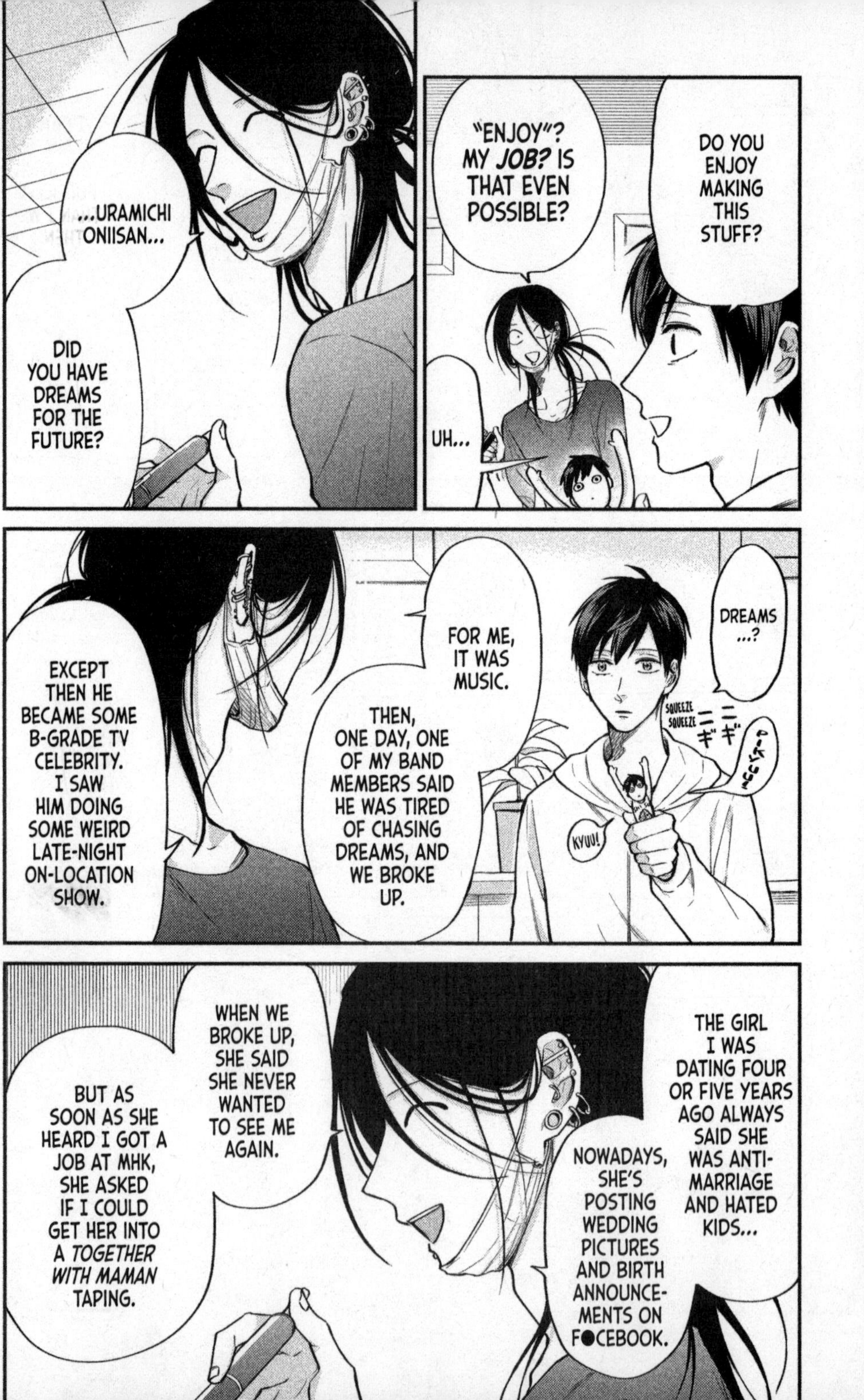
DO YOU ENJOY MAKING THIS STUFF?
"ENJOY"? MY *JOB?* IS THAT EVEN POSSIBLE?
UH...
...URAMICHI ONIISAN...
DID YOU HAVE DREAMS FOR THE FUTURE?
DREAMS ...?
SQUEEZE SQUEEZE
ニギニギ
PIKYUUU!
KYUU!
FOR ME, IT WAS MUSIC.
THEN, ONE DAY, ONE OF MY BAND MEMBERS SAID HE WAS TIRED OF CHASING DREAMS, AND WE BROKE UP.
EXCEPT THEN HE BECAME SOME B-GRADE TV CELEBRITY. I SAW HIM DOING SOME WEIRD LATE-NIGHT ON-LOCATION SHOW.
THE GIRL I WAS DATING FOUR OR FIVE YEARS AGO ALWAYS SAID SHE WAS ANTI-MARRIAGE AND HATED KIDS...
NOWADAYS, SHE'S POSTING WEDDING PICTURES AND BIRTH ANNOUNCE-MENTS ON F●CEBOOK.
WHEN WE BROKE UP, SHE SAID SHE NEVER WANTED TO SEE ME AGAIN.
BUT AS SOON AS SHE HEARD I GOT A JOB AT MHK, SHE ASKED IF I COULD GET HER INTO A *TOGETHER WITH MAMAN* TAPING.

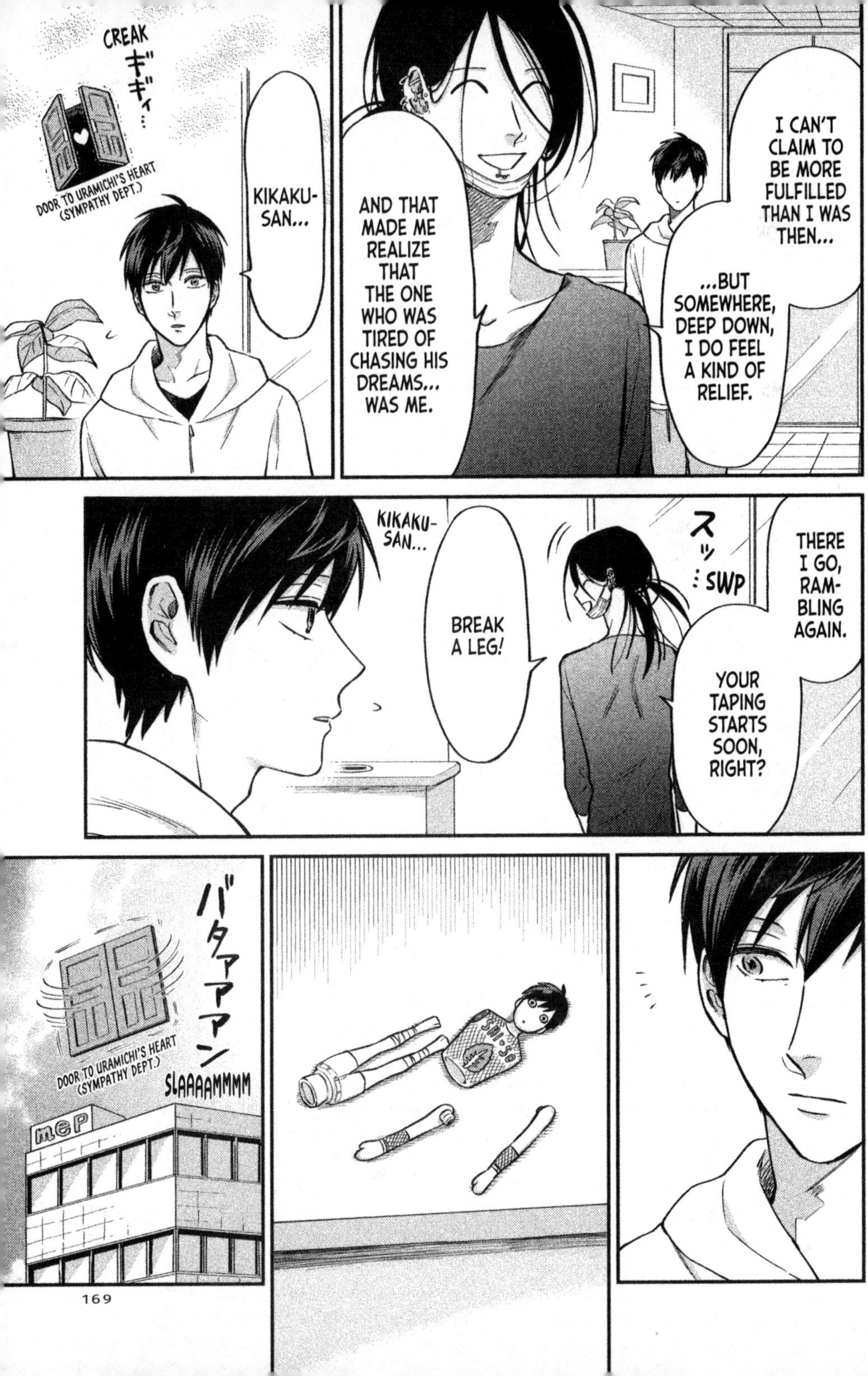

I CAN'T CLAIM TO BE MORE FULFILLED THAN I WAS THEN...
...BUT SOMEWHERE, DEEP DOWN, I DO FEEL A KIND OF RELIEF.
AND THAT MADE ME REALIZE THAT THE ONE WHO WAS TIRED OF CHASING HIS DREAMS... WAS ME.
KIKAKU-SAN...
CREAK
ギギィ…
DOOR TO URAMICHI'S HEART (SYMPATHY DEPT.)
THERE I GO, RAMBLING AGAIN.
YOUR TAPING STARTS SOON, RIGHT?
スッ…
SWP
KIKAKU-SAN...
BREAK A LEG!
バタアアン
SLAAAAMMMM
DOOR TO URAMICHI'S HEART (SYMPATHY DEPT.)
mep

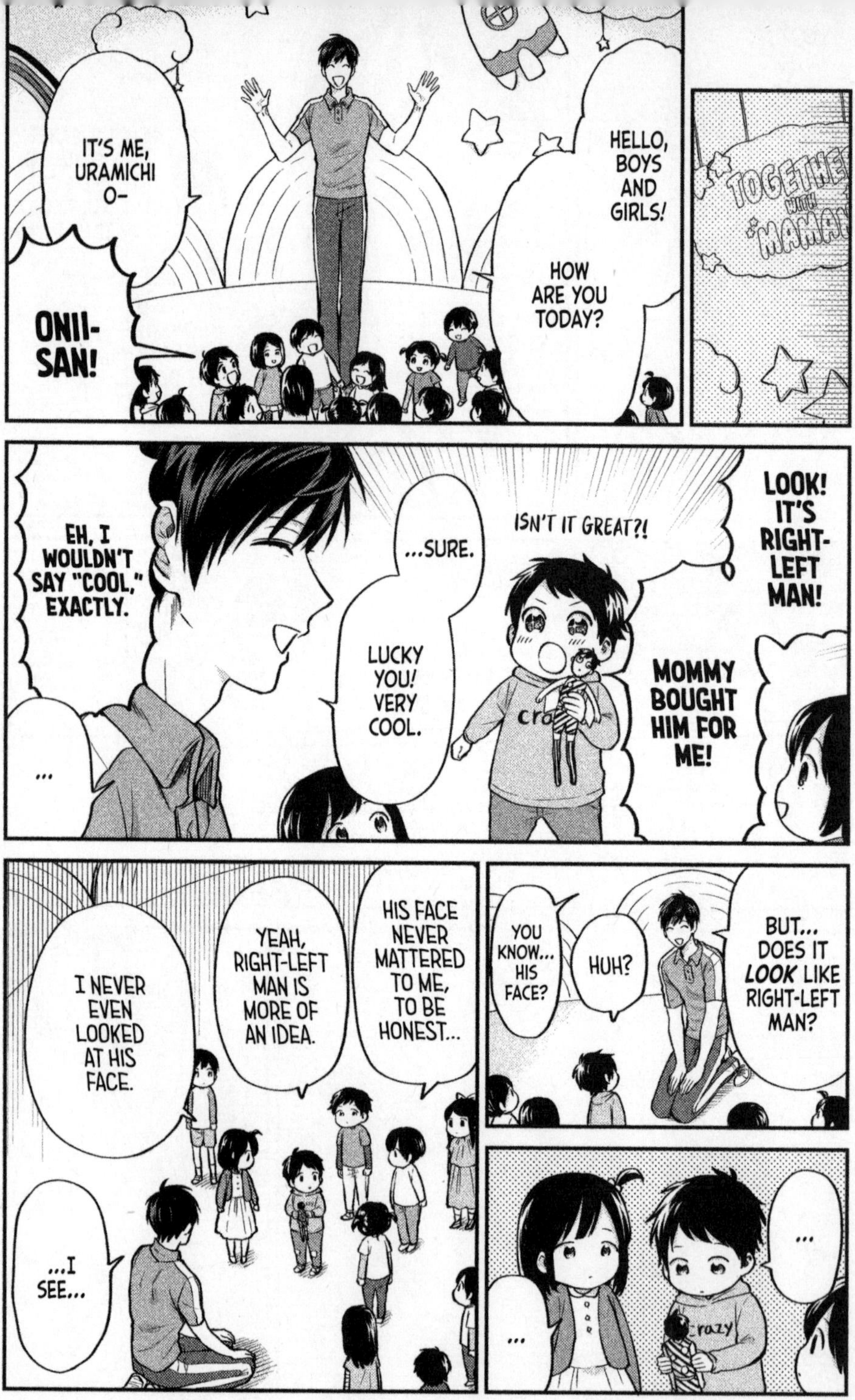
HELLO, BOYS AND GIRLS!
HOW ARE YOU TODAY?
IT'S ME, URAMICHI O-
ONII-SAN!
LOOK! IT'S RIGHT-LEFT MAN!
MOMMY BOUGHT HIM FOR ME!
ISN'T IT GREAT?!
...SURE.
LUCKY YOU! VERY COOL.
EH, I WOULDN'T SAY "COOL," EXACTLY.
...
BUT... DOES IT *LOOK* LIKE RIGHT-LEFT MAN?
HUH?
YOU KNOW... HIS FACE?
...
...
HIS FACE NEVER MATTERED TO ME, TO BE HONEST...
YEAH, RIGHT-LEFT MAN IS MORE OF AN IDEA.
I NEVER EVEN LOOKED AT HIS FACE.
...I SEE...

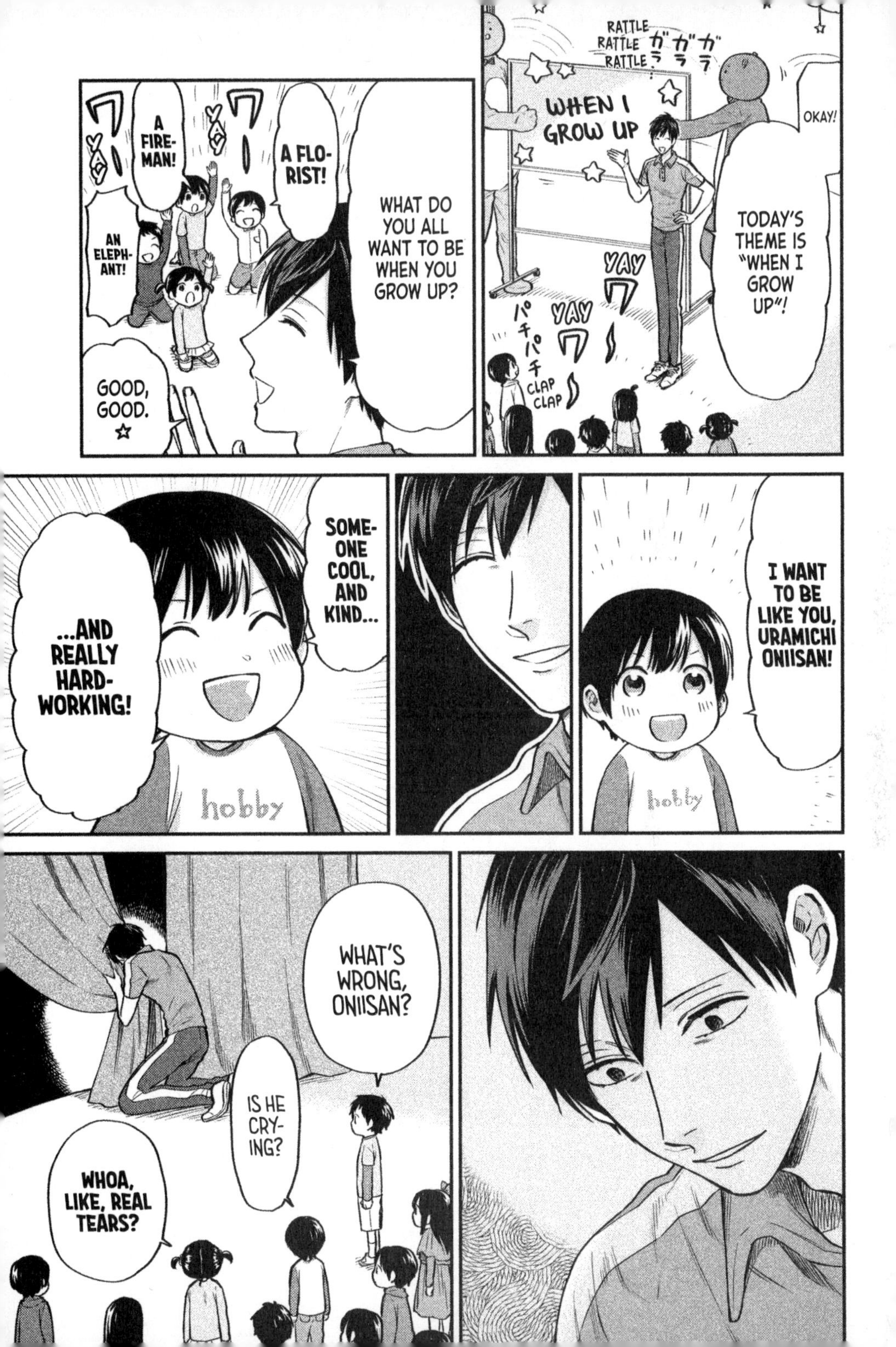
RATTLE RATTLE RATTLE ガガガラララ
WHEN I GROW UP
OKAY!
TODAY'S THEME IS "WHEN I GROW UP"!
YAY ワ
YAY ワ
パチパチ CLAP CLAP
WHAT DO YOU ALL WANT TO BE WHEN YOU GROW UP?
A FLORIST!
ワー YAY
A FIREMAN!
ワー YAY
AN ELEPHANT!
GOOD, GOOD. ☆
I WANT TO BE LIKE YOU, URAMICHI ONIISAN!
hobby
SOMEONE COOL, AND KIND...
...AND REALLY HARDWORKING!
hobby
WHAT'S WRONG, ONIISAN?
IS HE CRYING?
WHOA, LIKE, REAL TEARS?

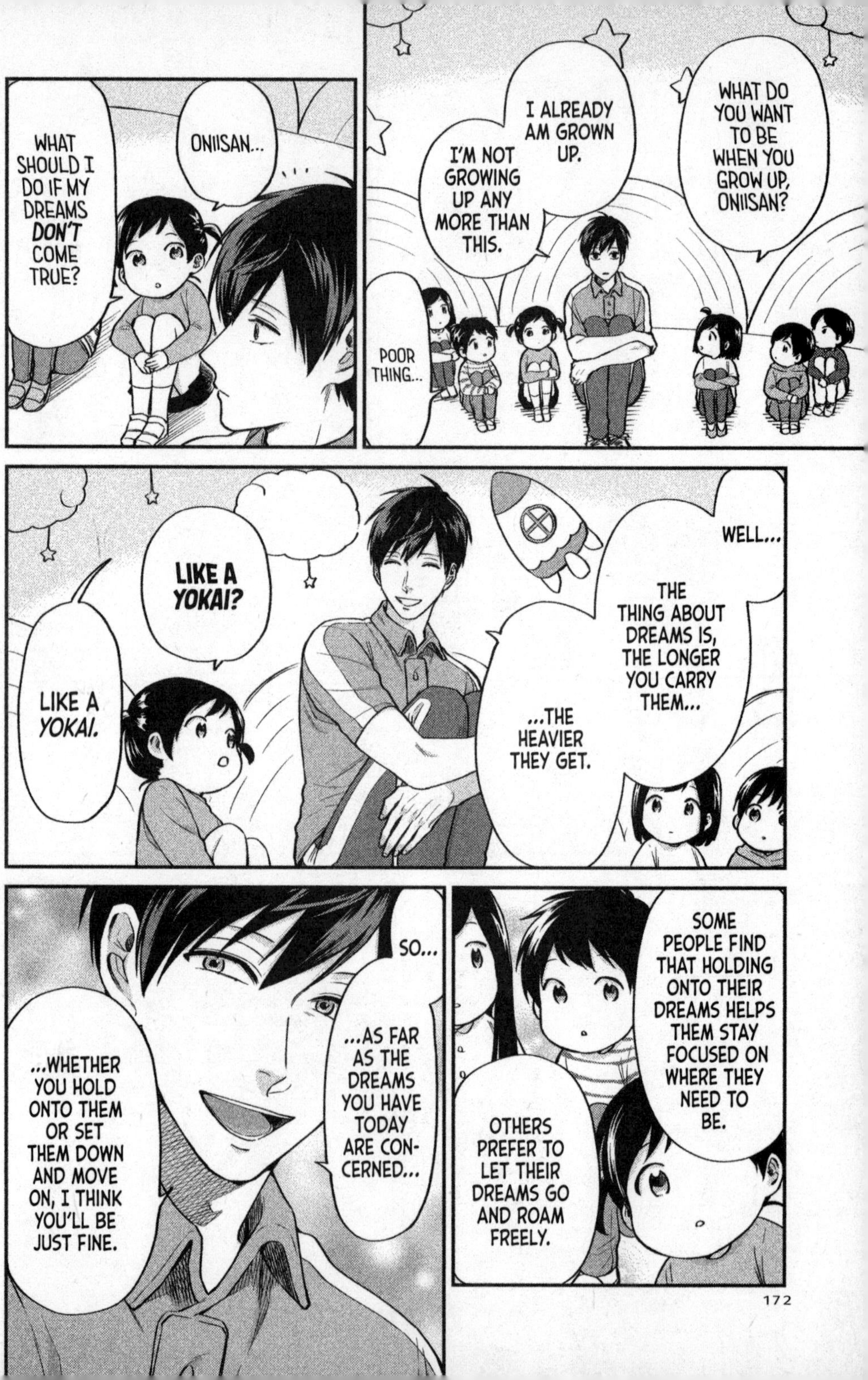
WHAT DO YOU WANT TO BE WHEN YOU GROW UP, ONIISAN?
I ALREADY AM GROWN UP.
I'M NOT GROWING UP ANY MORE THAN THIS.
POOR THING...
ONIISAN...
WHAT SHOULD I DO IF MY DREAMS *DON'T* COME TRUE?
WELL...
THE THING ABOUT DREAMS IS, THE LONGER YOU CARRY THEM...
...THE HEAVIER THEY GET.
LIKE A *YOKAI?*
LIKE A *YOKAI.*
SOME PEOPLE FIND THAT HOLDING ONTO THEIR DREAMS HELPS THEM STAY FOCUSED ON WHERE THEY NEED TO BE.
OTHERS PREFER TO LET THEIR DREAMS GO AND ROAM FREELY.
SO...
...AS FAR AS THE DREAMS YOU HAVE TODAY ARE CON-CERNED...
...WHETHER YOU HOLD ONTO THEM OR SET THEM DOWN AND MOVE ON, I THINK YOU'LL BE JUST FINE.

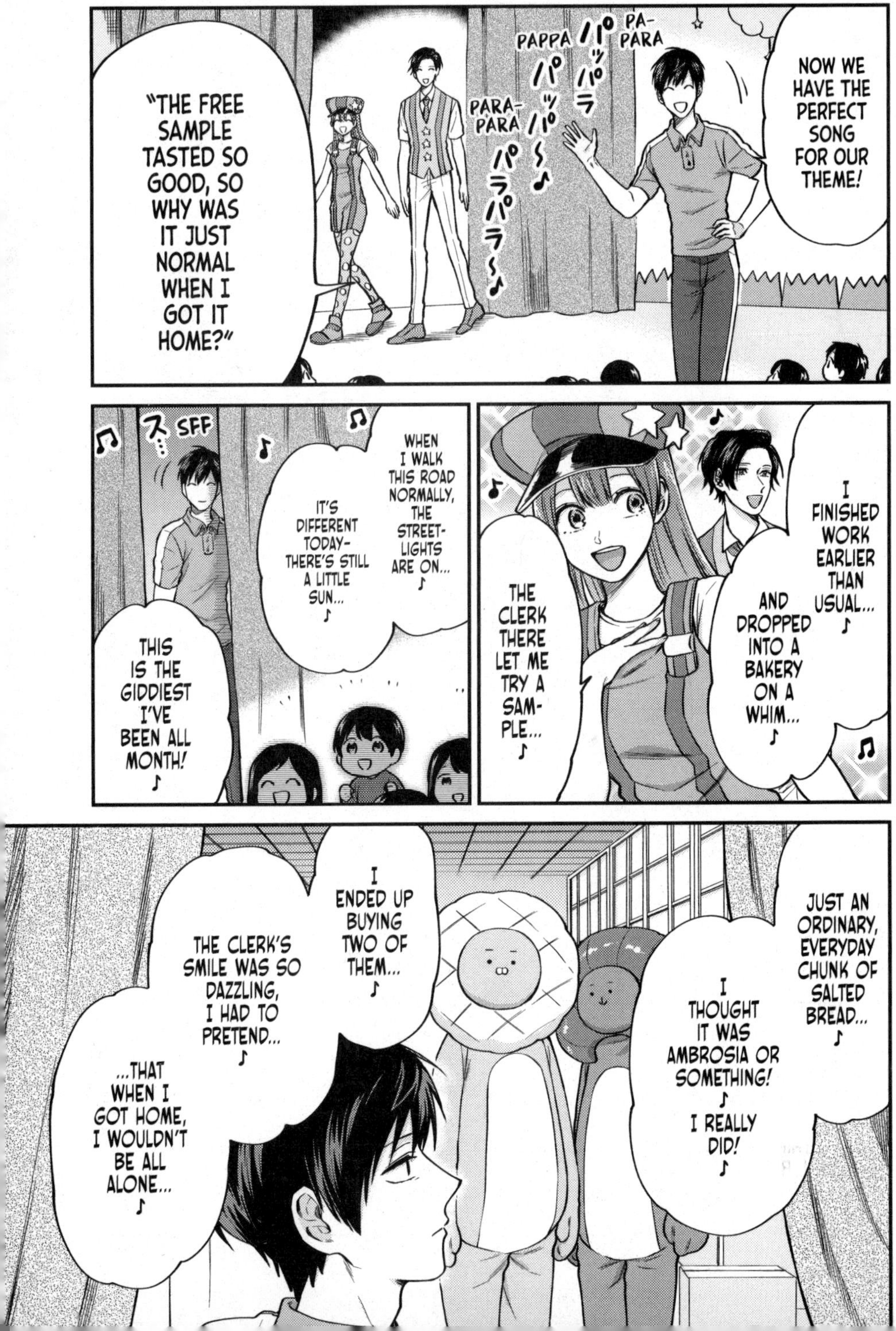
NOW WE HAVE THE PERFECT SONG FOR OUR THEME!
PA-PARA
パッパラ
PAPPA
パッパ~♪
PARA-PARA
パラパラ~♪
"THE FREE SAMPLE TASTED SO GOOD, SO WHY WAS IT JUST NORMAL WHEN I GOT IT HOME?"
I FINISHED WORK EARLIER THAN USUAL...♪
AND DROPPED INTO A BAKERY ON A WHIM...♪
THE CLERK THERE LET ME TRY A SAMPLE...♪
ス…
SFF
WHEN I WALK THIS ROAD NORMALLY, THE STREET-LIGHTS ARE ON...♪
IT'S DIFFERENT TODAY–THERE'S STILL A LITTLE SUN...♪
THIS IS THE GIDDIEST I'VE BEEN ALL MONTH!♪
JUST AN ORDINARY, EVERYDAY CHUNK OF SALTED BREAD...♪
I THOUGHT IT WAS AMBROSIA OR SOMETHING!♪ I REALLY DID!♪
I ENDED UP BUYING TWO OF THEM...♪
THE CLERK'S SMILE WAS SO DAZZLING, I HAD TO PRETEND...♪
...THAT WHEN I GOT HOME, I WOULDN'T BE ALL ALONE...♪

IT WASN'T AMBROSIA, BUT JUST NORMAL BREAD... ♪

WHY? ♪

(WHY?)

(JUST NORMAL BREAD!) ♪

BACK HOME, IT WAS JUST COMPLETELY NORMAL BREAD... ♪

I ONLY CHANGED THE LIGHTBULB YESTERDAY. ♪

WHY IS MY PLACE SO GLOOMY? ♪

THE WORLD THAT SEEMED TO GLITTER, MY HEART ALL AFLUTTER... ♪

WHERE DID IT GO? ♪

I LONG TO ONCE MORE SEE THE WORLD ALL AGLEAM. ♪

'CAUSE EVEN IF IT'S JUST A FLEETING DREAM... ♪

WHEN I NEXT GET OFF EARLY, I'LL GO BACK TO THE BAKERY... ♪

LA LA LA LA LA LA LA LA LA LA LA... ♪

IT WASN'T THE BREAD, IT WAS HOW I FELT INSIDE. ♪

BUT DEEP DOWN, I KNEW WHY... ♪

174

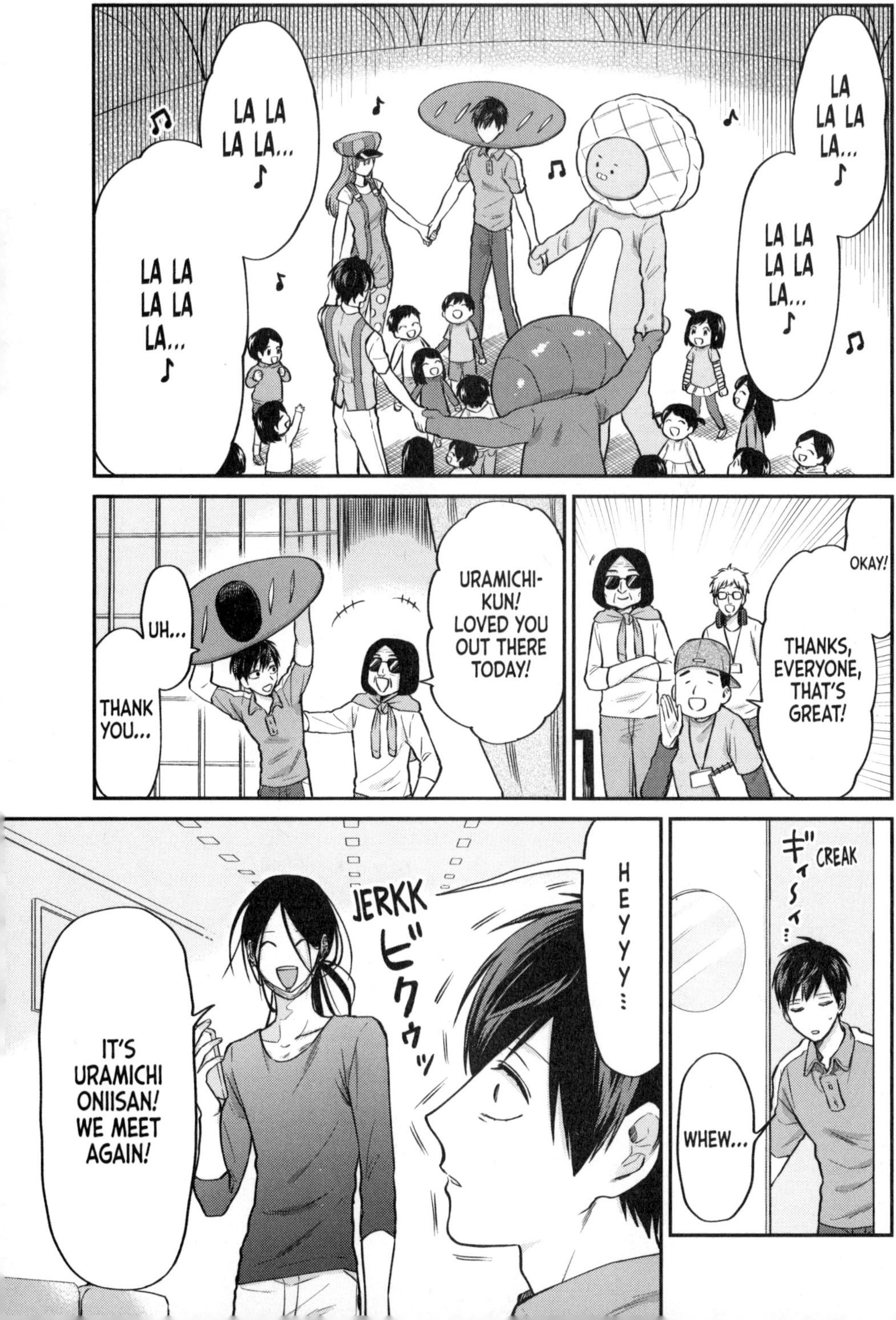
LA LA LA LA... ♪
LA LA LA LA LA... ♪
LA LA LA LA... ♪
LA LA LA LA LA... ♪
OKAY!
THANKS, EVERYONE, THAT'S GREAT!
URAMICHI-KUN! LOVED YOU OUT THERE TODAY!
UH...
THANK YOU...
CREAK
WHEW...
HEYYY...
JERKK
ビクゥッ
IT'S URAMICHI ONIISAN! WE MEET AGAIN!

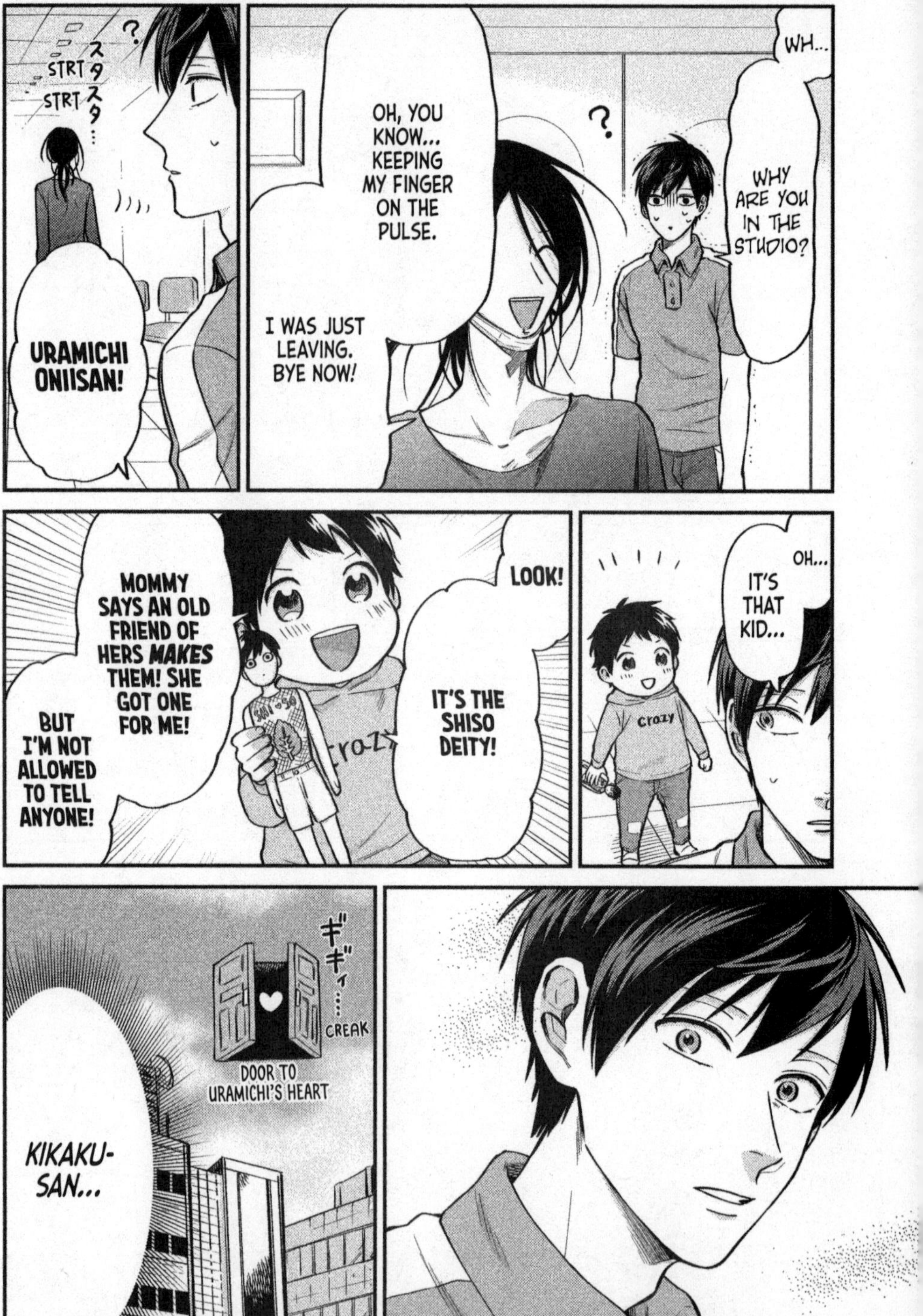
WH...
WHY ARE YOU IN THE STUDIO?
OH, YOU KNOW... KEEPING MY FINGER ON THE PULSE.
I WAS JUST LEAVING. BYE NOW!
スタスタ…
STRT STRT
URAMICHI ONIISAN!
OH...
IT'S THAT KID...
LOOK!
IT'S THE SHISO DEITY!
MOMMY SAYS AN OLD FRIEND OF HERS *MAKES* THEM! SHE GOT ONE FOR ME!
BUT I'M NOT ALLOWED TO TELL ANYONE!
ギギィ…
CREAK
DOOR TO URAMICHI'S HEART
KIKAKU-SAN...

Life Lessons with
Uramichi Oniisan

The Free Sample Tasted So Good, So Why Was It Just Normal When I Got It Home?

Sung by Iketeru Oniisan and Utano Oneesan

I finished work earlier than usual
And dropped into a bakery on a whim
The clerk there let me try a sample

When I walk this road normally, the streetlights are on
It's different today
There's still a little sun
This is the giddiest I've been all month

Just an ordinary, everyday chunk of salted bread
I thought it was ambrosia or something
I really did

I ended up buying two of them
The clerk's smile was so dazzling
I had to pretend

That when I got home
I wouldn't be all alone

Why? (Why?)
Back home, it was just completely normal bread

It wasn't ambrosia
But just normal bread (Just normal bread)

Where did it go?
The world that seemed to glitter, my heart all aflutter
Why is my place so gloomy?
I only changed the lightbulb yesterday

But deep down, I knew why
It wasn't the bread, it was how I felt inside

When I next get off early
I'll go back to the bakery

'Cause even if it's just
a fleeting dream
I long to once more see
the world all agleam

La la la la, la la la la...

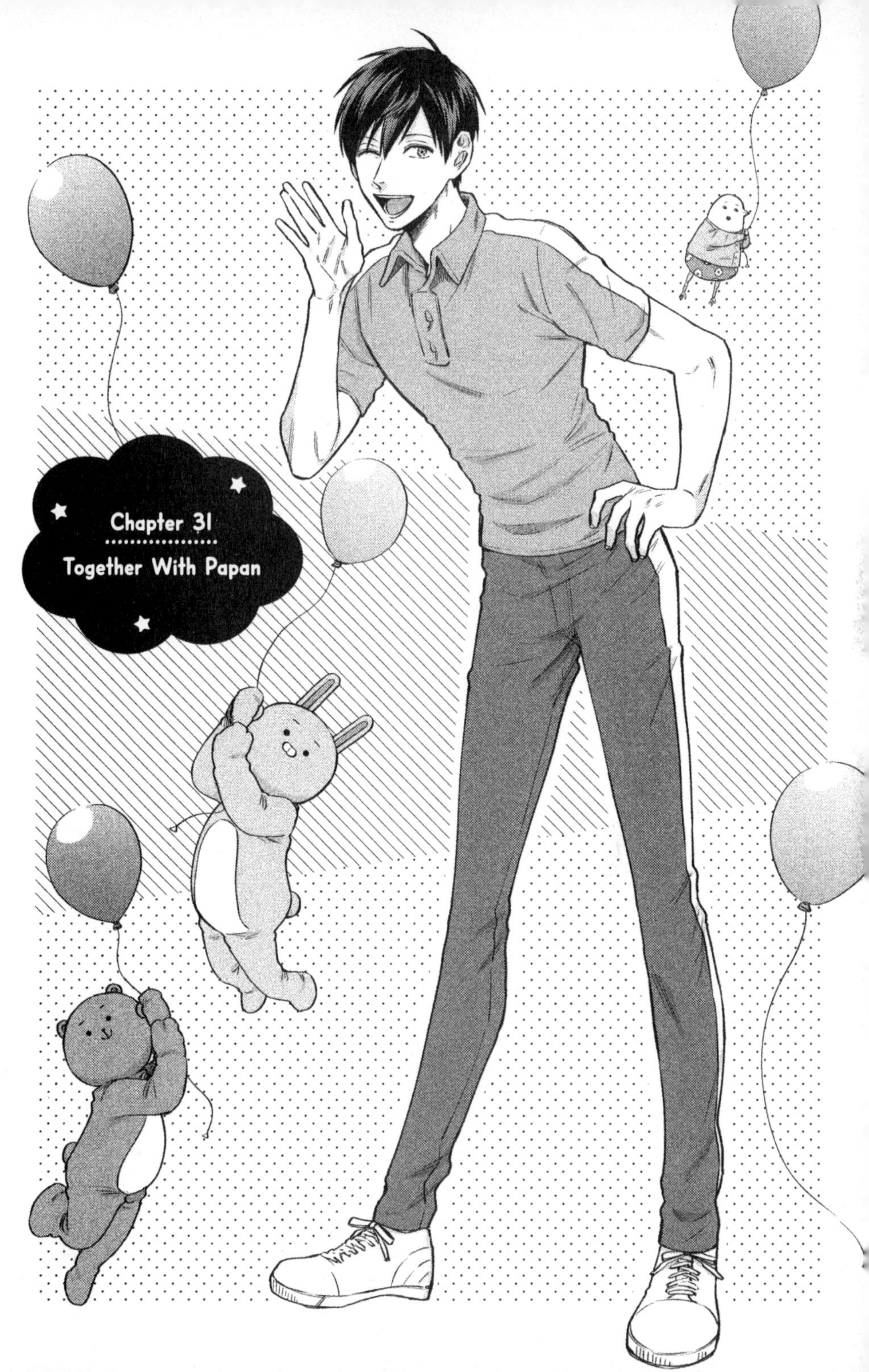
Chapter 31
Together With Papan

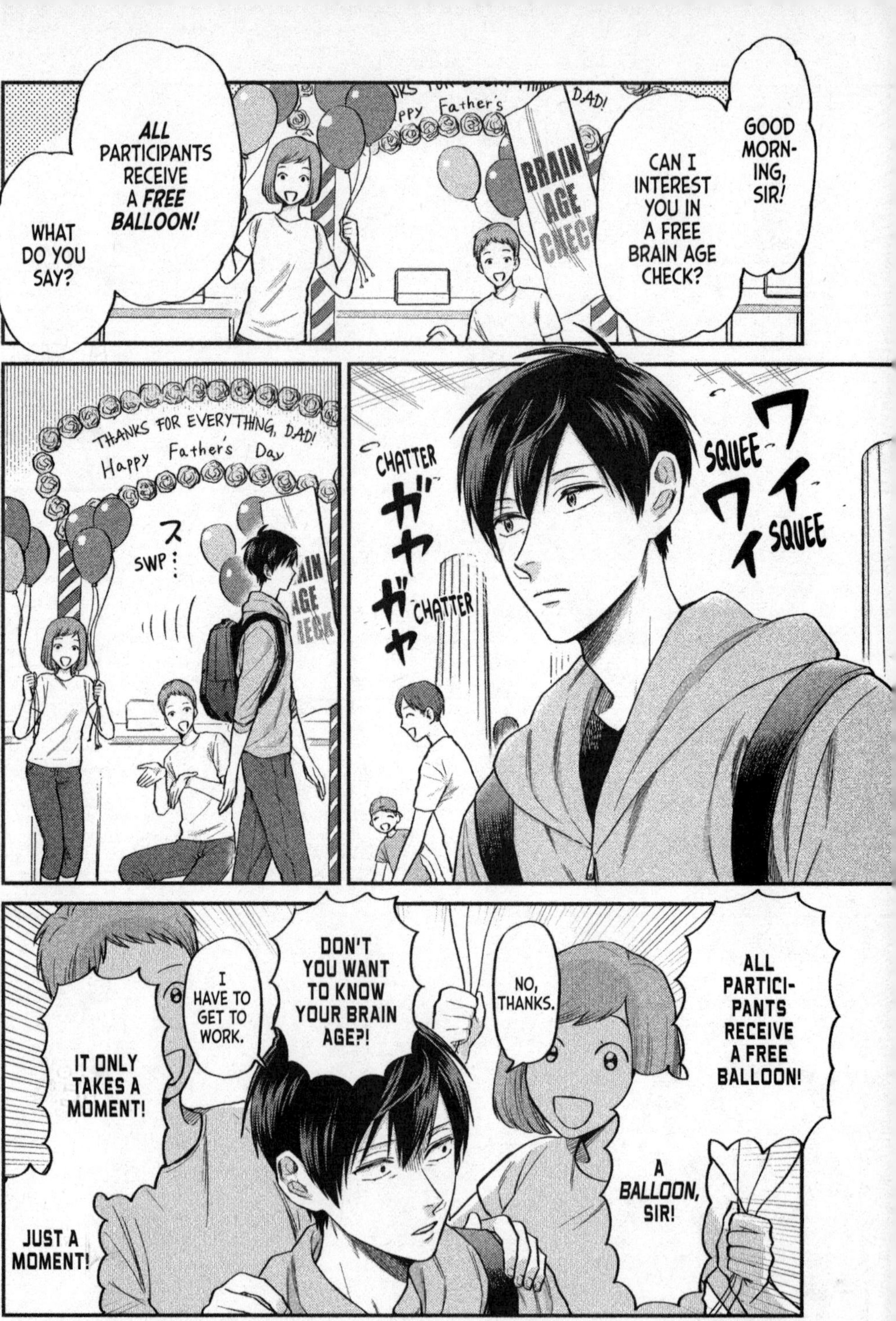

GOOD MORNING, SIR!
CAN I INTEREST YOU IN A FREE BRAIN AGE CHECK?
BRAIN AGE CHECK
DAD!
Happy Father's
ALL PARTICIPANTS RECEIVE A FREE BALLOON!
WHAT DO YOU SAY?
ワイワイ
SQUEE
SQUEE
ガヤガヤ
CHATTER
CHATTER
THANKS FOR EVERYTHING, DAD!
Happy Father's Day
ス
SWP...
ALL PARTICI-PANTS RECEIVE A FREE BALLOON!
A BALLOON, SIR!
NO, THANKS.
DON'T YOU WANT TO KNOW YOUR BRAIN AGE?!
I HAVE TO GET TO WORK.
IT ONLY TAKES A MOMENT!
JUST A MOMENT!

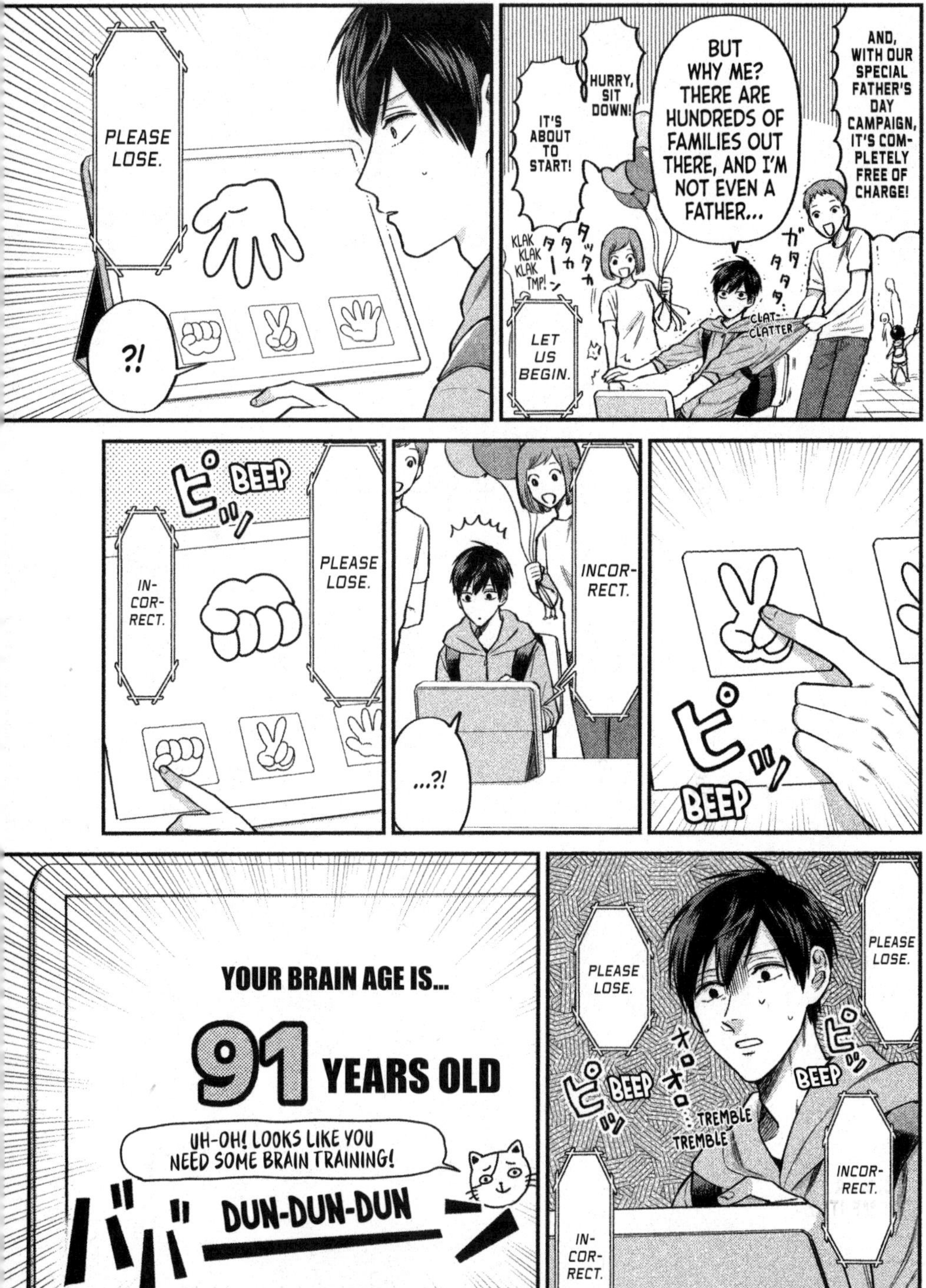
AND, WITH OUR SPECIAL FATHER'S DAY CAMPAIGN, IT'S COMPLETELY FREE OF CHARGE!
BUT WHY ME? THERE ARE HUNDREDS OF FAMILIES OUT THERE, AND I'M NOT EVEN A FATHER...
HURRY, SIT DOWN!
IT'S ABOUT TO START!
CLAT-CLATTER
KLAK KLAK KLAK TMP!
LET US BEGIN.
PLEASE LOSE.
?!
BEEP
INCORRECT.
...?!
PLEASE LOSE.
BEEP
INCORRECT.
PLEASE LOSE.
PLEASE LOSE.
BEEP
TREMBLE TREMBLE
BEEP
INCORRECT.
INCORRECT.
YOUR BRAIN AGE IS...
91 YEARS OLD
UH-OH! LOOKS LIKE YOU NEED SOME BRAIN TRAINING!
DUN-DUN-DUN

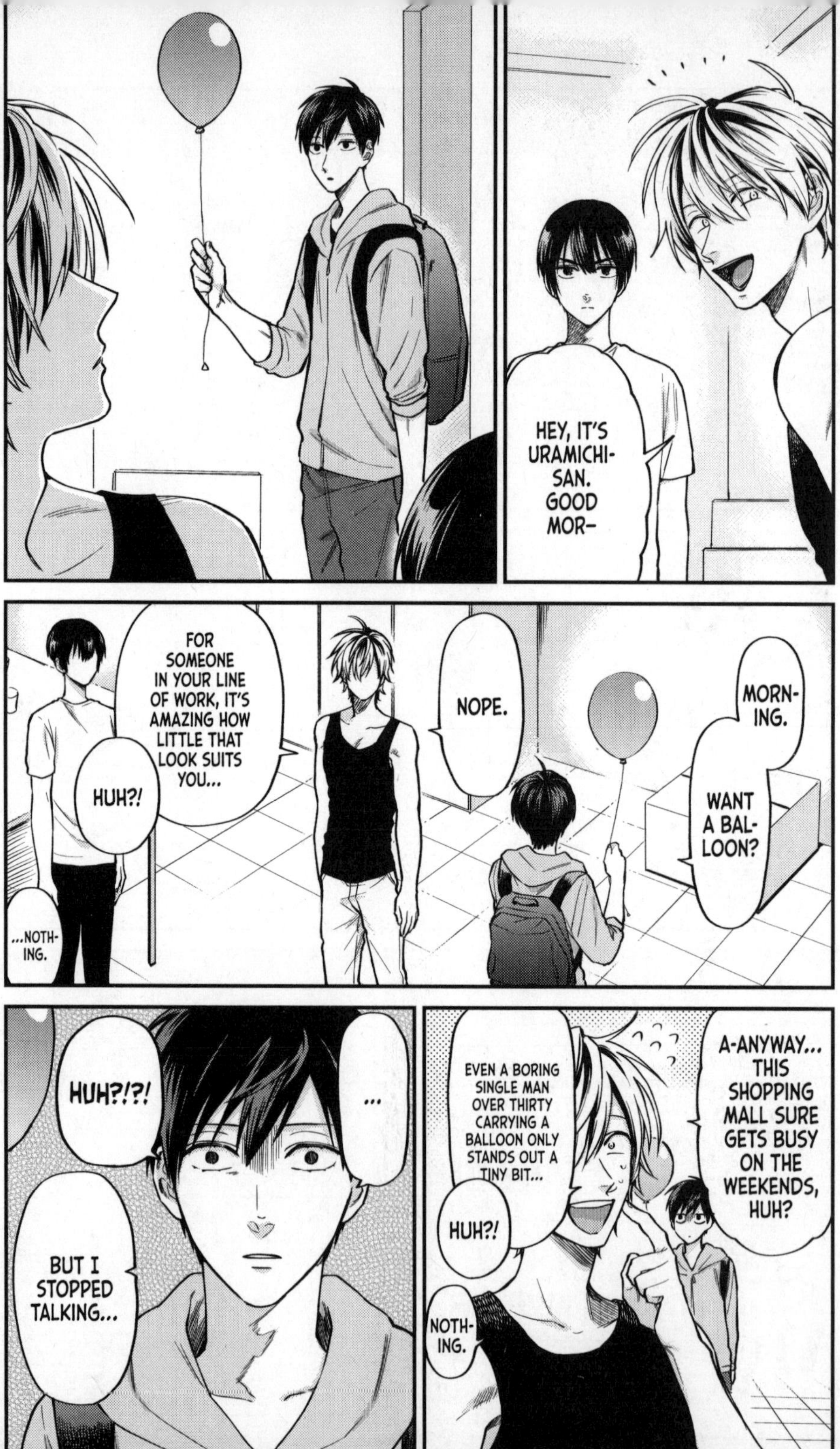
HEY, IT'S URAMICHI-SAN. GOOD MOR–
MORN-ING.
WANT A BAL-LOON?
NOPE.
FOR SOMEONE IN YOUR LINE OF WORK, IT'S AMAZING HOW LITTLE THAT LOOK SUITS YOU...
HUH?!
...NOTH-ING.
A-ANYWAY... THIS SHOPPING MALL SURE GETS BUSY ON THE WEEKENDS, HUH?
EVEN A BORING SINGLE MAN OVER THIRTY CARRYING A BALLOON ONLY STANDS OUT A TINY BIT...
HUH?!
NOTH-ING.
...
HUH?!?!
BUT I STOPPED TALKING...

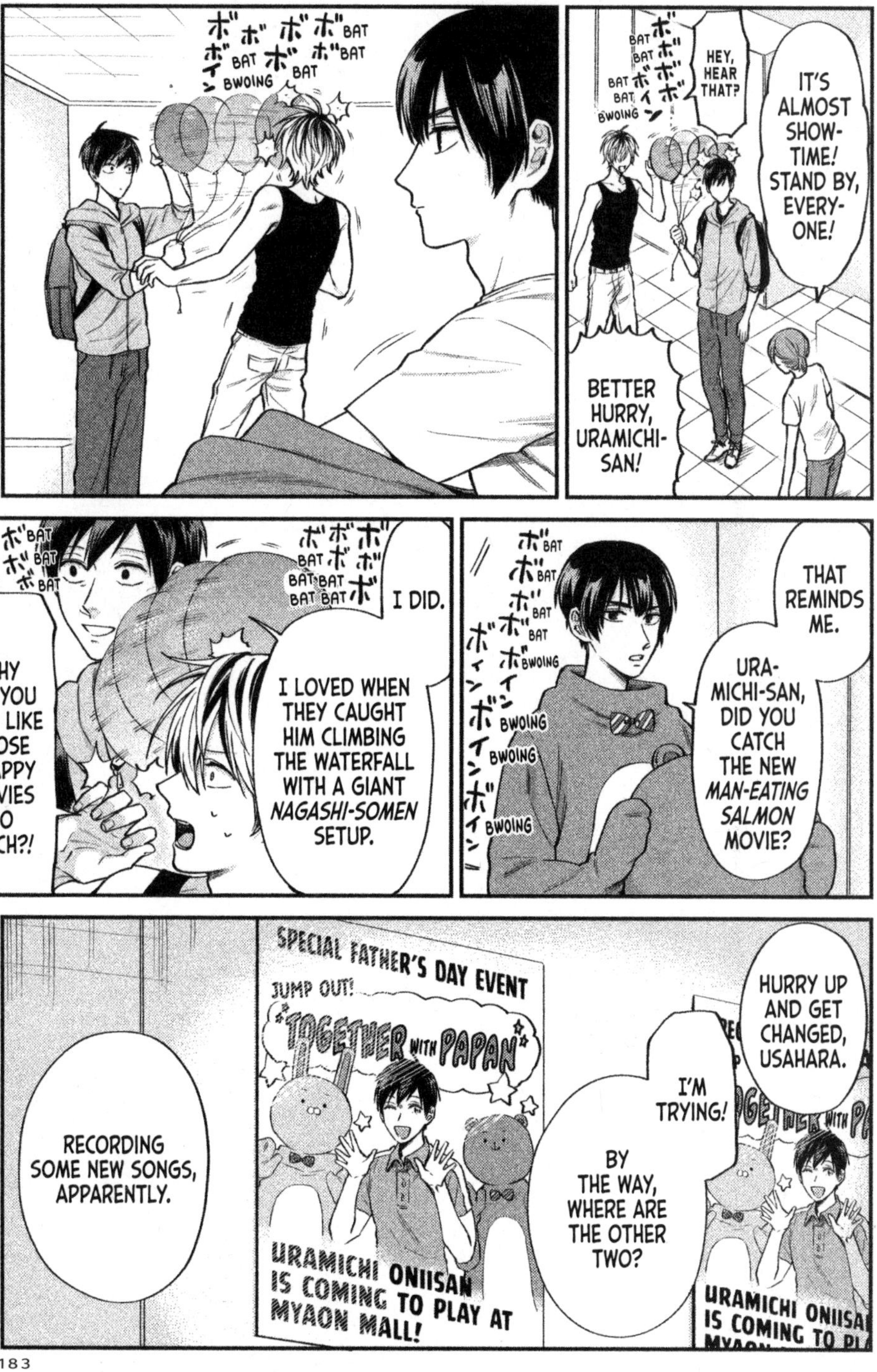

IT'S ALMOST SHOW-TIME! STAND BY, EVERY-ONE!
HEY, HEAR THAT?
BAT BAT BAT BAT BWOING
BETTER HURRY, URAMICHI-SAN!
BAT BAT BAT BAT BAT BWOING
THAT REMINDS ME.
URA-MICHI-SAN, DID YOU CATCH THE NEW *MAN-EATING SALMON* MOVIE?
BAT BAT BAT BAT BWOING BWOING BWOING BWOING
I DID.
BAT BAT BAT BAT BAT BAT
I LOVED WHEN THEY CAUGHT HIM CLIMBING THE WATERFALL WITH A GIANT *NAGASHI-SOMEN* SETUP.
BAT BAT BAT BWOING
WHY DO YOU TWO LIKE THOSE CRAPPY MOVIES SO MUCH?!
HURRY UP AND GET CHANGED, USAHARA.
I'M TRYING!
BY THE WAY, WHERE ARE THE OTHER TWO?
SPECIAL FATHER'S DAY EVENT
JUMP OUT! "TOGETHER WITH PAPAN"
URAMICHI ONIISAN IS COMING TO PLAY AT MYAON MALL!
RECORDING SOME NEW SONGS, APPARENTLY.

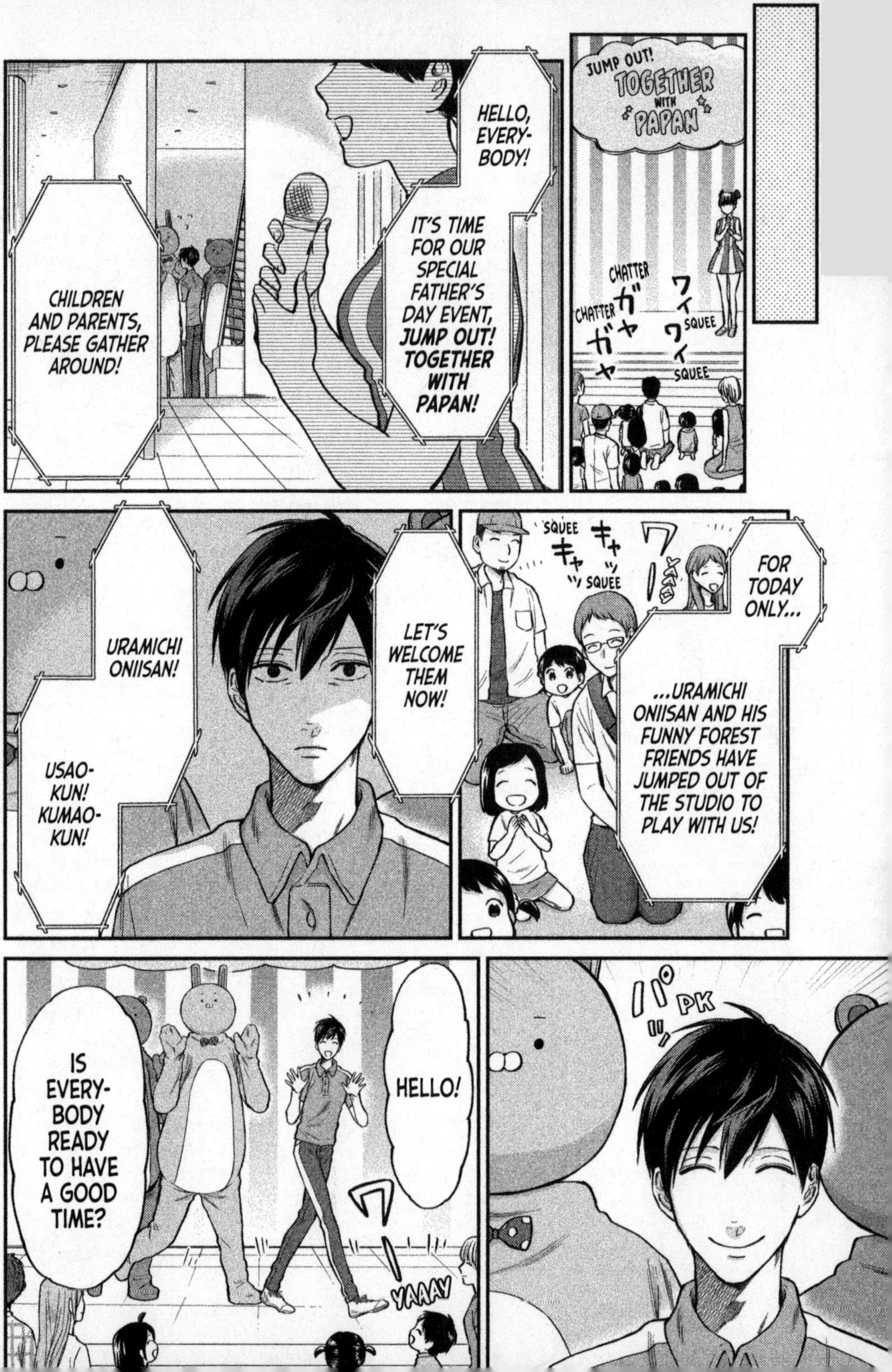
JUMP OUT! TOGETHER WITH PAPAN
ワイワイ SQUEE SQUEE
ガヤガヤ CHATTER CHATTER
HELLO, EVERY-BODY!
IT'S TIME FOR OUR SPECIAL FATHER'S DAY EVENT, JUMP OUT! TOGETHER WITH PAPAN!
CHILDREN AND PARENTS, PLEASE GATHER AROUND!
ワー
キャッキャッ SQUEE SQUEE
FOR TODAY ONLY...
...URAMICHI ONIISAN AND HIS FUNNY FOREST FRIENDS HAVE JUMPED OUT OF THE STUDIO TO PLAY WITH US!
LET'S WELCOME THEM NOW!
URAMICHI ONIISAN!
USAO-KUN! KUMAO-KUN!
パッ PK
HELLO!
IS EVERY-BODY READY TO HAVE A GOOD TIME?
ワー YAAAY

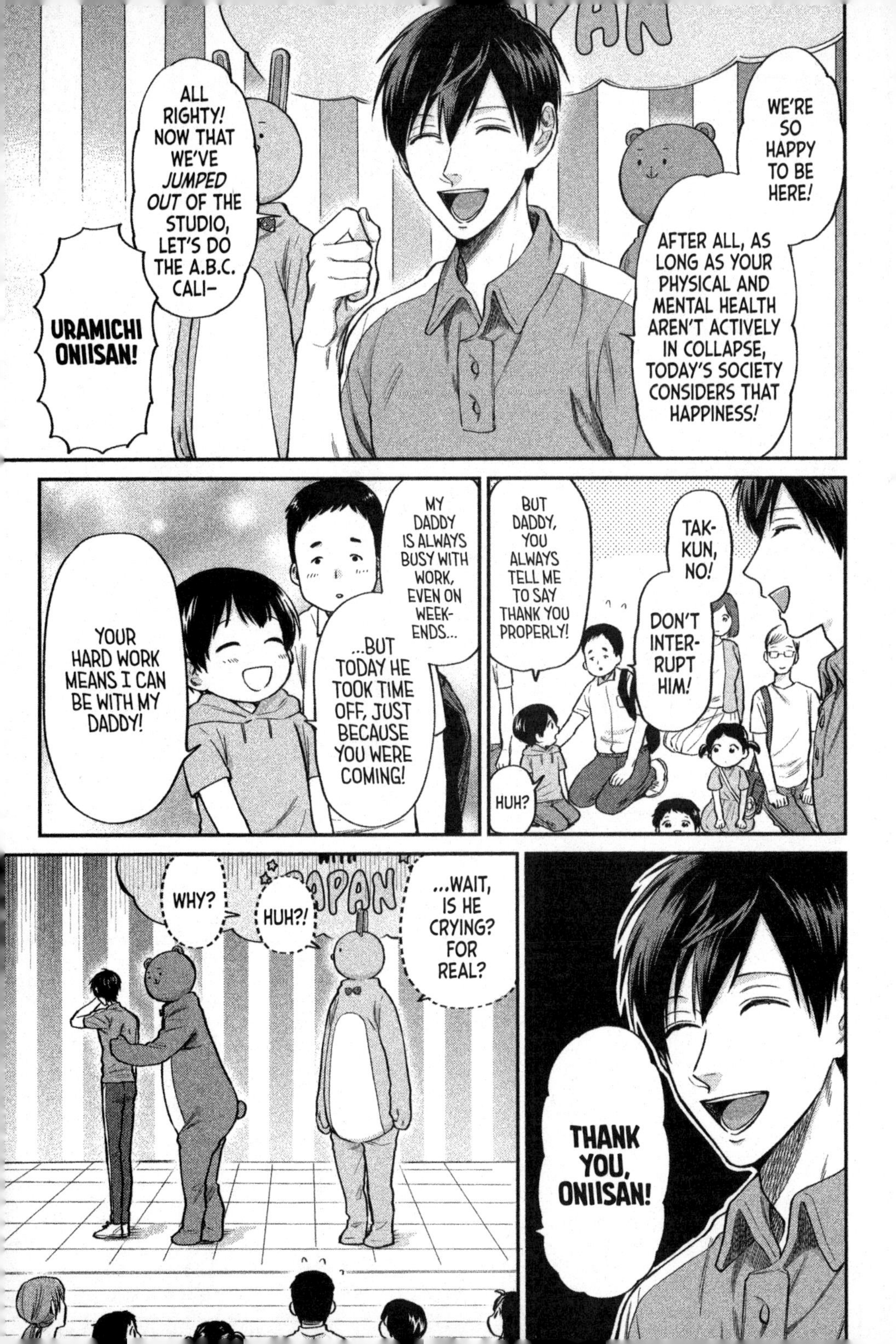
WE'RE SO HAPPY TO BE HERE!
AFTER ALL, AS LONG AS YOUR PHYSICAL AND MENTAL HEALTH AREN'T ACTIVELY IN COLLAPSE, TODAY'S SOCIETY CONSIDERS THAT HAPPINESS!
ALL RIGHTY! NOW THAT WE'VE *JUMPED OUT* OF THE STUDIO, LET'S DO THE A.B.C. CALI–
URAMICHI ONIISAN!
TAK-KUN, NO!
DON'T INTERRUPT HIM!
BUT DADDY, YOU ALWAYS TELL ME TO SAY THANK YOU PROPERLY!
HUH?
MY DADDY IS ALWAYS BUSY WITH WORK, EVEN ON WEEKENDS...
...BUT TODAY HE TOOK TIME OFF, JUST BECAUSE YOU WERE COMING!
YOUR HARD WORK MEANS I CAN BE WITH MY DADDY!
THANK YOU, ONIISAN!
...WAIT, IS HE CRYING? FOR REAL?
HUH?!
WHY?

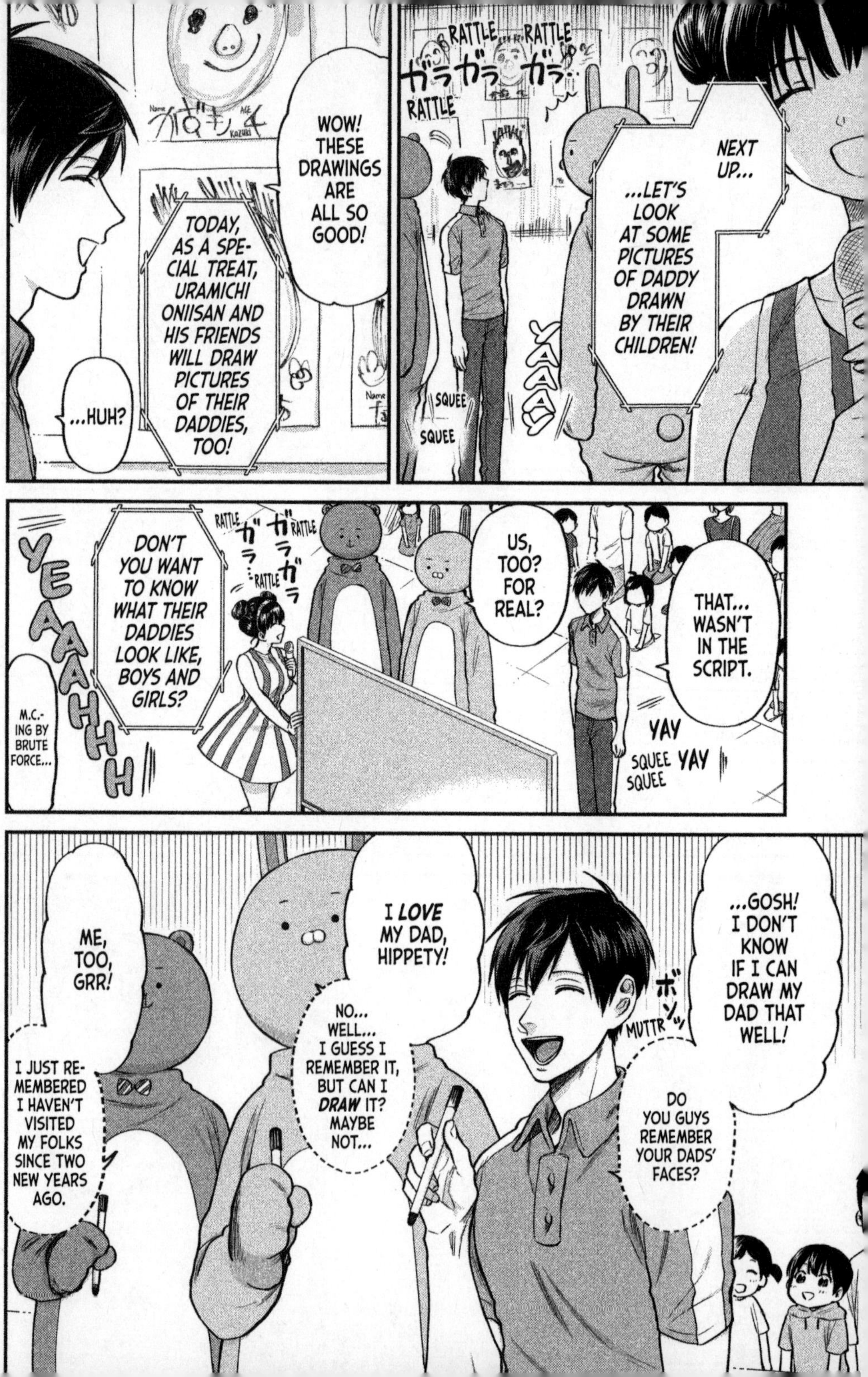
RATTLE RATTLE
ガラガラガラ
RATTLE
NEXT UP...
...LET'S LOOK AT SOME PICTURES OF DADDY DRAWN BY THEIR CHILDREN!
YAAAY
SQUEE
SQUEE
WOW! THESE DRAWINGS ARE ALL SO GOOD!
TODAY, AS A SPE-CIAL TREAT, URAMICHI ONIISAN AND HIS FRIENDS WILL DRAW PICTURES OF THEIR DADDIES, TOO!
...HUH?
THAT... WASN'T IN THE SCRIPT.
YAY YAY
SQUEE SQUEE
US, TOO? FOR REAL?
RATTLE RATTLE
ガラガラガラ
RATTLE
DON'T YOU WANT TO KNOW WHAT THEIR DADDIES LOOK LIKE, BOYS AND GIRLS?
YEAAAAHHH
M.C.-ING BY BRUTE FORCE...
...GOSH! I DON'T KNOW IF I CAN DRAW MY DAD THAT WELL!
ボソッ
MUTTR
DO YOU GUYS REMEMBER YOUR DADS' FACES?
I *LOVE* MY DAD, HIPPETY!
NO... WELL... I GUESS I REMEMBER IT, BUT CAN I *DRAW* IT? MAYBE NOT...
ME, TOO, GRR!
I JUST RE-MEMBERED I HAVEN'T VISITED MY FOLKS SINCE TWO NEW YEARS AGO.

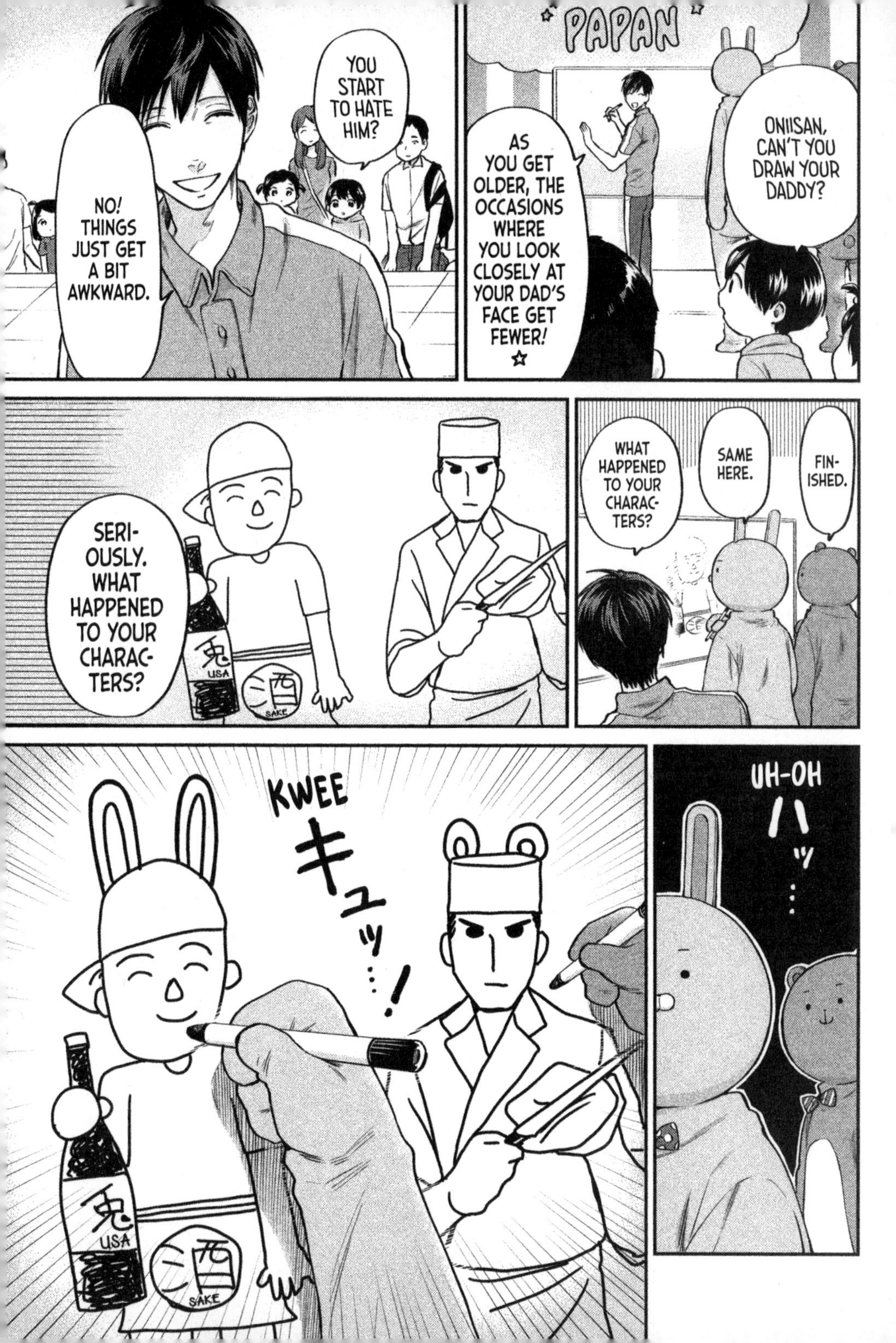
PAPAN
ONIISAN, CAN'T YOU DRAW YOUR DADDY?
AS YOU GET OLDER, THE OCCASIONS WHERE YOU LOOK CLOSELY AT YOUR DAD'S FACE GET FEWER! ☆
YOU START TO HATE HIM?
NO! THINGS JUST GET A BIT AWKWARD.
FIN-ISHED.
SAME HERE.
WHAT HAPPENED TO YOUR CHARAC-TERS?
SERI-OUSLY. WHAT HAPPENED TO YOUR CHARAC-TERS?
兎
USA
酒
SAKE
UH-OH
ハッ…
KWEE
キュッ…!
兎
USA
酒
SAKE

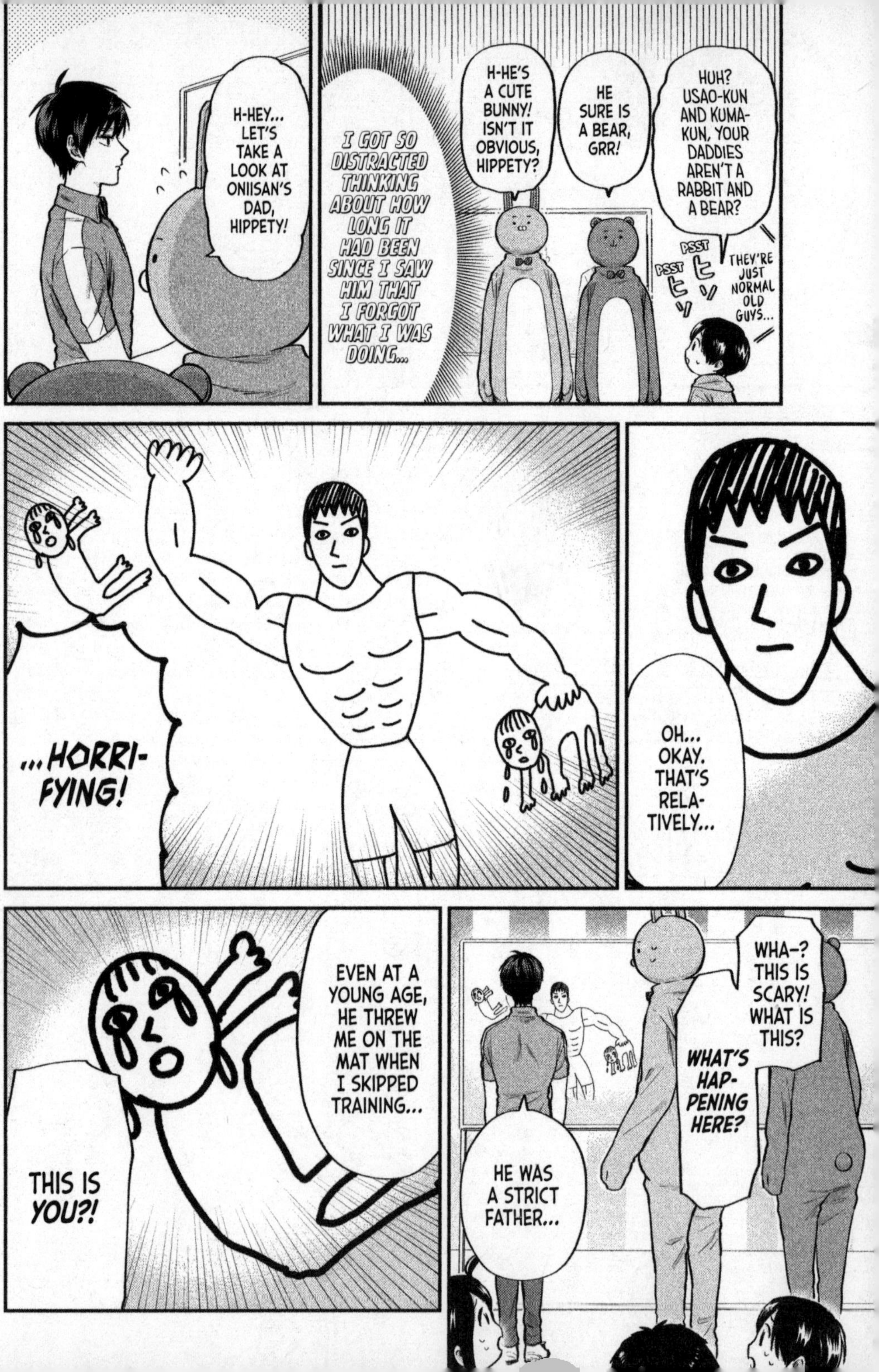
HUH? USAO-KUN AND KUMA-KUN, YOUR DADDIES AREN'T A RABBIT AND A BEAR?
PSST ヒソ
PSST ヒソ
THEY'RE JUST NORMAL OLD GUYS...
HE SURE IS A BEAR, GRR!
H-HE'S A CUTE BUNNY! ISN'T IT OBVIOUS, HIPPETY?
I GOT SO DISTRACTED THINKING ABOUT HOW LONG IT HAD BEEN SINCE I SAW HIM THAT I FORGOT WHAT I WAS DOING...
H-HEY... LET'S TAKE A LOOK AT ONIISAN'S DAD, HIPPETY!
OH... OKAY. THAT'S RELATIVELY...
...HORRIFYING!
WHA-? THIS IS SCARY! WHAT IS THIS?
WHAT'S HAPPENING HERE?
HE WAS A STRICT FATHER...
EVEN AT A YOUNG AGE, HE THREW ME ON THE MAT WHEN I SKIPPED TRAINING...
THIS IS YOU?!

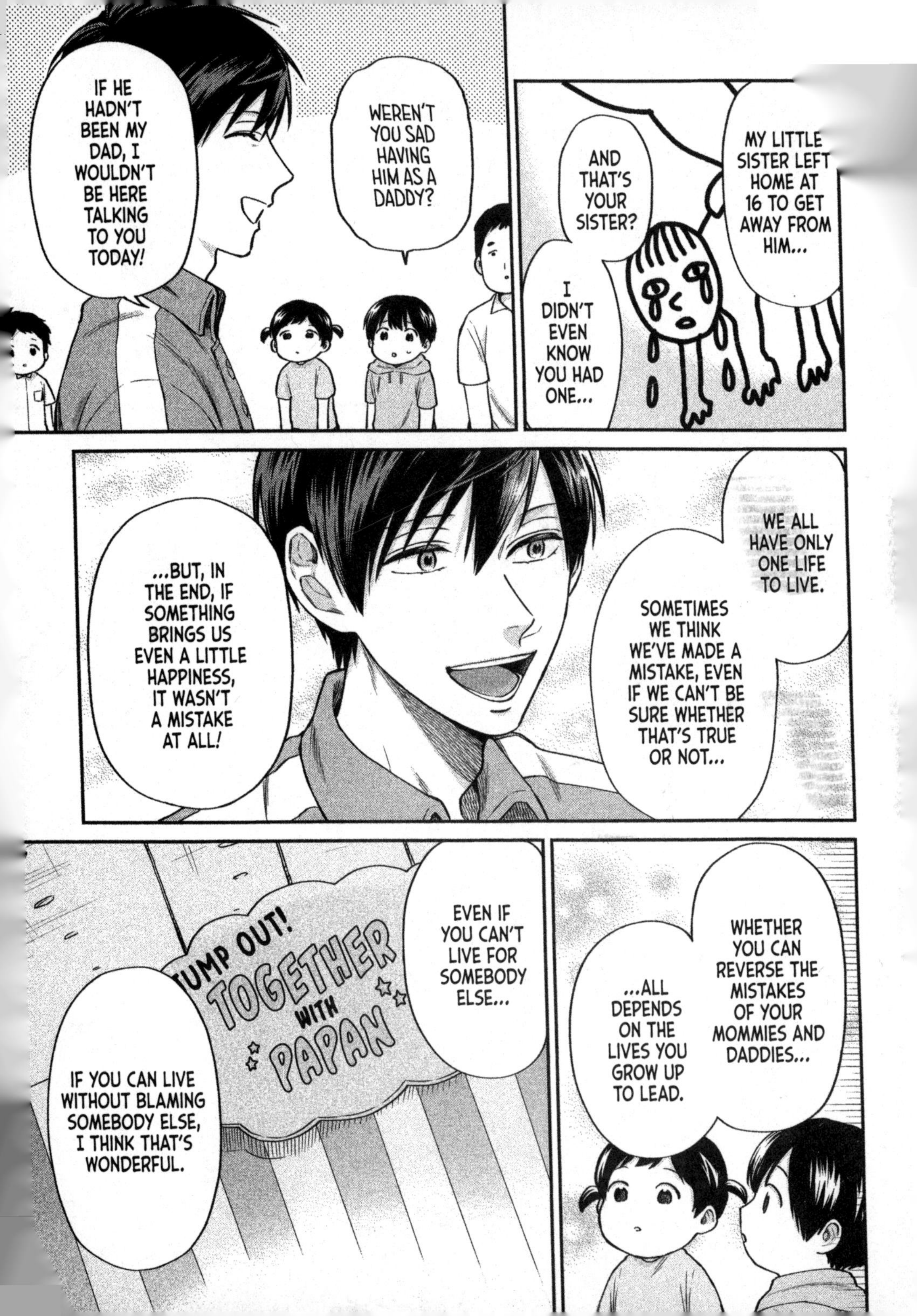
MY LITTLE SISTER LEFT HOME AT 16 TO GET AWAY FROM HIM...
AND THAT'S YOUR SISTER?
I DIDN'T EVEN KNOW YOU HAD ONE...
WEREN'T YOU SAD HAVING HIM AS A DADDY?
IF HE HADN'T BEEN MY DAD, I WOULDN'T BE HERE TALKING TO YOU TODAY!
WE ALL HAVE ONLY ONE LIFE TO LIVE.
SOMETIMES WE THINK WE'VE MADE A MISTAKE, EVEN IF WE CAN'T BE SURE WHETHER THAT'S TRUE OR NOT...
...BUT, IN THE END, IF SOMETHING BRINGS US EVEN A LITTLE HAPPINESS, IT WASN'T A MISTAKE AT ALL!
WHETHER YOU CAN REVERSE THE MISTAKES OF YOUR MOMMIES AND DADDIES...
...ALL DEPENDS ON THE LIVES YOU GROW UP TO LEAD.
EVEN IF YOU CAN'T LIVE FOR SOMEBODY ELSE...
JUMP OUT! TOGETHER WITH PAPAN
IF YOU CAN LIVE WITHOUT BLAMING SOMEBODY ELSE, I THINK THAT'S WONDERFUL.

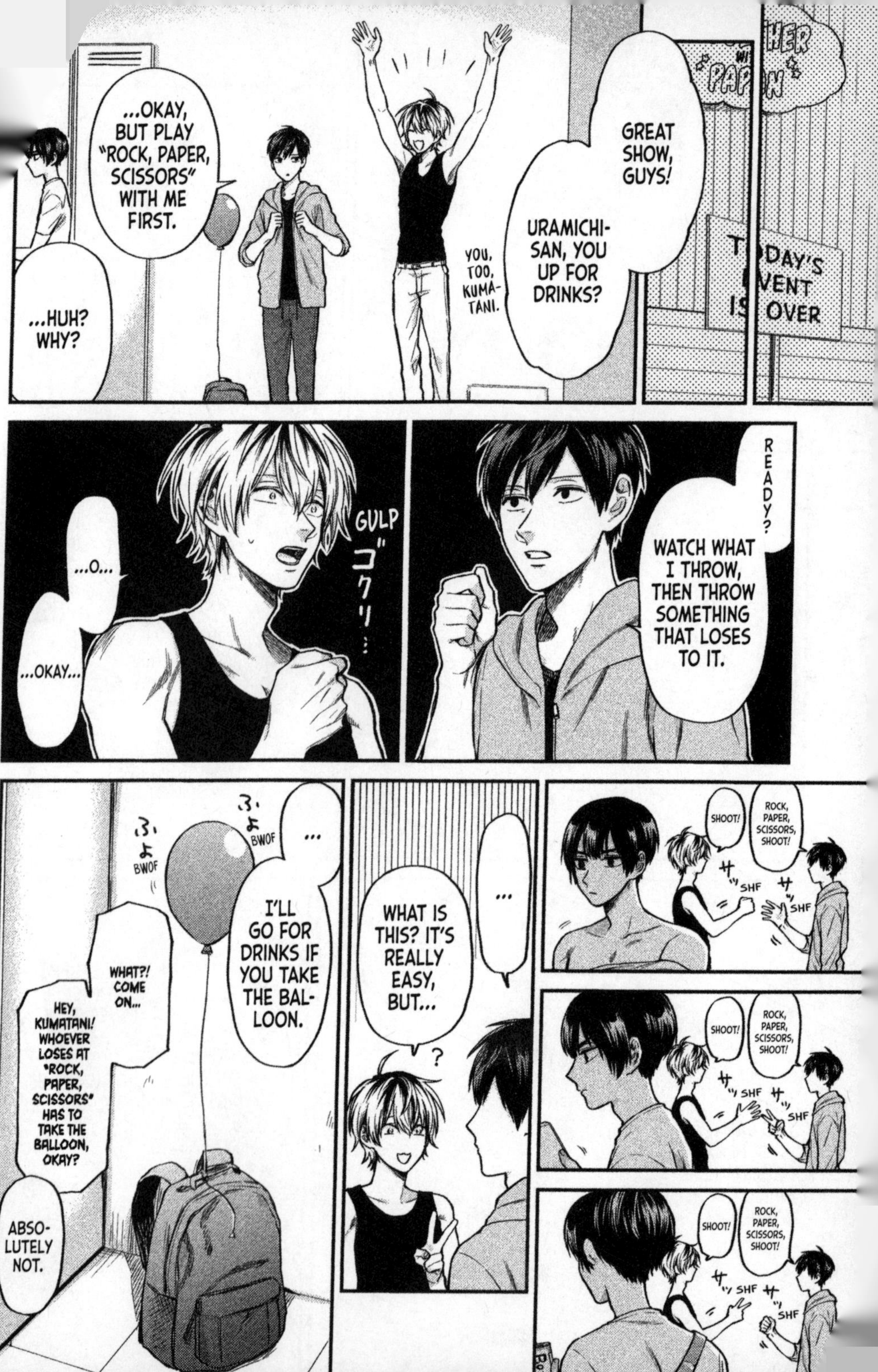
GREAT SHOW, GUYS!
URAMICHI-SAN, YOU UP FOR DRINKS?
YOU, TOO, KUMATANI.
...OKAY, BUT PLAY "ROCK, PAPER, SCISSORS" WITH ME FIRST.
...HUH? WHY?
READY?
WATCH WHAT I THROW, THEN THROW SOMETHING THAT LOSES TO IT.
ゴクリ GULP
...O...
...OKAY...
ROCK, PAPER, SCISSORS, SHOOT!
SHOOT!
サッ SHF
サッ SHF
ROCK, PAPER, SCISSORS, SHOOT!
SHOOT!
サッ SHF
サッ SHF
ROCK, PAPER, SCISSORS, SHOOT!
SHOOT!
サッ SHF
サッ SHF
...
WHAT IS THIS? IT'S REALLY EASY, BUT...
?
...
ふよ BWOF
ふよ BWOF
I'LL GO FOR DRINKS IF YOU TAKE THE BALLOON.
WHAT?! COME ON...
HEY, KUMATANI! WHOEVER LOSES AT "ROCK, PAPER, SCISSORS" HAS TO TAKE THE BALLOON, OKAY?
ABSOLUTELY NOT.

Life Lessons with
Uramichi Oniisan

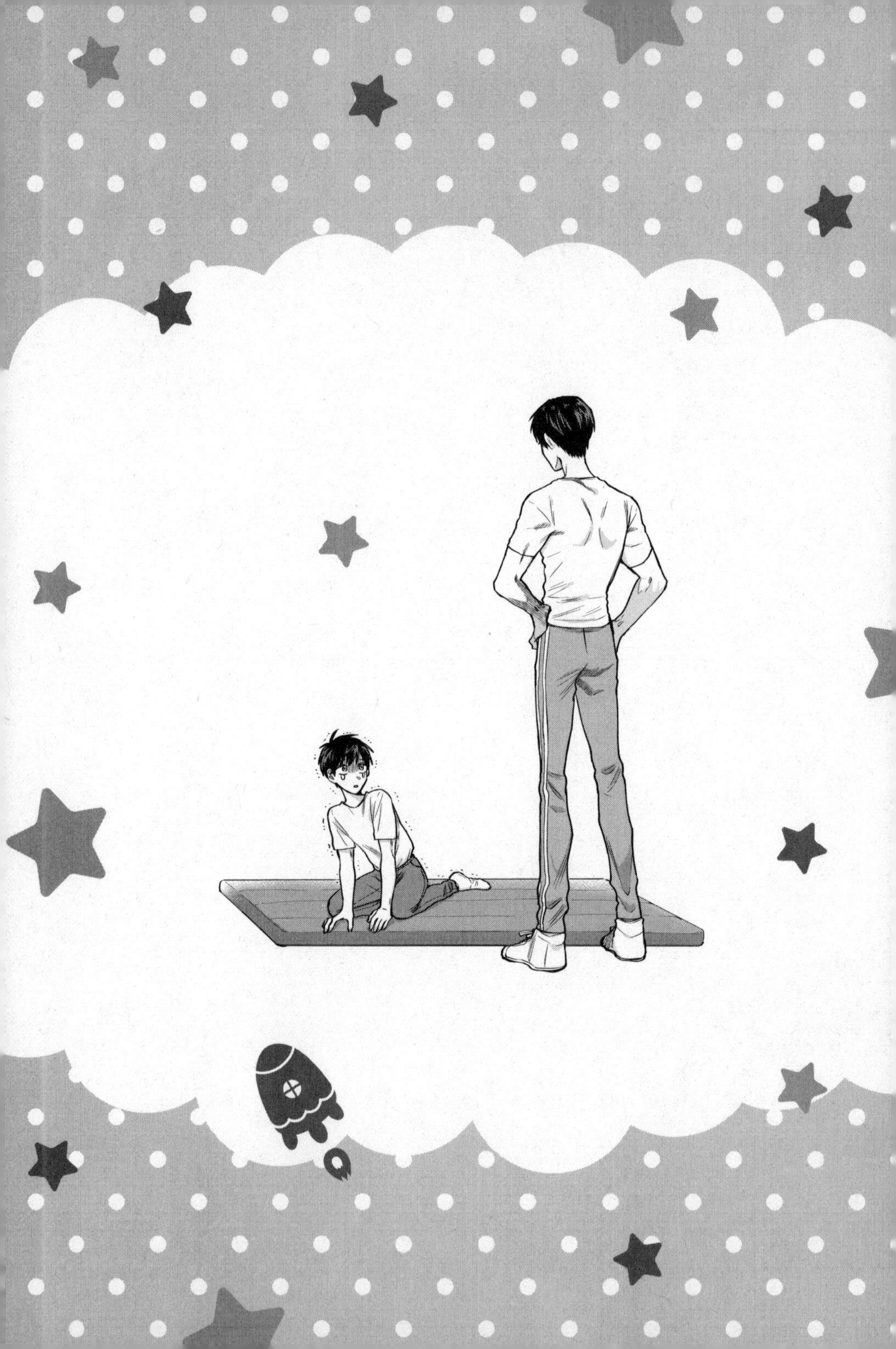

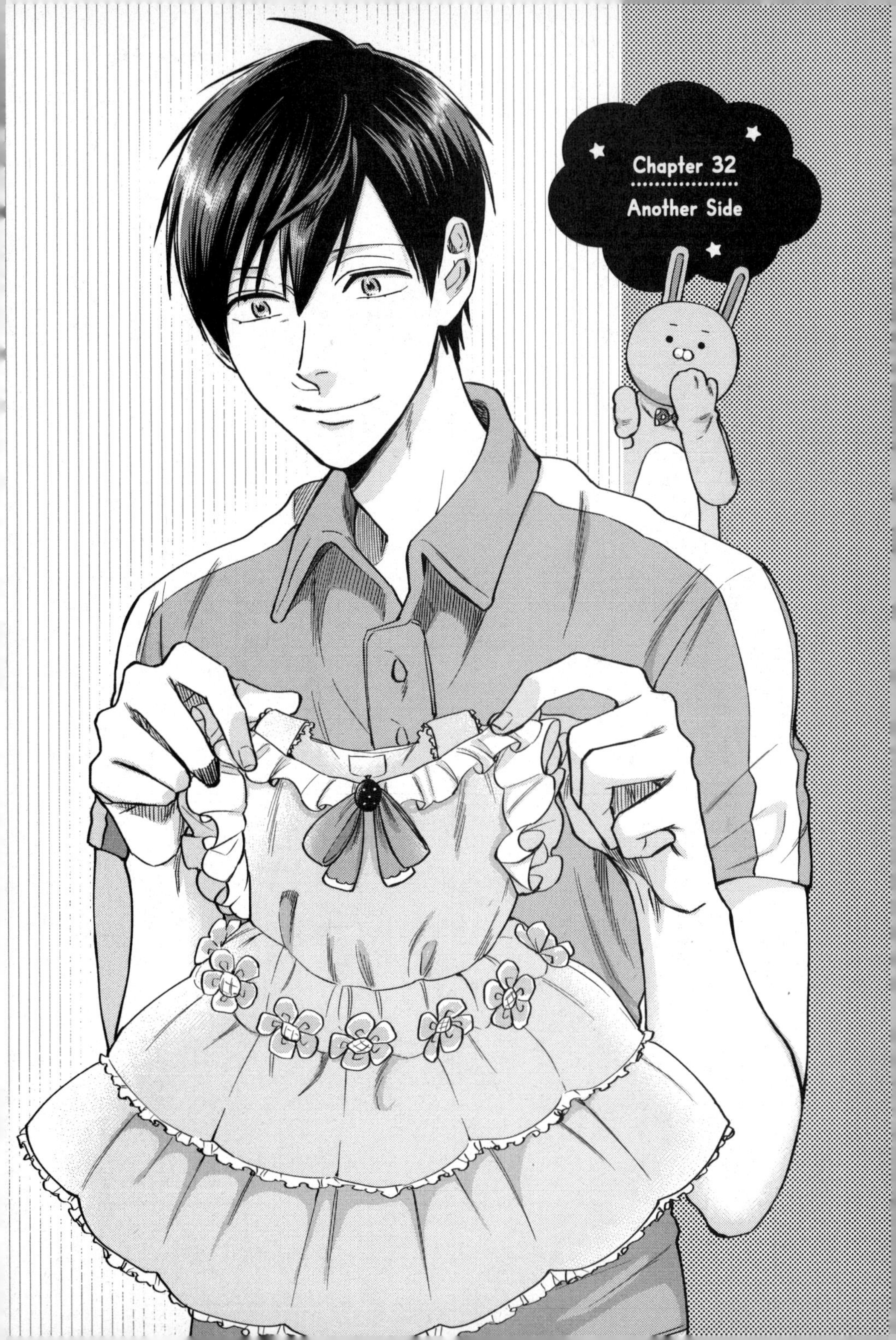
Chapter 32
Another Side

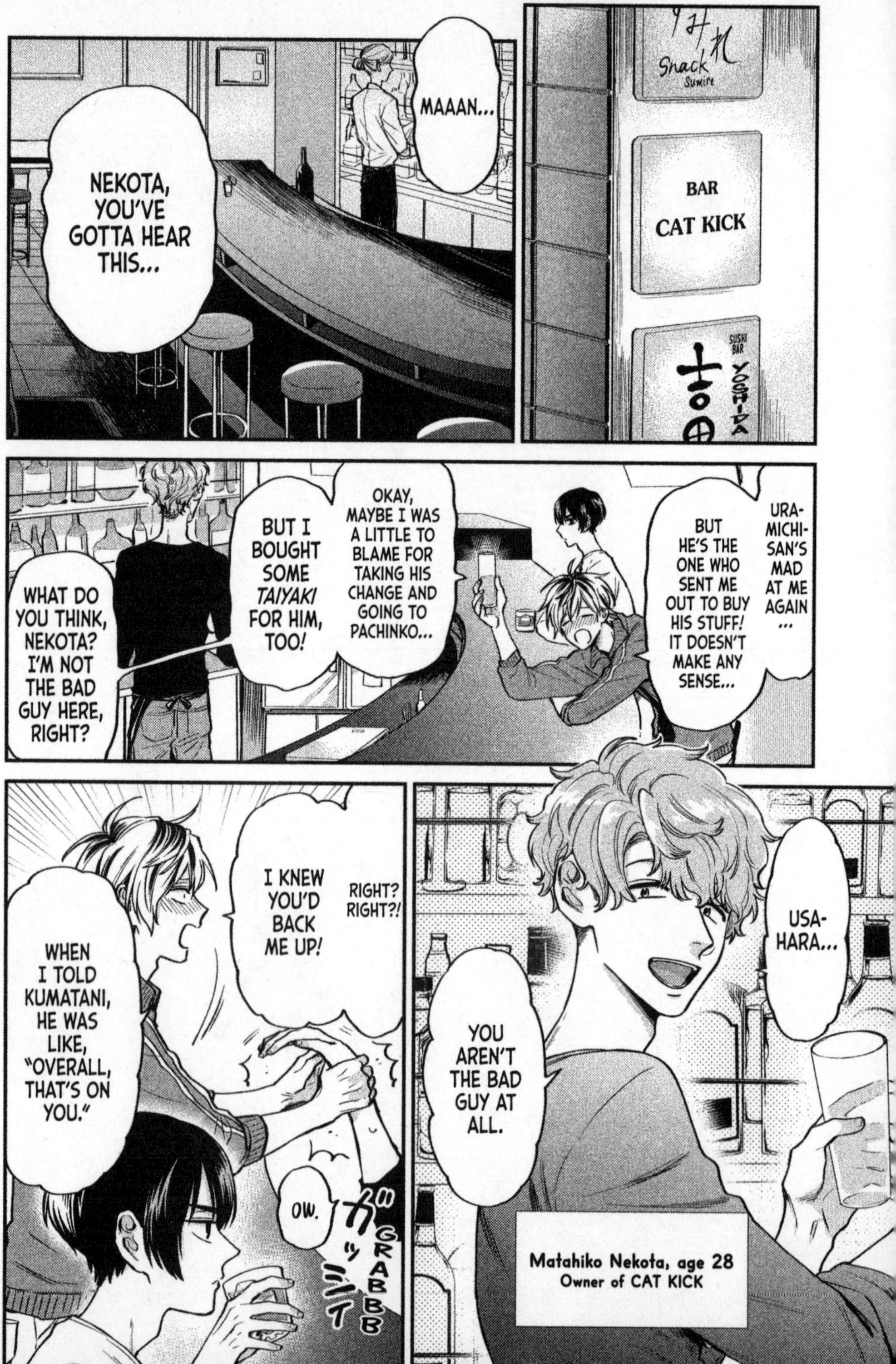
Snack
Sumire
BAR
CAT KICK
SUSHI BAR
YOSHIDA
MAAAN...
NEKOTA, YOU'VE GOTTA HEAR THIS...
URA-MICHI-SAN'S MAD AT ME AGAIN...
BUT HE'S THE ONE WHO SENT ME OUT TO BUY HIS STUFF! IT DOESN'T MAKE ANY SENSE...
OKAY, MAYBE I WAS A LITTLE TO BLAME FOR TAKING HIS CHANGE AND GOING TO PACHINKO...
BUT I BOUGHT SOME *TAIYAKI* FOR HIM, TOO!
WHAT DO YOU THINK, NEKOTA? I'M NOT THE BAD GUY HERE, RIGHT?
USA-HARA...
YOU AREN'T THE BAD GUY AT ALL.
Matahiko Nekota, age 28
Owner of CAT KICK
RIGHT? RIGHT?!
I KNEW YOU'D BACK ME UP!
WHEN I TOLD KUMATANI, HE WAS LIKE, "OVERALL, THAT'S ON YOU."
OW.
GRABBB

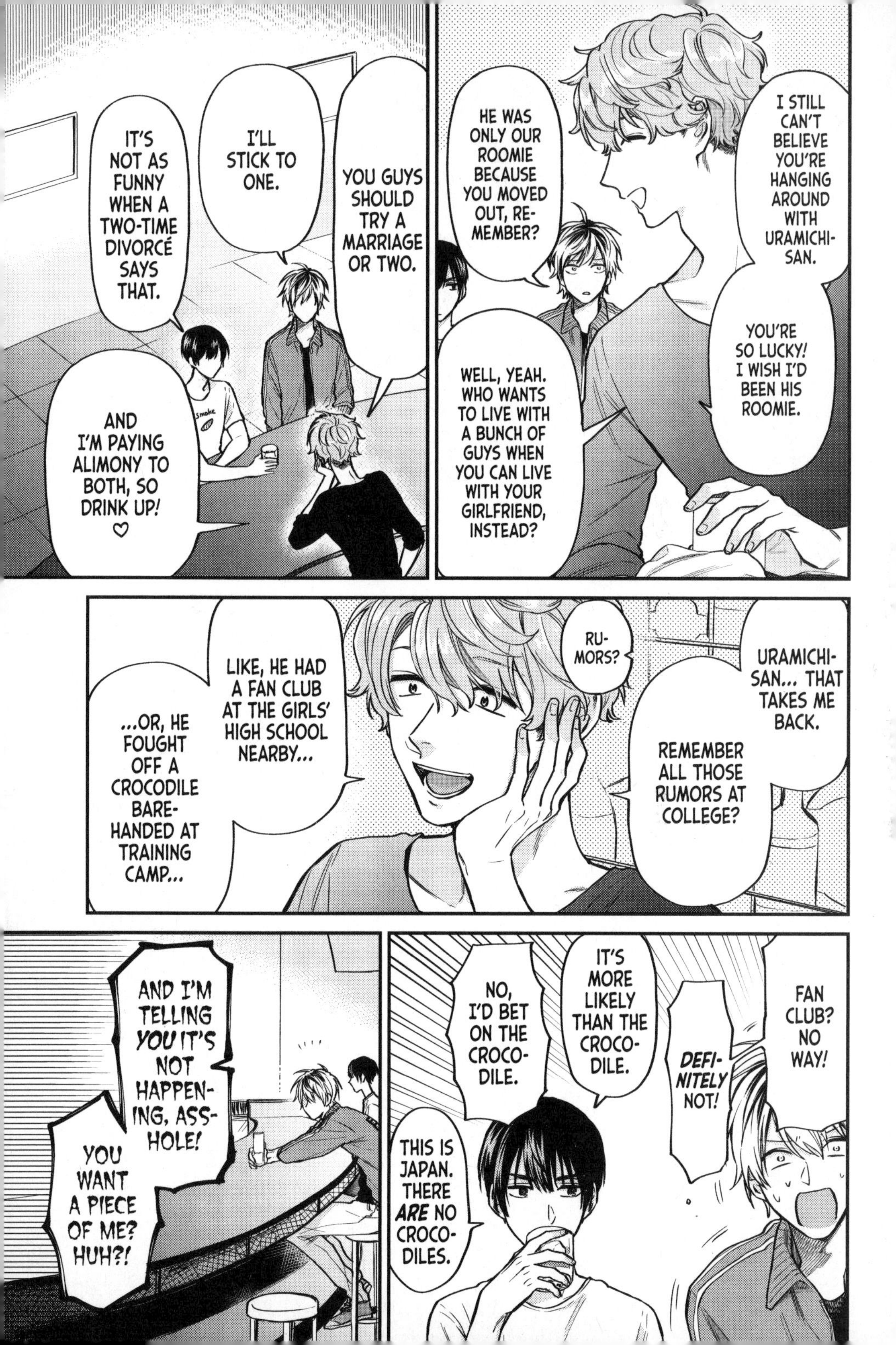
I STILL CAN'T BELIEVE YOU'RE HANGING AROUND WITH URAMICHI-SAN.
YOU'RE SO LUCKY! I WISH I'D BEEN HIS ROOMIE.
HE WAS ONLY OUR ROOMIE BECAUSE YOU MOVED OUT, REMEMBER?
WELL, YEAH. WHO WANTS TO LIVE WITH A BUNCH OF GUYS WHEN YOU CAN LIVE WITH YOUR GIRLFRIEND, INSTEAD?
YOU GUYS SHOULD TRY A MARRIAGE OR TWO.
I'LL STICK TO ONE.
IT'S NOT AS FUNNY WHEN A TWO-TIME DIVORCÉ SAYS THAT.
AND I'M PAYING ALIMONY TO BOTH, SO DRINK UP! ♡
URAMICHI-SAN... THAT TAKES ME BACK.
REMEMBER ALL THOSE RUMORS AT COLLEGE?
RUMORS?
LIKE, HE HAD A FAN CLUB AT THE GIRLS' HIGH SCHOOL NEARBY...
...OR, HE FOUGHT OFF A CROCODILE BAREHANDED AT TRAINING CAMP...
FAN CLUB? NO WAY!
DEFINITELY NOT!
IT'S MORE LIKELY THAN THE CROCODILE.
NO, I'D BET ON THE CROCODILE.
THIS IS JAPAN. THERE *ARE* NO CROCODILES.
AND I'M TELLING *YOU* IT'S NOT HAPPENING, ASSHOLE!
YOU WANT A PIECE OF ME? HUH?!

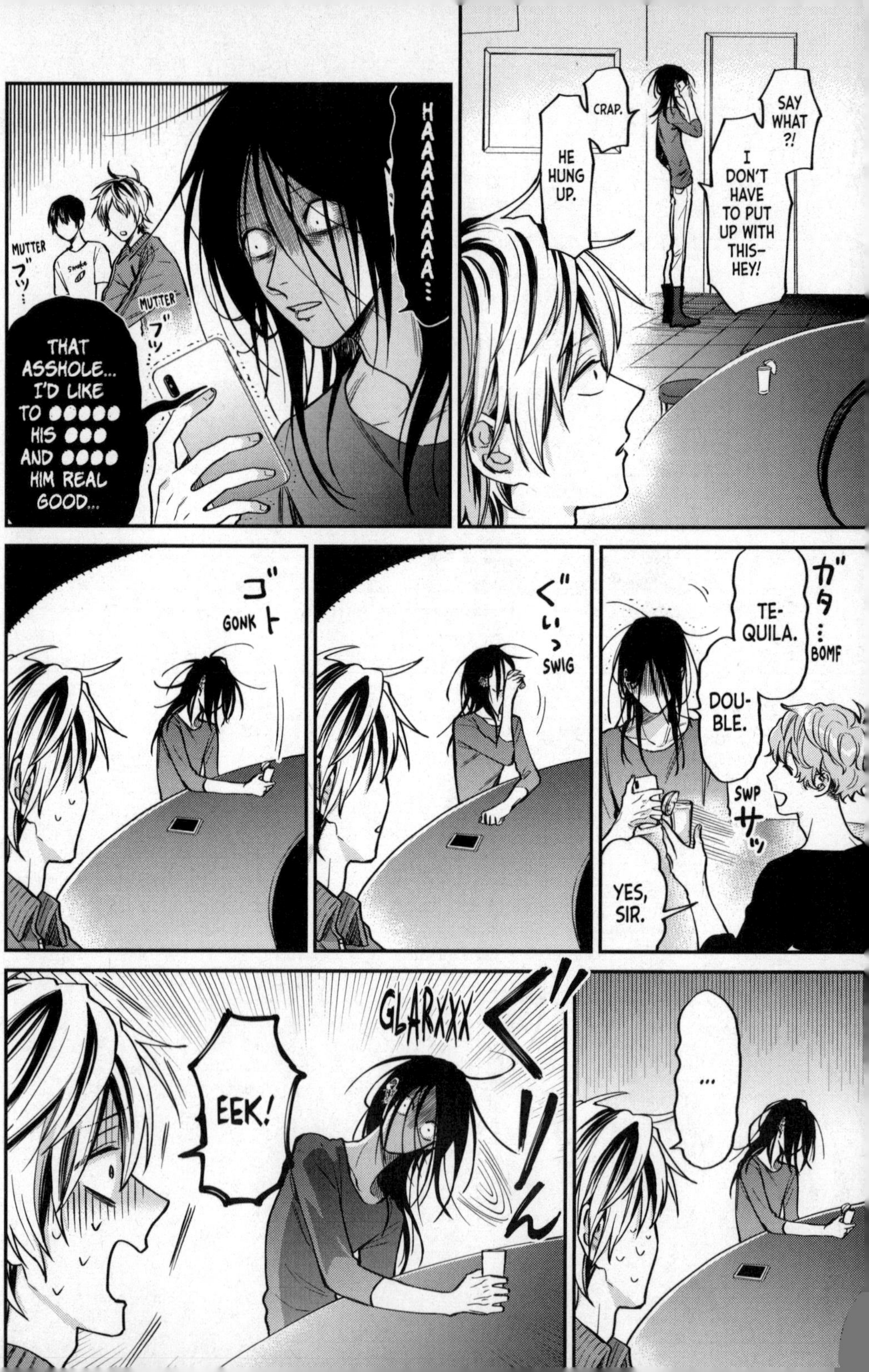
SAY WHAT?!
I DON'T HAVE TO PUT UP WITH THIS—HEY!
CRAP.
HE HUNG UP.
HAAAAAAAAAA...
MUTTER
MUTTER
THAT ASSHOLE... I'D LIKE TO ●●●●● HIS ●●● AND ●●●● HIM REAL GOOD...
ガタ…
BOMF
TEQUILA.
DOUBLE.
SWP
サッ
YES, SIR.
ぐいっ
SWIG
ゴト
GONK
...
GLARXXX
ぐりん
EEK!

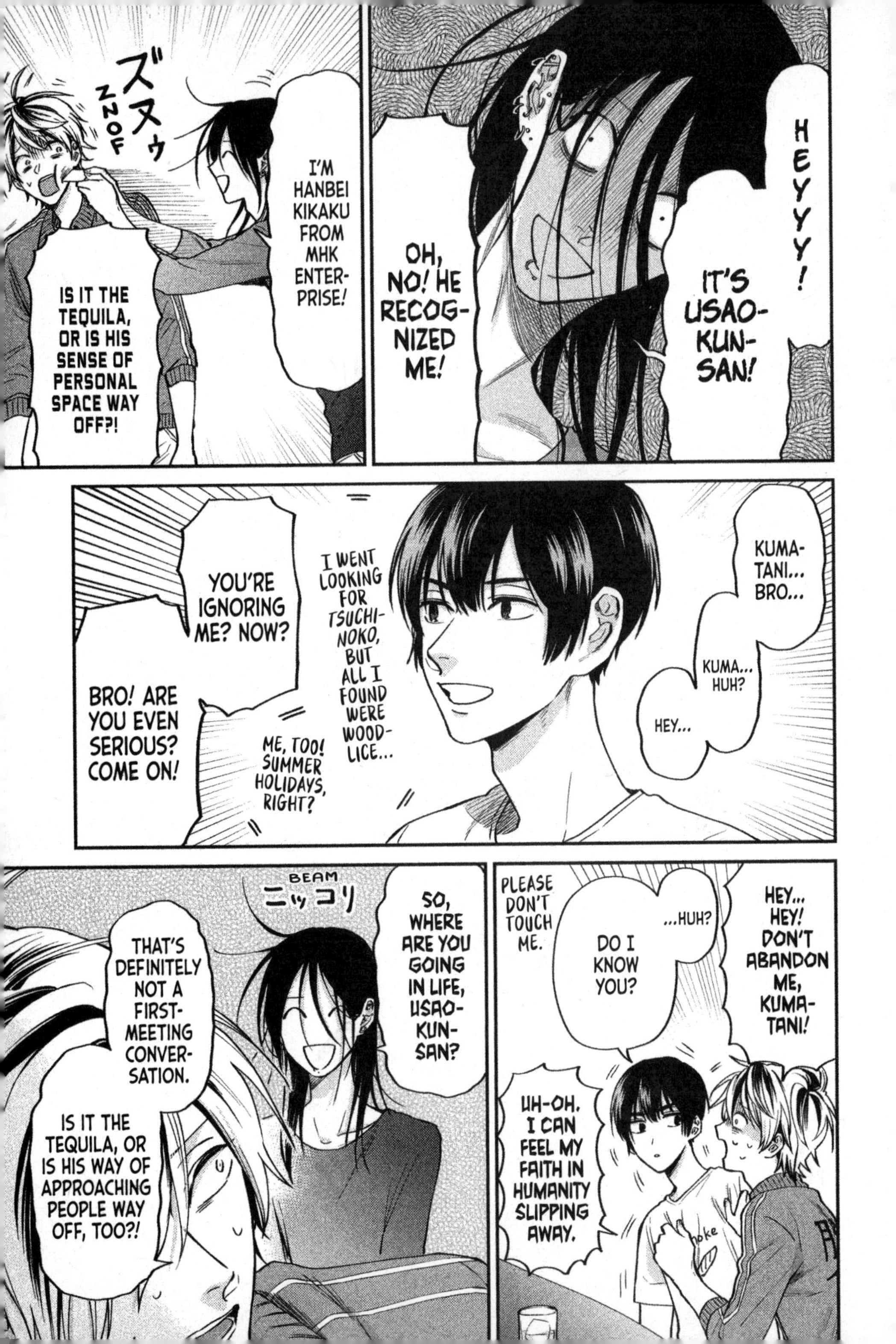
HEYYYY!
IT'S USAO-KUN-SAN!
OH, NO! HE RECOGNIZED ME!
ズヌゥ
ZNOF
I'M HANBEI KIKAKU FROM MHK ENTERPRISE!
IS IT THE TEQUILA, OR IS HIS SENSE OF PERSONAL SPACE WAY OFF?!
KUMATANI... BRO...
KUMA... HUH?
HEY...
I WENT LOOKING FOR TSUCHINOKO, BUT ALL I FOUND WERE WOODLICE...
ME, TOO! SUMMER HOLIDAYS, RIGHT?
YOU'RE IGNORING ME? NOW?
BRO! ARE YOU EVEN SERIOUS? COME ON!
HEY... HEY! DON'T ABANDON ME, KUMATANI!
...HUH?
PLEASE DON'T TOUCH ME.
DO I KNOW YOU?
UH-OH. I CAN FEEL MY FAITH IN HUMANITY SLIPPING AWAY.
SO, WHERE ARE YOU GOING IN LIFE, USAO-KUN-SAN?
ニッコリ
BEAM
THAT'S DEFINITELY NOT A FIRST-MEETING CONVERSATION.
IS IT THE TEQUILA, OR IS HIS WAY OF APPROACHING PEOPLE WAY OFF, TOO?!

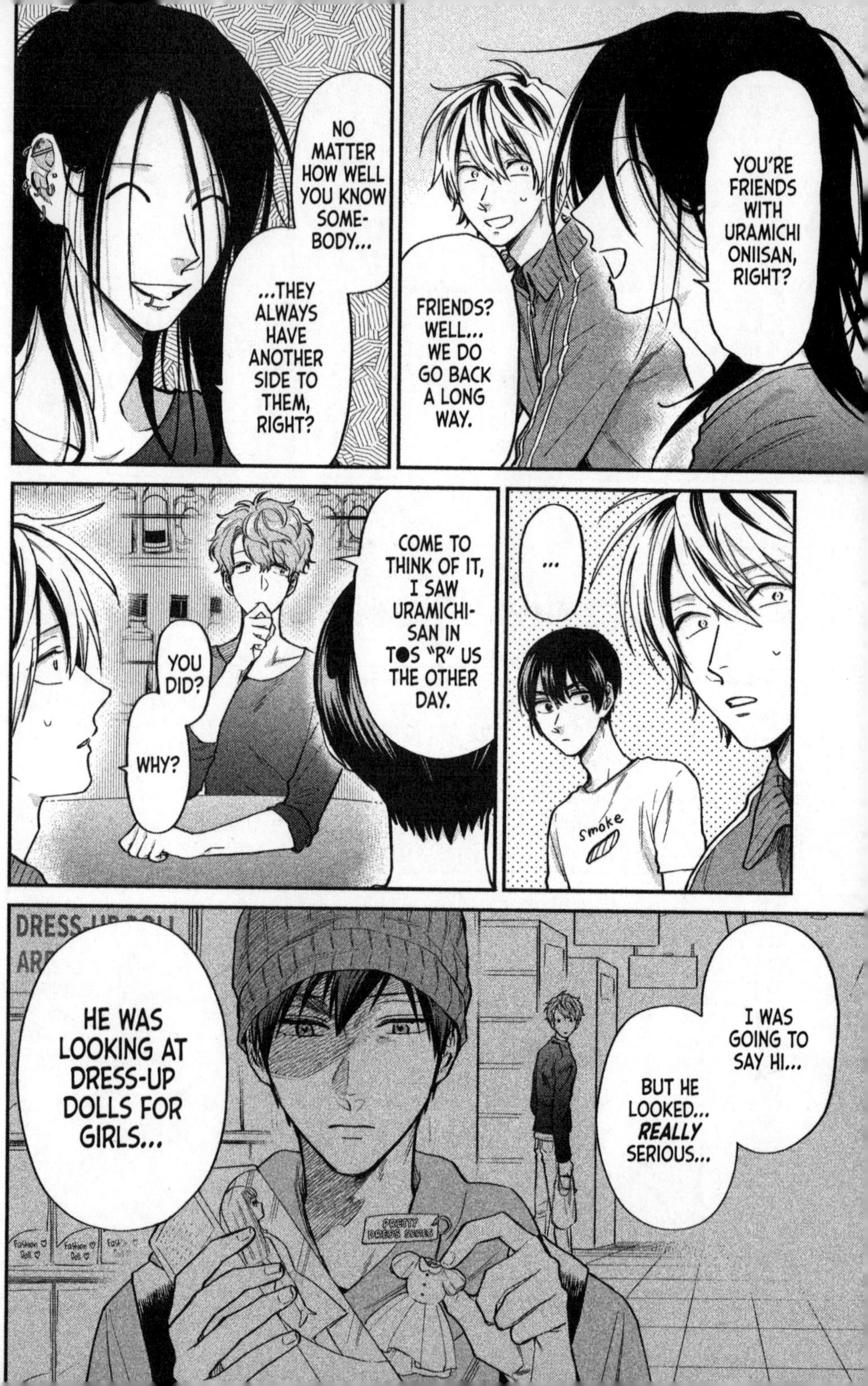
YOU'RE FRIENDS WITH URAMICHI ONIISAN, RIGHT?
FRIENDS? WELL... WE DO GO BACK A LONG WAY.
NO MATTER HOW WELL YOU KNOW SOME-BODY...
...THEY ALWAYS HAVE ANOTHER SIDE TO THEM, RIGHT?
...
smoke
COME TO THINK OF IT, I SAW URAMICHI-SAN IN T●S "R" US THE OTHER DAY.
YOU DID?
WHY?
I WAS GOING TO SAY HI...
BUT HE LOOKED... *REALLY* SERIOUS...
HE WAS LOOKING AT DRESS-UP DOLLS FOR GIRLS...
PRETTY DRESS SERIES

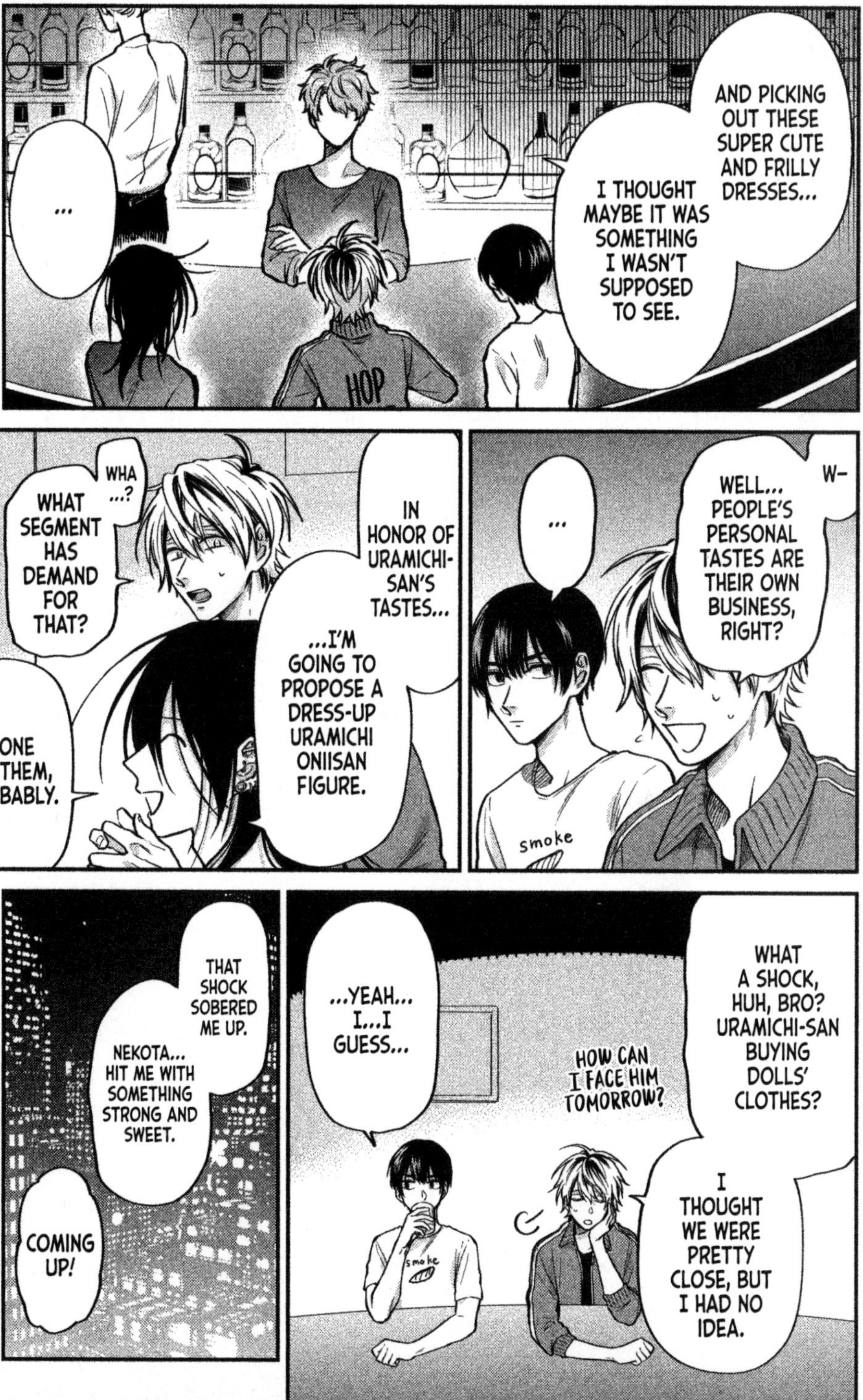
AND PICKING OUT THESE SUPER CUTE AND FRILLY DRESSES...
I THOUGHT MAYBE IT WAS SOMETHING I WASN'T SUPPOSED TO SEE.
...
W–
WELL... PEOPLE'S PERSONAL TASTES ARE THEIR OWN BUSINESS, RIGHT?
...
IN HONOR OF URAMICHI-SAN'S TASTES...
...I'M GOING TO PROPOSE A DRESS-UP URAMICHI ONIISAN FIGURE.
WHA ...?
WHAT SEGMENT HAS DEMAND FOR THAT?
NONE OF THEM, PROBABLY.
WHAT A SHOCK, HUH, BRO? URAMICHI-SAN BUYING DOLLS' CLOTHES?
I THOUGHT WE WERE PRETTY CLOSE, BUT I HAD NO IDEA.
HOW CAN I FACE HIM TOMORROW?
...YEAH... I...I GUESS...
THAT SHOCK SOBERED ME UP.
NEKOTA... HIT ME WITH SOMETHING STRONG AND SWEET.
COMING UP!

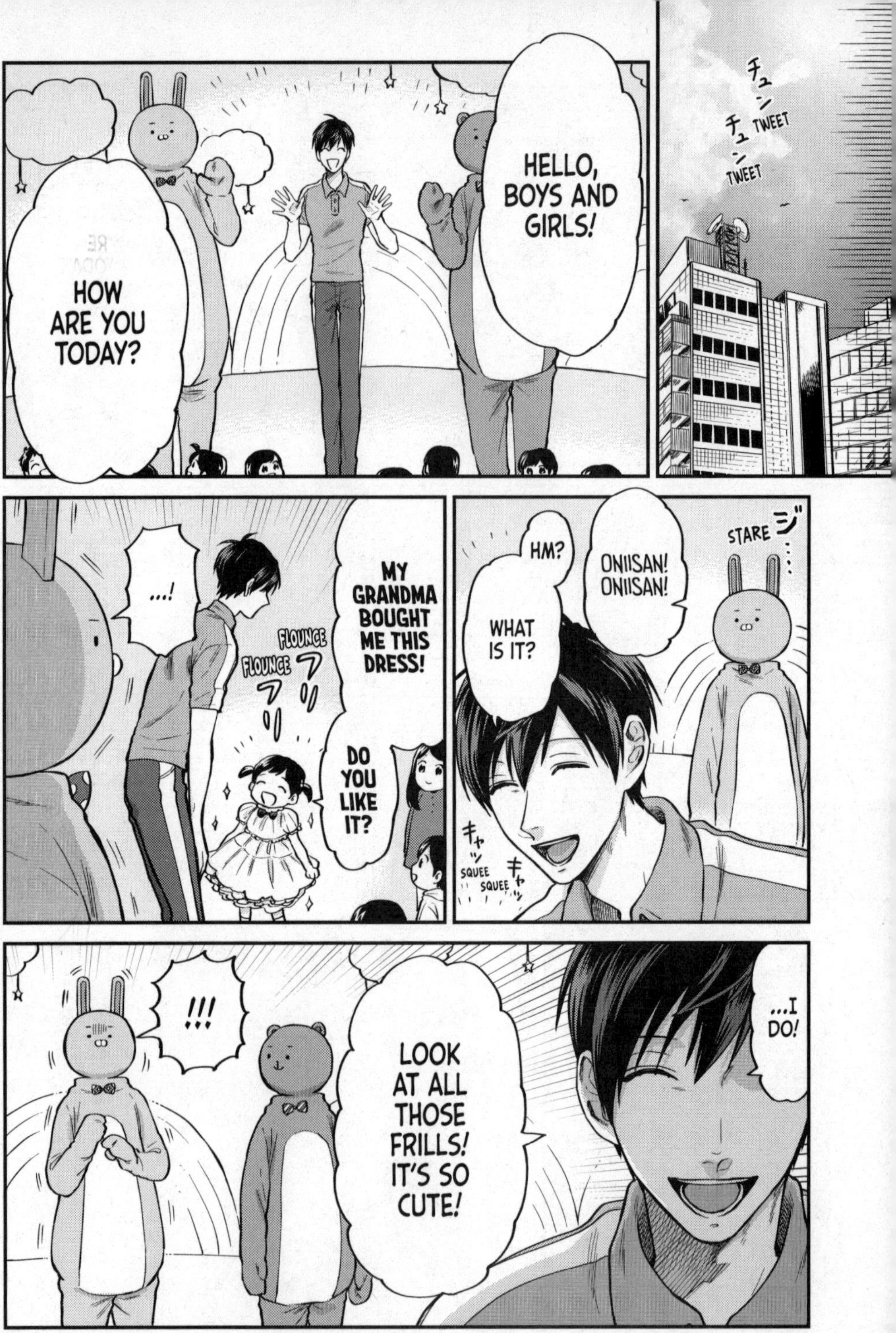
チュン TWEET
チュン TWEET
HELLO, BOYS AND GIRLS!
HOW ARE YOU TODAY?
STARE ジ…
ONIISAN! ONIISAN!
HM?
WHAT IS IT?
キャッ SQUEE
SQUEE キャッ
MY GRANDMA BOUGHT ME THIS DRESS!
FLOUNCE
FLOUNCE
DO YOU LIKE IT?
...!
...I DO!
LOOK AT ALL THOSE FRILLS! IT'S SO CUTE!
!!!

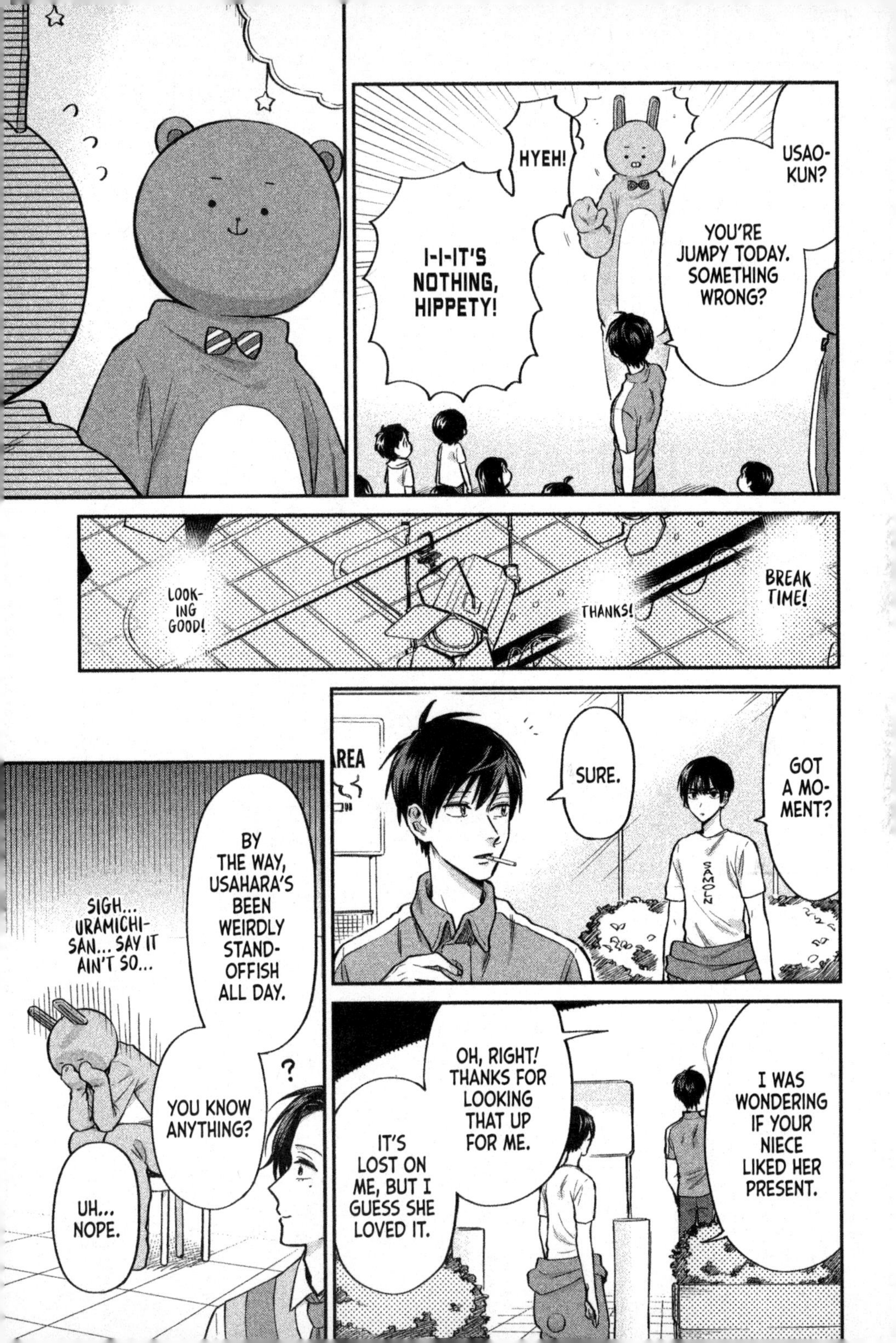
USAO-KUN?
YOU'RE JUMPY TODAY. SOMETHING WRONG?
HYEH!
I-I-IT'S NOTHING, HIPPETY!
BREAK TIME!
THANKS!
LOOKING GOOD!
GOT A MOMENT?
SURE.
AREA
I WAS WONDERING IF YOUR NIECE LIKED HER PRESENT.
OH, RIGHT! THANKS FOR LOOKING THAT UP FOR ME.
IT'S LOST ON ME, BUT I GUESS SHE LOVED IT.
BY THE WAY, USAHARA'S BEEN WEIRDLY STANDOFFISH ALL DAY.
SIGH... URAMICHI-SAN... SAY IT AIN'T SO...
YOU KNOW ANYTHING?
?
UH... NOPE.

Character file

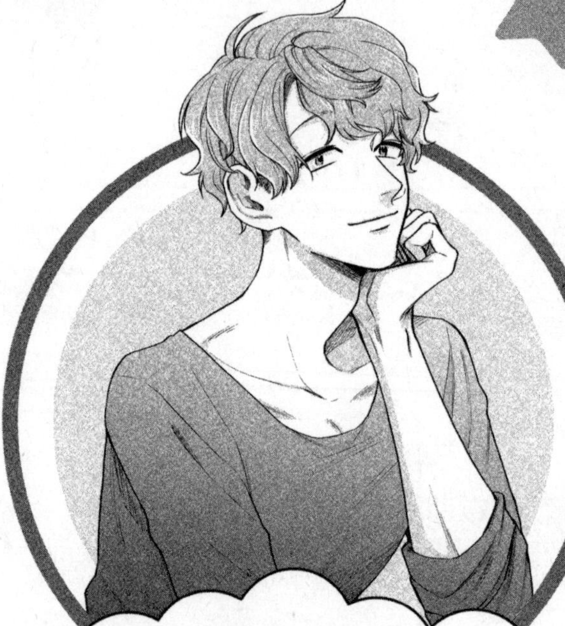

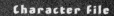

MATAHIKO NEKOTA

AGE: 28
HEIGHT: 181 CM (5' 11")
BLOOD TYPE: O
BIRTHDAY: FEBRUARY 22
SMOKER: YES
DRINKER: HEAVY-ISH

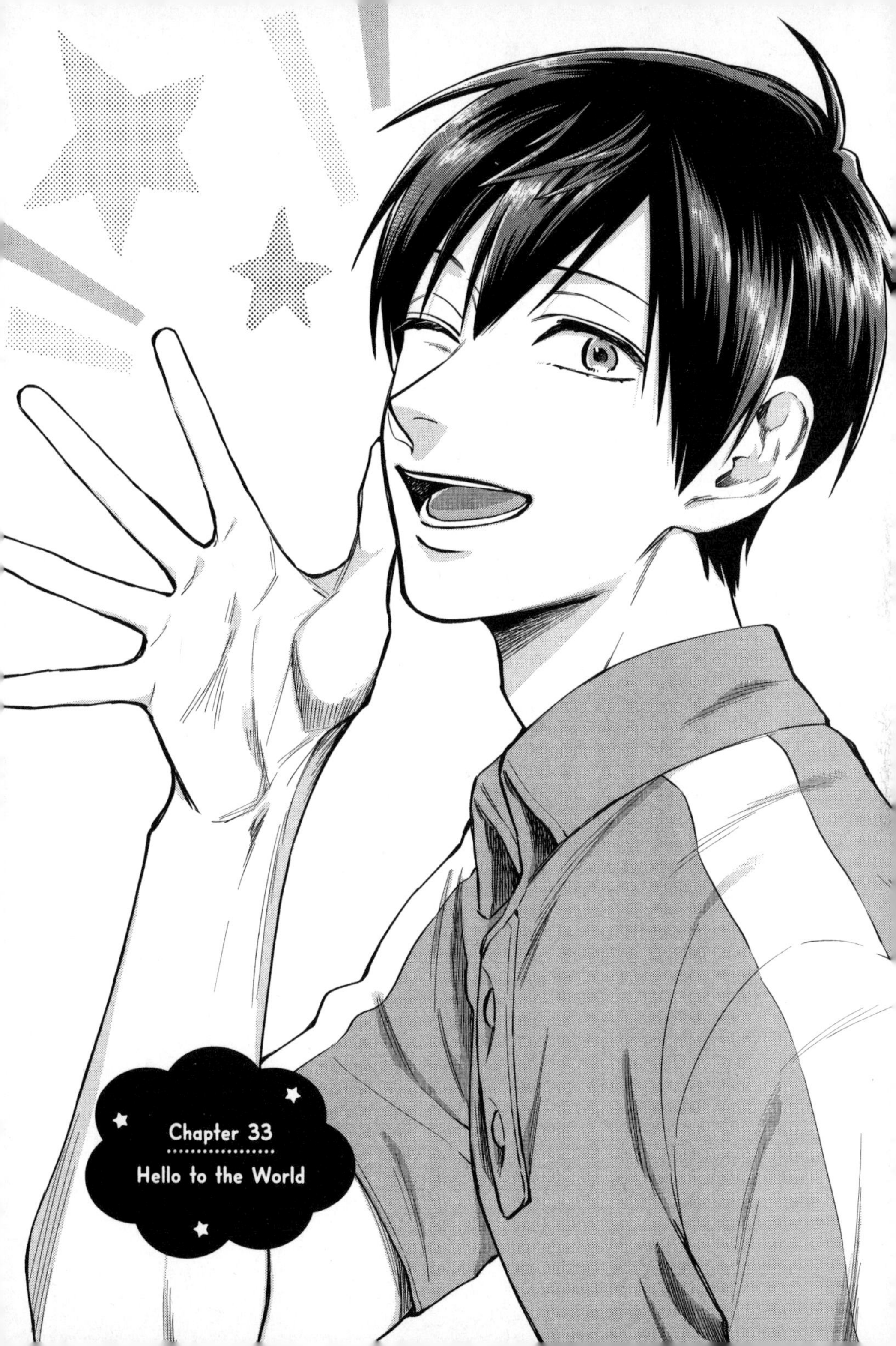
Chapter 33
Hello to the World

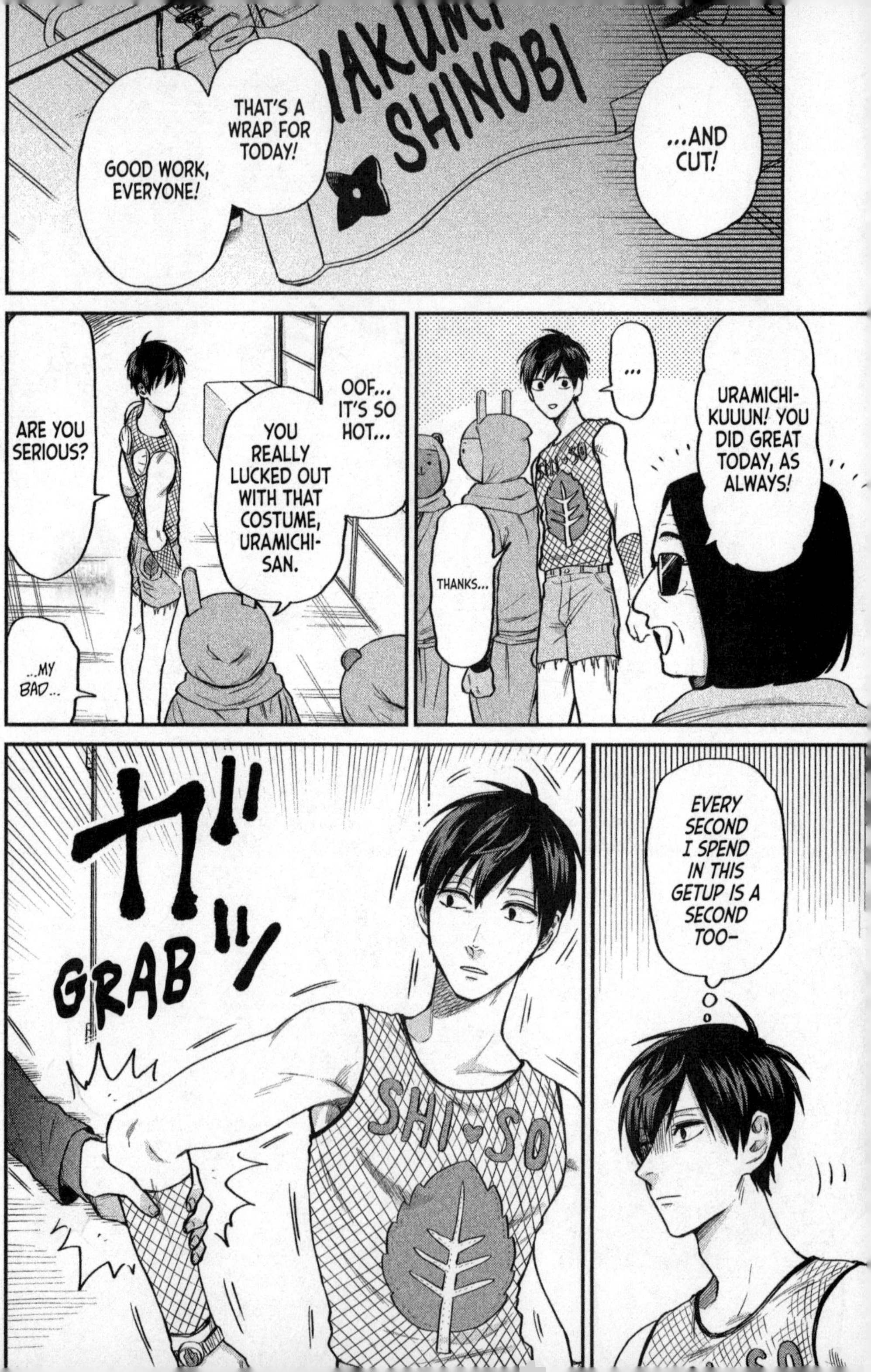
...AND CUT!
SHINOBI
THAT'S A WRAP FOR TODAY!
GOOD WORK, EVERYONE!
URAMICHI-KUUUN! YOU DID GREAT TODAY, AS ALWAYS!
...
THANKS...
OOF... IT'S SO HOT...
YOU REALLY LUCKED OUT WITH THAT COSTUME, URAMICHI-SAN.
ARE YOU SERIOUS?
...MY BAD...
EVERY SECOND I SPEND IN THIS GETUP IS A SECOND TOO—
ガッ
GRAB

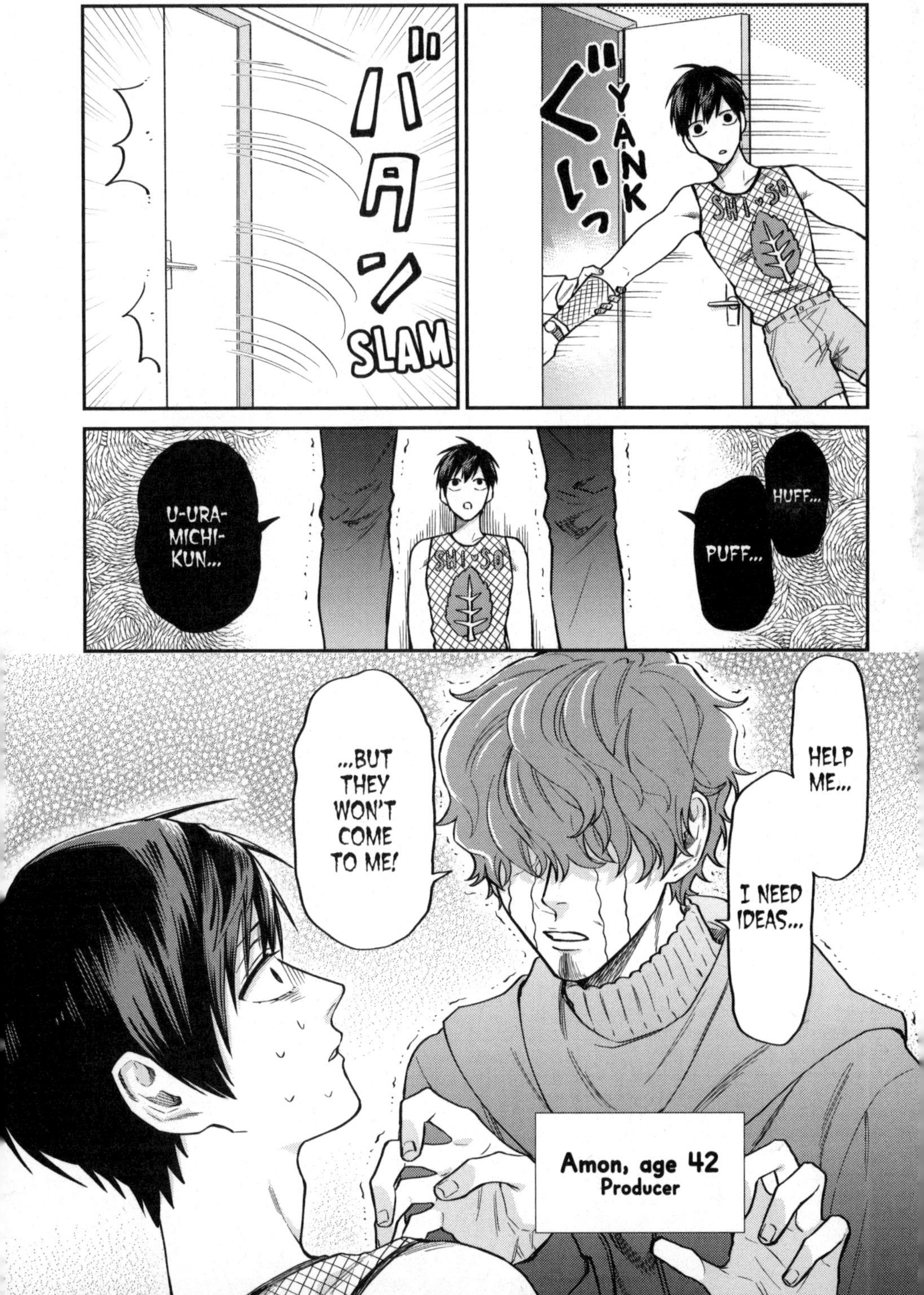
ぐいっ
YANK
バタン
SLAM
HUFF...
PUFF...
U-URA-MICHI-KUN...
HELP ME...
I NEED IDEAS...
...BUT THEY WON'T COME TO ME!
Amon, age 42
Producer

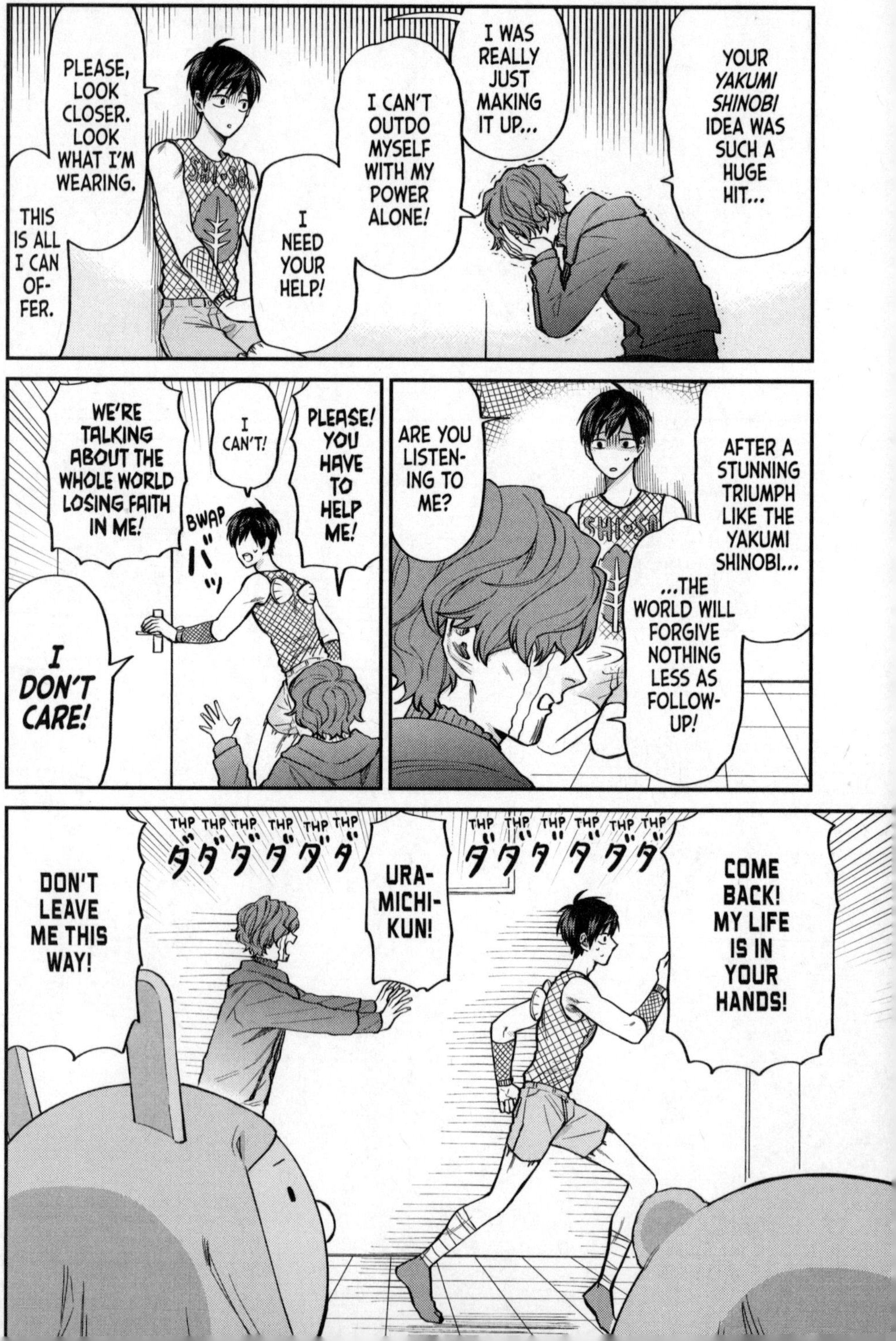
YOUR YAKUMI SHINOBI IDEA WAS SUCH A HUGE HIT...
I WAS REALLY JUST MAKING IT UP...
I CAN'T OUTDO MYSELF WITH MY POWER ALONE!
I NEED YOUR HELP!
PLEASE, LOOK CLOSER. LOOK WHAT I'M WEARING.
THIS IS ALL I CAN OF-FER.
AFTER A STUNNING TRIUMPH LIKE THE YAKUMI SHINOBI...
...THE WORLD WILL FORGIVE NOTHING LESS AS FOLLOW-UP!
ARE YOU LISTEN-ING TO ME?
PLEASE! YOU HAVE TO HELP ME!
I CAN'T!
WE'RE TALKING ABOUT THE WHOLE WORLD LOSING FAITH IN ME!
BWAP バッ
I DON'T CARE!
COME BACK! MY LIFE IS IN YOUR HANDS!
THP THP THP THP THP THP ダダダダダダ
URA-MICHI-KUN!
THP THP THP THP THP THP ダダダダダダ
DON'T LEAVE ME THIS WAY!

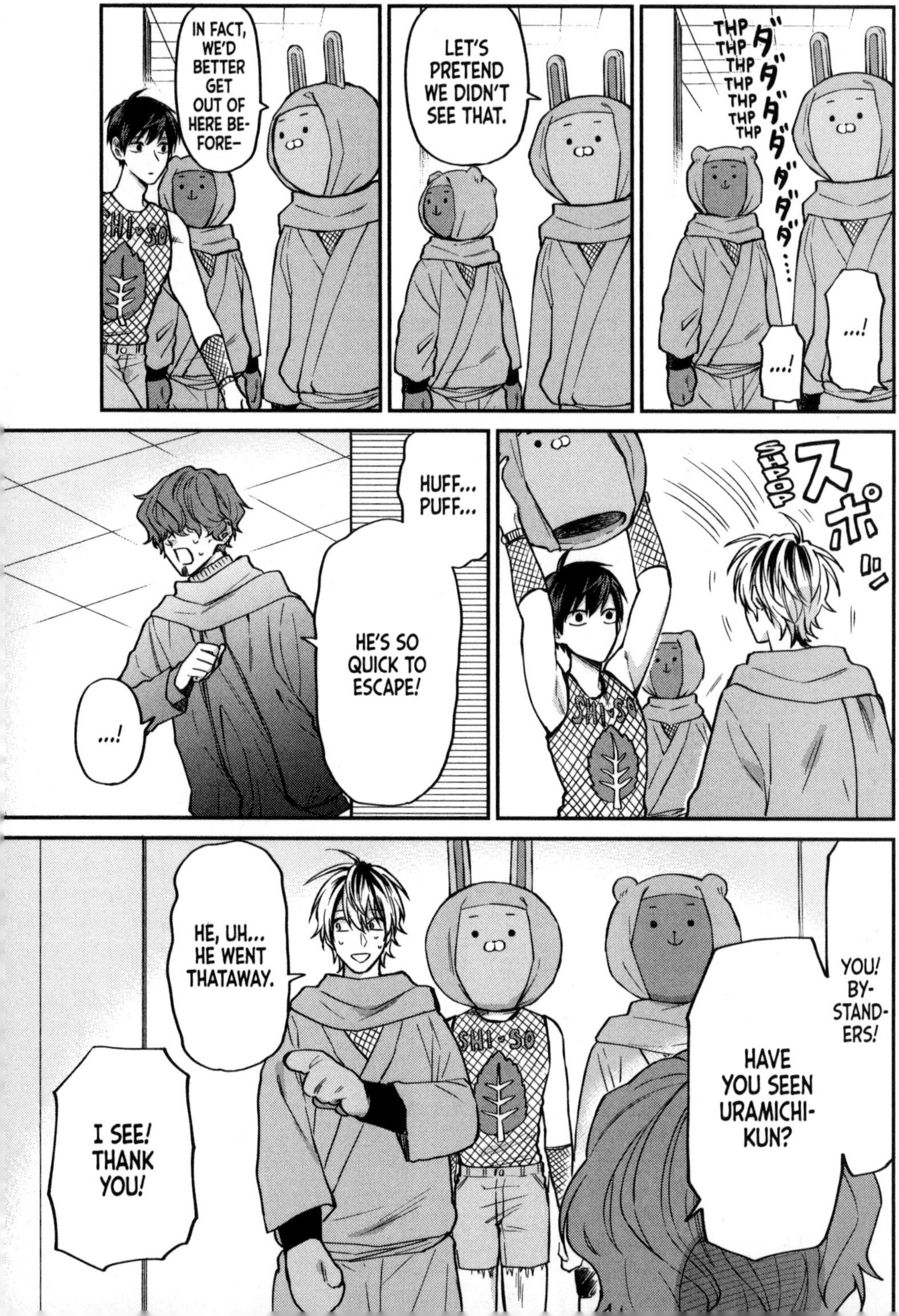
THP THP THP THP THP THP THP
ダダダダダダダ……
…!
…!
LET'S PRETEND WE DIDN'T SEE THAT.
IN FACT, WE'D BETTER GET OUT OF HERE BEFORE–
SHPOOP
スポッ
HUFF… PUFF…
HE'S SO QUICK TO ESCAPE!
…!
YOU! BYSTANDERS!
HAVE YOU SEEN URAMICHI-KUN?
HE, UH… HE WENT THATAWAY.
I SEE! THANK YOU!

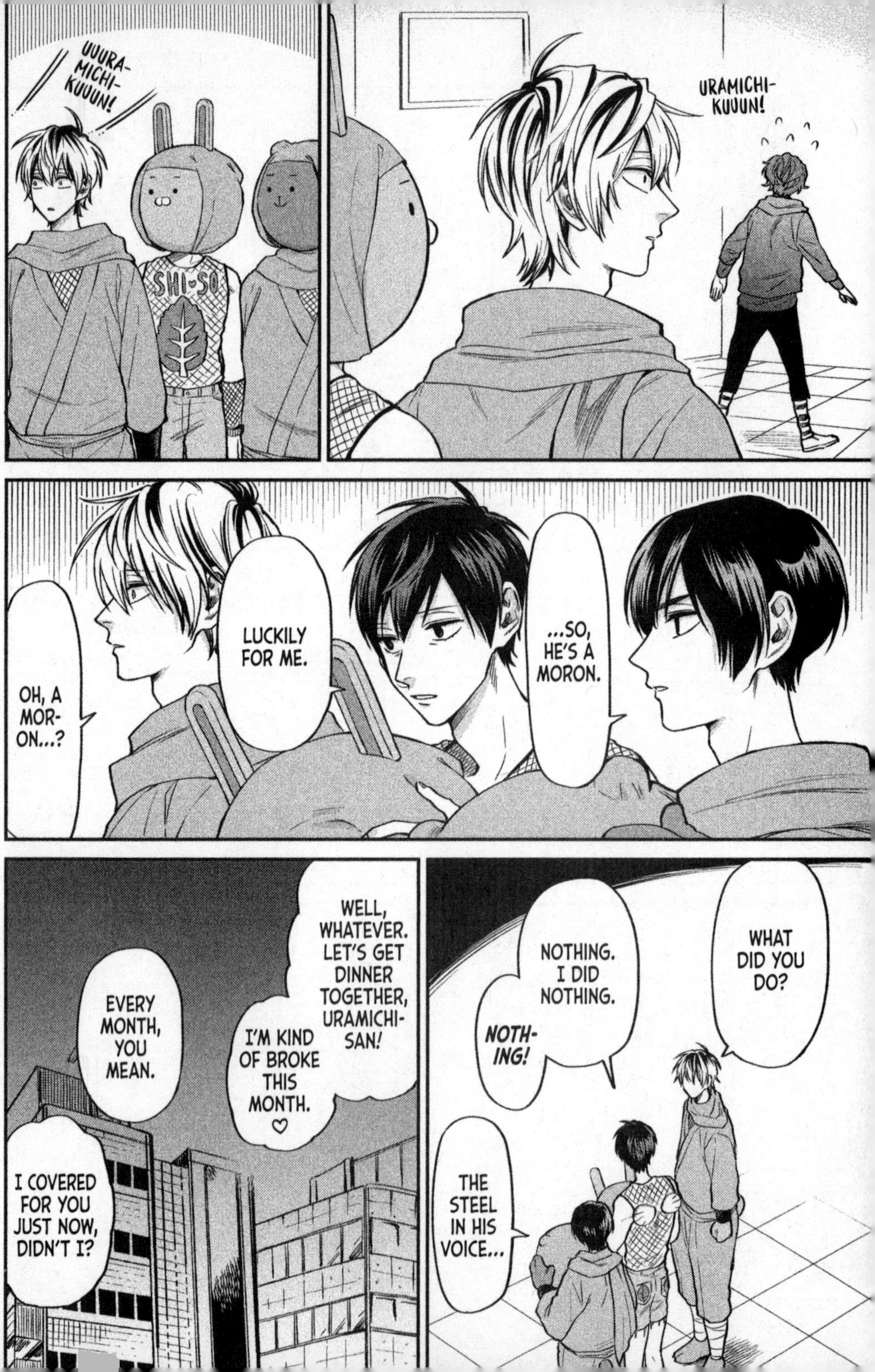
URAMICHI-KUUUN!
UUURA-MICHI-KUUUN!
...SO, HE'S A MORON.
LUCKILY FOR ME.
OH, A MOR-ON...?
WHAT DID YOU DO?
NOTHING. I DID NOTHING.
NOTH-ING!
THE STEEL IN HIS VOICE...
WELL, WHATEVER. LET'S GET DINNER TOGETHER, URAMICHI-SAN!
I'M KIND OF BROKE THIS MONTH. ♡
EVERY MONTH, YOU MEAN.
I COVERED FOR YOU JUST NOW, DIDN'T I?

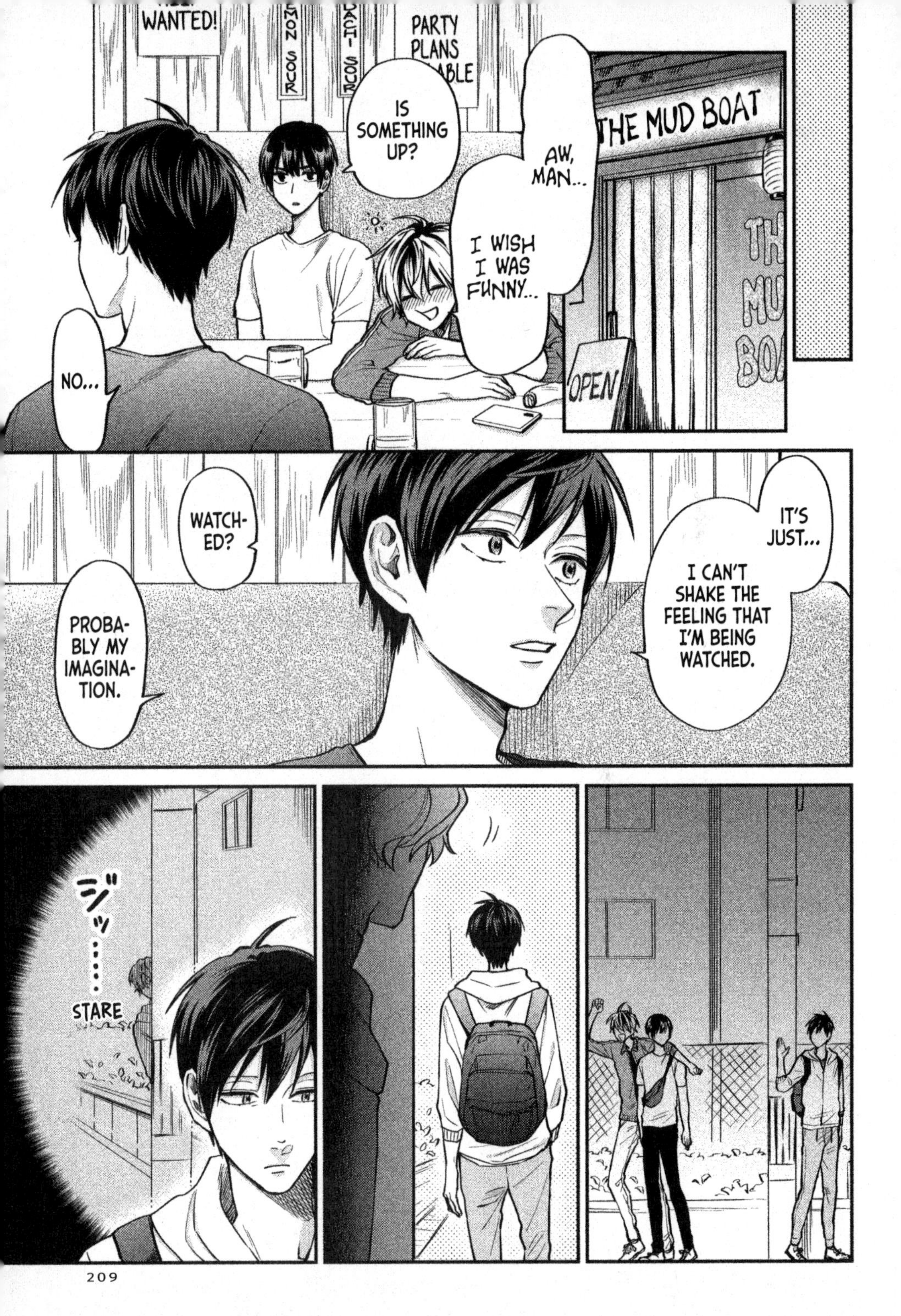
THE MUD BOAT
OPEN
AW, MAN...
I WISH I WAS FUNNY...
IS SOMETHING UP?
WANTED!
NO...
IT'S JUST...
I CAN'T SHAKE THE FEELING THAT I'M BEING WATCHED.
WATCH-ED?
PROBA-BLY MY IMAGINA-TION.
ジッ……
STARE

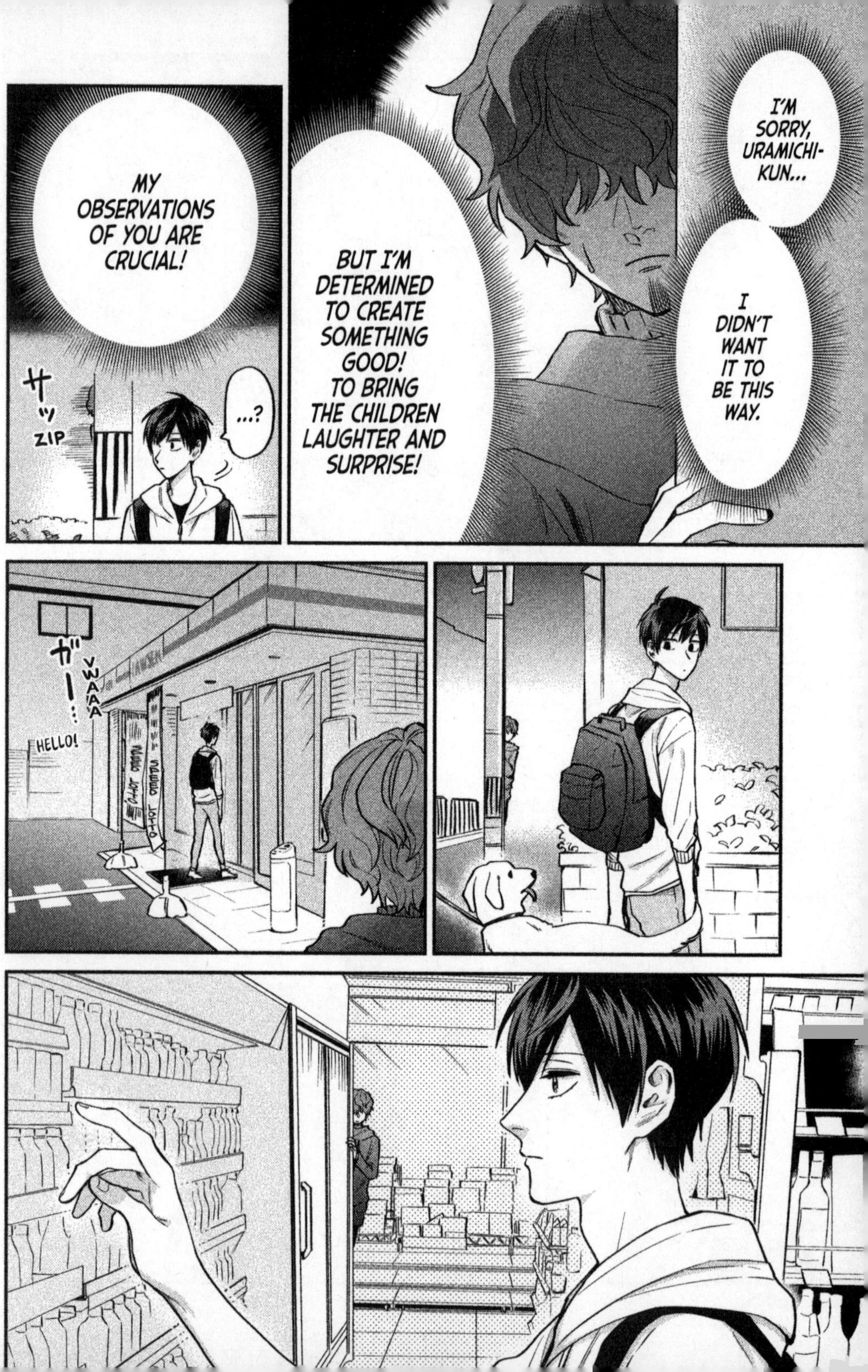
I'M SORRY, URAMICHI-KUN...
I DIDN'T WANT IT TO BE THIS WAY.
BUT I'M DETERMINED TO CREATE SOMETHING GOOD! TO BRING THE CHILDREN LAUGHTER AND SURPRISE!
MY OBSERVATIONS OF YOU ARE CRUCIAL!
サッ
ZIP
...?
ガー…
VWAAA
HELLO!
SPEED LOTTO

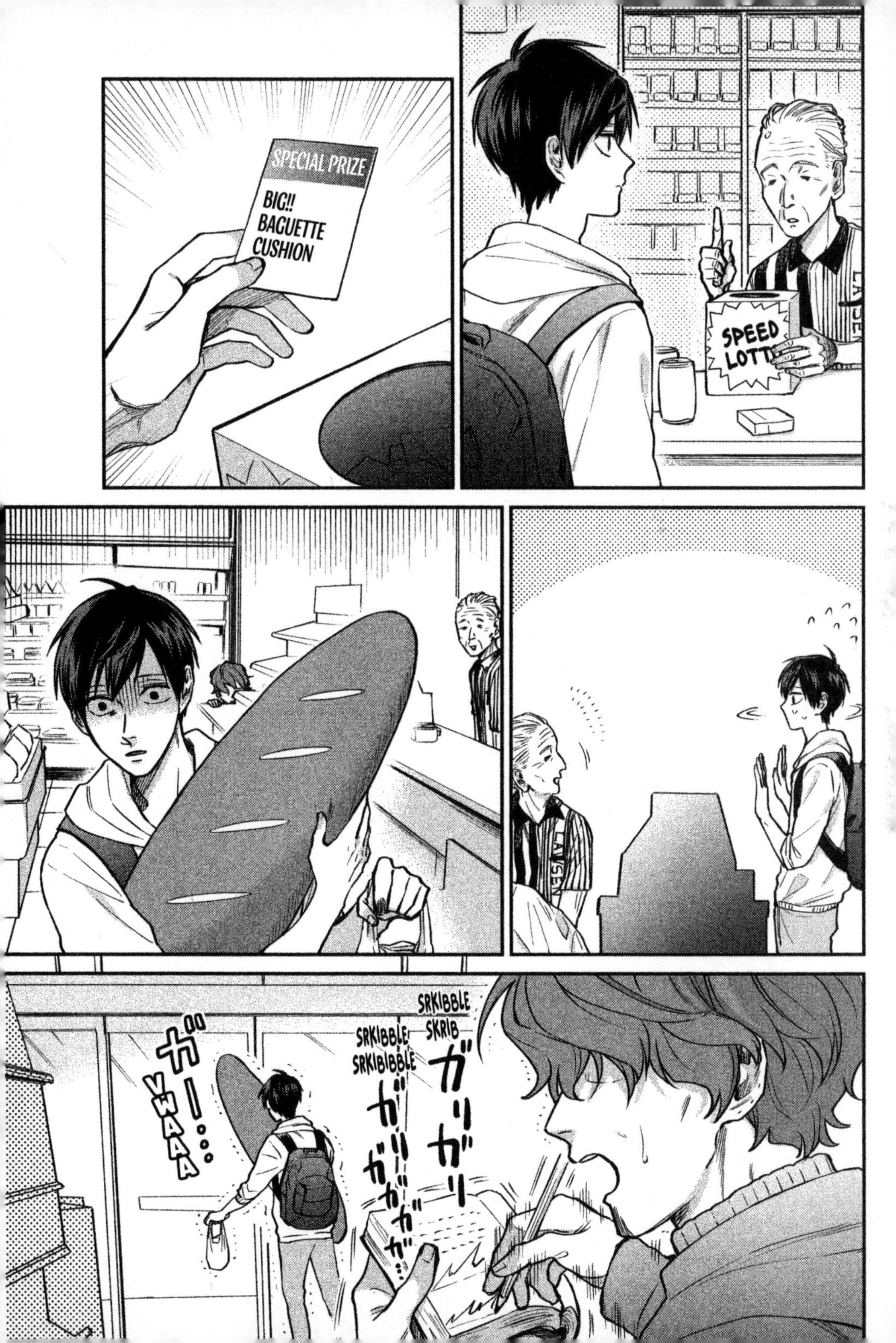
SPEED LOTT
SPECIAL PRIZE
BIG!! BAGUETTE CUSHION
SRKIBBLE SKRIB
ガリガリ
SRKIBBLE SRKIBIBBLE
ガリガリガガガ…
ガー…
VWAAA

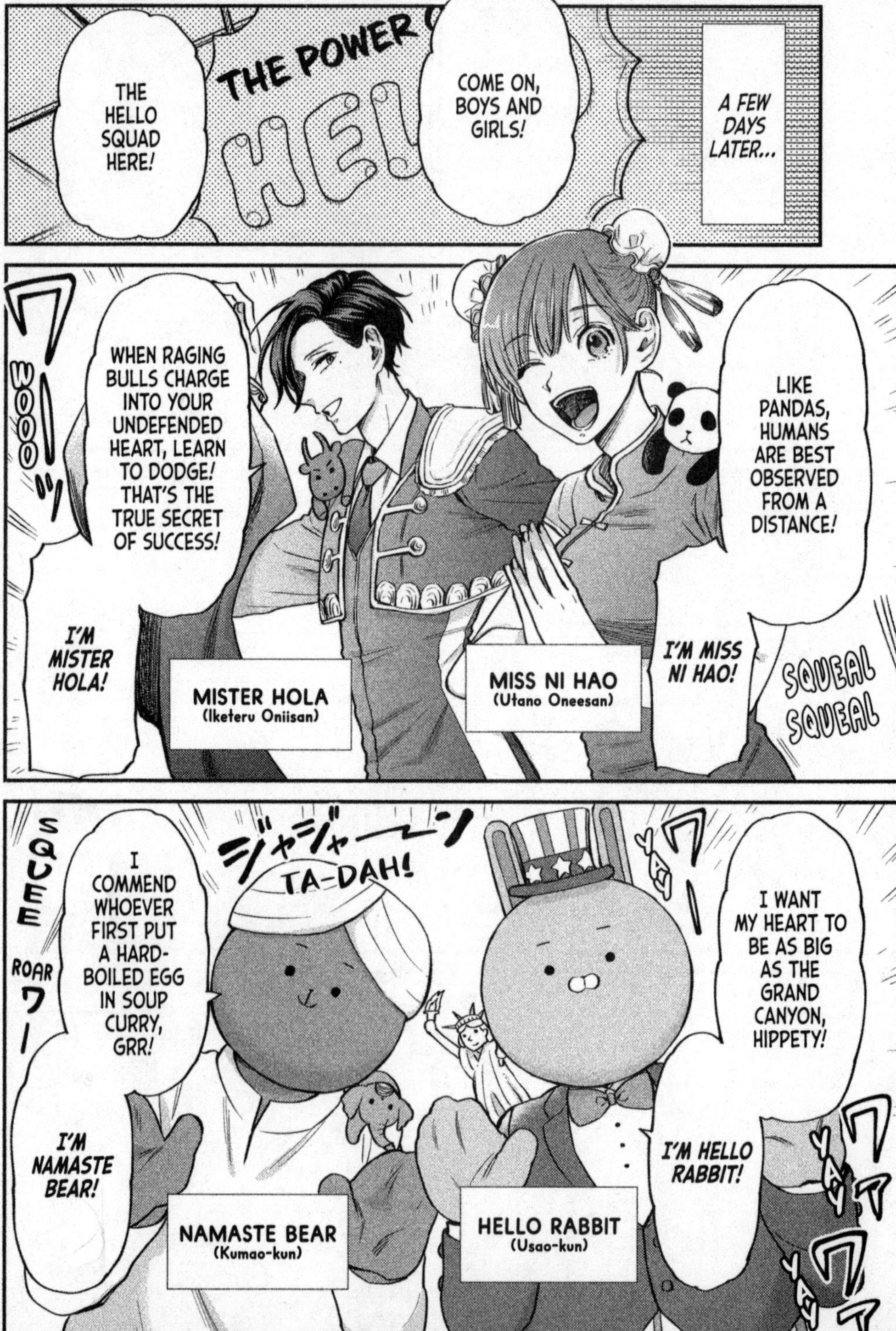
A FEW DAYS LATER...
COME ON, BOYS AND GIRLS!
THE POWER
HE
THE HELLO SQUAD HERE!
LIKE PANDAS, HUMANS ARE BEST OBSERVED FROM A DISTANCE!
SQUEAL SQUEAL
I'M MISS NI HAO!
MISS NI HAO
(Utano Oneesan)
WHEN RAGING BULLS CHARGE INTO YOUR UNDEFENDED HEART, LEARN TO DODGE! THAT'S THE TRUE SECRET OF SUCCESS!
I'M MISTER HOLA!
MISTER HOLA
(Iketeru Oniisan)
ワーッ
WOOO
ワァワァ
YAY YAY
I WANT MY HEART TO BE AS BIG AS THE GRAND CANYON, HIPPETY!
I'M HELLO RABBIT!
HELLO RABBIT
(Usao-kun)
ワー
YAY
ジャジャーン
TA-DAH!
I COMMEND WHOEVER FIRST PUT A HARD-BOILED EGG IN SOUP CURRY, GRR!
I'M NAMASTE BEAR!
NAMASTE BEAR
(Kumao-kun)
SQUEE
ROAR
ワー

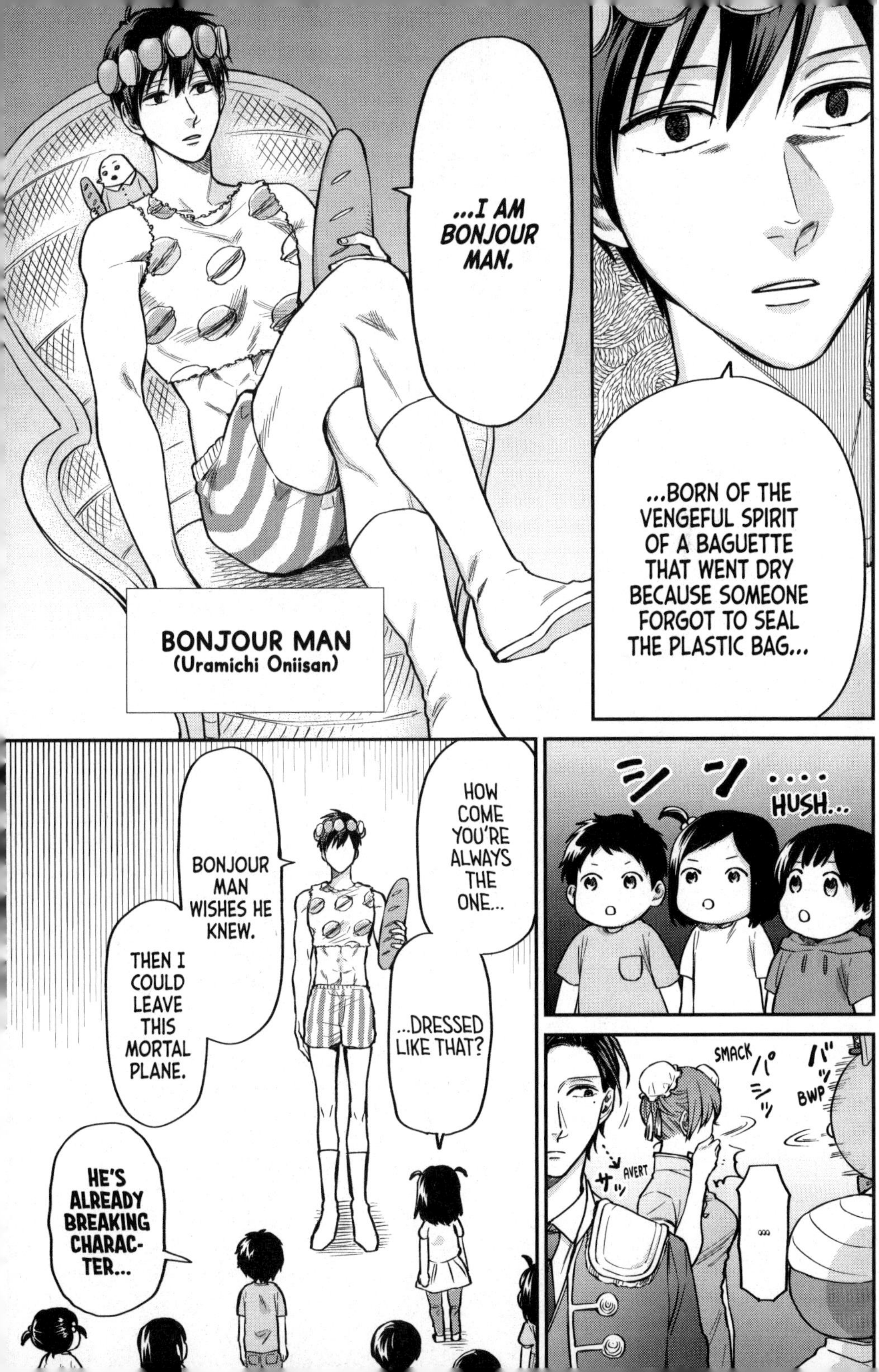

...BORN OF THE VENGEFUL SPIRIT OF A BAGUETTE THAT WENT DRY BECAUSE SOMEONE FORGOT TO SEAL THE PLASTIC BAG...
...I AM BONJOUR MAN.
BONJOUR MAN
(Uramichi Oniisan)
シン....
HUSH...
バッ
BWP
パシッ
SMACK
サッ
AVERT
HOW COME YOU'RE ALWAYS THE ONE...
...DRESSED LIKE THAT?
BONJOUR MAN WISHES HE KNEW.
THEN I COULD LEAVE THIS MORTAL PLANE.
HE'S ALREADY BREAKING CHARAC-TER...

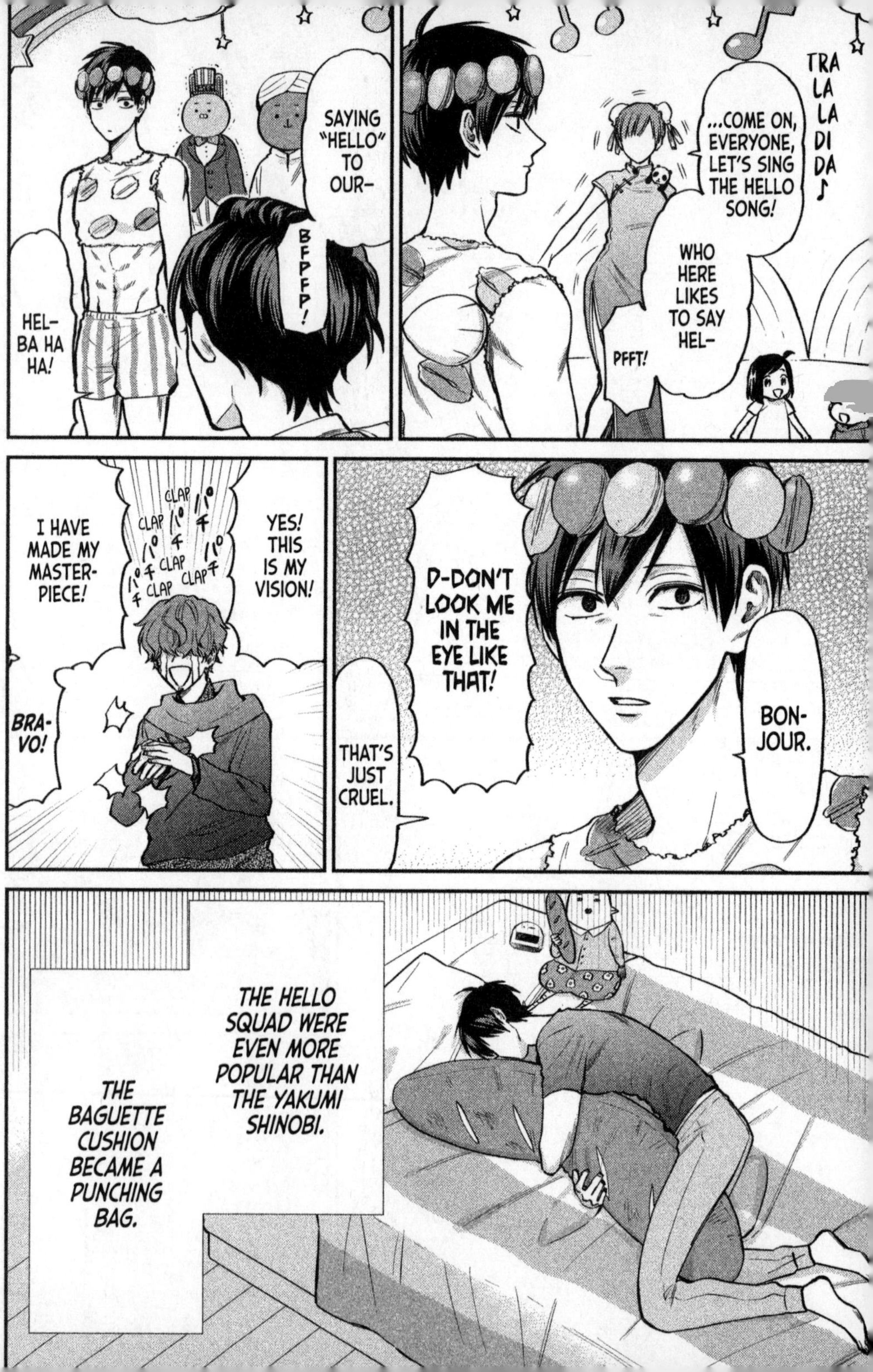
TRA LA LA DI DA ♪
...COME ON, EVERYONE, LET'S SING THE HELLO SONG!
WHO HERE LIKES TO SAY HEL–
PFFT!
SAYING "HELLO" TO OUR–
BFPFP!
HEL– BA HA HA!
BON-JOUR.
D-DON'T LOOK ME IN THE EYE LIKE THAT!
THAT'S JUST CRUEL.
YES! THIS IS MY VISION!
CLAP パチ CLAP パチ CLAP パチ CLAP パチ CLAP
I HAVE MADE MY MASTER-PIECE!
BRA-VO!
THE HELLO SQUAD WERE EVEN MORE POPULAR THAN THE YAKUMI SHINOBI.
THE BAGUETTE CUSHION BECAME A PUNCHING BAG.

Life Lessons with
Uramichi Oniisan

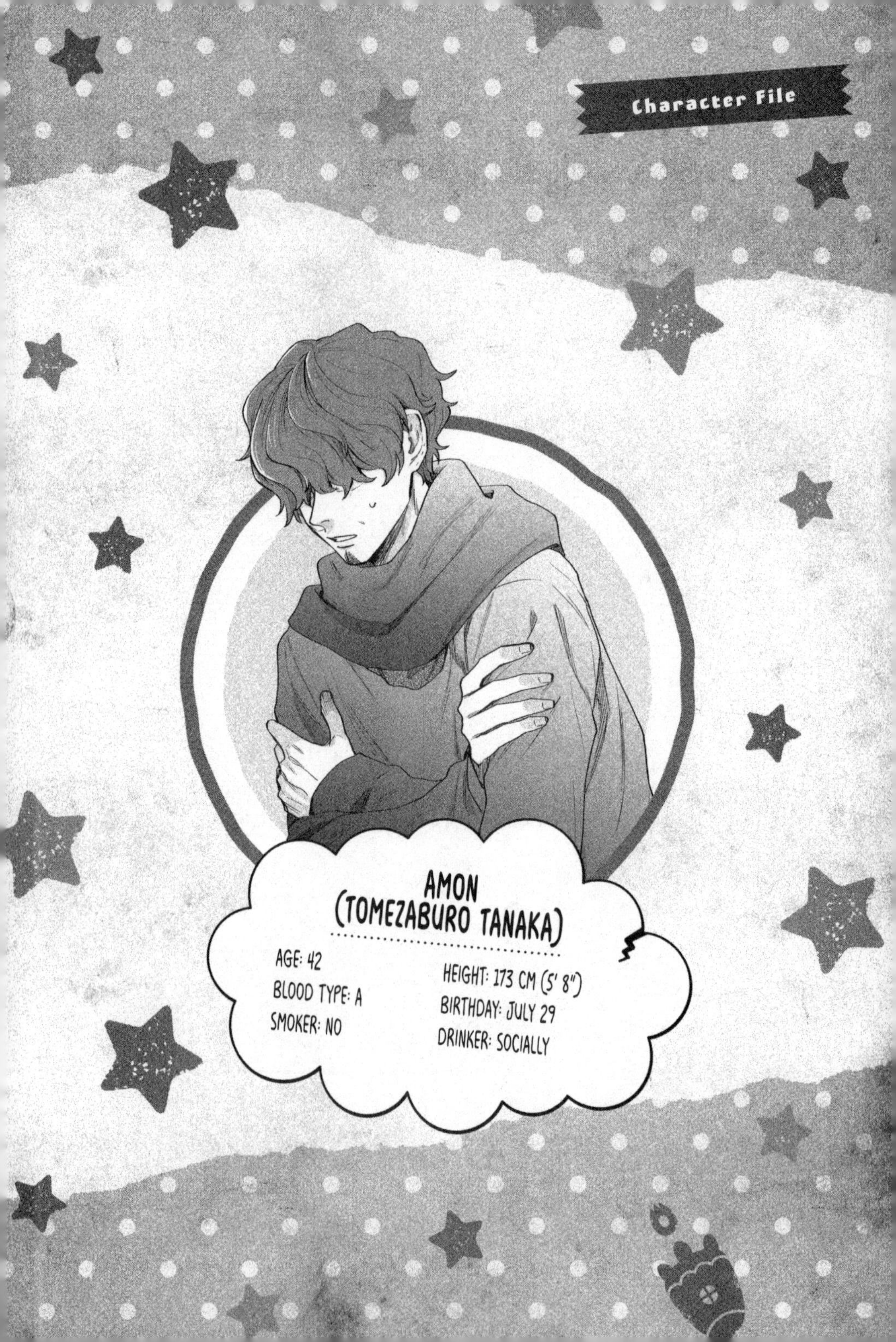
Character File
AMON
(TOMEZABURO TANAKA)
AGE: 42
BLOOD TYPE: A
SMOKER: NO
HEIGHT: 173 CM (5' 8")
BIRTHDAY: JULY 29
DRINKER: SOCIALLY

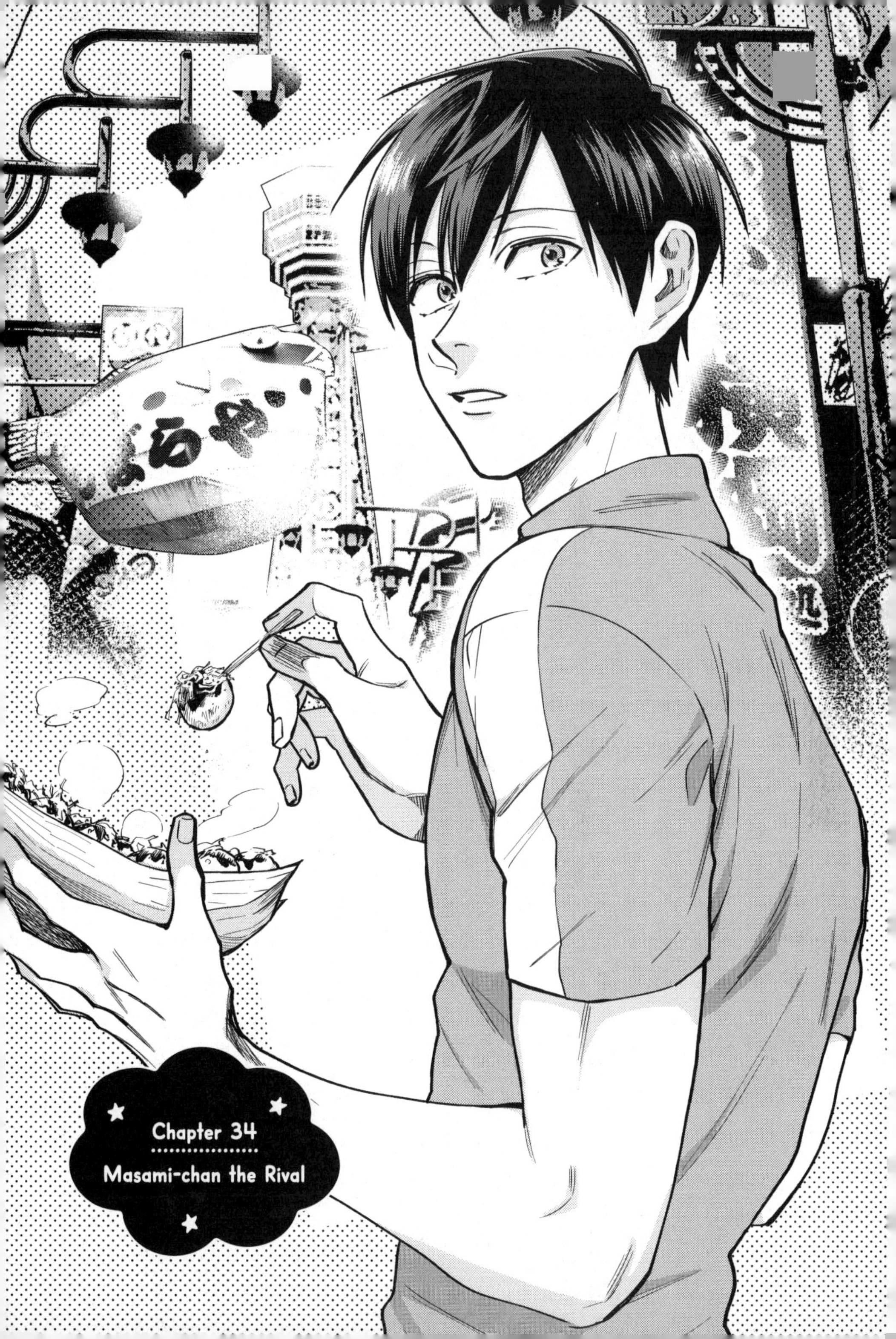
Chapter 34
Masami-chan the Rival

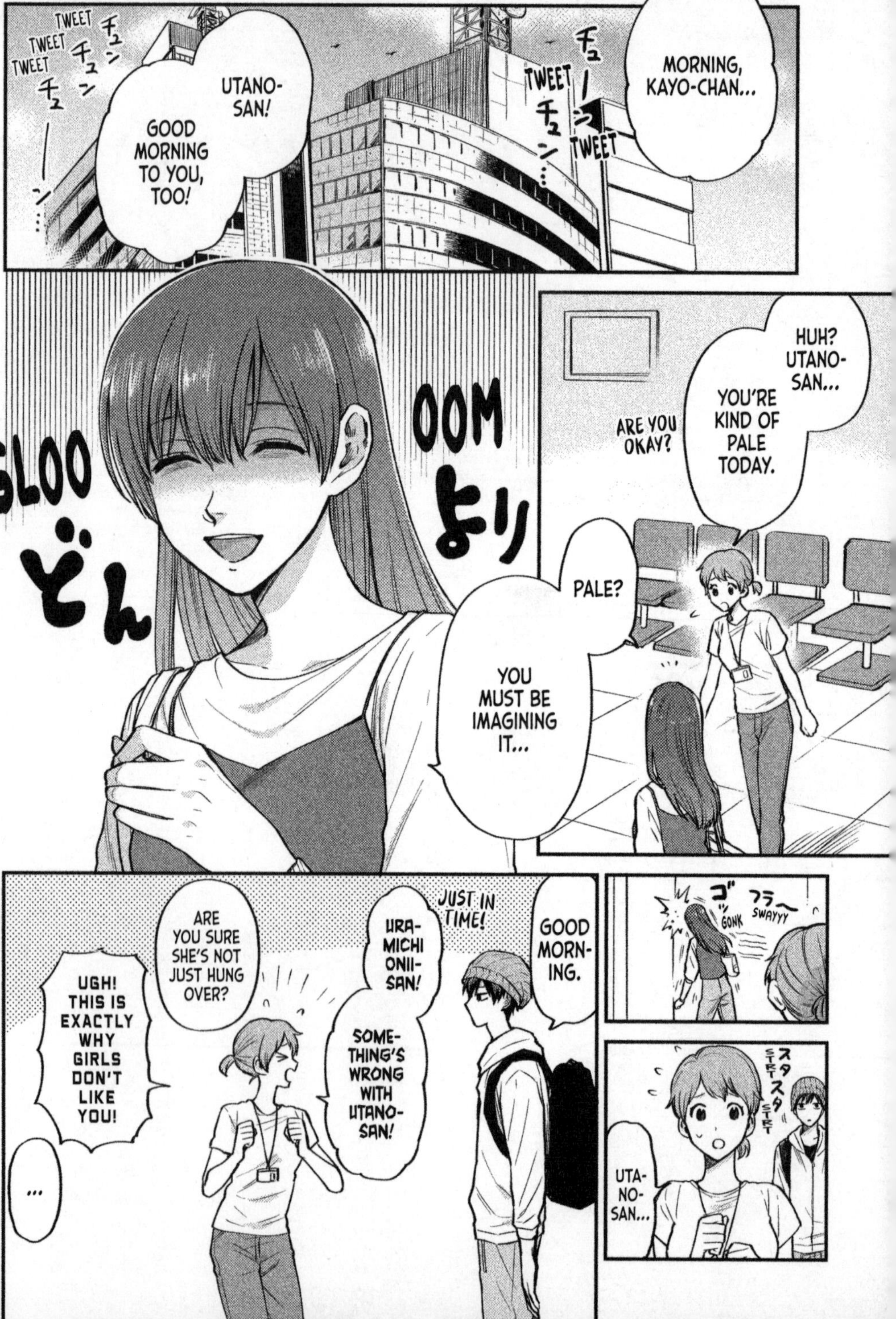
MORNING, KAYO-CHAN...
チューン
TWEET
チュン
TWEET
チューン…
UTANO-SAN!
GOOD MORNING TO YOU, TOO!
TWEET
チュン
TWEET
チュン
TWEET
HUH? UTANO-SAN...
YOU'RE KIND OF PALE TODAY.
ARE YOU OKAY?
PALE?
YOU MUST BE IMAGINING IT...
OOM
より
GLOO
どん
ゴッ
GONK
フラ〜
SWAYYY
スタ
STRT
スタ
STRT
UTA-NO-SAN...
GOOD MORN-ING.
JUST IN TIME!
URA-MICHI ONII-SAN!
SOME-THING'S WRONG WITH UTANO-SAN!
ARE YOU SURE SHE'S NOT JUST HUNG OVER?
UGH! THIS IS EXACTLY WHY GIRLS DON'T LIKE YOU!
...

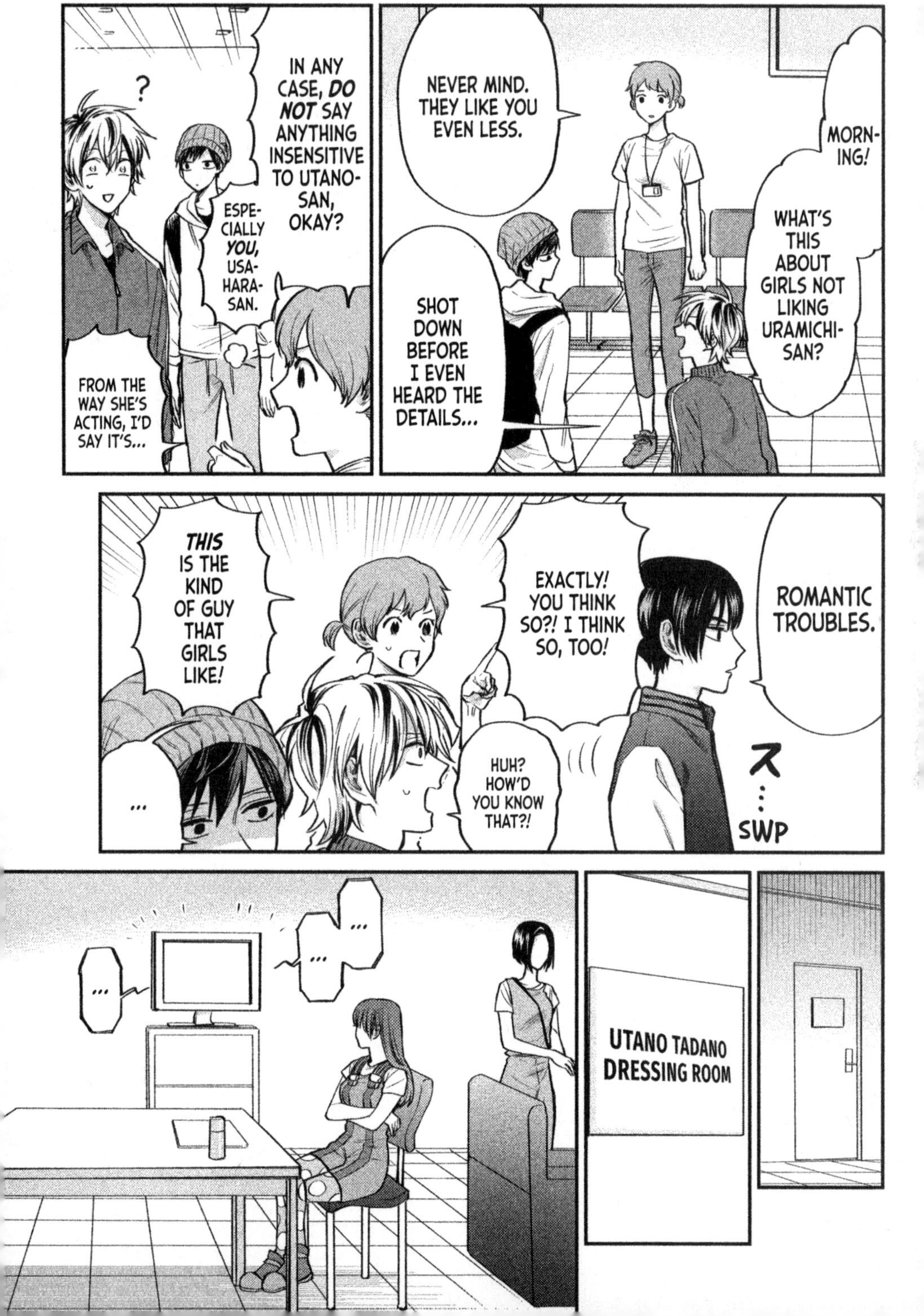
MORNING!
WHAT'S THIS ABOUT GIRLS NOT LIKING URAMICHI-SAN?
NEVER MIND. THEY LIKE YOU EVEN LESS.
SHOT DOWN BEFORE I EVEN HEARD THE DETAILS...
IN ANY CASE, DO NOT SAY ANYTHING INSENSITIVE TO UTANO-SAN, OKAY?
ESPECIALLY YOU, USAHARA-SAN.
?
FROM THE WAY SHE'S ACTING, I'D SAY IT'S...
ROMANTIC TROUBLES.
ス...
SWP
EXACTLY! YOU THINK SO?! I THINK SO, TOO!
HUH? HOW'D YOU KNOW THAT?!
THIS IS THE KIND OF GUY THAT GIRLS LIKE!
...
UTANO TADANO DRESSING ROOM
...
...
...

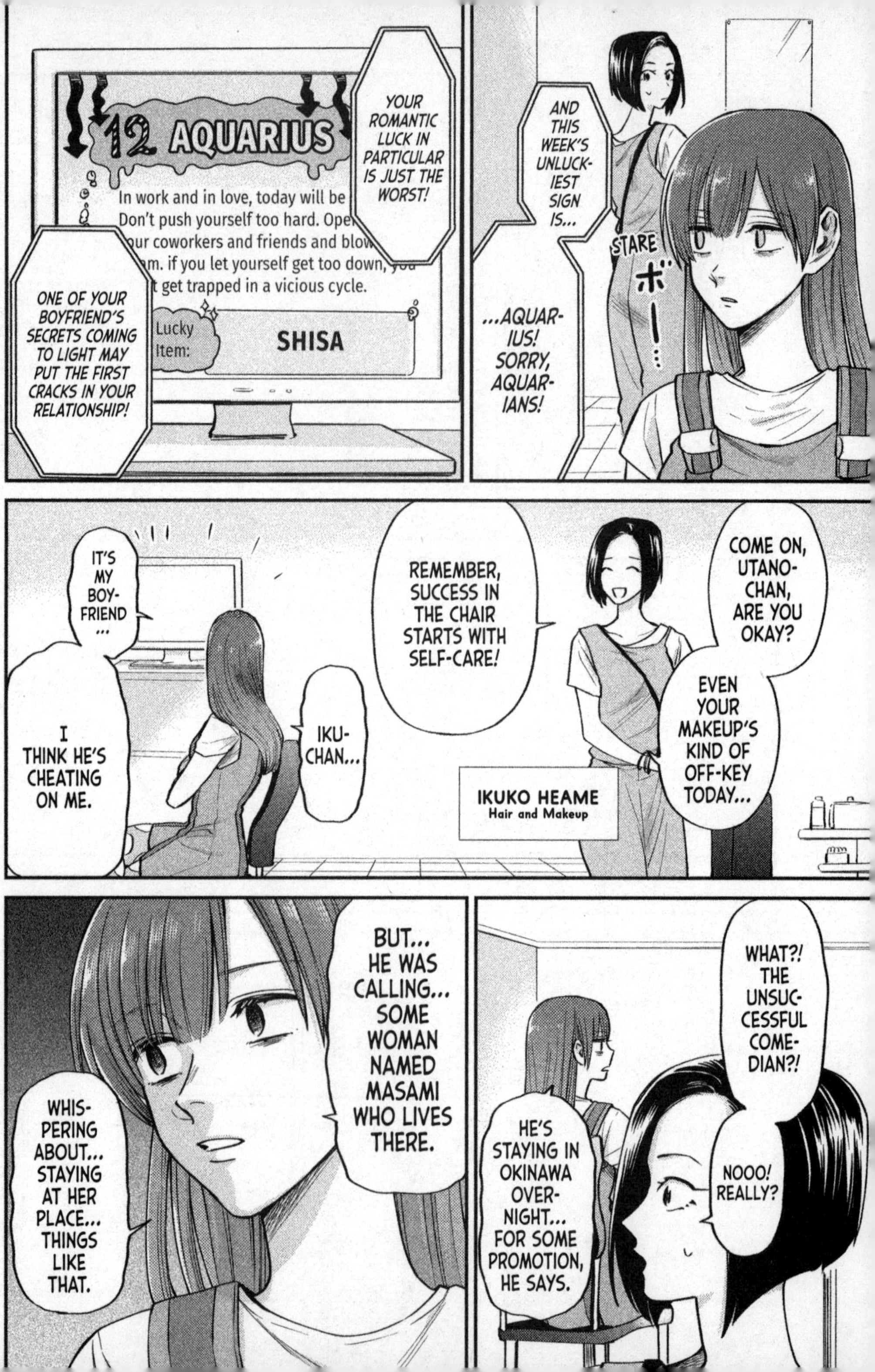
AND THIS WEEK'S UNLUCKIEST SIGN IS...
STARE
ボー…
...AQUARIUS! SORRY, AQUARIANS!
YOUR ROMANTIC LUCK IN PARTICULAR IS JUST THE WORST!
12 AQUARIUS
In work and in love, today will be
Don't push yourself too hard.
our coworkers and friends and
if you let yourself get too down,
get trapped in a vicious cycle.
Lucky Item:
SHISA
ONE OF YOUR BOYFRIEND'S SECRETS COMING TO LIGHT MAY PUT THE FIRST CRACKS IN YOUR RELATIONSHIP!
COME ON, UTANO-CHAN, ARE YOU OKAY?
EVEN YOUR MAKEUP'S KIND OF OFF-KEY TODAY...
REMEMBER, SUCCESS IN THE CHAIR STARTS WITH SELF-CARE!
IKUKO HEAME
Hair and Makeup
IKU-CHAN...
IT'S MY BOYFRIEND...
I THINK HE'S CHEATING ON ME.
WHAT?! THE UNSUCCESSFUL COMEDIAN?!
HE'S STAYING IN OKINAWA OVERNIGHT... FOR SOME PROMOTION, HE SAYS.
NOOO! REALLY?
BUT... HE WAS CALLING... SOME WOMAN NAMED MASAMI WHO LIVES THERE.
WHISPERING ABOUT... STAYING AT HER PLACE... THINGS LIKE THAT.

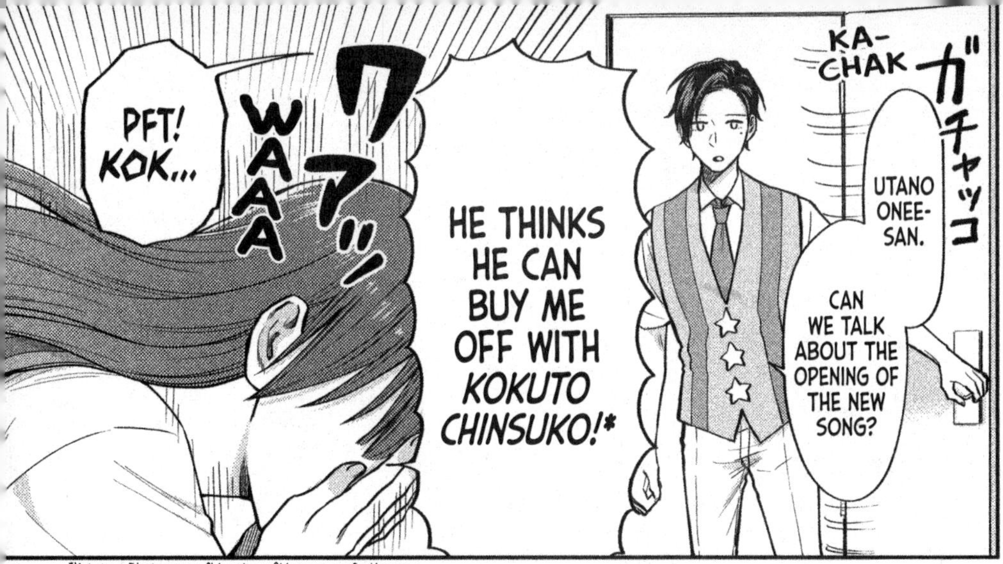
KA-CHAK
ガチャッコ
UTANO ONEE-SAN.
CAN WE TALK ABOUT THE OPENING OF THE NEW SONG?
HE THINKS HE CAN BUY ME OFF WITH *KOKUTO CHINSUKO!**
WAAA
ワァッ
PFT! KOK...

*Kokuto = Black sugar. Chinsuko = Okinawan confectionery.

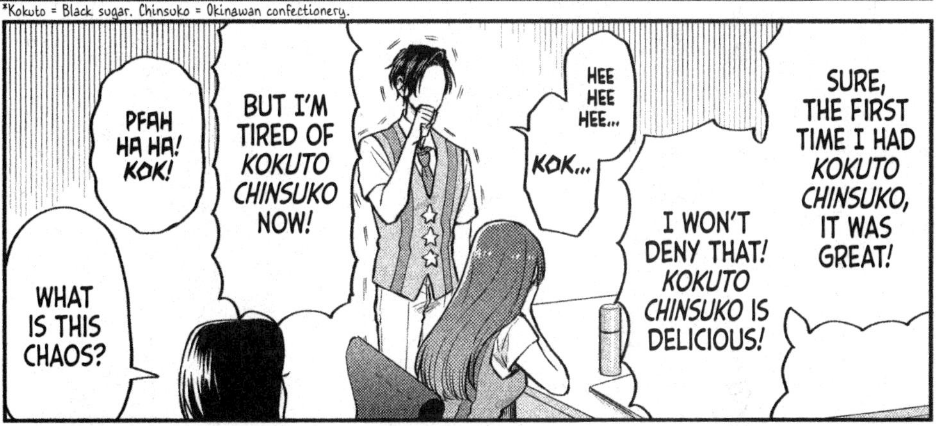
SURE, THE FIRST TIME I HAD *KOKUTO CHINSUKO*, IT WAS GREAT!
I WON'T DENY THAT! *KOKUTO CHINSUKO* IS DELICIOUS!
HEE HEE HEE...
KOK...
BUT I'M TIRED OF *KOKUTO CHINSUKO* NOW!
PFAH HA HA! KOK!
WHAT IS THIS CHAOS?

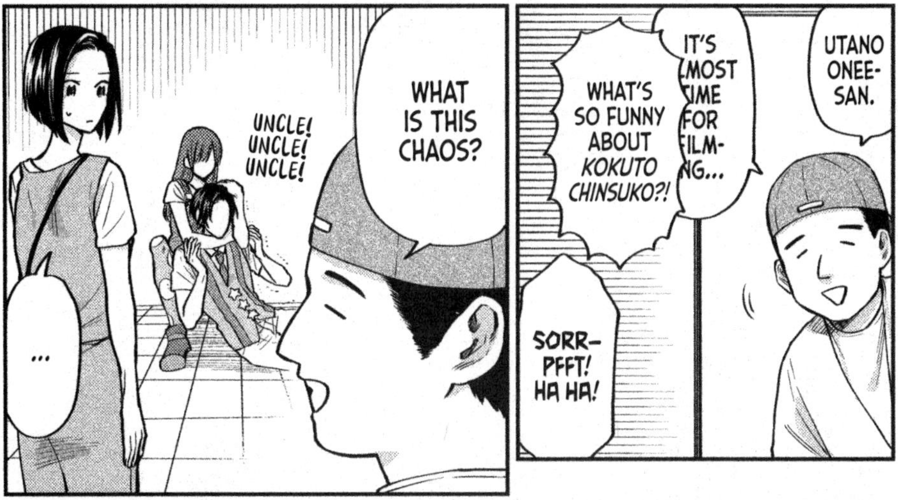
UTANO ONEE-SAN.
IT'S LMOST IME FOR FILM- NG...
WHAT'S SO FUNNY ABOUT *KOKUTO CHINSUKO?!*
SORR-PFFT! HA HA!
WHAT IS THIS CHAOS?
UNCLE! UNCLE! UNCLE!
...

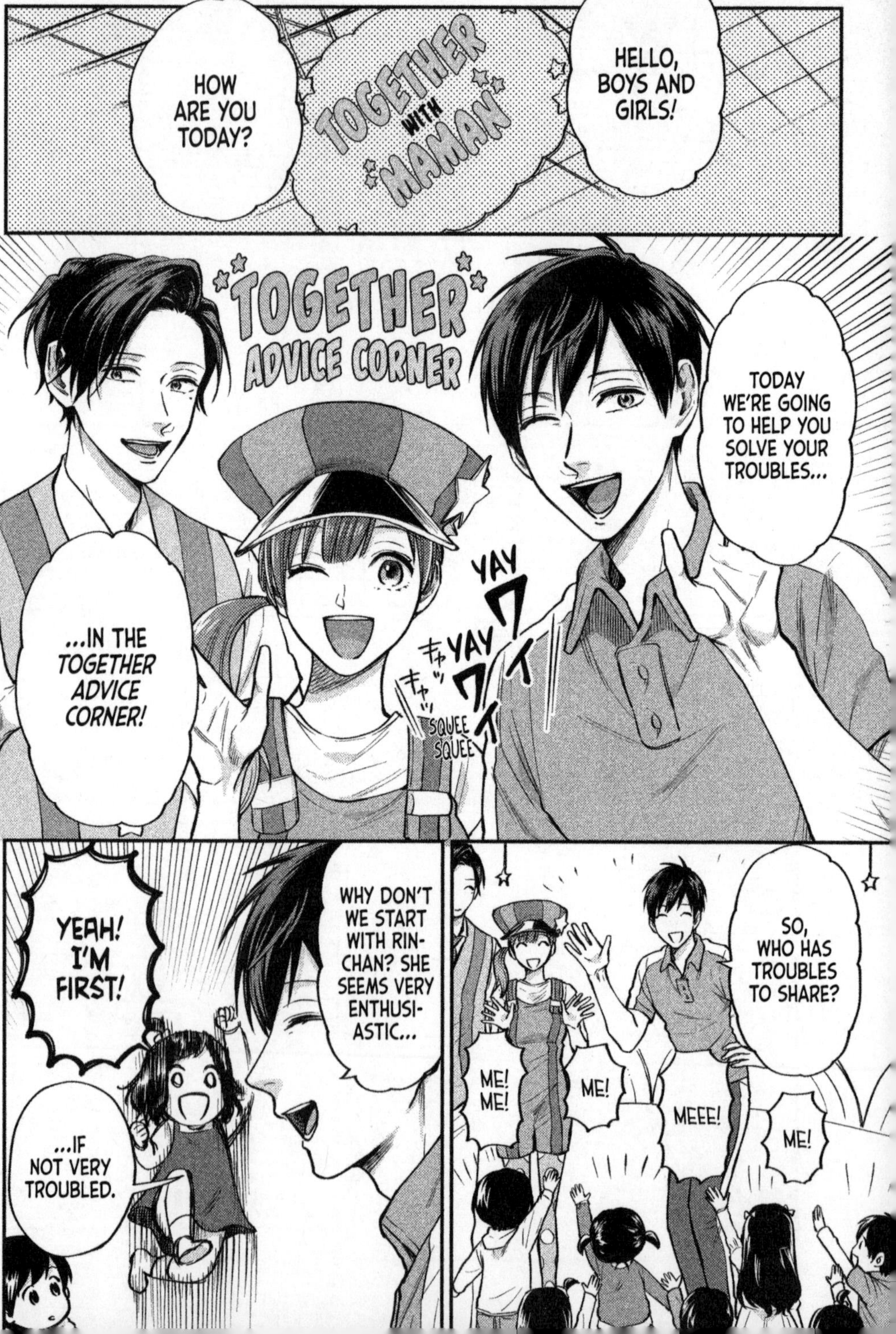
HELLO, BOYS AND GIRLS!
TOGETHER WITH MAMAN
HOW ARE YOU TODAY?
TOGETHER ADVICE CORNER
TODAY WE'RE GOING TO HELP YOU SOLVE YOUR TROUBLES...
YAY ワイ
YAY ワイ
キャッ キャッ
SQUEE SQUEE
...IN THE *TOGETHER ADVICE CORNER*!
SO, WHO HAS TROUBLES TO SHARE?
ME!
MEEE!
ME!
ME! ME!
WHY DON'T WE START WITH RIN-CHAN? SHE SEEMS VERY ENTHUSI-ASTIC...
YEAH! I'M FIRST!
...IF NOT VERY TROUBLED.

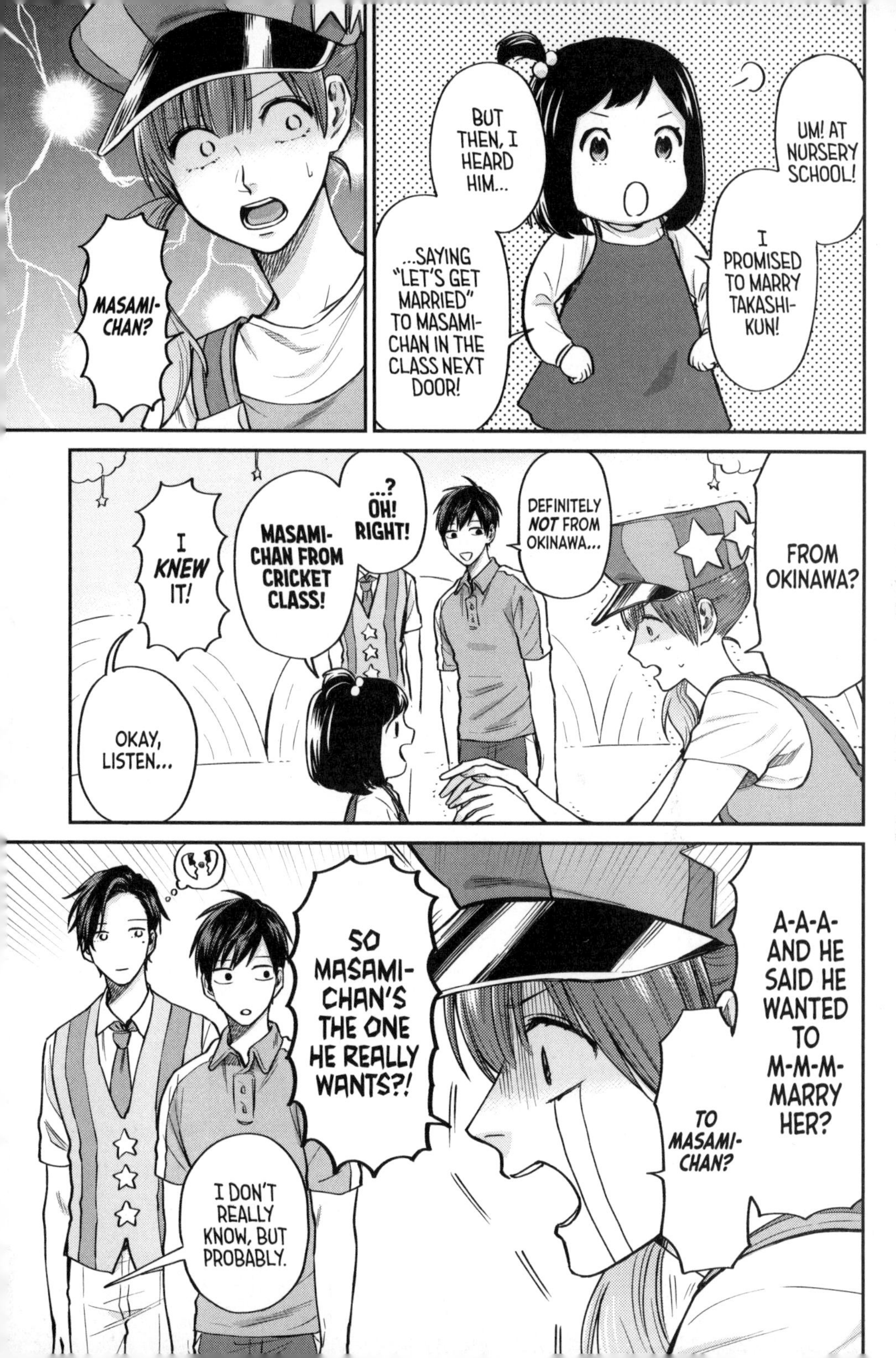
UM! AT NURSERY SCHOOL!
I PROMISED TO MARRY TAKASHI-KUN!
BUT THEN, I HEARD HIM...
...SAYING "LET'S GET MARRIED" TO MASAMI-CHAN IN THE CLASS NEXT DOOR!
MASAMI-CHAN?
FROM OKINAWA?
DEFINITELY NOT FROM OKINAWA...
...? OH! RIGHT!
MASAMI-CHAN FROM CRICKET CLASS!
I KNEW IT!
OKAY, LISTEN...
A-A-A-AND HE SAID HE WANTED TO M-M-M-MARRY HER?
TO MASAMI-CHAN?
SO MASAMI-CHAN'S THE ONE HE REALLY WANTS?!
I DON'T REALLY KNOW, BUT PROBABLY.

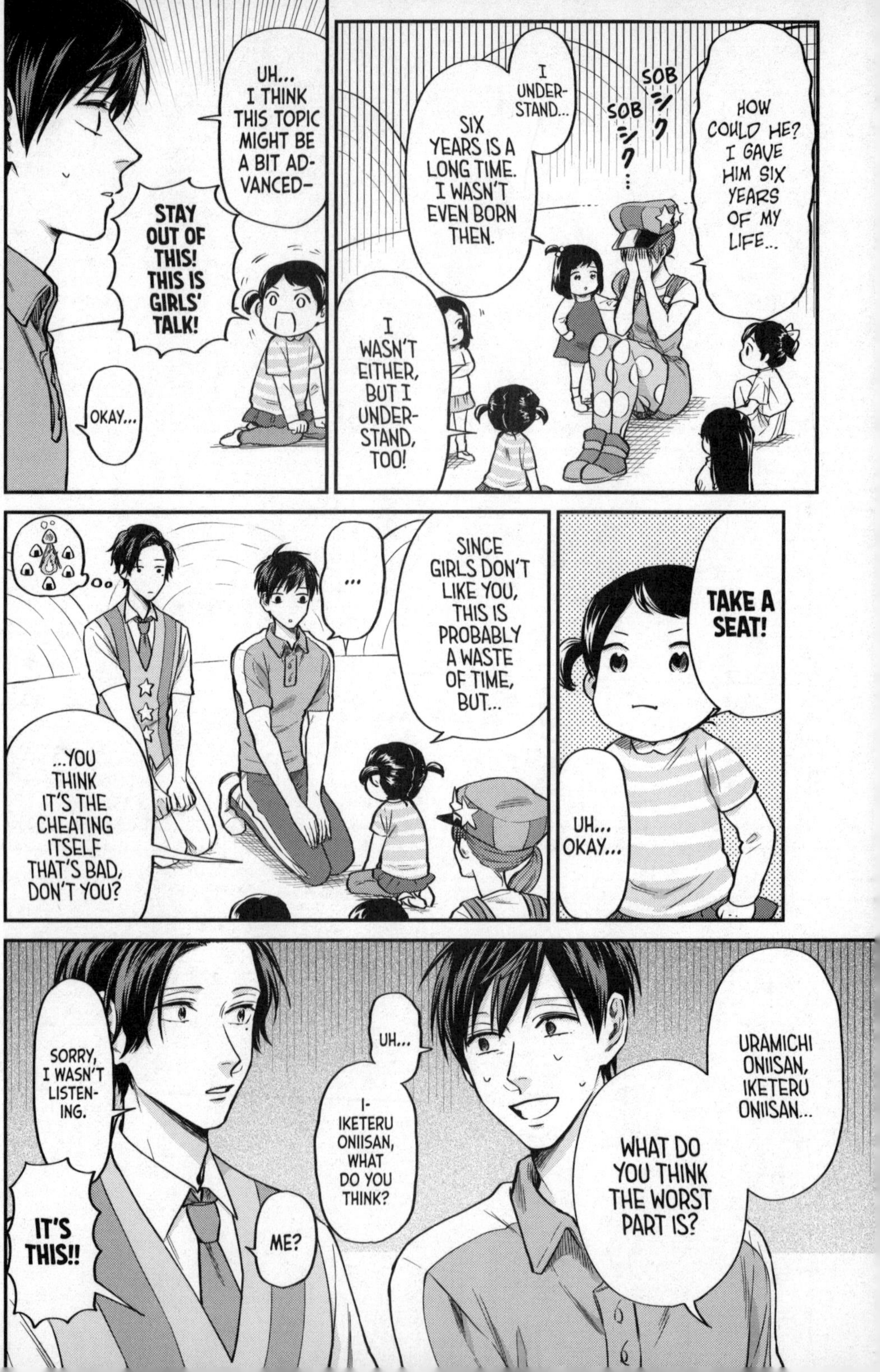
HOW COULD HE? I GAVE HIM SIX YEARS OF MY LIFE...
SOB シク
SOB シク...
I UNDERSTAND...
SIX YEARS IS A LONG TIME. I WASN'T EVEN BORN THEN.
I WASN'T EITHER, BUT I UNDERSTAND, TOO!
UH... I THINK THIS TOPIC MIGHT BE A BIT ADVANCED–
STAY OUT OF THIS! THIS IS GIRLS' TALK!
OKAY...
TAKE A SEAT!
UH... OKAY...
SINCE GIRLS DON'T LIKE YOU, THIS IS PROBABLY A WASTE OF TIME, BUT...
...
...YOU THINK IT'S THE CHEATING ITSELF THAT'S BAD, DON'T YOU?
URAMICHI ONIISAN, IKETERU ONIISAN...
WHAT DO YOU THINK THE WORST PART IS?
UH...
I- IKETERU ONIISAN, WHAT DO YOU THINK?
SORRY, I WASN'T LISTENING.
ME?
IT'S THIS!!

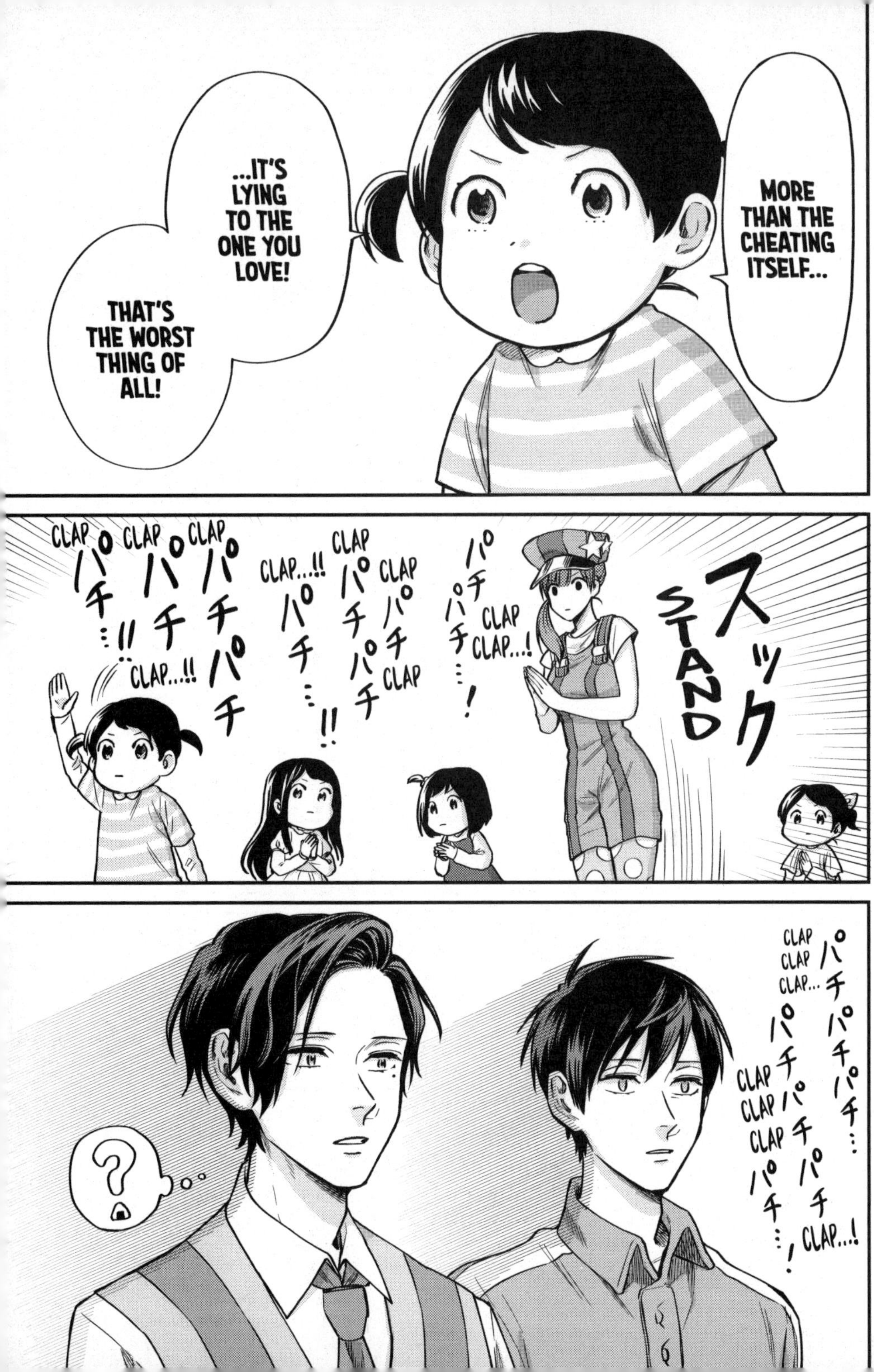
MORE THAN THE CHEATING ITSELF...
...IT'S LYING TO THE ONE YOU LOVE!
THAT'S THE WORST THING OF ALL!
スック
STAND
パチパチ…!
CLAP CLAP...!
パチパチパチ
CLAP CLAP
パチ…!!
CLAP...!!
パチパチパチ
CLAP
パチパチ
CLAP
パチ…!!
CLAP...!!
CLAP
CLAP
CLAP
パチパチパチ…
CLAP CLAP CLAP...
パチパチパチ
CLAP CLAP CLAP
パチ…!
CLAP...!
?

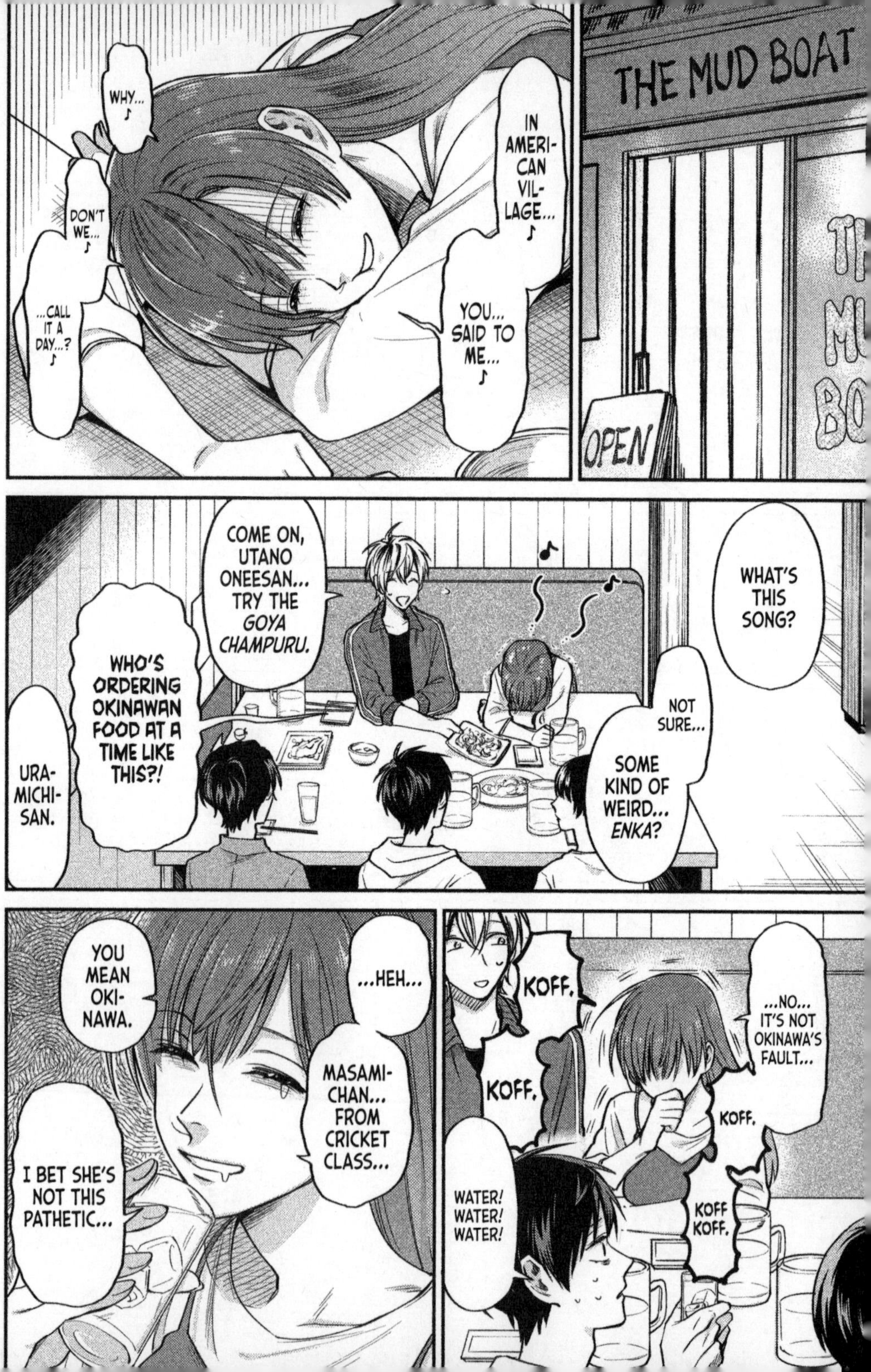
THE MUD BOAT
THE MUD BOAT
OPEN
IN AMERICAN VILLAGE... ♪
YOU... SAID TO ME... ♪
WHY... ♪
DON'T WE... ♪
...CALL IT A DAY...? ♪
WHAT'S THIS SONG?
NOT SURE...
SOME KIND OF WEIRD... *ENKA*?
COME ON, UTANO ONEESAN... TRY THE *GOYA CHAMPURU*.
WHO'S ORDERING OKINAWAN FOOD AT A TIME LIKE THIS?!
URAMICHI-SAN.
...NO... IT'S NOT OKINAWA'S FAULT...
KOFF.
KOFF.
KOFF.
KOFF KOFF.
WATER! WATER! WATER!
...HEH...
YOU MEAN OKINAWA.
MASAMI-CHAN... FROM CRICKET CLASS...
I BET SHE'S NOT THIS PATHETIC...

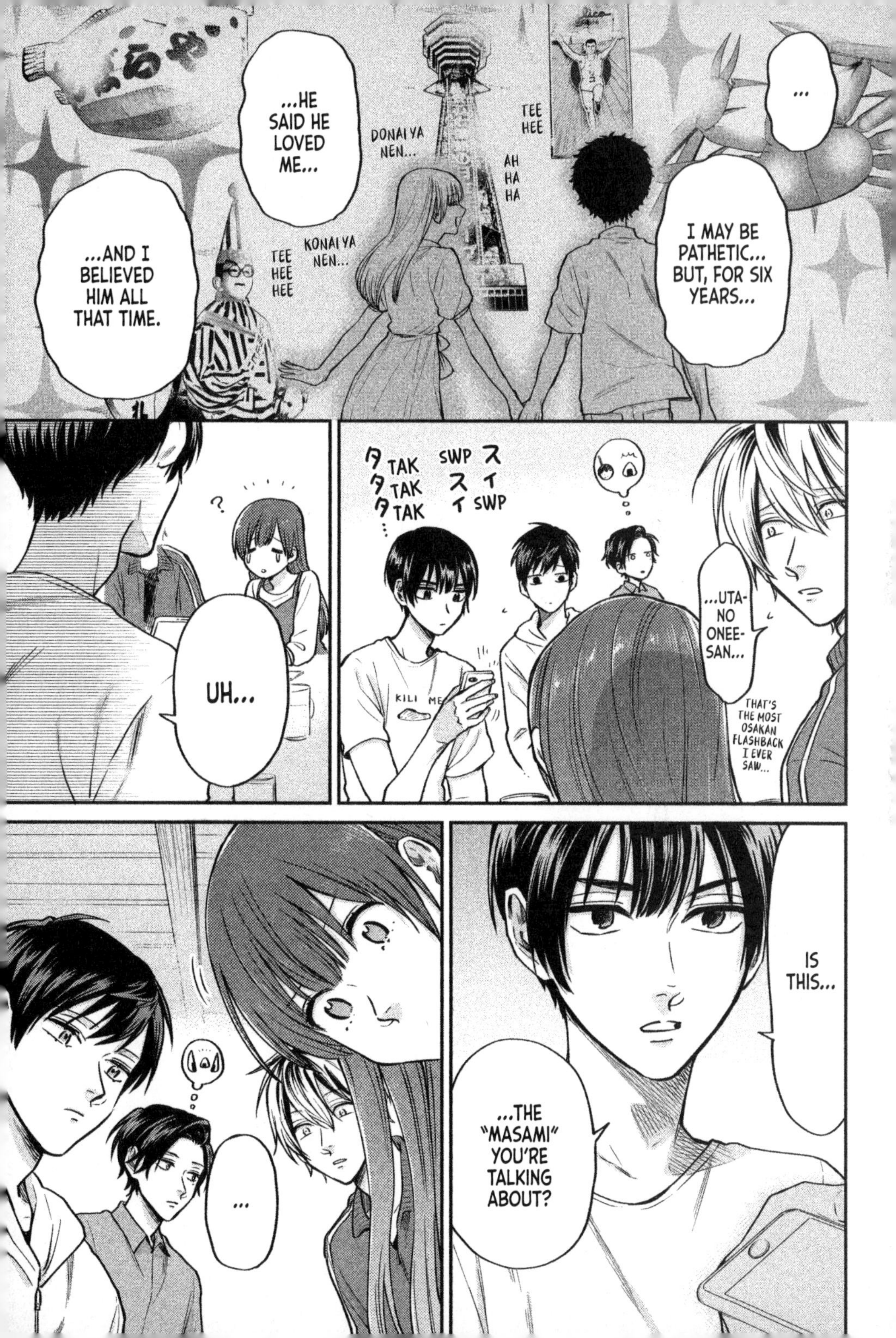
...
I MAY BE PATHETIC... BUT, FOR SIX YEARS...
TEE HEE
AH HA HA
...HE SAID HE LOVED ME...
DONAI YA NEN...
KONAI YA NEN...
TEE HEE HEE
...AND I BELIEVED HIM ALL THAT TIME.
...UTA-NO ONEE-SAN...
THAT'S THE MOST OSAKAN FLASHBACK I EVER SAW...
スイスイ SWP SWP
タタタ TAK TAK TAK...
KILI ME
UH...
IS THIS...
...THE "MASAMI" YOU'RE TALKING ABOUT?
...

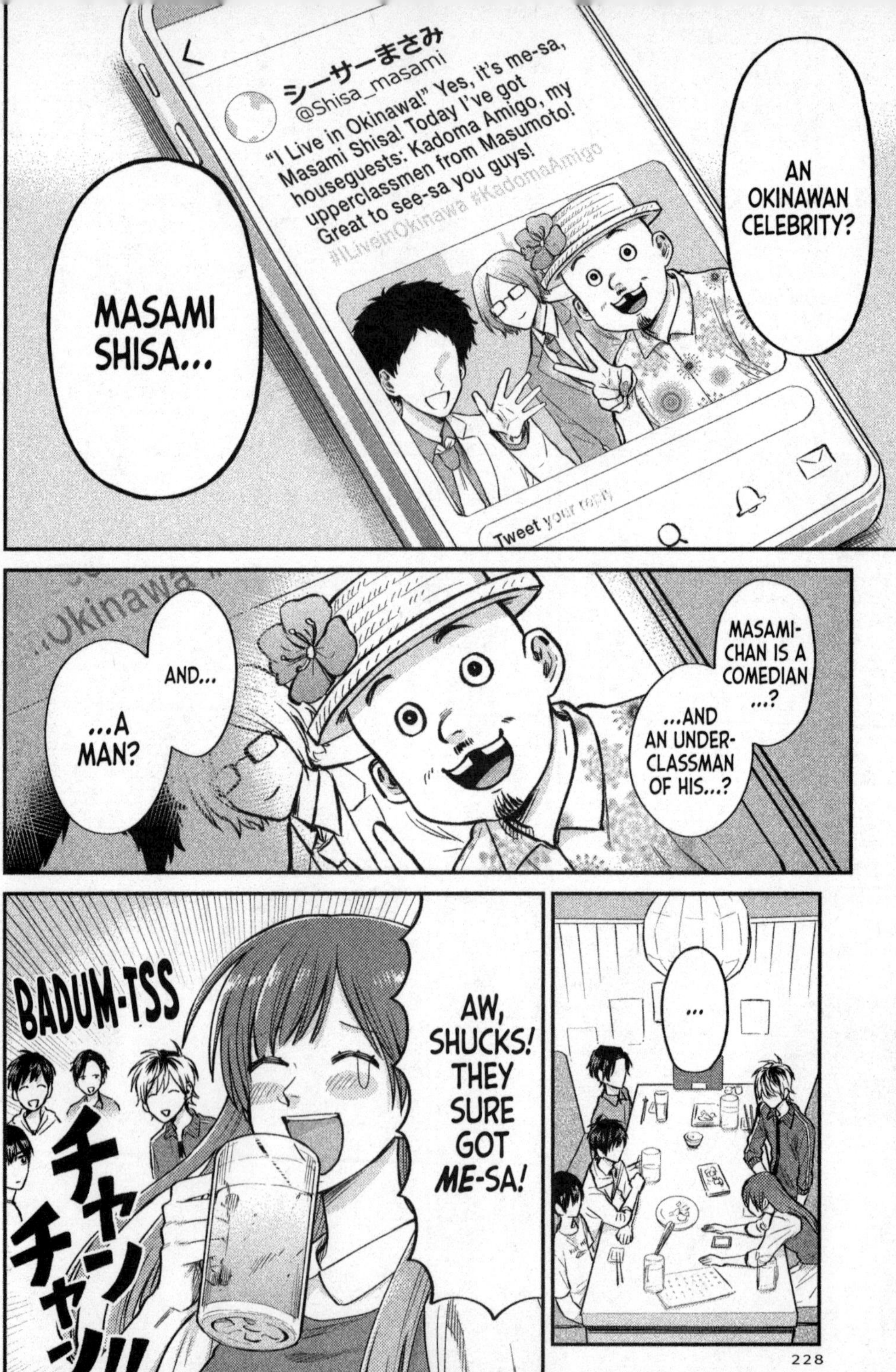
AN OKINAWAN CELEBRITY?
シーサーまさみ
@Shisa_masami
"I Live in Okinawa!" Yes, it's me-sa, Masami Shisa! Today I've got houseguests: Kadoma Amigo, my upperclassmen from Masumoto! Great to see-sa you guys!
#ILiveinOkinawa #KadomaAmigo
Tweet your reply
MASAMI SHISA...
MASAMI-CHAN IS A COMEDIAN ...?
...AND AN UNDER-CLASSMAN OF HIS...?
AND...
...A MAN?
...
AW, SHUCKS! THEY SURE GOT *ME*-SA!
BADUM-TSS
チャンチャン!!

Life Lessons with
Uramichi Oniisan

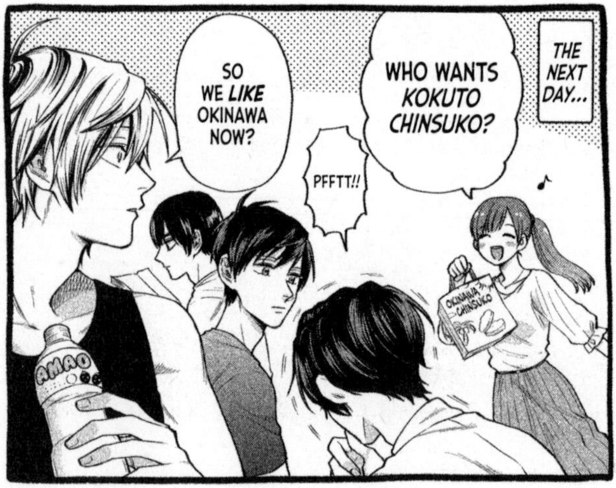
THE NEXT DAY...
WHO WANTS KOKUTO CHINSUKO?
OKINAWA CHINSUKO
PFFTT!!
SO WE *LIKE* OKINAWA NOW?
AMAO

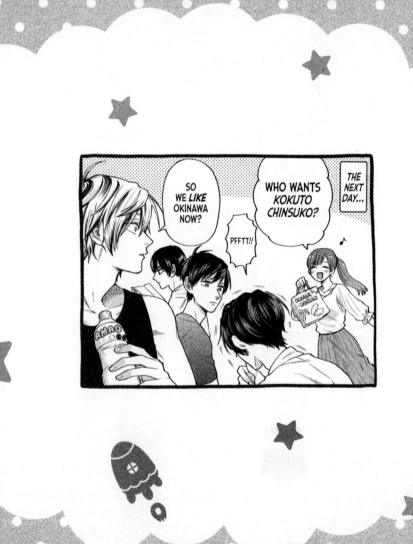

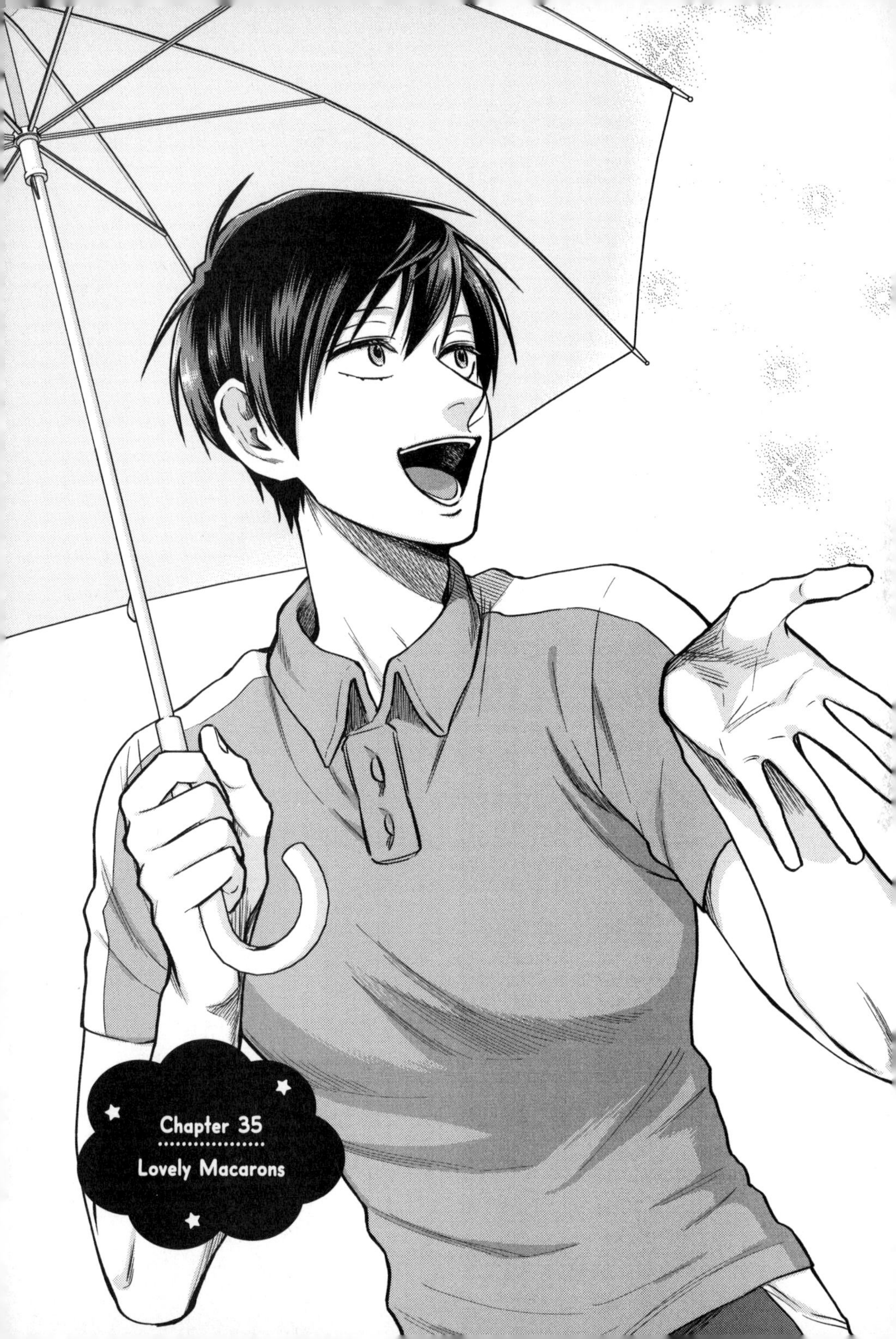
Chapter 35
Lovely Macarons

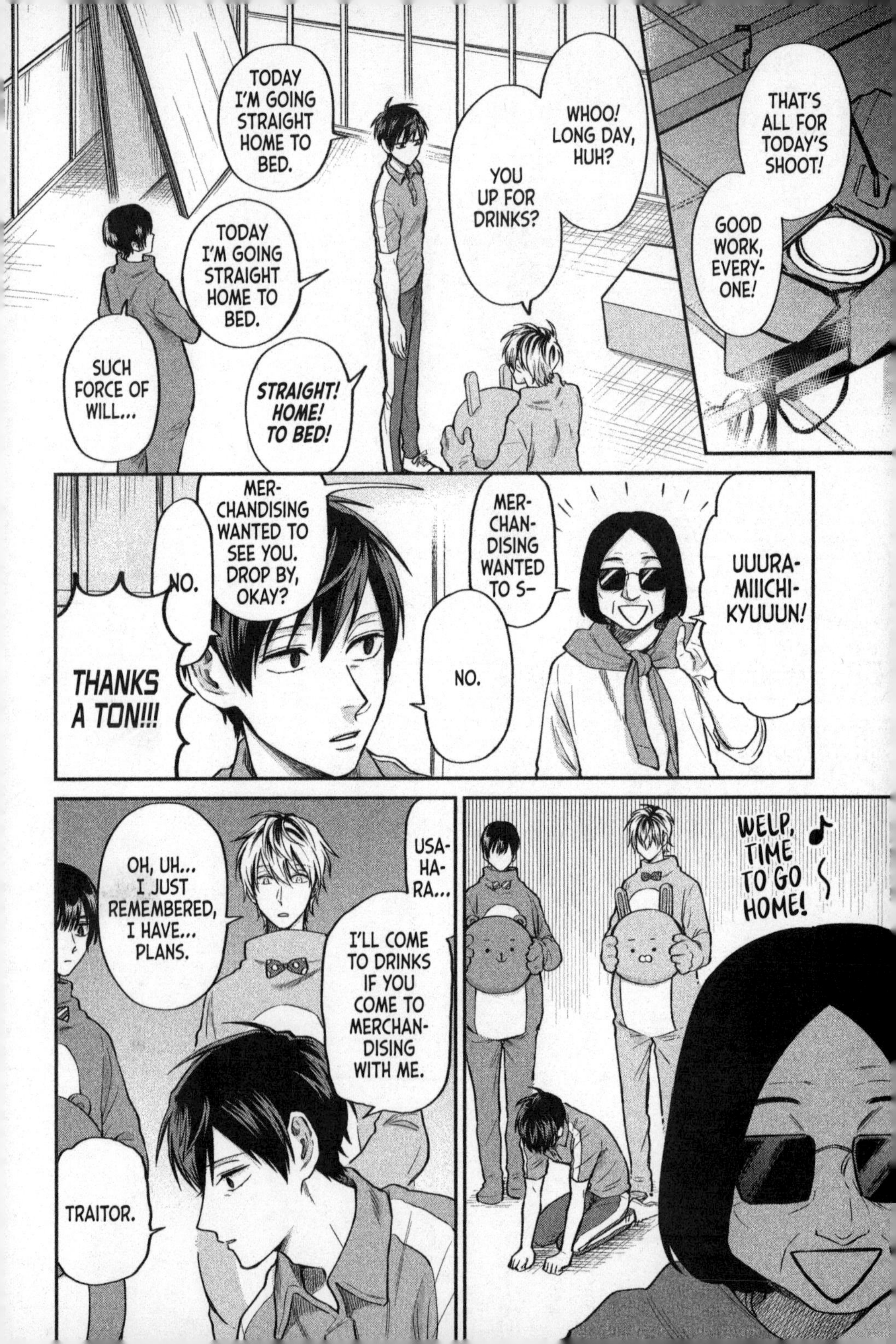
THAT'S ALL FOR TODAY'S SHOOT!
GOOD WORK, EVERY-ONE!
WHOO! LONG DAY, HUH?
YOU UP FOR DRINKS?
TODAY I'M GOING STRAIGHT HOME TO BED.
TODAY I'M GOING STRAIGHT HOME TO BED.
STRAIGHT! HOME! TO BED!
SUCH FORCE OF WILL...
UUURA-MIIICHI-KYUUUN!
MER-CHAN-DISING WANTED TO S—
NO.
MER-CHANDISING WANTED TO SEE YOU. DROP BY, OKAY?
NO.
THANKS A TON!!!
WELP, TIME TO GO HOME! ♪
USA-HA-RA...
I'LL COME TO DRINKS IF YOU COME TO MERCHAN-DISING WITH ME.
OH, UH... I JUST REMEMBERED, I HAVE... PLANS.
TRAITOR.

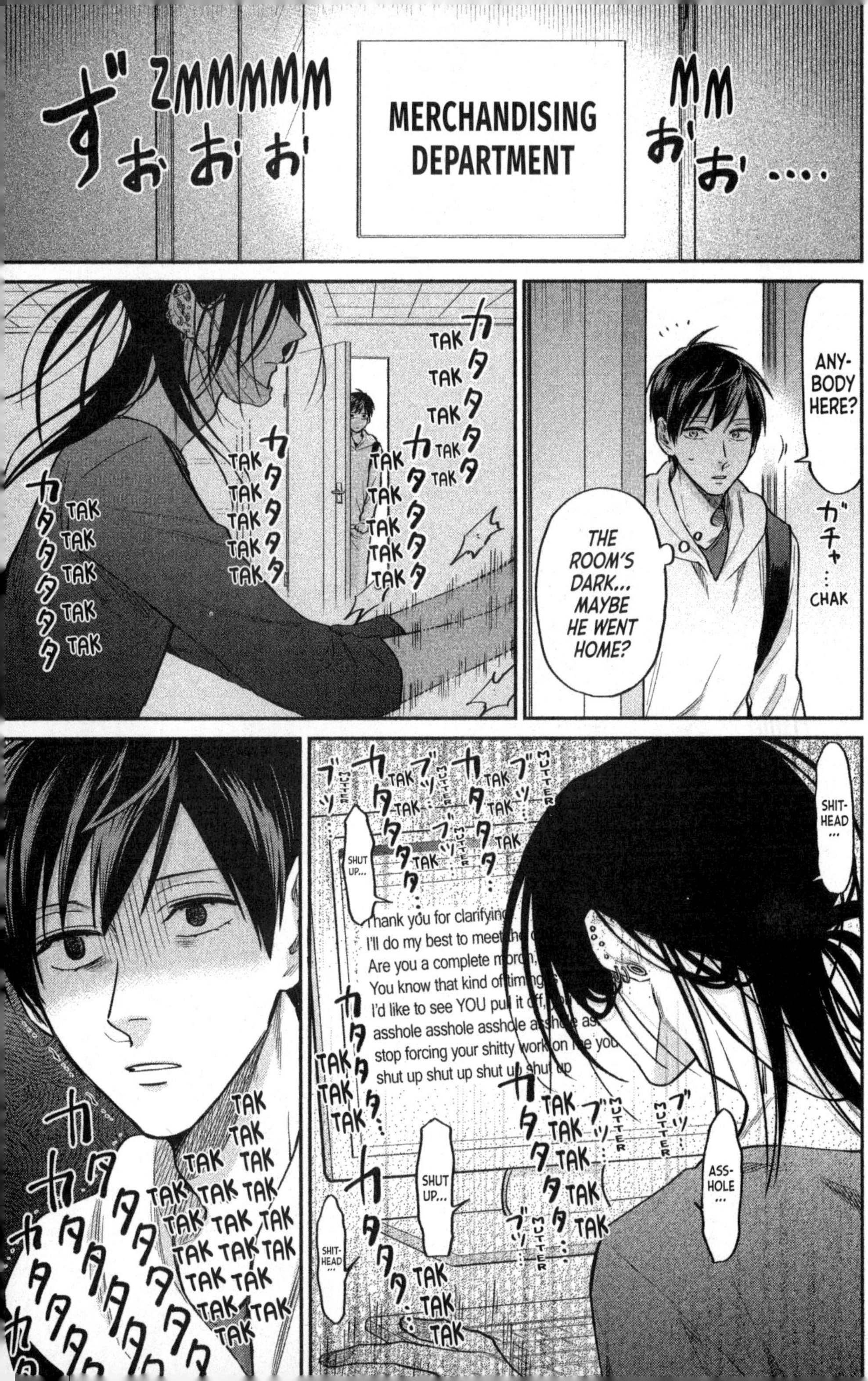

MM おぉ....
MERCHANDISING DEPARTMENT
ずぉぉぉ ZMMMMMM
ANY-BODY HERE?
ガチャ… CHAK
THE ROOM'S DARK... MAYBE HE WENT HOME?
カタタタタ TAK TAK TAK TAK TAK
カタタタタ TAK TAK TAK TAK TAK
カタタタタ TAK TAK TAK TAK TAK
SHIT-HEAD...
ブツ… MUTTER
カタタタ… TAK TAK TAK
ブツ… MUTTER
カタタタ… TAK TAK TAK
ブツ… MUTTER
SHUT UP...
Thank you for clarifying
I'll do my best to meet the
Are you a complete moron
You know that kind of timing
I'd like to see YOU pull it off
asshole asshole asshole asshole as
stop forcing your shitty work on me you
shut up shut up shut up shut up
カタタタ… TAK TAK TAK
ブツ… MUTTER
ブツ… MUTTER
カタタタ… TAK TAK TAK
ASS-HOLE...
SHUT UP...
ブツ… MUTTER
カタタタ… TAK TAK TAK
SHIT-HEAD...
カタタタタ TAK TAK TAK TAK TAK TAK
カタタタタタタ TAK TAK TAK TAK TAK TAK TAK TAK TAK TAK TAK TAK TAK TAK TAK

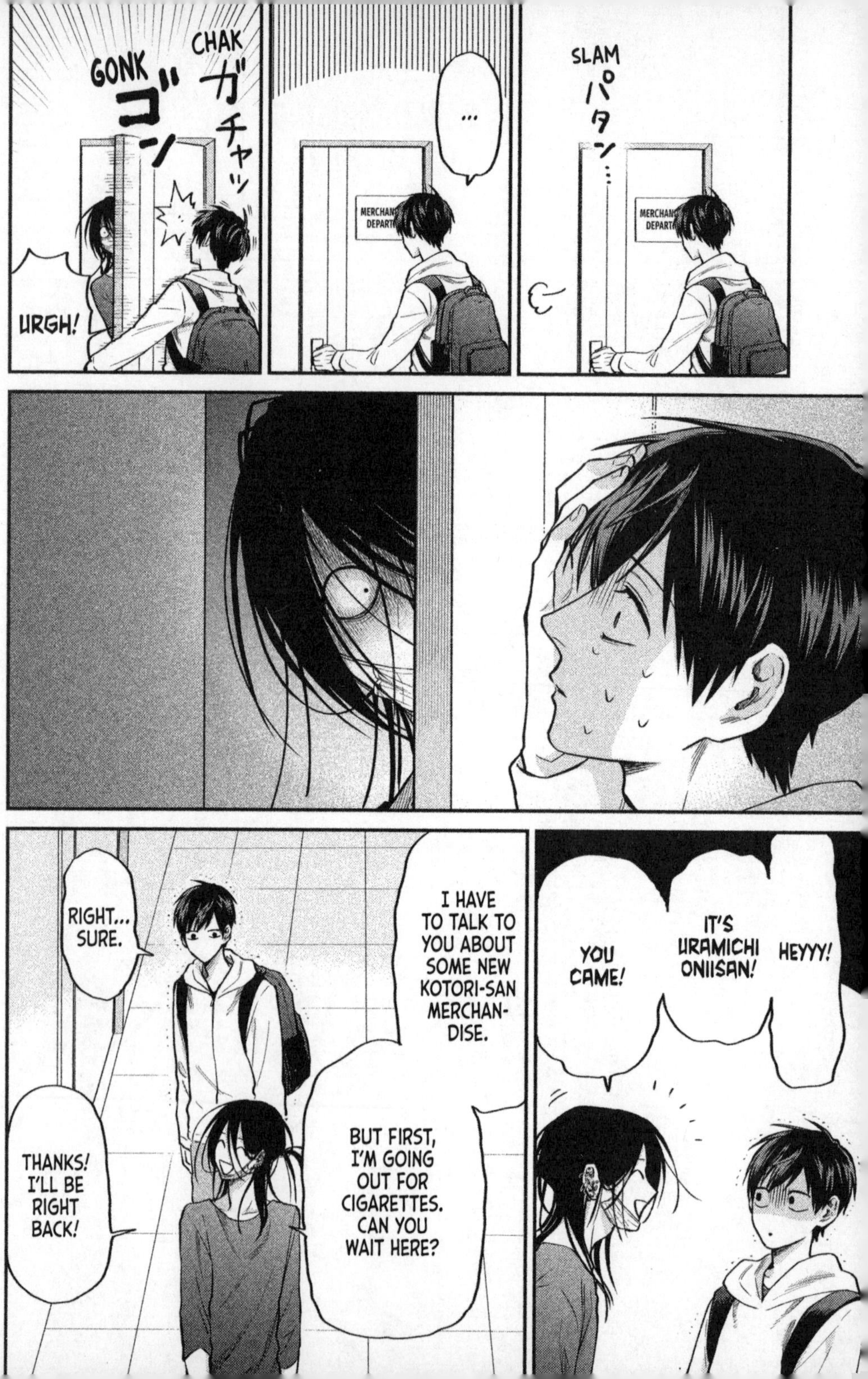
SLAM
パタン…
…
CHAK
ガチャッ
GONK
ゴン
URGH!
HEYYY!
IT'S URAMICHI ONIISAN!
YOU CAME!
I HAVE TO TALK TO YOU ABOUT SOME NEW KOTORI-SAN MERCHANDISE.
RIGHT... SURE.
BUT FIRST, I'M GOING OUT FOR CIGARETTES. CAN YOU WAIT HERE?
THANKS! I'LL BE RIGHT BACK!

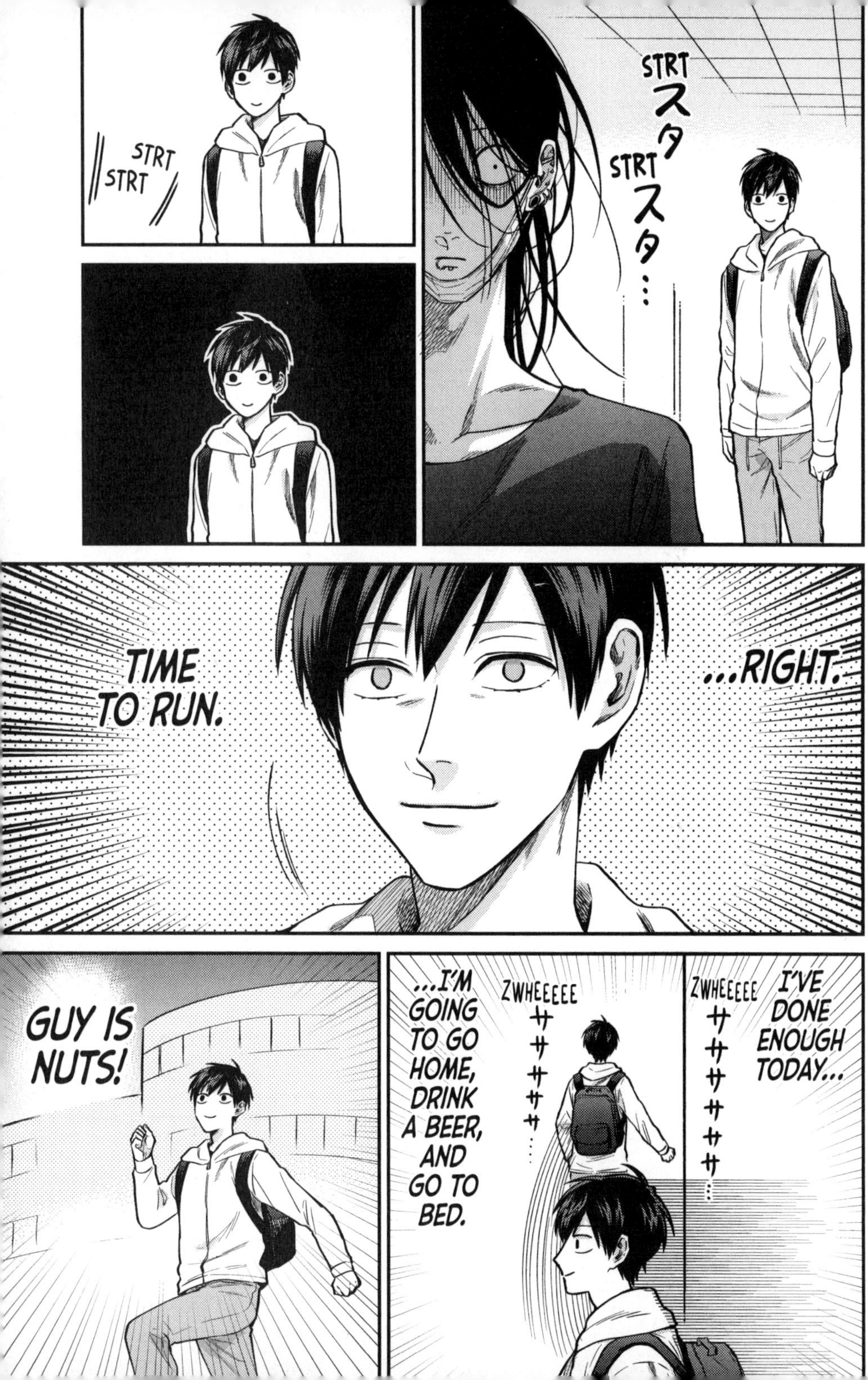
STRT
スタ
STRT
スタ…
STRT
STRT
...RIGHT.
TIME TO RUN.
I'VE DONE ENOUGH TODAY...
ZWHEEEEE
ササササササ…
ZWHEEEEE
サササササ…
...I'M GOING TO GO HOME, DRINK A BEER, AND GO TO BED.
GUY IS NUTS!

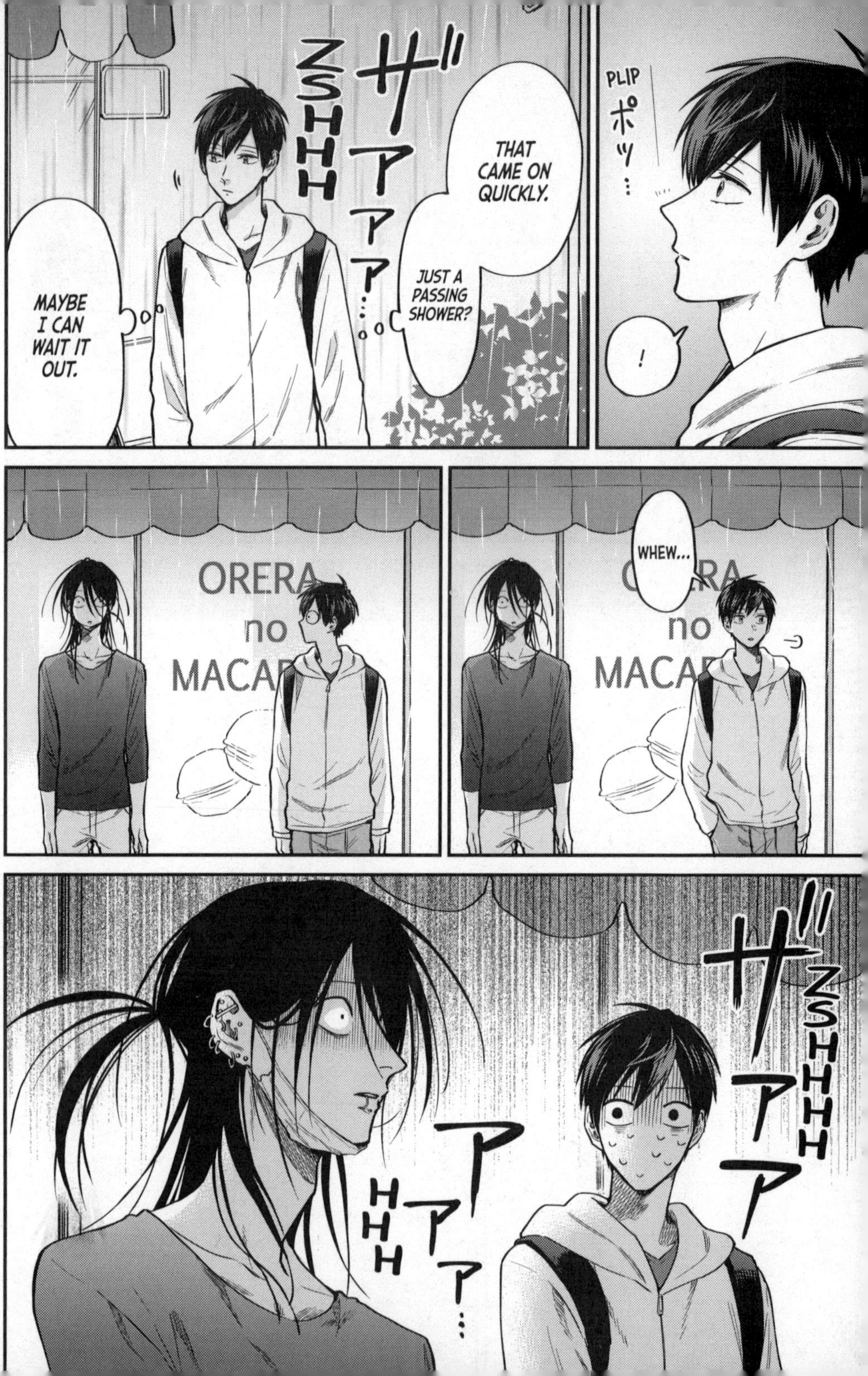
PLIP
ポツ…
!
ZSHHH
ザアア…
THAT CAME ON QUICKLY.
JUST A PASSING SHOWER?
MAYBE I CAN WAIT IT OUT.
WHEW…
ORERA no MACA
ZSHHHH
ザアア
HHHH
アアア…

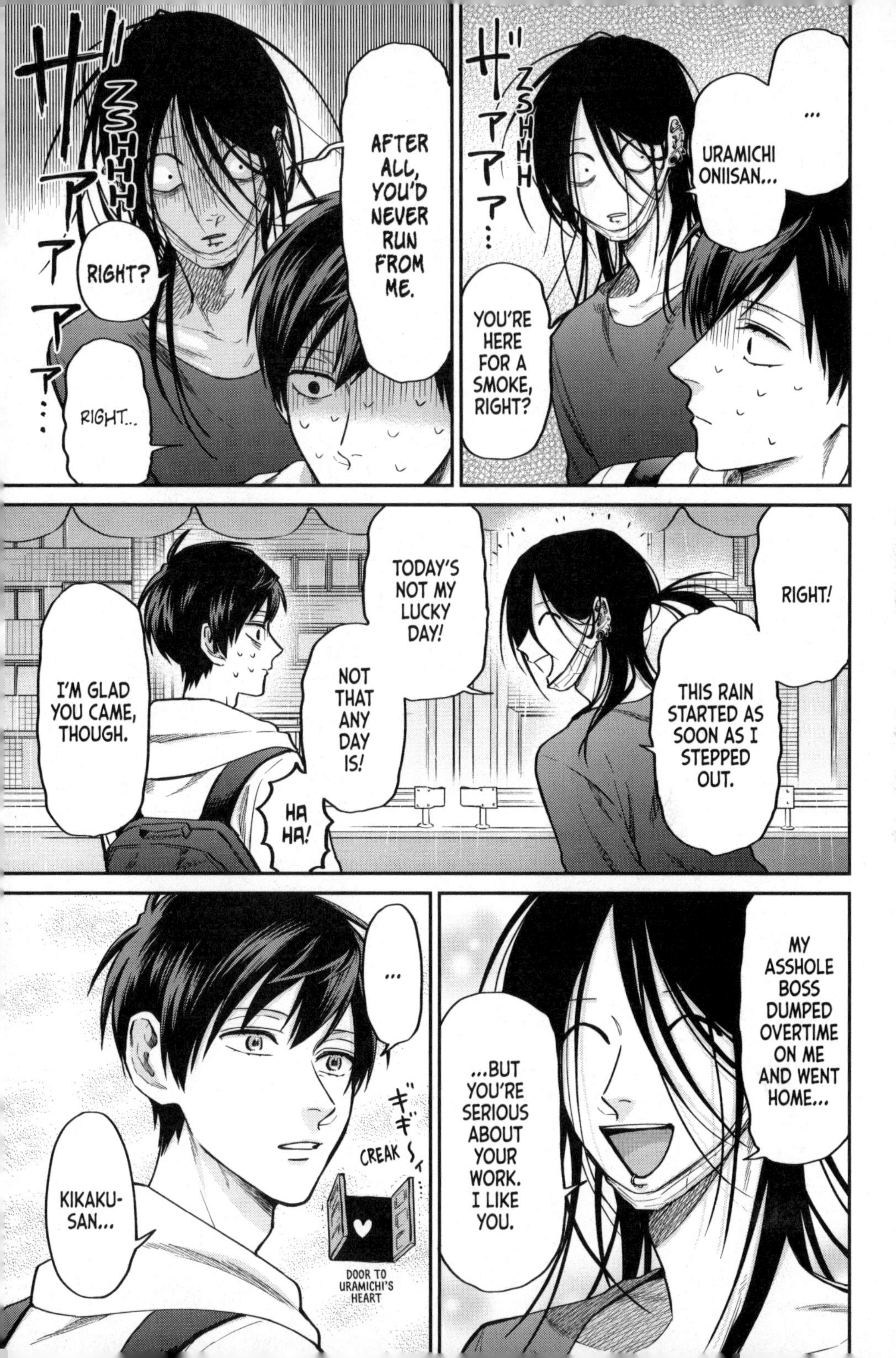
ZSHHH
...
URAMICHI ONIISAN...
YOU'RE HERE FOR A SMOKE, RIGHT?
ZSHHH
AFTER ALL, YOU'D NEVER RUN FROM ME.
RIGHT?
RIGHT...
RIGHT!
THIS RAIN STARTED AS SOON AS I STEPPED OUT.
TODAY'S NOT MY LUCKY DAY!
NOT THAT ANY DAY IS!
HA HA!
I'M GLAD YOU CAME, THOUGH.
MY ASSHOLE BOSS DUMPED OVERTIME ON ME AND WENT HOME...
...BUT YOU'RE SERIOUS ABOUT YOUR WORK. I LIKE YOU.
...
CREAK
KIKAKU-SAN...
DOOR TO URAMICHI'S HEART

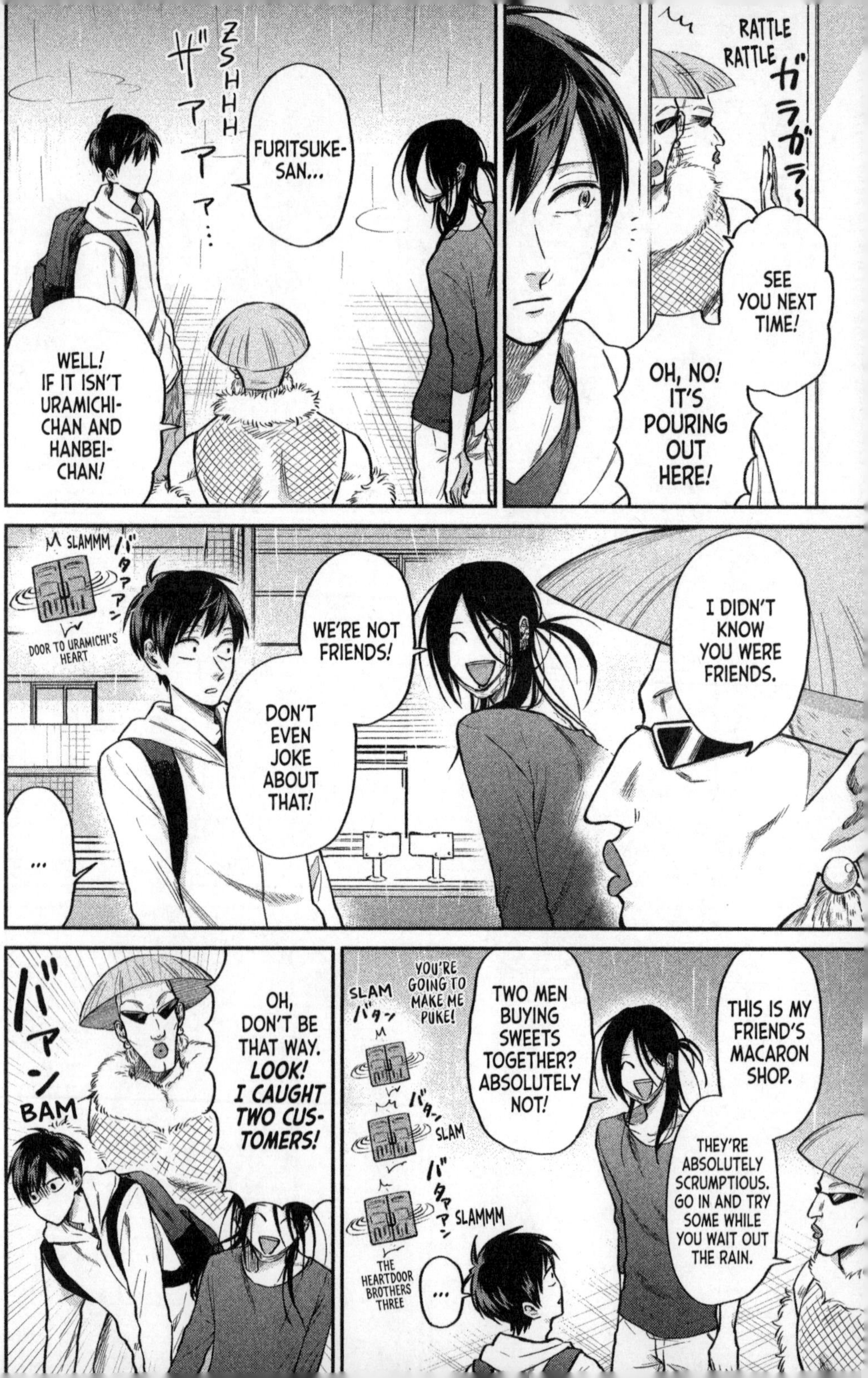
RATTLE RATTLE
ガラガラ~
SEE YOU NEXT TIME!
OH, NO! IT'S POURING OUT HERE!
ZSHHH
ザアア…
FURITSUKE-SAN...
WELL! IF IT ISN'T URAMICHI-CHAN AND HANBEI-CHAN!
I DIDN'T KNOW YOU WERE FRIENDS.
WE'RE NOT FRIENDS!
DON'T EVEN JOKE ABOUT THAT!
...
SLAMMM
バタアン
DOOR TO URAMICHI'S HEART
THIS IS MY FRIEND'S MACARON SHOP.
THEY'RE ABSOLUTELY SCRUMPTIOUS. GO IN AND TRY SOME WHILE YOU WAIT OUT THE RAIN.
TWO MEN BUYING SWEETS TOGETHER? ABSOLUTELY NOT!
YOU'RE GOING TO MAKE ME PUKE!
SLAM
バタン
バタン
SLAM
バタアン
SLAMMM
THE HEARTDOOR BROTHERS THREE
...
OH, DON'T BE THAT WAY. LOOK! I CAUGHT TWO CUS- TOMERS!
バァン
BAM

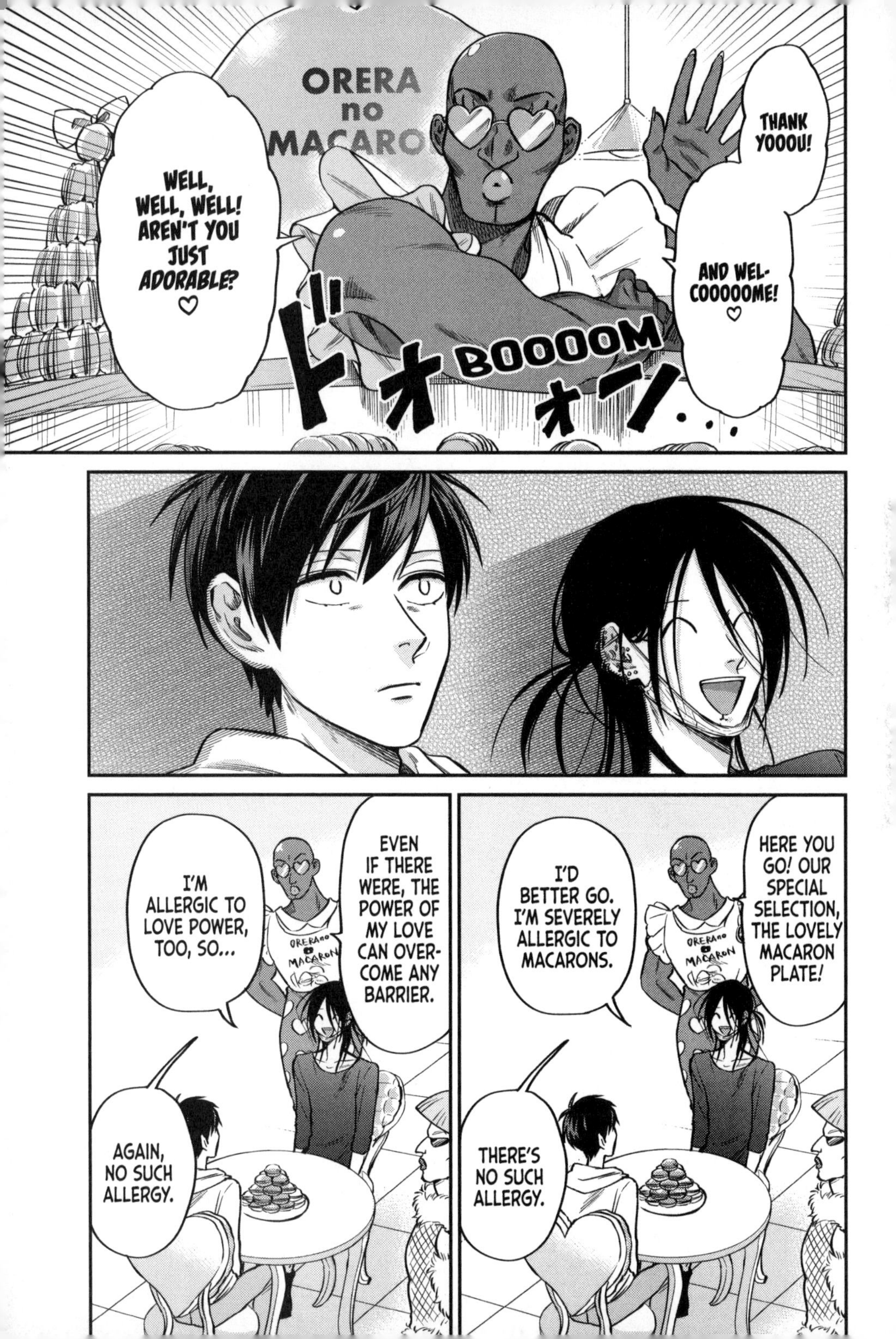
ORERA no MACARO
THANK YOOOU!
AND WEL-COOOOOME! ♡
BOOOOM
WELL, WELL, WELL! AREN'T YOU JUST ADORABLE? ♡
HERE YOU GO! OUR SPECIAL SELECTION, THE LOVELY MACARON PLATE!
I'D BETTER GO. I'M SEVERELY ALLERGIC TO MACARONS.
THERE'S NO SUCH ALLERGY.
EVEN IF THERE WERE, THE POWER OF MY LOVE CAN OVER-COME ANY BARRIER.
I'M ALLERGIC TO LOVE POWER, TOO, SO...
AGAIN, NO SUCH ALLERGY.

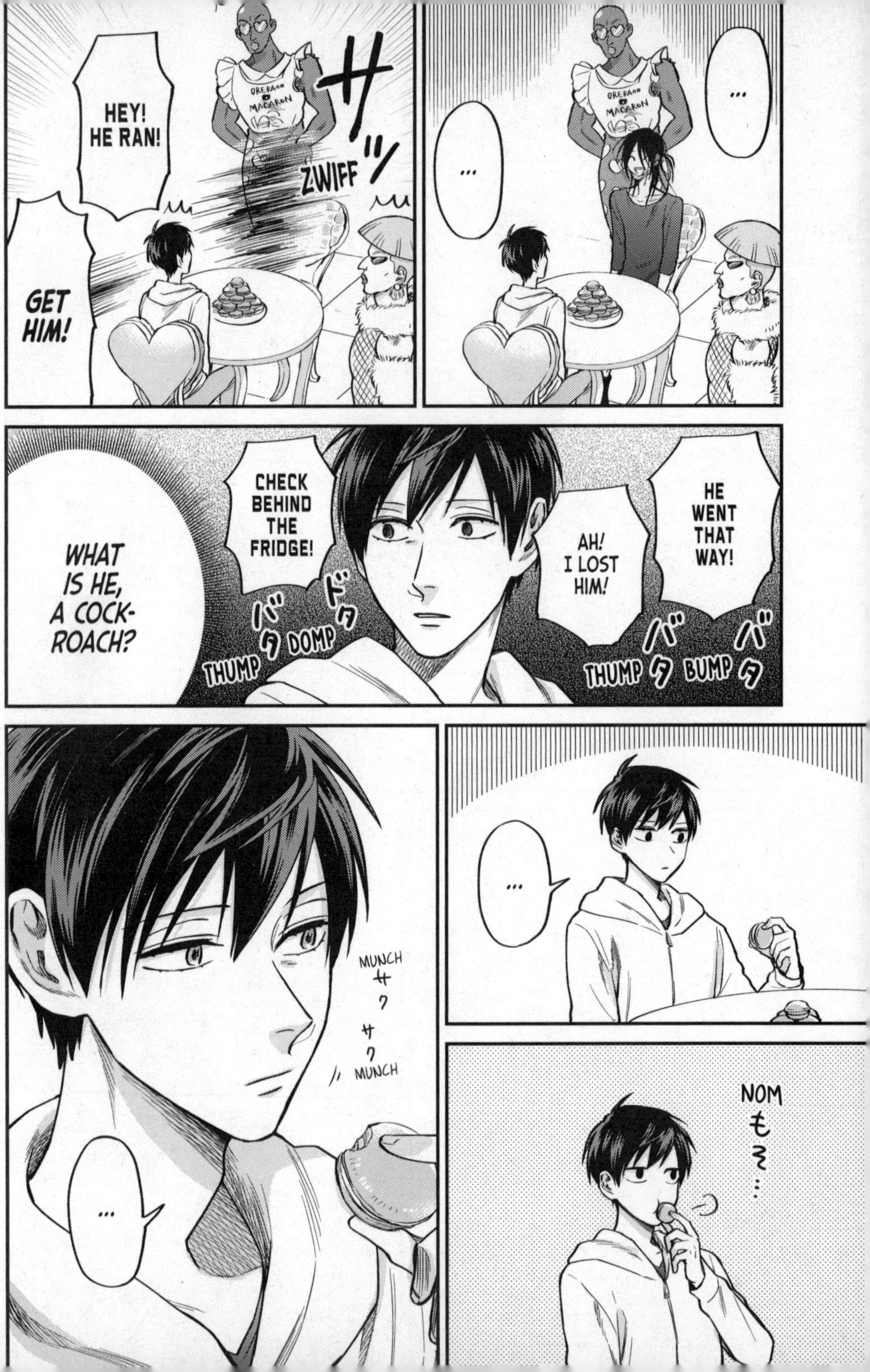
...
...
HEY! HE RAN!
サッ
ZWIFF
GET HIM!
HE WENT THAT WAY!
AH! I LOST HIM!
バタ THUMP バタ BUMP
CHECK BEHIND THE FRIDGE!
バタ ドタ THUMP DOMP
WHAT IS HE, A COCK-ROACH?
...
NOM もそ…
MUNCH サク サク MUNCH
...

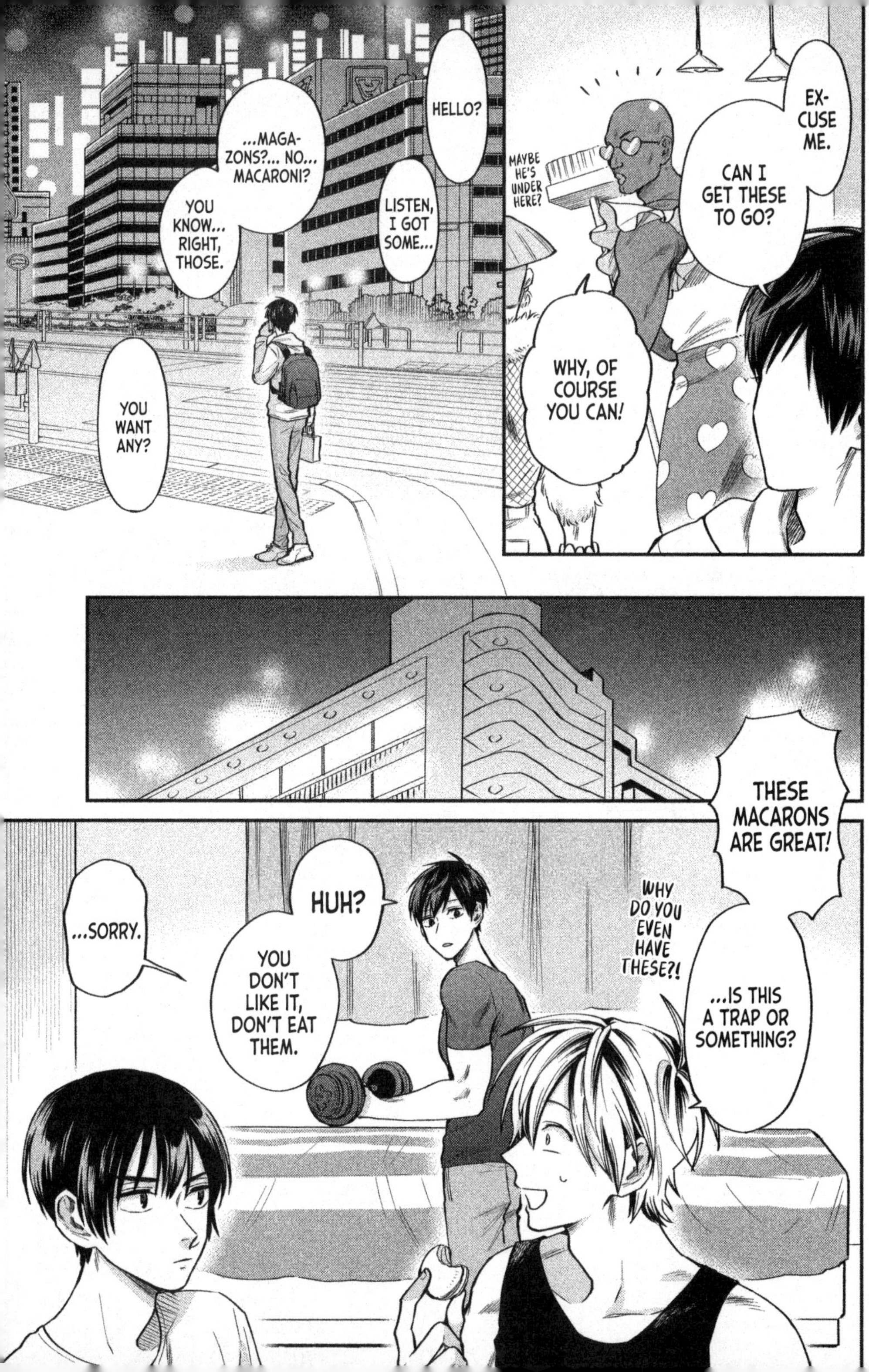
EX-CUSE ME.
CAN I GET THESE TO GO?
MAYBE HE'S UNDER HERE?
WHY, OF COURSE YOU CAN!
HELLO?
LISTEN, I GOT SOME...
...MAGA-ZONS?... NO... MACARONI?
YOU KNOW... RIGHT, THOSE.
YOU WANT ANY?
THESE MACARONS ARE GREAT!
WHY DO YOU EVEN HAVE THESE?!
...IS THIS A TRAP OR SOMETHING?
HUH?
YOU DON'T LIKE IT, DON'T EAT THEM.
...SORRY.

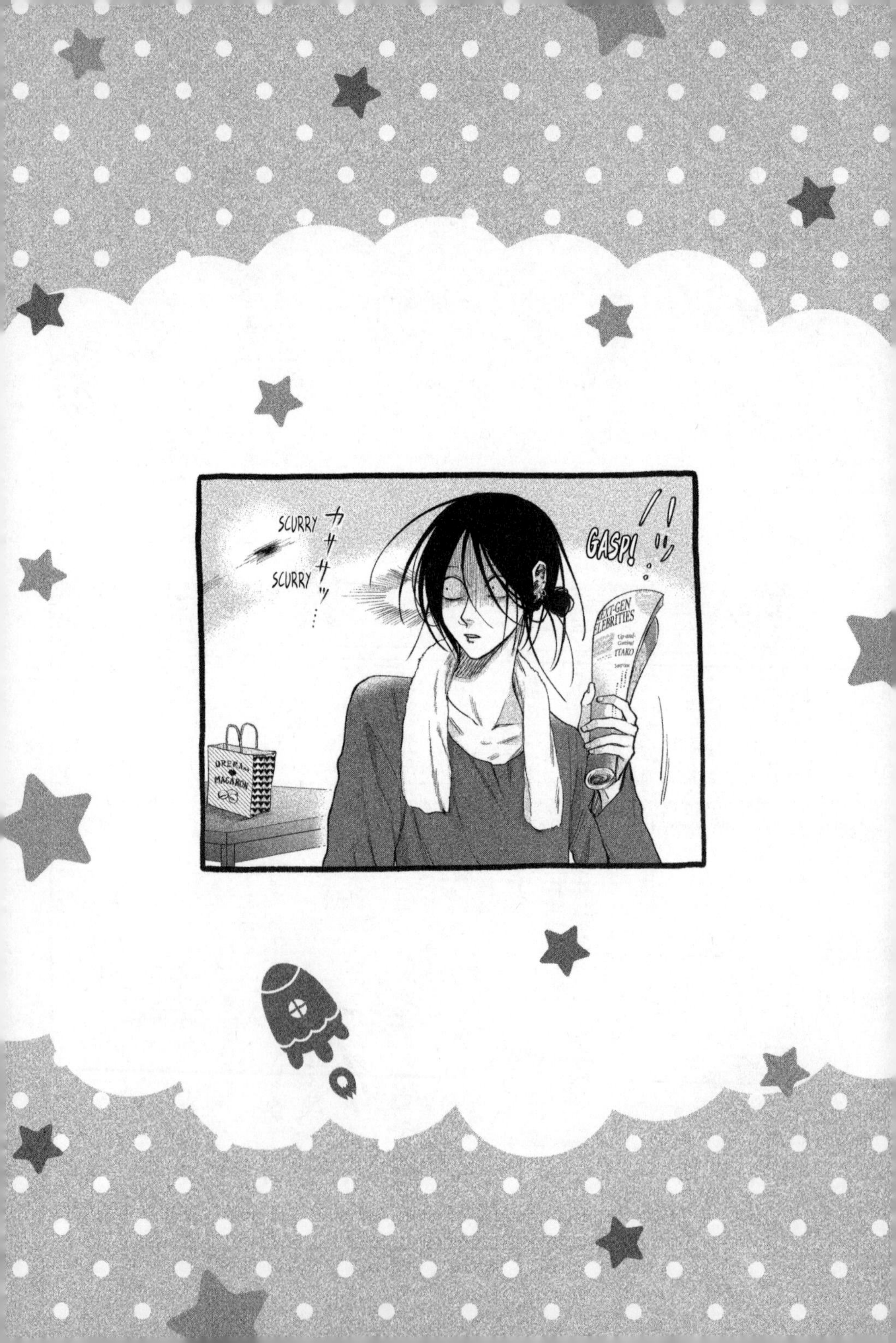
ハッ
GASP!
EXT-GEN
ELEBRITIES
Up-and-Coming!
ITAKO
カサカサッ…
SCURRY
SCURRY
MACARON

Life Lessons with
Uramichi Oniisan

Chapter 36
Winter Break Alone

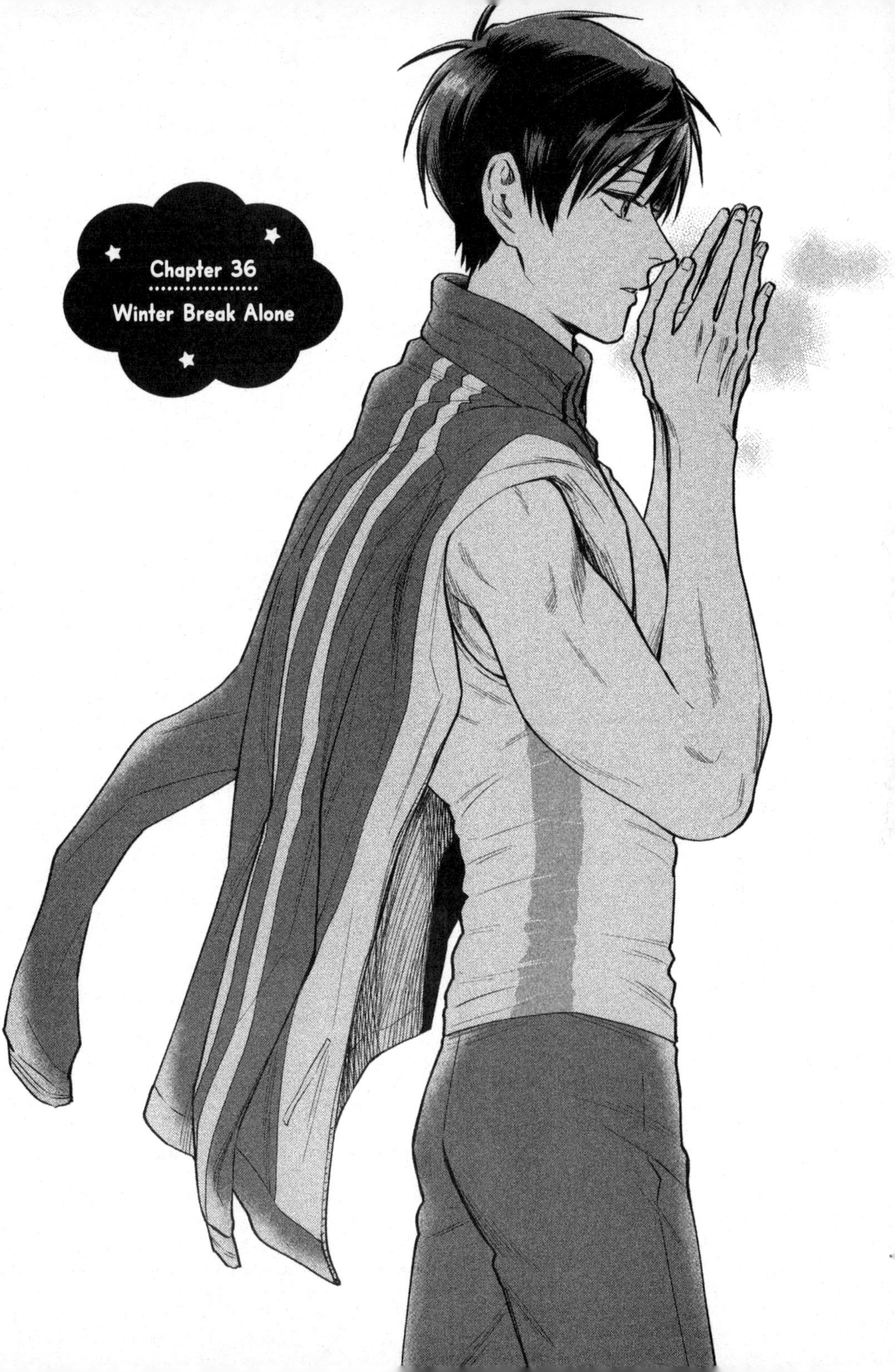

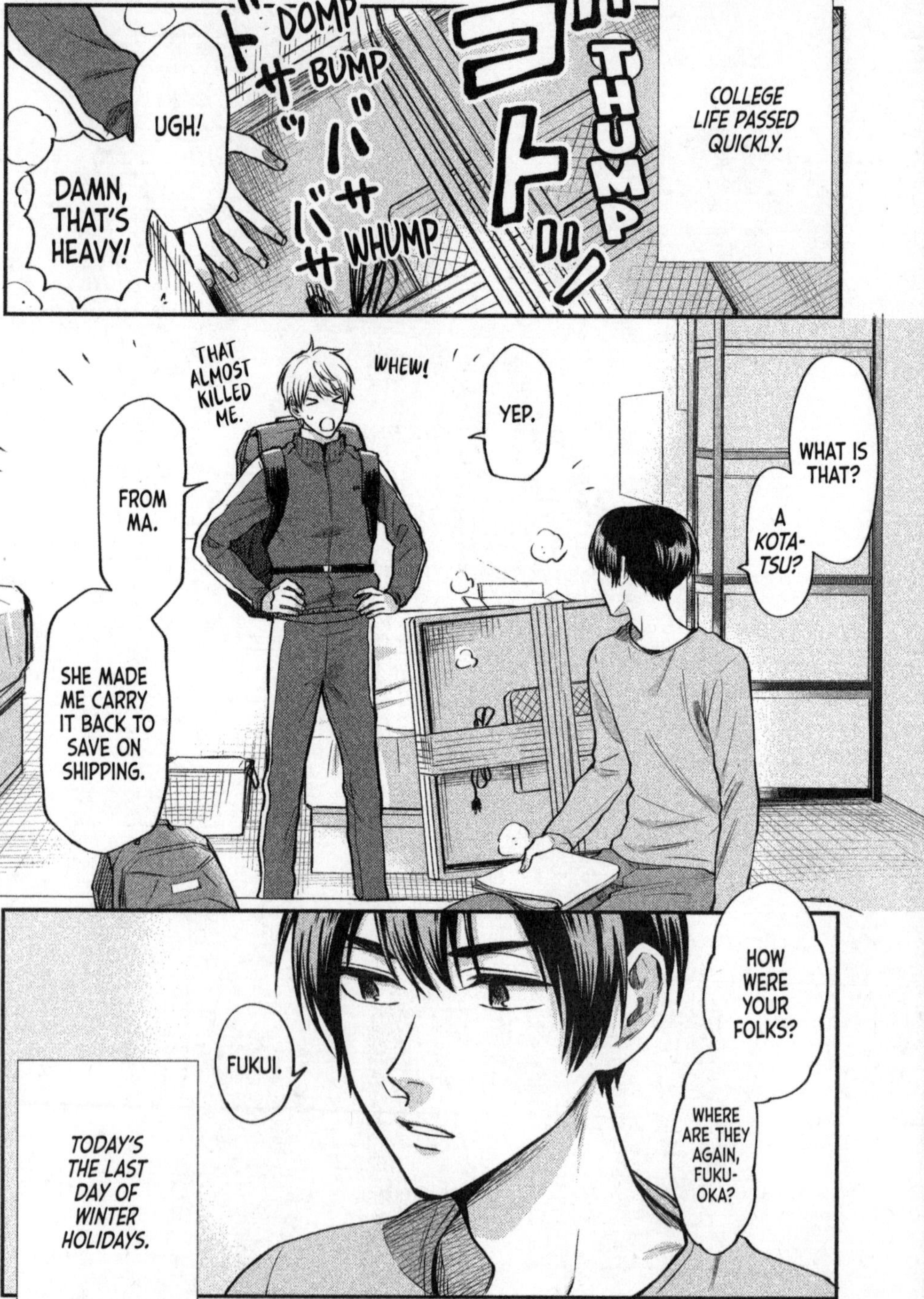
COLLEGE LIFE PASSED QUICKLY.
THUMP
WHUMP
BUMP
DOMP
UGH!
DAMN, THAT'S HEAVY!
WHAT IS THAT?
A KOTATSU?
YEP.
WHEW!
THAT ALMOST KILLED ME.
FROM MA.
SHE MADE ME CARRY IT BACK TO SAVE ON SHIPPING.
HOW WERE YOUR FOLKS?
WHERE ARE THEY AGAIN, FUKUOKA?
FUKUI.
TODAY'S THE LAST DAY OF WINTER HOLIDAYS.

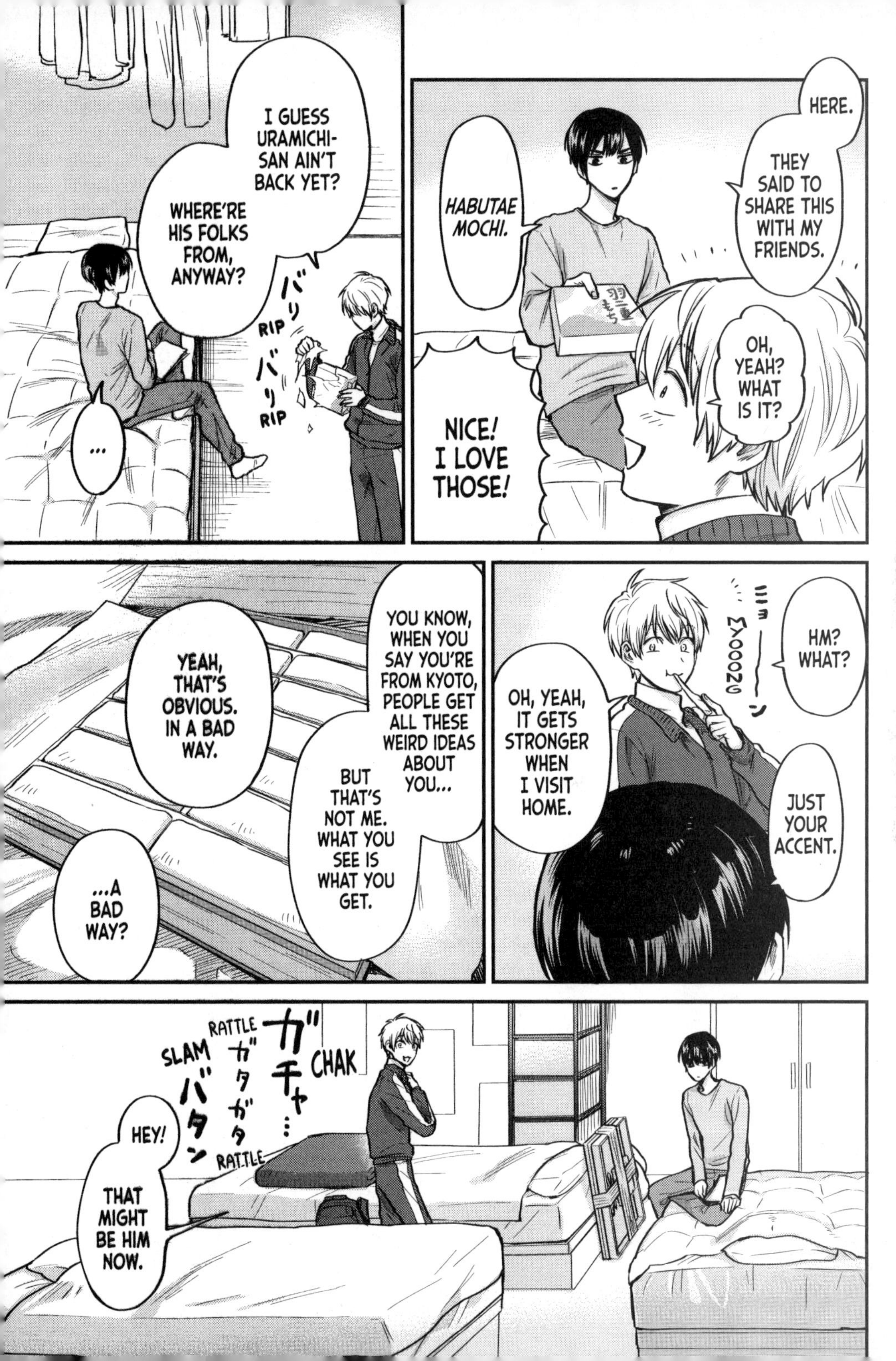
HERE.
THEY SAID TO SHARE THIS WITH MY FRIENDS.
OH, YEAH? WHAT IS IT?
HABUTAE MOCHI.
羽二重もち
NICE! I LOVE THOSE!
I GUESS URAMICHI-SAN AIN'T BACK YET?
WHERE'RE HIS FOLKS FROM, ANYWAY?
バリ RIP
バリ RIP
...
ニョーーン MYOOONG
HM? WHAT?
JUST YOUR ACCENT.
OH, YEAH, IT GETS STRONGER WHEN I VISIT HOME.
YOU KNOW, WHEN YOU SAY YOU'RE FROM KYOTO, PEOPLE GET ALL THESE WEIRD IDEAS ABOUT YOU...
BUT THAT'S NOT ME. WHAT YOU SEE IS WHAT YOU GET.
YEAH, THAT'S OBVIOUS. IN A BAD WAY.
...A BAD WAY?
ガチャ… CHAK
ガタガタ RATTLE RATTLE
バタン SLAM
HEY!
THAT MIGHT BE HIM NOW.

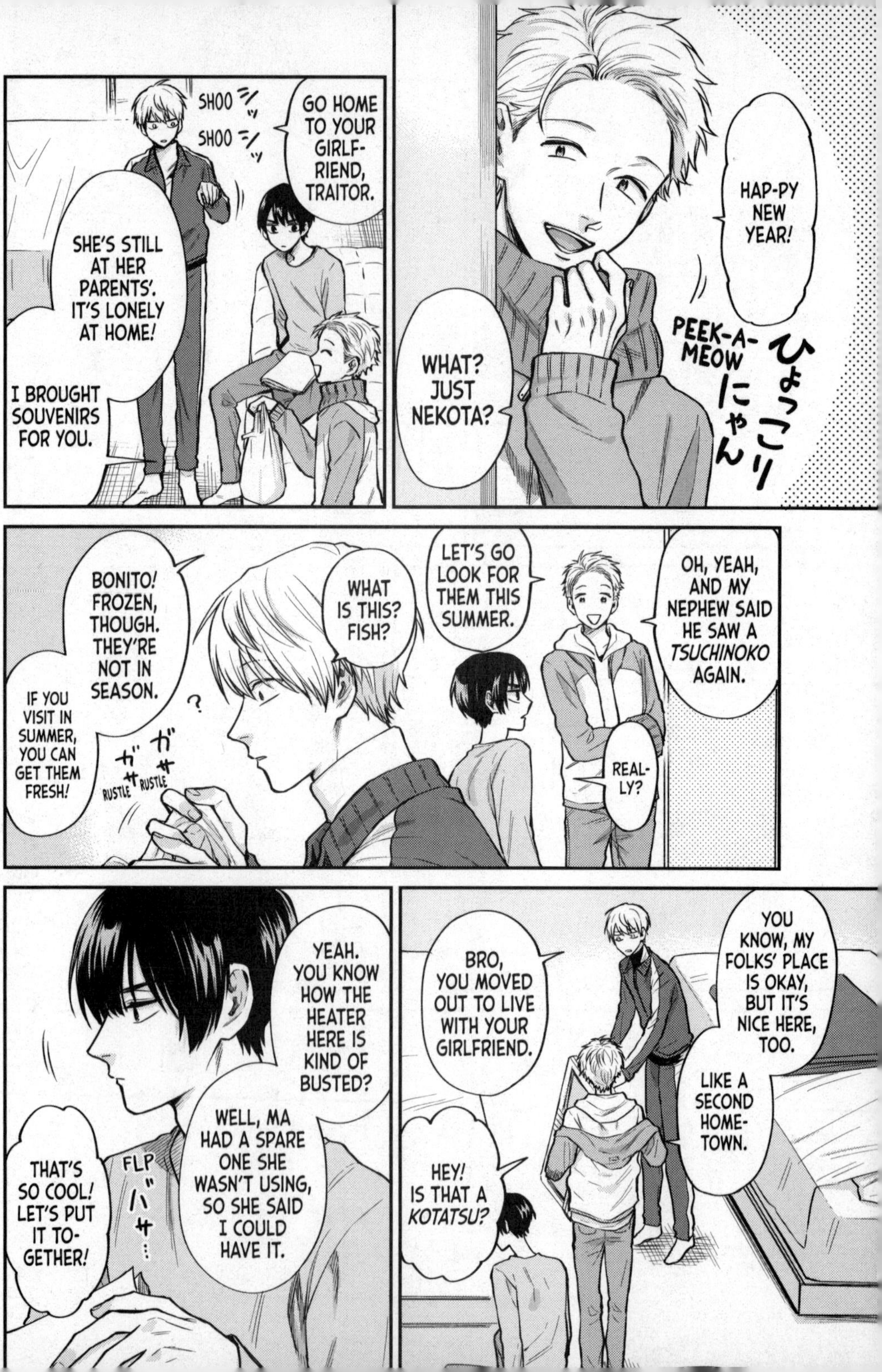
HAP-PY NEW YEAR!
PEEK-A-MEOW
ひょっこりにゃん
WHAT? JUST NEKOTA?
SHOO シッ
SHOO シッ
GO HOME TO YOUR GIRLF-RIEND, TRAITOR.
SHE'S STILL AT HER PARENTS'. IT'S LONELY AT HOME!
I BROUGHT SOUVENIRS FOR YOU.
OH, YEAH, AND MY NEPHEW SAID HE SAW A *TSUCHINOKO* AGAIN.
REAL-LY?
LET'S GO LOOK FOR THEM THIS SUMMER.
WHAT IS THIS? FISH?
BONITO! FROZEN, THOUGH. THEY'RE NOT IN SEASON.
?
IF YOU VISIT IN SUMMER, YOU CAN GET THEM FRESH!
ガサ ガサ
RUSTLE RUSTLE
YOU KNOW, MY FOLKS' PLACE IS OKAY, BUT IT'S NICE HERE, TOO.
LIKE A SECOND HOME-TOWN.
BRO, YOU MOVED OUT TO LIVE WITH YOUR GIRLFRIEND.
HEY! IS THAT A *KOTATSU*?
YEAH. YOU KNOW HOW THE HEATER HERE IS KIND OF BUSTED?
WELL, MA HAD A SPARE ONE SHE WASN'T USING, SO SHE SAID I COULD HAVE IT.
FLP バサ…
THAT'S SO COOL! LET'S PUT IT TO-GETHER!

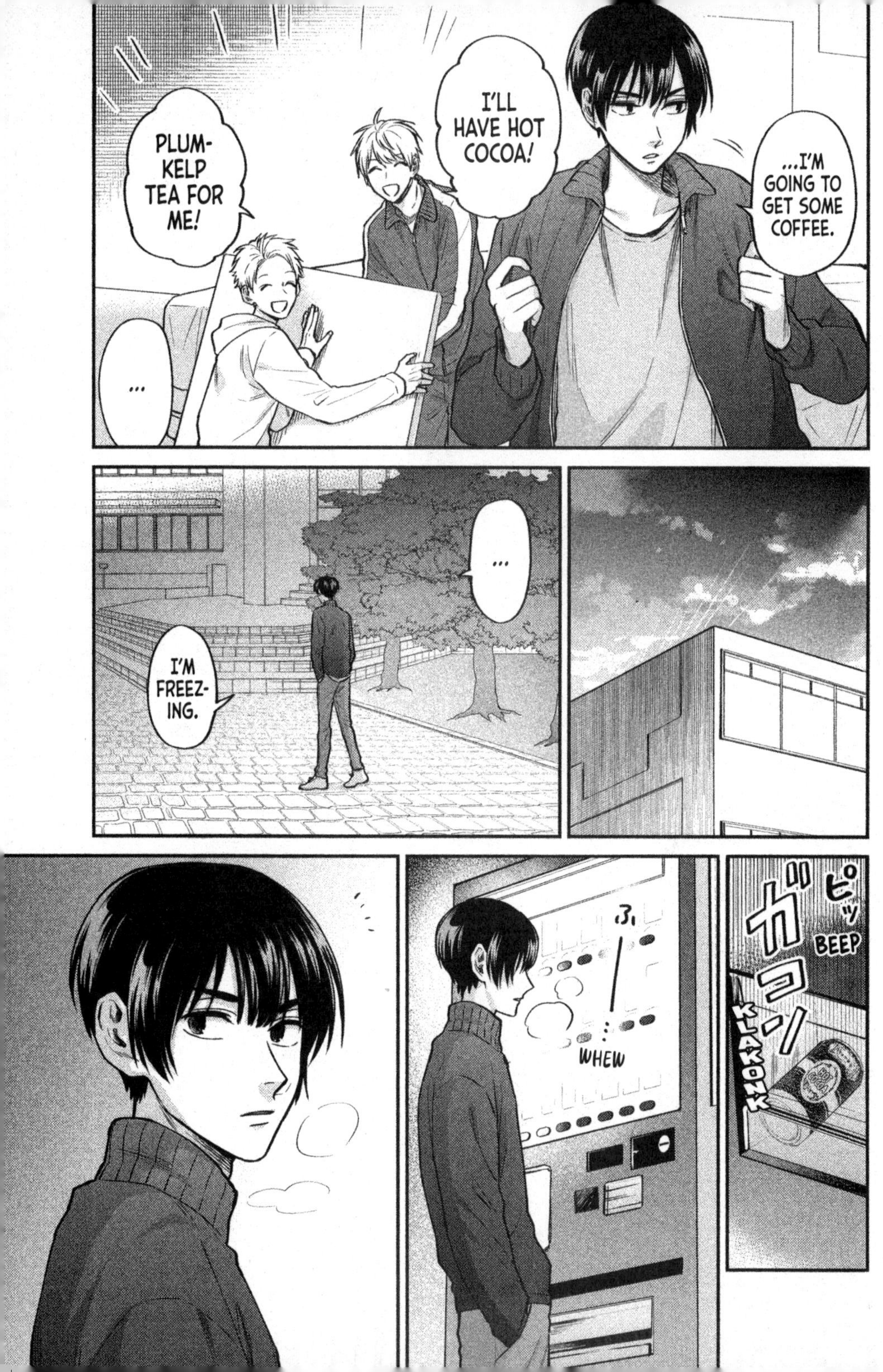
...I'M GOING TO GET SOME COFFEE.
I'LL HAVE HOT COCOA!
PLUM-KELP TEA FOR ME!
...
...
I'M FREEZING.
ピッ BEEP
ガコーン KLAKONK
ふー WHEW

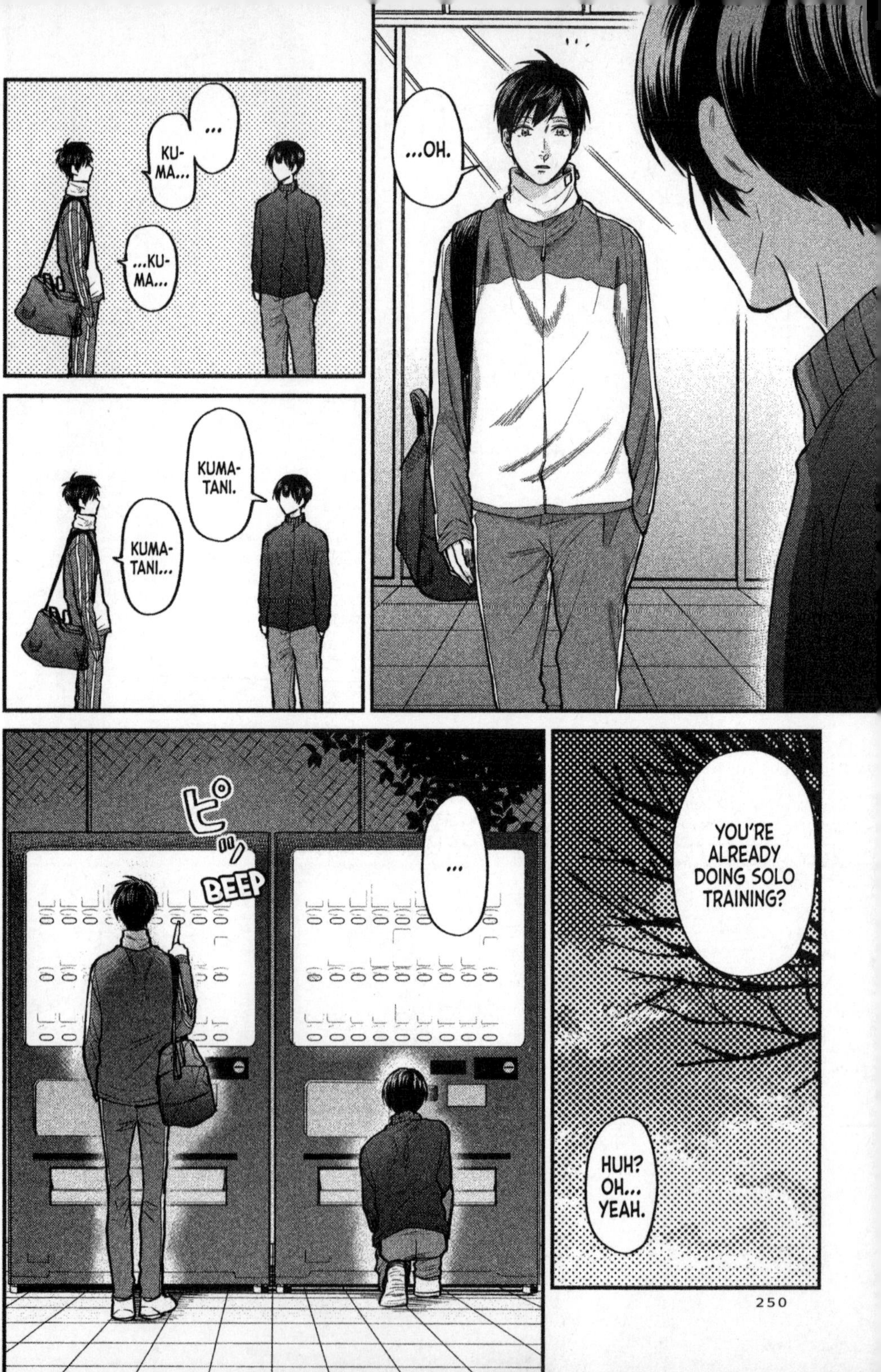
...OH.
...
KU-MA...
...KU-MA...
KUMA-TANI.
KUMA-TANI...
YOU'RE ALREADY DOING SOLO TRAINING?
HUH? OH... YEAH.
...
ピッ
BEEP

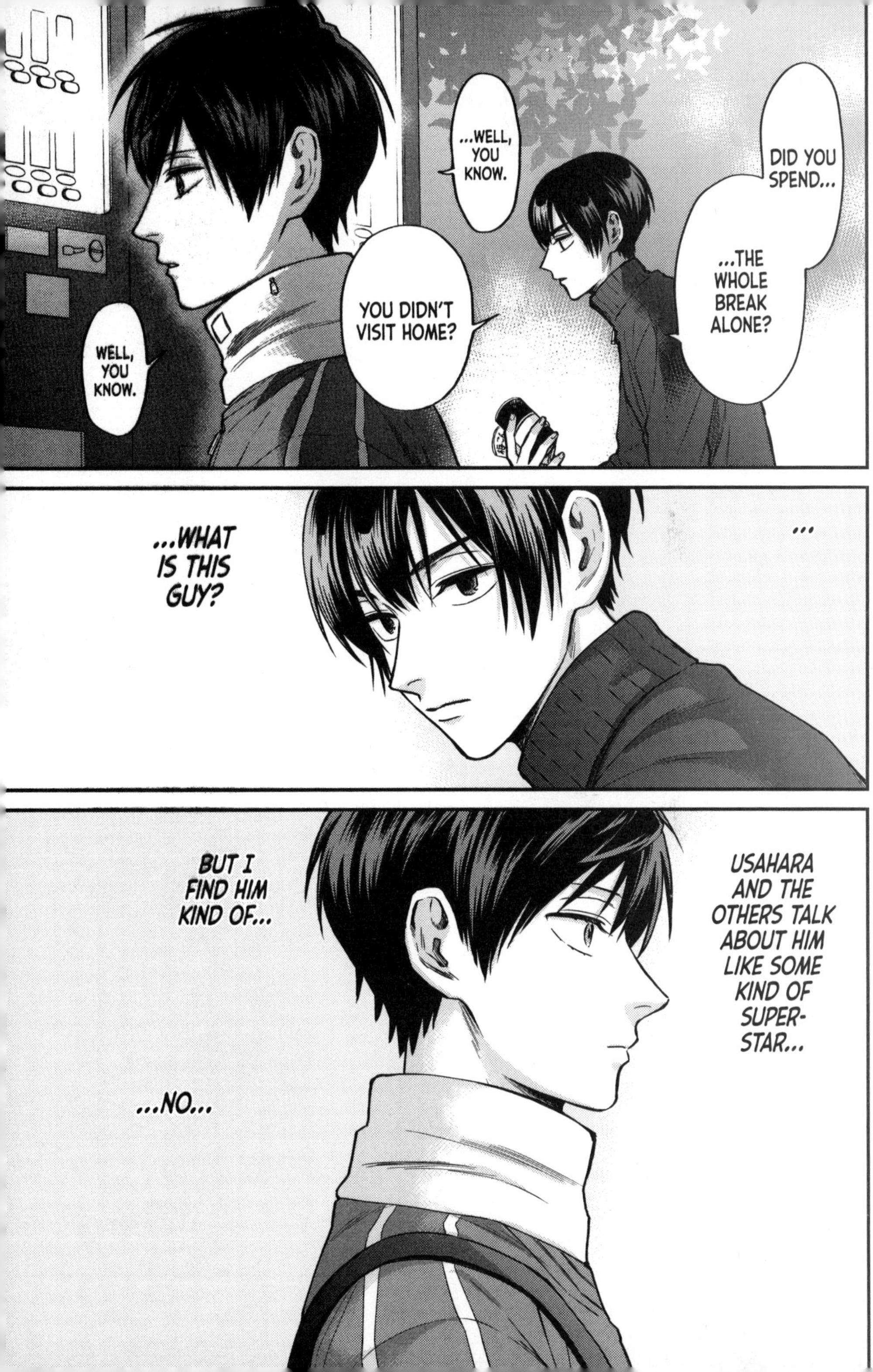
DID YOU SPEND...
...THE WHOLE BREAK ALONE?
...WELL, YOU KNOW.
YOU DIDN'T VISIT HOME?
WELL, YOU KNOW.
...
...WHAT IS THIS GUY?
USAHARA AND THE OTHERS TALK ABOUT HIM LIKE SOME KIND OF SUPER-STAR...
BUT I FIND HIM KIND OF...
...NO...

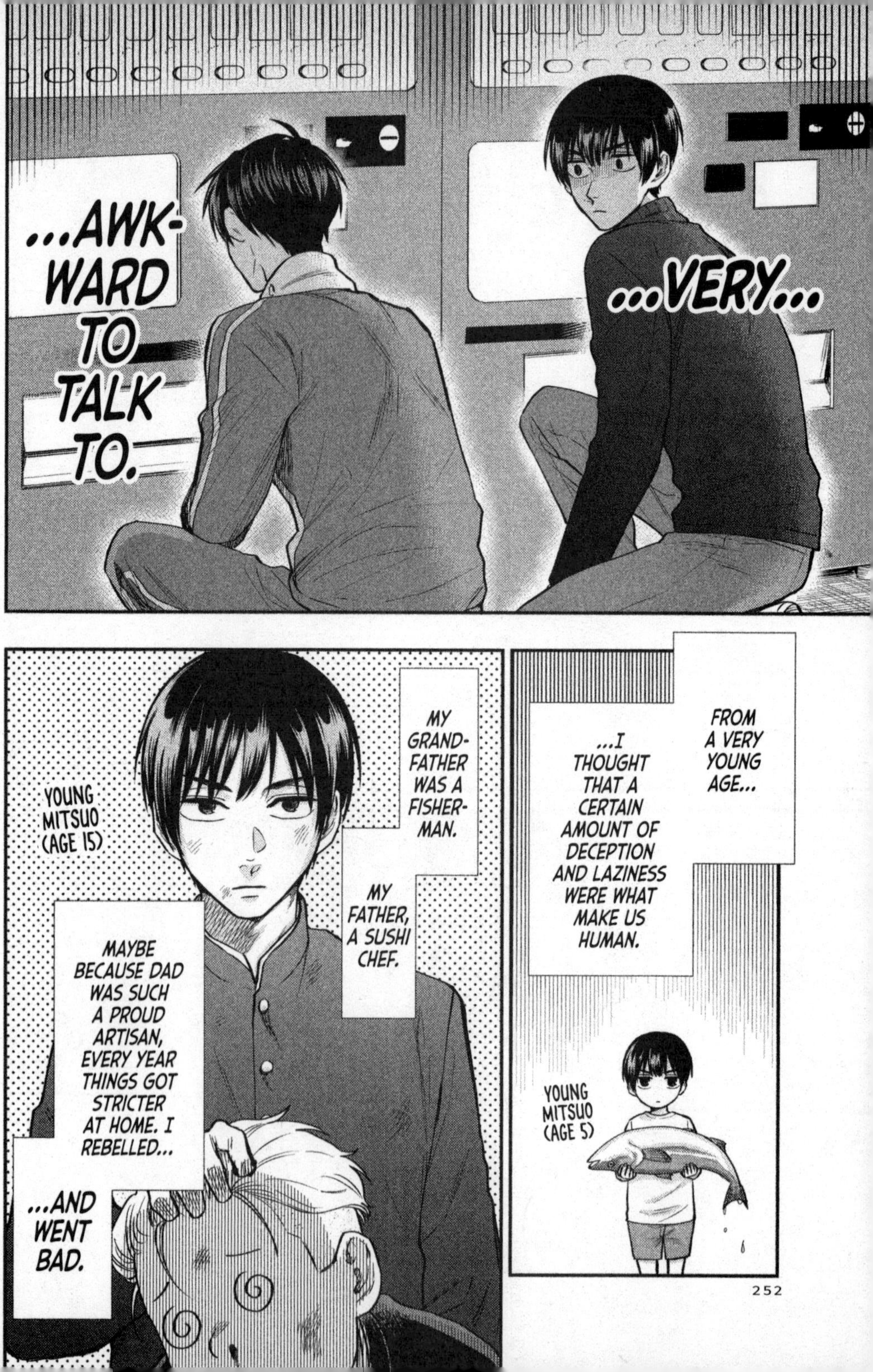
...VERY...
...AWK-WARD TO TALK TO.
FROM A VERY YOUNG AGE...
...I THOUGHT THAT A CERTAIN AMOUNT OF DECEPTION AND LAZINESS WERE WHAT MAKE US HUMAN.
YOUNG MITSUO (AGE 5)
MY GRAND-FATHER WAS A FISHER-MAN.
MY FATHER, A SUSHI CHEF.
YOUNG MITSUO (AGE 15)
MAYBE BECAUSE DAD WAS SUCH A PROUD ARTISAN, EVERY YEAR THINGS GOT STRICTER AT HOME. I REBELLED...
...AND WENT BAD.

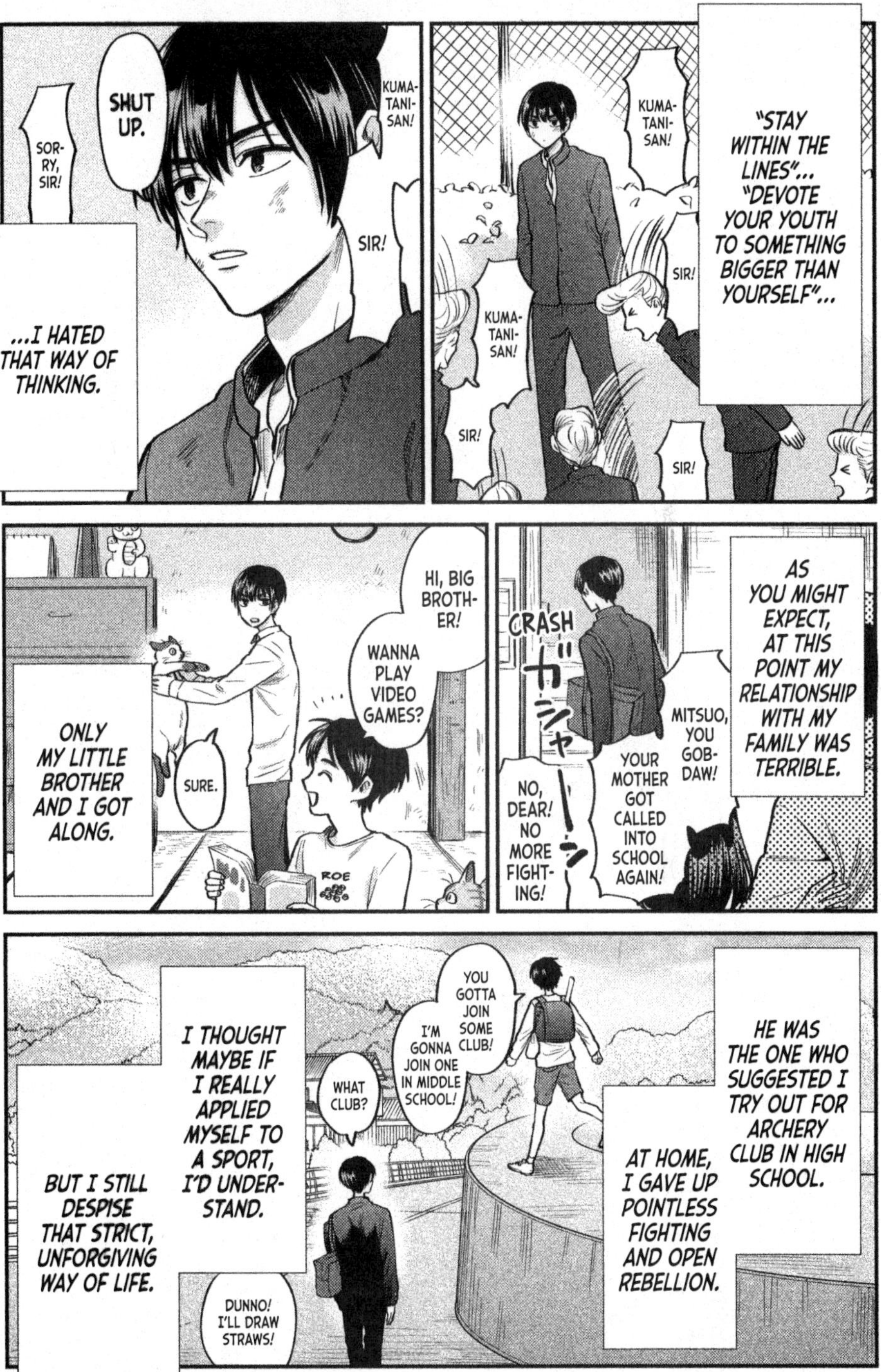
"STAY WITHIN THE LINES"... "DEVOTE YOUR YOUTH TO SOMETHING BIGGER THAN YOURSELF"...
KUMA-TANI-SAN!
SIR!
KUMA-TANI-SAN!
SIR!
SIR!
KUMA-TANI-SAN!
SHUT UP.
SIR!
SOR-RY, SIR!
...I HATED THAT WAY OF THINKING.
AS YOU MIGHT EXPECT, AT THIS POINT MY RELATIONSHIP WITH MY FAMILY WAS TERRIBLE.
CRASH
ガシャーン
MITSUO, YOU GOB-DAW!
YOUR MOTHER GOT CALLED INTO SCHOOL AGAIN!
NO, DEAR! NO MORE FIGHT-ING!
HI, BIG BROTH-ER!
WANNA PLAY VIDEO GAMES?
SURE.
ROE
ONLY MY LITTLE BROTHER AND I GOT ALONG.
HE WAS THE ONE WHO SUGGESTED I TRY OUT FOR ARCHERY CLUB IN HIGH SCHOOL.
AT HOME, I GAVE UP POINTLESS FIGHTING AND OPEN REBELLION.
YOU GOTTA JOIN SOME CLUB!
I'M GONNA JOIN ONE IN MIDDLE SCHOOL!
WHAT CLUB?
DUNNO! I'LL DRAW STRAWS!
I THOUGHT MAYBE IF I REALLY APPLIED MYSELF TO A SPORT, I'D UNDER-STAND.
BUT I STILL DESPISE THAT STRICT, UNFORGIVING WAY OF LIFE.

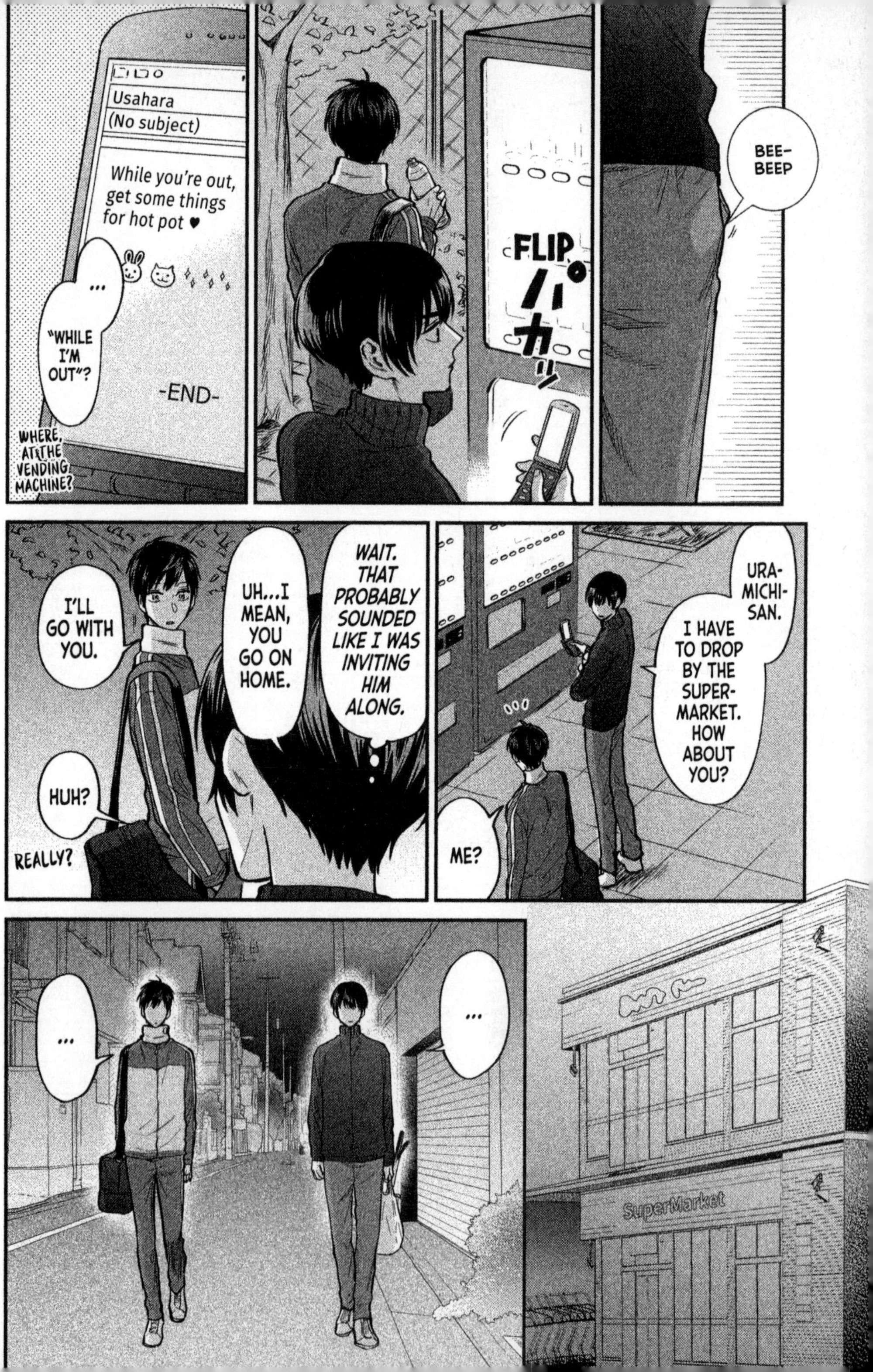
BEE-BEEP
FLIP
パカッ
Usahara
(No subject)
While you're out, get some things for hot pot ♥
-END-
...
"WHILE I'M OUT"?
WHERE, AT THE VENDING MACHINE?
URA-MICHI-SAN. I HAVE TO DROP BY THE SUPER-MARKET. HOW ABOUT YOU?
ME?
WAIT. THAT PROBABLY SOUNDED LIKE I WAS INVITING HIM ALONG.
UH...I MEAN, YOU GO ON HOME.
I'LL GO WITH YOU.
HUH?
REALLY?
SuperMarket
...
...

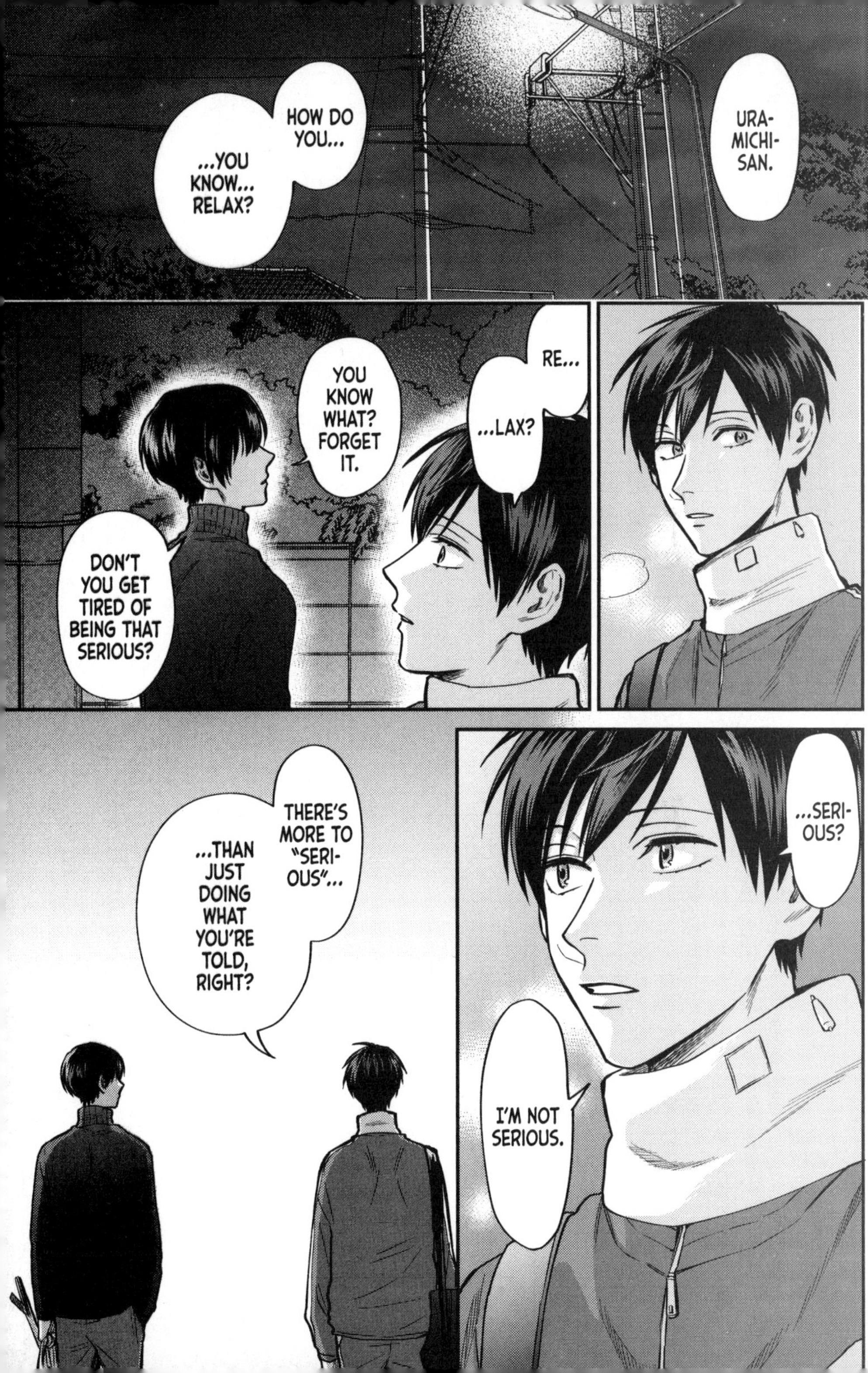
URA-MICHI-SAN.
HOW DO YOU...
...YOU KNOW... RELAX?
RE...
...LAX?
YOU KNOW WHAT? FORGET IT.
DON'T YOU GET TIRED OF BEING THAT SERIOUS?
...SERI-OUS?
I'M NOT SERIOUS.
THERE'S MORE TO "SERI-OUS"...
...THAN JUST DOING WHAT YOU'RE TOLD, RIGHT?

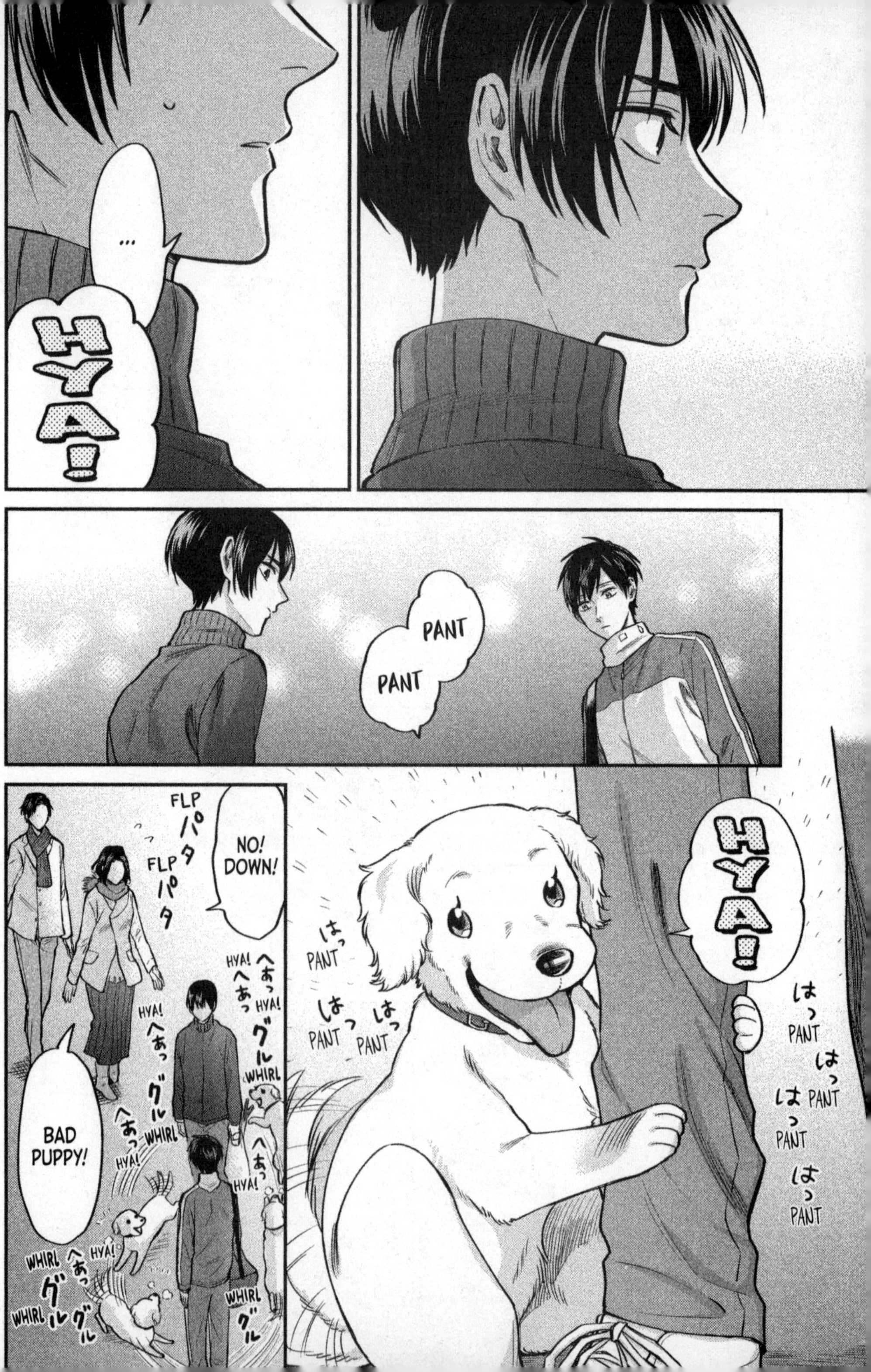
...
HYA!
PANT
PANT
HYA!
はっ PANT
はっ PANT
はっ PANT
はっ PANT
はっ PANT
はっ PANT
はっ PANT
FLP パタ
FLP パタ
NO! DOWN!
HYA! へあっ
HYA! へあっ
HYA! へあっ
グル WHIRL
グル WHIRL
へあっ HYA!
へあっ HYA!
BAD PUPPY!
WHIRL グル
WHIRL グル
WHIRL グル

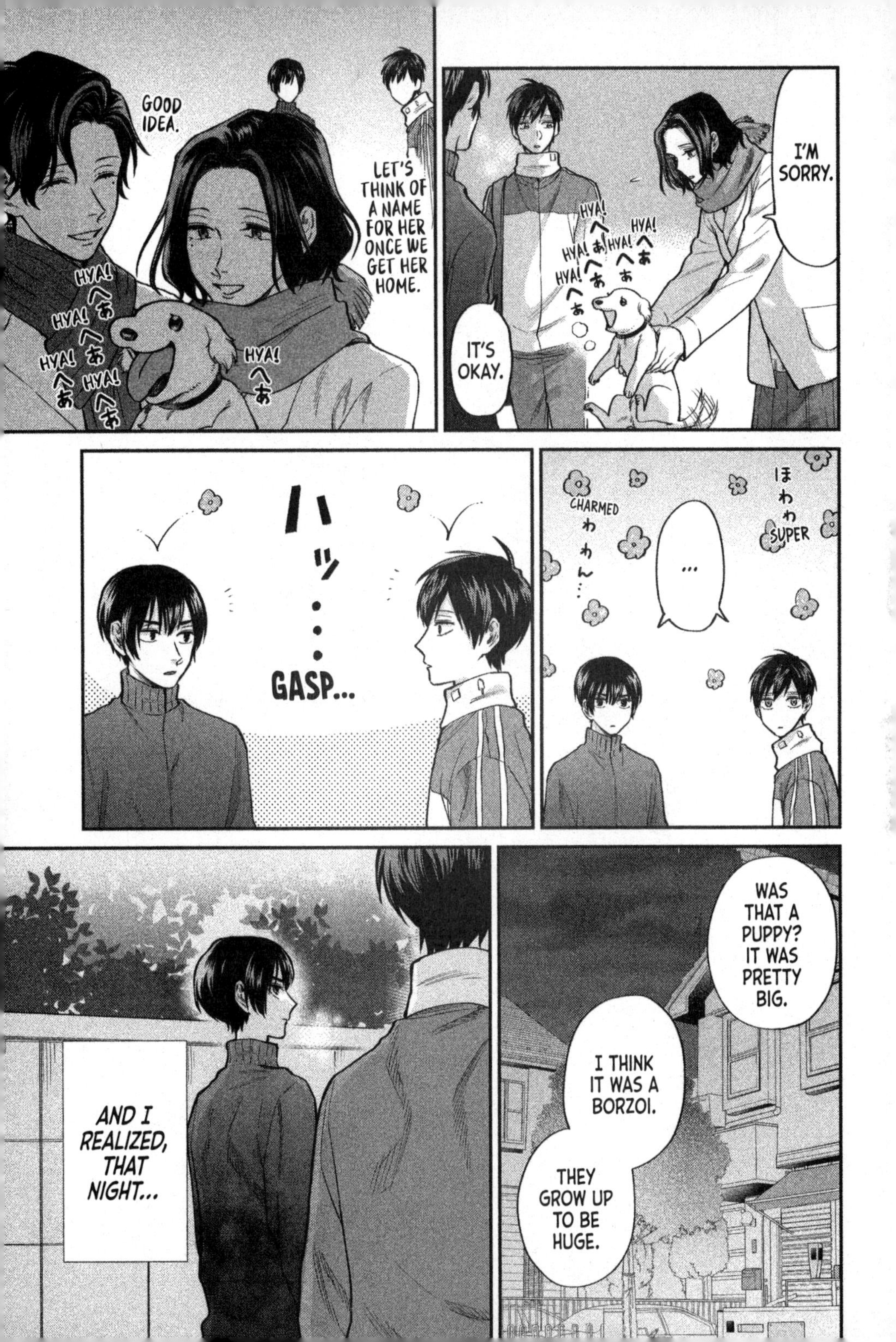
I'M SORRY.
HYA! へぁ
HYA! へぁ
HYA! へぁ
HYA! へぁ
IT'S OKAY.
LET'S THINK OF A NAME FOR HER ONCE WE GET HER HOME.
GOOD IDEA.
HYA! へぁ
HYA! へぁ
HYA! へぁ
HYA! へぁ
HYA! へぁ
ほわわ SUPER
...
CHARMED わわん...
ハッ...
GASP...
WAS THAT A PUPPY? IT WAS PRETTY BIG.
I THINK IT WAS A BORZOI.
THEY GROW UP TO BE HUGE.
AND I REALIZED, THAT NIGHT...

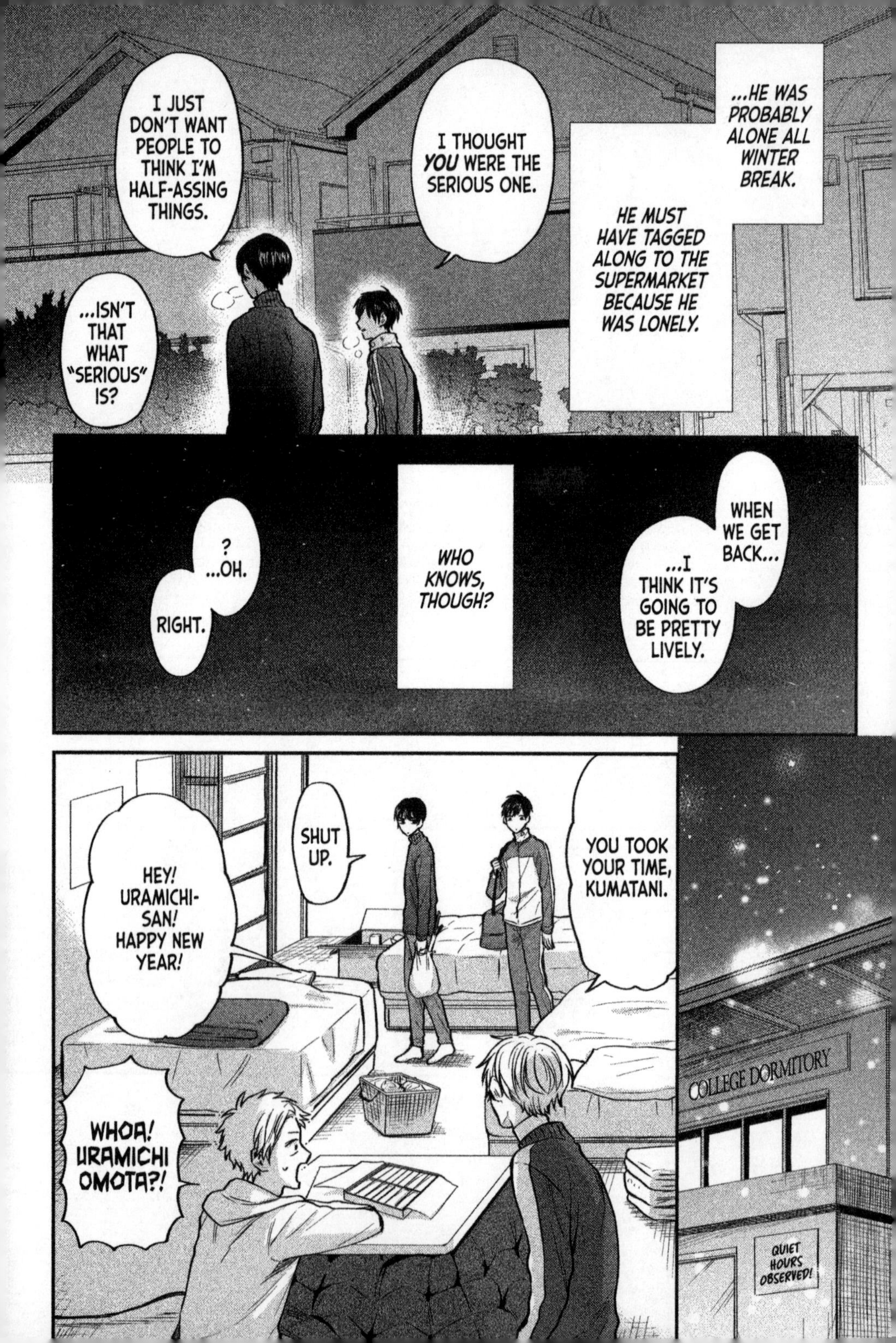
...HE WAS PROBABLY ALONE ALL WINTER BREAK.
HE MUST HAVE TAGGED ALONG TO THE SUPERMARKET BECAUSE HE WAS LONELY.
I THOUGHT *YOU* WERE THE SERIOUS ONE.
I JUST DON'T WANT PEOPLE TO THINK I'M HALF-ASSING THINGS.
...ISN'T THAT WHAT "SERIOUS" IS?
WHEN WE GET BACK...
...I THINK IT'S GOING TO BE PRETTY LIVELY.
WHO KNOWS, THOUGH?
? ...OH.
RIGHT.
COLLEGE DORMITORY
QUIET HOURS OBSERVED!
YOU TOOK YOUR TIME, KUMATANI.
SHUT UP.
HEY! URAMICHI-SAN! HAPPY NEW YEAR!
WHOA! URAMICHI OMOTA?!

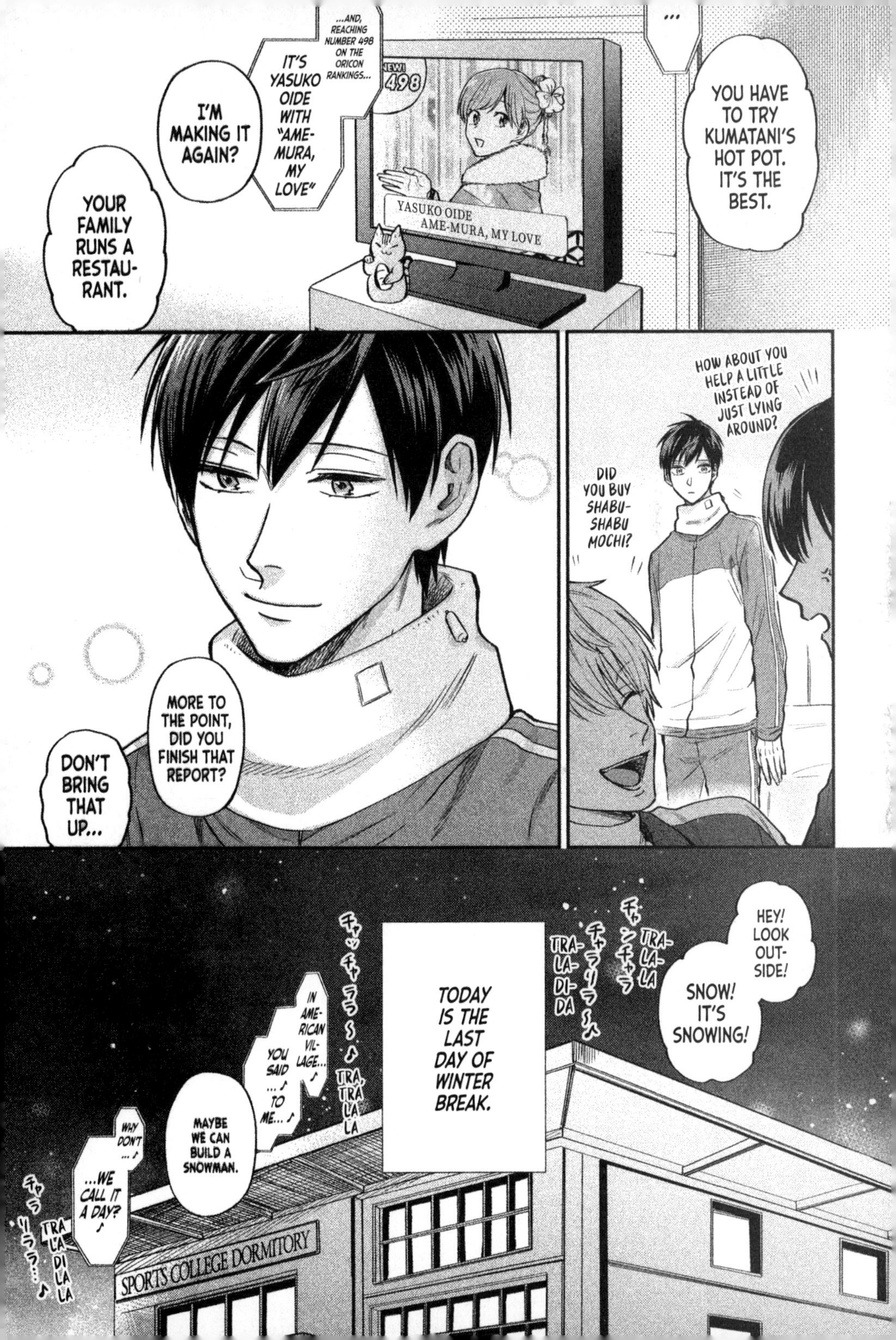
...
YOU HAVE TO TRY KUMATANI'S HOT POT. IT'S THE BEST.
...AND, REACHING NUMBER 498 ON THE ORICON RANKINGS...
IT'S YASUKO OIDE WITH "AME-MURA, MY LOVE"
NEW! 498
YASUKO OIDE AME-MURA, MY LOVE
I'M MAKING IT AGAIN?
YOUR FAMILY RUNS A RESTAURANT.
HOW ABOUT YOU HELP A LITTLE INSTEAD OF JUST LYING AROUND?
DID YOU BUY SHABU-SHABU MOCHI?
MORE TO THE POINT, DID YOU FINISH THAT REPORT?
DON'T BRING THAT UP...
HEY! LOOK OUT-SIDE!
SNOW! IT'S SNOWING!
チャンチャラ TRA-LA-LA
チャラリラ～♪ TRA-LA-DI-DA
TODAY IS THE LAST DAY OF WINTER BREAK.
チャッチャララ～♪ TRA, TRA LA LA
IN AMERICAN VILLAGE... ♪
YOU SAID ... ♪ TO ME... ♪
MAYBE WE CAN BUILD A SNOWMAN.
WHY DON'T ... ♪
...WE CALL IT A DAY? ♪
SPORTS COLLEGE DORMITORY
チャラリララ…♪ TRA DI LA LA

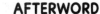

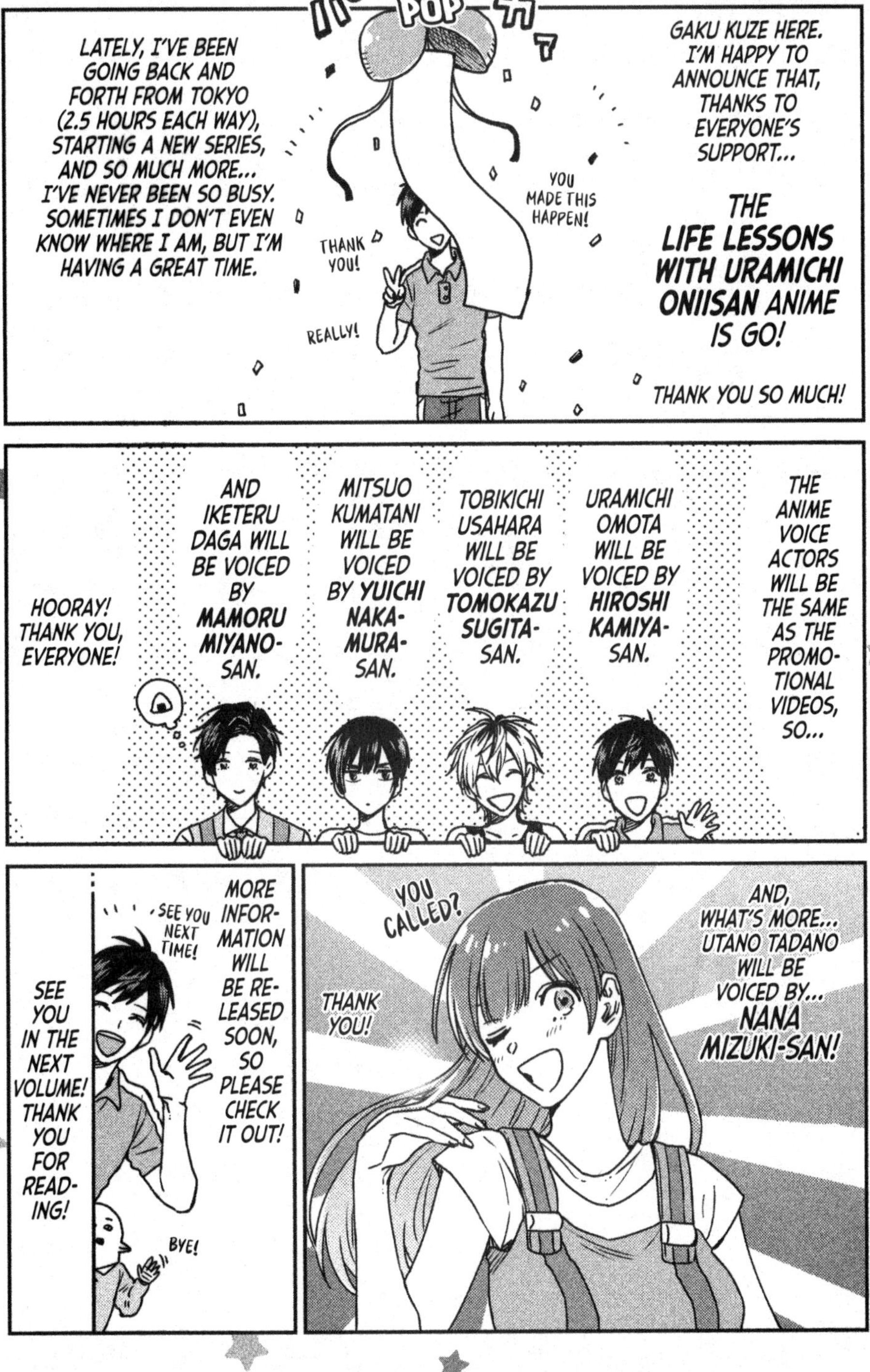
GAKU KUZE HERE. I'M HAPPY TO ANNOUNCE THAT, THANKS TO EVERYONE'S SUPPORT...
THE LIFE LESSONS WITH URAMICHI ONIISAN ANIME IS GO!
THANK YOU SO MUCH!
パ POP カァ
YOU MADE THIS HAPPEN!
THANK YOU!
REALLY!
LATELY, I'VE BEEN GOING BACK AND FORTH FROM TOKYO (2.5 HOURS EACH WAY), STARTING A NEW SERIES, AND SO MUCH MORE... I'VE NEVER BEEN SO BUSY. SOMETIMES I DON'T EVEN KNOW WHERE I AM, BUT I'M HAVING A GREAT TIME.
THE ANIME VOICE ACTORS WILL BE THE SAME AS THE PROMOTIONAL VIDEOS, SO...
URAMICHI OMOTA WILL BE VOICED BY HIROSHI KAMIYA-SAN.
TOBIKICHI USAHARA WILL BE VOICED BY TOMOKAZU SUGITA-SAN.
MITSUO KUMATANI WILL BE VOICED BY YUICHI NAKAMURA-SAN.
AND IKETERU DAGA WILL BE VOICED BY MAMORU MIYANO-SAN.
HOORAY! THANK YOU, EVERYONE!
AND, WHAT'S MORE... UTANO TADANO WILL BE VOICED BY... NANA MIZUKI-SAN!
YOU CALLED?
THANK YOU!
MORE INFORMATION WILL BE RELEASED SOON, SO PLEASE CHECK IT OUT!
SEE YOU NEXT TIME!
SEE YOU IN THE NEXT VOLUME! THANK YOU FOR READING!
BYE!

Translation Notes

Names

Many of the character names in the series include some kind of joke or pun, often based on the order in which the name is read, or what *kanji* (logographic Chinese characters adopted into the Japanese writing system) it contains. Here are the ones in this volume.

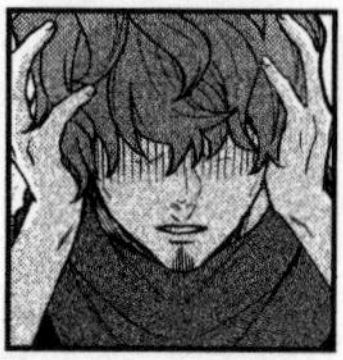

Amon (Tanaka Tomesaburo): The sleek, stylish pen name "Amon" contrasts sharply with the very traditional real name "Tanaka Tomesaburo."

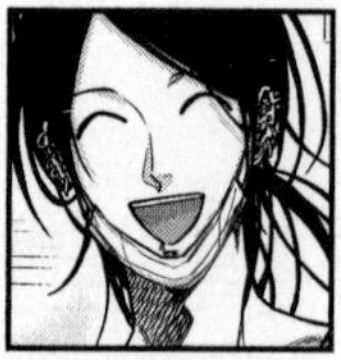

Kikaku Hanbei
"Planning and sales."

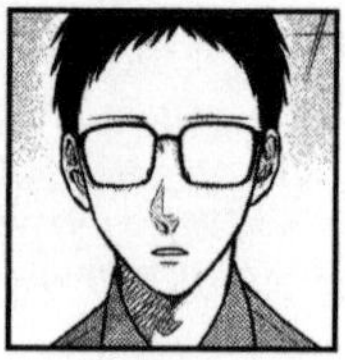

Uebu Saito
"Website."

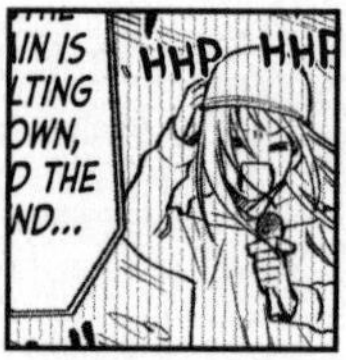
HHP HHP

Doshabu Riko
"Downpour girl."

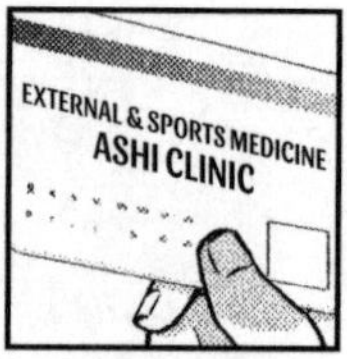
EXTERNAL & SPORTS MEDICINE
ASHI CLINIC

Ashi Clinic
"Leg clinic."

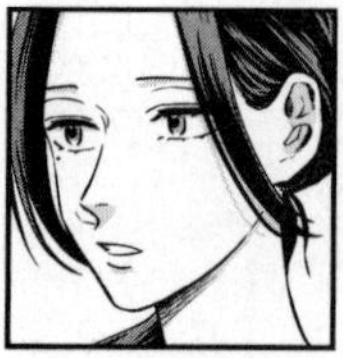

Daga Mabui
"But she's dazzling."

Nekota Matahiko: Literally "Cat-field Fork-boy." The *mata* (fork) is a reference to the *yokai* known as a *nekomata,* a kind of monstrous cat.

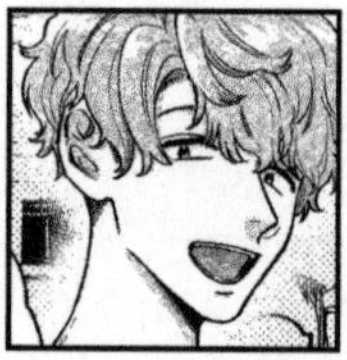

Kotatsu, page 38
A kind of low table with a built-in heater underneath and a blanket on top to keep the heat in. As indicated by Usahara on page 246, this can be an economical way to keep warm in winter without having to heat an entire room.

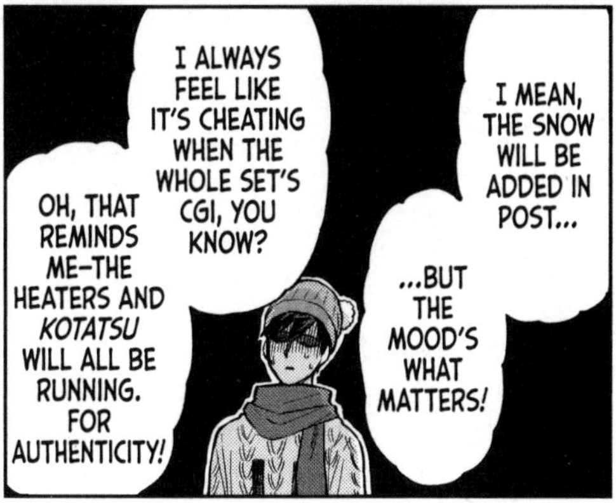
I MEAN, THE SNOW WILL BE ADDED IN POST...
...BUT THE MOOD'S WHAT MATTERS!
I ALWAYS FEEL LIKE IT'S CHEATING WHEN THE WHOLE SET'S CGI, YOU KNOW?
OH, THAT REMINDS ME—THE HEATERS AND *KOTATSU* WILL ALL BE RUNNING. FOR AUTHENTICITY!

Girl's bar, page 50
A bar with an all-female bartending and serving staff, catering to a clientele willing to pay extra for friendly female companionship.

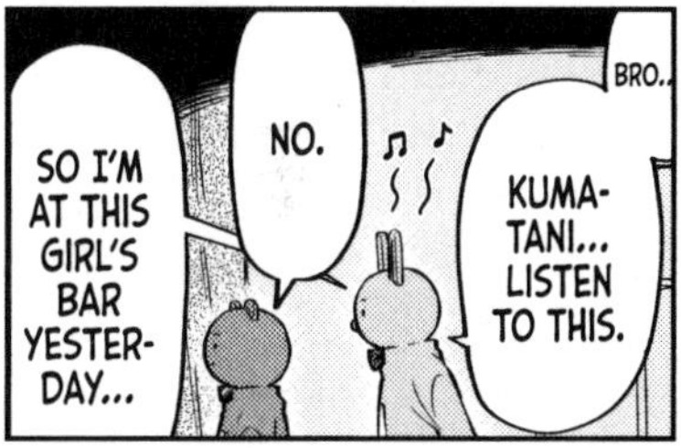
BRO..
KUMA-TANI... LISTEN TO THIS.
NO.
SO I'M AT THIS GIRL'S BAR YESTER-DAY...

It was fun, page 62
A reference to the be-all-end-all stock phrase many school-age children in Japan use when asked to write about topics like "how I spent my summer vacation," the implication being, of course, that the writer lacks imagination/creativity.

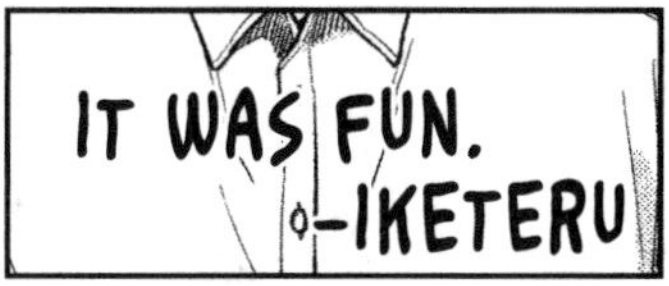
IT WAS FUN.
—IKETERU

Momiji the Kunoichi, page 65
Momiji, literally "fall foliage," is grated daikon radish with red chili peppers. When Utano says she's the "lady of the team," she's actually using a Japanese idiom for being the only woman among a group of men that literally translates as "one point of red"—another pun (since *momiji* is spelled using a Chinese character for "red").

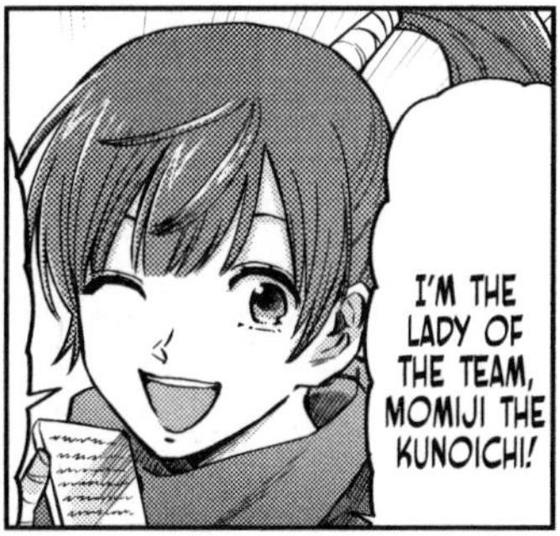
I'M THE LADY OF THE TEAM, MOMIJI THE KUNOICHI!

No-mind, page 65
A literal translation of the word *mushin*, which refers to a mental state in which the mind is "free" and open to anything.

Alone on Christmas, page 74
In Japan, Christmas is popularly regarded as a couples' holiday rather than a family one. When Kumatani refuses to attend the (singles') Christmas party, Usahara becomes increasingly concerned that his friend may be going on a date instead.

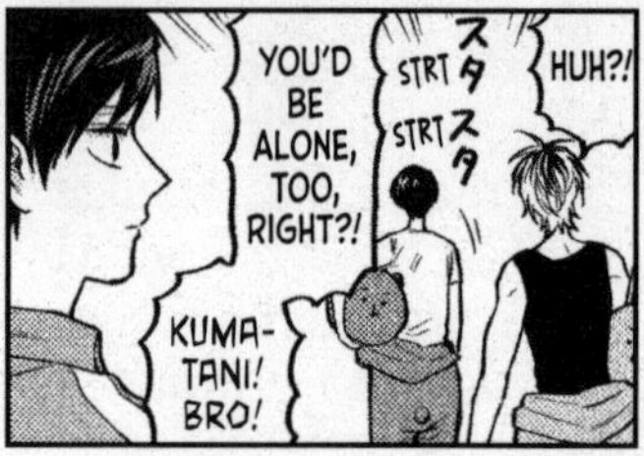
HUH?!
スタ STRT
スタ STRT
YOU'D BE ALONE, TOO, RIGHT?!
KUMA-TANI! BRO!

***Takoyaki*, page 109**
Commonly known as "octobus balls" in English, this popular Osakan street food consists of batter fried into a ball shape and filled with octopus (*tako*) or other ingredients. An at-home *takoyaki* maker is typically a hot plate-type device made with half-spherical indents into which batter is poured, then quickly turned to form a ball shape. This setup makes for a fun activity to do with friends, and the mold is versatile enough to use for other spherical foods (such as mini hotcakes).

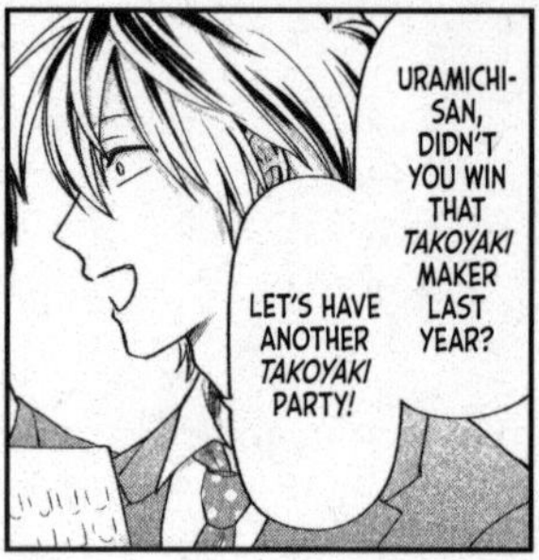
URAMICHI-SAN, DIDN'T YOU WIN THAT *TAKOYAKI* MAKER LAST YEAR?
LET'S HAVE ANOTHER *TAKOYAKI* PARTY!

***Yokai*, page 172**
A general Japanese term for a whole class of monsters and spirits, some rooted in folklore, others invented as jokes. The girl here is probably thinking of the *konaki jijii* ("Old man that cries like a child") in particular, a yokai that disguises itself as a crying baby to trick people into picking it up, then transforms into an extremely heavy old man who can't be put down.

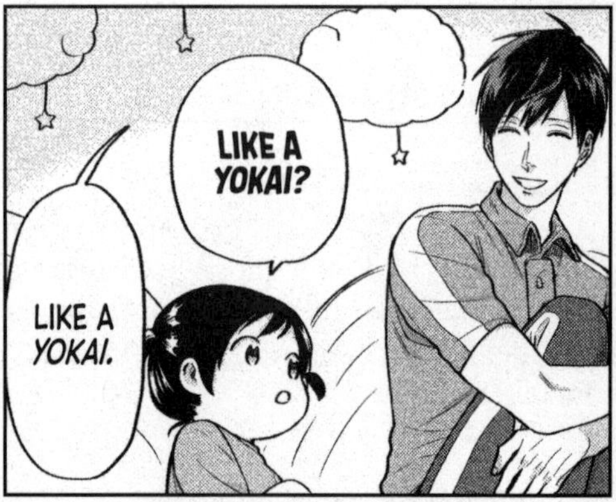
LIKE A *YOKAI?*
LIKE A *YOKAI.*

Giant *nagashi-somen* setup, page 183
Nagashi-somen means noodles (*somen*) served flowing (*nagashi*) down a chute filled with ice-cold water. Diners have to grab some noodles for their plate as they flow past. (How this setup was used to catch the man-eating salmon remains a mystery.)

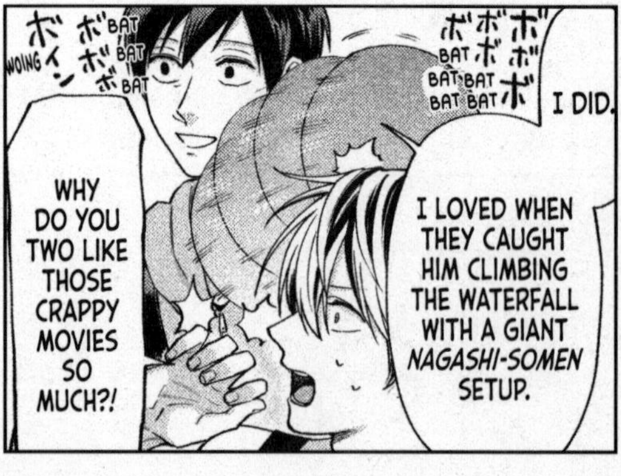
BAT BAT BAT BAT BAT BAT
I DID.
I LOVED WHEN THEY CAUGHT HIM CLIMBING THE WATERFALL WITH A GIANT *NAGASHI-SOMEN* SETUP.
BAT BAT BAT
WOING
WHY DO YOU TWO LIKE THOSE CRAPPY MOVIES SO MUCH?!

***Tsuchinoko,* page 197**
Cryptids said to live in Japanese forests. They look like fat snakes.

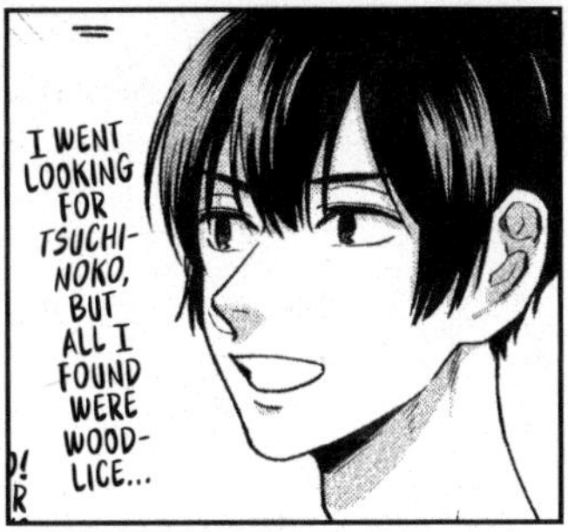
I WENT LOOKING FOR TSUCHI-NOKO, BUT ALL I FOUND WERE WOOD-LICE...

***Shisa,* page 220**
Sometimes spelled *shiisaa,* this term refers to a kind of stone guardian lion unique to Okinawa. They are usually placed in pairs, one on either side of a gate or door.

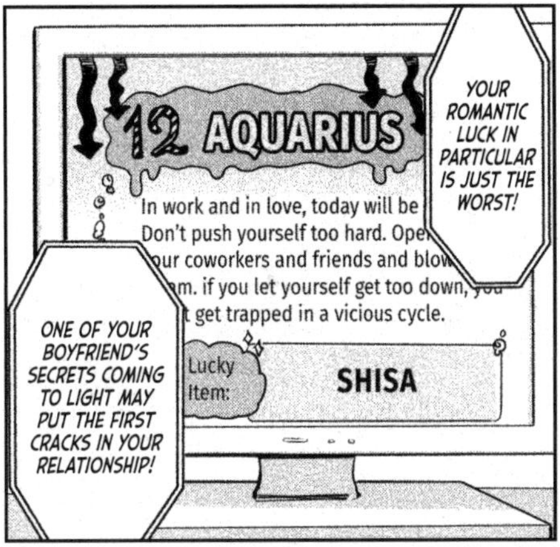
YOUR ROMANTIC LUCK IN PARTICULAR IS JUST THE WORST!
12 AQUARIUS
In work and in love, today will be
Lucky Item:
SHISA
ONE OF YOUR BOYFRIEND'S SECRETS COMING TO LIGHT MAY PUT THE FIRST CRACKS IN YOUR RELATIONSHIP!

American Village, page 226
A literal translation of the Japanese *Amerikamura* (which is abbreviated to *Ame-mura* in the song's title), this neighborhood in Osaka is a center of youth culture and creativity.

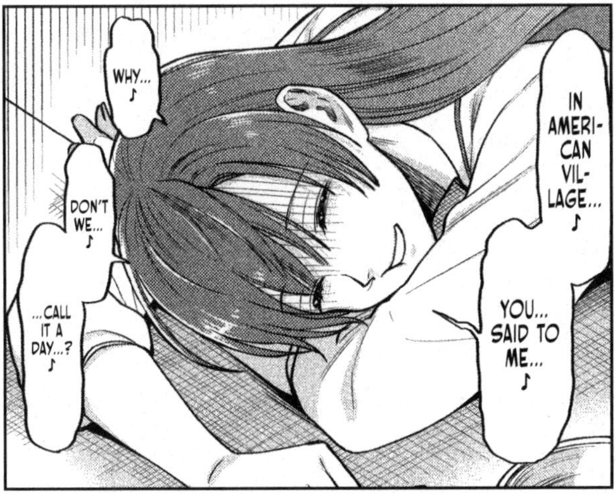
IN AMERI-CAN VIL-LAGE... ♪
WHY... ♪
YOU... SAID TO ME... ♪
DON'T WE... ♪
...CALL IT A DAY...? ♪

***Goya champuru*, page 226**
Champuru is an Okinawan stir-fry packed with ingredients locally available to the island. *Goya* is the Japanese word for "bitter melon," a staple in Okinawan cuisine.

The most Osakan flashback, page 227
The background of this panel contains images of 5 iconic Osaka landmarks (the Glico Man sign, *Kani Doraku* crab restaurant sign, and *Kuidaore Taro* clown in the Dotonbori area, and Tsutenkaku Tower and the Zuboraya puffer fish lantern in the Shinsekai area). The phrases *konai ya nen* and *donai ya nen* said by the couple are stereotypical of Osakan dialect, but don't carry much actual meaning on their own (literally "like this" and "how," respectively).

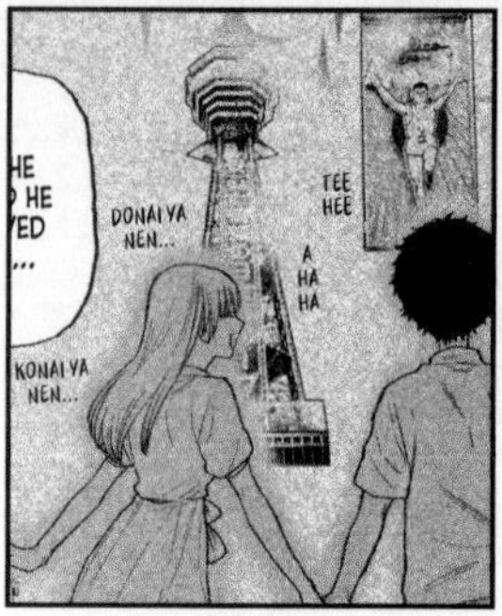
TEE HEE
A HA HA
DONAI YA NEN...
KONAI YA NEN...

***Orera no Macaron,* page 236**
Literally "Our Macarons." The personal pronoun *ore* is considered to be extremely masculine/crude, so this store name may represent the duality of femininity (macarons, or sweets in general) and crudity (*ore*) characteristic of the *onee* identity (see volume 1 translation notes).

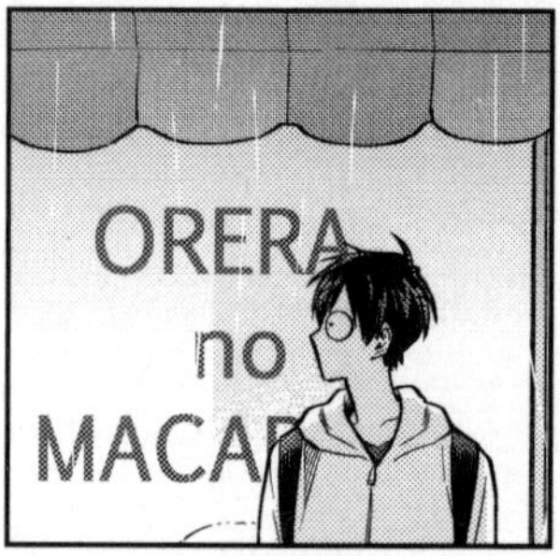
no

***Habutae mochi*, page 247**
This traditional confectionery is a sweet, glutinous rice cake formed into thin sheets. The texture may be said to imitate the *habutae* silk Fukui is known for producing.

People from Kyoto, page 247
Unsurprisingly, regions of Japan have become stereotyped over time. For Kyoto in particular, inhabitants are thought to harbor dark thoughts beneath a mask of politeness, and may not say what they truly think aloud. In essence, quite the opposite of Usahara's personality.

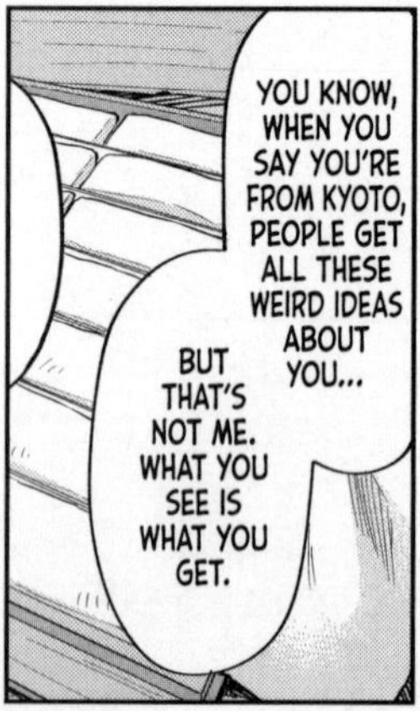
YOU KNOW, WHEN YOU SAY YOU'RE FROM KYOTO, PEOPLE GET ALL THESE WEIRD IDEAS ABOUT YOU...
BUT THAT'S NOT ME. WHAT YOU SEE IS WHAT YOU GET.

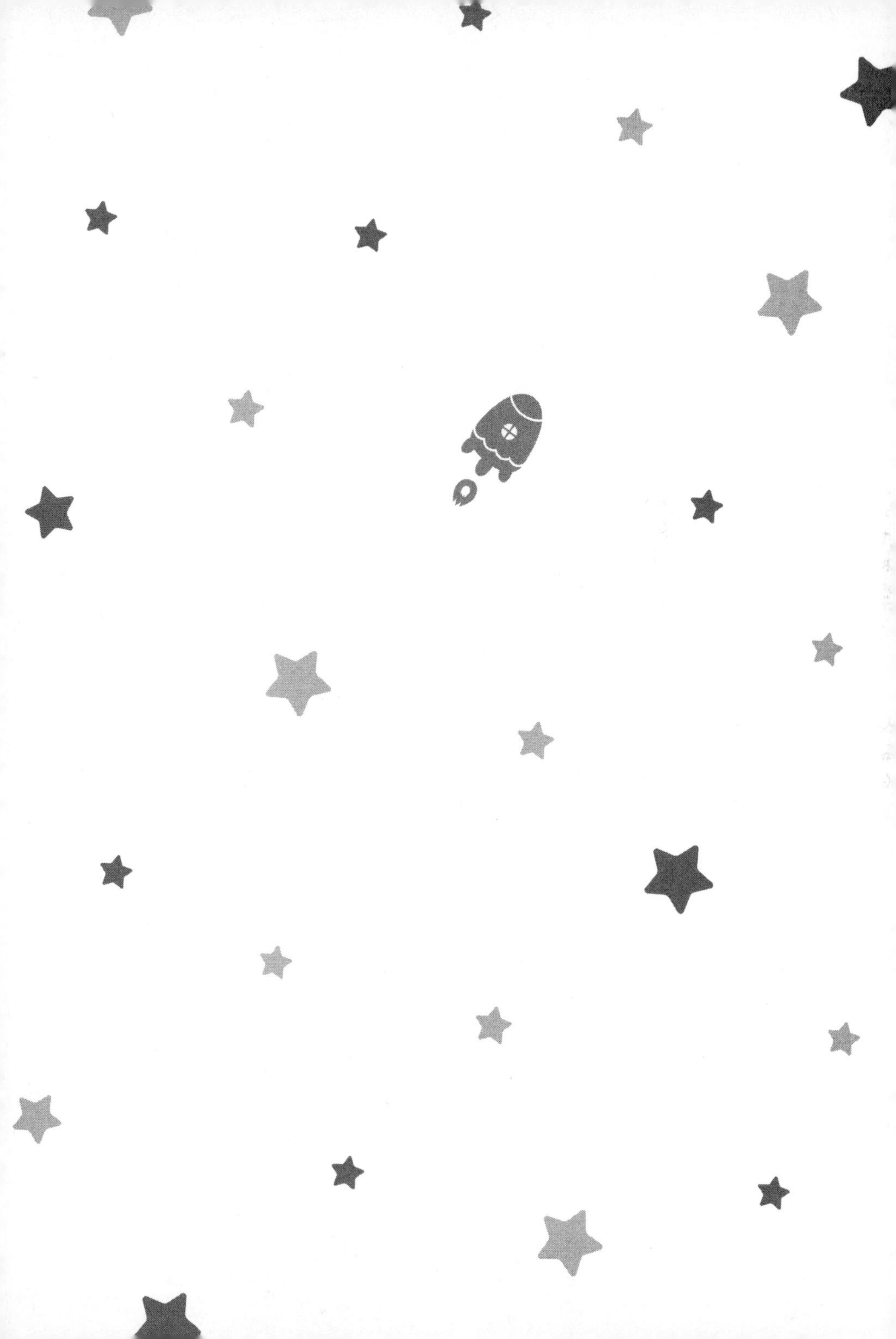

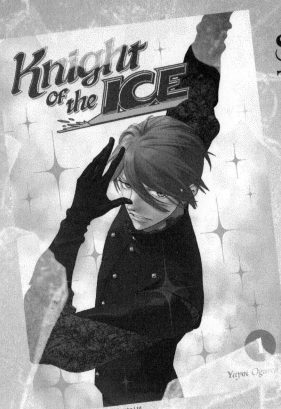

Knight of the ICE

Yayoi Ogawa

Knight of the Ice ©Yayoi Ogawa/Kodansha Ltd.

SKATING THRILLS AND ICY CHILLS WITH THIS NEW TINGLY ROMANCE SERIES!

A rom-com on ice, perfect for fans of *Princess Jellyfish* and *Wotakoi*. Kokoro is the talk of the figure-skating world, winning trophies and hearts. But little do they know... he's actually a huge nerd! From the beloved creator of *You're My Pet* (*Tramps Like Us*).

Chitose is a serious young woman, working for the health magazine *SASSO*. Or at least, she would be, if she wasn't constantly getting distracted by her childhood friend, international figure skating star Kokoro Kijinami! In the public eye and on the ice, Kokoro is a gallant, flawless knight, but behind his glittery costumes and breathtaking spins lies a secret: He's actually a hopelessly romantic otaku, who can only land his quad jumps when Chitose is on hand to recite a spell from his favorite magical girl anime!

KC KODANSHA COMICS

Young characters and steampunk setting, like *Howl's Moving Castle* and *Battle Angel Alita*

Beyond the Clouds © 2018 Nicke / Ki-oon

A boy with a talent for machines and a mysterious girl whose wings he's fixed will take you beyond the clouds! In the tradition of the high-flying, resonant adventure stories of Studio Ghibli comes a gorgeous tale about the longing of young hearts for adventure and friendship!

PERFECT WORLD

Rie Aruga

A TOUCHING NEW SERIES ABOUT LOVE AND COPING WITH DISABILITY

An office party reunites Tsugumi with her high school crush Itsuki. He's realized his dream of becoming an architect, but along the way, he experienced a spinal injury that put him in a wheelchair. Now Tsugumi's rekindled feelings will butt up against prejudices she never considered — and Itsuki will have to decide if he's ready to let someone into his heart...

"Depicts with great delicacy and courage the difficulties some with disabilities experience getting involved in romantic relationships... Rie Aruga refuses to romanticize, pushing her heroine to face the reality of disability. She invites her readers to the same tasks of empathy, knowledge and recognition."
—Slate.fr

"An important entry [in manga romance]... The emotional core of both plot and characters indicates thoughtfulness... [Aruga's] research is readily apparent in the text and artwork, making this feel like a real story."
—Anime News Network

KC
KODANSHA
COMICS

A SMART, NEW ROMANTIC COMEDY FOR FANS OF *SHORTCAKE CAKE* AND *TERRACE HOUSE!*

A romance manga starring high school girl Meeko, who learns to live on her own in a boarding house whose living room is home to the odd (but handsome) Matsunaga-san. She begins to adjust to her new life away from her parents, but Meeko soon learns that no matter how far away from home she is, she's still a young girl at heart — especially when she finds herself falling for Matsunaga-san.

Something's Wrong With Us

NATSUMI ANDO

The dark, psychological, sexy shojo series readers have been waiting for!

A spine-chilling and steamy romance between a Japanese sweets maker and the man who framed her mother for murder!

Following in her mother's footsteps, Nao became a traditional Japanese sweets maker, and with unparalleled artistry and a bright attitude, she gets an offer to work at a world-class confectionary company. But when she meets the young, handsome owner, she recognizes his cold stare...

KC
KODANSHA
COMICS

THE SWEET SCENT OF LOVE IS IN THE AIR! FOR FANS OF OFFBEAT ROMANCES LIKE *WOTAKOI*

Sweat and Soap © Kintetsu Yamada / Kodansha Ltd.

In an office romance, there's a fine line between sexy and awkward... and that line is where Asako — a woman who sweats copiously — meets Koutarou — a perfume developer who can't get enough of Asako's, er, scent. Don't miss a romcom manga like no other!

CUTE ANIMALS AND LIFE LESSONS, PERFECT FOR ASPIRING PET VETS OF ALL AGES!

For an 11-year-old, Yuzu has a lot on her plate. When her mom gets sick and has to be hospitalized, Yuzu goes to live with her uncle who runs the local veterinary clinic. Yuzu's always been scared of animals, but she tries to help out. Through all the tough moments in her life, Yuzu realizes that she can help make things all right with a little help from her animal pals, peers, and kind grown-ups.

Every new patient is a furry friend in the making!

The adorable new odd-couple cat comedy manga from the creator of the beloved *Chi's Sweet Home*, in full color!

Sue & Tai-chan

Konami Kanata

Sue is an aging housecat who's looking forward to living out her life in peace... but her plans change when the mischievous black tomcat Tai-chan enters the picture! Hey! Sue never signed up to be a catsitter! *Sue & Tai-chan* is the latest from the reigning meow-narch of cute kitty comics, Konami Kanata.

KC KODANSHA COMICS

SAINT ☆ YOUNG MEN

A LONG AWAITED ARRIVAL IN PREMIUM 2-IN-1 HARDCOVER

After centuries of hard work, Jesus and Buddha take a break from their
heavenly duties to relax among the people of Japan, and their adventures in this
lighthearted buddy comedy are sure to bring mirth and merriment to all!

"Brilliant…the physical comedy
and facial expressions will
make you literally LOL."

—Sam Humphries
(host of *DC Daily*;
writer, *Green Lanterns*,
Legendary Star-Lord)

Saint Young Men © Hikaru Nakamura/Kodansha Ltd.

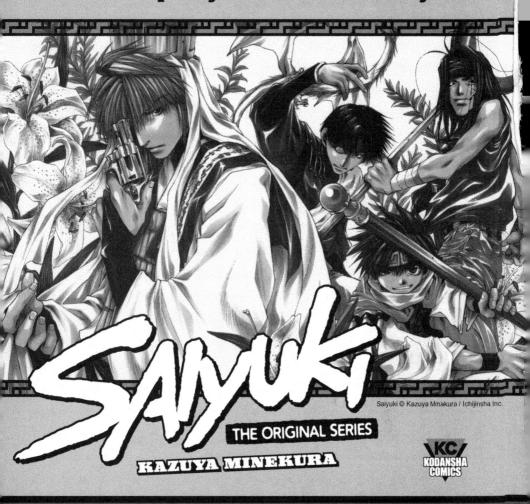

A Kodansha Comics Trade Paperback Original
Life Lessons with Uramichi Oniisan 2 copyright © 2019 Gaku Kuze
English translation copyright © 2020 Gaku Kuze

Published in the United States by Kodansha Comics, an imprint of Kodansha USA Publishing, LLC, New York.

Publication rights for this English edition arranged through Kodansha Ltd., Tokyo.

First published in Japan in 2019 by Ichijinsha Inc., Tokyo as *Uramichi oniisan*, volumes 3 and 4.

Original cover design by Kohei Nawata Design Office

ISBN 978-1-64651-140-2

Printed in Mexico.

www.kodansha.us

9 8 7 6 5 4 3 2
Translation: Matt Treyvaud
Lettering: Michael Martin
Editing: Vanessa Tenazas
Kodansha Comics edition cover design by Phil Balsman

Publisher: Kiichiro Sugawara

Director of publishing services: Ben Applegate
Associate director of operations: Stephen Pakula
Publishing services managing editor: Noelle Webster
Assistant production manager: Emi Lotto, Angela Zurlo
Logo and character art ©Kodansha USA Publishing, LLC